51

CHRISTIANITY AND RELIGIOUS PLURALITY

CHRISTIANITY AND RELIGIOUS PLURALITY

EDITED BY

CHARLOTTE METHUEN
ANDREW SPICER
JOHN WOLFFE

PUBLISHED FOR
THE ECCLESIASTICAL HISTORY SOCIETY
BY
THE BOYDELL PRESS
2015

First published 2015

A publication of the Ecclesiastical History Society
in association with The Boydell Press
an imprint of Boydell & Brewer Ltd
PO Box 9, Woodbridge, Suffolk IP12 3DF, UK
and of Boydell & Brewer Inc.
668 Mt Hope Avenue, Rochester, NY 14620-2731, USA
website: www.boydellandbrewer.com

ISBN 978-0-95468-103-6

ISSN 0424-2084

A CIP catalogue record for this book is available
from the British Library

The publisher has no responsibility for the continued existence or accuracy
of URLs for external or third-party internet websites referred to in this
book, and does not guarantee that any content on such websites is, or will
remain, accurate or appropriate.

Details of previous volumes are available from Boydell & Brewer Ltd

This publication is printed on acid-free paper

Printed and bound in Great Britain by
TJ International Ltd, Padstow, Cornwall

CONTENTS

CONTENTS

PREFACE

Christianity and Religious Plurality is the subject of the fifty-first volume of Studies in Church History. This was the theme of the Summer Conference of the Ecclesiastical History Society held at the University of Chichester in July 2013 and the Winter Meeting in January 2014, presided over by Professor John Wolffe. This volume collects the plenary lectures from both events and a selection of the communications offered at Chichester.

We would like to thank Professor Wolffe for his choice of this fascinating and challenging subject, which (as will become apparent from the essays) has considerable relevance for understanding some of today's world conflicts, and for his contribution to the completion of the volume. Thanks are due also to the authors for their engagement in the editorial process, to all those who chaired sessions at the Summer Conference and peer-reviewed the communications, and in particular to Dr Tim Grass for his able and assiduous work as assistant editor. We are grateful to the Ecclesiastical History Society for its ongoing funding of Dr Grass's post, which is essential to the production of the volume. We are grateful too to the University of Chichester conference team and to Dr Andrew Chandler, who helped to ensure the success of the Summer Conference; to Dr Williams's Library, for hosting the Winter Meeting; and to Professor Michael Walsh, who organized both with his usual good humour and efficiency.

Charlotte Methuen
University of Glasgow

Andrew Spicer
Oxford Brookes University

ILLUSTRATIONS

CONTRIBUTORS

Gareth ATKINS
Postdoctoral Research Fellow, Centre for Research in Arts,
Social Science and Humanities, University of Cambridge

Angela BERLIS
Ordinary Professor in the History of Old Catholicism
and General Church History, Departement für
Christkatholische Theologie, Universität Bern

Clyde BINFIELD
Professor Emeritus in History, University of Sheffield

Marion BOWMAN
Senior Lecturer in Religious Studies, The Open University

Frans CIAPPARA
Senior Lecturer in History, University of Malta

Kristian GIRLING
Postgraduate student, Heythrop College, London

Bernard HAMILTON
Professor Emeritus of Crusading History, University of
Nottingham

A. D. R. HAYES
Postgraduate student, King's College, London

W. M. JACOB
Visiting Research Fellow, King's College, London

John MAIDEN
Lecturer in Religious Studies, The Open University

Nabil MATAR
Professor of English, University of Minnesota

Charlotte METHUEN
Senior Lecturer in Church History, University of Glasgow

Stuart MEWS
Reader Emeritus in Religious Studies, University of
Gloucestershire

James T. PALMER
Lecturer in Medieval History, University of St Andrews

Konstantinos PAPASTATHIS
Postdoctoral researcher, Identités, Politiques, Sociétés,
Espaces Research Unit, University of Luxembourg

Ariana PATEY
Visiting Assistant Professor, Departments of History and
Religious Studies, Memorial University, Newfoundland

Jonathan PHILLIPS
Professor of Crusading History, Royal Holloway, University
of London

Amanda POWER
Senior Lecturer in Medieval History, University of Sheffield

Mona SIDDIQUI
Professor of Islamic and Interreligious Studies, University of
Edinburgh

Brian STANLEY
Professor of World Christianity, University of Edinburgh

Guy G. STROUMSA
Emeritus Professor of the Study of the Abrahamic
Religions, University of Oxford; Martin Buber Professor
Emeritus of Comparative Religion, Hebrew University of
Jerusalem

Todd M. THOMPSON
Assistant Professor of History, Torrey Honors Institute, Biola University

Christine WALSH
Independent scholar, London

Peter WEBSTER
Independent scholar, Chichester

Martin WELLINGS
Methodist minister, Oxford

John WOLFFE
Professor of Religious History, The Open University

Angeliki ZIAKA
Assistant Professor, Study of Religion and Interreligious Dialogue, Aristotle University of Thessaloniki

ABBREVIATIONS

BJRL	*Bulletin of the John Rylands Library*, vols 1–50; *Bulletin of the John Rylands Library of Manchester*, vols 51–4; *Bulletin of the John Rylands University Library of Manchester*, vol. 55 on (1903–)
Bodl.	Bodleian Library
BN	Bibliothèque nationale de France
CChr.CM	Corpus Christianorum, continuatio medievalis (1966–)
CHC	*Cambridge History of Christianity*, 9 vols (Cambridge, 2005–9)
ChH	*Church History* (1932–)
CSM	*Corpus scriptorum Muzarabicorum*, ed. Juan Gil, 2 vols (Madrid, 1973)
CTT	Crusade Texts in Translation
DOP	*Dumbarton Oaks Papers* (1941–)
EHR	*English Historical Review* (1886–)
EME	*Early Medieval Europe* (1992–)
ET	English translation
IRM	*International Review of Missions*, vols 1–57; *International Review of Mission*, vols 58 on (1912–)
JAAR	*Journal of the American Academy of Religion* (1967–)
JEH	*Journal of Ecclesiastical History* (1950–)
JMedH	*Journal of Medieval History* (1975–)
LPL	Lambeth Palace Library
LW	*Luther's Works*, ed. J. Pelikan and H. Lehmann, 55 vols (St Louis, MO, 1955–75)
MGH	Monumenta Germaniae Historica inde ab a. *c.* 500 usque ad a. 1500, ed. G. H. Pertz et al. (Hanover, Berlin, etc., 1826–)
MGH AA	Monumenta Germaniae Historica, Auctores antiquissimi, 15 vols (1877–1919)
MGH Conc.	Monumenta Germaniae Historica, Concilia (1893–)

MGH Epp. Sel.	Monumenta Germaniae Historica, Epistolae Selectae (1916–)
MGH S	Monumenta Germaniae Historica, Scriptores, 29 vols (1826–94)
MGH SRG i.u.s.	Monumenta Germaniae Historica, Scriptores rerum Germanicarum in usum scholarum seperatum editi (1871–)
MGH SRM	Monumenta Germaniae Historica, Scriptores rerum Merovingicarum (1884–1951)
MGH SS	Monumenta Germaniae Historica, Scriptores (in folio) (1826–)
MW	Moslem World, vols 1–37; Muslim World, vols 38 on (1911–)
n.d.	no date
n.s.	new series
ODNB	Oxford Dictionary of National Biography, ed. H. C. G. Matthew and Brian Harrison (Oxford, 2004)
OMT	Oxford Medieval Texts
PG	Patrologia Graeca, ed. J.-P. Migne, 161 vols (Paris, 1857–66)
PL	Patrologia Latina, ed. J.-P. Migne, 217 vols + 4 index vols (Paris, 1844–65)
RHC Or.	Recueil des Historiens des Croisades: Historiens orientaux, 5 vols (Paris, 1872–1906)
RS	Rerum Britannicarum medii aevi scriptores, 99 vols (London, 1858–1911) = Rolls Series
s.a.	sub anno ('under the year')
SCH	Studies in Church History
SCM	Student Christian Movement
SHCM	Studies in the History of Christian Missions
s.n.	sub nomine ('under the name')
TNA	The National Archives
WA	D. Martin Luthers Werke: Kritische Gesamtausgabe, ed. J. K. F. Knaake, G. Kawerau et al. (Weimar, 1883–)
YMCA	Young Men's Christian Association

INTRODUCTION

In the half-century since its formation in 1961 the Ecclesiastical History Society, which publishes Studies in Church History, has been slow to explore religious worlds beyond Christianity. It is true that the society's central aim 'to foster interest in, and to advance the study of, all areas of the history of the Christian Churches' implies that the internal history of other traditions is outside its scope, but as is abundantly clear from the contributions to the present volume, throughout its history Christianity itself has been profoundly influenced by wider religious encounters. An early volume, *The Mission of the Church and the Propagation of the Faith* (SCH 6, 1970), and a more recent Subsidia volume, *Missions and Missionaries* (SCH Subsidia 13, 2000), both touched on such issues, but as their titles imply they limited themselves to just one dimension of interreligious encounter. When the late Barrie Dobson chose *Christianity and Judaism* (SCH 29, 1992) as the theme for his presidential year, he found it 'perhaps surprising' that the society had not already engaged with that subject.[1] More than two decades later, however, this has remained the only volume in the series that has focused centrally on relations between Christianity and another major world religion. When it fell to me, in my turn, to propose a theme for the society's conferences in 2013–14 it seemed urgent by then to endeavour to do something to address that omission.

My first thought was to propose the theme of 'Christianity and Islam', but that would have had two obvious disadvantages. First, it would effectively have excluded contributions concerned with the six centuries of church history that preceded the beginning of Muḥammad's prophetic career, an unacceptable limitation for a society that has always sought to pursue its chosen themes across the whole chronological sweep of organized Christianity. Second,

---

[1] Barrie Dobson, 'Introduction', in Diana Wood, ed., *Christianity and Judaism*, SCH 29 (Oxford, 1992), xv. It is timely to pay tribute to Barrie Dobson, a most distinguished president of the EHS, who died in 2013, and to whom I am personally much indebted.

the very topicality of such a theme would have risked reinforcing an academic and journalistic 'tunnel vision', driven by anxieties stemming from the recent rapid growth of Muslim communities in the West and by the perceived need to 'explain' events such as the terrorist outrages of 11 September 2001 in the United States and 7 July 2005 in London. Accordingly, while recognizing and welcoming the prospect of a substantial proportion of contributions concerned with Christianity and Islam, it seemed better to encourage a wider perspective under the theme of 'Christianity and Religious Plurality'.

The choice of the word 'plurality' rather than 'pluralism' was intended to steer contributors, and the expectations of readers, primarily towards exploration of the practical experience of Christians in a world of manifold belief systems and religious practices, rather than discussion of the philosophical and theological issues raised by the concept of pluralism. Analysis of the implications of plurality *beyond* Christianity is moreover a natural development from earlier volumes that have explored diversity *within* Christianity, both in organizational and theological terms in *Unity and Diversity in the Church* (SCH 32, 1996) and in varied social and cultural milieus in *Elite and Popular Religion* (SCH 42, 2006).

If one takes a long view of the historiography of Christianity, the theme of this volume is by no means a novel one.[2] Edward Gibbon's *Decline and Fall of the Roman Empire* (1776–88) gives extensive attention to interactions between Christianity, Judaism and paganism, and later to the impact of Islam on the Byzantines. The leading Scottish churchman and historian William Robertson insightfully explored pre-Columbian religion in his *History of America* (1777) and Hinduism in his *Historical Disquisition ... of India* (1791). Such wider interests were also pursued by nineteenth-century church historians such as Henry Hart Milman in his *History of the Jews* (1829) and Arthur Penrhyn Stanley in his *Lectures on the History of the Eastern Church* (1861), which devoted substantial space to encounters with Islam.

For much of the twentieth century, however, the development of 'ecclesiastical history' as an academic subdiscipline seeking to

---

[2]   For a more extended discussion, see John Wolffe, 'Religious History', in John R. Hinnells, ed., *The Routledge Companion to the Study of Religion*, 2nd edn (London, 2010), 56–72.

serve an increasingly introspective and embattled Western Church tended to limit the further pursuit of such lines of enquiry. They were seen rather as the preserve of historians of Christian missions or of those of comparative religion, both perspectives that offered substantial insights but also their own inherent limitations. Only in recent decades, with the growing awareness that contemporary Western societies are now characterized by a plurality of religions rather than by Christian near-monopoly, has the importance of seeing Christianity in its wider religious context become once more apparent to historians of the Churches themselves. There remains much research to be done in this field, but it is hoped that the essays in this volume will serve as a valuable summation of existing work, and as a stimulus to new enquiries.

The arrangement of the volume is broadly chronological, so it will be helpful in introducing the essays that follow to suggest some threads of comparison and continuity across time and space. The contributions fall into four main categories.

First, there are studies of Christianity in contexts where it was itself a minority faith. In a suggestive opening essay Guy Stroumsa locates early Christianity in the evolving religious landscape of the eastern Mediterranean in late antiquity, arguing against the conventional view of a Constantinian 'revolution' that transformed it almost overnight from marginality to dominance. Andrew Hayes's case study of Justin Martyr well illustrates the challenge of establishing a distinctive Christian identity in this environment, while arguing that Justin's philosophical approach enabled him to find significant common ground with both Graeco-Romans and Jews. Both these essays emphasize religious coexistence in the early Christian centuries and hence are a useful balance to more familiar narratives of persecution. Martyrdom, however, receives due attention in Ariana Patey's analysis of the later context of ninth-century Islamic Córdoba, although here, to a greater extent even than under the pre-Constantinian Roman Empire, Christians deliberately provoked their own fate, as a radical means of asserting their religious identity. On the other hand, as Amanda Power shows in her study of captive Latin Christians in the mid-thirteenth-century Mongol Empire, although these also faced acute problems in maintaining a distinctive identity in an environment of intriguing and complex religious encounters, amidst an underlying tolerance of diversity they did not find themselves driven to such extreme measures. Elsewhere, indeed, as Angeliki Ziaka explores in her analysis of the writings of two leading Greek Christians who lived under Ottoman rule after 1453, dialogue with representatives of the now dominant faith could be a viable strategy. Nevertheless the limited toleration accorded to Christian minorities could quickly be rescinded, whether (as under Diocletian) due to the changed attitude of rulers or (as in Córdoba) by the actions of Christians themselves.

Three case studies of much more recent history – by Kristian Girling of Iraq and by Brian Stanley of Egypt and Indonesia – illustrate a similar instability. In all three countries Christians found ways both to gain acceptance and to cooperate with Muslims, especially in nationalist movements against colonial rule. However, in the face of the growth of militant Islamism and the unfortunate tendency for local Christians to be compromised in the eyes of their neighbours by the neo-crusading rhetoric of Western leaders, their situation subsequently became much more insecure. Ongoing events in Iraq and Syria at the time of writing indicate, as did the genocide of Armenian Christians a century ago, that the long-standing peaceful existence of a Christian minority is no guarantee of indefinite security.

Second, and conversely, a number of contributors explore responses to religious minorities in predominantly Christian societies. Here too, as the experience of Jews in the 1090s as well as the 1930s graphically illustrates, toleration could never be taken for granted. Nevertheless the essays in this volume in general highlight degrees of acceptance rather than persecution. As Christine Walsh indicates in her study of Vikings in tenth-century Francia, the distinction between Christian and non-Christian was not always clear-cut, with baptism sometimes more a political than a spiritual act, which could be followed by lapses into 'paganism' and consequent dilemmas for the ecclesiastical authorities. Ambivalences of a different kind are illustrated by Frans Ciappara's study of Muslim slaves in early modern Malta: they were allowed actively to practise their religion, but they were deliberately isolated from the Christian population and sometimes subjected to considerable pressure to convert. My own essay argues, however, that in nineteenth- and twentieth-century London there was no simple polarity between proselytism and acceptance of plurality, as those Christians in the forefront of efforts to evangelize minorities were also increasingly committed to their material welfare and to the combating of popular prejudices against them. Indeed, as W. M. Jacob demonstrates, the tacit response of Anglican clergy to late Victorian Jewish settlement in the East End was acceptance of the inevitability of coexistence.

Over the course of the twentieth century religious minorities in Britain became much more conspicuous. This was not merely a matter of numerical growth. In 1909, the small number of Hindu students in Britain received unwelcome notoriety due to the assassination of Sir Curzon Wyllie by Madan Lal Dhingra. Stuart Mews sets this event in context, and explores its implications for Christian attitudes to Hindus, and for the campaign for Indian independence. It is true that even in the 1960s there were still those who denied or challenged the reality of plurality, but, as Peter Webster shows, Archbishop Michael Ramsey was not among them and sought to lead the Anglican Communion in a constructive response to a rapidly changing religious landscape, both in England and abroad. Implications at a local level are explored by John Maiden in his case study of the controversy arising from proposals to sell the redundant church of St Leonard's, Bedford to the Ramgarhia Sikh Society. Bedford in the 1970s at first sight is a very different context from the Rouen of the tenth century discussed by Christine Walsh, but a thread running through the six essays in this second strand is the tension between maintaining the integrity of Christian witness and living with the reality of religious plurality.

Third, there are analyses of religious encounters in situations where no one tradition was obviously dominant. An interesting common feature of these essays is the manner in which they indicate a range of responses *within* Christianity to plurality *beyond* it. James Palmer draws out the complexities of the religious landscape of early medieval Europe, showing how religious difference was not necessarily a barrier to cooperation, and how the internal diversity and insecurities of Christendom were reflected in attitudes to Jews, Muslims and 'pagans'. Moreover, as Jonathan Phillips shows, such cross-currents continued even in the face of the apparent polarities of the crusading era, when military confrontation did not preclude trading links. Although some Christians pursued theological polemic, others attained a more sympathetic understanding of Islam and engaged in discussion with Muslims.

There were even attempts to settle the vexed question of the status of Jerusalem, with its plurality of religious associations, by diplomacy rather than military action. The painful intractability of this problem, which seems no closer to resolution the greater part of a millennium later, should not obscure the seriousness of endeavours to resolve it. One such initiative is described by Clyde Binfield in his account of the building of the West Jerusalem YMCA in the early 1930s: a Christian construction, but one explicitly seeking to reach out to Jews and Muslims. Glastonbury's religious plurality has been much less contentious than Jerusalem's, but, as Marion Bowman shows, it had its own considerable complexities, especially in highlighting the fluid relationships between 'official' Christianity and the pluralities of vernacular religion. Such studies grounded in particular localities and specific periods – also represented in this volume by Patey's account of Córdoba, Ciappara's of Malta, Wolffe's of London and Maiden's of Bedford – bring the practical implications of religious plurality into especially sharp focus.

A final substantial group of essays examine Christian views of other religious traditions. Bernard Hamilton complements Amanda Power's analysis of the situation of Christians in the Mongol Empire by examining the perceptions and misperceptions of Buddhism disseminated by Western visitors such as William of Rubruck and Marco Polo. Western interest in Buddhism was long to remain limited by remoteness, but the fall of Constantinople in 1453 and the subsequent Ottoman military challenge to Europe brought consciousness of Islam much more to the fore. Konstantinos Papasthathis analyses the ideas of George of Trebizond (actually a Cretan living in Italy), who proposed a visionary scheme for an accommodation between Christianity and Islam grounded in the universal political monarchy of the sultan and the universal spiritual authority of the pope. German responses in the first half of the sixteenth century, as explored by Charlotte Methuen, were, however, much more negative, in the face of the growing 'Turkish' threat to a now divided Christendom. In later seventeenth-century England, on the other hand, Henry Stubbe and John Locke, discussed by Nabil Matar, developed discourses that showed a more sympathetic understanding of Islam, and pointed the way forward to an emergent Enlightenment framework for toleration.

Christian views in the nineteenth and twentieth centuries were shaped by more explicit missionary agendas than were apparent in earlier eras. Gareth Atkins describes William Jowett's travels in the eastern Mediterranean between 1815 and 1830, which raised awareness both of the Eastern Churches and of Judaism and Islam and were intended to prepare the ground for Protestant evangelism. By contrast, Hyacinthe and Emilie Loyson's travels over similar territory in the 1890s, discussed by Angela Berlis, were motivated by a 'truly missionary zeal', not for making converts to Christianity but for bringing about the reunion of Churches and faiths in the cause of world peace. For J. H. Moulton, however, whose book *Religion and Religions* (1913) is analysed by Martin Wellings, there was no incompatibility between the better appreciation of other traditions and the ongoing mission of Christians to propagate their own faith. Finally, Todd Thompson's study of the Lebanese scholar Charles Malik (1906–87) shows how in his mind Christianity, far from endorsing the supposed 'civilizing' mission of the West, served as the mainspring for his critique of orientalism.

It is inevitable that a volume of this nature, made up primarily of a selection of essays offered for publication around a common theme rather than from articles systematically commissioned to cover a predetermined agenda, contains significant lacunae. One might wish, for example, for more contributions exploring the religious pluralities of late antiquity, and the multifarious other contexts in which Christianity subsequently established itself, from China to the Americas. The complex transitions in Western Christian attitudes to other faiths, from the polemics of the Reformation era, through the advent of Enlightenment toleration, to the missionary zeal of the nineteenth century and the widespread acceptance of plurality as a local as well as global reality in the twentieth, also merit further research and elucidation. However, if this volume serves to map out a territory for further work and to inspire future enquiry in a field that will surely become increasingly central to the study of the history of Christianity, it will have served its purpose.

In the concluding essay a leading Muslim scholar, Mona Siddiqui, reflects on the long-term development of Christian-Muslim relations. She highlights the significance of different views of the person of Jesus, but nevertheless argues for the abiding viability of dialogue in a post-9/11 world where some see a fundamental divide between the 'West' and a stereotyped conception of Islam. Her argument is consistent with the consensus of the other contributors to this volume, whose essays offer substantial historical evidence to refute a 'clash of civilizations'[3] narrative of interreligious relations. Granted that the historical record contains many instances of persecution, prejudice and sheer incomprehension, it also reveals that peaceful coexistence and acknowledgement of the reality of religious plurality on local, national and global stages was widespread. The past thus offers significant resources for constructive thinking about the future.

John Wolffe
The Open University

---

[3]   Cf. Samuel P. Huntington, *The Clash of Civilizations and the Remaking of World Order* (New York, 1996).

FROM QUMRAN TO QUR'ĀN: THE RELIGIOUS WORLDS OF ANCIENT CHRISTIANITY*

by GUY G. STROUMSA

This essay seeks to present, in a nutshell, a number of reflections on the long trajectory of ancient Christianity, particularly in the East, from its beginnings until the coming of Islam. As is well known, the Islamic conquests transformed the Christian self-understanding in the East, on both sides of the border between Byzantium and the Caliphate. In the West, too, the consciousness of the new, powerful challenge to the Christian empire was never very far away. Hence the advent of Islam constitutes the first real challenge to the belief in the ecumenical destiny of Christianity.[1]

While the trajectory of ancient Christianity is usually studied by church historians, it may be worthwhile to approach it also from the outside. To borrow the categories famously invented by the American linguist and anthropologist Kenneth Lee Pike, I propose to reflect here from an etic – external, or uninvolved – rather than an emic – internal or involved – viewpoint. Although I have spent much effort over decades in order to understand better the religious and intellectual worlds of early Christianity, I have done that not as an ecclesiastical historian or a patristics scholar but as a comparative historian of religion in late antiquity. My research has focused mainly on the contacts of Christians with Jews and pagans, as well as on the formation and development of those internal challenges which the Church Fathers (the intellectuals of the winning party) called 'the heresies', in particular Gnosticism and Manichaeism.[2]

* I should like to thank Professor John Wolffe for his generous invitation to present this work in the form of a keynote lecture at the conference of the Ecclesiastical History Society held in Chichester in July 2013.

[1] For a panoramic vision of the perception of nascent Islam by contemporary Christians, see James Howard-Johnston, *Witnesses to a World Crisis: Historians and Histories of the Middle East in the Seventh Century* (Oxford, 2010).

[2] See, for instance, G. G. Stroumsa, *Savoir et salut: traditions juives et tentations dualistes dans le christianisme ancien* (Paris, 1992); idem, *Barbarian Philosophy: The Religious Revolution of Early Christianity* (Tübingen, 1999).

As is well known, the Constantinian revolution usually remains, together with its sequels throughout the fourth century, the obvious and unavoidable turning point of any ancient Christian historiography. From a despised and forbidden minority religion, Christianity moved very fast, in the fourth century, to the status of a legitimate religion, and then to that of the imperial official religion. While Judaism would remain tolerated in the Christian Roman Empire, all public forms of paganism – and in particular animal sacrifices – were forbidden by law after the publication of the edict of Thessaloniki (*Cunctos Populos*) in 380. For the theologian and sociologist of religion Ernst Troeltsch a century ago, the first chapter in ecclesiastical history, which ended in the fourth century, represented the passage from sect to church, while for his friend Max Weber this transformation represented the passage from a charismatic to a routinized religion.[3] To a great extent, such conceptions still inform much contemporary historiography of ancient Christianity. However, one could ask whether this traditional narrative is really compelling, and this essay is in part a response to that question.

The traditional vision of the religious context of ancient Christianity is constituted by both its Jewish matrix, mainly until the so-called 'parting of the ways' in the first half of the second century, and Roman paganism thereafter, until the fourth century.[4] After the fourth-century watershed, Christian historiography usually functioned in an autarkic way, with other religions relegated to a dark, indistinct background about which there is little to say, or at least little to say that directly impinges on ecclesiastical history.

I shall seek here to offer another approach to ancient Christianity in its multiple religious milieux, by taking the long view, from the birth of Christianity to that of Islam. A view from the Near East offers a perspective different from that of traditional historiography. It shows, rather than the transformation of a Jewish

---

3   For Troeltsch's main work on sociology of religion, see his *The Social Teachings of the Christian Churches*, transl. Olive Wyon (Louisville, KY, 1992; first publ. in German 1912 and in English 1931). Weber's concepts of charisma and routine were mainly developed in his *The Theory of Social and Economic Organizations*, transl. A. M. Henderson and Talcott Parsons (New York, 1947; first publ. in German 1921).

4   See Adam H. Becker and Annette Yoshiko Reed, eds, *The Ways that never Parted: Jews and Christians in Late Antiquity and the Early Middle Ages* (Minneapolis, MN, 2007; first publ. Tübingen, 2003).

sect into the triumphant Catholic Church, that of a forbidden sect in the Roman Empire into a tolerated one under the caliphate. Both in those areas that had been part of the Sasanian Empire and in those that had belonged to Byzantium, the Christian communities would become, in the Islamic realm, tolerated minorities, together with the Jews and the Zoroastrians. One can say that the Christians had now reverted, to some extent, to the sociological status of their sectarian beginnings, although not quite, since Christianity had achieved under the Muslims an official recognition as a religious community possessing a prophetic Scripture (*ahl al-kitab*) and was thus tolerated, although Christians were required to pay a special tax (*ahl al-dhimma*) that they had escaped under the pagan Roman Empire.[5] In that sense, one can trace a trajectory of ancient Christianity which leads it from Qumran to Qur'ān.[6]

For the comparative historian of religion, the Near East and the whole Mediterranean, from the first to the seventh century, constitute a rare laboratory in which a number of religious communities were in constant contact and conflict.[7] Rather than referring to 'sects', a quite loaded word, alluding to doctrines deviating from a reigning orthodoxy, we should perhaps speak of communities, which were connected through a highly complex web which offered a kaleidoscope of sorts, in which the various crystals constantly restructured themselves in a seemingly infinite number of new combinations.

Beyond the many differences between the various world views, a religious *koinē* of sorts can be discerned in the Roman Empire and beyond. The numerous religious communities might well have been constantly fighting one another, but they nonetheless shared a number of presuppositions (usually implicit rather than explicit)

---

5   See Yohanan Friedmann, *Tolerance and Coercion in Islam: Interfaith Relations in the Muslim Tradition* (Cambridge, 2003).

6   For a brilliant work of *haute vulgarisation* describing the different religious worlds of the late antique Near East up to the coming of Islam, see Tom Holland, *In the Shadow of the Sword: The Battle for Global Empire and the End of the Ancient World* (London, 2012).

7   On the use of 'laboratory' for describing the emergence of various theological schools in Early Christianity, see Winrich Löhr, 'Epiphanes' Schrift *Peri diakaiosynês* (= Clemens Alexandrinus, Str. III,6,1–9,3)', in *Logos. Festschrift für Luise Abramowski*, ed. H. C. Brennecke, E. L. Grasmück and C. Markschies (Berlin and New York, 1993), 12–29, at 29.

which constituted the structures of their religious world.[8] These structures evolved with time, although the consciousness of this evolution was not always clear. We should search for the rules of the transformative grammar which accounts for the historical evolution of these structures.

While the Roman world in which the new religion grew and blossomed could be aptly described, by the late Keith Hopkins, as 'a world full of gods', it is important to remember that these gods were not only the Roman gods.[9] The religious context of ancient Christianity included, besides Judaism and Roman religion, and not only in the East, a number of Oriental cults from Asia and Egypt (such as Isis, Cybele or Mithras), and various Gnostic trends, such as Hermeticism, Manichaeism, Mandaeism and Zoroastrianism.

The Jewish world in which Christianity was born can certainly be defined as a sectarian milieu. Side by side with the Pharisees and the Essenes, Josephus Flavius names the 'party' (*hairesis*) of the elite, the Sadducees, and that of the partisans of radical revolt against Rome, the Zealots, in the spectrum of Palestinian Jewry. Qumran, the community of Jewish sectarians on the north-western shores of the Dead Sea, was destroyed by the Romans during the Jewish war in the first century, but, as is well known, many of the sectarians' writings were found after the Second World War, which permit us a glimpse of their beliefs and rituals.[10] While the specialists still argue vehemently about the exact identity of the Qumran covenanters, it stands to reason to assume that they were Essenes, or close to the Essenes, and that there were some striking similarities between their religious world and that of John the Baptist. Jesus himself seems to have had some sympathy for aspects of the Essenes' religious attitude (in particular in his eschatological expectations and his social sensitivity), while in other ways he was

8   See, for instance, G. G. Stroumsa, 'Religious Dynamics between Christians and Jews in Late Antiquity', in Augustine Casiday and Frederick W. Norris, eds, *CHC*, 2: *Constantine to c.600* (Cambridge, 2007), 151–72.

9   Keith Hopkins, *A World Full of Gods: The Strange Triumph of Christianity* (New York, 2001).

10   See, for instance, Geza Vermes, *The Dead Sea Scrolls in English*, 3rd edn (London, 1987); also idem, *The Dead Sea Scrolls: Qumran in Perspective* (Philadelphia, PA, 1977).

probably very close to the Pharisees, a fact which also explains the anti-Pharisee polemics in the Gospels.[11]

Among the first followers of Jesus, who were of course all Jewish, not all gave up, with Paul, on the traditional Jewish patterns of behaviour. Those Jews who believed that the Messiah had come but who refused to relinquish Jewish religious law are traditionally referred to in scholarship as 'Jewish Christians'. 'Ebionites' (from Hebrew *evyon*, poor), is only one of the various names of the sect. Both the Church Fathers and the rabbis sought to minimize their presence and to argue that the sect had fundamentally disappeared by the fourth century.[12] However, we know from a number of testimonies that the Ebionites were still present, even if marginally from a sociological viewpoint, in the seventh century. I mean to call attention to the surprising continuity of sectarian milieux in relation to which I propose to look at the development of Christianity in antiquity.

For the traditional narrative, reflecting patristic perceptions, the sectarian milieu of the Christian beginnings would soon be absorbed into the new structures created in the *oikoumene* by victorious Christianity. The Ebionites, like the various Gnostic groups, would have disappeared, for all practical purposes, by the fourth century. Of all the sects which had, according to Irenaeus, 'popped up like mushrooms on the earth', only the Manichaeans, who had established a real ecumenical Church, like the Christians themselves, would remain a real, powerful threat to Catholic Christianity.[13]

Such a view, however, does not reflect reality on the ground. A number of indices reveal the traces of various sects even in much later times, and offer evidence that the Jewish-Christians had not really disappeared. Even if these sects seem to have been rather insignificant from a sociological viewpoint, the important

---

[11] The literature is of course immense. On John the Baptist and the Essenes, see, for instance, Hartmut Stegemann, *Die Essener, Johannes der Täufer und Jesus* (Freiburg im Breisgau, 1998). For two classics, see Geza Vermes, *Jesus and the World of Judaism* (London, 1983); E. P. Sanders, *The Historical Figure of Jesus* (London, 1995).

[12] See, for instance, Simon Claude Mimouni, *Le judéo-christianisme ancien: essais historiques* (Paris, 1998).

[13] Irenaeus, *Against Heresies* 1.29 (transl. A. Rousseau and L. Doutreleau, Sources Chrétiennes 264 [Paris, 1979], 358–9). For an authoritative presentation, see David Brakke, *The Gnostics: Myth, Ritual, and Diversity in Early Christianity* (Cambridge, MA, and London, 2010).

fact is that we can now assume with real confidence that some marginal Jewish-Christian communities remained active in the Near East, in particular in various areas of Palestine, Syria and Arabia, throughout late antiquity.[14]

This rich religious mosaic remained that of the Near East, within and without the borders of the Roman Empire, until at least the seventh century. In this regard, the Arabist John Wansbrough has been able to speak about the 'sectarian milieu' within which Islam was born, thinking not only about the Arabian Hejaz, but, more broadly, about greater Syria (the Arabic *Bilad al-Sham*).[15] This 'sectarian milieu' included not only Christians and Jews, but also a number of religious communities on the margins of the leading traditions.

The religious world in which Christianity developed, from its beginnings and throughout late antiquity, remained pluralistic by nature. I am not arguing, of course, that Constantine and his successors did not transform the status of Christianity in the empire. What I am saying is that a continuous thread nonetheless links Christian discourse from the origins to the eve of the medieval age. In that sense, the fourth century, despite its undeniable significance, does not constitute in the East a radical paradigm shift, as the history of the Christian communities there cannot be understood in isolation from that of other religious communities. Constant interface entailed a dialectic of reciprocal impact between the different religious identities, identities characterized by their fluidity. One could speak here of intertwined or connected histories – to use a term coined by the historian of early modern India Sanjay Subramanian – of an essentially plural history of religion.[16]

If the birth of Islam constitutes a religious revolution, comparable *mutatis mutandis* to the birth of Christianity, we should be able to reconstitute the vector leading from one to the other. A religious revolution entails a paradigm change: various elements

[14] See, for instance, G. G. Stroumsa, 'Jewish Christianity and Islamic Origins', in *Islamic Cultures, Islamic Contexts: Essays in Honor of Patricia Crone*, ed. Benham Sadeghi et al., Islamic History and Civilization 114 (Leiden and Boston, MA, 2014), 72–96.

[15] John Wansbrough, *The Sectarian Milieu: Content and Composition of Islamic Salvation History* (Oxford, 1978).

[16] Sanjay Subrahmanyam, *Explorations in Connected History: From the Tagus to the Ganges* (Delhi, 2004); idem, *Explorations in Connected History: Mughals and Franks* (Delhi, 2004).

which were expressed by a number of religious agents suddenly coalesce, and their sum creates a new reality. Since Thomas Kuhn's seminal book on scientific revolutions,[17] historians and philosophers of science have learned that the paradigm changes reflected in scientific revolutions do not appear *ex nihilo*, but rather are prepared by a number of smaller-scale changes effected by various agents. We should perhaps learn to approach religious revolutions in a similar way.[18]

I propose to call the religious transformations of late antiquity a *praeparatio coranica*, referring metaphorically to *Praeparatio Evangelica*, the title of Eusebius of Caesarea's book on pagan pre-Christian Greek ideas as having in a sense prepared the way for the development of Christian concepts. This expression highlights the dramatic pace with which the new Islamic realm succeeded not only in conquering lands throughout the Near East, but also in converting populations (mainly, but not only, Christian).[19] This pace is not really explainable without taking into account the fact that some of the main traits of the Qur'ān's message had not only been circulating for centuries, but had to some extent been internalized, becoming part of the religious and ethical ethos of late antique Christianity (and also Judaism). Prophecy, eschatological expectations, asceticism and fear of sin were all part and parcel of the late antique religious *koinē*.

What we have recently learned to call 'the Abrahamic religions', which were previously referred to as 'the religions of the book' or 'the monotheistic religions', are usually conceived as referring to (at least) Judaism, Christianity and Islam; the term itself is a modern plural rooted in the Qur'ānic expression about *dīn Ibrāhīm*,

---

[17] Thomas S. Kuhn, *The Structure of Scientific Revolutions* (Chicago, IL, 1962).

[18] What the anthropologist Dan Sperber, together with the psychologist Deirdre Wilson, has called the 'epidemiology of representations' might prove here a useful conception: Dan Sperber, 'Anthropology and Psychology: Towards an Epidemiology of Representations', *Man* n.s. 20 (1984), 73–89. Sperber researches the ways in which microprocesses of cultural transmission affect the macro-structure of culture, its contents and its evolution. In other words, he asks how social phenomena related to psychological, mental phenomena. On our side, we should ask how both *theologoumena* and modes of religiosity are transformed in history: see G. G. Stroumsa, 'Patterns of Rationalization in Late Antique Religion', forthcoming.

[19] For a grand and authoritative overview of the Islamic conquests, see Hugh N. Kennedy, *The Great Arab Conquests: How the Spread of Islam Changed the World we live in* (Philadelphia, PA, 2007).

'the religion [singular] of Abraham'. Actually, we should realize that in order to speak about 'the Abrahamic religions', a plurality of two (Judaism and Christianity) is enough. Indeed, the Christian competition with Judaism in the first centuries is clearly centred on the issue of who the true heirs of Abraham are, as a number of texts, from Justin Martyr to Eusebius of Caesarea, show.[20] In many ways, emergent Islam replicated the model developed earlier by Christians. Just as Christians considered themselves, from the first century on, to be the true sons and legitimate inheritors of Abraham, while the Jews had turned away from the core message of their forefathers, so for the Qur'ān, applying also to Christians the logic of the latter's argument against the Jews, both Jews and Christians had perverted the deep kernel of the true religion of Abraham, which the Qur'ān reclaimed.[21]

In many ways, one can therefore conceive late antiquity as being the true crucible of the Abrahamic religions: it is in the polemics between Jews and Christians and in the Christian attitudes to a number of crucial religious problems that the conceptions which would soon become identified with Islam were forged. The emergence, mainly among Christians, but also among Jews, Zoroastrians and dualists, of modes of thought which would be instrumental in permitting the rise of Islam represents the *praeparatio coranica*.[22]

To some extent, therefore, the common perception of the Constantinian revolution may lead to a slanted understanding of the Christianization process in the Roman Empire. From J. B. Bury to Paul Veyne, a whole tradition of historiography insists on the imperial *fiat* which made Christianity into a *religio licita*, soon to be the preferred one, and eventually the only legitimate state religion. To Veyne's restatement of this approach in *Quand notre monde est devenu chrétien* (2007), Marie-Francoise Baslez objected the following year, in a brilliant book, *Comment notre*

---

[20] See, for instance, G. G. Stroumsa, 'Athens, Jerusalem and Mecca: The Patristic Crucible of the Abrahamic Religions', in Markus Vinzent, ed., *Studia Patristica 62, Papers presented at the Sixteenth International Conference on Patristic Studies held in Oxford 2011, 10: The Genres of Late Antique Literature; Foucault and the Practice of Patristics; Patristic Studies in Latin America; Historica* (Leuven, 2013), 153–68.

[21] On the concept of the Abrahamic religions, see G. G. Stroumsa, 'From Abraham's Religion to the Abrahamic Religions', in *Historia Religionum 3* (2011), 11–22.

[22] For a detailed historical study of the conflict between empires in the late antique Near East, see Peter Saris, *Empires of Faith: The Fall of Rome to the Rise of Islam, 500–700* (Oxford, 2011).

monde est devenu chrétien.[23] Baslez describes how throughout the first three centuries, the Christian communities, originally close to the Qumran covenanters, gradually adopted different identities according to the various areas and cities of the empire. She shows how, from the second century to the fourth, Christianity gradually became a religion of the book. For Baslez, explaining the Christianization of the empire through a sudden and total conversion of Constantine, as Veyne does, remains unconvincing.

Despite this sobering approach, the leading paradigm in contemporary historiography of religion in late antiquity seems to remain that of the radical revolution. Following a recent fashion according to which *ioudaismos* refers to geographical or ethnic, rather than religious, identity, the rabbinic scholar Daniel Boyarin has claimed that religion itself, as a concept, was invented in the fourth century CE.[24] Although Boyarin rightly detects a real mutation of the concept of religion in the fourth century, his claim is obviously quite odd, as if the Greeks, the Romans or the Egyptians had had only rituals but no beliefs.[25] For Boyarin, Constantine is thus in a sense the inventor of two religions, rabbinic Judaism side by side with Christianity. However, as with most far-fetched views, there is a kernel of truth in this vision of things, namely that religion underwent in the Roman Empire, throughout the Mediterranean, a series of major changes which do amount to a radical transformation.

In *The End of Sacrifices: Religious Transformations of Late Antiquity*, I have sought to identify a number of these changes, as well as the nature of this transformation.[26] A series of major political, cultural and social changes affected all aspects of life in the Near East

---

[23] P. Veyne, *Quand notre monde est devenu chrétien* (Paris, 2007); Marie-Françoise Balnez, *Comment notre monde est devenu chrétien* (Paris, 2008). On patterns of Christianization, see Hervé Inglebert, Sylvain Destephen and Bruno Dumézil, eds, *Le problème de la christianisation du monde antique* (Paris, 2010).

[24] Boyarin has expressed his views in a number of essays; see in particular his *Border Lines: The Partition of Judeo-Christianity* (Philadelphia, PA, 2004).

[25] I assume here that any definition of religion would include a mixture of words and deeds, of myths and rituals.

[26] G. G. Stroumsa, *The End of Sacrifice: Religious Transformations in Late Antiquity* (Chicago, IL, 2009), first publ. as *La fin du sacrifice: Mutations religieuses de l'antiquité tardive* (Paris, 2005). For a succinct presentation of the book's main theses, see my 'The End of Sacrifice: Religious Mutations of Late Antiquity', in J. Arnason and K. Raaflaub, eds, *The Roman Empire in Context: Historical and Comparative Perspectives* (London, 2011), 134–47.

as well as around the Mediterranean under the Roman Empire. Religious beliefs and attitudes, in particular, underwent some dramatic transformations. Indeed, those scholars who, rejecting the Gibbonian paradigm of decline and fall, have taught us to look at the Roman Empire in the *longue durée* as an epoch in which new cultural frameworks were developed, have all insisted on the religious dimensions of late antique creativity. Each in his own way, Henri-Irénée Marrou, Eric R. Dodds, Peter Brown and Robin Lane Fox have been able to speak of the religious revolution of late antiquity.[27] One might argue that the period of late antiquity was no less important for future developments than the 'Axial Age' (*Achsenzeit*) identified by Karl Jaspers with the middle of the first millennium BCE.[28] In order to do justice to the dramatic nature of the transformations in this period, from, say, Jesus to Muḥammad, one can also speak of 'religious mutations'. By borrowing this metaphor from the field of biology, I intend to highlight the fact that we do not only witness the passage from paganism to Christianity (to follow the traditional perception), or that from polytheism to monotheism. Rather, I wish to claim that we can observe nothing less than a transformation of the very concept of religion. To encapsulate the nature of this transformation, one may perhaps speak of 'the end of sacrifice', in reference to the fact that at the time of Jesus, religion meant, for Jews and Greeks alike, the offering of sacrifice, while the situation had changed in some radical ways in the sixth century. But the multi-faceted nature of this revolution encompassed other areas than ritual and its transformations. This is true, for instance, for psychological conceptions, for the place and role of books in religious life, and for the passage

[27] See, for instance, Henri-Irénée Marrou, *Décadence romaine ou antiquité tardive? IIIᵉ–IVᵉ siècle* (Paris, 1977); for Marrou, the new religiosity constituted the main originality of late antiquity. See also Eric R. Dodds, *Pagan and Christian in an Age of Anxiety: Some Aspects of Religious Experience from Marcus Aurelius to Constantine* (Cambridge, 1965); Robin Lane Fox, *Pagans and Christians* (Harmondsworth, 1986); Peter Brown, 'Brave Old World' (a review of Lane Fox's book), *New York Review of Books*, 12 March 1987, 27.
[28] For a new analysis of Jaspers's thesis, see S. N. Eisenstadt, ed., *The Origins and Diversity of Axial Age Civilizations* (Albany, NY, 1986); cf. G. G. Stroumsa, 'Robert Bellah on the Origins of Religion – A Critical Review', *Revue de l'histoire des religions* 229 (2012), 467–77. See further Robert N. Bellah and Hans Joas, eds., *The Axial Age and tts Consequences* (Cambridge, MA, and London, 2012).

from an essentially civic to a mainly communitarian nature of religion.

Since Gibbon, various explanations have been offered of the rise of religious intolerance and violence (two different but connected phenomena) in the world of late antiquity. As such violence and intolerance was mainly the work of Christians, it is in either the nature of Christianity (i.e. its origins in Jewish exclusivism) or in its history (i.e. in the collusion, not before the fourth century, between state and Church) that the roots of Christian violence and intolerance have been sought. It seems to me that both approaches err in their static character: they are unable to account for the deep transformation of mental patterns within Christian communities from the first century to the fourth. Early Christian communities, which remained *entpolitisiert* in the strongest sense of this Weberian expression, could, like the Qumran community, develop freely, upon a radical interpretation of their Scriptures, some violent ideas about the *Endzeit* and the final eschatological war. The trouble began when they were suddenly put in a position of power. Most were unable to realize at once that the new political fortune demanded a new hermeneutics. As we know too well, similar phenomena are known elsewhere, including in contemporary history.[29]

In order to understand the growth in religious intolerance and violence in late antiquity, one must recognize the new fact of an identity defined, more than ever before, in religious terms. People now perceived themselves as belonging to a community identified by a common faith, rather than by ethnic identity. While Jewish exclusivism made space for non-Jews (for instance as 'Godfearers', fellow travellers of sorts, or as 'pious among the nations'), Christian universalism could not easily tolerate outsiders. By definition, such outsiders were heretics, pagans or Jews. Only the latter could be, to a certain extent, tolerated on the fringes of society. With time, these fringes had a tendency to shrink. Justinian could no longer tolerate their use of Hebrew,[30] and in the early seventh century, forced baptism was demanded in the Byzantine Empire.[31]

Jews and Christians knew exactly the stakes of the conflict

---

[29] For further developments, see Stroumsa, *Barbarian Philosophy*, 8–26.
[30] On this, see Stroumsa, 'Religious Dynamics'.
[31] For an excellent study of religious violence in late antiquity, see Thomas

GUY G. STROUMSA

between them, and the rules of the game (the definition of true
prophecy and the correct understanding of the common Scriptures). Between Christians and 'pagans', on the other hand, a
dialogue de sourds was soon established. On both sides, it seems,
there was a total lack of understanding of the nature of the other
side's religion. Both Christians and 'pagans' sought to understand
one another in their own terms. From one of the most impressive
intellectual testimonies to this conflict, Origen's *Contra Celsum*, at
least (a text written around the mid-third century), it would appear
that the main argument between them focused on the idea of civic
religion, or on the relationship between state and religion.[32]

To the extent that it claimed to be the sole representative
of true prophecy, Islam was similar to Christianity. However, its
success in transforming the community of the faithful (the *umma*)
into imperial society, a transformation probably due mainly to the
fast pace of the Arab conquests, permitted the Muslims to set a
relationship between state and religion that ever evaded Christian
rulers, East and West.

In this essay, I have sought to present, in a rather impressionistic
way, a series of examples showing how ancient Christianity must
also be understood from the viewpoint of the history of religions in late antiquity. Prophecy runs like a thread from Jesus to
Muḥammad. And yet, this thread, arguably the single most important
characteristic of the Abrahamic movement, often remains outside
the mainstream, hidden, as it were, since it generates heresy. The
figures of the Gnostic, the holy man and the mystic are all sequels
of the Israelite prophet.[33] They reflect a mode of religiosity which
is characterized by high intensity. It is centrifugal by nature and
emphasizes sectarianism and polemics, esoteric knowledge (*gnosis*)
and charisma. The other mode of religiosity, obviously much more
common than the first one, is centripetal. It favours an ecumenical
attitude, contents itself with a widely shared faith (*pistis*), and reflects,
in Weberian parlance, the routinization of the new religious movement. This is the mode of priests and bishops, rather than that of
martyrs and holy men. These two main modes of religiosity, high-

Sizgorich, *Violence and Belief in Late Antiquity: Militant Devotion in Christianity and Islam* (Philadelphia, PA, 2009).
32 This is developed in Stroumsa, *Barbarian Philosophy*, 44–56.
33 Cf. Stroumsa, *End of Sacrifice*, ch. 1.

versus low-intensity, exist simultaneously and cross the boundaries of religious communities. They offer a tool permitting us to follow the transformations of religion in late antiquity in general, and in ancient Christianity in particular, without becoming prisoners of the traditional categories of patristic literature. Through the dialectical relationship between these two modes of religiosity, one can follow the complex transformations of ancient Christianity in its broad religious context.

Christianity, which had started as a Jewish heresy, soon turned the tables and made the Jews into the first Christian heretics, who had rejected the correct understanding of their own Scriptures. This transformation would be completed in the sixth century with Justinian's legal measures, which transformed the Jews into a community (or more precisely a web of communities) of tolerated heretics. The 'cunning of reason', to use Hegel's pregnant phrase, would then see the early Muslims apply this approach to the Christians themselves. Under the caliphate, the Christians would also become a community (or web of communities) of tolerated heretics, who, like the Jews, had intentionally distorted the one, true message of God, first proclaimed by Abraham and last retrieved by Muḥammad.

Hebrew University of Jerusalem and University of Oxford

JUSTIN'S CHRISTIAN PHILOSOPHY: NEW POSSIBILITIES FOR RELATIONS BETWEEN JEWS, GRAECO-ROMANS AND CHRISTIANS

by A. D. R. HAYES

I dentity is always a complicated and negotiated reality, whether personal or communal, and this is certainly true for Christian identity in the second century CE. This century was the setting for many complicated changes that gave birth to Christianity as it is commonly understood. Naming, and the use of the terms 'outsiders' and 'followers of Christ' to define those we would call 'Christians', were important parts of this process. Examining how early Christians presented themselves can help us to understand the development of both Christianity and Judaism, and also to appreciate better how the early Christians saw themselves. Justin Martyr (100–65) is a central figure in this task. This essay will analyse his presentation, at a crucial point in history, of what it meant to be a follower of Christ.

Information about Justin's life and background is limited and comes almost exclusively from his own texts. Justin describes himself as a Samaritan, but there is little to suggest he was ever actually part of the Samaritan religious tradition; on the contrary, the evidence suggests a pagan upbringing.[1] While the distinctions between pagan, Jewish and Christian in Justin's period may not be as stratified as once thought, and their definitions can be seen to have a certain amount of fluidity, Justin nonetheless was uniquely qualified to address these traditions: he was a philosophically trained pagan, brought up around the Jewish tradition (as practised by the Samaritans), and a late convert to become a follower of Jesus.[2] He was the inventor of the tradition of genuine engagement with non-Christians on their own terms, using the instruments of their own ideological heritage.[3]

---

[1] Justin's grandfather, Bacchius, had a Greek name, while his father, Priscus, had a Latin name, as did Justin.

[2] Indeed, the term 'Christian' must be used loosely with reference to this period, as representing something which is only beginning to become established as what modern readers would recognize by the term.

[3] Sara Parvis, 'Justin Martyr and the Apologetic Tradition', in Denis Minns and

Recent years have brought something of a revival in Justin studies. As Minns and Parvis note, Justin has been called a philosopher ever since Tertullian.[4] However, recent Justin scholarship has been moving away from the examination of his philosophical credentials – the 'Justin of the Apologies', in Slusser's phrase – to focus on the ways in which Justin reveals the contemporaneous and reciprocal development of two new traditions,[5] 'Judaism' and 'Christianity' – the 'Justin of the Dialogue with Trypho'.[6] Yet Justin saw himself as both a philosopher and a Christian, without any sense of necessary incompatibility: he saw himself as a Christian philosopher in a very natural way. It is important that Justin is not seen as a cynical evangelical exporter of Christianity under the guise of philosophy.[7] Such an assumption, which has been fairly common in Justin scholarship, assumes too easy and mutually exclusive a distinction between philosophy and Christianity (or Judaism) as religious systems or cultures.[8] Such a distinction between philosophy and 'faith' is more appropriate with reference to later writers such as Tatian, Irenaeus and Tertullian than is the case for Justin.[9] Nonetheless, Hyldahl and Joly wanted to deny that Justin could be considered a genuine philosopher at all,[10] while

Paul Foster, eds, *Justin Martyr and his Worlds* (Minneapolis, MN, 2007), 115–27, at 123.

4 *Justin, Philosopher and Martyr: Apologies*, ed. Denis Minns and Paul Parvis, Oxford Early Christian Texts (Oxford, 2009), 59.

5 Daniel Boyarin has argued that the nature of heresy is not only emerging at this time but is being created dialectically by 'Christians' and 'Jews' ruling each other in and out and forming new standards of belonging in the process. Boyarin's thesis is not that these two groups witness to one another's existence; these are not two religions or obvious diametric poles of one, but rather they are differing strands, wide and varied with different points of overlap in different places, and in the course of their conversation they invent one another as new identities: Daniel Boyarin, 'Justin Martyr invents Judaism', *ChH* 70 (2001), 427–61, at 438; idem, 'Rethinking Jewish Christianity: An Argument for dismantling a Dubious Category (to which is appended a Correction of my Border Lines)', *Jewish Quarterly Review* 99 (2009), 7–36.

6 Michael Slusser, 'Justin Scholarship: Trends and Trajectories', in Minns and Foster, eds, *Justin Martyr and his Worlds*, 13–21. Trypho appears to have been a Hellenistic Jew.

7 Rebecca Lyman, 'Justin and Hellenism: Some Postcolonial Perspectives', ibid. 160–8, at 163.

8 Ibid. 163–5.

9 Rebecca Lyman, 'The Politics of Passing: Justin Martyr's Conversion as a Problem of "Hellenization"', in Kenneth Mills and Anthony Grafton, eds, *Conversion in Late Antiquity and the Early Middle Ages; Seeing and Believing* (Rochester, NY, 2003), 36–60, at 45.

10 Niels Hyldahl, *Philosophie und Christentum. Eine Interpretation der Einleitung zum*

Barnard and Henry Chadwick confidently understood Justin as presenting a vision of Christianity which was compatible and in continuity with philosophy.[11] These two positions, one denying Justin's philosophical credentials and one endorsing them, are really two sides of the same coin; both proceed on the basis of what these authors think philosophy is, rather than by noticing the subtlety of the ways in which Justin uses the category of philosophy.[12]

This essay will argue that what matters is not the extent to which Justin was a philosopher, middle Platonist or otherwise, or whether he appears to present a continuity between philosophy and faith. Justin is not offering a translation of one complete (Christian) tradition into another complete (philosophical) tradition. The argument Justin makes about the nature and source of truth – which arguably reflects contemporary approaches in non-Christian Hellenic authors such as Atticus and Numenius[13] – necessitates the presence of honour and truth in philosophy. For Justin, Christian faith is the highest form of a Hellenistic project, which is to say that it inhabits the same cultural space, not standing completely outside it, and yet offers an alternative account of the manner in which the aims, the virtues and cultural goals of Hellenism, such as truth, wisdom and philosophy, ought to be realized.[14] It is this presentation of a Christian truth internal to the philosophical project which is most interesting and which underpins Justin's attempt to clarify what a follower of Christ is to Graeco-Romans and to Jews (who, of course, are also Graeco-Romans).[15]

Dialog Justins (Copenhagen, 1966); Robert Joly, *Christianisme et philosophie. Études sur Justin et les Apologistes grecs du deuxième siècle* (Brussels, 1973).

[11] Thus Leslie Barnard thought Justin evidenced Platonism as a 'valid preparation for the Gospel': *Justin Martyr: His Life and Thought* (Cambridge, 1967), 38; see also Henry Chadwick, *Early Christian Thought in the Classical Tradition: Studies in Justin, Clement and Origen* (Oxford, 1966).

[12] *Apologies*, ed. Minns and Parvis, 59.

[13] Lyman, 'Justin and Hellenism', 167.

[14] Ibid. 168.

[15] Christians ought also to be considered Graeco-Romans, just as people of many traditions who have grown up in Europe ought to be considered 'Western': sharing a transnational cultural history, even if they have strong roots in traditions that might present challenges to elements of Western culture. Being 'westernized', say a westernized Yemeni or Iranian, does not make that person only Western. There is a hybridity involved that allows the person to stand both within and at a distance from the 'Western tradition'. This is how I am using the terms 'Christian' and 'Jew' in relation

SHAME-NAME

Justin's texts are not only appeals to authorities and defences of Christianity; they are also attempts at definition, gestures towards clarifying what a follower of Christ is and who can and who cannot be considered to be such. Attention to Justin's texts reveals that his audiences appear to share an understanding that the name Christian implies wrongdoing; it is primarily a shame-name. Justin suggests that Christians are considered by the authorities to be intrinsically bad, which is why the name itself is cause enough for prosecution without inquiry into behaviour or beliefs:[16]

> Now something is not to be judged to be either good or bad by the name it is called without consideration of the actions which are associated with that name. In fact, in so far as you can draw anything from the name alleged against us, we are most kind hearted ... if any of those accused becomes a denier and simply says that he is not a Christian you release him, as though you were in no way able to convict him if doing wrong.[17]

Justin's use of the term 'Christian' (*Christianos*) often reads as though he is reflecting reported speech about his own people.[18] The majority of uses are in relation to things done against the Christians by outsiders, reflecting the manner in which outsiders see them. In the *Dialogue* Justin implores Trypho not to be put off by the death 'which awaits every Christian'.[19] This reads as if Justin may be quoting a non-Christian source rather than offering his own description. In a similar manner, he uses the phrase 'the godless heresy of the Christians' (*hairēsin atheon Christianōn*), which appears to be of Jewish origin since it is the title that the Jewish leaders sent out representatives to announce.[20] This is the

to 'Graeco-Roman'; part of that world, deeply so, yet with alternative perspectives inherent in their position.

[16] Justin, *First Apology* [hereafter: *1 Apol.*] 4; *Second Apology* [hereafter: *2 Apol.*] 2.

[17] *1 Apol.* 4.1, 6 (*Apologies*, ed. Minns and Parvis, 87).

[18] Justin and other early Fathers often speak of Christians as a distinct people or race, an ethnicity defined by faith but an ethnicity all the same: see Denise K. Buell, *Why this New Race? Ethnic Reasoning in Early Christianity* (New York, 2005).

[19] Justin, *Dialogue with Trypho* 44.1 (*The Writings of Saint Justin Martyr*, transl. Thomas B. Falls, Fathers of the Church [Washington DC, 1977], 213).

[20] *Dial.* 17.1 (*Writings*, ed. Falls, 173).

first appearance in the *Dialogue* of the term 'Christian', which is introduced as connoting ignominy attributed by a community of people who are not part of the group who follow Christ. Justin's account of this persecution of Christians by Jews may be exaggerated to make the rhetorical point that the Jews always kill the messengers of their God, thus proving the truth of who Christ was.[21] However, there is no reason to doubt that some propaganda against Christians was a reality among the Jews, and so the shame-name status of the term 'Christian' ought to be taken seriously, albeit balanced by an awareness of Justin's rhetorical aims.[22]

'Christian' is not yet a fixed title. First and foremost Christians participate in the name of Christ: people become 'disciples in the name of Christ' (*matheteuomenous eis to onoma tou Christou*)[23] and it is his name that followers will not deny.[24] Those who follow Jesus share in his name by association with him. But Justin suggests that many who claim to follow Jesus and who are considered by outsiders to be Christians are in fact abusing the name of Christ by their association with it. It is true that there are examples of Justin speaking of 'us Christians',[25] but in general he prefers to talk about 'those taught by Christ' or 'who follow Christ's teaching'; this allows him to exclude those do not follow Christ's teachings but only appear to be his followers. Similarly, although not uncontroversially, Peter Tomson has suggested that the term 'Jew' (*Ioudaios*) in the Graeco-Roman period is a designation used by non-Jews, and only deployed by Jews when speaking of themselves from a non-Jewish perspective in non-Jewish contexts; he contrasts it with the insider name of 'Israel'.[26] Citing numerous counter-examples, Margaret Williams believes that Tomson has overstated his case, but she acknowledges that he has identified one of a legitimate 'range of connotations' of a term not easily defined in

[21] Judith M. Lieu, 'Accusations of Jewish Persecution in Early Christian Sources, with particular Reference to *Justin Martyr* and the *Martyrdom of Polycarp*', in Graham Stanton and Guy Stroumsa, eds, *Tolerance and Intolerance in Early Judaism and Christianity* (Cambridge, 1998), 279–95, at 281.

[22] Daniel Boyarin, 'Justin Martyr invents Judaism', *ChH* 70 (2001), 427–61, at 434–5.

[23] *Dial.* 39.2 (*Writings*, transl. Falls, 206).

[24] *Dial.* 96.2 (*Writings*, transl. Falls, 299).

[25] *Dial.* 78.10, 110.2 (*Writings*, transl. Falls, 273, 317). .

[26] Peter J. Tomson, *'If this be from Heaven ...': Jesus and the New Testament Authors in their Relationship to Judaism*, Biblical Seminar 76 (Sheffield, 2001), 110.

this period.[27] Something similar may perhaps be said of 'Christian' (*Christianos*) in Justin's time: a range of meanings are possible, one of which is externally orientated. Justin sometimes uses the name in a way that implies a level of internal identification with it but, as noted above, he generally uses it in ways which seem to reflect a pejorative definition from outside the Christian community and himself prefers to describe followers of Christ as pupils of a master.

Justin demonstrates the derogatory function of the name 'Christian' for those who do not believe in Christ by recounting his pre-conversion understanding: 'For I myself, too, when I was delighting in the doctrines of Plato, and heard the Christians slandered, and saw them fearless of death, and of all other things which are counted fearful, perceived that it was impossible that they could be living in wickedness and pleasure.'[28] Here Justin describes himself as an outsider, delighting in Plato, recalling speech he heard about a group called 'Christians' and observing them. By portraying himself in this way he is attempting to report what appears to be the case to outsiders. His point is that Christians are considered by outsiders to be a unified group under a single name (hence his claim that all are called Christians whether they agree with each other or not[29] and that all are cast together as irreligious and unjust, regardless of conduct[30]), worthy of being maligned, either because they are immoral or because they do not keep the law.

Though the use of the term 'Christian' by outsiders appears to be pejorative, it also appears to lack clear definition. In the *Second Apology* 2.1 an unnamed woman becomes a Christian and seeks a divorce from her licentious husband. As a rebuttal he brings the charge of being a Christian against her. As Thorsteinsson notes, the charge brought against her is nothing more than that she was a Christian; it is otherwise devoid of content.[31] As the other characters in this drama come forward, it becomes obvious that further charges or evidence are not required to secure a conviction. We

[27] Margaret H. Williams, *Jews in a Graeco-Roman Environment*, Wissenschaftliche Untersuchungen zum Neuen Testament I 312 (Tübingen, 2013), 267–79.

[28] *2 Apol.* 12.1 (*Apologies*, ed. Minns and Parvis, 317).

[29] *1 Apol.* 7.3; 26.6 (*Apologies*, ed. Minns and Parvis, 93, 151).

[30] *1 Apol.* 4.8 (*Apologies*, ed. Minns and Parvis, 89).

[31] Runar M. Thorsteinsson, 'The Literary Genre and Purpose of Justin's Second Apology: A Critical Review with Insights from Ancient Epistolography', *Harvard Theological Review* 105 (2012), 91–114, at 108.

know that confessing to the name 'Christian' is guilt enough, but we also know that there are those who are considered by outsiders to be Christian whom Justin wants to exclude from that category. In his view, it is the existence of such people – who would later be termed heretics – that obscures what is true and good about what Christ taught, because they claim to follow Christ but in reality follow different teachings. These non-Christian 'Christians' present a threat to Justin's attempt to give positive content to what a Christian is. Thorsteinsson has recently argued that Justin's comment in the *Second Apology* 1.2 that those who have accepted that the fruit of injustice and licentiousness is punishment are known as Christians ought to be considered evidence for the independence of the *Second Apology* from the *First Apology* as a separate composition because it is, he believes, perfectly obvious that such people are Christians within the context of the *First Apology*.[32] This, I would argue, is mistaken: the opposite is the case. This is why Justin tries so hard in the *First Apology*, with much repetition, to establish who Christians are, and who they are not. The comment made in the *Second Apology* is perfectly consistent with this definition, explaining that those who are to be considered followers of Christ are those who live the virtuous Christlike life. Christian identity, Justin implies, is internally disputed, but it is also externally undifferentiated in a pernicious way. Justin attempts to change this situation, for, as Moll suggests, '[h]is mission is to clear the Christian name.'[33] He does this by presenting faith in Christ as falling within the shape of Graeco-Roman philosophy, not in order to supplement but to reinforce and modify Jewish theology, producing a version of Christianity that appears more attractive and intelligible to both Graeco-Romans and Jews. Early Christian apologetics may usefully be thought of as an attempt to clarify and define what Christianity is, as much as defence of the faith. That is, apologetics should not be thought of as an attempt to defend Christianity against persecution only but also, by its appeal to outsiders, it should be seen as attempting to gain recognition for one position as Christian to the necessary exclusion of others. It is as much a matter of internal politics as external.

---

[32] Ibid. 96.
[33] Sebastian Moll, 'Justin and the Pontic Wolf', in Parvis and Foster, eds, *Justin Martyr and his Worlds*, 145–51, at 149.

PHILOSOPHER OF CHRIST

Justin's method in circumventing this prejudicial understanding of Christians is to emphasize the ways in which Christian discipleship has the same aspirations as the Graeco-Roman traditions; in short, the ways in which it is a philosophy:

> But my spirit was immediately set on fire, and an affection for the prophets, and for those who are friends of Christ, took hold of me; while pondering on his words, I discovered that his was the only sure and useful philosophy. Thus it is that I am now a philosopher.[34]

Justin does not say here that he is a Christian but rather that he is a philosopher. People are called, accused of, or charged with being Christians, and it can be a more or less accurate description of certain groups of people, depending on the doctrines they follow. The doctrines are the centre. Philosophers have doctrines and the doctrines Justin keeps are those of Christ. At its most basic, 'philosophy was the guide of life and practical ethics its most important object'.[35] Justin has a practical approach to philosophy. Philosophy to him is that which is safe and profitable. That is, the results of philosophy represent its value. This was an authentic and dominant perspective at the time.[36] In short, philosophy was a way or path of life, very close to what in modern times is seen as a religion.

It cannot be said that Hellenistic philosophical culture was atheistic and non-religious, for if it were then the charge of atheism against Christians would be nonsensical. Philosophers were not isolated from religious practice of one kind or another. However, the Jews were outsiders because of the exclusivity of their cult,[37] and the cultic traditions of nations – like the Jews – were exclusive enterprises in which a people's own god or gods were worshipped to the exclusion of all others. If such cultic practices could be shown to be ancestral they were generally protected, but exclusive ancestral cults entailed an alternative vision of life and were thus

---

34 *Dial.* 8.1 (*Writings*, transl. Falls, 160).
35 J. C. M. van Winden, ed., *An Early Christian Philosopher: Justin Martyr's Dialogue with Trypho Chapters One to Nine*, Philosophia Patrum 1 (Leiden, 1971), 119.
36 Ibid.
37 Tomson, *'If this be from Heaven'*, 37.

to some extent inherently political.[38] The difference, at least theoretically, between philosophy and cultic nations was that one automatically belonged to the cultic nation but philosophical doctrines were things that could be acquired, combined and abandoned much more freely, as is shown by Justin's progression through the philosophical schools recounted in the introduction to the *Dialogue*. The philosophy of Justin's age was characterized by an eclecticism that allowed it to imbue and to criticize a wide collection of traditions and in which philosophical speculation could stand apart, at least theoretically, from cultic practice.[39] That is, it was open rather than closed. This is why Justin can repeatedly say that philosophers widely disagree, and that some even insult the gods yet do not have their philosophical credentials doubted.[40] Moving between philosophical traditions was not, then, as dangerous or as criminal as converting to a non-indigenous cult.

Yet in understanding Christianity as philosophy Justin is not condoning a pluralistic approach in which Christianity might be one philosophical option among others of equal standing. For Justin, Christian faith is in fact the primordial form of philosophy rediscovered; the original and ancient purity over and against its decaying progeny in Greek systems.[41] Justin travelled through other philosophies before reaching their culmination in Christianity, which contains all that is good but rejects anything that contradicts its core tenets. As well as being a practical mode of life, philosophy, for Justin, has at its heart the following of the universal truth. Any true philosopher – which he flatters rulers by asserting that they are[42] – must seek reasonableness and truth, and must recognize it on seeing it. In presenting Christianity, Justin is presenting the truth rather than a private national cult, and he believes that the rulers ought to be able to see this and to recognize not only its similarity to other philosophies, but also its superiority and ultimate truth.[43]

---

[38] Williams, *Jews in a Graeco-Roman Environment*, 42.
[39] Barnard, *Justin Martyr*, 35; G. E.M. de Sainte Croix, *Christian Persecution, Martyrdom and Orthodoxy*, ed. Michael Whitby and Joseph Streeter (Oxford, 2006).
[40] *1 Apol.* 4.8–9; 7.3–4; 26.6 (*Apologies*, ed. Minns and Parvis, 89, 93, 151).
[41] Van Winden, ed., *Early Christian Philosopher*, 17.
[42] *1 Apol.* 2.2; 3.2; 12.5; *2 Apol.* 15.4 (*Apologies*, ed. Minns and Parvis, 81, 85, 105, 269).
[43] *2 Apol.* 15.3 (*Apologies*, ed. Minns and Parvis, 269).

This understanding of Christianity as part of the universal enterprise of philosophy achieves a great deal for Justin. It is put to work to remove obstacles in the way of the relationship of Christians to both Graeco-Romans and Jews by acquitting Christianity of the appearance of being a radical form of Jewish proselytism, a relevant complaint to both Jew and Graeco-Roman, to the Jew because they appear incomplete or blasphemous proselytes and to the Graeco-Roman because they appear to have betrayed their own heritage and gods. Indeed, Justin goes so far as to claim the best Greek philosophers as honorary Christians. Smith draws on Skarsaune to argue that Justin did not necessarily believe that they would be saved but was making a counter-charge: Graeco-Romans call Christians atheists and Justin retorts that they (or the best of their tradition at least) are in fact Christian; Christianity is internal to their own tradition because the philosophers have borrowed the revelation through Moses and the prophets.[44] All philosophy, or at least all good philosophy, is Christian, because what is Christian is that which is universal and true.

In order to reach the point of claiming that all philosophies are parasitic upon the true Christian philosophy, Justin must first ground the claim that Christianity is a philosophy. To do this, he must rely on the popular reverence for the life and *dicta* of the founders of philosophical schools and demonstrate that Christianity, whose founder is Christ, ought to be considered no different from these in this respect.[45] However this should not imply an acceptance of the plurality of philosophical schools. For Justin there is only one true and profitable philosophy, which comes through the prophets of Israel; it contrasts with the contemporary philosophical scene, which has become a celebrity-obsessed patronage system. In Justin's view, philosophy ought to be unified rather than divided into competing schools. It ought to be one because it has been designed to be a means by which the one true God is revealed.

CHRISTIAN PHILOSOPHY

To Justin's mind, truth and philosophy are almost synonymous. By

44 Shawn C. Smith, 'Was Justin Martyr an Inclusivist?', *Stone-Campbell Journal* 10 (2007), 193–212, at 199–200.
45 Barnard, *Justin Martyr*, 28.

virtue of being true, Christianity shows up all the pseudo-philoso-
phies, but also, because it values truth in itself, acknowledges where
they have come close to the truth which God revealed through
the prophets and in Christ.

> I will explain to you, I replied, my views on this subject.
> Philosophy is indeed one's greatest possession, and is most
> precious in the sight of God, to whom it alone leads us and
> to whom it unites us, and they in truth are holy men who
> have applied themselves to philosophy. But, many have failed
> to discover the nature of philosophy, and the reason why it
> was sent down to men; otherwise, there would be no Platon-
> ists, or Stoics, or Peripatetics, or Theoretics, or Pythagoreans,
> since this science of philosophy is always one and the same.
> Now, let me tell you why it has at length become so diversi-
> fied. They who first turned to philosophy, and, as a result, were
> deemed illustrious men, were succeeded by men who gave no
> time to the investigation of truth, but, amazed at the courage
> and self-control of their teachers as well as with the novelty
> of their teachings, held that to be the truth which each had
> learned from his own teacher. And they transmitted to their
> successors such opinions, and others like them, and so they
> became known by the name of him who was considered the
> father of the doctrine.[46]

Clearly for Justin the chain of truth in philosophy has been
corrupted. No longer is philosophy practised as it should be.
Justin does know of an exception to this, however. He will reveal
another chain of practitioners who have preserved faithfully the
truth which leads to God – the prophets of Israel.

The prophets spoke by inspiration of the divine spirit (indeed,
Justin sometimes speaks as if the Spirit itself speaks rather than the
prophets) and so their philosophy is that of God; furthermore they
spoke about Christ, who completed their work. This, then, is the
philosophy Justin follows. It is styled after Christ – the founder –
but it goes back beyond the ancients, because it is from the one
true God. The prophets bear witness to this philosophy and Christ
fulfils and exemplifies it. Indeed, Justin's primary description of

---

[46] *Dial.* 2.1-2 (*Writings*, transl. Falls, 149).

Christ is that of a teacher (*didaskalos*). He makes two references to being friends of Christ (*philoî*),[47] two to becoming acquaintances (*epiginōskein*) of Christ, those who come to know him fully,[48] and a few to being disciples (*mathētaí*)[49] – as distinct from discussion of the twelve – which in any case really means those who follow a teacher. By contrast, the instances in which Christ is spoken of as having taught, or as being a teacher, number nearly thirty.[50] Without overemphasis, since the contrast between teachers and worshippers under the episcopate in the second century has perhaps been somewhat overdrawn,[51] this places Christ in the context of wider Hellenistic practice rather than treating Christianity as a separate 'religious' phenomenon. In the *Second Apology* it is not said of the woman who converts that she became a 'Christian', but rather that:

> she came to the knowledge of the teachings of Christ; she became soberminded, and endeavoured to persuade her husband likewise to be temperate, citing the teaching of Christ. And likewise … Lucius in the same chapter when asked whether he was a Christian? … being conscious of his duty, and the nobility of it through the teaching of Christ, he confessed his discipleship in the divine virtue. Lucius was a disciple [one under the rule and discipline] of the teachings of Christ.[52]

The woman was persuaded, and attempted to persuade, on the basis of these teachings. These converts are made, not by ritual, custom or birth rite of an *ethnos*, but by becoming disciples and pupils under their one and only master, just as Pythagoreans have their master and Marcionites theirs. For Justin, however, Christ is the only master who has genuine knowledge of God that he can pass on.

---

47 *Dial.* 8.1; 139.4 (*Writings*, transl. Falls, 160, 361).
48 *Dial.* 8.2; 44.4 (*Writings*, transl. Falls, 160, 214).
49 *Dial.* 35.2; 39.2 (*Writings*, transl. Falls, 201, 206); *1 Apol.* 15.6 (*Apologies*, ed. Minns and Parvis, 115).
50 *Dial.* 18.1; 32.5; 48.4; 49.3; 53.1; 76.3; 96.3; 105.5; 107; 108.2 (*Writings*, transl. Falls, 160, 195, 220, 221, 228, 269, 300, 312, 314, 315); *1 Apol.* 4.7; 6.2; 8.3; 12.9; 13.3; 14.4; 15.9; 16.4; 19.6; 21.1; 23.2; 32.2; 33.5; 46.1; 67.8 (*Apologies*, ed. Minns and Parvis, 89, 91, 95, 107, 111, 113, 115, 119, 129, 131, 139, 169, 173, 199, 261); *2 Apol.* 2.2; 3.1; 8.5; 10.8 (*Apologies*, ed. Minns and Parvis, 273, 281, 301, 313).
51 Lyman, 'Politics of Passing', 41.
52 *2 Apol.* 2.2 (*Apologies*, ed. Minns and Parvis, 273).

Philosophical Acquittal

Justin's insistence on Christ being a teacher, and on the following of Christ being a philosophy, undermines (at least in his view) much of what stands against Christians. Graham Stanton has argued that Trypho's friends were probably Graeco-Roman proselytes to Judaism[53] – which is why Trypho identifies himself early in the *Dialogue* as a Hebrew born of the circumcision and thus as belonging to the Jewish community – and that conversion is a key background topic in the *Dialogue*.[54] The *Dialogue* needs to be understood against the background of the illegality of converting to any novel sect, which was seen as betraying one's Graeco-Roman roots. As de Sainte Croix remarks: 'Gibbon expressed the contrast perfectly when he wrote, "The Jews were a people which followed, the Christians a sect which deserted, the religion of their fathers".'[55] The genius of understanding Christianity as a philosophy is that it allows Justin, at least theoretically, to circumvent suspicions of conversion because the path he follows is not a private cultic devotion but is one of devotion to the universal truth, recorded in the ancient writings of the prophets, and taught by Christ, who approached God in truth and righteousness, as all philosophy ought to do.

Presenting Christians as philosophers rather than as a rival national or novel cultic group also saves Christians from another Graeco-Roman accusation. The *First Apology* suggests that those to whom Justin speaks expect Christians to pose a nationalistic threat:

> And when you hear that we look for a kingdom, you suppose, without making any inquiry, that we speak of a human kingdom; whereas we speak of that which is with God, as appears also from the confession of their faith made by those who are charged with being Christians, though they know that death is the punishment awarded to him who so confesses.

---

[53] Graham Stanton, 'Justin Martyr's Dialogue with Trypho: Group Boundaries, "Proselytes" and "God-fearers"', in idem and Stroumsa, eds, *Tolerance and Intolerance*, 263–78, at 265.

[54] Ibid. Stanton sees much of the discussion as reflecting degrees of adherence by Christians to Judaism and understands Justin to be attempting to work within that perspective to win over those who are undecided.

[55] De Sainte Croix, *Christian Persecution*, 8.

> For if we looked for a human kingdom, we should also deny
> our Christ, that we might not be slain …[56]

The Graeco-Romans assumed that Christians were seeking to establish an earthly kingdom, presumably one that could rival Rome. This fear was understandable when placed against the background of recent war in Judaea, in which Rome had been challenged and at times embarrassed by people who claimed the same God and heritage as Christians did. Justin is quick to deny this and to assert that any such claim would be contrary to what it means to trust in Christ and his teachings. The followers of Christ are not a nation, a people of the land or government; they are disciples of a philosophy, and disciples of philosophies do not attempt to found nations but seek only to live by truth.

As a defence against another common charge, that of atheism, Justin's philosophical position is somewhat weaker. Jews were tolerated — to the extent that they were — because their religion was perceived as belonging to their ancestral culture and because they would still, in the time of the temple, offer sacrifices on behalf of the emperor.[57] Christians resembled Jews in their radical monotheism (seen by the Graeco-Romans as atheism), but could not claim that their religion was their culture. De Sainte Croix argues that it was chiefly for this reason that Christians faced charges before Roman governors:

> except to a limited extent in the time of Valerian, and more
> seriously under Diocletian, what I have called the positive
> side of Christianity is never officially attacked: persecution did
> not extend to any aspect of the Christian religion other than
> its refusal to acknowledge other gods. No attempt was ever
> made, even in the general persecutions, to prohibit Christians
> from worshipping their own god in private, although Valerian
> and Diocletian, but not Decius, forbade them to assemble for
> common worship, and Diocletian also ordered the destruction
> of churches and the confiscation of sacred books and church
> property. As the deputy prefect of Egypt said to Bishop Diony-
> sius of Alexandria in 257, 'Who prevents you from worship-

---

56 *1 Apol.* 11.1–2 (*Apologies*, ed. Minns and Parvis, 101).
57 De Sainte Croix, *Christian Persecution*, 135.

ping your own god also, if he is a god, along with the natural gods?'[58]

Justin's appeal against this sort of thinking proceeds on the basis of the indulgence given to philosophers on such topics:

> For of philosophy, too, some assume the name and the garb who do nothing worthy of their profession; and you are well aware, that those of the ancients whose opinions and teachings were quite diverse, are yet all called by the one name of philosophers. And of these some taught atheism; and the poets who have flourished among you raise a laugh out of the uncleanness of Jupiter with his own children. And those who now adopt such instruction are not restrained by you; but, on the contrary, you bestow prizes and honours upon those who euphoniously insult the gods.[59]

Indeed, Justin even tries to present himself and Christians in a similar light to the best philosophers, as in the *Second Apology* 3.4, where he relates that he has questioned Crescens and found him to know nothing. There, as Thorsteinsson notes,

> the reader would presumably also have understood that Justin was assuming the role of Socrates as 'the question' par excellence (referred to in 3.6), who, as Justin reminds his readers in 10.5 was (unreasonably) charged and put to death for the very same crimes as the Christians, namely, atheism and impiety.[60]

The charge of atheism against Socrates and its similarity to that levelled at Christians also appear twice in the *First Apology*.[61]

Furthermore, Justin thinks that the Christian philosophy should be respected by rulers as much as the best of their own tradition: As he says in the *First Apology*: 'Receive us, at least like these [Empedocles, Pythagoras, Plato and Xenocrates], since we believe in God not less, but rather more, than they do.'[62] In his identity as a follower of the philosophy of Christ, then, Justin sees himself as at least an equal of other philosophers and of the rulers whom

58   Ibid.
59   *1 Apol.* 4.8–9 (*Apologies*, ed. Minns and Parvis, 89).
60   Thorsteinsson, 'Justin's Second Apology', 111.
61   *1 Apol.* 5.3; 46.3 (*Apologies*, ed. Minns and Parvis, 91, 201).
62   *1 Apol.* 18.6 (*Apologies*, ed. Minns and Parvis, 125).

he flatters as philosophers in order to emphasize his equality with them.[63] In establishing this, Justin quotes the famous dictum from the *Republic* which says that a city-state will only find prosperity when both rulers and subjects are philosophers.[64]

Being a philosopher is no real defence against charges of atheism, however. As de Sainte Croix points out, 'the vital difference [between Christians and philosophers] was, of course, that the philosophers, whatever they might believe, and even write down for circulation among educated folk, would have been perfectly willing to perform any cult act required of them and that was what mattered'.[65] The use of Socrates as philosopher-victim is inspired, but Justin's ruse is not likely to work here because philosophical speculation is not equal to atheism for Graeco-Romans. Many philosophers may say and do things that seem insulting to the gods but, as de Sainte Croix makes clear, they still make offerings to the gods. Christians are non-conformists and threaten the communal spiritual life which sustains Roman society. On these grounds Christians may make themselves more vulnerable even than Jews.

Although most probably unsuccessful, it is apparent that Justin's presentation of Christianity as a philosophical project had the potential to solve various problems in the relationships between Christians and Graeco-Romans and to make Christianity seem like a true and original version of the Graeco-Roman philosophical tradition. Christians should no longer be thought of as shameful because Christians are not converts to something new, nor are they atheists or nationalists; rather they are philosophers who know the original philosophy. Without philosophical truth Justin would not have a legitimate approach to Graeco-Romans because Christians are de facto disreputable. However, as redefined, Christians, borrowing from the Graeco-Roman tradition, are the paragon of virtue.

THE DIVINE PHILOSOPHY AND THE JEWS

The utility of this presentation does not end there, however. It has particular power when it comes to Christian-Jewish relations. At the beginning of the *Dialogue* Trypho recognizes Justin as a philos-

---

[63] *Apologies*, ed. Minns and Parvis, 60.
[64] *1 Apol.* 3.3 (*Apologies*, ed. Minns and Parvis, 85); cf. Plato, *Republic* 5.473c–d.
[65] De Sainte Croix, *Christian Persecution*, 136–7.

opher and beckons him over on this understanding, explaining that he and his friends would like to learn from him, revealing some philosophical education and a predilection never to despise philosophers.[66] Here Justin deliciously anticipates that Trypho will later reveal that Jews are supposed to have no communication with Christians, but at this point Trypho does not know Justin is a Christian.[67] Trypho and Justin both agree that philosophy is truly concerned with God and his care for the world. It is obvious, then, that in adopting philosophy Justin has found ground which both Christians and Jews can inhabit and which is as attractive to Jews as it is to Graeco-Romans. Furthermore, being an exponent of the concept of the divine philosopher affords Justin a route out of a number of predicaments. Trypho reveals that he cannot understand how Christians can claim to follow God and not keep his commandments.[68] They do not separate themselves or live differently from Graeco-Romans, nor are they circumcised. These are not incidental quibbles for Trypho: as Bruce Chilton has pointed out, purity was a central concern for the Judaism emerging in the second century.[69] To be in the people of God, it had to be evident that one was in the people of God. Indeed, Justin admits directly to Trypho that the law is not the basis of the relationship with God of the follower of Christ. There is no other God but the God of Abraham, Isaac and Jacob, but for Christians 'our hope is not through Moses or through the Law, otherwise our customs would be the same as yours'.[70] Trypho's complaint and Justin's admission neatly do the work of emphasizing that Christians are not proselytes to Judaism and have thus not contravened Roman law by converting. To Trypho, they appear to be incomplete or interrupted proselytes to Judaism. For Justin, however, Christians are not proselytes but followers of Christ, who taught them the ways of the Father and how to please him. This being the case, Christians have access to God and the promises he made to the Jews without having to be Jews:

---

[66] *Dial.* 1.2 (*Writings*, transl. Falls, 147).
[67] *Dial.* 38.1 (*Writings*, transl. Falls, 204).
[68] *Dial.* 10.1 (*Writings*, transl. Falls, 162).
[69] Bruce D. Chilton, 'Justin and Israelite Prophecy', in Parvis and Foster, eds, *Justin Martyr and his Worlds*, 77–87, at 82.
[70] *Dial.* 11.1 (*Writings*, transl. Falls, 160).

Now, we are the children and co-heirs of Christ, though you cannot understand it, because you are unable to drink from the living fountain of God, but only from the broken wells which retain no water, as the Scriptures [Jer. 2.13] tell us ... Besides this, those teachers deceive themselves and you when they suppose that those who are descendants of Abraham according to the flesh will most certainly share in the eternal kingdom, even though they be faithless sinners and disobedient to God, suppositions which the Scriptures show have no foundation in fact.[71]

Christians are like Jews, they know and follow God, who is the creator and no new god of a novel cult; they inherit the promises made by him to the ancients and with all this the respectability of antiquity in the Roman world (indeed Justin's use of *presbutēs* for the 'certain old man' who converts Justin in the *Dialogue* is, as Chilton notes, designed to emphasize the antiquity and traditional nature of his wisdom rather than his temporal age),[72] but crucially they are not converts to Judaism. They are disciples or pupils of Christ in the divine philosophy[73] and this gains them those elements of Judaism which otherwise they could not legitimately claim as non-Jews. Justin has licence to speak to Jews like Trypho only as one who shows the wisdom and learning of a philosopher. Trypho would not listen simply to a 'Christian' – a half-hearted proselyte. For Justin the opportunity to relate to Jews is afforded only by his particular philosophy, which is the divine philosophy. Being the philosophy of God, Justin has the same revelation as the Jews, and indeed deeper revelation; so he can treat them as brethren, erring brethren but brethren nonetheless. A connection has been forged through philosophy that makes dialogue a possibility where it would not otherwise exist.

CONCLUSION

Justin has presented the following of Christ as the highest form of philosophical enterprise, a way of life by definition pious and true, by virtue of being the only genuine and universal philosophy. This has enabled him to engage Graeco-Romans on their own

---

[71] *Dial.* 140.1, 2 (*Writings*, transl. Falls, 363).
[72] Chilton, 'Justin', 77.
[73] *2 Apol.* 12.5 (*Apologies*, ed. Minns and Parvis, 319).

terms and to call them back to their own aspirations to truth and philosophy, and at the same time to remain a child of God without having to become a Jewish proselyte. Justin inhabits a new space where, although one changes under the tutelage of Christ, it is not required to betray one's heritage by becoming a proselyte. This also redefines the Christian-Jewish relationship, as it opens a new space for followers of God who are not failed candidates for proselytes, or at least it opens up the possibility for discussion on these grounds. Justin has not only defended Christianity, as has often been discussed, but he has redefined it, in order to change the relationship of Christians to Jews and Graeco-Romans. No more should discussion of philosophy in Justin be limited to his own educational history or his relation to the contemporary philosophical scene. The significance of philosophy in Justin is the holistic approach which such an orientation makes possible and the potential new terms of engagement it provides Christians in their encounters with Graeco-Romans and Jews.

King's College, London

THE OTHERNESS OF NON-CHRISTIANS IN THE EARLY MIDDLE AGES

by JAMES T. PALMER

Non-Christian 'others' were crucial to the definition of early medieval Christendom.[1] Many groups certainly found it important to generate a sense of belonging through shared practice, history and ideals. But the history of Christianity was a story of conflict, which from the very beginning saw a community of believers struggling against Jews and 'pagan' Romans. At the end, too, Christ warned there would be 'false prophets' and tribulations, and John of Patmos saw the ravages of Gog and Magog against the faithful.[2] When many early medieval Christians looked at 'religious others', they saw not so much 'members of religions', as they did people defined by typologies and narratives designed to express the nature and trajectory of Christendom itself.[3] This has been a recurring theme in scholarship which has sought to understand Christian views of pagans, Muslims and Jews in the period, but the effect and purpose of such rhetoric is not always fully appreciated.[4] It is the purpose of this essay, therefore, to provide a survey of attitudes towards Christendom's 'others' and, in the process, to argue for the importance of otherness for defining the early Middle Ages.

The religious and political maps of Europe changed dramatically in the early Middle Ages, redefining contrasts between Christians and non-Christians. As late as the fifth century, there was

---

[1]   Hans-Werner Goetz, *Die Wahrnehmung anderer Religionen und christlich-abendländisches Selbstverständnis im frühen Mittelalter (5.–12. Jahrhundert)* (Berlin, 2012), 10–11.

[2]   For further analysis of the importance of apocalypse for early medieval 'otherness', see James T. Palmer, 'Apocalypse Outsiders and their Uses in the Early Medieval West', in Felicitas Schnieder, Rebekka Voss and Wolfram Brandes, eds, *Völker der Endzeit: Apokalyptische Vorstellungen und politische Szenarien* (Berlin, forthcoming 2015).

[3]   Haimo, *In Apocalypsin* 2.6 (PL 117, 1028).

[4]   Robert Hoyland, *Seeing Islam as others saw it: A Survey and Evaluation of Christian, Jewish and Zoroastrian Writings on Early Islam* (New York, 1997); John Tolan, *Saracens: Islam in the Medieval European Imagination* (New York, 2002). On pagans, see Ian Wood, 'The Pagans and the Other: Varying Presentations in the Early Middle Ages', *Networks and Neighbours* 1 (2013), 1–22. On Jews, see Wolfram Drews, *The Unknown Neighbour: The Jew in the Thought of Isidore of Seville* (Leiden, 2006).

a coherent, if diverse, Roman Empire which was mostly Christian.[5] There were still pagans, and some of the classic responses to the Goths' 'Sack of Rome' in 410 – Augustine's *City of God* and Orosius's *Seven Books of History against the Pagans* – were written at least in part to meet the accusations by pagans that the empire's woes were Christianity's fault. Otherness was also supplied by the various pseudo-barbarian groups who entered and settled in the empire at this time, both because they were culturally non-Roman and because many groups rejected Roman Christianity for a while to come. The transformation of the Roman world – its fragmentations and new combinations of socio-cultural groups – meant that by the seventh century the old imagined frontiers of the Rhine and Danube had become lines to break through, as targets for political and episcopal expansion. Pagan cultures in the north and east, once far from Christian centres of gravity, were now drawn more colonially into the Christian universal.[6] And this reorientation of horizons occurred just as the Arabs spread from the Middle East as far as Spain by 711, taking Islam with them.[7] Things had changed dramatically, and fast.

There are many narratives germane to our topic which historians like to see running through these events. Such transformations naturally meant that new cultural identities were pursued and developed; and how can new groups form a sense of 'us' without a sense of 'them'?[8] For a long time we looked at *the* spread of *the* Church institutionally, often in terms of the rise of the papacy or the origins of national Churches; but in keeping with the new cultural history paradigms we might now look for the emergence and mutations of multiple 'micro-Christendoms',

---

[5]   Ramsay MacMullen, *Christianity and Paganism in the Fourth to Eighth Centuries* (New Haven, CT, 1997).

[6]   Richard Fletcher, *The Conversion of Europe: From Paganism to Christianity, 371–1386 AD* (London, 1997).

[7]   For a history drawn almost exclusively from the Latin sources, see Roger Collins, *The Arab Conquest of Spain: 710–797* (Oxford, 1989). Nicola Clarke, *The Muslim Conquest of Iberia: Medieval Arabic Narratives* (London, 2012), offers a stimulating appraisal of the Arabic sources.

[8]   Walter Pohl and Gerda Heydemann, eds, *Strategies of Identification: Ethnicity and Religion in Early Medieval Europe* (Turnhout, 2013); Walter Pohl and Helmut Reimitz, eds, *Strategies of Distinction: The Construction of Ethnic Communities, 300–800* (Leiden, 1998). Different positions are argued for in Andrew Gillett, ed., *On Barbarian Identity: Critical Approaches to Ethnicity in the Early Middle Ages* (Turnhout, 2002).

defined by the local experience and appropriation of universality.[9] Different cultural encounters generate multiple Christendoms, all coexisting. Important variables include the role of women as transmitters of culture and the ways in which institutions shaped social organization and behaviour, aristocratic and peasant.[10] I would also argue for the importance of different reading patterns, resources and levels of access from centre to centre affecting how people were conditioned to respond.[11] The shape of cultural interaction and its consequences is determined by various factors, and works at a number of levels.

Just glancing at Western Europe around the year 700 should make the importance of regional variation obvious.[12] The south of the Frankish kingdoms, which experienced the Arab conquests most directly, had a longer Roman past and more developed sociocultural links with Spain, Italy and the rest of the Mediterranean. The north-east, where most Christian expansion into pagan territory occurred, was the least Romanized and urban, except that it included the major ancient centres of Cologne and Mainz. The English kingdoms were still relatively new to Christianity and provided a unique melting pot of ideas, not least in response to Pope Gregory the Great's suggestion that they should develop practices as seemed best on the ground. Much about southern Germany is unclear but the mountains of Rhaetia witnessed some of the strongest Roman traditionalism, the greatest import of Irish culture and, by the end of the eighth century, the beginnings of some impressive and eclectic libraries. One could offer more examples, but the crucial point is this: while we may seek to generalize about Christian attitudes towards non-Christians, we

[9] The paradigm shift is best represented by Peter Brown, *The Rise of Western Christendom: Triumph and Diversity, AD 200–1000*, 2nd edn (Oxford, 2003). Old classics include Albert Hauck, *Kirchengeschichte Deutschlands*, 5 vols (Leipzig, 1898–1913); Erich Caspar, *Geschichte des Papsttum von den Anfängen bis zur Höhe der Weltherrschaft*, 2 vols (Tübingen, 1930–3); and, for the context of the present essay, J. Michael Wallace-Hadrill, *The Frankish Church* (Oxford, 1983).

[10] Julia Smith, *Europe after Rome: A New Cultural History, 500–1000* (Oxford, 2005); Chris Wickham, *Framing the Early Middle Ages: Europe and the Mediterranean 400–800* (Oxford, 2005).

[11] Rosamond McKitterick, *The Carolingians and the Written Word* (Cambridge, 1989).

[12] For an account of the period sensitive to local variations, in addition to Brown, *Rise of Western Christendom*, see Chris Wickham, *The Inheritance of Rome: A History of Europe from 400–1000* (London, 2009).

have to remember that Christendom was not homogeneous. All our examples, as we proceed, will be seen to have their own situational logic.

We begin with the case of Germanic paganism. At one level there are many references to the 'Days of the Week Gods' (Tiw, Woden, Thor, Freya), lot casting, and other beliefs and practices in sources across Northern Europe, which have encouraged modern scholars to see a relatively stable pan-Germanic religious cosmology existing for centuries.[13] Linguistic and material evidence has certainly reinforced the sense that peoples across Germania and Scandinavia were culturally similar. But at the same time the written sources pose something of a conundrum, because they were produced almost exclusively by Christians. Most Christians were not interested in the details of non-Christian practice and not a few used clichés derived from things they had read rather than seen.[14] Some writers, however, did supply more distinctive detail and, as long as we avoid appealing to an imaginary unchanging pan-Germanic pantheon of gods to fill in gaps, useful observations about the character of pagan practices can be made.[15] Nevertheless, we are always dealing with accounts of paganism in contact with Christianity, in communities in dialogue, where the presence of external observers has changed the dynamics of what is going on. These are cultural encounters in which both sides are changing. While we could extract the 'distinctive detail' from the narratives of our sources, we must also take care to understand the value of the commonplace, the misunderstood and the polemical. For that reason, we must turn to the uses of representations of 'others'.

For many writers, the otherness of pagans allowed them to

---

[13] Hilda Ellis Davidson, *Gods and Myths of Northern Europe* (London, 1964); John D. Niles, 'Pagan Survivals and Popular Belief', in Michael Herren and Michael Lapidge, eds, *The Cambridge Companion to Old English Literature* (Cambridge, 1991), 126–41; Richard North, *Heathen Gods in Old English Literature* (Cambridge, 1997). For more caution, see Alexandra Sanmark, *Power and Conversion: A Comparative Study of Christianization in Scandinavia* (Uppsala, 2004), 143–79.

[14] James T. Palmer, 'Defining Paganism in the Carolingian World', *EME* 15 (2007), 402–25. Goetz, *Wahrnehmung*, 144–63, defends the level of knowledge about pagan practices.

[15] Instructive is Ian Wood, 'Pagan Religion and Superstition East of the Rhine from the Fifth to the Ninth Century', in Giorgio Ausenda, ed., *After Empire: Towards an Ethnology of Europe's Barbarians* (Woodbridge, 1995), 253–68; see also Goetz, *Wahrnehmung*, 144–63.

critique contemporary society. We see this clearly in book four of *On the Governance of God* by Salvian of Marseilles, in which he lambasted his fellow Romans for their sinfulness in the wake of the fifth-century 'barbarian invasions'. All barbarians, Salvian argued, were either pagans or heretics, and most sinned just like the Romans did through gluttony, violence and perjury. At the same time, he continued, pagans could not be accused of violating God's law because of they were generally ignorant of it.[16] The Romans needed to look at their own behaviour to explain their fall from grace. Such polemics reverberated with the words of Old Testament prophets warning Israel of sin, and they proved popular, from Gildas's attack on the Britons who were losing control to the pagan English, to Alcuin of York's attack on the monks of Lindisfarne two hundred and fifty years later, after their monastery was raided by Vikings in 793. The success of pagans was a warning.

The Arab conquests of the seventh century could be fitted into the same kind of providential discourse. Few commentators, in East or West, seem to have seen religion as a defining feature of the Arabs; instead these groups were seen as barbarians, and popularly as the Saracens, the descendants of Ishmael, a people genealogically separated from salvation.[17] Their success as a stimulus for change can be seen in a range of polemics, from the anti-Jewish *Doctrina Jacobi* to the chronicle of John bar Penkaye.[18] The most famous textual response to their successes against the Byzantine Empire was the *Revelation* of Pseudo-Methodius, composed as a sermon-cum-history around 690 in Syria after half a century of Arab dominance. The angry author squarely blamed the sinfulness of the Christian population for their defeat and asked whether those who compromised with the Arabs were truly Christians.[19] The text proved popular and was translated into Greek and then

---

[16] Especially Salvian, *De gubernatione Dei* 4.16 (MGH AA I/I, 51–2).

[17] Clarke, *Muslim Conquest*, 16.

[18] Hoyland, *Seeing Islam*, 55–61 (on the *Doctrina Jacobi*), 195 (on bar Penkaye); James Howard-Johnston, *Witnesses to a World Crisis: Historians and Histories of the Middle East in the Seventh Century* (Oxford, 2010).

[19] Gerrit Reinink, 'Pseudo-Methodius: A Concept of History in Response to the Rise of Islam', in Averil Cameron and Lawrence I. Conrad, eds, *The Byzantine and Early Islamic East: Problems in the Literary Source Material* (Princeton, NJ, 1992), 149–87, especially 157–9; *Apocalypse of Pseudo-Methodius. An Alexandrian World Chronicle*, ed. and transl. Benjamin Garstad, Dumbarton Oaks Medieval Library 14 (Cambridge, MA, 2012), 2–139.

into Latin, possibly within twenty years, fuelling apocalyptic imaginations East and West for centuries.[20] But it had no monopoly on this way of thinking. Half a generation earlier, the Frankish chronicler Fredegar had attributed Saracen successes to the moral failings and fall into heresy of the Emperor Herakleios (d. 641).[21] And, after the Arab conquest of Spain, the English missionary Boniface and his Rhineland colleagues used the fate of the Visigoths as an example to King Æthelbald of Mercia to illustrate what the punishment for sexual excess could be.[22] Otherness did not have to be clearly defined for the message to work.

That same letter by Boniface illustrates the potential for providential discourse to be blended with the less common 'noble savage' critique. Æthelbald had refused to take a wife and, what was worse as far as the bishops were concerned, preferred to amuse himself with nuns. Boniface sought to shame the king by telling him how even the pagans of Saxony abhorred adultery to such an extent that they would expect adulteresses to kill themselves, with the adulterer then being hanged over the funeral pyre; or else the adulteress would be flogged through the streets, stripped half naked, until nearly dead. In Wendish society, Boniface continued, women were praised for refusing to outlive their husbands, such was their commitment to matrimony. It probably tells us more about Boniface, rather than Æthelbald, that he hoped the king to be moved by stories of *female* purity in this regard, but maybe his intention was to shame the nuns who had betrayed Christ at court. Also striking is Boniface's apparent source material: not just empirical observation of Saxon and Wendish society but rather an extract from Tacitus's *Germania*, written to illustrate to the Romans the ways in which they were less moral than the savages to the north.[23] There was a strong literary tradition which helped to shape writing about pagans as moral discourse.

There was, unsurprisingly, still a rhetoric which firmly categorized pagans simply as the enemies of Christendom. This is perhaps

[20] Paul Alexander, 'Byzantium and the Migration of Literary Works and Motifs: The Legend of the Last Roman Emperor', *Medievalia et Humanistica* n.s. 2 (1971), 47–68; Paul Alexander, *The Byzantine Apocalyptic Tradition*, ed. Dorothy Abrahamse (Berkeley, CA, 1985).

[21] Fredegar, *Chronica* 4.66 (MGH SRM 2, 154).

[22] Boniface, *Epistola* 73 (MGH Epp. Sel. 1, 151); Tolan, *Saracens*, 77–8.

[23] James T. Palmer, *Anglo-Saxons in a Frankish World, 690–900* (Turnhout, 2009), 124.

most striking with regard to the assaults of the Vikings in the ninth century. Frankish chroniclers were significantly more likely to call Vikings *Nordmanni* than *pagani*, which suggested that religion was not always a significant factor in their identity.[24] But in royal and episcopal legislation the word 'pagans' was more common – they should be resisted as 'enemies' (*inimici*), like Jews they should not have power over Christians, and so on.[25] People groaned at the infestations and persecutions of the pagans, and the challenges they posed to order and the security of churches. This could be combined explicitly with providential rhetoric, as famously happened following the Viking sack of Paris in 845, when bishops identified the Northmen with the punishment from the north prophesied by Jeremiah (1: 14).[26] But even when not so explicit, people were ready to identify 'pagans' as a particular type of enemy in a legal setting, where the emphasis was on reform of Christians.

This language could be turned on the Saracens as well. In 846 Rome and St Peter's were sacked in a Saracen raid.[27] Emperor Lothar responded by marching south to restore the church and to establish provisions for defence. In the records of a council which discussed matters we find the Saracens described as *pagani*: 'on account of our sins and offences, this year the church of St Peter was laid waste and plundered by pagans'.[28] It is a turn of language which reflected transgression in law, heightening the sense of opposition between the Christian community at large and religious others. Lothar underscored this by talking about summoning a great army to eject from Beneventum 'the enemies of Christ, the Saracens and Maurs'.[29] In chronicles, ethnic labels dominated the accounts of what happened, underscoring the importance of the legal setting for nomenclature.

---

[24] Simon Coupland, 'The Rod of God's Wrath or the People of God's Wrath? The Carolingian Theology of the Viking Invasions', *JEH* 42 (1991), 535–54.

[25] Council of Meaux (846), c. 73 (MGH Conc. 3, 119–20); Council of Pîtres (869), c. 15 (MGH Conc. 4, 360).

[26] Council of Meaux (846), pref. (MGH Conc. 3, 82); Council of Quirzy (857; ibid. 385); Council of Quirzy (858), c. 15 (ibid. 423); Council of Troyes (860/1), pref. (MGH Conc. 4, 44); Council of Pîtres (869), c. 15 (ibid. 360).

[27] *Annales Bertiniani, s.a.* 846 (MGH SRG i.u.s. 5, 34); *Annales Fuldenses, s.a.* 846 (MGH SRG i.u.s. 7, 36).

[28] Council of Francia (846), c. 7 (MGH Conc. 3, 136): 'quia pro peccatis nostris et offensionibus aecclesia beati Petri hoc anno a paganis vastata est a direpta'.

[29] Council of Francia, c. 8 (ibid. 137).

If we look at attitudes towards Jews, canon law helps to illumi-
nate other dynamics of religious otherness – and this will lead us
into consideration of issues about the nature of cultural diversity
in early medieval communities.[30] In Christian theology, of course,
Jews had a clearer identity than pagans or Muslims.[31] But they
also posed less of a military threat. They were more likely to live
amongst Christian communities, although we must remember to
invoke regional difference here, because one was more likely to
encounter Jews in places such as Lyon than in, say, Britain.[32] Either
way, the threat in many imaginations was that Jews and Jewish
practices could corrupt Christian belief and ritual. This was vividly
put in regulations concerning the importance of not celebrating
Easter 'with the Jews' on Passover, particularly in seventh-century
Britain, where it was feared that Irish observances contravened
this tradition.[33] Legislation in Gaul and Spain sought to regulate
relations between Jewish and Christian communities, especially
concerning slavery and other power relations. Persecution and
forcible conversion of Jews was not without controversy, however,
and seemed to go beyond the spirit of canon law.[34]

What made such legislation pressing? Frankish law is notable for
not dealing with aspects of Jewish-Christian relations for nearly
two hundred years. This changed at the Council of Meaux (846),
the acts of which contained a significant compilation of extracts
on precisely that subject. The change is often associated with
the conversion of a deacon, Eleazar Bodo, to Judaism while on

[30] Bernard Bachrach, *Early Medieval Jewish Policy in Western Europe* (Ann Arbor,
MI, 1977); Michael Toch, 'The Jews in Europe, 500–1050', in Paul Fouracre, ed., *The
New Cambridge Medieval History*, 1: *c.500 – c.700* (Cambridge, 2005), 547–70; Bat-Sheva
Albert, 'Christians and Jews', in Thomas F. X. Noble and Julia M. H. Smith, eds, *CHC*,
3: *Early Medieval Christianities, c.600 – c.1100* (Cambridge, 2008), 157–77.

[31] But again the 'paganization' of religious others could be an issue: Wolfram
Drews, 'Jews as Pagans? Polemical Definitions of Identity in Visigothic Spain', *EME*
11 (2002), 189–207.

[32] Elisheva Baumgarten, 'Daily Commodities and Religious Identity in the Medieval Jewish Communities of Northern Europe', in John Doran, Charlotte Methuen
and Alexandra Walsham, eds, *Religion and the Household*, SCH 50 (Woodbridge, 2014),
97–121.

[33] Clare Stancliffe, *Bede, Wilfrid, and the Irish*, Jarrow Lecture 2003 (Jarrow, 2003).

[34] Brian Brennan, 'The Conversion of the Jews of Clermont in AD 576', *Journal
of Theological Studies* 36 (1985), 321–37; Rachel Stocking, 'Early Medieval Christian
Identity and Anti-Judaism: The Case of the Visigothic Kingdom', *Religion Compass* 2
(2008), 642–58; Jamie Wood, *The Politics of Identity in Visigothic Spain: Religion and Power
in the Histories of Isidore of Seville* (Leiden, 2012), 195–208.

pilgrimage to Rome in 838 and his subsequent flight to Córdoba in 840.[35] But it cannot be coincidence that this compilation formed part of the response to the Viking sack of Paris the previous year. The sense of anxiety and introspection caused by pagan success actualized other, related anxieties. The Viking attack also provided opportunity: Amulo of Lyon and his predecessors had been at odds with the Jewish community of their episcopal city for a while, and it seems that he seized the chance to promote his minority agenda against Jews at a time when the sense of 'otherness' was heightened.[36] The growing air of suspicion can be seen in the report of Prudentius of Troyes in 848 that Jews had betrayed Bordeaux to the Vikings.[37]

It was certainly possible for Christians to work with religious others; political crisis often made the difference. Before the conversion of Frisia, the region's 'gentile duke' Radbod (d. 719) allied with different Frankish factions to the south, supported Duke Ragamfred in battle, and even gave his daughter to marry mayor Grimoald II.[38] He also welcomed missionaries, although he refused to convert himself. Religion was no barrier to cooperation and, in this example, we get hints about the potential for people to support and tolerate non-violent interaction between different cultural groups. Radbod's worldview was, in a sense, multicultural, with political and social ideals which tolerated diversity if not embracing it outright. The paganism of figures in Frisia, Saxony or Thuringia had rarely been a political issue, as we can see if we look at the purely political account of the 'rebellion' of Duke Radulf of Thuringia against the Franks in 641, a generation before Thuringia's conversion.[39] But after he had come into conflict with Duke Charles Martel and lost, Radbod and his values were reimagined.[40] The terms of encounter were being redesigned by English outsiders in the Rhineland who wanted more episcopal

35 Albert, 'Christians and Jews', 175–6. On the incident, see Frank Reiss, 'From Aachen to al-Andalus: The Journey of Deacon Bodo', *EME* 13 (2005), 131–57.
36 On the situation in Lyon, see Johannes Heil, 'Agobard, Amolo, das Kirchengut und die Juden von Lyon', *Francia* 25 (1998), 39–76.
37 *Annales Bertiniani, s.a.* 848 (MGH SRG i.u.s. 5, 66–7).
38 Continuator of Fredegar, *Chronica* 7 (MGH SRM 2, 172–3).
39 Fredegar, *Chronica* 87 (ibid. 164–5).
40 Wolfert van Egmond, 'Radbod van de Friezen, een aristocrat in de periferie', *Millennium: Tijdschrift voor middeleeuwse studies* 16 (2005), 24–44.

and cultural authority in Frisia on the back of missionary work there. Now, despite early good Frankish-Frisian relations, Radbod's opposition to Charles was remembered as a battle between Christian and pagan kingdoms – the upgrade from duchy intensifying the sense of opposition – with churches the focus of dispute.[41]

Charles is perhaps more famous for fighting the 'Saracens' who attacked Gaul in the 730s.[42] Here, strikingly, we see similar processes of cooperation at work. According to one chronicler, the Saracens were invited into Gaul by Duke Eudo of Aquitaine, forming a strategic alliance intent on restoring Eudo to lands he had lost to Charles.[43] This was the background to the famous battle of Poitiers or Tours in 732/3. Apart from some church-burning – which surely did not include an attack on the Burgundian monastery of Luxeuil, despite modern claims otherwise[44] – religion was neither a barrier to cooperation nor a motivation to fight defensively. Strikingly, the next year, Charles invaded Burgundy and quashed the resistance of 'rebellious and unfaithful peoples'. Wallace-Hadrill, in his idiosyncratic translation of 1960, assumed here that the use of 'unfaithful' indicated that 'pagan practices' were being eradicated, by which he meant a spread of Islam in the region following the turmoil of the previous years.[45] But surely, in context, this meant political infidelity, not least because Charles completed his work by handing Lyon over to 'faithful' men to restore justice. He needed to return to Lyon, and then move onto Marseille and Arles to do the same thing only a year later. The Saracens, as 'others', had become involved in rebellion against Carolingian (or northern) dominion, not a religious war. We may wonder just how much Frankish attitudes towards otherness were shaped by opposition to one secular leader.

The role of religious otherness in rebellion is a complicated issue in the sources we have available, but this reminds us to be

---

[41] Willibald, *Vita Bonifatii* 4 (MGH SRG i.u.s. 57, 16–17).

[42] For more detail and context on the campaigns of Charles Martel discussed, see Paul Fouracre, *The Age of Charles Martel* (Harlow, 2000), 86–99; Andreas Fischer, *Karl Martell. Der Beginn karolingischer Herrschaft* (Stuttgart, 2012), 110–36.

[43] Continuator of Fredegar, *Chronica* 13 (MGH SRM 2, 175).

[44] G. Cugnier, *Histoire du monastère de Luxeuil à travers ses abbés 590–1790*, 3 vols (Langres, 2003), 1: 238–9.

[45] *The Fourth Book of the Chronicle of Fredegar with its Continuations*, ed. and transl. J. Michael Wallace-Hadrill, Nelson's Medieval Texts (London, 1960), 91; see also Fischer, *Karl Martell*, 131.

careful of perspective. The same chronicler, a Burgundian Carolingian sympathizer, described Saxons and Saracens explicitly as
'rebellious' in the following years as they fought against Charles.[46]
Their otherness was signalled differently. In 738, the distant
Saxons were *paganissimi*, the most pagan. They were *gens illa saevis-
sima*, 'that most savage people'. But they were forced back into
their customary tributary position, and that was satisfactory. The
Muslims were understood differently, not least because they were
active on the doorstep of the chronicler. In 737 they allied with the
unfaithful (*infidelis*) Maurontus and gave arms to a revolt of Christian Provençals against northern rule.[47] The chronicler called the
Muslims 'Ismaelites' and quoted Isidore of Seville, saying that they
were called Saracens through a corruption. If this denoted religious difference, it did so in a language of politicized ethnography
which pre-dated Islam.[48] Charles was indeed a conquering Christian hero but the chronicler compared him to Joshua at Jericho
(Josh. 6), a comparison which established the triumph of the righteous, not the fall of the unfaithful.[49] Much about otherness here
was political and designed to support the Carolingian infiltration
of the south; not everything was about religious otherness.

The potential for cooperation is important to bear in mind,
because of the sheer volume of diplomatic exchange between
kingdoms of different religion in the period. Such interaction draws our attention to the potential for both honorific and
pragmatic engagement. Indeed, the former had the capability to
revel in the exoticism of the other: we need think only of the
evident joy of the Frankish court when Harun al-Rashid, caliph
of Baghdad, sent Charlemagne an elephant.[50] (Just as noteworthy
is the religious identity of the intermediary, the otherwise undocu-
mented Frankish representative Isaac 'Iudeus', the Jew.) But while a

---

[46] Continuator of Fredegar, *Chronica* 19–20 (MGH SRM 2, 177–8).

[47] Support for a political reading of *infidelis* can be gained from looking at the will
of Abbo, edited and analysed in Patrick Geary, *Aristocracy in Provence: The Rhône Basin
at the Dawn of the Carolingian Age* (Stuttgart, 1985), 38–79.

[48] John Tolan, '"A Wild Man, whose Hand will be against All": Saracens and
Ishmaelites in Latin Ethnographical Traditions, from Jerome to Bede', in Walter Pohl,
Clemens Gantner and Richard Payne, eds, *Visions of Community in the Post-Roman
World* (Farnham, 2012), 513–30.

[49] Cf. Fischer, *Karl Martell*, 131–2.

[50] *Annales regni Francorum, s.aa.* 801, 802 (MGH SRG i.u.s. 6, 116–17); Einhard, *Vita
Karoli* 16 (MGH SRG i.u.s. 25, 19), on friendship.

distant caliph could be cast as a wealthy, friendly and anachronistic 'King of the Persians', pagans from the north offered little oriental magic. Consequently, one finds little excitement in historical notes recording Frankish diplomacy with the pagan Danes Sigifrid or Horik I over more pressing concerns relating to peace on the frontiers. Dealing with northerners was everyday stuff.[51]

However, just as there was a complex 'orientalism' in play, there were notable prejudices against the north that had their own character. In a letter on missionary strategy in the early eighth century, Daniel of Winchester encouraged Boniface to point out to pagans that it could be no coincidence that they had possession of only frozen lands, while Christians inhabited lands rich in oil and wine.[52] A few years later the author of the satirical *Cosmography of Aethicus Ister* cast northern Germany and Scandinavia as barbarous lands, full of monsters and brutes; he even included a short poem: 'And you, O North | mother of dragons | and nurse of scorpions | pit of vipers | and lake of demons'.[53] The north was the antithesis of the civilization of the south. This played into the hands of a teleological missionary narrative which anthropologists will find familiar: to convert to Christianity was to modernize and to become cultured.[54] The rejection of paganism was literally the rejection of the countryside, the *pagus*, in favour of the cult of the city.

But there was a practical problem here because the north, beyond the old Roman *limes*, was not often structured around *civitates* or *urbes*. The institutions which competed for jurisdiction over Saxony in the eighth and ninth centuries, such as the monastery of Fulda, had to participate in an imperial project of reinventing the north in the image of the south, with the building of towns encouraged where there had only been small communities or forts before.[55] Paderborn, the *Urbs Karoli*, city of Charles the Great, was devised for this purpose as a symbol of Christian triumph over

---

[51] See also Wood, 'Pagans and the Other', 18.

[52] Daniel, *Epistola* 23 (MGH Epp. Sel. 1, 40).

[53] *The Cosmography of Aethicus Ister* 33, ed. and transl. Michael Herren, Publications of the *Journal of Medieval Latin* 8 (Turnhout, 2011), 34–5.

[54] Webb Keane, *Christian Moderns: Freedom and Fetish in the Mission Encounter* (Berkeley, CA, 2007).

[55] Caspar Ehlers, *Die Integration Sachsens in das fränkische Reich (751–1024)* (Göttingen, 2007); Palmer, *Anglo-Saxons*, 166–8.

pagan superstition, a short distance north of the Irminsul shrine near Eresburg.[56] The challenges were signalled early on by Pope Zacharias in 743, when he objected to the founding of a bishopric in the Thuringian border fortress of Erfurt because, from what he had heard, it was not sufficiently urban to support the dignity of episcopal office.[57] Only once missionaries got to the Elbe and beyond did they find networks of relatively stable trading settlements, which then provided the targets for Anskar (d. 865) and his successors for the next century.[58]

This is, of course, to view the alterity of the pagan north from the perspective of Roman habits of ecclesiastical organization. One of the things which made mission to these regions so compelling was how familiar they were in some ways. We know that culturally and linguistically there was much to facilitate ready communication. (How much wonder and hostility towards Jewish or Arab culture stemmed from linguistic and cultural differences?) Many people who came together to become 'the English' had ancestors from the pagan Germanic north, and this became part of the legitimizing tradition which encouraged missionary and episcopal involvement there during the course of the eighth century.[59] And just as well documented are the lively trade links which crisscrossed the North Sea world, adding an economic dimension to interaction.[60] Scandinavians 'prime-signing' (being marked with the cross but not yet accepting baptism) so that they could trade at Christian ports, and invertible crosses which became pagan hammers, are famous enough to be part of the standard narrative of the period.[61] Christian and pagan iconographies could overlap and inspire each other. It was not, then, the fact that the pagan north was completely unfamiliar which defined its alterity. By

---

[56] Karl Hauck, 'Paderborn: Das Zentrum von Karls Sachsen-Mission 777', in *Adel und Kirche. Gerd Tellenbach zum 65. Geburtstag*, ed. Josef Fleckenstein and Karl Schmid (Freiburg im Breisgau, 1968), 92–140; Rosamond McKitterick, *Charlemagne: The Formation of a European Identity* (Cambridge, 2008), 165–6.

[57] Pope Zacharias, *Epistola* 51 (MGH Epp. Sel. 1, 87).

[58] On Viking Age towns, see Søren Sindbæk, 'Networks and Nodal Points: The Emergence of Towns in Early Viking Age Scandinavia', *Antiquity* 81 (2007), 119–32.

[59] Palmer, *Anglo-Saxons*, 46–59.

[60] Stéphane Lebecq, *Marchands et navigateurs frisons du haut Moyen Âge*, 2 vols (Lille, 1983); Christopher Loveluck, *Northwest Europe in the Early Middle Ages, c.AD 600–1150* (Cambridge, 2013), ch. 9.

[61] Fletcher, *Conversion of Europe*, 373–4.

joining the world Christian community with centres in Rome and the Holy Land, northern peoples found that they now inhabited a peripheral space, where once they had been more central to their own religious universe.[62] Cultural dissonance followed for both sides as they sought to adjust.

One could contrast here expansion into the north with the way that Islam came to occupy places more familiar to Christian narratives, including the Holy Land itself. One of the most striking features of the Arab conquests of the seventh century is the fact that Western commentators did not consider them more shocking and that it took until the eleventh century for Christians really to object. In many respects this was because the holy places proved the truth of the New Testament regardless of who was in charge, and most were treated with respect, at least until al-Hakim destroyed the Church of the Holy Sepulchre in 1009.[63] One of Boniface's colleagues, Willibald, visited the region in the 720s and his account of his experiences is testament to this relative harmony. At one point he was arrested as a cultural outsider but a Spaniard vouched for him in front of Caliph Hisham 'Abd al-Malik, who released him and sent him on his way with a letter of protection.[64] Later on, in Nazareth, Willibald heard that Muslims wished to destroy the church on the site where Gabriel had visited Mary, but that the local Christians had reached an agreement to keep it safe.[65] It appears that such agreements were not unusual: we find Charlemagne sending money 'for the Saracens' to support such churches eighty years later.[66] Strikingly, even so, the Muslims were

---

[62] On a similar modern process, see Joel Robbins, 'Is the "Trans-" in "Transnational" the "Trans-" in "Transcendent"? On Alterity and the Sacred in the Age of Globalization', in Thomas Csordas, ed., *Transnational Transcendence* (Berkeley, CA, 2009), 55–72.

[63] On the exegetical contexts of the *Vita Willibaldi*, see Palmer, *Anglo-Saxons*, ch. 7; R. Aist, The *Christian Topography of Early Islamic Jerusalem: The Evidence of Willibald of Eichstätt (700–787 CE)* (Turnhout, 2009). On the events and context of 1009, see Ralph-Johannes Lilie, ed., *Konfliktbewältigung vor 1000 Jahren: Die Zerstörung der Grabeskirche in Jerusalem im Jahre 1009* (Berlin, 2011).

[64] *Vita Willibaldi* 4 (MGH S 15/1, 94).

[65] Ibid. 95.

[66] *Basel Roll* 3, ed. Michael McCormick, in idem, *Charlemagne's Survey of the Holy Land: Wealth, Personnel, and the Building of a Mediterranean Church between Antiquity and the Middle Ages* (Cambridge, MA, 2011), 216.

called 'pagan Saracens' twice by Willibald to signal their otherness to the Christian audience in Heidenheim.[67]

This is to consider the matter from the position of external observers and visitors, of course. Many Eastern Christians were not so inclined to accept religious diversity. Perhaps the most extreme text, and also the one with the most enduring influence, was again the *Revelation* of Pseudo-Methodius. In this apocalypse, it was retrospectively prophesied that Christians would be handed over to Arabs ('barbarians' and 'the sons of Ishmael' in the text) as punishment for their sins; but it would be the Christians' collaboration with their new overlords which would bring their final ruin. Clearly the Syrian author disapproved of the acceptance of *dhimmi* status which his contemporaries found easier.[68] He prophesied that the Saracens would be destroyed by a last 'king of the Romans/ Greeks/Christians' (depending on the version), but that this would lead to an even less merciful attack by the godless hordes of the north. Apocalyptic fantasy helped Pseudo-Methodius to find a way to explain Muslim successes against Christians and to imagine a worse, final adversary defined by northernness. With Latin versions of Pseudo-Methodius circulating in the West at least as early as 750, it was no wonder that the author of the *Cosmography of Aethicus Ister* looked at Scandinavia with such mock horror.[69]

A similar mixture of providential ire and collaboration anxiety can be seen concerning the Iberian peninsula after the Arab conquest of 711. The *Chronicle of 754* reflected on the conquest in these terms, comparing it to the assaults on Jerusalem and the Sack of Rome.[70] Just over a century later, the so-called *Prophetic Chronicle of 883* made play of similar ideas, when the author explained that the peninsula had been lost through sin, but would now be reclaimed by the righteous Alfonso III.[71] In between, accepting *dhimmi* status and collaborating harmoniously was probably a reality for most Christians in Muslim Spain.[72] Indeed, over the last

---

[67] Tolan, *Saracens*, 77.

[68] Reinink, 'Pseudo-Methodius', 180–1.

[69] For a fuller discussion, see James T. Palmer, *The Apocalypse in the Early Middle Ages* (Cambridge, 2014), ch. 4.

[70] *Chronicle of 754* 45 (*CSM* 1: 33); Clarke, *Muslim Conquest*, 17–18.

[71] *Chronica prophetica* 2.2 (Yves Bonnaz, ed., *Chroniques Asturiennes (fin IXe siècle)* [Paris, 1987], 3).

[72] Clarke, *Muslim Conquest*, 20–1. For interest in taxation, see *Chronicle of 754* 52, 60, 75 (*CSM* 1: 36, 39, 51); *Treaty of Tudmīr*, transl. Olivia Remie Constable, in eadem, ed., *Medieval*

decade or so it has become apparent that the supposedly Visigothic churches which scholars assumed must have predated the conquest of 711 more likely belong to the ninth or tenth century, indicating that it was possible for Christians to build and develop their lives under Muslim rule.[73] It was to Spain that Louis the Pious's deacon, Eleazar Bodo, fled in 838 when he converted to Judaism. And we know that Mozarabic practices – Arabized Christian rituals and culture – developed out of this melting pot of culture.[74] It does not seem to have been a hostile environment because of religious differences.

Eschatological visions of peace and salvation did not thrive on such cultural harmony, however, but rather worked against it. As we have already seen with Pseudo-Methodius, Christians were just as adept at fantasizing about liberation from cultural-political constraints. In Spain, this manifested itself in a martyrs' movement.[75] Over a number of years in Córdoba, a number of Christians – many, I think not coincidentally, new converts – took it upon themselves to provoke Muslim officials to arrest, intimidation and ultimately murder.[76] Just how radical this was can be seen by the treatment of one of the ringleaders, Eulogius, who was arrested by the Christian bishop Reccafred of Seville in an attempt to preserve peace. Eulogius took the opportunity to write a treatise in defence of the martyrs, and later his friend and correspondent Paul Alvar – an opponent of Eleazar Bodo – composed his own defences of the movement.[77] Both appealed to apocalyptic traditions to cast Muḥammad as one of the many antichrists that would come before the end times, a *praecursor Antichristi* who denied the divinity of Christ.[78] Their imaginations may have been stoked by the circulation of a satirical *Life of Muḥammad* which cast the Prophet as a sinful heresiarch.[79] But it could not change what was

---

Iberia: Readings from Christian, Muslim, and Jewish Sources, 2nd edn (Philadelphia, PA, 2012), 45–6. See also Collins, *The Arab Conquest of Spain*, 39–50.

[73] Roger Collins, *Visigothic Spain*, 2nd edn (Oxford, 2004), 186–96.

[74] For a recent long-term view, see Richard Hitchcock, *Mozarabs in Medieval and Early Modern Spain: Identities and Influences* (Aldershot, 2008).

[75] See, in this volume, Ariana Patey, 'Asserting Difference in Plurality: The Case of the Martyrs of Córdoba', 53–66.

[76] Kenneth Baxter Wolf, *Christian Martyrs in Muslim Spain* (Cambridge, 1988).

[77] Paul Alvar, *Indiculus luminosus* (*CSM* 1: 270–315); *Vita Eulogii* (ibid. 330–43).

[78] Tolan, *Saracens*, 90–1.

[79] Janna Wasilewski, 'The "Life of Muhammad" in Eulogius of Córdoba: Some

obvious: the opponents of a broad cultural harmony were in the minority.

One of the most important ways in which Christian communities dealt with religious others was through the project of evangelization. Here we find ways of thinking in which action was directed against pagans rather than Muslims, Jews or heretics. Indeed, while there was little or no interest in converting Muslims or Jews, significant resources were dedicated to missionary work in the far north and east in the period that concerns us.[80] The contrast with the eleventh and twelfth centuries could not be clearer, with the Crusades and widespread anti-Semitism but relatively modest progress in the Christianization of Scandinavia. The pursuit of missionary work was one of the great projects which shaped the earlier Middle Ages because, with the expansion of Christendom, frontiers changed, new cultural worlds developed and economic patterns were redrawn. The reasons for Western Christendom's priorities are crucial for our analysis.

A central issue here which we have already touched on is the intersection of geography, history and Scripture. Muslims, Jews and heretics lived in lands which had already been evangelized, even if there had been some kind of retreat; and all, in some sense, had rejected or 'misunderstood' Christ. Their Christian neighbours belonged to communities with long Christian histories and there is often, in ecclesiastical history, a sense in which it is the newer institutions and collectives which seem more energized towards missionary work. (Institutions in Burgundy, for instance, only seem to have been engaged in mission in the generation after the Irishman Columbanus [d. 615] had unsettled them.) The worlds beyond the northern and eastern frontiers of Western Christendom were different because they represented a 'clean slate' with energetic new Christian institutions on the edge. Christ had foretold that the gospel would be preached in the whole world to all peoples before the end of the world would come (Matt. 24: 14, 28: 19). It was therefore, in a global sense, more important to move into new lands to preach to new peoples, than to work in old ones against people who had already heard the message. And, as one

Evidence for the Transmission of Greek Polemic to the Latin West', *EME* 16 (2008), 333–53.

[80] On conversions of Jews, see n. 34 above.

cynical ninth-century exegete wrote, preaching to all peoples was more essential than converting all people in this context, because human beings themselves were too fallible to remain constant in their faith.[81] The existence of pagans posed a compelling challenge to many, and with an apocalyptic edge.

Martyrdom narratives helped to shape attitudes here.[82] To die for the faith at the hands of a pagan was a long-standing ideal of sanctity, institutionalized into the infrastructure of Christendom through commemorative churches and shrines. We need only think of the importance of St Denis, the murdered missionary from Rome in the third century, whose burial site became the focal point for the cult of France's 'special patron'.[83] Mission may have been more popular at some times than others (for instance in the eighth century compared to the sixth) but hagiographies and martyrologies provided a steady bedrock of legends about people facing pagans without fear. Many inspirational figures, including Amandus of Maastricht in the seventh century, Boniface in the eighth and Anskar of Hamburg-Bremen in the ninth, fantasized about being martyred by pagans.[84] It is little surprise that such feelings also fuelled a 'psychological otherness', in which people associated distant lands with monsters and strange practices.[85] There was opposition to prioritizing pagans, to be sure: Pope Martin I (d. 655) was supposed to have condemned this as self-indulgent compared to struggling against heretics.[86] But even so, there was a strong cultural basis in the West for an impulse to seek out and challenge pagans in a way that was different to that for dealing with Jews, Muslims or heretics. Martyrdom fuelled mission, and the presence of pagans was a crucial ingredient.

The longer-term impact of mission perhaps helped to change the terms of religious encounter. Missionary work saw the frontiers of Christendom expanded far from earlier centres, with two main

---

[81] Paschasius, *Expositio in Matheo* 11 (CChr.CM 56B, 1164).

[82] James T. Palmer, 'Martyrdom and the Rise of Missionary Hagiography in the Merovingian World', in Nancy Edwards, Roy Flechner and Máire Ní Mhaonaigh, *Converting the Isles*, Cultural Encouters in Late Antiquity and the Midde Ages (Turnhout, forthcoming).

[83] *Passio Dionysii, Rustici et Eleutherii* (MGH AA 4/2, 101–5).

[84] For a survey, see Ian Wood, *The Missionary Life: Saints and the Evangelisation of Europe 400–1050* (Harlow, 2001).

[85] Ibid. 250–4.

[86] Audoin, *Vita Eligii* 1.34 (MGH SRM 4, 691).

consequences. First, expansion meant that there were multiple cultural shifts as former frontiers became part of the 'middle' (e.g. Cologne) and new outposts were established (e.g. Magdeburg). Second, the proliferation of micro-Christendoms and the sheer scale of the Frankish Church made it harder to maintain any sense of unity, politically, ideologically or practically. The pagans of the north and east were in many ways more distant than ever to old centres of Christian political power; they were, as Wood has suggested, now 'outsiders' more than they were 'others'.[87] The situation was complicated, but this may well be one reason why 'old Christendom' became more concerned with Jews, heretics and Muslims as the year 1000 passed. But it makes sense: if early medieval Christendom was partly defined by its 'others', then changing the 'others' redefined the rest.

Let us draw together some of the issues we have seen. At the beginning we saw how early medieval Christians imagined their unity defined in relation to struggles against potential enemies. But a general sense of opposition does not explain the otherness of paganism – not least because, in many ways, the Germanic and Slavic pagans whom Christians encountered in the early Middle Ages were often culturally understandable as neighbours, relatives and trading partners. Jews and Muslims were, in many respects, both more alien and, therefore, less troubling. All groups, in fact, seemed to have been able to coexist with Christian communities without trouble for long periods of time until there was some kind of political crisis or someone provoked an incident of intolerance. People may not always like 'politically correct' histories, but there was peace and willingness to cooperate far more than there was conflict based on prejudice and ignorance.

This was only part of the story. The very fact that Christian unity in this period was defined so crucially by its struggles meant that religious (or cultural) encounters were catalysts to action. Christian trials and defeats encouraged polemicists to argue for internal moral reform, not crusades. Even where things seemed less tolerant, as in the councils of 846 where the rights of Jews were restricted and an army was summoned against the Saracens, it is striking that such actions were at best backdrops to episcopal reform programmes. Partly this is to do with impulses to create

---

[87] Wood, 'The Pagans and the Other'.

identities. To establish a community of belief based on a moral code required affirmation of both what to believe and what not to believe. For a long time in the early Middle Ages, pagans represented the closest and clearest 'other' – northern, uncivilized and likely to cause trouble. The Middle Ages changed when this otherness became more distant.

University of St Andrews

ASSERTING DIFFERENCE IN PLURALITY: THE CASE OF THE MARTYRS OF CÓRDOBA

by ARIANA PATEY

Between the years 850 and 859 forty-eight Christians were decapitated for offences against Islam in Córdoba, the capital of the Islamic Umayyad dynasty in Al-Andalus, Spain (756–1031). The majority of those executed had deliberately instigated their own deaths by making derogatory comments about the Prophet Muḥammad, a known capital offence. The calculated nature of their behaviour, in action against rulers considered by their contemporaries to be fellow monotheists, and without the super- natural support of widely accepted miracles, strained the already fractured Christian community.[1] While the Córdoban bishop and the metropolitan of Seville worked closely with the emirs to stop the would-be martyrs,[2] Eulogius, a Córdoban priest and bishop- elect of Toledo, and his friend Paul Alvar composed martyrologies and apologies for the group.[3] Written for prisoners preparing for martyrdom and for circulation amongst the religious communities surrounding the city,[4] the works allow insight into a movement of martyrs composed of men and women, lay and religious, with Christian and non-Christian backgrounds. The works of Eulogius and Alvar reflect an intense preoccupation with public behaviour as an expression of identity in a religiously diverse society. This emphasis on the bodies of Muslims, Christians and martyrs in both hagiography and act draws attention to the movement's motives by highlighting its relationship with the strictly ascetic monastic communities of Córdoba, where monks and nuns used their own

---

[1]   Kenneth Baxter Wolf, *Christian Martyrs in Muslim Spain* (Cambridge, 1998), 77–96.

[2]   The relationship between the bishops and the government, and between the bishops and the martyrs' movement, was probably far more complex than the narra- tive provided by the movement indicates. For an analysis of the role of the bishop of Córdoba, see Jessica A. Coope, *The Martyrs of Córdoba: Community and Family Conflict in an Age of Mass Conversion* (London, 1995), 61–4.

[3]   The known works of Eulogius and Alvar can be found in *CSM*. For a discussion of the texts, see E. P. Colbert, *The Martyrs of Córdoba* (Washington DC, 1962).

[4]   Eulogius, *Memoriale sanctorum* 1.4 (*CSM* 2: 363–459, at 371), Alvar, *Vita Eulogii* 2.4 (*CSM* 1:330–43, at 332–3).

bodies as means of preserving and articulating Christian culture in early medieval Spain.[5]

Martyrdom is an inherently contested topic. Its appearance in communities speaks to an existing plurality of understanding regarding self- and group identification. The politics of interreligious engagement, especially within the last decade, have promoted a historiography of Al-Andalus as a time and place when a plurality of religions flourished in coexistence.[6] The martyrs' movement has been a foil to this narrative, and the martyrs are often described as people who 'feared diversity' and 'despised anyone who did not conform to their beliefs'.[7] The venomous nature of their polemic, both in the texts and in the behaviour designed to offend Muslims and provoke their martyrdoms, certainly displays hatred of Islam.[8] But they also engaged in attacking a pluralism that did not promote diversity, but rather uniformity. Their concerns about Islam included its similarity to Christianity, which other Christians saw as a reason to cooperate with the Muslims.[9] The martyrs were angered by difference in the form of Islam, but this difference

---

[5] Scholarly material dealing with the medieval body is vast and greatly indebted to Peter Brown, *The Body and Society: Men, Women and Sexual Renunciation in Early Christianity* (New York, 1988); Caroline Walker Bynum, *Holy Feast and Holy Fast* (Berkeley, CA, 1987); Sarah Kay and Miri Rubin, eds, *Framing Medieval Bodies* (Manchester, 1977). See also Caroline Walker Bynum, 'Why All the Fuss about the Body? A Medievalist's Perspective', *Critical Inquiry* 22 (1995), 1–33. While studies have focused predominantly on a Christian context, recent work has been done on Muslim bodies: see Shahzad Bashir, *Sufi Bodies: Religion and Society in Medieval Islam* (New York, 2011); Scott S. Kugle, *Sufis and Saints' Bodies: Mysticism, Corporeality and Sacred Power in Islam* (Chapel Hill, NC, 2007).

[6] For an example of this kind of history, see Maria Rosa Menocal, *The Ornament of the World* (Boston, MA, 2002). For discussion of the historiography, see Anna Akasoy, 'Convivencia and its Discontents', *International Journal of Middle East Studies* 42 (2010), 489–99; Maria Jesús Rubiera Mata and Mikel de Epalza, 'Al-Andalus: Between Myth and History', *History and Anthropology* 18 (2007), 269–73.

[7] Coope, *Martyrs of Córdoba*, xii. The historiography of the movement also reflects concerns about Spanish nationalism and religious identity; for an overview, see Wolf, *Martyrs*, 36–50.

[8] Norman Daniel, *The Arabs and Medieval Europe* (London, 1975), 39–45; Janna Wasilewski, 'The "Life of Muhammad" in Eulogius of Cordoba', *EME* 16 (2008), 333–53; John V. Tolan, *Saracens: Islam in the Medieval European Imagination* (New York, 2002), 85–97.

[9] Eulogius, *Liber apologeticus martyrum* 12 (*CSM* 2: 475–95, at 481). Wolf sees this response as inspired by Islamic attitudes to Christianity and Judaism: *Martyrs*, 86–7.

was perceived as all the more dangerous because of assimilation between religious communities in the public sphere.[10]

Within Al-Andalus, the survival of Christian and Jewish communities was seen by the Umayyads as an indicator of the state's success.[11] These communities were *ahl al-dhimma*, meaning 'people under protection'. The protection in question was that afforded under Islamic law to those of other religions who acknowledged Islamic authority through the paying of a special tax, the *jizya*. These communities were also made distinctive by restrictions. Under law, Christians were forbidden to construct new churches. Chanting, bells and processions were prohibited. *Dhimmī* were also bound to wear distinctive clothing.[12] With the exception of taxation, these laws were not enforced in Córdoba at the time the voluntary martyrdoms began, although they would be enforced later in an attempt to quell the movement.[13] Before the martyrs, bells were rung for the canonical hours, Christian funeral processions were allowed to move through Muslim neighbourhoods, monasteries and churches were constructed and the only reference to distinctive Christian dress is to clerical vestments.[14] Eulogius and Alvar were vehemently opposed to the existing taxation and decried the imposition of these laws after the martyrdoms began.[15] Yet the failure to implement the laws in the beginning may have created the identity crisis that precipitated the movement. *Dhimmī* laws, while encoding the dominant position of Islam, also upheld the religious and cultural identity of other communities. Mikel de Epalza has argued that a Christian community's ability to achieve *dhimmī* status in Al-Andalus was determinative for its survival during the Umayyad period.[16]

Early medieval Spain was a volatile ideological landscape that fostered a multiplicity of identities. Even discounting the dominant

---

[10] Wolf, *Martyrs*, 86–95.

[11] Mikel de Epalza, 'Mozarabs: An emblematic Christian Minority in Islamic al-Andalus', in Salma Khadra Jayyusi, ed., *The Legacy of Muslim Spain*, 2 vols (Leiden, 1994), 1: 149–70, at 155.

[12] See A. S. Tritton, *The Caliphs and the Non-Muslim Subjects* (London, 1970).

[13] The *jizya* probably increased with the other taxes under the reign of 'Abd al-Rahman II (822–52): Wolf, *Martyrs*, 122.

[14] Ibid. 11–13.

[15] Eulogius, *Memoriale* 1.21 (*CSM* 2: 385); *Documentum martyriale* 18 (*CSM* 2: 459–75, at 470); Paul Alvar, *Indiculus luminosus* 3 (*CSM* 1: 270–315, at 275).

[16] De Epalza, 'Mozarabs', 155.

(in politics if not in numbers) Islamic presence from 711,[17] Christian identity was neither stable nor uniform.[18] The presence of the emiral court and lack of legal differentiation in ninth-century Córdoba only aided the fluidity of religious identity.[19] A century and a half of coexistence had begun to give rise to assimilation and conversion, creating societal changes that affected the different religious communities and prompted some to reiterate their boundaries.[20] The milieu from which the martyrs emerged was marked by this tension. A number of the martyrs had been 'secret Christians', that is to say, practising their religion privately while appearing outwardly neutral or even passing as Muslim.[21] Within the movement itself, many cases of this behaviour represented apostasy from Islam, a crime punishable by death.[22] The complicated nature of inter-faith relations is revealed in the status of children of mixed marriages who were legally Muslim from birth but had been raised as Christians.[23] Other martyrs were people who had outwardly converted to Islam but privately converted back to Christianity.[24] The accepted separation of public and private identity is high-

[17]   Thomas F. Glick, *Islamic and Christian Spain in the Early Middle Ages* (Princeton, NJ, 1979), 33–5; Jessica A. Coope, 'Religious and Cultural Conversion to Islam in Ninth-Century Umayyad Cordoba', *Journal of World History* 4 (1993), 47–68; Kenneth Baxter Wolf, 'The earliest Spanish Christian Views of Islam', *ChH* 55 (1986), 281–96, at 286–7.

[18]   For a brief discussion of the Christian Church in eighth-century Spain, see Juan Francisco Rivera Recio, 'La iglesia mozárabe', in Ricardo García Villoslada, ed., *Historia de la iglesia en España*, 2 (Madrid, 1982), 21–60. For larger surveys of these issues, see Ann Rosemary Christys, *Christians in Al-Andalus 711–1000* (Richmond, 2002); Richard Hitchcock, *Mozarabs in Medieval and Early Modern Spain: Identities and Influences* (Aldershot, 2008).

[19]   Robert Hillenbrand, '"The Ornament of the World": Medieval Córdoba as a Cultural Centre', in Jayyusi, ed., *Legacy of Muslim Spain*, 1: 112–35.

[20]   Janina M. Safran has approached these issues from the existing Muslim and Jewish sources: see her 'Identity and Differentiation in Ninth-Century Al-Andalus', *Speculum* 76 (2002), 573–98; eadem, *Defining Boundaries in Al-Andalus* (Ithaca, NY, 2013).

[21]   Alvar, *Indiculus* 9 (*CSM* 1: 281).

[22]   The legal proceedings of the cases are discussed by Adriano Duque, 'Claiming Martyrdom in the Episode of The Martyrs of Córdoba', *Collectanea Christiana Orientalia* 8 (2011), 23–48, at 27–34.

[23]   Coope, *Martyrs of Córdaba*, is an excellent study of the family dynamics of the martyrs' movement; see also Daniel, *Arabs and Medieval Europe*, 35–6. Safran also explores inter-faith marriage in Islamic law in al-Andalus: *Defining Boundaries*, 125–67.

[24]   Such as the martyrs Felix, Witesindus, Rudericus and Salmon: Eulogius, *Memoriale* 2.10.1–4, 3.10 (*CSM* 2: 416–17, 455); *Liber apologeticus martyrum* 21–35 (*CSM* 2: 488–96).

lighted by the charge levelled against the martyrs of being 'indiscreet and unwilling to suffer with the weaker Christians'.[25]

Contemporary Christian sources claimed that it was not uncommon for Córdoban Christians to pass as Muslims. This involved a range of physical modifiers from refraining from making the sign of the cross in public, keeping Islamic food laws and speaking Arabic through to circumcision.[26] Particular scorn was reserved for those Christians who were circumcised. Samson, the abbot of a nearby monastery which housed relics of the martyrs, described the surgery in lurid detail and referred to one circumcised Christian as Judas Iscariot.[27] Alvar said that circumcised Christians had willingly taken on the mark of the Antichrist.[28] The physicality and permanence of the act made it the ultimate sign of collusion.

The desire to participate publicly in the dominant Córdoban culture was felt not only by those Christians most closely associated with the emiral court, but also by average Christians and even by the clergy. The tensions created by these conflicting identities are brought into sharp relief by the cases of two protomartyrs. These men were tried and punished for crimes against Islam several years before the first wave of voluntary martyrdoms. One, a merchant named John, was accused by Muslim members of the public of trying to pass as a Muslim in the market place, possibly to aid his business. He did this by swearing on the name of the Prophet Muḥammad. When confronted, John lost his temper and cursed the Prophet. He was dragged to the judge, given four hundred lashes and paraded around town on a donkey.[29] The other protomartyr was a priest named Perfectus. While he was shopping in Córdoba, some Muslims approached him to ask him about religion. In the course of the discussion he insulted the Prophet, for which he was then executed.[30] Perfectus was likely approached because he was identifiably Christian. According to Alvar, identifiable priests were sometimes harassed verbally in the streets or had rocks thrown at

[25] Eulogius, *Memoriale* 2.15.1 (*CSM* 2: 434).
[26] Alvar, *Indiculus* 9, 35 (*CSM* 1: 281, 313); Samson, *Apologeticus* 2, pref. (*CSM* 2: 506–658, at 547–55).
[27] Samson, *Apologeticus* 2, pref., 3, 4.9 (*CSM* 2: 550)
[28] Alvar, *Indiculus* 35.4–9 (*CSM* 1: 313).
[29] Eulogius, *Memoriale* 1.9 (*CSM* 2: 377–8); Alvar, *Indiculus* 5 (*CSM* 1: 277–8).
[30] Eulogius, *Memoriale* 2 (*CSM* 2: 397–401); Alvar, *Indiculus* 3 (*CSM* 1: 275–6).

them by children.[31] This could have contributed to the circumstances surrounding a ninth-century manuscript bemoaning the declining standards of dress amongst the clergy.[32] This harassment of those who wore 'the symbols of our sacred order' made even priests unwilling to display their religious identity.[33]

The anthropologist Clifford Geertz has defined culture as 'an ordered system of meaning and of symbols'.[34] In the *Liber de habitu clericorum* the author outlined the symbolic significance of each piece of priestly clothing, and in doing so alluded to the cultural importance of maintaining the dress code. For the movement, the decline in Christian symbols in the public sphere existed within a self-perpetuating cycle leading to cultural extinction. Negative associations, or the desire for positive advancement, made the public display of Christian symbols unpopular. As their visibility declined, the meanings of the symbols were forgotten, and there was even less impetus to display them as they, and Christianity, lost their importance. The public sphere was important to the martyrs because it was where symbols were displayed and explained.[35] As Alvar argued: 'What could be a greater persecution, what more severe kind of degradation is to be feared when a person cannot say in public what he believes by reason in his heart?'[36]

The display of religious identity through the public performance of symbolic action was a central concern of the martyrs' movement. This concern was part of their collective motivation, and it formulated their response.[37] The medieval body, which participated in the shared space of the community, 'was *the* preeminent symbol of community'.[38] Bodies were the medium by which individuals could articulate their personal religious identities as

---

[31] Alvar, *Indiculus* 6 (*CSM* 1: 278).

[32] *Liber de habitu clericorum* (*CSM* 2: 667–84).

[33] Eulogius, *Memoriale* 1.21.22 (*CSM* 2: 385).

[34] Clifford Geertz, *The Interpretation of Cultures* (New York, 1973), 144.

[35] Ibid, 12.

[36] Alvar, *Indiculus* 6.2–5 (*CSM* 1: 278).

[37] Jan Willem van Henten and Friedrich Avemarie have drawn attention to the importance of the public spectacle of martyrdom as self-sacrifice in early Christianity: *Martyrdom and Noble Death* (London, 2002), 1; see also G. W. Bowersock, *Martyrdom and Rome* (Cambridge, 1995), 41–58.

[38] Suzanne Conklin Akbari and Jill Ross, 'Limits and Teleology: The Many Ends of the Body', in eaedem, eds, *The Ends of the Body: Identity and Community in Medieval Culture* (Toronto, ON, 2013), 3–24, at 3.

vehicles of voluntary collusion or disobedience, but they could also be dominated in displays of power.[39] Access to the public sphere was already highly contested, but execution in Córdoba was a public affair. The heads of rebels were usually mounted on the gates of the city, including those of defeated Christians in the north that were sent back to the capital for the purpose of exhibition. The emirate even occasionally practised public crucifixion.[40]

Displaying the bodies of the executed for the viewing public was important to Córdoban officials and the bodies of the martyrs were no exception.[41] The movement attempted to appropriate this display and subvert normative concepts of authority.[42] The apologists of the movement reported that the expositions of the bodies were accompanied by visible signs, to which they ascribed meaning. In some cases storm clouds darkened the sky,[43] in others the bodies emanated a heavenly glow.[44] Rather than viewing the corpses of those who had failed to conform to the religious laws and expectations of the people, the crowds witnessed divine displeasure at the rulers and collaborators, or approbation of the martyrs. The word 'martyr' means 'witness', and the group believed that their actions bore witness to a divinely sanctioned Christianity in the face of Muslims and other, 'weaker' Christians.[45] These signs not only changed criminals into victors but undermined the religious identification assigned by the government, and consequently the Muslims' right to rule. Those who had been seen as Muslims in life were, in death, vindicated in Christian bodies.[46] Attempts to destroy the dead bodies or impede the acquisition of relics,[47]

---

[39] For a discussion of public execution and the body see Danielle M. Westerhof, 'Amputating the Traitor: Healing the Social Body in Public Executions for Treason in Late Medieval England', in Akbari and Ross, eds, *Ends of the Body,* 177–92.

[40] Roger Collins, *Early Medieval Spain: Unity in Diversity, 400–1000* (London, 1983), 189, 191; Wolf, *Martyrs,* 125.

[41] Eulogius, *Memoriale* 1, pref., 2–3 (*CSM* 2:367–8).

[42] Bruce Malina, 'Pain, Power, and Personhood: Ascetic Behavior in the Ancient Mediterranean', in Vincent L. Wimbush and Richard Valantasis, eds, *Asceticism* (New York, 1995), 162–77, at 171.

[43] Eulogius, *Memoriale* 2.12 (*CSM*: 2: 432).

[44] Eulogius, *Liber apologeticus martyrum* 31 (*CSM* 2: 492).

[45] Eulogius, *Memoriale* 2.15.1 (*CSM* 2: 434).

[46] Ibid.

[47] Relics were distributed amongst the churches and religious houses of the movement's supporters and in demand as far away as Paris: Coope, *Martyrs of Córdoba*, 53; Wolf, *Martyrs*, 60.

a mark of some of the later executions,[48] were stopped by divine assistance. Alvar relates that a dove landed on Eulogius's body after his execution and refused to move, and that the body of his fellow martyr Leocritia, disposed of in the river by the authorities, refused to sink, demanding to be seen.[49]

If their concern was the disappearance of Christian bodies from the public sphere in Córdoba, then the executions allowed the martyrs to display their bodies for all to see. The opportunity to view the spectacle of the dead, along with the attendant signs, was emphasized by Eulogius and Alvar. The sight of the bodies had the power to bring about miracles. When Perfectus was decapitated the crowds were so immense that two men took to the river in a boat to allow themselves a better view; in the course of their attempt to catch sight of the priest's body God caused their boat to capsize and they drowned.[50] Several of the martyrs reported that seeing the public punishment of the protomartyrs was an impetus to their own decisions to join the movement.[51] The martyrologies reveal the expectation of a similar response from the wider Christian population to the witness of the martyrs. But the exposure of the bodies did not always work in the movement's favour. The only criticism against the martyrs, that did not have its basis in the movement's inability to establish its authenticity in relation to traditional Roman martyrdom, was that the bodies of the martyrs decomposed.[52]

Narratives of martyrdom were popular amongst Christians in the Islamic world of the early Middle Ages.[53] They were intended to strengthen the identity of the Christian communities in which they circulated, defining the persecutor and the persecuted,[54] by reiterating the Christian history of survival and triumph.[55] In Córdoba, the movement hoped that the history of the Roman

---

[48] Eulogius, *Liber apologeticus martyrum* 31 (*CSM* 2: 492).

[49] Alvar, *Vita Eulogii* (*CSM* 1: 330–43, at 341).

[50] Eulogius, *Memoriale* 2.4 (*CSM* 2: 400).

[51] Ibid. 2.10.7 (*CSM* 2: 418).

[52] Ibid. 1.26 (*CSM* 2: 389).

[53] Sidney H. Griffith, 'Christians, Muslims, and Neo-Martyrs: Saints' Lives and Holy Land History', in Arieh Kofsky and Guy G. Stroumsa, eds, *Sharing the Sacred* (Jerusalem, 1998), 163–207; idem, *The Church in the Shadow of the Mosque: Christians and Muslims in the World of Islam* (Princeton, NJ, and Oxford, 2008), 147–51.

[54] Griffith, *Mosque*, 150.

[55] Martyrologies constructed a similar narrative for the early Church: see Lucy

persecutions would help to explain their actions. The *passio* narratives of the Roman martyrs were part of the Visigothic liturgy,[56] and a number of Córdoban churches were dedicated to martyrs, including the Church of St Vincent upon which the Great Mosque of Córdoba was built. Eulogius invoked the language of the classic martyrologies in his writings, and argued for a visible continuum between the experience of the Christian community under Islamic and Roman rule.[57] Yet the persecutions were not the only shared cultural memory that the martyrs hoped to evoke in their co-religionists. Their preoccupation with bodies (both their own and those of others) as the medium for the Christian message may also have drawn on a Spanish narrative of bodily asceticism as a source of orthodox authority and instruction.

Although lacking the support of the ecclesiastical hierarchy and the wider Christian community, the movement was closely aligned with the monasteries surrounding the city. It was to these 'holy brothers and sisters in Christ' that Eulogius dedicated his work.[58] The relationship between the martyrs and the strictly ascetic monastic communities of Córdoba provides insight into the origins and methodologies of the movement.

The martyrs' movement emerged out of the rural monasteries surrounding Córdoba. Although Spanish monasticism was not organized under a single rule but manifested a variety of different expressions,[59] possibly as many as nine monasteries around Córdoba were connected to each other through the movement of priests (such as Eulogius and Perfectus) and students from house to house and in and out of the city.[60] Twenty-one of the martyrs are specifically identified as monks or nuns, including the first voluntary martyr and five others who were executed just four days later, making the religious the largest subgroup of the movement.[61] If one considers that the second largest subgroup is composed of

Grig, *Making Martyrs in Late Antiquity* (London, 2004); Candida Moss, *The Myth of Persecution* (New York, 2013).

56 M. C. Díaz y Díaz, 'Literary Aspects of the Visigothic Liturgy', in Edward James, ed., *Visigothic Spain: New Approaches* (Oxford, 1980), 61–76.
57 Wolf, *Martyrs*, 96–104.
58 Eulogius, *Memoriale* 1.4 (*CSM* 2: 371).
59 José Orlandis, *Estudios sobre instituciones monásticas medievales* (Pamplona, 1971).
60 Wolf, *Martyrs*, 13, 62–74.
61 Coope, *Martyrs of Córdoba*, 23.

apostates, whose family tragedies were inherently tied to Islamic law, then the ideological importance of the monasteries is brought into sharper relief. The apostates were criminals regardless of their association with the other martyrs. They could conceivably be arrested and executed independent of any individual or collective action. The fact that, of those who chose to instigate their own deaths,[62] the vast majority were religious indicates that any attempt to investigate group motivation or ideology needs to begin with the monasteries.

The monasteries also acted as a preparation for several of the lay martyrs, who retired to them before embarking on their martyrdom. The first voluntary martyr, Isaac, an assimilated high-ranking official in the government, left his job and moved to a double monastery, Tabanos, established by members of his family.[63] He lived there for three years before he presented himself to the judge and insulted the Prophet Muḥammad. Another lay couple, who lived as secret Christians, spent at least a year in contact with members of the movement before deciding to spend their last days in a monastery prior to their public denunciation of Islam and execution.[64] It appears that the lay martyrs viewed the monasteries as a stronghold for Christianity and as a source for those who wanted to rediscover or affirm their Christian identity.

The relationship between the martyrs and the surrounding monasteries has been explored before.[65] Any connection discovered between the asceticism of the monasteries and the voluntary deaths of the martyrs has been based on a negative understanding of asceticism as penitential and world-rejecting.[66] The martyrs' affiliation with the monasteries has contributed to a historiography which views the movement equally as apocalyptic, suicidal

---

[62] For a discussion of 'voluntary martyrdom', see Candida R. Moss, 'The Discourse of Voluntary Martyrdom', *ChH* 81 (2012), 531–51.

[63] Eulogius, *Memoriale* 1, pref., 2, 2.1 (*CSM* 2: 367, 402).

[64] Ibid., 2.10.15 (*CSM* 2: 422).

[65] Notably by Wolf, *Martyrs*, 107–19; Franz R. Franke, 'Die freiwilligen Märtyrer von Cordova und das Verhältnis des Mozarabes zum Islam', *Spanische Forschungen der Görresgesellschaft* 3 (1953), 1–170, at 18.

[66] 'Psychologists who see asceticism as a death-wish and suicide as an aggression must see in this movement the epitome of their theories': Daniel, *Arabs and Medieval Europe*, 35. A synopsis of modern interpretations of asceticism can be found in Lawrence Wills, 'Ascetic Theology before Asceticism? Jewish Narratives and the Decentering of Self', *JAAR* 84 (2006): 902–25.

and 'self-destructive'.[67] Yet an understanding of asceticism as an act of culture creation both explains the group's emphasis on bodies and physical acts and allows further insight into the relationship between the movement and the monasteries. Without denying the possibility that a variety of personal motivations inspired individual martyrs,[68] an understanding of the role of asceticism and monasticism allows us to see the martyrs' movement, as a whole, as an extension of the Christian culture of Córdoba.

Although Spanish monasticism established itself later than its Western European counterparts,[69] the monasteries quickly became essential transmitters of Christianity in early medieval Spain.[70] Set apart, their cultural authority rested on their role as material carriers for ascetic behaviours which acted as the cultural framework of orthodox Christianity.[71] Richard Valantasis has defined asceticism as '[physical] performances designed to inaugurate an alternative culture, to enable different social relations, and to create a new identity'.[72] The systematic training and retraining through acts, that is, the patterning of behaviour, moulds someone into a different person for a different culture that they, through their participation, then help to create and perpetuate.[73] As places that translated the theology of Christianity into practical performances,

---

[67] Clayton J. Drees, 'Sainthood and Suicide: The Motives of the Martyrs of Córdoba, A.D. 850–859', *Journal of Medieval and Renaissance Studies* 20 (1990), 59–89. This attitude exists in discussions of early Christian martyrdom, especially in cases of voluntary martyrdom, which are seen as 'spontaneous acts of self-destruction': Arthur J. Droge and James D. Tabor, *A Noble Death* (New York, 1992), 132; see also Arik Greenber, *My Share of God's Reward* (New York, 2009); Donald Riddle, *The Martyrs: A Study in Social Control* (Chicago, IL, 1931).

[68] However, in at least one case the nuns of the monastery of St Salvador tried to convince their sister not to present herself to be martyred: Eulogius, *Memoriale* 3.11 (*CSM* 2: 452–4).

[69] Collins, *Early Medieval Spain*, 80.

[70] Neil Allies, 'The Monastic Rules of Visigothic Iberia: A Study of their Text and Language' (PhD thesis, University of Birmingham, 2009), 41–52; Roger Collins, *Visigothic Spain: 409–711* (Oxford, 2004), 153, 170, 202–6.

[71] Bernard McGinn, 'Asceticism and Mysticism in Late Antiquity and the Early Middle Ages', in Wimbush and Valantasis, eds, *Asceticism*, 58–74, at 58.

[72] Richard Valantasis, 'A Theory of the Social Function of Asceticism', in Wimbush and Valantasis, eds, *Asceticism*, 544–52, at 548. Valantasis's definition is indebted to the work of Geoffrey Harpham, who views asceticism as the common feature of all cultures: *The Ascetic Imperative in Culture and Criticism* (Chicago, IL, 1987).

[73] Valantasis, 'Social Function of Asceticism', 548.

the monasteries acted as a repository for the cultural codes of Spanish Christianity in a fluid religious landscape.

This definition of asceticism as a creative physical performance implies an audience. In the Spanish context the performance was not confined to fellow monks as part of the perpetuation of an exclusively monastic culture. The monasteries continually connected with, and replenished, the wider Christian community, not least through their role as the breeding ground for bishops.[74] It was in the monastery that the bishops learned the ascetic behaviours that invested them with the authority to lead the Christian population in right behaviour.[75] Reflecting the changing nature of both the religious landscape and the discipline of the monasteries, Spanish episcopal councils focused their attention on the correct performance of correct Catholic rituals in the face of 'cultic anomalies'.[76] Ascetic ideals are diffused in a variety of ways. As a system of symbols, literacy or theological understanding is not necessarily a prerequisite.[77] Due to their visibility, the bodies of monks and bishops were essential to the instruction of the Christian population. Emerging from the monasteries, their bodies were marked by ascetic discipline, physically moulded into symbols of Christianity.[78]

Like monastic asceticism, the martyrdoms were premeditated, and many were highly stylized. Isaac, mirroring the ques-

[74] De Epalza, 'Mozarabs', 154–6. As elsewhere, bishops were essential to the survival of Spanish Christianity because without bishops to perform sacramental functions, there could be no Church.

[75] Similar situations occurred throughout the late antique and early medieval Mediterranean: see Peter Brown, *Power and Persuasion in Late Antiquity: Towards a Christian Empire* (Madison, WI, 1992); Conrad Leyser, *Authority and Asceticism from Augustine to Gregory the Great* (Oxford, 2000); Philip Rousseau, *Ascetics, Authority, and the Church in the Age of Jerome and Cassian* (Notre Dame, IN, 2010); Andrea Stark, *Renouncing the World yet Leading the Church* (London, 2004). For a wider discussion of asceticism and power, see Richard Valantasis, 'Constructions of Power in Asceticism', *JAAR* 63 (1995), 775–821.

[76] Brown, *Western Christendom*, 221.

[77] Averil Cameron, 'Ascetic Closure and the End of Antiquity', in Wimbush and Valantasis, eds, *Asceticism*, 147–61, at 155.

[78] For a discussion of the role of the body in religious education, see Talal Asad, *Genealogies of Religion: Discipline and Reasons of Power in Christianity and Islam* (Baltimore, MD, 1993); Linda G. Jones, 'Bodily Performances and Body Talk in Medieval Islamic Preaching', in Akbari and Ross, eds, *Ends of the Body*, 211–39; Derek Krueger, 'Hagiography as an Ascetic Practice in the Early Christian East', *Journal of Religion* 79 (1999), 216–32.

tions posed to Perfectus, asked the judge to instruct him in Islam moments before attacking it himself.[79] Sabigotho and Liliosa unveiled themselves in a dramatic public display of their identity as Christian women.[80] Rogelius and Servus Dei announced their decision to become martyrs by preaching in the mosque.[81] Others simply presented themselves to the judge and launched into their polemics without fanfare.[82] Monastic asceticism is repetitious. Acts are performed over and over to discipline and develop habit but also, in the process, to create and participate in the culture which gives the repetitive actions meaning.[83] One after another the martyrs repeated the same acts, blasphemy against Islam and death, participating in a Christian culture which rejected Islam and was marked by self-denial. At the same time, by taking their asceticism into the public sphere they hoped to stop the cycle of cultural extinction by presenting their own bodies as the Christian symbols that others had chosen to deny.

Like the bishops, the martyrs came from the monasteries prepared to teach the community in right Christianity. They must have considered their work all the more essential in light of the failures of some clerics to maintain Christian symbols and the perceived collusion of the bishops with the Umayyads.[84] Invested with monastic authority, they performed their ascetic rituals for the public. This is most obvious in the cases of monks and nuns who were known for their feats of asceticism prior to becoming martyrs. One of the earliest martyrs was the monk Habentius, who practiced self-flagellation with iron bars and 'showed himself through breaches in the wall to visitors'.[85] Like the bodies of the dead, the bodies of those dying to the world were meant to be seen by the people. Christian ascetic practice, with roots in the early theologies of martyrdom, is intended to act as a witness for

---

[79] Eulogius, *Memoriale* 1, pref., 2 (*CSM* 2: 367).

[80] Ibid. 2.10.30 (*CSM* 2: 428).

[81] Ibid. 2.13 (*CSM* 2: 432–3).

[82] Ibid., 2.4 (*CSM* 2:403–4).

[83] Asad, *Genealogies*, 72–7; Valantasis, 'Social Function of Asceticism', 548–9.

[84] In fact, both Alvar and Eulogius had disputes with the ecclesial authorities, with Eulogius going as far as refusing to celebrate mass in protest: see Coope, *Martyrs of Córdoba*, 61–9; Wolf, *Martyrs*, 55–8.

[85] Eulogius, *Memoriale* 2.4.3 (*CSM* 2: 403–4). Similar stories were told about the nun Columba: ibid. 3 10 (*CSM* 2: 447–52).

the community to God, and for God to the community.[86] By extending his ascetic discipline into the public sphere through martyrdom, Habentius and the other martyred monks and nuns were allowing the symbols of their disciplined bodies to be seen by a wider audience.

Eulogius was the last martyr recorded by Alvar. While there may have been other deaths in later decades, the movement seems to have died out with their main chronicler,[87] and indeed with the destruction of the monasteries brought about by the implementation of the *dhimmī* laws regarding new church construction.[88] While it existed, the movement caused considerable concern for the Umayyads and the local Christian hierarchy, who never accepted it. It is ironic that, by punishing preaching against the Prophet with execution, the emiral government inadvertently allowed a form of bodily pedagogy access to the public sphere. The martyrs' obsession with the body reflects not only the shifting nature of public religious identity in ninth-century Córdoba, but also Spanish methods of transmitting authority and orthodoxy. The monastic communities from which the movement emerged existed within the Spanish tradition of ascetic cultural transmission for which they were the loci. The fluid nature of religious identity had only solidified the role of the monasteries in maintaining and perpetuating Christian symbols through the training of bishops and martyrs. Within the context of Spanish monasticism, the motivation of the martyrs can be understood not as perverted self-destruction but as an extreme attempt at culture creation and preservation.

Memorial University, Newfoundland

---

[86] Bowersock, *Martyrdom*, 41–58, 67–70. Isabelle Kinnard, '*Imitatio Christi* in Christian Martyrdom and Asceticism', in Oliver Freiberger, ed., *Asceticism and its Critics: Historical Accounts and Comparative Perspectives* (Oxford, 2006), 91–116.

[87] Wolf, *Martyrs*, 35.

[88] Ibid, 31.

BAPTIZED BUT NOT CONVERTED: THE VIKINGS IN TENTH-CENTURY FRANCIA

by CHRISTINE WALSH

This essay focuses on one particular encounter between pagan and Christian in tenth-century Western Europe, namely the aftermath of the Viking settlement in Rouen and its environs in or around the year 911. There is little contemporary evidence for the early settlement and such as exists was written from a Christian perspective.[1] The Vikings left no records, although their descendants wrote several romanticized accounts of their origins, again from a Christian perspective.[2] Despite this bias in the sources, it is possible to use them to examine the interaction between the two groups. In particular, two letters survive, one from Pope John X (914–28/9) and one from Archbishop Hervé of Reims (900–22), which together give a unique perspective on what it was like at the sharp end of the Viking influx.

Bands of Vikings had been raiding Francia[3] from the 830s onwards.[4] To those they attacked the Vikings were the ultimate 'other': violent and non-Christian.[5] However, while contemporary

---

[1]   The principal sources are Dudo of St Quentin (fl. 960s–1020s) and Flodoard of Reims (893/7–966). See *De Moribus et actis primorum Normanniae ducem, auctore Dudone Sanctii Quintini decano*, ed. Jules Lair (Caen, 1865); *Dudo of St Quentin, History of the Normans*, ed. and transl. Eric Christiansen (Woodbridge, 1998); Flodoard of Reims, *Historia Remensis Ecclesiae* (MGH S 36); idem, *Les Annales de Flodoard*, ed. Philippe Lauer (Paris, 1905); *The Annals of Flodoard of Reims 919–966*, ed. and transl. Steven Fanning and Bernard Bachrach, Readings in Medieval Civilizations and Cultures 9 (Toronto, ON, 2011); David Bates, *Normandy before 1066* (Harlow, 1982), xii–xiii, 6, 8–12; Leah Shopkow, *History and Community: Norman Historical Writing in the Eleventh and Twelfth Centuries* (Washington DC, 1997), 68–79; Emily Albu, *The Normans in their Histories: Propaganda, Myth and Subversion* (Woodbridge, 2001), 9–11.

[2]   Ralph H. C. Davis, *The Normans and their Myth* (London, 1976), 49–69.

[3]   By *Francia* I mean the western Frankish lands which ultimately coalesced to form modern France.

[4]   *The Annals of St-Bertin*, transl. Janet Nelson, Ninth-Century Histories 1 (Manchester, 1991), 60, 65–6; Angelo Forte, Richard Oram and Frederic Pederson, *Viking Empires* (Cambridge, 2005), 59–63; Lucien Musset, 'Naissance de la Normandie (Vᵉ–XIᵉ siècles)', in Michel de Boüard, ed., *Histoire de la Normandie* (Toulouse, 1970), 75–130, at 119; Michel Mollat, *Histoire de Rouen* (Toulouse, [c.1979]), 38.

[5]   *St-Bertin*, transl. Nelson, 51, where the Vikings are described as demon-worshippers.

writers emphasize Viking 'paganism', little specific information is given as to the form it took. This is typical of medieval writing on 'paganism', which tended to follow generic stereotypes, often derived from classical writing.[6] It is also the case that Christianity as a universal religion with a relatively consistent set of beliefs and practices found it hard to understand the multiplicity of pagan beliefs and practices.[7] In addition, the term could also be used of Christians whose behaviour was considered unorthodox and there-fore 'non-Christian'.[8] 'Pagan' is perhaps best understood, then, as a nonspecific, pejorative term for 'non-Christian'. Those designated as 'pagans' were by definition outside regular society. Conversion thus becomes a way of enrolling or re-enrolling someone into society.

The Vikings were born opportunists and found themselves drawn into Frankish regional politics as various war-bands devel-oped a lucrative sideline as mercenaries.[9] There were also attempts by some groups to establish permanent settlements.[10] Against this background, at some point around 911 Charles the Simple, Caro-lingian king of the western Franks from 893 until 922, when he was deposed, dying in prison in 929, made a grant of land, centred on Rouen, to a Viking band led by Rollo.[11] Rollo may have already seized Rouen by 911, but not everything had gone his way, as he

---

[6] James T. Palmer, 'Defining Paganism in the Carolingian World', *EME* 15 (2007), 402–25, esp. 403–5; Ian Wood, *The Missionary Life: Saints and the Evangelisation of Europe 400–1050* (Harlow, 2001), 5–6; idem, 'Pagan Religions and Superstitions East of the Rhine from the Fifth to the Ninth Century', in Giorgio Ausenda, ed., *After Empire: Towards an Ethnology of Europe's Barbarians* (Woodbridge, 1993), 253–68.

[7] Przemysław Urbańczyk, 'The Politics of Conversion in North Central Europe', in Martin Carver, ed., *The Cross goes North: Processes of Conversion in Northern Europe, AD 300–1300* (York, 2003), 15–27, at 23.

[8] James T. Palmer, *Anglo-Saxons in a Frankish World, 690–900* (Turnhout, 2009), 121–4.

[9] Forte, Oram and Pederson, *Viking Empires*, 61; Janet Nelson, *Charles the Bald* (London, 1992), 151, 170, 187, 183, 193–4.

[10] Forte, Oram and Pederson, *Viking Empires*, 60, 62, 64–6.

[11] *Dudo*, transl. Christiansen, 48–9; Flodoard, *Historia*, 407; idem, *Annals*, ed. and transl. Fanning and Bachrach, 9. In 918 Charles the Simple confirmed certain lands of the monks of Saint-Germain-des-Prés, with the exception of lands already granted to Rollo, so the settlement must have existed by then: *Recueil des Actes de Charles III le Simple, Roi de France (893–923)*, ed. Philippe Lauer (Paris, 1949), no. 92; *Dudo*, transl. Christiansen, xiii–xxiii; Bates, *Normandy before 1066*, xii–xiii, 6, 8–12; Shopkow, *History and Community*, 68–79; Albu, *Normans in their Histories*, 9–11; David Douglas, 'Rollo of Normandy', *EHR* 57 (1942), 417–36, at 425.

had been defeated while besieging Chartres.[12] The situation was probably something of a stalemate, with Charles trying to stabilize his western front. A condition of the grant was that Rollo and his followers were baptized as Christians.

There were precedents for mass baptisms. Some, such as those that occurred during Augustine's mission to England, were more or less voluntary.[13] Others, such as Charlemagne's forcible conversion of the Saxons, were not.[14] In the latter case baptism was used as a political tool to reinforce conquest.[15] The mass baptism of the Saxons had deeply troubled Alcuin (*c.*735–804), and in a letter to Charlemagne and other writings he emphasized the need for conversion through instruction prior to baptism.[16] However, for the Carolingians baptism continued to have significance as an entry rite into Frankish society and an acknowledgement of political allegiance.[17] Baptism was a way of managing the Christian-pagan relationship in circumstances where the political imperative to create an alliance outweighed any consideration of a meaningful personal conversion. So we find in 826 Louis the Pious offering baptism and support to Harold, an exiled claimant to the Danish throne, and in 882 Charles the Fat became godfather to Godafrid, leader of an aggressive war-band.[18] It is likely, although unprovable, that Rollo and his followers also saw the political implications of

---

[12] *Dudo*, transl. Christiansen, 36–46, 43; Janet Nelson, 'Normandy's Early History since *Normandy Before 1066*', in *Normandy and her Neighbours, 900–1250: Essays for David Bates*, ed. David Crouch and Kathleen Thompson (Turnhout, 2011), 3–15, at 5; Douglas, 'Rollo', 427.

[13] Barbara Yorke, *The Conversion of Britain 600–800* (Harlow, 2006), 122–8; Henry Mayr-Harting, *The Coming of Christianity to Anglo–Saxon England* (London, 1972), 61–8.

[14] Timothy Reuter, *Germany in the Early Middle Ages* (Harlow, 1991), 65–7.

[15] Wood, *Missionary Life*, 58.

[16] Donald Bullough, 'Alcuin and the Kingdom of Heaven: Liturgy, Theology, and the Carolingian Age', in Uta-Renate Blumenthal, ed., *Carolingian Essays: Andrew W. Mellon Lectures in Early Christian Studies* (Washington DC, 1983), 1–69, at 41–5; Douglas Dales, *Alcuin: Theology and Thought* (Cambridge, 2013), 112–18; Peter Cramer, *Baptism and Change in the Early Middle Ages c.200 – c.1150* (Cambridge, 1993), 46.

[17] Susan Keefe, *Water and the Word: Baptism and the Education of the Clergy in the Carolingian Empire*, 2 vols (Notre Dame, IN, 2002), 1: 3; eadem, 'Carolingian Baptismal Expositions: A Handlist of Tracts and Manuscripts', in Blumenthal, ed., *Carolingian Essays*, 169–237, at 171–2.

[18] For Harold, see Thegan of Trier, *Vita Hludowici Imperatoris*.33 (MGH SS 2, 597); *Anonymi Vita Hludowici Imperatoris* 40 (MGH SS 2, 629). For Godafrid, see *Annales Fuldenses sive Annales Regni Francorum Orientalis* (MGH SRG i.u.s., 99); ET *The Annals of Fulda*, transl. Timothy Reuter, Ninth-century Histories 2 (Manchester, 1992), 92–3.

baptism as more significant than the religious ones. They may have been baptized; they had yet to be converted.

Milis, in the context of the Christianization of the Franks, has argued that conversion has to be regarded as a process leading from initial baptism to full acceptance of the Christian faith and that, despite its emphasis on conversion before baptism, in practice the medieval Church was pragmatic and recognized that the process of conversion continued after baptism.[19] In this context, Wood has suggested that Boniface, best known today as a missionary and martyr, actually spent more time on episcopal and monastic organization to strengthen the Church in recently Christianized lands than on preaching to the unconverted.[20] Wood has also distinguished between mission and Christianization – the latter consisting of cultural, political and economic processes which continued long after formal conversion.[21] In the case of the Rouen Vikings, this process of acculturation was probably more significant in the conversion process than actual baptism, as succeeding generations grew up within a Christian society.

It has been argued that the Vikings also used conversion as a political tool. Wallace-Hadrill quotes the example of Pippin II of Aquitaine, a grandson of Louis the Pious, who succeeded to the throne of Aquitaine in 838. There was considerable infighting amongst the descendants of Louis during the middle of the ninth century for control of the constituent parts of the Carolingian Empire and Pippin was one of the losers in this contest.[22] Deposed and forced to enter a monastery in 852, Pippin escaped in 854 and, in an attempt to regain his inheritance, allied himself with a Viking band that had settled on the Loire in the 840s. He is said to have adopted pagan ways, and when he was recaptured in 864 he was condemned to death for treason and apostasy.[23] Wallace-Hadrill suggests that the Vikings may have insisted that Pippin

See also Simon Coupland, 'The Rod of God's Wrath or the People of God's Wrath? The Carolingian Theology of the Viking Invasions', *JEH* 42 (1991), 535–54, at 552.

[19] Ludo Milis, 'La Conversion en profondeur: un processus sans fin', *Revue du Nord* 68 (1986), 487–98, at 494–6.

[20] Wood, *Missionary Life*, 57–73.

[21] Ibid. 4.

[22] J. Michael Wallace-Hadrill, *The Vikings in Francia: The Stenton Lecture 1974* (Reading, 1975), 12–13.

[23] His fate is unknown but he is thought to have died in prison: *St-Bertin*, transl. Nelson, 74, 79, 111, 119.

renounce Christianity as a sign of loyalty.[24] However, Coupland interprets the evidence as showing that Pippin's association with pagans was considered equivalent to worshipping idols rather than that he actually embraced paganism.[25] Nelson has also argued that the text means that Pippin followed the Vikings' way of life rather than converting.[26] It seems most likely that Pippin's real crime was losing the power struggle, and that his alliance with non-Christians provided a convenient way of discrediting him.

The process by which Rollo and his followers became Christians is unclear. The only detailed account is in Dudo of St Quentin, who recounts how Rollo was first instructed in the faith and then baptized. On the eighth day after his baptism Rollo 'took off his baptismal and chrismal vestments'.[27] This is similar to Asser's account of the baptism of the Viking leader Guthrum following his defeat by Alfred in 878, and follows known practice for adult converts, especially the wearing of white robes for eight days.[28] So, although the description is written in Dudo's characteristic literary style, with much of the detail springing from his imagination, it may well reflect something of what took place.

In Asser's account of Guthrum's baptism there is no mention of any prior instruction in the Christian faith. It is clearly a political act of submission and alliance. This is further emphasized by Alfred becoming Guthrum's godfather, creating a relationship of spiritual kinship.[29] In Rollo's case, Dudo says he was instructed in the faith before baptism and that Robert, duke of the Franks, became his godfather.[30] The extent of any instruction is glossed over. Dudo goes on to say that Rollo's followers were also baptized and 'instructed in the observances of the Christian faith by preaching', which sounds plausible. However, in order to preach successfully a preacher has to have a language in common with his audience. The Vikings had been in Francia long enough for some of them to

---

[24] Wallace-Hadrill, *Vikings in Francia*, 12–13.

[25] Coupland, 'Rod of God's Wrath', 546.

[26] *St-Bertin*, transl. Nelson, 111 n. 3.

[27] *Dudo*, transl. Christiansen, 50–1.

[28] *Alfred the Great: Asser's Life of Alfred and other Contemporary Sources*, transl. Simon Keynes and Michael Lapidge (Harmondsworth, 1983), 85; Joseph Lynch, *Christianizing Kinship: Ritual Sponsorship in Anglo-Saxon England* (Ithaca, NY, 1998), 128–34.

[29] Lynch, *Christianizing Kinship*, 81–98, 215–17.

[30] *Dudo*, transl. Christiansen, 50–1. Robert (d. 923) was a leading noble whose descendants became the Capetian kings of France.

have picked up the local language, but their grasp of this is likely to have been fairly basic. Charles and Rollo must have been able to communicate in order to reach agreement. Interpreters may have existed. However, any instruction in the tenets of Christianity is likely to have been brief and simple.[31]

The unlucky cleric who was archbishop of Rouen at this time was one Guy (b. 892).[32] He faced a local regime which was busy consolidating and expanding its position. King Charles was a long way away, with other preoccupations; the Vikings were on Guy's doorstep, fully armed and only nominally converted. Canon law demanded severe penalties for converts who relapsed into paganism; pragmatism said he should tread carefully. Isolated and in need of support, Guy sought advice from Hervé, archbishop of Reims and chancellor to Charles the Simple.[33] Guy knew Hervé from ecclesiastical councils at Reims in 900 and Trosly in 909; Flodoard implies that Hervé already had some experience in converting Vikings, but there is no evidence that this was so.[34] Certainly Hervé seems to have had doubts about how to proceed, and to have written to the pope for advice. A letter from John X to Hervé and one from Hervé to Guy survive in a tenth-century manuscript from Reims.[35] The letter from Hervé includes twenty-three extracts from various authorities intended to give Guy some guidance.

Although the papal letter cannot be directly linked to Hervé's letter, its content suggests that it was related to the same problems. Some scholars have argued that the pope's letter was written by John IX, for example the seventeenth-century editors of the

---

[31] The Church could be pragmatic about such matters: see Urbańczyk, 'Politics of Conversion', 23.

[32] It is not known when Guy died.

[33] Olivier Guillot, 'La conversion des Normands peu après 911: Des reflets contemporains à l'historiographie ultérieure (X^e–XIe s.)', *Cahiers de civilisation médiévale* 24 (1981), 101–16, 181–219, at 102; Michel Sot, *Un Historien et son église au Xe siècle: Flodoard de Reims* (Paris, 1993), 221.

[34] Isolde Schröder, *Die westfränkischen Synoden von 888 bis 987 und ihre Überlieferung* (Munich, 1908), 153–7, 189–97; Flodoard, *Historia*, 407; Sot, *Un Historien*, 224–6.

[35] Paris, BN, MS 4280A, fols 102^r–107^r. For the Reims provenance of this manuscript, see Frederick M. Carey, 'The Scriptorium of Reims during the Archbishopric of Hincmar (845–882 A.D.)', in *Classical and Medieval Studies in Honor of Edward Kennard Rand: Presented upon the Completion of his Fortieth Year of Teaching*, ed. Leslie Webber Jones (New York, 1938), 41–60.

documents.[36] But, as Prentout has pointed out, they dated John IX's pontificate to 901–5, whereas later scholarship has dated it to 898–900.[37] Although the exact date of John's death is unknown, his successor, Benedict IV, was elected in May/June 900.[38] Hervé only became archbishop of Reims in July 900, making it unlikely that the letter is from John IX.[39]

Similar exchanges of letters exist between several popes and missionaries. Amongst the best known is the correspondence between Boniface (*c.*675–754) and successive popes concerning the behaviour of the pagan and semi-pagan Germanic peoples.[40] There is also the exchange between Pope Gregory the Great (590–604) and Augustine (d. 604) recorded in Bede, in which Gregory gives advice on a number of issues of morals and behaviour.[41] This latter is of particular interest as an extract from Gregory's advice to one of Augustine's companions, Mellitus, is included with Hervé's letter.

We can glean some idea of the problems facing Guy from the letters of John X and Hervé. The pope's letter says that Hervé has asked what ought to be done with people who were 'baptized and rebaptized and after baptism have lived as heathens, and killed Christians in the manner of pagans, who have slaughtered priests and offered sacrifice to idols, eating the food sacrificed to idols'.[42] Hervé's letter to Guy similarly repeats the problem as put to him by Guy: 'you ask … about those who have been rebaptized and in like manner as before baptism follow pagan customs, as they return to wallow like pigs and like dogs to their vomit [and] perform unspeakable pagan rituals as recreational pleasures'.[43]

[36] *Sacrosancta Concilia ad Regiam Editionem exacta quae nunc quarta parte prodit auctior,* ed. Philip Labbei et Gabriel Cossartii, 17 vols (Paris, 1671–2), 9: cols 483–94.

[37] Henri Prentout, *Étude critique sur Dudon de Saint-Quentin et son histoire des premiers ducs normands* (Paris, 1916), 255; J. N. D. Kelly, ed., *Oxford Dictionary of Popes,* (Oxford, 1968), 116–17.

[38] Kelly, ed., *Oxford Dictionary of Popes,* 117.

[39] Prentout, *Étude critique,* 256.

[40] See for example, *Die Briefe des heligen Bonifatus und Lullus* (MGH Epp. Sel. 1, 44–7; letter 26).

[41] *Bede's Ecclesiastical History of the English People,* ed. Bertram Colgrave and R. A. B. Mynors, OMT (Oxford, 1992; first publ. 1969), 27, 79–103 (hereafter: *HE*).

[42] '[Q]uid agendum sit quod fuerint baptizati et rebaptizati et post baptismum gentiliter vixerint atque paganorum mores Christianos interfecerint, sacerdotes trucidaverint atque simulacris immolantes, idolythyta comederint': MS 4280A, fol. 106[v].

[43] '[R]ogatis … his qui rebaptizati sunt et aeque ut ante baptismum juxta pagan-

The two passages are similar in content although the second is harsher in tone. Too much should not be read into this, as the imagery used follows a common theme that has been used elsewhere and draws upon biblical sources.[44] The key issues are the same in both letters and divide into two main areas: the nature of baptism and the behaviour of supposed converts.

As far as baptism is concerned the main issue seems to be that some Vikings had been baptized more than once. The surviving documents do not say why rebaptisms occurred. It may have been because it was difficult to know who had been baptized in a mass ceremony. It was not unknown for individuals to present themselves on numerous occasions.[45] Alternatively, there may have been uncertainty about whether it was necessary to rebaptize individuals who had reverted to paganism and subsequently wanted to be reconciled to the Church.

Although neither letter deals with rebaptism directly, the extracts sent by Hervé address the issue, but they do not give consistent advice. Chapter 14, from the Council of Carthage (345–8), and chapter 19, from the writings of Pope Leo the Great (440–61) say that rebaptism is forbidden by canon law.[46] Chapter 10, an extract from Bede, and chapter 11, another extract from Pope Leo, both say that rebaptism should not take place except where the baptizer was a heretic or schismatic (Bede) or there is genuine doubt that an adult was baptized as a child (Leo).[47] Chapter 8, taken from the *Passio* of St Lawrence, tells of someone baptized by Lawrence and later catechized and rebaptized by St Hippolytus.[48] There is an echo here of the debate in the patristic period as to whether someone baptized by heretics needed to be rebaptized before being admitted into the established Church.[49] This was not really the issue facing Guy, as it was not the validity of an individual's first baptism that was in question. Taken together, though,

---

ismi morem quemadmodum sues suum reversi ad volutabrum et canes ad vomitum ludicras voluptates nefando paganorum ritu exercuere': ibid., fol. 102ʳ.

44 Prov. 26: 11; 2 Pet. 2: 22; Guillot, *Conversion*, 110–11, esp. n. 59; Nelson, 'Normandy's Early History', 6.

45 Balbulus Notker, *Gesta Karoli Magni* 2.19 (MGH SS n.s. 12, 90).

46 MS 4280A, fols 105ʳ⁻ᵛ.

47 Ibid., fol. 105ʳ.

48 Ibid., fol. 104ʳ.

49 Cramer, *Baptism and Change*, 127.

the general impression given is that rebaptism should not know-ingly be performed.

The second broad area addressed in the documents is the problem of backsliding converts. Before examining the detailed charges, the response in the correspondence will be considered. John X's letter is couched in terms of general encouragement and reassurance. Indeed, in the opening part of his letter John almost seems to be missing the point when he rejoices 'that the Normans who were once enjoying human blood are by the inspi-ration of divine mercy converted to the faith'.[50] Here he appears to be equating baptism with conversion, although when he turns to the problem of backsliding converts he does recognize that it is a process. He offers three pieces of advice. Firstly, Hervé should concentrate on bringing the influential back into the fold. Secondly, because they are new to the faith Hervé should be gentle with them.[51] Thirdly, if they have repented they should be allowed to perform penance.[52]

It is often said that John's letter to Hervé shows deep pastoral concern for the problems he faced.[53] There is an element of hind-sight in this interpretation. A modern historian reviewing the situ-ation knows that the conversion was successfully completed. From the standpoint of Hervé and Guy in the early tenth century this was a far from certain outcome. Whilst the fact that the pope seemed willing to take the long view might have given Hervé some reassurance, in terms of practical advice on steps to take the papal letter gives no real guidance. This is not surprising when one considers the conditions John X faced in Rome. His pontifi-cate was problem-strewn. In Rome itself he was involved in some extremely murky political infighting amongst various noble factions and in 928 was deposed and imprisoned in the Castel Sant'Angelo, where he died, probably murdered, in 929.[54] Given this, dealing with pastoral problems on the western fringes of Christendom was not going to be high on his agenda and I would argue that John's letter reads like that of a man with other things on his mind. It is

---

[50] '[D]e ipsa gente Northmannorum quae ad fidem divina inspirante clementia conversa olim humano sanguine grassata laetabatur': MS 4280A, fol. 106ᵛ.

[51] Ibid., fol. 106ᵛ.

[52] Ibid., fol. 107ʳ.

[53] Guillot, *Conversion*, 109.

[54] Kelly, ed., *Oxford Dictionary of Popes*, 121–2.

a classic bureaucratic response to a problem: lots of sympathy but little in the way of practical help.

Hervé's letter to Guy is shorter and is little more than a covering note to the extracts he has sent him. The only indications of Hervé's approach are two biblical quotations emphasizing that God will be merciful to repentant sinners.[55] This follows the line taken in the pope's letter that converts who have lapsed from the faith should be allowed to do penance and be reconciled. The appended extracts reinforce this approach, which Hervé further emphasizes by saying that he has placed a story of St John the Evangelist first as it is 'a wonderful and most merciful deed'.[56] The story is of a young man, converted by St John, who later falls into bad company and becomes a thief and murderer. John persuades him to repent and reconciles him with the Church.[57] Chapter 7 tells a similar tale of an apostate brought back to the faith by St Basil.[58] In both cases the individual is brought to repentance by the eloquence of the saint and his own sense of shame. A further nine chapters deal with repentance, of which four spell out appropriate penances.[59] An additional four chapters give details of the penances to be imposed on people who have fallen into pagan ways.[60]

The cumulative effect of these chapters is to give Guy reassurance that he could readmit repentant Vikings into the Church, and to suggest suitable penances. What they do not give him are many suggestions as to how to achieve this happy outcome. Only one extract out of the twenty-three gives any practical advice. It consists of three passages from Gregory the Great. In one, a letter to Bishop Peter of Corsica, Gregory recommends 'scaring them over the coming judgement and ... explaining why they should not worship ... stones'.[61] In another from a letter to Abbot Mellitus, he recommends turning pagan customs into Christian ones. In particular, instead of sacrificing animals to the devil, they should be allowed to 'kill animals for eating in praise of God ...

---

[55] MS 4280A, fol. 102[r]. The Scripture passages are Ps. 32: 5; Wisd. 11: 24.
[56] MS 4280A, fol. 102[r].
[57] Ibid., fols 102[r–v].
[58] Ibid., fols 103[v]–104[r].
[59] Ibid., chs 2–5, 12, 13, 15, 21–22.
[60] Ibid., chs 16–19.
[61] MS 4280A, fol. 103[r]; *The Letters of Gregory the Great*, transl. John R. C. Martyn, 3 vols, Medieval Sources in Translation 40 (Toronto, ON, 2004), 2: 497 (*Epistola* 8.1).

for there is no doubt that it is impossible to cut away everything at the same time from hardened minds, because anyone who strives to ascend to the highest place relies on ladders or steps. He is not lifted up in one leap'.[62] I have already referred to Gregory's advice to Augustine and it is a testament to the practical approach to conversion taken by Gregory that his advice, by Rollo's time some three hundred years old, was still being used.[63]

This all begs the question of how real the problems were which the two letters describe. The first charge is the general one of 'living like heathens'. This may have been a matter of perception. We have already noted that the term 'pagan' or 'heathen' could be used of nominally Christian people who followed some unapproved practices. The Vikings were not suddenly going to start behaving like Franks. The settler group was comprised largely of men used to a roving warrior life who came from a non-Frankish cultural and linguistic background. A more settled existence focused on the urban centre of Rouen required them to work out new or modified patterns of behaviour.[64] There is some evidence for continuing paganism; Rollo himself is said to have asked for pagan rites at his funeral as well as Christian ones.[65] While this story may be apocryphal, it does reflect the eclectic nature of pagan religion.[66] There is also some evidence for a short-lived pagan revival at the time of the assassination of Rollo's son and heir William Longsword in 942.[67] However, once settled, linguistic assimilation seems to have taken place relatively quickly: William is said to have sent his son Richard to Bayeux to learn Danish as he could not do so in Rouen.[68] Once the chaos that followed the death of Longsword had died down and Duke Richard I of Normandy had reached maturity and come into his inheritance, there is little

[62] MS 4280A, fol. 103ʳ; *Letters of Gregory the Great*, transl. Martyn, 3: 803 (*Epistola* 11.56).

[63] For Gregory's views on conversion, see Marilyn Dunn, *The Christianization of the Anglo–Saxons c.597–c.700: Discourses of Life, Death and Afterlife* (London, 2009), 44–54.

[64] Mollat, *Histoire de Rouen*, 40.

[65] Adémar de Chabannes, *Chronique*, ed. Jules Chavanon (Paris, 1897), 139–40.

[66] Similarly, Bede recounts how Raedwald of East Anglia, even though baptized, kept both a Christian and a pagan altar: *HE* 2.15 (transl. Colgrave and Mynors, 190–1).

[67] Flodoard, *Annals*, ed. and transl. Fanning and Bachrach, 38; Bates *Normandy before 1066*, 13.

[68] *Dudo*, transl. Christiansen, 97.

evidence for substantial pagan survival and rather more evidence for the Normans, as the Vikings had by then become, being active Christians.[69]

The second charge, of killing Christians and priests, may also not be what it seems. Once settled in Rouen the Vikings continued to expand their territory through aggressive behaviour towards their neighbours. However, this was mirrored by their neighbours' aggressive behaviour towards them. In other words, they were behaving like their Christian neighbours, who were also busy killing each other and not necessarily respecting church property in the process.[70] Indeed, Hervé had had experience of this, as his predecessor, Archbishop Fulk of Reims, had been assassinated on the orders of Baldwin of Flanders in 900.[71] Orderic Vitalis records how in the late 940s Hugh the Great ordered his men to attack Normandy and 'wreck churches', and how they subsequently sacked the monastery of St-Évroul.[72] The perception that the Vikings' behaviour was somehow worse could have derived from memories of their pagan past.

The final charge, of sacrificing to idols and afterwards eating the food, is a common trope found elsewhere in Christian writings. We have already seen Gregory the Great writing on the subject in the early seventh century. Boniface also makes the same complaint.[73] It is hard to tell whether it is true or just an assumption of likely behaviour, but it does seem to have been a sensitive issue, more so than establishing church control over other important social practices such as marriage.[74]

---

[69] Cassandra Potts, *Monastic Revival and Religious Identity in Early Normandy* (Woodbridge, 1997), 5–7.

[70] John Le Patourel, *The Norman Empire* (Oxford, 1976), 12–20.

[71] Flodoard, *Historia*, 102–3.

[72] *The Ecclesiastical History of Orderic Vitalis*, ed. and transl. Marjorie Chibnall, 6 vols, OMT (Oxford, 1969–80), 3: 314–17. Coupland, 'Rod of God's Wrath', 543, gives other examples.

[73] *Die Briefe des heligen Bonifatus und Lullus* (MGH Epp. Sel. 1, 44–7; letter 26).

[74] It took some hundred and fifty years to establish control over marriage. Of the seven counts or dukes from Rollo to William the Conqueror (duke 1035–87), only the brothers Richard III (duke 1026–7) and Robert I (duke 1027–35) were born in wedlock.

Guy's response to Hervé's letter and inclusions is not known. There is no way of telling if he followed Gregory the Great's advice or whether he found any of the other extracts helpful. In the end I suspect that he and his successors preached and persuaded and quietly pointed out the political benefits of working with the Church. Whether he realized it or not, his efforts would contribute to the ultimate success of the Christian Duchy of Normandy.

London

WESTERN CHRISTIAN CONTACTS WITH BUDDHISM, c.1050–1350

by BERNARD HAMILTON

The existence of Buddhism was known to some people in the Graeco-Roman world. Writing about two centuries after the birth of Christ, Clement of Alexandria recorded: 'Some of the Indians obey the precepts of Buddha, whom, on account of his extraordinary sanctity, they have raised to divine honours.'[1] No Latin translation was made of this part of Clement's work, and nothing was known of Buddhism in Western Europe in the early Middle Ages. In 1048 an anonymous Western scholar living in Constantinople made a Latin translation from the Greek of a story called *Barlaam and Ioasaph*, which was wrongly attributed to John of Damascus (d. *c.*750). This appeared to be a saint's life: it told how the Indian prince Ioasaph had renounced the world and embraced an austere ascetic life under the direction of the hermit Barlaam. In fact, this was a life of Prince Gautama, the Buddha. This version had originated in the kingdom of Bactria and had been translated into Arabic and later into Georgian, from which the Greek version was made in the early eleventh century. In the process of transmission the text had been Christianized. Prince Ioasaph, who renounced earthly glory to lead the contemplative life, fitted easily into the pattern of Christian hagiography, and his life proved popular because of its exotic setting in the Indies.[2] During the Middle Ages the Latin version was translated into most Western languages, but Western people remained ignorant of Buddhism until the rise of the Mongol Empire in the thirteenth century made it possible for them to travel to central and eastern Asia.

The empire founded by Chinggis (Genghis) Khan (d. 1227) and expanded by his successors stretched at its greatest extent from China, through central Asia, to Russia in the west and to Iran and

---

[1] Clement of Alexandria, *Miscellanies* 1.15 (William Wilson, *The Writings of Clement of Alexandria*, 2 vols [Edinburgh, 1867], 1: 399).

[2] St John Damascene, *Barlaam and Ioasaph*, ed. and transl. G. R. Woodward and H. Mattingly, intro. D. M. Lang, Loeb Classical Library 34 (London and New York, 1914).

Iraq in the south-west. From the mid-1240s Western diplomats, merchants and missionaries travelled to the court of the Great Khans, initially in Mongolia and after 1261 in north China, along the land route from southern Russia through central Asia. After the Mongol conquest of south-west Asia in the 1250s it also became possible for Western travellers to use the sea route to China from the ports of the Persian Gulf. This period of unrestricted Asiatic travel came to an end in the mid-fourteenth century with the disintegration of Mongol power.[3]

This essay will examine what the West learned about Buddhism in that period and how far Western travellers understood that religion. The sources cited are selective, because of considerations of length, but I consider them to be the fullest and best-informed accounts of Buddhism produced by medieval Western writers.

The first Western traveller to make a written report about the Mongol Empire was Pope Innocent IV's envoy, the Franciscan John of Plano Carpini, who visited the Mongol court at Karakorum in 1245–6. Although he was interested in the religion of the Mongol Empire, he says nothing about Buddhists, but classifies the Great Khan's subjects as Christians, Muslims and idolaters.[4]

The first to identify Buddhism as a separate religion was another Franciscan friar, William of Rubruck, who reached the court of the Great Khan Möngke at Karakorum in Mongolia in December 1253, and stayed there for over six months.[5] William wrote a detailed account of his journey and of the peoples whom he met, among whom were those he called *tuins*.[6] This was his

---

[3]   An excellent survey of the history of the Mongol Empire is David Morgan, *The Mongols*, 2nd edn (Oxford, 2007); a detailed study particularly relevant to the present essay is Peter Jackson, *The Mongols and the West, 1221–1410* (Harlow, 2005).

[4]   John of Plano Carpini, *Historia Mongalorum*, in Anastasius van den Wyngaert, ed., *Sinica Franciscana*, 1: *Itinera et relationes fratrum minorum saeculi xiii et xiv* (Florence, 1929), 27–130; ET in *The Mongol Mission: Narratives and Letters of the Franciscan Missionaries in Mongolia and China in the Thirteenth and Fourteenth Centuries*, transl. by a nun of Stanbrook Abbey, ed. C. Dawson (London, 1955), 3–72.

[5]   William of Rubruck, *Itinerarium*, in *Sinica Franciscana* 1, 145–332; ET *The Mission of Friar William of Rubruck: His Journey to the Court of the Great Khan Möngke 1253–1255*, transl. Peter Jackson, intro., notes and appendices by Peter Jackson and David Morgan, Hakluyt Society 2nd ser. 173 (London, 1990). On William's visit to the Mongol court, see also, in this volume, Amanda Power, 'Encounters in the Ruins: Latin Captives, Franciscan Friars and the Dangers of Religious Plurality in the early Mongol Empire', 115–36.

[6]   See Peter Jackson's note on this usage: *Mission*, transl. Jackson, 164 n. 3.

attempt to render their Chinese name, *tao-jen* or *daoren*, 'men of the path': we should describe them as Buddhist monks. By the thirteenth century two major schools of Buddhism had developed: the Theravadin school of Ceylon and south-east Asia, which venerated the Buddha Gautama and was custodian of his teaching, and the Mahayana school found in east Asia and the Himalayas, especially in Tibet.[7] The northern Buddhists recognized Gautama as the most recent Buddha, but also paid cult to a huge number of other Buddhas, those who had preceded him, those who had lived in different ages of this world, and those who had lived in other worlds. In addition they recognized a vast pantheon of gods and demons as protectors of the doctrine of enlightenment, and this gave rise to very elaborate forms of iconography in their temples. This was a particularly complex religious system to understand, and William was hampered by the fact that he had to rely on interpreters, who were not trained in Buddhist theology. He reports that on one occasion while he was discussing their beliefs with some Buddhist monks, 'when I wanted to argue further with them, my interpreter, who was tired and incapable of finding the right words, made me stop talking'.[8]

William's understanding of this alien faith was further complicated by the fact that the first Buddhist monasteries he encountered were not really Buddhist at all. They were in the territory of the Uighurs, who lived to the south-west of Lake Balkash. They had been converted to Manichaeism in the eighth century, and, as Manicheans were accustomed to do, had adapted their cult to the prevalent local form of worship, in this case Buddhism.[9] William met true Buddhists when he reached the court of the Great Khan, and he comments that there were two kinds of *tuins*, those who were monotheists, that is the Manichaean Uighurs, who believed that there was only one Good God, and those who worshipped many gods, that is the Tibetan Buddhists.[10]

William did not know it, but he had arrived at Karakorum at a critical time for the future of religion at the Mongol court. The

---

7 Donald K. Swearer, *The Buddhist World of South-East Asia*, 2nd edn (Albany, NY, 2010); David Snellgrove, *Indo-Tibetan Budddhism* (Boston, MA, 2002).

8 William of Rubruck, *Itinerarium* 25.8 (*Mission*, transl. Jackson, 156).

9 S. N. C. Lieu, *Manichaeism in the Later Roman Empire and Medieval China* (Manchester, 1985), 189–201.

10 William of Rubruck, *Itinerarium* 25.7, 33.16 (*Mission*, transl. Jackson, 155, 232–3).

Mongol rulers were Shamanists, while some tribes in the Mongol confederacy were Christians, members of the Church of the East, sometimes wrongly called the Nestorian Church, a term which William himself uses. Among the Great Khan's subjects in central Asia there were many Muslims, but the Khans had only recently become aware of Buddhism. Tibet had submitted to the Mongols in 1244. The dominant religious leader in Tibet at that time was the head of the Sakya Order, whose members were outwardly distinguished from other Tibetan monastic orders by the red hats that they wore. The Great Khans recognized the Sakya Lama as regent of Tibet, and he was an influential member of the Mongol government. Throughout the Mongol Empire all religions enjoyed toleration, but Möngke Khan was undecided about which faith he should himself profess.[11] He therefore arranged for a public debate to be held between representatives of Buddhism, Islam, the Church of the East and the Latin Church, which took place on 30 May 1254.[12]

William was the Latin representative, and the Eastern Christian and Muslim representatives were both present at court, but the Buddhist speaker (presumably chosen by the Sakya Lama) travelled there from northern China, which was already part of the Mongol Empire. He was a Tibetan speaker, and brought an interpreter with him who could translate his discourse into Mongolian. William also had a translator, the son of the Khan's French goldsmith, Guillaume Boucher, who knew both French and Mongolian.[13] Möngke Khan appointed three members of his chancery, an Eastern Christian, a Muslim and a Buddhist, as adjudicators. The Buddhist spokesman wished to begin the discussion by debating either how the world had come into being or what becomes of souls after death. These are fundamental Buddhist concerns: the recognition that the phenomenal world is illusory and the need for guidance in how to escape from the endless round of reincarnation in that world. William refused to accept this proposal and argued that the debate should begin with a discussion of the nature of

---

[11] David Snellgrove and Hugh Richardson, *A Cultural History of Tibet* (Boulder, CO, 1968), 144–55.

[12] William of Rubruck, *Itinerarium* 33–4 (*Mission*, transl. Jackson, 226–39).

[13] Ibid. 33.13 (*Mission*, transl. Jackson, 232); Leonardo Olschki, *Guillaume Boucher, a French Artist at the Court of the Khans* (Baltimore, MD, 1946).

God. Although the Buddhist spokesman protested about that, the adjudicators upheld William's request.

This put the Buddhist at a disadvantage. Buddhists believed that there were many gods, but considered that they were part of the transitory world, just as men and animals and demons were. Their religion was not interested in how the phenomenal world had come into being, but in how to attain enlightenment and be freed from the world of illusion. From William's description it appears that the discussion subsequently lost its structure. The Buddhist denied that there was only one God, and questioned William about the origin of evil, a question he sidestepped by saying: 'you should ask first what evil is, before asking where it comes from'. William claimed to have emerged victorious in the debate, but had the candour to add: 'But for all that, no one believed and said "I wish to become a Christian". When it was all over, the Nestorians and Saracens alike sang in loud voices, while the *tuins* remained silent; and after that everyone drank heavily.'[14]

William did not use the word 'Buddha' in his description of this religious system. He called its practitioners either *tuins* or idolaters, supposing that they worshipped the images with which their temples were filled. He had no understanding of the aims and beliefs of the Buddhists he met, but he drew a very clear picture of their way of life. Their public worship was conducted by communities, sometimes very large communities, of monks and also of nuns, who sang liturgies each day in their temples, just as Christian monks did. William described their dress, their use of prayer beads, and the interiors of their temples, decorated with frescoes of gods and demons, and housing statues, some very large. He learned that there were Buddhist hermits 'who lived in the forests and mountains, leading lives which are extraordinarily ascetic', although he did not meet any of them.[15] He also sought to reproduce the prayer of the Tibetan Buddhists: 'They keep repeating the words "*On mani battan*", which means, "God, you know". This was the translation which one of them gave me'. This was obviously an attempt to render the prayer '*Om mani padme hum*', generally translated as 'Hail to the jewel in the lotus'.[16]

[14] William of Rubruck, *Itinerarium* 33.22–3 (*Mission*, transl. Jackson, 235).
[15] Ibid. 26.11 (*Mission*, transl. Jackson, 163).
[16] Ibid. 25.2 (*Mission*, transl. Jackson, 153–4).

William did understand the importance of reincarnation in Buddhist teaching. This was not an alien concept to him, since it had been held in antiquity by some pagan thinkers like Pythagoras, and condemned by some Church Fathers, such as Augustine. William reports that an Eastern Christian priest, who had clearly been influenced by contact with Buddhists, asked him whether he thought 'it was possible for the souls of animals to escape after death to any place where they would not be compelled to suffer'. In other words, could an animal attain enlightenment without first being reincarnated as a human being?[17] This would seem to be a perennial Buddhist topic of discussion: the mountaineer Marco Pallis reports how he talked about it to the monks of Spituk in Ladak in 1936.[18] The holders of certain offices in the Tibetan Buddhist hierarchy claim to be reincarnated after death as the new office holder: this is true, for example, of the Dalai Lama and the Panchen Lama. This was a medieval development in Tibetan religion, and it is therefore interesting to find this comment in Rubruck: 'Master William [the goldsmith] told me, a boy was brought from Cathay, who to judge by his physical size was not three years old, yet was fully capable of rational thought: he said of himself that he was in his third incarnation, and he knew how to read and write'.[19]

Some twenty years after William of Rubruck returned to the West, the young Venetian traveller Marco Polo arrived in China. The Mongol Empire was then ruled by Möngke's brother Khubilai, who had moved his capital from Karakorum to Khanbaligh (near Beijing). Khubilai had been initiated into Tantric Buddhism in 1264 and Buddhism was therefore the religion of his court, although the Mongols remained tolerant of all other faiths.[20] Marco Polo was a layman. Unlike all the other Western witnesses to Buddhism in this period he had no theological training. John Critchley points out that Marco did distinguish between Taoists and Buddhists in China, but made no attempt to explore that difference in any detail.[21]

---

[17] Ibid. 33.15 (*Mission*, transl. Jackson, 232).
[18] Marco Pallis, *Peaks and Lamas* (London, 1939), 323.
[19] William of Rubruck, *Itinerarium* 33.15 (*Mission*, transl. Jackson, 232).
[20] Jacob P. Dalton, *The Taming of the Demons* (London, 2011), 128.
[21] John Critchley, *Marco Polo's Book* (Aldershot, 1992), 122–3.

Marco had a clear understanding of the Buddhist teaching on reincarnation: that as soon as a human being dies his or her soul enters into another body, and that bad conduct in this life might lead an individual to be reincarnated as an animal. What he failed to grasp was the concept of Nirvana: he who did good in successive incarnations, he thought, 'would be always ascending until he be taken into God', which reflects a Christian framework of thought.[22] Marco praised the Buddhists for having taught the Great Khan that 'provision for the poor was a good work for him'.[23] He knew about Tibet, the home of court Buddhism, and commented: 'in this province they have many of the most clever charmers and the best astrologers in all the provinces which are about'.[24] This is an early example of Western belief in the paranormal powers of some Tibetan lamas, which still persists among the credulous.

Marco was sent on a mission to South-east Asia and Ceylon by the Great Khan, and there he had experience of southern Buddhism. He was told that Buddhists believe that the sepulchre of Sakyamuni Borgan is situated on Adam's Peak in Ceylon. Sakyamuni, the Sakya Sage, was a common description of the Buddha Gautama, while Burkhan ('the divine one') was the title which the Mongols gave him. Marco gave a synopsis of Prince Gautama's life and concluded that, if he had been a Christian, 'he would have been a great saint with Our Lord Jesus Christ for the good and pure life which he led'. Marco reported how his shrine was a focus of pilgrimage, and that his relics, his teeth, his hair and his dish were objects of veneration. Marco also reported that Sakyamuni was believed to have been reincarnated eighty-four times before becoming a god.[25]

Marco spent seventeen years in the service of the Great Khan before returning to Venice. The textual history of his book is extremely complex, but it has no bearing on this essay, since even if any of the passages about Buddhism in his work are interpolations made by translators and editors drawing on different sources, they remain evidence of information about Buddhism which had reached the West at this time. One piece of evidence is incontro-

---

[22] Marco Polo, *The Description of the World*, ed. A. C. Moule and P. Pelliot, 2 vols (London, 1938), 1: 255–6 (ch. 104).

[23] Ibid. 1: 252 (ch. 104).

[24] Ibid. 273 (ch. 115).

[25] Ibid. 407–10 (ch. 178).

vertibly Marco's own: among the possessions listed in his will was a set of Buddhist prayer-beads, 108 in number, probably the first example of this devotional aid to reach Western Europe.[26]

The Mongol Il-Khans of Persia, who from the 1260s sought an alliance with the Christian powers of Europe against their common enemy, the Egyptian Mamluks, opened the Indian Ocean to Western travellers, and merchants, diplomats and missionaries took ship from the Persian Gulf to India and China. Among them was Odoric of Pordenone, a Franciscan from Friuli, who spent over twelve years in Asia, from 1316/18 to 1330, travelling by sea from Persia to India and China and returning to the West by the overland route through central Asia. He was struck by the huge size of Buddhist monastic communities in China: 'In one of these monasteries there were three thousand monks and eleven thousand idols', he commented.[27] No medieval Western monastery approached that size. When Odoric reached Cansay (Hang-chou), the former capital of the Sung Emperors, his host took him to visit a Buddhist monastery, and introduced him by saying: 'This is a Frankish monk who has come from the land of the setting sun and is on his way to Khanbaligh to pray for the life of the great Khan'. Each day one of the brethren went out to the foot of a hill and banged a gong, which was a signal for wild animals to come and be fed. The monk explained to Odoric that this was done because the souls of dead men were reincarnated in animals.[28]

Friar Odoric wrote of Tibet:

> The chief and royal city is all built with walls of black and white, and all its streets are very well paved. In this city no one shall dare to shed the blood of any, whether man or beast, for the reverence they bear to a certain idol which is there worshipped. In that city dwells the *Abassi*, that is in their tongue the Pope, who is the head of all idolaters ...[29]

David Snellgrove considers justly that Odoric's account of Tibet is 'just generalised hearsay'. He thinks that the friar's reference to

---

[26] John Larner, *Marco Polo and the Discovery of the World* (London, 1999), 87.

[27] Odoric of Pordenone, *Relatio*, in *Sinica Franciscana* 1, 379–495; ET *The Travels of Friar Odoric of Pordenone*, in Henry Yule, *Cathay and the Way Thither*, rev. Henri Cordier, 4 vols, Hakluyt Society 2nd ser. 33, 37, 38, 41 (London, 1913–16), 2: 184.

[28] Yule, *Cathay*, 2: 201–3.

[29] Ibid. 247–50.

'the idol which is worshipped there' probably relates to the image in the Jo-khang temple of Lhasa, although, as he points out, in Odoric's day Lhasa was not the capital of Tibet: it had not been so since 842, and did not regain that status until the mid-fourteenth century. The *Abassi*, Snellgrove suggests, may probably be a reference to the Grand Lamas of Sakya who in the Mongol period were vice-regents of Tibet.[30]

The last Westerner to make the full circuit of Asia in the Mongol period, travelling overland to China and returning by sea to Persia, and to write an account of it was John of Marignolli, a Franciscan from Naples, sent by Pope Benedict XII as part of a delegation to oversee the Catholic missionary province in China. The party left Avignon in 1338, travelled by the overland route to Khanbaligh, where they arrived in 1342, stayed there for four years and returned by sea to the Persian Gulf, reaching Avignon in 1352. In his memoirs, Marignolli recounted how he visited the shrine of the Buddha Gautama in Ceylon. On the slope of Adam's Peak he found 'a statue of a sitting figure with the left hand resting on the knee and the right hand extended towards the West'.[31] The monks who served the shrine venerated certain trees, which were 'encircled with crowns of gold and jewels, and there are lights placed before them'. Yule and Cordier suggested that these were pipul trees, sacred because of the pipul tree of Bodhgaya, beneath which Gautama and all other Buddhas were said to have received enlightenment.[32] Marignolli described the life of the community:

> The monks ... never keep any food in their house till the morrow. They sleep on the bare ground; they walk barefoot carrying a staff; and are contented with a habit like one of our Friars Minor (but without a hood), and with a mantle cast in folds over the shoulder ... They go about in procession every morning begging rice for their day's dinner. The princes and others go forth to meet them with the greatest rever-

---

[30] I asked David Snellgrove's advice about the value of Friar Odoric's evidence, and the opinion I cite is contained in his letter to me of 12 May 1976.

[31] John of Marignolli, *Relatio*, in *Sinica Franciscana* 1, 513–60; Yule translated the excerpts relating to Asia: *Marignolli's Recollections of Eastern Travel*, in Yule, *Cathay*, 3: 177–269, quotation at 232–3.

[32] Yule, *Cathay*, 3: 242–3; on the sacred tree of Bodhgaya, see David Snellgrove, *Buddhist Himalaya* (Oxford, 1957), 1–5.

ence, and bestow rice upon them in measure proportionate to their numbers; and this they partake of, steeped in water, with coconut milk and plantains. These things I speak of as an eye-witness; and indeed, they made me a *festa* as though I was one of their own order.[33]

John admired the austere life of the Buddhist monks: he wrote of the community of Cansay that 'their rigid attention to prayer and fasting and other religious duties, if they but held the true faith, would far surpass any strictness and self-denial that we practise'.[34]

Soon after John's return to Europe the Mongol Empire disintegrated, which led to warfare and made the land route to the Far East too dangerous to use, and then in 1368 the Ming revolution in China was accompanied by a xenophobic reaction, because foreigners were associated with Mongol patronage. It was not until the late fifteenth century that a new sea route to the Indies was established by the Western powers and contact re-established with Buddhist communities.

What had the West learned about that faith during the century of Mongol supremacy? That some real attempt was made to understand Buddhist doctrine is suggested by a passage in *The Book of the Estate of the Great Caan*, written *c.*1330 by John, archbishop of Sultaniyya, head of the Dominican province of Persia, at the request of Pope John XXII. The author related that the religious head of Cathay was the Grand Trutius, a term which appears to mean 'the chief *tuin*'. 'He is the pope of the Buddhists, dresses in red and is honoured by the Emperor.' This was a description of the Sakya Lama. His report continued that they worshipped various idols, but then stated: 'and over these idols they say there are four gods; and these four gods they carve in gold and silver ... And above these four gods they say that there is a greater God who is over all the gods great and small.'[35]

An important role in the spiritual training provided by the Tantric Buddhists of Tibet was taken by the mandala, a painted scroll or fresco, designed as an aid to meditation on spiritual truths.

[33] Yule, *Cathay*, 3: 243–4.
[34] Ibid. 260.
[35] John of Sultaniyya, *Libellus de Notitia Orbis*, ed. A. Kern, *Archivum fratrum praedicatorum* 8 (1938), 82–123; ET of part of the text as *The Book of the Estate of the Great Caan*, in Yule, *Cathay*, 3: 89–103, quotation at 93–4.

The Sakya school used the iconography of a pentad of Buddhas in their mandalas, which were chosen from the huge number of Buddhas revered in Tibetan tradition. Four Buddhas were placed in the four points of the compass: Akshobya, the Blue Buddha, to the east; Ratnasambhava, the Yellow Buddha, to the south; Amitabha, the Red Buddha, to the west; and Amoghasiddhi, the Green Buddha, to the north. In the centre of the mandala was Vairacona, the White Buddha.[36] It is this iconography which *The Book of the Estate of the Great Khan* was trying to describe, but the designation of the five Buddhas as gods reveals a total misunderstanding of Buddhist faith.

Thus, although Western visitors learned a good deal about the outward practice of Buddhism in both its south Asian and Tibetan forms, they failed to grasp the substance of that faith. The Buddhists had many images in their temples, but they did not worship any of them. They sought enlightenment which would free them from the wheel of being and admit them to Nirvana, the Other. Part of the difficulty which Western observers experienced sprang from their inability to read the sacred books or to master the theological terminology which Buddhists used. Although some of them did learn the vernacular languages which Buddhists spoke, this did not help them to read the books of the south Asian Buddhists written in Sanskrit, or the 108 books of the Tibetan canon written in classical Tibetan.

The central problem, though, was that clergy trained in the Western tradition, particularly in the scholastic tradition, could not conceive of a religion which did not consider the concept of God relevant. Only Byzantine Hesychasts, trained in the apophatic tradition, a position shared by a few medieval Western mystics, might have been able intuitively to understand Buddhist spirituality, but they had no contact with Buddhism at that time.[37]

Most people in Western Europe failed to identify the life of

---

[36] Snellgrove, *Buddhist Himalaya*, 64–6.

[37] Apophatic theology teaches that the Godhead cannot be an object of knowledge; this entails the rejection of all human concepts and images of God, who makes himself known to us through his divine energies. St Gregory Palamas, the champion of Hesychasm, was trained in this tradition and his teaching was endorsed as orthodox by the Byzantine Church at a synod at Constantinople in 1351: Dirk Krausmüller, 'The Rise of Hesychasm', in Michael Angold, ed., *CHC*, 5: *Eastern Christianity* (Cambridge, 2006), 101–26.

Sakyamuni described by Marco Polo with the life of Prince Ioasaph in the romance of Barlaam and Ioasaph, and this had an unexpected consequence.[38] The cult of those two saints continued to spread,[39] and when, as part of the liturgical reform initiated by the Council of Trent, Cardinal Baronius revised the text of the Roman Martyrology in 1584, he added to the entries for 27 November: 'In the Indies bordering on Persia the feast of Sts. Barlaam and Josaphat, whose wonderful deeds have been recounted by St. John of Damascus'.[40] Baronius was undoubtedly influenced in accepting the authenticity of this legend by its attribution to a very orthodox church father. In that way the Buddha Gautama came to enjoy the honours of a saint in the modern Catholic Church.

University of Nottingham

[38] One exception is the gloss written on the section about the life of Sakyamuni in one manuscript of Marco Polo: 'This is like the life of St. Josafat ... converted to the Christian faith by means of Barlaam': Marco Polo, *Description*, 1: 410 (ch. 178).

[39] The spread of this cult is discussed by Hippolyte Delehaye as part of his examination of the cult of St Barlaam of Antioch, in 'S. Barlaam martyr à Antioche', *Analecta Bollandiana* 22 (1903), 129–45.

[40] 'Ad Indos Persis finitimos sanctorum Barlaam et Josaphat quorum actus mirandos sanctus Iohannes Damascenus conscripsit': *Martyrologium Romanum* (Mechlin, 1899), 223. This text is found among the entries for 27 November in all editions of the Roman Martyrology issued between 1584 and its revision by the Second Vatican Council.

THE THIRD CRUSADE IN CONTEXT: CONTRADICTION, CURIOSITY AND SURVIVAL*

by JONATHAN PHILLIPS

This essay will explore a few of the myriad competing tensions of motive, ideology and practicality that were created by, and existed during, the time of the Crusades. The First Crusade was launched in 1095 when Pope Urban II called for the liberation of Jerusalem from the Muslims of the Near East. Four years later, the knights of Western Europe captured the holy city and established a series of territories in the Levant. Over time the Muslims began to fight back and by 1187, under the leadership of Saladin, they defeated the Franks (as the settlers were known) and recovered Jerusalem. The particular focus here is on the Third Crusade (1187–92), the campaign called in the aftermath of this seismic event. Popular history books often characterize this as the great clash between Richard the Lionheart and Saladin, and between Christianity and Islam.[1] They describe battles and sieges; they might also highlight the divisions between Richard and Philip Augustus, and the failure of the crusade to recover Jerusalem. Such points are certainly central to a discussion of the Third Crusade but they are symptomatic of more detailed treatments of the expedition that have not, to date, placed the subject in a fuller context.[2] One aspect of this broader approach is to emphasize the diversity of participants within the Christian and Muslim forces, to take the crusade beyond the Richard and Saladin binary. Thanks to Anne-Marie Eddé, the acute divisions (religious and political in form) within Saladin's dominions are coming into clearer focus, while on the Latin Christian side, away from the usual spotlight on Richard and Philip, the work of Graham Loud has brought

---

* This essay is dedicated to the memory of Dr John Doran (1966–2012), a fine scholar and a truly warm-hearted man, who was taken from us far too soon.

[1] James Reston Jr, *Warriors of God: Richard the Lionheart and Saladin in the Third Crusade* (London, 2001), is one such example. See Bernard Lewis, *Islam and the West* (Oxford, 1993), 12–13, for a more scholarly perspective, albeit one that follows the 'clash of civilizations' line.

[2] This is my longer term purpose regarding a study of the Third Crusade for Yale University Press.

Frederick Barbarossa into the picture.[3] The German emperor led what was probably the largest army from the West, and the military and strategic threat that he posed to the Muslim Near East is only one example of matters that need to be carefully evaluated. The significant contributions of Sicily, Pisa and Flanders to the crusade are further topics that require detailed research. Taking a wider perspective can reveal a multifarious range of motives and once these are identified we can see how they affected the involvement of particular individuals or groups in the crusade, and then review their dealings and decision-making both with their co-religionists (be they Christian or Muslim) and regarding those against whom they struggled.

It has to be said that contemporaries were sometimes confused by what was happening. Ibn Jubayr, a Spanish Muslim pilgrim who passed through the kingdom of Jerusalem in August–September 1184, wrote:

> One of the astonishing things that is talked of is that though the fires of discord burn between the two parties, Muslim and Christian, two armies of them may meet and dispose themselves in battle array, and yet Muslim and Christian travellers will come and go between them without interference. In this connection, we saw … the departure of Saladin with all the Muslim troops to lay siege to the fortress of Kerak … but still the caravans passed successively from Egypt to Damascus, going through the lands of the Franks without impediment from them. In the same way the Muslims continuously journeyed from Damascus to Acre (through Frankish territory), and likewise not one of the Christian merchants was stopped or hindered in Muslim territories.[4]

Similarly, many of the English crusaders who responded to the desperate pleas for help from Patriarch Heraclius of Jerusalem during his visit to the West of 1184–5 chose to return home when

3   Anne-Marie Eddé, *Saladin*, transl. Jane-Marie Todd (Cambridge, MA, 2011), 67–270; *The Crusade of Frederick Barbarossa: The History of the Expedition of the Emperor Frederick and related Texts*, transl. Graham A. Loud, CTT 19 (Farnham, 2010).

4   Ibn Jubayr, *The Travels of Ibn Jubayr*, transl. Roland J. C. Broadhurst (London, 1952), 300–1.

they discovered, on their arrival in the Levant the following Easter, a three-year truce in operation between the Franks and Saladin.[5]

Two subjects are of key interest to this essay: firstly, Christian-Muslim trade, and secondly, Latin Christian understanding of Islam around the time of the Third Crusade. This latter point will consider cultural and diplomatic interactions in order to explore the divergence in perception of Muslims between crusaders coming over from Europe and the Frankish settlers in the Levant.

The first concern of this essay is well illustrated by a case study of a particularly intriguing group: the Genoese. By reason of its basic *raison d'être* as a trading city, Genoa had a complex series of relationships that stretched out from its location on the Ligurian coastline of north-western Italy to include dealings with Muslim powers in Iberia, North Africa and the Near East. Yet at the same time the Genoese were, of course, Latin Christians and Genoa was the seat of an archbishopric. Through fairly extensive participation in the First Crusade and its immediate aftermath, the Genoese had acquired a strong presence in the Holy Land via trade and settlement in cities such as Antioch, Jaffa, Acre and Caesarea.[6] Furthermore, the city of Jubayl (better known as Byblos, today Jubail in Lebanon) was owned and ruled by the Genoese Embriaci family. Thus, when Saladin crushed the Franks at the Battle of Hattin in July 1187 the Genoese were amongst those directly affected. By reason of their seafaring capabilities they were at the forefront of relaying news of these terrible events back to the West. A letter from the Genoese in August 1187 begged Pope Urban III to help the settlers in the Levant; it also noted losses to their own lands and 'the shedding of the blood of some of our most distinguished citizens'.[7] The only city to withstand Saladin's advance was Tyre. The contemporary Genoese annalist Ottobono Scriba argued that his colleagues had taken a prominent role in the defence of Tyre, a

---

[5] Roger of Howden, *Gesta Henrici II et Ricardi I*, ed. William Stubbs, 2 vols, RS 49 (London, 1867), 1: 359; Jonathan P. Phillips, *Defenders of the Holy Land: Relations between the Latin East and the West, 1119–1187* (Oxford, 1996), 251–64.

[6] These events are outlined in the introduction to *Caffaro, Genoa and the Twelfth-Century Crusades*, transl. Martin A. Hall and Jonathan P. Phillips, CTT 26 (Farnham, 2013), 11, 32–6. The texts can be found in *I Libri Iurium della Repubblica di Genova*, ed. Dino Puncuh et al., 9 vols (Rome, 1992–2002), 1/1: 97–102, 182–3; 1/2: 152–60.

[7] Roger of Howden, *Gesta Henrici II et Ricardi I*, ed. Stubbs, 2: 11–13 (*Caffaro*, transl. Hall and Phillips, 213–15).

point echoed and recognized in a charter given by the remaining
barons of Outremer in late 1187, who

> seeing that they would lose the Holy Land, by common
> consent granted freedom of passage in and out of Tyre to the
> Genoese, on the basis that they paid no customary dues what-
> soever on the goods and transactions forming their imports
> and exports by land or sea, on the grounds that they found the
> Genoese alert and in a state of preparedness to defend the city,
> and of a mind to serve the king and queen loyally.

Various properties in Tyre were also given to the Genoese.[8] Thus,
intertwined with the wish of the Genoese as good Christians to
resist the Muslims was the desire to advance the city's economic
standing. In fact, the Ligurians had held no privileges or territorial
concessions in Tyre prior to this time and, as the generous terms
of the deal indicated, they were able to enhance their position
as a consequence of the sheer urgency of the situation and their
willingness to engage with the enemy.

Genoa's need to boost its status in the kingdom of Jerusalem
was given greater impetus by the severe challenge posed to the
city's rights during the reigns of Baldwin III (1143–63) and
Amalric (1163–74). Back at the start of the century, in recognition
of their role in the conquest of the Latin East during the First
Crusade, King Baldwin I (1100-18) had awarded Genoa a series of
commercial privileges inscribed in golden letters inside the Holy
Sepulchre, a remarkable juxtaposition of the sacred and the secular,
although not without parallel elsewhere in the Latin world.[9]
Amalric, however, was closely aligned with Genoa's bitter rivals,
the Pisans, and this relationship led to an effort to marginalize the

---

[8]   Ottobono Scriba, 'Annals', ed. Luigi Belgrano and Cesare Imperiale, in *Annali
genovesi di Caffaro e de' suoi continuatori*, Fonti per la storia d'Italia, 118 vols (Rome,
1887–1993), 12: 23–4 (*Caffaro*, transl. Hall and Phillips, 145). The document is in *I
Libri Iurium*, ed. Puncuh et al., 1/2: 135–7 (*Caffaro*, transl. Hall and Phillips, 215–16).
For a discussion of the award of privileges to Genoa and Pisa at this time, see David
Jacoby, 'Conrad, Marquis of Montferrat and the Kingdom of Jerusalem, 1187–92', in
idem, *Trade, Commodities and Shipping in the Medieval Mediterranean* (Aldershot, 1997),
187–238.
[9]   For example, the cathedrals of Mainz and Speyer had privileges inscribed on
them, see *Quellen zur Verfassungsgeschichte der deutschen Stadt im Mittelalter*, ed. Bernd-Ul-
rich Hergemöller (Darmstadt, 2000), 118–23, 184–8. My thanks to Professor Felicitas
Schmieder for this reference.

Ligurians. In the 1160s, 1170s and 1180s successive popes wrote to the rulers and the senior figures of the kingdom attempting to resolve this. As recently as 1186, Pope Urban III had urged the patriarch of Jerusalem and the prior and canons of the Holy Sepulchre to restore the position of the Genoese.[10] With this in mind, the traumatic circumstances of 1187–8 offered the chance to reformulate the political and economic balance in the Holy Land, a situation seemingly given further impetus by the facts that the defence of Tyre had been led by Conrad of Montferrat and that the Montferrese were relatively local to Genoa and (generally) got on well with their neighbours.

We learn from Ottobono Scriba that in 1189–90, Guido Spinola, the Genoese consul, took part in both the defence of Tyre and the subsequent siege of Acre, and that other important citizens participated in the ongoing struggle, most notably the diplomat Rosso della Volta and members of the Embriaci family, as well as other groups of knights and foot-soldiers.[11] Support could be financial too: in March 1191, from the £186 Genoese that he sent to Syria, Ruggero Noxenzio set aside £20 Genoese 'for the service of God and of Ultramare', showing his wish to provide financial assistance for the crusade.[12] Ansaldo Buonvico became the castellan of Tyre; it was in his ship that Conrad had reached the Levant in the summer of 1187. In April 1189, Conrad gave the Genoese a charter which assured them of one-third of the revenue from import and export duties at the chain of the harbour of Tyre.[13] Just over a year later, King Guy of Jerusalem, now leading the assault on Acre, promised the Genoese similar incentives in that city, although it was under close siege from August 1189, and the deal could not

---

[10]   This struggle is discussed in the introduction to *Caffaro*, transl. Hall and Phillips, 24–7. The relevant papal letters are translated ibid. 207–11; for the texts, see *I Libri Iurium*, ed. Puncuh et al., 1/2: 113–16, 119–26.

[11]   See the important article by Merav Mack, 'A Genoese Perspective of the Third Crusade', *Crusades* 10 (2011), 45–62. See also Scriba, 'Annals', ed. Belgrano and Imperiale, 32 (*Caffaro*, transl. Hall and Phillips, 148–9).

[12]   *Guglielmo Cassinese (1190–1192)*, ed. Margaret W. Hall, Hilmar C. Krueger and Robert L. Reynolds, 2 vols (Turin, 1938), 1: 129–30.

[13]   On Conrad's journey, see the anonymous *Regni Ierosolymitani brevis historia*, ed. Luigi Belgrano, in *Annali genovesi di Caffaro e de' suoi continuatori*, 11: 144–5 (*Caffaro*, transl. Hall and Phillips, 164–5). For the charter, see *I Libri Iurium*, ed. Puncuh et al., 1/2: 137–40 (*Caffaro*, transl. Hall and Phillips, 216–18).

become operative until it eventually fell in July 1191.[14] Yet in giving out these privileges, which encouraged Genoese presence in the area, and which helped to ensure the basic economic survival of the remnants of the Frankish East, there was an implicit need for the resumption of trade. The 1187 charter from the nobles of Outremer noted above mentioned trade 'by land and sea'; presumably this meant Muslim lands too. Obviously no commercial trade took place through Acre during the siege, but was this the case in the period after the siege ended and before the final settlement between Richard and Saladin fifteen months later? A document from the cartulary of Genoese merchant Guglielmo Cassinese of 29 December 1190 excludes going to 'Ultramare' and Alexandria, yet an agreement of 30 August 1191 explicitly includes Ultramare, thus raising this possibility.[15]

What this account reveals is a tension between the simple binary encouraged by the rhetoric of holy war, the needs of a trading city in the Mediterranean and the basic economic requirements of the Latin East. The latter two points did not sit well with the former, either on the Christian side or, to some extent, on the Muslim (as we will see below). Godfrey of Bouillon, the first Frankish ruler of Jerusalem, recognized the practicalities as early as 1100 when, as Ekkehard of Aura reported, he 'maintained firm peace with Ascalon and Damascus for the sake of commerce'.[16] Godfrey, of course, had within the previous twelve months arrived at Jerusalem with the armies of the First Crusade, a body of men urged by the papacy to cleanse the city of barbaric, impious creatures, and he had taken part in the massacre of the defenders of the holy city.[17]

---

[14] *I Libri Iurium*, ed. Puncuh et al., 1/2: 140–2 (*Caffaro*, transl. Hall and Phillips, 220–1).

[15] *Guglielmo Cassinese*, ed. Hall, Krueger and Reynolds, 1: 6, 365. William of Tyre's comments after King Amalric's failed attack on Egypt in late 1168 included a lament regarding the negative impact of this outcome on Egyptian traders who had come to the Latin kingdom and spent large sums of money. In other words, usually there was a substantial level of trade between the Christians and Muslims of the Near East: William of Tyre, *Historia* 20.10 (CChr.CM 63A, 924); ET William of Tyre, *A History of Deeds done Beyond the Sea*, transl. Emily A. Babcock and August C. Krey, 2 vols (New York, 1943), 2: 358.

[16] Ekkehard of Aura, *Frutolfi et Ekkehardi chronica necnon anonymi chronica imperatorum*, ed. and transl. Franz-Joseph Schmale and Irene Schmale-Ott, Ausgewählte Quellen zur deutschen Geschichte des Mittelalters 15 (Darmstadt, 1972), 158–9.

[17] See Marcus G. Bull, 'Views of Muslims and of Jerusalem in Miracle Stories, *c.*1000–*c.*1200: Reflections on the Study of First Crusaders' Motivations', in idem and

Since the eleventh century, Genoese involvement in holy war had played out against a blend of religion and commerce particular to the Latin trading cities of the day. Caffaro, the great civic annalist and a crusader himself, elided conflicts in Iberia and North Africa with the First Crusade: 'As with the first Frankish army against Antioch in 1097, in the African expedition in 1088 [i.e. the expedition to Mahdia in 1087], in the first expedition to Tortosa [in Spain] in 1093 and when Jerusalem was taken in 1099'.[18] It is clear that the Genoese should be seen as genuine First Crusaders, hosting the preaching of papal representatives in the cathedral of San Siro in 1096, wearing the cross on their shoulders during the capture of Caesarea, acquiring relics and helping to conquer the Holy Land for the Christian faith. Yet at the same time they were comfortable with securing clear profit, as at Ascalon in 1099 and Caesarea in 1101, as well as commercial privileges across the Latin East.[19] Meanwhile trade continued with Alexandria, for example, as it had done prior to the First Crusade.[20] Likewise, there was a substantial level of commerce with Muslim Iberia, coupled with diplomatic arrangements, such as a non-aggression pact with Morocco in 1138. A Genoese document from 1143 showing tithes owed to the archbishop indicates trade with Egypt, the Maghreb, Tunis and Bougie; in 1161 the Genoese concluded truces with Ibn Mardanish of the Levante (or his brother Yusuf) and 'Abd al-Mu'min of Morocco. Yet with no irony, in his entry for the same year, Caffaro reported welcoming Pope Alexander III to Genoa immediately afterwards. In 1169 and 1170, the civic annals mention further visits to Morocco, and so on; the point is made.[21]

Norman Housley, eds, *The Experience of Crusading*, 1: *Western Approaches* (Cambridge, 2003), 13–38, at 23.

[18]   Caffaro, 'Annals', 13 (*Caffaro*, transl. Hall and Phillips, 56).

[19]   For a broader discussion of Genoa and the First Crusade, see Jonathan P. Phillips, 'Caffaro of Genoa and the Motives of the Early Crusaders', forthcoming in Per Ingesman, ed., *Religion as an Agent of Change* (Leiden, 2015). For the acquisition of relics, see Valeria Polonio, 'Devozioni di lingo corso: lo scalo genovese', in Gheradro Ortelli and Dino Puncuh, eds, *Genova, Venezia, il Levante nei secoli xii–xiv* (Venice, 2001), 349–94.

[20]   Samuel M. Stern, 'An Original Document from the Fatimid Chancery concerning Italian Merchants', in *Studi orientalistici in onore di Giorgio Levi della Vida*, 2 vols, Pubblicazioni dell'Istituto per l'Oriente 52 (Rome, 1956), 2: 529–38.

[21]   Oberto Cancelliere, 'Annals', ed. Luigi Belgrano and Cesare Imperiale, in *Annali genovesi di Caffaro e de' suoi continuatori*, 11: 228, 237 (*Caffaro*, transl. Hall and Phillips, 142–5).

The Genoese were certainly not alone in practising this blend of holy war and commerce. The Pisans were the prime Western trading partner with the Fatimids, while the Venetians were engaged in diplomacy and commerce in Alexandria, most notably from the early 1170s once Saladin came to power.[22] In the context of the apparent tension between holy war and the requirements of trade, it is worth noting that Saladin himself felt the need to explain his dealings with the Italians. He wrote to the caliph of Baghdad in 1175:

> Among the [enemy] armies were also Venetians, Pisans and Genoese. They sometimes behaved like invaders … and sometimes like travellers, imposing their law on Islam with their imported goods and escaping strict regulation. Yet there is not a single one of them who does not come today to bring us the weapons with which they fought and conducted the holy war … I established alliances and peace accords with them all, on the conditions that we set, in keeping with our interests against their interests.[23]

The Genoese envoy Rosso della Volta concluded a peace agreement with Saladin in 1177 and the latter's envoys are known to have passed through Genoa during discussions with Frederick Barbarossa.[24]

Yet as early as the 1150s, perhaps not coincidentally after the failure of the Second Crusade and at a time when the Muslim counter-crusade began to gather momentum, we see pressure on the Latin side concerning trade with the lands of Islam. Intriguingly, some of this came from within Genoa itself, suggesting that there was tension amongst the citizens themselves on this matter. In 1151 this proclamation was issued:

> In the church of San Lorenzo, before a full *parlamentum*, the consuls … proclaim and declare that no one without the

---

[22] David Jacoby, 'The Supply of War Materials to Egypt in the Crusader Period', *Jerusalem Studies in Arabic and Islam* 25 (2001), 102–32, especially 104–10; Yaacov Lev, 'A Mediterranean Encounter: The Fatimids and Europe, Tenth to Twelfth Centuries', in *Shipping, Trade and Crusade in the Medieval Mediterranean: Studies in Honour of John Pryor*, ed. Ruthy Gertwagen and Elizabeth Jeffreys (Farnham, 2012), 131–56, at 135–7.
[23] From Abu Shama, in Eddé, *Saladin*, transl. Todd, 449.
[24] Ibid. 451; Scriba, 'Annals', ed. Belgrano and Imperiale, ii (*Caffaro*, transl. Hall and Phillips, 143).

specific authority of the consuls *de comuni* of Genoa shall transport oars, spears, timber for constructing galleys, or weapons to the territory of the Saracens. The person and all the goods of anyone who contravenes this order shall be placed under an interdiction. The above-named consuls made this proclamation because they recognise that this is our duty to God, to the whole of Christendom and to the commune of Genoa. May 1151, in the thirteenth year of the indiction.[25]

Such efforts notwithstanding, the evidence noted above indicates that this legislation seemingly had little effect.

Ecclesiastical bodies began to publish similar measures. In 1162 the Council of Montpellier prohibited the delivery of arms, naval wood and iron to Muslim lands.[26] Most notably of all, the Third Lateran Council of March 1179 issued this powerful declaration:

> Cruel avarice has so seized the hearts of some that though they glory in the name of Christians they provide the Saracens with arms and wood for helmets … and supply them with arms and necessaries to attack Christians. There are even some who for gain act as captains or pilots in galleys or Saracen pirate vessels … such persons should be cut off from the communion of the church and be excommunicated for their wickedness, … catholic princes and civil magistrates should confiscate their possessions, and … if they are captured they should become the slaves of their captors. We order that throughout the churches of maritime cities frequent and solemn excommunication should be pronounced against them …[27]

There had been bans on Christians trading with Muslims before, yet in spite of these ever tighter curbs on certain forms of commerce there is little doubt that shipping and trade between the Italians and the Muslim Near East certainly continued at some levels.[28] Ibn Jubayr travelled on a Genoese ship from Ceuta in

---

[25] *I Libri Iurium*, ed. Puncuh et al., 1/1: 223 (*Caffaro*, transl. Hall and Phillips, 191).

[26] Cited in Jacoby, 'Supply of War Materials', 109.

[27] *Decrees of the Ecumenical Councils*, ed. and transl. Norman J. Tanner, 2 vols (New York, 1990), 1: 223; Sophia Menache, 'Papal Attempts at a Commercial Boycott of the Muslims in the Crusader Period', *JEH* 63 (2012), 236–59.

[28] David Jacoby, 'Venetian Commercial Expansion in the Eastern Mediterranean, 8th–11th Centuries', in Marlia M. Mango, ed., *Byzantine Trade, 4th–12th Centuries: The*

North Africa to Alexandria in 1183, and the cartulary of Oberto Scriba reveals a number of further voyages in between 1184 and 1186.[29] In the winter of 1187, no less than thirty-eight Genoese, Pisan and Venetian ships were impounded in Alexandria and forced to take Christian refugees away.[30] In the year after the fall of Jerusalem the Ligurians seemingly found little problem in making a twenty-year truce with another Muslim group, those of the Mediterranean island of Majorca, a party whose Almohad overlord, Abu Yusuf Ya'qub, was certainly in contact with Saladin and therefore connected to the struggles in the Middle East.[31]

As Jacoby points out, once Acre was recovered by the Christians in 1191 the volume of trade between Genoa and the Levant grew dramatically. Access to the best port on the coast was clearly one part of this, and in the autumn of 1191 there was a substantial investment in business with the Near East, presumably fuelled by the privileges granted by Conrad and Guy, coupled with an expectation that trade with Saladin's lands would resume.[32] Mack has drawn attention to the remarkable story of Rubaldo di Buontommaso, who was being held prisoner in Alexandria. His wife Leona struck a deal with the trader Ansaldo da Castello to travel to Egypt and to pay her husband's ransom. Ansaldo's willingness to undertake this commission – in early 1192, long before the final peace treaty – shows that at least one trader was prepared to go to Alexandria. This, along with the need repeatedly to exclude Alexandria as a destination for journeys to the Eastern Mediterranean, perhaps indicates that some merchants were visiting, or wished to visit, Egypt.[33] Again, it is worth noting that Genoese traders were permitted to go to Bougie in Almohad North Africa, a place from

Archaeology of Local, Regional and International Exchange, Publications of the Society for the Promotion of Byzantine Studies 14 (Farnham, 2009), 371–92, at 380.

[29] Ibn Jubayr, *Travels*, transl. Broadhurst, 26.

[30] *La continuation de Guillaume de Tyr (1184–97)*, ed. M. Ruth Morgan (Paris, 1982), 74–5; 'The Old French Continuation of William of Tyre', in *The Conquest of Jerusalem and the Third Crusade*, transl. Peter W. Edbury, CTT 1 (Aldershot, 1996), 66.

[31] Ottobono Scriba mentioned the agreement with Majorca: 'Annals', ed. Belgrano and Imperiale, 26. See also Eddé, *Saladin*, transl. Todd, 252–5.

[32] Jacoby, 'Conrad of Montferrat', 220–1; David Abulafia, *The Two Italies* (Cambridge, 1977), 182. See also *Guglielmo Cassinese*, ed. Hall, Krueger and Reynolds, 1: 365.

[33] Mack, 'Genoese Perspective', 57–8. For the charters, see *Guglielmo Cassinese*, ed. Hall, Krueger and Reynolds, 1: 174, 365; 2: 36–8, 77, 154, 180, 187.

whose overlord Saladin was trying hard to secure help.[34] After May 1192 Henry of Troyes, the new ruler of Jerusalem, published a charter making it clear that trade with Muslim lands was taking place by land and sea.[35]

Holy war in the East was, by this time, especially focused on possession of Jerusalem, but this was a struggle that had to fit into an existing pattern of territorial rivalries, economic realities and pragmatism, all of which incorporated and reflected over ninety years of Latin presence in the Levant. Enormous flexibility and contradiction rendered the seemingly obvious Christian-Muslim divide problematic. Outsiders to the region were brought up on the charged rhetoric of accounts of the First Crusade, and, after the loss of Jerusalem in 1187, infused with powerful polemics about the fall of the holy city (see below). Such texts formed the preconceptions of crusaders and, in part, had propelled them to the Levant in the first place. Thus, when, in accordance with local custom, the Franks accepted payment from the Muslim defenders of Damascus in 1148 the Western crusaders were infuriated and felt betrayed in both military and religious terms.[36]

Westerners needed to spend some time in the area if they were to assimilate their own prejudgements to the situation in the Levant. Burchard of Strasbourg, a chaplain in the German imperial court, went on a diplomatic mission to Saladin in 1175. He sailed on a Genoese ship via Sicily to Alexandria and, once in the sultan's lands, in tune with the positive tenor of his journey, chose (or was directed) to visit shrines venerated by both Christians and Muslims. First, he went to the shared Marian sanctuary of Matariyya near Cairo. He then travelled to the monastery of Saidnaya, about twenty-seven kilometres north of Damascus. There, as Bernard Hamilton and Benjamin Kedar have outlined, he reflected upon the shared devotion of Muslim and Christian pilgrims to Christ and most particularly to the Virgin Mary, in whose honour

---

[34] *Guglielmo Cassinese*, ed. Hall, Krueger and Reynolds, 1: 174; Eddé, *Saladin*, transl. Todd, 252–5.

[35] *Caffaro*, transl. Hall and Phillips, 224–5; *I Libri Iurium*, ed. Puncuh et al., 1/2: 146–52.

[36] Michael A. Köhler, *Alliances and Treaties between Frankish and Muslim Rulers in the Middle East: Cross-Cultural Diplomacy in the Period of the Crusades*, transl. Peter M. Holt, rev., ed. and intro. Konrad Hirschler (Leiden, 2013), 155–62; Jonathan P. Phillips, *The Second Crusade: Extending the Frontiers of Christendom* (London, 2007), 269–78.

there stood a shrine with an image that lactated holy oil which was (and still is) regarded by both faiths as having miraculous quali- ties.[37] Burchard clearly spent a fair amount of time debating with Muslim holy men and he reported – calmly – on some of the objections that they held to Christianity. He also depicted very good relations between the Egyptian and Syrian Christians and the Muslims. As Tolan indicates, this mission was conducted in a diplomatic context; given this positive environment we see a more overt nod to the similarities between the two faiths, and even the Virgin's granting of miracles to the Muslims at Matariyya and Saidnaya was not described by Burchard as entirely wrong.[38]

A further strand of the interaction between Christians and Muslims at the time of the Third Crusade was, in a limited fashion, at the level of religious debate. This, it will be suggested, broadened the understanding of Islam, at least amongst some of those present on the Third Crusade. This operated alongside, and intertwined with, the issue of diplomacy, which also required a far greater level of religious understanding than had been seen on earlier crusades. By way of context, there follows a brief outline of Muslim-Chris- tian relations in the decades prior to the Third Crusade.

The rise of European intellectual interest in Islam is fairly well documented. Around the year 1110 Petrus Alfonsi produced the strongest and best informed critique of Islam and Muhammad to date in his *Dialogues*. This was an immensely popular text, with numerous copies circulating across Europe during the twelfth century.[39] A few decades later (1142–3), Peter the Venerable commissioned Robert of Ketton to undertake a landmark transla- tion of the Qur'ān from Arabic to Latin, to enable him to refute

---

[37] Bernard Hamilton, 'Our Lady of Saidnaya: An Orthodox Shrine revered by Muslims and Knights Templar at the Time of the Crusades', in Robert N. Swanson, ed., *The Holy Land, Holy Lands and Christian History*, SCH 36 (Woodbridge, 2000), 207–15; Benjamin Z. Kedar, 'Convergences of Oriental Christian, Muslim and Frankish Worshippers: The Case of Aydnâyâ and the Knights Templar', in Zsolt Hunyadi and Józef Laszlovsky, eds, *The Crusades and the Military Orders: Expanding the Frontiers of Medieval Latin Christianity* (Budapest, 2001), 89–100.

[38] John V. Tolan, '"Veneratio Sarracenorum": Shared Devotion among Muslims and Christians, according to Burchard of Strasbourg, Envoy from Frederick Barbarossa to Saladin (c.1175)', in idem, *Sons of Ishmael: Muslims through European Eyes in the Middle Ages* (Gainesville, FL, 2008), 101–12.

[39] Petrus Alfonsi, *Dialogue against the Jews*, transl. Irven M. Resnick, Fathers of the Church, Medieval Continuation 8 (Washington DC, 2006); John V. Tolan, *Petrus Alfonsi and his Medieval Readers* (Gainesville, FL, 1993), 27–33, 98.

the ideas therein. The abbot also composed his polemical works against Islam: *Sum of the Entire Heresy or Demonic Sect of the Saracens or Ishmaelites* (1143–4) and *Against the Sect of the Saracens* (1155–6).[40]

These two authors represent a very theological and confrontational approach, that of clerics writing in Latin in the West. Prior to this, the most important access point for the wider public's understanding of Islam had been the numerous narrative histories of the First Crusade (almost all of which were in Latin) and the *Chansons de Geste.* While it was reasonably common for these texts to acknowledge the bravery and strength of their Muslim opponents, most tended to depict them as pagan idolaters, in line with the concept of a centuries-old struggle ending in Christian triumph and possibly the second coming. Thus, argues Tolan, the 'image of Islam as paganism helps justify the crusade', that is, to put it in the context of Christian history.[41] Muslims were described as barbarous, diabolical creatures; the crusaders were the new apostles; 'Saracen' was a synonym for 'pagan'.[42] When we recognize the scale of copying and retelling of the First Crusade, it is logical that such images became deeply embedded in the mental landscape of Western Europeans.[43] Robert the Monk's *Historia Iherosolimitana* was the most popular of these texts, with at least thirty-four surviving manuscripts dating from the twelfth century, far and away the largest number for a First Crusade narrative.[44] He described the Muslims as sons of the devil, and as users of divination, spells and astrology.[45] A neat continuity between this narrative and the Third Crusade itself can be seen in Provost Henry of Schäftlarn's

[40]   John V. Tolan, 'Peter the Venerable on the "Diabolical Heresy of the Saracens"', in idem, *Sons of Ishmael*, 46–63; Thomas E. Burman, *Reading the Qur'ān in Latin Christendom, 1140–1560* (Philadelphia, PA, 2007).

[41]   John V. Tolan, *Saracens: Islam in the Medieval European Imagination* (New York, 2002), 105–34, quotation at 111. For an example of a First Crusade text acknowledging the martial virtues of Muslim warriors, see *Gesta Francorum et aliorum Hierosolimitanorum*, ed. and transl. Roger A. B. Mynors, intro. Rosalind M. T. Hill, Nelson's Medieval Texts (London, 1962), 21.

[42]   Tolan, *Saracens*, 126–8. See also Margaret Jubb, 'The Crusaders' Perception of their Opponents', in Helen J. Nicholson, ed., *Palgrave Advances in the Crusades* (Basingstoke, 2005), 225–44.

[43]   On the flowering of crusade texts in the early twelfth century, see Phillips, *Second Crusade*, 17–36.

[44]   Robert the Monk, *The Historia Iherosolimitana of Robert the Monk*, ed. Damien Kempf and Marcus G. Bull (Woodbridge, 2013), lxv–lxxiv, lists 84 manuscripts, dating from the twelfth to the sixteenth centuries.

[45]   Ibid. 43, 63–4; ET in *Robert the Monk's History of the First Crusade*, transl. Carol

presentation of a (beautifully illustrated) manuscript of Robert the Monk's account to Frederick Barbarossa just before the emperor departed for the East in 1189.[46]

That said, such a negative picture was not born out of complete ignorance and there was certainly some understanding of Islam in the West prior to the First Crusade.[47] In 1076, Pope Gregory VII had written to the al-Nasir, the sultan of Bougie in North Africa thus: 'you and we ought to love each other … more than other races of men because we believe and confess in one God, albeit in different ways'.[48] Similarly, after 1099 we can see glimpses of accuracy. Otto of Freising (*c*.1146) stated that Muslims were not idolaters, but that they worshipped one God

> and do not even reject Christ and the apostles and the apos-
> tolic men; they are cut off from salvation by one thing alone,
> the fact that they deny that Jesus Christ … is God or the Son
> of God, and hold in reverence and worship as a great Prophet
> of the Supreme God, Mahomet, a deceiver.[49]

William of Malmesbury knew that Muslims were monotheists, but still claimed they had a statue of Muḥammad in the Temple. As Cole shows, however, his general tone towards Islam was extremely hostile indeed.[50] On a more pragmatic note, as argued earlier, areas of Latin Christendom bordered on Muslim lands (Iberia), or had Muslim trading partners (such as the Italian seafaring cities), or ruled over an indigenous Muslim population (such as Sicily).

Sweetenham, CTT 11 (Aldershot, 2005), 130, 156; see also the discussion in the Introduction, at 56.

[46] Damien Kempf, 'Towards a Textual Archaeology of the First Crusade', in Marcus G. Bull and Damien Kempf, eds, *Writing the Early Crusades: Text, Transmission and Memory* (Woodbridge, 2014), 116–26, at 123–4.

[47] Benjamin Z. Kedar, *Crusade and Mission: European Approaches towards the Muslims* (Princeton, NJ, 1984), 3–41.

[48] Cited in Bernard Hamilton, 'Knowing the Enemy: Western Understanding of Islam at the Time of the Crusades', *Journal of the Royal Asiatic Society* 3rd ser. 7 (1997), 373–87, at 373–6.

[49] Otto of Freising, *Chronica sive Historia de duabus civitatibus* (MGH SRG i.u.s. 45, 510); ET *The Two Cities: A Chronicle of Universal History to the year 1146*, transl. Charles M. Mierow (New York, 1928), 412; Tolan, *Saracens*, 109.

[50] Penny J. Cole, '"O God, the Heathen have come into your Inheritance" (Ps. 78.1): The Theme of Religious Pollution in Crusade Documents', in Maya Shatzmiller, ed., *Crusaders and Muslims in Twelfth-Century Syria* (Leiden, 1993), 84–111, at 86–8; Rodney M. Thomson, 'William and Some other Western Writers on Islam', in idem, *William of Malmesbury*, rev. edn (Woodbridge, 2003), 168–77.

Given the cultural and geo-political circumstances of the Latin East, the Frankish settlers might be expected to have acquired some insight into the various forms of religion practised by their neighbours, and the multiplicity of belief systems found amongst the indigenous population under Latin rule. That said, simple presence (and we know of mosques in Frankish towns such as Tyre and Acre) does not necessarily mean a seeking of, or a wish to seek, insight or understanding.[51] Ralph of Caen travelled out with the First Crusade and wrote his *Gesta Tancredi* in the Levant prior to 1118. He claimed that Tancred found and destroyed a huge silver idol of Mahomet in the Temple of Solomon.[52] That Ralph was writing an account of one of the heroes of the First Crusade may explain this passage. Walter the Chancellor composed his largely eye-witness account, the *Bella Antiochena*, from 1115 to 1122. He suggested that the Muslims used divination, something strictly forbidden in Islam, and on one occasion he accused them of enjoining 'false gods to appear for them', implying that they were polytheists.[53]

It is in the work of William of Tyre, the great chronicler of the Latin East, later royal chancellor of Jerusalem and archbishop of Tyre, that we find the most detailed information. Born in the Holy Land around 1130, William was educated in Europe for almost twenty years before he returned to the Levant to begin his stellar career.[54] He was, therefore, certainly exposed to the crude stereotypes noted above, yet these are largely absent from his own work. William also chose to describe his fellow-Franks as *orientales latini*, indicating, as Schwinges cogently argues, his distinctive standpoint compared to his co-religionists in the West.[55]

[51] Ibn Jubayr noted mosques in Acre and Tyre: Ibn Jubayr, *Travels*, transl. Broadhurst, 318, 321.

[52] Ralph of Caen, *Tancredus* (CChr.CM 231, 107, lines 3633–5); ET *The Gesta Tancredi of Ralph of Caen: A History of the Normans on the First Crusade*, transl. Bernard S. Bachrach and David S. Bachrach, CTT 12 (Aldershot, 2005), 143–4.

[53] Walter the Chancellor, *Bella Antiochena*; ET *Walter the Chancellor's The Antiochene Wars*, transl. Susan B. Edgington, commentary by Thomas S. Asbridge, CTT 4 (Aldershot, 1999), 101. On Islam and polytheism, see Daniella Talmon-Heller, *Islamic Piety in Medieval Syria: Mosques, Cemeteries and Sermons under the Zangids and Ayyubids (1146–1260)* (Leiden, 2007), 228–32.

[54] For an overview of William's life, career and writings, see Peter W. Edbury and John G. Rowe, *William of Tyre: Historian of the Latin East* (Cambridge, 1988).

[55] Ranier C. Schwinges, 'William of Tyre, the Muslim Enemy and the Problem of Tolerance', in Michael Gervers and James M. Powell, eds, *Tolerance and Intolerance:*

William produced a 'Deeds of the Rulers of the East', a history of the Muslim world from the Prophet down to 1182.[56] This contained Arabic texts, but sadly does not survive.[57] William's main work did endure and, of course, it rejects what was for him the false doctrine of Islam. The initial chapters, those based on earlier chroniclers, display the most hostile treatment of Muslims; but once we reach William's own time in the Levant, the polemical edge largely disappears. He knew that Muslims revered Muḥammad as a prophet and did not worship idols. He was well aware of the split between Sunnī and Shī'ite Muslims and explained the matter in detail – in part accurate, in other parts not.[58] Interestingly he did not use the word 'pagan', which as Schwinges observed, is the usual semantic term employed by Western churchmen. Pagans, in William's writings, deny God; for him, Muslims were *infidelis*, holding a different attitude to God from Christians.[59]

In a more practical fashion we can see the extent to which some contemporary Frankish nobles engaged in close diplomatic contacts with the local Muslims. The evidence for this derives not only from writers such as William of Tyre, but from Muslim sources too. Various individuals, such as the lords of Toron, often acted as diplomats and might be described as having acquired a particular skill and standing as such. In 1175, Humphrey III was said to have become too friendly with Saladin in the course of negotiations to free Frankish prisoners. William of Tyre regarded this as dangerous because, as he wrote, 'this prince [Saladin] won our goodwill'.[60] Humphrey's son, Humphrey IV of Toron, conducted multiple negotiations between the crusaders and Saladin during the early 1190s, in part because he was fluent in Arabic.[61] With that

---

Social Conflict in the Age of the Crusades (Syracuse, NY, 2001), 124–32. See also Nicholas E. Morton, 'William of Tyre's Attitude Towards Islam: Some Historiographical Reflections', in *Deeds done Beyond the Sea: Essays on William of Tyre, Cyprus and the Military Orders Presented to Peter Edbury*, ed. Susan B. Edgington and Helen J. Nicholson, Crusades – Subsidia 6 (Farnham, 2014), 13–23.

[56]   William of Tyre, *Historia*, 1: 109 (*History*, transl. Babcock and Krey, 1: 65).

[57]   Edbury and Rowe, *William of Tyre*, 23–4.

[58]   William also regarded the Shī'ites as closer to Christian doctrine than the Sunnī: William of Tyre, *Historia* 1.4 (CChr.CM 63, 109–10; *History*, transl. Babcock and Krey, 1: 65).

[59]   Schwinges, 'William of Tyre', 126–7.

[60]   William of Tyre, *Historia* 21.8 (CChr.CM 63A, 972; *History*, transl. Babcock and Krey, 2: 410).

[61]   Humphrey met with al-Adil, Saladin's brother, on several occasions: see Beha

in mind, it is intriguing to read a section of Beha ad-Din's largely eye-witness biography of Saladin. One story concerns Reynald of Sidon, a senior figure in the Frankish nobility.[62] By the late spring of 1189, that is, as the Third Crusade was gathering steam in the West, Saladin had conquered the majority of the Frankish lands in the south of the Levant; one place that still held out was the castle of Beaufort (now just inside the south-eastern border of Lebanon). In mid-May the sultan began to increase pressure on the fortress and in an attempt to avoid capitulating Reynald started to open diplomatic negotiations and call upon his diplomatic contacts. Beha ad-Din records that he was received with honour and respect and allowed to come into the sultan's tent. 'He was one of the Frankish nobles' ... wise heads who knew Arabic and had some familiarity with histories and Hadith collections. I heard that he kept a Muslim who read to him and explained things. He was a man of cautious deliberation.'[63] In part, Reynald was clearly playing for time because he suggested that if he surrendered the castle he might go and live in Damascus for his own safety. He wanted land from the sultan, three months to get the remainder of his family and retainers from Tyre, as well as to collect the annual revenue from the harvest. Saladin agreed to this, presumably seeing Beaufort as a difficult target and worth waiting for. Most intriguing of all, however, was Beha ad-Din's observation that 'all the time he [Reynald] continued to frequent the sultan's presence, disputing with us about his religion while we argued for its falsity. He was an excellent conversationalist and cultured in his talk.'[64] The author seems to have been present at these events, which took place over a series of weeks, and he was keen to praise Reynald as a man of words, presumably acknowledging the virtues in him as an *adib*, or cultivated man, displaying qualities so valued

ad-Din Ibn Shaddad, *The Rare and Excellent History of Saladin*, tr. Donald S. Richards, CTT 7 (Aldershot, 2001), 174, 179, 198, 231. See also Hussein M. Attiya, 'Knowledge of Arabic in the Crusader States in the Twelfth and Thirteenth Centuries', *JMedH* 25 (1999), 203–13.

[62] Malcolm Barber, *The Crusader States* (London, 2013), 308.

[63] Ibn Shaddad, *Rare and Excellent History*, transl. Richards, 90. The story is also included in Abu Shama, 'Two Gardens', *RHC Or.* 4: 396–7.

[64] Ibn Shaddad, *Rare and Excellent History*, transl. Richards, 91. This episode might well be labelled a *majlis*, that is, an interreligious debate: see Hava Lazarus-Yafeh et al., eds, *The Majlis: Interreligious Encounters in Medieval Islam*, Studies in Arabic Language and Literature 4 (Wiesbaden, 1999).

in the courts of the Near East.[65] The willingness of a contemporary Latin Christian, especially of a secular background, to engage in an intellectual debate on matters of religion has been ignored by historians. Reynald himself was evidently pretty well educated: aside from being fluent in Arabic, his familiarity with histories and Hadith collections mark him out as someone who was manifestly curious about Islam. This episode thus had both a theological and a cultural aspect.[66]

To put this in context, and to add to its broader plausibility, there was an interest in the Muslim Near East in discussing and writing about the 'errors' of Christianity. For example, Ibn al-Jawzi, a prolific Hanbali scholar in Baghdad from the 1160s to *c.*1180 produced *The Devil's Deception*, a work that showed how people, including Shī'ites, Ṣūfīs and Christians, could be led astray.[67] Likewise, the Damascene scholar Ibn 'Asakir (d. 1176) was an important scholar in the ideology of the counter-crusade who included biographical entries on Jesus, John the Baptist and Mary within his huge *History of Damascus*, which ran to over eighty volumes. In one section he suggested that Jesus might return and join the Muslims against the crusaders, because the latter had deserted the true message of Jesus.[68] Elsewhere Ibn 'Asakir urged his co-religionists to fight the Christian infidels.[69] Inevitably, perhaps, the picture is not entirely clear. An apologetic commentary on the Nicene Creed written in Arabic in Baghdad drew upon a range of literature to address Muslim objections to Christian belief.[70] As Kedar has argued, contemporary Muslims had a much better

---

[65] Paul M. Cobb, *Usama ibn Munqidh: Warrior Poet of the Age of the Crusades* (Oxford, 2005), 59–62.

[66] The Old French continuation of William of Tyre described this, including a scene in which Reynald was tortured in front of the fortress, leading to its capitulation. There is, however, a sense of Reynald being (at first) well entertained; there is no explicit statement that he spoke Arabic, although an exchange between the count and Saladin is part of the narrative: *La continuation*, ed. Morgan, 79–82 ('Old French Continuation', transl. Edbury, 70–3).

[67] Ibn al-Jawzi, in *Christian-Muslim Relations: A Bibliographical History, Volume 3 (1050–1200)*, ed. David Thomas and Alex Mallett (Leiden, 2011), 733.

[68] Ibn 'Asakir, ibid. 683–9. For more on Ibn 'Asakir and his views of Jesus, see Suleiman A. Mourad and James E. Lindsay, *The Intensification and Reorientation of Sunni Jihad Ideology in the Crusader Period* (Leiden, 2013), 8–9.

[69] Mourad and Lindsay, *Sunni Jihad Ideology*, 57, 80.

[70] 'Apologetic Commentary on the Creed', in *Christian-Muslim Relations 3*, ed. Thomas and Mallett, 671–5.

understanding of Christianity than Western Europeans did of Islam.[71] Nonetheless, the debate between Reynald and Saladin was evidently a big step up from the usual level of contemporary discussion.

Insight into the faith of one's opponent also manifested itself and, from a Western perspective, evolved during some of the diplomatic exchanges of the Third Crusade. The loss of Jerusalem in 1187 was, of course, a body-blow to Christendom. Letter writers related a terrible slaughter of Christians, and Saladin himself was said to be thirsting after Christian blood while the Muslims defamed the holy places.[72] The text known as *De expugnatione Terrae Sanctae per Saladinum*, based upon an eye-witness account of the fall of Jerusalem, described the Muslims as servants of evil, thirsty for Christian blood and encouraging apostasy, with Saladin himself being a cruel tyrant and the son of Satan.[73] The *Passio Reginaldi* of Peter of Blois, an incendiary Western text, imagined Reynald of Châtillon, who was executed by Saladin in the aftermath of the Battle of Hattin, vainly defying the sultan, who was labelled as the 'profane, impious and cruel antichrist', 'the dog of Babylon, the son of perdition', and a man who wanted to terminate the Christian religion.[74] Providing an especially close link to the actual campaign is Joachim of Fiore, the Cistercian abbot famed for his interpretation of the Book of Revelation. Joachim met King Richard in Messina as the latter journeyed to the East and he argued that Saladin was the sixth of the seven great persecutors of the Church.[75]

For all this aggressive rhetoric, once Richard had spent a period of time in the Holy Land, the deadlocked military situation, coupled with the king's pragmatic personality, meant that a more nuanced, better-informed perspective came into play. Diplomacy played a far greater role in the Third Crusade than it had in earlier expeditions: it was practically negligible in the First

---

[71] Benjamin Z. Kedar, 'Croisade et jihad vus par l'ennemi: une étude des perceptions mutuelles des motivations', in Michel Balard, ed., *Autour de la première croisade* (Paris, 1996), 345–55.

[72] See the letter mentioned in n. 7 above, along with, for example, 'Two *excitationes* for the Third Crusade: The Letters of Brother Thierry of the Temple', ed. John H. Pryor, *Mediterranean Historical Review* 25 (2010), 147–68.

[73] *De Expugnatione Terra Sanctae per Saladinum*, in Ralph of Coggeshall, *Chronicon Anglicanum*, ed. Joseph Stevenson, RS 66 (London, 1875), 209–62.

[74] Peter of Blois, *Passio Raginaldi principis Antiochie* (CChr.CM 194, 40, 57).

[75] Roger of Howden, *Gesta Henrici II et Ricardi I*, ed. Stubbs, 2: 151–5; John B. Gillingham, *Richard I* (London, 1999), 138–9.

and Second Crusades.[76] Of course, this was one aspect of both sides' recognizing that they lacked the military strength to remove their opponent in a single go. More pertinently for the discussion here, religious insight played a part too. Thus, early on, Saladin's brother al-Adil (known to the crusaders as Saphadin) met Richard, with the Frankish noble Humphrey of Toron acting as interpreter. At this stage, in early September 1191, the king's demands were uncompromising: 'The basic condition is that you should restore all the lands to us and return to your own countries.' This was not well received by al-Adil and resulted in the break-up of the meeting.[77] Several weeks later, little had changed, although Richard now outlined the importance of Jerusalem and the True Cross to the Christians, and indicated that the return of both was necessary for peace. Saladin responded that he would not give up Jerusalem because of its importance as the location of the Prophet's Night Journey. He noted the role of the True Cross as a diplomatic card.[78]

By March 1192, however, the crusaders had made an abortive attempt to besiege Jerusalem and morale was low. The news that Prince John was causing serious trouble at home was an added complication.[79] With Humphrey of Toron acting as his envoy, King Richard put forward further proposals. The Muslims would keep the Dome of the Rock and the citadel; the remainder of Jerusalem would be divided in two, with the villages around the city shared.[80] Another Western text, the *Itinerarium*, reported a comparable scheme on offer between Saladin and Conrad of Montferrat, who at this stage, was engaged in a bitter political struggle with Richard.[81]

By the summer of 1192, with both leaders in poor health and facing their own political and financial difficulties, a similar

---

[76] An important analysis of the diplomatic encounters of the Third Crusade is in Thomas S. Asbridge, 'Talking to the Enemy: The Role and Purpose of Negotiations between Saladin and Richard the Lionheart during the Third Crusade', *JMH* 39 (2013), 275–96, although the bulk of the analysis concerns strategic matters.

[77] Ibn Shaddad, *Rare and Excellent History*, transl. Richards, 173–4.

[78] Ibid. 185–6.

[79] Ambroise, *The History of the Holy War*, ed. and transl. Marianne Ailes and Malcolm C. Barber, 2 vols (Woodbridge, 2003), 2: 146–7.

[80] Ibn Shaddad, *Rare and Excellent History*, transl. Richards, 198.

[81] *Itinerarium peregrinorum et Gesta Regis Ricardi*, in *The Chronicle of the Third Crusade*, transl. Helen J. Nicholson, CTT 3 (Aldershot, 1997), 303–4; Ambroise, *Holy War*, ed. and transl. Ailes and Barber, 148–9.

proposal reappeared, with Beha ad-Din explicitly mentioning that the Holy Sepulchre would be returned to the Christians. It was the destruction (or not) of the castle of Ascalon that proved to be the sticking point at this time.[82] Further negotiations ensued, during which, according to Beha ad-Din, Richard met and knighted various Muslim emirs, which, if true, indicates a further level of cultural interaction.[83] By the early autumn, the king could no longer remain in the Levant, and with the sultan unmoving on Jaffa and Ascalon the diplomatic initiative swung towards the Muslims. The final agreement yielded a truce of three years, gave the Christians the coastline from Tyre to Jaffa and, most importantly of all, permitted Saladin full control over Jerusalem, which meant that the crusaders could only visit the city as pilgrims.[84] At the very least, the various conditions outlined in these negotiations seem to have made plain to the Westerners the significance of particular religious sites to their opponents. For those, such as the bishop of Salisbury, who took advantage of the opportunity to enter Jerusalem and who even met with Saladin himself, this was even more likely to have been the case.[85]

Back in the 1130s the Syrian poet and diplomat Usama ibn Munqidh had commented: 'Anyone who is recently arrived from the Frankish lands is rougher in character than those who have become acclimated and have frequent company with the Muslims.' He then recounted a tale in which a newcomer tried aggressively to prevent him from praying in the al-Aqsa mosque, a Templar friend of the author having to step in and protect his right to worship.[86] It was a combination of hostility and ignorance of Muslim beliefs that presumably provoked this episode. By the end of the Third Crusade, and with people such as Humphrey of Toron and Reynald of Sidon (who acted as interpreter and chief negotiator for Conrad of Montferrat, himself a very recent arrival in the Levant), this was less of an issue for some of the Latins. Notwith-

---

[82] Ibn Shaddad, *Rare and Excellent History*, transl. Richards, 214–15.

[83] Ibid. 227. Frederick II was reported as knighting Fakhr al-Din, a Muslim noble and diplomat in the 1220s: see Jean de Joinville, *Vie de saint Louis*, ed. and transl. Jean Monfrin (Paris, 1995), 96–9; ET in *Joinville and Villehardouin: Chronicles of the Crusades*, transl. Caroline Smith (London, 2008), 194–5.

[84] Ambroise, *Holy War*, ed. and transl. Ailes and Barber, 187–91.

[85] Ibn Shaddad, *Rare and Excellent History*, transl. Richards, 223.

[86] Usama ibn Munqidh, *The Book of Contemplation: Islam and the Crusades*, transl. Paul M. Cobb (London, 2008), 147.

standing their apparently crude and limited understandings of Islam prior to the campaign, the crusaders engaged in diplomacy with increasing insight into the faith of their opponents. The simple 'return everything to us' starting point of Richard's negotiations could now, coupled with the basic issues of political and military expediency, reflect some sense of the importance of Jerusalem to the Islamic world and hence its place in the wider jihad and the motivation of Saladin and his men.

In conclusion, crusading was a hugely complex affair. While the basic idea of Christianity versus Islam was, during the twelfth century at least, the position of the Church (whose leaders had the loudest voice in the written record), it was not that of all the other participants. Crusading exposed the clash between ideology and practice through variables, such as the mercantile cities, a group that became so important that they could not be wholly overruled or ignored. We have glimpsed the considerable tensions between the powerful rhetoric of the Latin Church and the commercial imperatives of Genoa, the religious aspirations of the Genoese themselves and the realities of life in the Levant.

In essence, the First Crusade had worked because of an alliance of interests between the Church and the lay nobility; such an alliance did not fit so comfortably between the papacy and the trading cities. As we have seen above, this is not to say that the latter were unaware of the tensions between holy war and commerce, and at times they clearly felt uneasy, but in the early, successful, decades of the crusading movement this pressure was less critical. As the thirteenth century wore on, however, in the face of a continued failure to recover Jerusalem, bans on commerce with the Muslim Near East grew. Pope Innocent III (1198–1216), a man obsessed with the recovery of Jerusalem from Islam, recognized the need for economic exchange with such lands, while excluding specified materials of war and shipbuilding.[87] But the trading cities became increasingly unresponsive and legislation at the Fourth Lateran Council in 1215 distinguished Ayyubid lands from other Muslim regions with which it was still permissible to trade.[88]

---

[87] *Die Register Innocenz' III*, ed. O. Hageneder et al., 11 vols (Graz, Cologne, Rome, Vienna, 1964–2010), 1: 775–6, no. 536 (539); ET in *Contemporary Sources for the Fourth Crusade*, tr. Alfred Andrea (Leiden, 2000), 23–4.

[88] Menache, 'Papal Attempts', takes the story through the thirteenth century.

It is a paradox that the event which generated the most violent religious rhetoric – the loss of Jerusalem – actually brought about, by reason of the duration of the Third Crusade, a substantial opportunity for the diffusion of knowledge concerning the Islamic faith to a number of Western Europeans.[89] For all that, well into the thirteenth century the continuing evolution of crusading would both sharpen engagement with Islam, through the powerful writing of men such as James of Vitry, and also see the creation of new avenues of contact with the age of mission.[90] Thus we have to recognize and to accommodate the complexities, contradictions and inconsistencies of the Crusades. As this essay shows – and as today's world leaders will eventually realize too – the closer you get to the Levant, the more complex the picture becomes.

Royal Holloway, University of London

---

[89] Obviously the border of Muslim and Christian Iberia, as well as the trading cities, saw much longer levels of contact: see Tolan, *Saracens*.

[90] Kedar, *Crusade and Mission*.

ENCOUNTERS IN THE RUINS: LATIN CAPTIVES, FRANCISCAN FRIARS AND THE DANGERS OF RELIGIOUS PLURALITY IN THE EARLY MONGOL EMPIRE[*]

by AMANDA POWER

Among the richest, and strangest, sites for religious encounter during the medieval period was the network of Mongol encampments on the Eurasian steppe. In the middle decades of the thirteenth century, a vast empire was administered from these itinerant cities. In consequence, they were crammed with a transient population of people drawn, summoned or seized from diverse societies across the continent. Within these cities, physical space, approved gestures and permitted actions were heavily ritualized according to shamanistic practice, but as long as these customs were respected, the Mongols encouraged an atmosphere of relative egalitarianism among the various faiths represented in the camps.[1] Indeed, they actively sought the services of the clerical classes of the different groups, requiring each to offer prayers and blessings within public and private ceremonies.[2] This meant the permanent presence in the camps of shamans, priests, monks, imams and others, who embodied the authority of their faith in that place. These individuals seem to have spent their time competing for the favour of powerful Mongols, forming brief alliances, differentiating themselves or exhibiting signs of syncretism, quarrelling and drinking together. How far the rest of the non-Mongol population of the camps participated in these peculiar

[*]   In writing this essay, I have benefited from discussions at the meetings of the AHRC-funded network, 'Defining the Global Middle Ages', conversations with Miles Larmer, Caroline Dodds Pennock and Miriam Dobson, and the opportunity to present a version at the University of Sheffield's Department of History research seminar.

[1]   See Peter Jackson, 'The Mongols and the Faith of the Conquered', in Reuven Amitai and Michal Biran, eds, *Mongols, Turks and Others: Eurasian Nomads and the Sedentary World* (Leiden, 2005), 245–90.

[2]   Christopher P. Atwood, 'Validation by Holiness or Sovereignty: Religious Toleration as Political Theology in the Mongol World Empire of the Thirteenth Century', *International History Review* 26 (1994), 237–56.

inter-faith relations, or identified with them, is less clear, given the nature of our sources. We can, nonetheless, be certain that there were sharp differences in experience of religious encounter that were conditioned by various factors, including the role or status of the person in the camp. The emphasis in the historiography on Mongol religious 'tolerance' should not be allowed to obscure the true nature of these curious micro-cosmopolitanisms of the steppes. They were the product of disrupted hegemonies, destroyed societies, brutal enslavement and opportunism in the ruins.

For the historian wishing to investigate forms of religious encounter, the complexities and ambiguities of life in the Mongol camps are enticing. They both force and facilitate much-needed reflection on the qualities and agendas of the groups or individuals encountering each other. Despite increasing sophistication in the broader study of encounters – now usually characterized as occurring between 'cultures' – medievalists still tend to explore contacts between groups defined primarily through their presumed religious beliefs and structures of religious authority.[3] There is, for example, a large literature on interactions between various combinations of 'Christians', 'Muslims', 'Jews', 'pagans' and 'heretics' in the Middle Ages. While these perceived communities are in practice treated more as cultures than as 'religions' in the modern sense – and this method of labelling undoubtedly reflects the worldview of many medieval authors – these are categories which, when used in scholarship, carry dangers of simplification, essentialism and reification. When treating more than one religion at once, it is all too easy to obliterate the immense diversity of practices, beliefs, loyalties, identities, levels of doctrinal awareness, individual commitment and much else which existed within each 'religion' – or even each member of a religious community over the course of a lifetime. There is a growing awareness (at least in some quarters) that the concept of 'religion' – as a distinctive but universal, and properly private, category of thought and behaviour – is an invention of Western scholarship, and more broadly, of secular moder-

---

[3]   Even so, historians' conceptualization of 'culture', especially the recognition of the instability, fluidity and mobility of 'cultures', remains problematic: Daniel T. Rodgers, 'Cultures in Motion: An Introduction', in idem et al., eds, *Cultures in Motion* (Princeton, NJ, 2013), 1–19; Serge Gruzinski, *The Mestizo Mind: The Intellectual Dynamics of Colonization and Globalization* (London, 2002), 17–31. Similar difficulties arise in the study of 'religions'.

nity.[4] Attention has been drawn to the dangers of using this idea of 'religion' as a 'normalising concept' to describe non-Christian traditions.[5] But I am not sure that these recognitions have entered as far as they might into the ways that historians discuss encounters between members of 'religions' in a global context. The medieval period is vulnerable to these problems in very specific ways, as it is imagined as a time of coexistence and exchange between distinct communities, and yet also as the static, autochthonous 'other' to the cultural hybridities and globalizing processes of modernity.[6] In these contexts, the value of the extant descriptions of the Mongol camps is that they at once use religious affiliations as markers of identity, but also show that more complicated dynamics were at work, especially as time and distance weakened the connections between Latin Christians and the authorities and teachings of their Church.[7]

In what follows, I would like to explore some of these issues by looking closely at Latin Christian experiences of encounter in this setting, especially those of the captives and slaves who were not free to leave. These were lived encounters, developing over decades. Each, as Subrahmanyam put it in relation to some later examples, 'represented a chronology and a series of events rather than a simple moment. If misunderstandings existed [between different parties], they did not remain stable'.[8] Most began in unrecorded

---

[4]   As an invention of Western scholarship, see Jonathan Z. Smith, *Relating Religion: Essays in the Study of Religion* (Chicago, IL, 2004); as a broader enterprise, Derek Peterson and Darren Walhof, eds, *The Invention of Religion: Rethinking Belief in Politics and History* (New Brunswick, NJ, 2002); Talal Asad, *Genealogies of Religion: Discipline and Reasons of Power in Christianity and Islam* (Baltimore, MD, 1993). In relation to medieval ideas, see Peter Biller, 'Words and the Medieval Notion of "Religion"', *JEH* 36 (1985), 351–69.

[5]   Asad, *Genealogies*, 1.

[6]   On the first view, see Rémi Brague, *The Legend of the Middle Ages: Philosophical Explorations of Medieval Christianity, Judaism, and Islam*, transl. Lydia G. Cochrane (Chicago, IL, 2009), especially 185–202; on the second, C. A. Bayly, '"Anarchic" and "Modern" Globalization in the Eurasian and African Arena, c.1750–1850', in A. G. Hopkins, ed., *Globalization in World History* (London, 2002), 47–72; and the challenge to the 'modernocentric' bias in Jerry H. Bentley, 'Hemispheric Integration, 500–1500 C.E.', *Journal of World History* 9 (1998), 237–54.

[7]   'Latin Christians' were those who considered themselves to belong to the Roman Church and acknowledged the primacy of the pope. During this period, there were ongoing negotiations to bring various Eastern Churches (notably the Russian, Armenian and Greek Churches) into union with Rome, but none had lasting success.

[8]   Sanjay Subrahmanyam, *Explorations in Connected History: Mughals and Franks*

circumstances that we can only infer from other sources. Let us begin with a brief account of this background.

It was with the violent assault on the Eastern kingdoms of Christendom in 1241–2 that the Latin West was abruptly brought into the ambit of the tribal conglomerate now known as the Mongols. In the later 1230s, a people previously unknown in the West had laid waste to the lands of the Rus', Georgia, Greater Armenia and the western steppes, destroying cities and massacring or enslaving their populations. Kiev had fallen in 1240. Rumours came to the Latin West of these and other attacks, but the danger seemed far away. Then, in the early months of 1241, nomad hordes advanced into Poland, Moravia and Hungary, plundering through the summer and crossing the Danube when it froze. They brought devastation wherever they went. Yet, without penetrating deeper into Europe, they unexpectedly withdrew and, in fact, never returned.[9] For the inhabitants of the affected regions, it was a prolonged experience of terror and privation. We know something of what occurred from the letters sent to beg help from the rulers of the West, but their recourse to eschatological imagery blunts the sense of real horrors befalling real people.[10] The most graphic and immediate account is that of Master Roger, then archdeacon of Waradinum in what was then eastern Hungary (modern Oradea in Romania). He was a fugitive in the wrecked landscape, and later a captive of the Mongols for a time. His report indicates that those left alive by the Mongols witnessed the gruesome murders of many people, including their own families, and endured appalling mistreatment, including sexual violence.[11] Such memories must

(Oxford, 2005), 6. Here he argues that the *topos* of encounter freezes 'rather complex processes into a memorable Kodak moment'.

[9]   Peter Jackson, *The Mongols and the West, 1221–1410* (Harlow, 2005), 38–44, 58–75.

[10]   Some were preserved by the English Benedictine chronicler Matthew Paris, although their authenticity has been questioned: James Ross Sweeney, 'Thomas of Spalato and the Mongols: A Thirteenth-Century Dalmatian view of Mongol Customs', *Florilegium* 4 (1982), 156–83, at 157.

[11]   'Master Roger's Epistle to the Sorrowful Lament upon the Destruction of the Kingdom of Hungary by the Tartars', transl. János M. Bak and Martyn Rady, in Martyn Rady et al., eds, *Anonymus and Master Roger*, Central European Medieval Texts 5 (Budapest, 2010), especially 164/5–224/5 (facing Latin and English text). Roger's picture of Mongol tactics is broadly confirmed in John of Plano Carpini, *Historia mongalorum* 8.2–6 (*Storia dei Mongoli*, ed. and transl. Enrico Menestò et al., Biblioteca del Centro per il collegamento degli studi medievali e umanistici dell'Università di Perugia 1 [Spoleto, 1989], 293–6). For scholarly assessment of the accuracy of the

have haunted those who survived to be enslaved in the steppe encampments.

In the grand narrative of global encounters, these years are presented as a brief bloody epoch before the *pax Mongolica* connected Europe into a 'world system' characterized by cultural and commercial exchange.[12] The focus shifts from the victims of the Mongol onslaught to the shiver of fear that these events inspired across Christendom, where there was speculation that the 'Tartars' were the harbingers of the Apocalypse, but little concrete action from the distracted and quarrelling leaders of the West.[13] It was not until 1245 that the pope sent representatives to the Mongol leaders. The envoys were members of the Franciscan and Dominican orders, who were also charged with finding out as much as possible about the new enemies. The results were not generally encouraging, but were interpreted to suggest that the Mongols were open to some kind of dialogue, and might be receptive to Christianity. It was the beginning of a century of Latin involvement in the Mongol Empire, an entity that soon stretched from China to the Russian steppes, and south into India. These experiences enabled people in the Latin West – through the reports of travellers and more material exchanges – to engage in a radical revision of their ancient geographical, ethnographical and cosmographical traditions. These shifts, in turn, had a considerable effect on the intellectual and cultural context for subsequent encounters and early colonialism.[14]

This understanding of the trajectory of Latin experience with the Mongols is, like so many other established narratives, almost entirely

chronicle accounts and the impacts of the invasion, see Nora Berend, *At the Gate of Christendom: Jews, Muslims and 'Pagans' in Medieval Hungary, c.1000–c.1300* (Cambridge, 2001), especially 34–8, 163–71.

[12] Janet L. Abu-Lughod, *Before European Hegemony: The World System AD 1250–1350* (New York, 1989), especially 143–4 (invasions discussed briefly); J. R. S. Phillips, *The Medieval Expansion of Europe*, 2nd edn (Oxford, 1998), 96–114. On exchange, see Thomas T. Allsen, *Commodity and Exchange in the Mongol Empire: A Cultural History of Islamic Textiles* (Cambridge, 2002).

[13] Peter Jackson, 'The Crusade against the Mongols (1241)', *JEH* 42 (1991), 1–18; Felicitas Schmieder, 'Christians, Jews, Muslims – and Mongols: Fitting a Foreign People into the Western Christian Apocalyptic Scenario', *Medieval Encounters* 12 (2006), 274–95, at 279–82.

[14] Stuart B. Schwartz, ed., *Implicit Understandings: Observing, Reporting, and Reflecting on the Encounters between Europeans and Other Peoples in the Early Modern Era* (Cambridge, 1994).

shaped by the writings and experiences of a male clerical elite and prioritizes intellectual and analytical responses over other kinds. We see the Mongols through the eyes of the educated men who travelled under the protection given to envoys, missionaries or merchants and returned to write and disseminate accounts of what they had seen.[15] This obscures the fact that captives supplied much of their information. The author of the most systematic report on the Mongols stated specifically: 'through these people, we were able to study everything carefully'.[16] Even less noted is the other fact: that most of the information came from the most privileged among the captives – the highly skilled artisans, captive clerics and other literate people – rather than the ordinary slaves. Nonetheless, it was the Latin cleric, with the full force of ecclesiastical authority behind him, who determined the epistemological status of the material and its meaning, while the enslaved captives and others in the Mongol encampments, who spoke the Mongol language and had in some cases lived among them for many years, were, perhaps, compromised witnesses.[17] They were no longer fully 'Latin' but lived in between cultures, without priests or pastoral care. The clerical observer, on the other hand, retained his agency – certainly within the texts, if not while in Mongol lands – and his cultural and religious 'purity' – and with all this, his capacity to serve as an effective representative of, and informant for, his society. This highlights the influence of a process within medieval society that is rarely connected explicitly with its gathering and managing of knowledge about the wider world: the hegemonistic agendas of the post-Gregorian Church. Orthodox interpretations were privileged; others were silenced.

Viewed with these observations in mind, the early reports on the Mongols are less straightforward records of Latin Christian perceptions than they might seem. This essay will consider two accounts, both written by Franciscan friars. The earlier of the two was that of John of Plano Carpini, one of the friars despatched by Pope

---

[15] For example, David Morgan, *The Mongols*, 2nd edn (Oxford, 2007), 155–9.

[16] '[A] quibus poteramus perscrutari omnia': John of Plano Carpini, *Historia mongalorum* 9.39 (*Storia*, ed. and transl. Menestò et al., 324).

[17] For the view that the captives were untrustworthy, see Gregory Guzman, 'European Captives and Craftsmen among the Mongols, 1231–1255', *The Historian* 72 (2010), 122–50, at 147–9. More broadly on the role of captives in the production of knowledge, see Lisa Voigt, *Writing Captivity in the Early Modern Atlantic: Circulations of Knowledge and Authority in the Iberian and English Imperial Worlds* (Chapel Hill, NC, 2009).

Innocent IV in 1245 to carry papal letters to the Mongols.[18] His
report assessed the history, society, morals, military techniques and
intentions of the Mongols and offered detailed recommendations
for how to deal with them. It was widely circulated.[19] The later
account, written in 1255, was that of William of Rubruck. William
was in the eastern Mediterranean, accompanying the crusade of
Louis IX of France, when he heard of a group of German slaves
adrift in the Mongol Empire and determined to go and settle with
them as their priest. Due to a series of misunderstandings, he was
sent to the court of the great *qaghan*, Möngke, in what is now
central Mongolia.[20] His report was written for Louis, who had
both attempted unsuccessfully to convert the Mongols and had
himself endured a period of captivity at the hands of the Egyptians
– a traumatic experience that probably intensified his commitment
to penance and reform.[21] The report was a candid description of
William's experiences, focusing especially on the 'religious' environment, his efforts to provide pastoral care to various scattered
Christians, and his attempts to convert non-Christians. It had a
limited audience.[22]

These texts present at least three layers of 'religious' encounter.
It is possible to use them to reconstruct something of the experiences of a variety of Latin captives and slaves living in the Mongol
encampments among representatives of many different faiths and

[18] His previous experiences included directing the establishment of the eastern
provinces of his order between 1221 and 1239: *Fratris Iordani a Iano: Chronica*, in
Analecta Franciscana, 1: *Ad historiam Fratrum Minorum spectantia* (Quaracchi, 1885), 16–17.
Biographical details can be found in Igor de Rachewiltz, *Papal Envoys to the Great
Khans* (Stanford, CA, 1971), 89–111; *Dizionario Biografico degli Italiani*, *s.n.* 'Giovanni da
Pian del Carpine', online at: <http://www.treccani.it/enciclopedia/giovanni-da-pi-
an-del-carpine_%28Dizionario-Biografico%29/>, accessed 18 June 2014. For further
context, see Jean Richard, *La papauté et les missions d'orient au Moyen Âge (XIIIe–XVe
siècles)* (Rome, 1998), 17–83.
[19] John of Plano Carpini, *Historia mongalorum* (*Storia*, ed. and transl. Menestò et al.,
226–333).
[20] On William's visit to the Mongol court, see also, in this volume, Bernard
Hamilton, 'Western Christian Contacts with Buddhism, *c.*1050–1350', 80–91.
[21] Cecilia Gaposchkin, 'The Captivity of Louis IX', *Quaestiones Medii Aevi Novae*
18 (2013), 85–114.
[22] On William, see *The Mission of Friar William of Rubruck: His Journey to the Court of
the Great Khan Möngke 1253–1255*, transl. Peter Jackson, intro., notes and appendices by
Peter Jackson and David Morgan, Hakluyt Society 2nd ser. 173 (London, 1990), 39–52;
his account (*Itinerarium*) is edited in *Viaggio in Mongolia*, ed. Paolo Chiesa (Milan, 2011).
Except where the Latin terminology is important, I have used Jackson's translation.

interpretations of faiths. The texts, partly based on this material, are also first-hand accounts of the perceptions of visitors who embodied the authority and the moral urgency – and yet the flexible, innovating impulses – of a very specific element in Latin Christianity.[23] Finally, John was travelling in order to facilitate a more remote encounter: that of the pope and the great *qaghan*. It is here, of course, on both sides, that we find the 'religious' identity that has traditionally been regarded as most stable and definitive. The pope defines Catholicism; Genghis *qaghan* and his successors define what it is to be 'Mongol'.[24] There is therefore the potential to discover multiple 'Latin Christianities' within the texts, each of which was connected with the others through a shared system of authority, belief and practice, but experienced and reacted to the challenge of religious plurality differently. Thus these are fertile materials for a critical investigation of the forms that might be taken by 'Christian' encounters with other religions.

What follows will offer at least some indication of the ways in which each 'layer' of Christianity experienced encounter and consequently attempted to act. We begin, briefly, with the papacy. Copies are extant of the papal letters that were despatched with John, and he expounded their contents several times in his text.[25] They outlined what were perceived at the time as the essential doctrines of the Christian faith, with particular emphasis on the power, authority and primacy of the pope as God's sole representative on earth. Innocent IV then expressed his desire for the salvation of the Mongols, which could only be achieved by their conversion to Christianity and repentance for their violence. They would otherwise go to hell. He explained that he had sent the friars because they were virtuous and knowledgeable men, able

[23] For background, see C. H. Lawrence, *The Friars: The Impact of the early Mendicant Movement on Western Society* (London, 1994).

[24] These were not necessarily asymmetrical categories for medieval observers. For Roger Bacon, the 'Mongol' religion (*secta* or *ritus Tartarorum*), was one of the six major *sectae* of the world: *Rogeri Baconis: Moralis philosophia*, ed. Eugenio Massa (Turin, 1953), e.g. 212–14. For 'Mongol' identity as communicated to Europeans by the *qaghans*, see Eric Voegelin, 'The Mongol Orders of Submission to European Powers, 1245–1255', *Byzantion* 15 (1941), 378–413.

[25] Karl-Ernst Lupprian, ed., *Die Beziehungen der Päpste zu islamischen und mongolischen Herrschern im 13. Jahrhundert anhand ihres Briefwechsels* (Vatican City, 1981), 141–9 (nos 20–1), For John's reference to the letters, see John of Plano Carpini, *Historia mongalorum* 9.8 (*Storia*, ed. and transl. Menestò et al., 306–7).

to instruct the *qaghan* in the faith. He requested the Mongols to desist from attacking people and to live in peace with the rest of humanity, and finally, asked that they should inform him regarding their intentions for the future. Although it is not usually characterized in such terms, this sounds like an attempt to place the Mongols within the structures of pastoral care upon which so much emphasis was being laid by the Church in this period. The pope's envoys were offered, in effect, as confessors, and the Mongols were imagined as potential converts and penitents. In some ways this was a pure abstraction, because of the sheer unreality of how the encounter was being envisaged, but it was also quite specific to the time and circumstances in which the letters were written. The aggrandizing claims of the thirteenth-century papacy were to be projected into the barbarous world of the Mongol Empire, as they had been into the eastern Mediterranean.[26] In practice, the audience for this self-positioning was principally domestic. For that reason, here, at the core of Latin Christianity imagined – in Asad's phrase – as possessing a trans-historical 'autonomous essence', there could be no accommodation, no transforming encounter.[27]

For all that they were representatives of this Christianity, the friars could not see things in the same light. They had the hard and hungry journey across a continent devastated by decades of savage war, with no easy means of communicating with those around them, and were wholly at the mercy of the uncongenial and arrogant world conquerors.[28] This was the theatre in which these members of an order dedicated to preaching their faith with humility through a combination of word and example had to perform.[29] John's position was complicated because he was a papal envoy as well as a kind of military scout. His party deliberately muted the more confrontational aspects of being a friar: wearing shoes, modifying their habits, and even covering them

---

[26] On the mechanisms of this projection, see Richard, *Papauté*; James Muldoon, *Popes, Lawyers and Infidels* (Liverpool, 1979).

[27] Asad, *Genealogies*, 28; see also Antti Ruotsala, *Europeans and Mongols in the Middle of the Thirteenth Century: Encountering the Other* (Helsinki, 2001), 100–9.

[28] On the devastation through which they passed, see John of Plano Carpini, *Historia mongalorum* 6.16 – 7.6; 7.9; 9.22–3 (*Storia*, ed. and transl. Menestò et al., 283–7, 289–90, 314); William of Rubruck, *Itinerarium* 19.2; 23.6; 12.6 respectively (*Mission*, transl. Jackson, 130, 147, 106).

[29] The guidance for friars 'going among infidels' was at 'Regula non bullata' 16, in *Opuscula Sancti Patris Francisci Assisiensis*, ed. Katejan Esser (Grottaferrata, 1978), 268–71.

with brocade in the presence of the *qaghan*.[30] They steered a careful path between accommodating the demands of Mongol custom and asserting their 'Christian' integrity where they could. William, on the other hand, made much of the performative aspects of being a friar. His party appeared in their habits, barefoot on the winter steppes, 'and presented quite a spectacle for them'. However, on other occasions they came before Mongol leaders in their best vestments, singing the *Salve regina* and carrying books: the Bible, an illuminated psalter and the missal.[31] These contrasting guises reflect two types of Christian authority that were present in William, who was at once a friar and a priest. Both men, in keeping with the conventions of their order and their society, attempted through their modest self-fashioning to shape the nature of their various encounters in the Mongol Empire.

When it came to verbal communication, both tried to express the core doctrines of the Church of their day. John's reports of his own preaching were concerned entirely with his recounting of the contents of the papal letter to people he met along the way. William's preaching was more varied and opportunist, but badly hampered by a poor interpreter. Nonetheless, William explained to a Muslim the doctrines of the incarnation, the resurrection of the dead and the last judgement, 'and how cleansing from sin lay in baptism', and nearly succeeded in baptizing him.[32] To the Mongols, he was harsher, saying as the pope had done: that they might have worldly power now, but without baptism they could only face damnation.[33] He went into Buddhist temples and argued with them about the notion that God had become human.[34] Sometimes he could do nothing more than write out the Creed and the Lord's Prayer on bits of paper that the Mongols then tucked in their hats and used as lucky charms.[35] He also tried to teach Latin doctrines and practices to the Eastern Christians, especially the

---

[30] *Relatio Fr. Benedicti Poloni*, in Anastasius van den Wyngaert, ed., *Sinica Franciscana*, I: *Itinera et relationes fratrum minorum saeculi xiii et xiv* (Florence, 1929), 133–43, at 139.

[31] William of Rubruck, *Itinerarium* 19.5; 15.6–7 respectively (*Mission*, transl. Jackson, 132, 116–17).

[32] Ibid. 12.1–2 (*Mission*, transl. Jackson, 104).

[33] Ibid. 19.7; 33.5–6 (*Mission*, transl. Jackson, 133, 228).

[34] Ibid. 25.7 (*Mission*, transl. Jackson, 155).

[35] Ibid. 27.4 (*Mission*, transl. Jackson, 166–7).

Nestorians – whose theology had been affected by centuries of syncretism among the religions of the East, and the great distance from their religious centres in Mesopotamia – and an unprincipled Armenian monk with whom he had to share accommodation.[36] Most famously, he had the opportunity to engage in a debate between Christians, Buddhists and Muslims before Möngke, in order, the *qaghan* said, to establish which was the true religion (*lex*). On this occasion, he employed the dialectical method that was fundamental to academic practice in the Latin West.[37] Yet even here, if we are looking for essentialized religions in contact, we will not find them: the whole debate was carried out in a highly idiosyncratic fashion with considerable disagreement among representatives of each of the 'religions'.

During his time in Möngke's camp, William was part of a 'Christian' community: a diverse, quarrelsome, unprepossessing group. He hated watching what he regarded as their various perversions, but he considered it risky and inappropriate to isolate himself from the other Christians.[38] Thus William trod a faltering course when encountering other forms of faith. He continually tried to preach, to offer pastoral care and to show by his example how a true (Latin) Christian should behave, but amid the diversity of the Mongol camps he was always having to defer to Mongol custom, to halt his proselytizing when his interpreter refused to continue, and to stand by while the holy office was chanted by Nestorian priests who were, in William's opinion, 'usurers and drunkards', ignorant of grammar, polygamous, who washed before entering church like Muslims and ate meat on Fridays.[39]

For John, clothed in the certainties of his mission and papal authority, this world was chiefly a military menace, and some of his conclusions included the standard reformers' criticisms of Latin society, suggesting that Christendom's best defence against inva-

---

[36] On the history of the 'Nestorian' or East Syrian Church, see Christoph Baumer, *The Church of the East: An Illustrated History of Assyrian Christianity* (London, 2006), especially 212–16 for Latin attitudes to Nestorians in this period.

[37] William of Rubruck, *Itinerarium*, 33.7–22 (*Mission*, transl. Jackson, 229–35); Hamilton, 'Western Christian Contacts with Buddhism'.

[38] William of Rubruck, *Itinerarium* 30.8 (*Mission*, transl. Jackson, 212).

[39] Ibid. 26.12–14 (*Mission*, transl. Jackson, 163–4).

sion lay in peace and unity among its leaders.[40] For William, it was a different matter entirely. To venture into a new world, a terrain unexplored since the original apostles took Christianity to the ends of the earth, believing that one's order, going barefoot and humble into the wilderness, represented that same bold apostolic power, and to be met with little but indifference, must have posed an unsettling existential threat. He concluded his report by recommending that no more friars be sent, but instead a bishop, 'in some style'.[41] Given the high status of the mendicant orders in the Church and in society and the considerable social investment in the efficacy of their 'apostolic' way of life, this psychological and moral defeat is significant. It seems that encounters with religious plurality posed the greater danger to the man whose mission, and perhaps disposition, required him to engage deeply with its complex effects. To put it in a different language: William perceived processes of syncretism at work and felt impotent to arrest them, while John adopted a more robust defence, by imposing normative interpretative models on the strange world of the camps.

This difference affected the friars' representations of the lives of the Latin captives. John gave a stark picture of their circumstances. He had seen people without fingers and toes, lost to the bitter cold; half-naked and barely fed. The women were forced into sexual slavery, while the men were sent ahead into dangerous situations; 'beaten like donkeys'. He was told that many had already died from this treatment.[42] He maintained that slavery of the type that the captives suffered at Mongol hands – which he considered extreme to an extent previously unknown – was 'intolerable for

---

[40] E.g. John of Plano Carpini, *Historia mongalorum* 8.6, 10 (*Storia*, ed. and transl. Menestò et al., 296, 299). The connection between peace and reform had been widely emphasized from at least the late tenth century: see T. Head and R. Landes, eds, *The Peace of God: Social Violence and Religious Response in France around the Year 1000* (Ithaca, NY, 1992); T. Mastnak, *Crusading Peace: Christendom, the Muslim World, and Western Political Order* (Berkeley, CA, 2002). For a later instance of the same argument, see, in this volume, Charlotte Methuen, '"And our Muḥammad goes with the Archangel Gabriel to Choir": Sixteenth-Century German Accounts of Life under the Turks', 166–80, at 174, 177–80.

[41] William of Rubruck, *Itinerarium*, Epilogue 5 (*Mission*, transl. Jackson, 278).

[42] '[U]t asini verberantur': John of Plano Carpini, *Historia mongalorum* 7.11–12 (*Storia*, ed. and transl. Menestò et al., 291–2); cf. ibid. 8.6 (*Storia*, ed. and transl. Menestò et al., 296); William of Rubruck, *Itinerarium* 8.2 (*Mission*, transl. Jackson, 93). Similar information was given by other envoys: Simon de Saint-Quentin, *Histoire des Tartares* 30.84 (ed. Jean Richard [Paris, 1965], 47–8).

our race [*nostre genti*]'. It was shameful because of the abominations that the Mongols practised, 'and because [in this captivity] the worship of God is reduced to nothingness, souls are lost, and bodies are afflicted in various ways, quite beyond belief'.[43] Here we have a very strong statement of the virtual impossibility of the 'Christianity' of the slaves surviving this kind of lived encounter, but was it accurate? By the time that William arrived at Möngke's court, just eight years later, the Latin captives from the original invasions had long since become part of the world of their captors. Their material conditions had not changed significantly. William's party was beset by numerous starving people who were not provided with food, but survived on the dregs of milk, dirty water, mice and carrion – whatever they could find.[44] Yet for all this, they had not lost their essential identities: it was, William reported, the 'poor Christians' in the camp who came to depend on the charity of the friars.[45] But in what form had they retained their 'Christianity', and what constituted its expression?

The slaves, like everyone else in the camps, had no choice but to live in the world of Mongol belief and custom, not least because of the ritualization of physical space. This was a constant theme in both friars' accounts. The friars were warned before meeting their first Mongol leader that they must avoid stepping on the threshold of his dwelling and that they had also to pass between two fires as a purification ritual.[46] Mongol dwellings contained idols, to which offerings were made before every meal, and there were various situations in which particular places could not be entered or things could not be removed from them. Failure to observe these customs led to severe punishment or to death.[47] The slaves were not exempt, and so had been obliged to adopt outward forms of Mongol practice in their daily lives. In addition, the shamans were extremely powerful, exercising an arbitrary tyranny over the

---

[43] '[Q]uasi intollerabilis nostre genti'; 'et quia in nichilum redigitur cultus Dei, et anime pereunt, et corpora ultra quam credi possit multimode affliguntur': John of Plano Carpini, *Historia mongalorum* 8.5, 3 respectively (*Storia*, ed. and transl. Menestò et al., 296, 294).

[44] William of Rubruck, *Itinerarium* 29.17; 4.4; 5.1; 11.2 respectively (*Mission*, transl. Jackson, 188, 82, 84, 102).

[45] Ibid. 36.18 (*Mission*, transl. Jackson, 252).

[46] John of Plano Carpini, *Historia mongalorum* 9.11, 14 (*Storia*, ed. and transl. Menestò et al., 308, 310).

[47] E.g. ibid. 3 (*Storia*, ed. and transl. Menestò et al., 235–44).

inhabitants of the camps, while their auguries and incantations seemed to many of the Christians to have an uncanny influence over the natural and demonic worlds.[48]

The experiences of some identified individuals, as described by John, provide examples of Mongols going further in forcing their social norms on those they had subjugated. Mikhail of Chernigov, the most important of the princes of Rus' – all of whom were subject to the Mongols – was executed by Batu, *qaghan* of the Golden Horde, ostensibly for his refusal to bow to an image of Genghis. While Batu's reasons for killing Mikhail were political, it is interesting that he made this particular form of submission his pretext; just as Mikhail apparently chose to make his inevitable death a martyrdom, saying that he would 'rather die, than do what was not lawful [to a Christian]'.[49] Another of the Russian princes was forced to marry his brother's widow, in accordance with Mongol practice, but in grave violation of the consanguinity rules of the Russian Church. John reported that the woman had said – like Mikhail – that she would rather die than go against her religion (*lex*), and described her 'crying out and weeping' as she was forced to consummate the marriage.[50]

These examples, although offered as illustrations in John's section on Mongol religion (*cultus*), probably relate more to the politics of Batu's subjugation of the elites of the Rus' and their strategies of resistance.[51] John claimed that the Mongols did not otherwise force people formally to deny 'their faith or law', but in practice that was exactly what was occurring in the rough, routine subordinations of the ordinary slaves.[52] William gives us

[48] Ibid. 3.10 (*Storia*, ed. and transl. Menestò et al., 240); William of Rubruck, *Itinerarium* 35 (*Mission*, transl. Jackson, 240–5).

[49] '[P]otius vellet mori, quam facere quod non licet': John of Plano Carpini, *Historia mongalorum* 3.4–5 (*Storia*, ed. and transl. Menestò et al., 237–8 and note at 415). The Russians, too, chose to understand what had happened in 'religious' terms. Mikhail was canonized, and Russian authors took care to avoid discussing the realities of the situation: Martin Dimnik, *The Dynasty of Chernigov, 1146–1246* (Cambridge, 2003), 366–75; Charles Halperin, *Russia and the Golden Horde: The Mongol Impact on Medieval Russian History* (London, 1985), 64–8.

[50] '[C]lamantem et plorantem': John of Plano Carpini, *Historia mongalorum* 3.6 (*Storia*, ed. and transl. Menestò et al., 238–9); Dimnik, *Dynasty*, 381–2.

[51] John of Plano Carpini, *Historia mongalorum* 3.1 (*Storia*, ed. and transl. Menestò et al., 235).

[52] '[S]uam fidem vel legem': ibid. 3.5 (*Storia*, ed. and transl. Menestò et al., 238 and note at 415).

a rare glimpse of this. He recounted that as Easter approached and the Nestorian priests prepared to celebrate, a great crowd of Hungarian, Alan, Russian, Georgian and Armenian Christians appeared, 'none of whom had set eyes on the sacrament since their capture'.[53] They begged William to celebrate mass. Before he could do this, he had to instruct them on the laws of their faith and hear their confessions. These concerned sins that could not be avoided, given their circumstances, and for which the slaves do not seem, by William's account, to have been particularly penitent. They explained to William that they had to steal because the Mongols did not provide them with food or clothes and some were forced to fight or be killed themselves. He found it hard to disagree with their assessment of their situation, although he did insist that they should choose martyrdom over killing fellow Christians.[54] What we see here are groups identifying themselves as Christians and being accepted as such by William, quite regardless of whether they were able to obey the laws of the faith within the terms of their enslavement.

The experiences of the captives were not uniform. At least some of the Latins and other Christians had adapted to their new lives and even prospered, which liberated them from the circumstances that oppressed others of their co-religionists. The Mongols paid their craftsmen, even if they would not free them, so those with the most refined skills were able to accrue substantial wealth.[55] John wrote of a Russian goldsmith called Cosmas, who was greatly esteemed by Güyük, and who gave the friars basic sustenance without which they might have starved. Cosmas had built the *qaghan*'s throne and made his personal seal. William met a woman called Pascha, from Metz, who told him that she had been in 'unheard-of destitution' before arriving in the Mongol camp, where she had joined the household of a Christian wife of Möngke, married a Russian artisan, and now had three 'very fine little boys'.[56] William also met a Parisian goldsmith, Guil-

[53] The Alans were an Iranian people, living in the Caucasus region. Like the Georgians, they were Eastern Orthodox Christians, but they may have held some Catholic doctrines in preference to those of the Greek Church: *Mission*, transl. Jackson, 102 nn. 1–2.

[54] William of Rubruck, *Itinerarium* 30.10–14 (*Mission*, transl. Jackson, 213–16).

[55] E.g. ibid. 29.3 (*Mission*, transl. Jackson, 183).

[56] Ibid. 29.2 (*Mission*, transl. Jackson, 182).

laume Boucher, who had been captured in Hungary, given to
Möngke's Christian mother, Sorqaghtani Beki, and inherited by
her youngest son, Ariq-böke. He was highly valued by the *qaghan*
for his skills and despite being a slave lived comfortably with his
wife, a Hungarian-born Frenchwoman.[57] They had a foster son,
whose origins William did not disclose, who seems to have been
at least bilingual and had a reputation as an 'excellent interpreter',
serving the *qaghan* in this capacity.[58]

Thus far, the focus has been on the effects of 'encounters' with
the Mongols themselves: the basic conditions of slavery and the
extent to which it was possible for different groups to exercise
agency within them. Yet the captives' experiences were greatly
complicated by living among the many distinct religious traditions
present in the camps. Möngke's capital of Karakorum contained a
Muslim quarter, with markets, and a Chinese quarter, notable for
its craftsmen. There were twelve Buddhist temples, two mosques
and a Christian church.[59] On feast days – as identified for him by
Mongol shamans or Nestorian clergy – Möngke would summon
in turn Christian, Muslim and Buddhist religious leaders to pray
for him and offer blessings.[60] William had many stories of members
of Möngke's family, even those who preferred the teaching of
the shamans and Buddhists, engaging in practices that Nestorians
had taught them.[61] The *qaghans* encouraged different groups to
believe that their own was favoured, with the effect, according to
William, that 'they all follow his court as flies do honey'.[62] This
policy, which operated in relation to all major religions encountered by the Mongols, has been much discussed, but here we shall
focus on the environment it generated in the camps. The Mongols
did not like the groups at court to quarrel over beliefs. Möngke's
brother intervened in an argument between the Armenian monk
and some Muslims, and later Möngke himself punished the monk
for hitting the Muslims with a whip when they taunted him.[63]

[57] Ibid. 32.4–5 (*Mission*, transl. Jackson, 223–4).
[58] Ibid. 29.3 (*Mission*, transl. Jackson, 183).
[59] Ibid. 32.1 (*Mission*, transl. Jackson, 221).
[60] Ibid. 29.15 (*Mission*, transl. Jackson, 187).
[61] Ibid. 22.2; 29.19–23 (*Mission*, transl. Jackson, 141–2, 189–91).
[62] Ibid. 29.15 (*Mission*, transl. Jackson, 187); see Richard Foltz, 'Ecumenical
Mischief under the Mongols', *Central Asiatic Journal* 43 (1999), 42–69.
[63] William of Rubruck, *Itinerarium* 32.8, 11 (*Mission*, transl. Jackson, 225).

On another occasion, a Muslim insulted William but the friar would not permit him to be denounced to Möngke for it, since the offender would have been 'either executed or beaten to a pulp'.[64] The Mongols enjoyed watching representatives of different faiths disputing over doctrine, but in general they demanded that everyone should live together respectfully.

One result was that the Latin captives had become culturally fluent, able to give detailed explanations of the practices and customs of the diverse communities of the camps. Cosmas, the Russian goldsmith, told John 'many secrets which were essential for us to know' about the Mongols, as did other Russian and Hungarian captives who either lived in the *qaghan's* camp or had accompanied their Mongol masters to the enthronement of Güyük. Some of these men knew Latin and French (*gallicum*). Some had been among the Mongols for decades, knew their language and had closely observed them in war and at other times. 'They reported everything to us willingly and sometimes spontaneously,' John wrote, 'because they understood our purpose [in being there]'.[65] Much of John's report was based on this material, especially his detailed descriptions of Mongol military tactics and his recommendations for how to repel them.[66] John emphasized that the captives were eager to act against the interests of their masters and in shaping Latin understanding of the Mongols and their empire.[67] However, it is worth noting that he thought he had brokered a union of the Russian and Roman Churches at a meeting in Kiev on his way home and, eager to promote this connection with a formerly schismatic group, now the subjects of the Mongols, had every reason to stress the loyalty and trustworthiness of the defeated Russians.[68]

In William's account, we can see that the Latin Christian captives actually served as cultural intermediaries, also providing information about Latin Christianity for others in the Mongol camps.

---

[64] Ibid. 33.3 (*Mission*, transl. Jackson, 227–8).

[65] '[A]lia multa secreta que nobis erant necessaria ad sciendum'; 'Et ipsi nobis voluntarie et aliquando sine interrogatione, quia sciebant nostram volontatem, omnia referebant': John of Plano Carpini, *Historia mongalorum* 9.38–9 (*Storia*, ed. and transl. Menestò et al., 324).

[66] Ibid. 5–8 (*Storia*, ed. and transl. Menestò et al., 252–302).

[67] Hence the argument in Guzman, 'European Captives'.

[68] John of Plano Carpini, *Historia mongalorum* 9.48 (*Storia*, ed. and transl. Menestò et al., 330).

William's party was greeted by a Cuman with a '*Saluete, domini*!' and discovered that the man had been baptized in Hungary by the Franciscans there.[69] After the friars arrived, Batu had asked this man 'many questions' about them and got him to explain the *conditiones* of their order – by which expression, perhaps, William meant the external perception of the order, rather than the rule itself.[70] Similarly, when they arrived at Möngke's court, people gathered around, looking at William's bare feet in astonishment – but a Hungarian recognized the men as Friars Minor and 'gave the reason to the crowd, describing the *conditiones* of our Order'. As in the case of the Cuman, this Hungarian was then questioned about them by Möngke's chief scribe, a Nestorian called Bolghai.[71]

Another feature of the intense cosmopolitanism of the camps was the use of 'religious' behaviour by groups and individuals in order to distinguish themselves from others. The further that the friars travelled into the Mongol Empire, the more complex became the landscape of belief, practice, language and identity.[72] William noted the efforts of each group to maintain distinct practices. He described how the Muslims refused to discuss Buddhists and were 'scandalised' by his interest in them. The Buddhists prayed with clasped hands, prostrate, with their forehead on their hands – so the Nestorians never prayed with their hands together, but spread their palms in front of their chests. The doors of their temples faced south, which was the opposite of the Muslims', and they had large bells – which, William surmised, was why the Eastern Christians would not use them.[73] While most of this practice was not new with the Mongols, it was clearly being deployed very consciously in the context of the camps. What is less clear is how far it was feasible for the Latin Christians to assert themselves through similar distinctive behaviour, in the absence of priests, and as a religious tradition entirely alien to the world in which they found themselves. On the occasion when William was asked to say

---

[69] The Cumans were a nomadic tribal grouping of Turkic, Mongol and Iranian origins. They had dominated the Eurasian steppe for two centuries before the Mongol invasions, and had close relations with the sedentary societies around them, some settling in Hungary: Berend, *At the Gate*, 68–73.

[70] William of Rubruck, *Itinerarium* 20.4 (*Mission*, transl. Jackson, 135–6; *Viaggio*, ed. Chiesa, 100, cf. 407).

[71] '[R]eddidit eis rationem, narrans ei conditiones Ordinis nostri': ibid. 28.4–5 (*Viaggio*, ed. Chiesa, 146–8 [my translation]; *Mission*, transl. Jackson, 173).

[72] E.g. ibid. 23.7 (*Mission*, transl. Jackson, 148).

[73] Ibid. 24 (*Mission*, transl. Jackson, 150–2).

mass, he hesitated because the proper equipment was not available in the camp. Boucher came to his assistance, and made the friars an iron so that they could bake their own unleavened wafers, since they could not use the leavened bread of the Nestorians. He also made them a triptych with a statue of the Virgin 'in the French style' and a silver casket in which to keep the consecrated hosts. All this was contained in a mobile oratory. The Nestorians lent William their altar.[74] It is perhaps worth noting that, while no doubt a product of conviction, the manufacture of these highly distinctive objects was exactly the kind of public performance of doctrinal difference that the other groups in the camps had been able, far more readily, to undertake. The presence of the friars in the camp, with their priestly status, specific liturgies and songs, their habits and books, and their supposed expertise in dialectical engagement with other faiths, made some difference to the Latin Christians there, but it was an ephemeral difference that would disappear as soon as they left.[75]

There were hints, however, of other strategies of differentiation. Boucher told William of an occasion when the court shamans were summoning demons and a Hungarian had hidden himself among them to witness the proceedings. But the demon sat on the top of the house and shouted that he was unable to enter because a Christian was present. The Hungarian ran out of the house as fast as he could, pursued by the shamans.[76] This story, as William recounted it, would not have been out of place in the collections of preaching *exempla* that were so popular among the friars in that period. It also indicates some of the aspects of the moral differentiation being employed by the Latin Christians, which perhaps depended more on narratives told among themselves than on public performance that might compete with that of more prominent Christian groups.

Nevertheless, the fact was that the Latin Christians in the camp, who lacked the influence of the Nestorians, and who were almost all slaves, were in a profoundly vulnerable position. Practically speaking, they had little recourse against anyone who wished to

---

[74] Ibid. 30.10–14 (*Mission*, transl. Jackson, 213–16; *Viaggio*, ed. Chiesa, 218–24, quotation at 224).

[75] Even so, the influence of Latin doctrines was curtailed by the Nestorians, as (for example) when they removed the figure of Christ from a crucifix made by Boucher for the Nestorian chief scribe Bolghai; William's indignation had no effect: ibid. 29.62 (*Mission*, transl. Jackson, 208).

[76] Ibid. 35.11–13 (*Mission*, transl. Jackson, 244–5).

subject them to other religious norms or practices. On one occasion, some shamans spoke incantations over a German slave girl who belonged to an ailing concubine, causing her to sleep for three days. When she woke, they questioned her about what she had seen in her sleep, and pronounced that everyone whom she had 'seen' would die soon. The object of the ritual was to discover whether the girl's mistress would die, and since the girl had not 'seen' her, it was concluded that she would live. William, prosaically, reported that he had met the girl afterwards, while she was still suffering from a headache caused by her prolonged sleep.[77] In this case, being a Christian was no protection from being manipulated into participation in alien ritualistic or magical practices.

One of the main reasons for the vulnerability of the Latins was that, in the absence of priests, there was no one to teach them authoritatively. This could lead to troubling uncertainties. The main drink of the Mongols was *comos*, fermented mare's milk. Those of the Russian, Greek and Alan Christians 'who wish strictly to observe their religion [*legem suam*]' did not drink it, 'indeed, they do not consider themselves Christians after drinking it, and their priests reconcile them as if they had denied the faith of Christ'.[78] They also believed that the standard food available to them in the camps – 'carrion and what had been slaughtered by Saracens and other infidels' – was 'tantamount to carrion or idol sacrifices'. Observing this, the Hungarian Christians in the camp of the Mongol commander, Scacatai, were worried, since they had little choice but to drink *comos* and eat such meats. Some of them asked William whether it was possible for them to be saved under these circumstances. He tried to reassure them but commented sadly that it had been almost impossible to counter the widespread fears about *comos*, and lamented to Louis: 'how far they are alienated from the faith [*fides*] because of this opinion'.[79] They were also conscious that they were not observing the feasts and fasts of the Church since they did not know the dates 'and were in no position to observe them even if they did know them'.[80]

---

[77] Ibid.

[78] '[I]mmo non reputant se christianos postquam biberint, et sacerdotes eorum reconciliant eos tamquam negassent fidem Christi': ibid. 10.5 (*Viaggio*, ed. Chiesa, 54 [my translation]; *Mission*, transl. Jackson, 101).

[79] Ibid. 12.2 (*Mission*, transl. Jackson, 104; *Viaggio*, ed. Chiesa, 58).

[80] Ibid. 11.2 (*Mission*, transl. Jackson, 102–3).

William encountered variants of the problem as he crossed the Mongol Empire. While travelling down the Volga, he met more Hungarian captives. These men had some degree of education, for William described them as *clericuli*. One, who could still 'chant many things by heart', was treated by the other Hungarians like a priest (*quasi sacerdos*) and was asked by them to carry out funeral rites for the dead. They asked for books, but William had none to spare, so they brought him parchment (*cartas*) and he copied out the Hours of the blessed Virgin and the office for the dead.[81] This meant that the Hungarians could once more pray in communion with the rest of the *ecclesia dei*, even without a priest, and the dead could be buried with the Latin rites. A Latin Christian with at least rudimentary learning could serve to guide the others, even if he could not administer sacraments.[82] This was a role undertaken by various individuals. The goldsmith, Boucher, had embraced it to the extent that he had made for himself some vestments, 'for', William explained, 'he has acquired some slight learning and conducts himself like a cleric [*ut clericus*]'.[83] He corrected the practices of the Eastern Christians, teaching his friend Bolghai, the chief scribe mentioned above, not to eat meat on Friday.[84] William emphasized that these men were not clerics, but then, as we have seen, he belonged to an order dedicated to improving the quality and rigour of pastoral care provision within a Church that increasingly insisted that only a narrow group of educated males could provide it.[85] Nonetheless, the episode in which he was asked to celebrate the mass indicates that the captives understood the importance of properly ordained priests and had been aware of the disadvantages of being without one.

This brings us back to the recurring question of what is a

---

[81] Ibid. 20.3 (*Mission*, transl. Jackson, 135; *Viaggio*, ed. Chiesa, 100).

[82] See note to ibid. 30.13 in *Viaggio*, ed. Chiesa, 462.

[83] Ibid. 30.13 (*Mission*, transl. Jackson, 215; *Viaggio*, ed. Chiesa, 222). On Boucher's knowledge of Christian theology and tradition, see Sarolta Tatár, 'The Iconography of the Karakorum Fountain', in Michael Knüppel and Aloïs van Tongerloo, eds, *Life and Afterlife and Apocalyptic Concepts in the Altaic World* (Wiesbaden, 2011), 77–105.

[84] William of Rubruck, *Itinerarium* 29.25 (*Mission*, transl. Jackson, 192).

[85] On the active discrediting of less educated clergy, see Jeffrey H. Denton, 'The Competence of the Parish Clergy in Thirteenth-Century England', in *The Church and Learning in Later Medieval Society: Essays in Honour of R. B. Dobson*, ed. Caroline Barron and Jenny Stratford, Harlaxton Medieval Studies 11 (Donington, 2002), 273–85.

'Christian' and how this identity related to observance, authority, orthodox doctrine and other issues. I would suggest that the determination of the Roman Church of this period to invest its pastoral authority in a clerical elite distinguished from the laity by its celibacy, education and exemption from secular control made Christianity beyond Latin Christendom far more fragile than it might otherwise have been. Routine access to the divine, according to the papacy, was mediated almost wholly through the priesthood, as the only people who could administer the sacraments. One could only be made a priest by a bishop. For the captives and slaves, adrift in a strange world without these structures, it was impossible to participate in the most fundamental rituals of their faith. We glimpse them relying on fading memory for their knowledge of what they were supposed to believe, on fragments retained haphazardly by the better educated – as William had it – among them. We also see them confused by the robust assertions of doctrine and custom by more dominant Christian groups, unsure of where the boundaries lay, still fearing for their salvation, but no longer secure in their sense of how they might enter into it. Yet if this was what John had meant by worship 'reduced to nothingness' and souls lost, he had underestimated the determination of at least some of even the most brutalized slaves to retain a sense of themselves as Latin Christians in the face of an overwhelming diversity of competing belief systems.

University of Sheffield

CHRISTIAN-MUSLIM ENCOUNTERS: GEORGE OF TREBIZOND AND THE 'INVERSION' OF EASTERN DISCOURSE REGARDING ISLAM IN THE FIFTEENTH CENTURY[*]

by KONSTANTINOS PAPASTATHIS

The capture of Constantinople (1453) by the Ottoman troops of Mehmed II was a historical turning point. The political reference point of Eastern Christianity was now in Muslim hands, the Ottomans representing in the eyes of late medieval Europeans not only an enemy of the true faith, and as such an obstacle for ecclesiastical unity, but also a potential rival of the papacy as a political power. In short, within the contemporary context and the socially dominant apocalyptic frame of mind, the Ottomans were viewed as an existential threat for Christianity as a whole. While the papal reaction to this development was to go on the offensive, expressed through the call for a new crusade, the emergence of a few voices expressing divergent theological content and political orientation had special significance. One of the voices which 'set off the politics of religious synthesis from different quarters'[1] was that of George of Trebizond (1395–1472/3), a Cretan emigrant to Italy who lived in Venice and Florence before moving to Rome. He had converted to Catholicism without losing his sense of belonging to the East, and became a prominent figure of the Italian intellectual elite and an editor of classical and theological literature, as well as a member of the Vatican bureaucracy.[2]

The topic of this essay is the endeavour of George of Trebizond to achieve a political paradigm shift towards Islam, opposed to the

---

[*]   The author is grateful to Angeliki Ziaka, Bishara Ebeid and the editors of Studies in Church History for their support.
[1]   Tijana Krstić, *Contested Conversions to Islam: Narratives of Religious Change in the Early Modern Ottoman Empire* (Stanford, CA, 2011), 62.
[2]   For more biographical details, see John Monfasani, *George of Trebizond: A Biography and a Study of his Rhetoric and Logic* (Leiden, 1976), 3–237; Thierry Ganchou, 'Le dilemme religieux de la famille crétoise de Géôrgios Trapézountios: Constantinople ou Rome?', in Chryssa Maltézou et al., eds, *I greci durante la venetocrazia: Uomini, spazio, idee (XIII–XVIII sec.)* (Venice, 2009), 251–75; Angeliki Ziaka, *La Recherche grecque contemporaine et l'Islam* (Lille, 2004), 111–13.

hegemonic polemical narrative. It explores his political project, seeks to identify the underlying ideas upon which he grounded his vision and considers their socio-political implications. To this end, the essay examines contextually George of Trebizond's perspective in approaching the Muslim 'other', as well as his distinct religious considerations and political programme. The main thesis is that George advocated a system of enlightened autocracy as the ideal form of governance under Mehmed. Nevertheless, he made clear neither how this might be established nor the details of its practical outworking, particularly in respect to the pope. He thus left room for a major revision of existing political hierarchies, probably with the intention of creating a bipolar system, the major axiom of which would be the principle of non-interference of one system in the affairs of the other. More specifically, the essay argues that George of Trebizond's vision of the conversion of Mehmed to Christianity and the subsequent unified global rule of the Ottoman sultan was not purely theological in character. Rather, George's discourse was substantially political, since he proposed a new plan of action and an inversion of established social loyalties, implicitly supporting a partial separation between the temporal and the religious spheres, and thus the secularity of social space.

George's theory should certainly be elaborated within an apocalyptic context.[3] If patriotism had been his only motive, he would have simply aligned himself with the advocates of a crusade, which was a more plausible and effective plan for ending Byzantine captivity; such a stance would not have caused him any problems with his superiors. But George's ambiguous and abstract proposal was also political, since it entailed, at its core, the restructuring of the balance of power of the Western Christian world at the expense of papal authority, through the establishment of a bipolar political framework. This development, however, presupposed the separation of temporal from religious power, envisaging that the former would be exercised by Mehmed and the latter by the pope. Consequently, given that contemporary temporal and religious spheres were generally conceived as a united and cohesive whole, George opposed both the dominant political systems of his

---

3   Monfasani, *George of Trebizond*, 130–6; M. Balivet, 'Deux partisans de la fusion religieuse des chrétiens et des musulmans au XVᵉ siècle: Le turc Bedreddin de Samavra et le grec Georges de Trebizonde', *Βυζαντινά* 10 (1980), 361–96.

time, papal theocracy and caesaropapism. Therefore his perspective might be regarded as ground-breaking, although that was not his intention.

This essay will examine the development of this discourse in three works: *On the Truth of the Faith of Christians to the Emir when he stormed Constantinople;*[4] *On the Eternal Glory of the Autocrat and his World Dominion;*[5] and *On the Divinity of Manuel.*[6] The two letters in which George praised the Sultan Mehmed will also be considered.[7] Unfortunately, relatively few modern scholars are interested in George's works on Islam, and although there have been several valuable studies, including those by John Monfasani, Georgios Zoras, Adel Theodor Khoury and Angelo Mercati, these have treated George's texts as principally theological, and the political aspect of George's texts as secondary.[8] For Monfasani, George's proposition had an instrumental character as serving God's purposes of salvation: it was a means to the end of the final victory of Christianity. A somewhat more politicized view was proposed by Zoras. Without opposing the primacy of theology, Zoras advocated an analysis of George's discourse as an expression of his national loyalty which sought to secure, in the long run, the liberation of the ethnic Greeks from the Ottomans.[9] Giorgio Ravegnani sought to explain George's change of opinion from an ardent proponent of a crusade against the Ottomans to a self-proclaimed servant of Mehmed.[10] These contributions, with their merits and misconceptions, have not focused on exploring systematically the political

---

4 Georgios Th. Zoras, ed., Γεώργιος ὁ Τραπεζούντιος καὶ αἱ πρὸς Ἑλληνοτουρκικὴν συνεννόησιν προσπάθειαι αὐτοῦ (Ἡ «Περὶ τῆς τῶν χριστιανῶν πίστεως» ἀνέκδοτος πραγματεία) (Athens, 1954). For a French translation with an insightful introduction and notes, see Adel Th. Khoury, 'Georges de Trébizonde: De la vérité de la foi des chrétiens', *Proche-Orient Chrétien* 18 (1968), 326–40; 19 (1969), 135–49, 320–34; 20 (1970), 238–71; 21 (1971), 235–61; this translation was later published by Khoury as *Georges de Trébizonde et l'union islamo-chrétienne* (Louvain, 1971).

5 John Monfasani, ed., *Collectanea Trapezuntiana: Texts, Documents, and Bibliographies of George of Trebizond* (Binghamton, NY, 1984), 492–563.

6 Ibid. 564–74.

7 Angelo Mercati, 'Le due lettere di Giorgio da Trebisonda a Maometto II', *Orientalia Christiana Periodica* 9 (1943), 65–99.

8 Monfasani, *George of Trebizond*, 125–36; M. Balivet, *Pour une concorde islamo-chrétienne. Démarches byzantines et latines à la fin du Moyen Âge. De Nicolas de Cues à Georges de Trébizonde* (Rome, 1997); Balivet, 'Deux partisans', 385–7.

9 Zoras, Γεώργιος, 15–16.

10 Giorgio Ravegnani, 'Nota sul pensiero politico di Giorgio da Trebisonda', *Aevum* 49 (1975), 310–29.

features of George's discourse. This essay endeavours to fill this lacuna, interpreting George's theory as calling for the politicization of the sacred instead of the sacralization of the political.

The method used for elucidating this material is the so-called Essex School pattern. Discourse is analyzed as a network of elements or signifiers, one of which functions as the 'nodal point' or centre of the discursive structure and thus determines its core meaning.[11] As mentioned above, it will be argued that the concept of universalism, namely the unified political control of the known world as incarnated in the *potestas* of the ruler, is the nodal point of George's discourse. In effect, universalism overrides the other privileged signifiers, the meaning of which is fixed precisely by their relation with it. For instance, the meaning of George's anti-heretical rhetoric was determined by universalism as the core feature of his discourse; that is, his condemnation of heresy was not so much because of its intrinsically false character, but mainly because he perceived it to be an obstacle to universalism.

George's Apocalyptic Discourse advocating Universal Governance

On the Truth of the Faith of Christians (July 1453) aimed to prove what George alleged to be an identification between the sacred texts of the two faiths. For George, minimizing the quality and quantity of their differences was not about providing a robust argument in favour of reconciliation, but essentially about creating a framework which would make possible their unification and hence the universal domination of the Ottoman leader. By proclaiming Mehmed as the 'King of Kings' or the 'Greatest of all Kings' and by acknowledging the divine origins of his power,[12] George legitimized Ottoman rule and accepted its symbolic authority. He viewed Mehmed's dominance not as a fundamental change but as being in historical continuity with the Roman Empire. As God's political representative, Mehmed was perceived as destined

---

[11] David Howarth, Yannis Stavrakakis and Aletta J. Norval, eds, *Discourse Theory and Political Analysis: Identities, Hegemonies and Social Change* (Manchester, 2000); Louise Phillips and Marianne W. Jørgensen, *Discourse Analysis as Theory and Method* (London, 2002).

[12] Zoras, Γεώργιος, 93.

to restore the unity of all people in one collective body, that is, to recreate the *pax romana*.[13]

Universalism, as the nodal point of George's discourse, was not conceptualized only in political terms, but also as a theological presupposition for the fulfilment of the Christian apocalyptic writings. Mehmed's absolute power was ascribed to him personally; in Weberian terms his rule had a 'charismatic' rather than an 'institutional' character. For George, Mehmed was divinely chosen, and as such had the sacred duty of transcending the cultural borders and redefining the new social entity on the basis of God's saving purpose. His power was distinguished from that of other kings, whether Christian or Muslim, because, unlike them, he did not use violence. In contrast, as George saw it, Mehmed called on people's minds, appealing to their reason, which was exactly the quality needed for accomplishing religious unification, the key to which was objective analysis of the two faiths.[14] Consequently, Mehmed's power was not represented oppressive monarchy but as benevolent leadership, which had the teleological function of guiding the body of the faithful to salvation. In short, George's utopia was not a mere reproduction of the authoritarian political system of his time, but a plea for the establishment of an enlightened autocracy. Mehmed's authority, as a signifier of George's discourse, did not have political domination as its signified, but rather it pointed to the actual redemption of the people of God, as a condition for God's final victory. Its virtue, therefore, was not founded so much on its content as on its universal character. For this reason, George could conceive of Mehmed as predestined to become the successor of Constantine the Great.[15] Just as Constantine, as God's tool for liberation from paganism, had played his part in the plan of salvation, so too Mehmed would have the sacred mission of bringing together the two faiths in order to establish God's power – and with it his own – over the whole world.

For George, there were three main alleged differences between Christianity and Islam: Trinitarian doctrine, perceived by the Muslims as polytheism; the hypostatic union of the two natures

---

[13] Ibid. 95.
[14] Ibid. 97.
[15] Ibid. 164.

in Jesus; and belief in Jesus's death and resurrection.[16] George's apologetic is not our priority here. What is of interest, though, is that the specification of the above differences was defined solely on the basis of Muslim perceptions of Christianity, as if the latter accepted Islam's authenticity and did not represent it as its hostile other. That is, George did not report on the extensive Christian literature against Islam, but accepted the Qur'ān as God's revelation.[17] Only when discussing the doctrine of the resurrection did he propose the possibility of a (partial) distortion of the doctrine by the Qur'ān. Indeed, his emphasis on the alleged textual identification between the Bible and the Qur'ān was such that, according to his modern editors, he made certain falsifications or deliberately misinterpreted the meaning in order to make the two texts correspond with each other.[18] At the same time, George suggested that the existence of diverse narratives should be attributed to differing customs and traditions.[19] He concluded that both belief systems should be viewed as presenting one message of God, expressed in variant forms in order to allow its expansion within diverse cultural frameworks. Monotheism played a significant role in George's thesis, as the core common feature of both religious structures and thus the foundation of what he imagined to be their consistency.

In this work George was obsessed with the Jews, whom he saw as the driving force behind the clash between the two faiths, seeking to obliterate both sides.[20] He accused the Jews of being the cause of evil, reproducing the hegemonic stereotype of the Middle Ages against the Jewish community. However, despite these repeated allegations, anti-Semitism was not a privileged signifier, that is a central ideological element, of George's discourse, since it is almost absent from his other works on Islam. Consequently, like other discursive features such as anti-Arianism or opposition to idolatry,[21] it did not acquire the status of a core concept of his theory. In contrast, Aristotelianism became the philosophical ground upon which George founded his arguments in favour

---

[16] Ibid. 99.
[17] Ibid. 113.
[18] Ibid. 76; Khoury, 'Georges de Trébizonde', 146–9.
[19] Zoras, Γεώργιος, 98–9.
[20] Ibid. 100.
[21] Ibid. 117, 115 respectively.

of the dual nature of Jesus.[22] By employing Aristotle, George defined him as a major source of religious authenticity. Such a status, however, should not be attributed to Aristotle on the basis of his significance within Islam, for the invocation of Aristotle was not instrumental but represents the fact that his teachings had become the normative basis for scholastic theology.[23] Consequently, although Aristotelianism worked as a permanent theme and a core element of the ideological background of George's discourse, its place within it was contingent, dependent on the issue at stake: while George drew on Aristotle's authority to indicate the validity of the doctrines of the Trinity and of the hypostatic union, he made no reference to Aristotelian philosophy in his discussion of the incarnation or the resurrection. Consequently, the use of Aristotle's thought here should be explained in conjunction with the nodal point of universalism; that is, as a philosophical tradition which had the potential to indicate the unity of the two faiths and thus the need for a global authority.

In general, George followed the same perspective in his other major essay, *On the Eternal Glory of the Autocrat*. Although written thirteen years later, in 1466, this second treatise is based almost on the same elements. Universalism retains its principal position, while other features, such as the identification of Christian and Muslim scriptures, monotheism, and Aristotelianism as the criterion of logicality, work as privileged signifiers of the discursive structure. However, the anti-Semitism of George's earlier work is not found here, probably because he had in the meantime been informed about Mehmed's employment of Jewish physicians.[24] Furthermore, in *On the Eternal Glory of the Autocrat* George developed a far more flattering rhetoric. Mehmed was represented not as Constantine's equal but as his superior, and the conquest of Constantinople was seen as a clear sign of God's election.[25] Another innovation was George's perception of the process of political integration as depending on ecclesiastical unity under the pope's supreme authority. This question had not been dealt with in his

---

[22] Ibid. 118–23, 126–31.
[23] Gerhard Podskalsky, *Griechische Theologie in der Zeit der Türkenherrschaft, 1453–1821* (Munich, 1988), 20.
[24] Monfasani, *Collectanea*, 492 (*On the Eternal Glory*).
[25] Ibid. 493–4.

previous work (*On the Truth of the Faith of Christians*), despite the fact that George viewed it as a central aspect of the plan of salvation. For him, the schism between Eastern and Western Churches was the primary cause of the downfall of Constantinople, and the responsibility for this should be borne by Constantinople, which had disputed Rome's primacy. The birth and expansion of Islam at the expense of Oriental Christianity was perceived, therefore, as God's punishment for breaking the unity of the Church, contrary to God's rule.[26] As the new sovereign of the schismatic city and the prospective conqueror of the West, Mehmed now had the sacred duty of remedying the injustice and gathering 'all the races into one faith and one church'.[27] Otherwise his political authority would be at stake. The clarity and cohesiveness of George's messianic scheme, which had previously been expressed in abstract terms, were directed to this end.

George's works suggest that he believed that God's plan for salvation consisted of five stages: the fall of humankind, the product of which was the Old Testament; the coming of Christ, the rejection of whom led to the destruction of the Second Temple; the dominance of Constantine and the victory of Christianity over paganism; the Great Schism, which had caused God's punishment and led to the growth of Islam;[28] and the capture of Constantinople by Mehmed, who would unite the whole world in one political and religious entity, thus paving the way for the Second Coming. Within this apocalyptic context, religious unity was represented, not as the final aim, but as the determinant of universal power. This messianic approach was in agreement with George's two letters addressed to Mehmed, also in 1466. In the first letter, he suggested that the sultan's political virtues were given by God for creating a universal empire under his monarchy.[29] In the second letter, George repeated his conviction that it would be Mehmed's destiny

---

[26] Ibid. 494–5.

[27] Ibid. 495.

[28] The chronological order of this step is clearly problematic, since the birth and growth of Islam in the seventh century long preceded the schism between the Roman Catholic and Orthodox Churches. On the other hand, it is likely that George perceived the events of 1054 as the cause of the gradual weakening of Byzantium and the defeat of the its army by the Seljuk Turks at Manzikert (1071), which opened the way for the Muslims to the heartland of the Christian empire, leading to its actual fall.

[29] Mercati, 'Le due lettere', 87–91.

to remedy the schism between Rome and Constantinople and to achieve religious unity and global governance.[30] In all George's works of this period, Mehmed was represented as the tangible embodiment of God's universal dominance, and thus as the decisive factor for the transition to the final stage of the economy of salvation: the union of all people in one society.

George's ideas were most fully expressed in his third treatise, *On the Divinity of Manuel* (1467–9). Here the authority of Mehmed was defined as the embodiment of God's rule. The name 'Manuel', which George ascribes to him, had a highly symbolic importance, being the name of Jesus himself according to the Scriptures.[31] In effect, divine grace was expressed through the acts of Mehmed; Mehmed was an agent of God. George based his theory on five presuppositions: the necessity of religious unity before the coming of the Antichrist; the conviction that this condition would be fulfilled 'through the agency of some descendant of Ishmael'; the belief that the time for its realization had come; his perception that Mehmed was the descendant of Ishmael destined to carry out this task; and the understanding that his rule would cover the whole world.[32] As Monfasani has argued, this scheme indicates that George's eschatological perception was based on the kind of apocalyptic prophecies which were highly influential in this period, and especially those of Pseudo-Methodius.[33] According to this text, the expansion of the 'sons of Ishmael' was an act of divine punishment. However, the last Roman emperor, as his agent, would save his people and Christianity from evil.[34] Following this pattern, George believed that the fall of Constantinople signified 'the horrible arrival of Gog and Magog', the ultimate enemies of God's people,[35] and the beginning of a period of terror and fear. Mehmed's conver-

---

[30] Ibid. 92–7.

[31] Matt. 1: 23.

[32] Monfasani, *Collectanea*, 565 (*On the Divinity*).

[33] Monfasani, *George of Trebizond*, 86–8.

[34] Sidney H. Griffith, *The Church in the Shadow of the Mosque: Christians and Muslims in the World of Islam* (Princeton, NJ, 2008), 32–9; Debié Muriel, 'Muslim-Christian Controversy in an Unedited Syriac Text: Revelations and Testimonies about Our Lord's Dispensation', in Emmanouela Grypeou and Mark N. Swanson, eds, *The Encounters of Eastern Christianity with Early Islam* (Leiden, 2006), 225–36; *Apocalypse of Pseudo-Methodius. An Alexandrian World Chronicle*, ed. and transl. Benjamin Garstad, Dumbarton Oaks Medieval Library 14 (Cambridge, 2012).

[35] Rev. 20: 7–10.

sion, fulfilling the role played by the Roman emperor in Pseudo-Methodius, would avert this prospect and transform this dreadful period into 'an age of universal bliss and peace'.[36]

On the other hand, the supreme authority ascribed by George to Mehmed 'as the ruler of the whole world',[37] in conjunction with his allegations of 'apostasy from Christ to Plato at the instigation of Cardinal Bessarion' that had 'occurred in Rome',[38] leaves room for a more synthetic interpretation. This would allow the diversion of the political order, directly linked with a religious-centred frame of reference, towards a more secular path, and in particular towards the disengagement of the temporal sphere from the spiritual, or even the subjection of what he saw as a declining religious institution to the 'charismatic' tool of sacred economy. In other words, the political content of George's plan diverged significantly from the dominant ideological structures established in Western Christendom, in that it implicitly indicated a reduction of clerical political authority. According to this line of thought, George's discourse had a substantial apocalyptic orientation, but its structure was not based on a theological nodal point; in contrast, its central signifier, universalism, did not signify religious authority so much as primarily absolute global governance in the name of God, to which the declining religious bureaucracy had – at least partially – to submit. Due to the ambiguity of his writings, however, it is not possible to reach a clear conclusion on this matter but only to make certain suggestions about George's approach, hidden as it is beneath his rhetoric.

CRITIQUE

Universalism worked as the nodal point of the discursive structure of George's works about Islam. Within the apocalyptic framework of the late Middle Ages, the ideal of universalism determined the significance of the other ideological features employed by the author. That is, although signifiers such as benevolent leadership, unity of faith or Aristotelianism, certainly hold a privileged role in his theory, their meaning is fixed in terms of their relation to universalism. But universalism as the central signifier of George's

---

[36] Monfasani, *George of Trebizond*, 133–5.
[37] Monfasani, *Collectanea*, 564 (*On the Divinity*).
[38] Ibid. 565.

discourse is 'empty' in and of itself; in other words, it is 'a signifier without a signified'.[39] In George's thought, it acquires its general meaning as autocracy, because it is combined contextually with religiously centred signs, such as unity of faith. At the same time, its emptiness has a special political function, since it allows diverse interpretations.[40]

More particularly, 'universalism' in George's case is 'empty' because the author did not specify its ideological content or political character. Within his scheme, it is not clear whether Mehmed would obtain absolute power, subduing the pope under his authority, or whether he would be under papal guidance as a member of the Church and thus obliged to serve and obey his ecclesiastical master. Consequently George left room for both sides, the Sublime Porte and the Holy See, to interpret the significance of the political hierarchy and to conceptualize it according to their own political traditions, as caesaropapism or as papal theocracy respectively. The fact that his treatise *Eternal Glory* spurred the Vatican to establish a commission, chaired by Cardinal Bessarion, to inquire into his newly expressed ideas and the implicit threat they presented to papal authority, demonstrates both the cold reception offered to George's theory and the Church's inability to judge it adequately. It might be argued that since George in his letter to the pope vindicated his writing as a technique for gaining Mehmed's favour and smoothing the way for his conversion,[41] the author had no intention of downgrading the papal primacy. If that had been the case, however, George could have invoked the letter of Pius II (1458–64) to Mehmed, in which the pope called on the sultan to convert to Christianity.[42]

It is possible that the underlying reason for George's divergence from the established ideology lies in his different perspective. Pius

[39] David Howarth, 'Hegemony, Political Subjectivity, and Radical Democracy', in Simon Critchley and Oliver Marchart, *Laclau: A Critical Reader* (Abingdon, 2004), 256–78, at 260; compare, for this understanding of this term, Phillips and Jørgensen, *Discourse Analysis*, 50.

[40] Ernesto Laclau, 'Why do Empty Signifiers matter to Politics?', in idem, ed., *Emancipation(s)* (New York, 1996), 36–46.

[41] Monfasani, *Collectanea*, 492 (*On the Eternal Glory*).

[42] Giuseppe Toffanin, ed., *Lettera a Maometto II (Epistola ad Mahumetem) di Pio II (Enea Silvio Piccolomini), L'idea umanistica nella sua sintesi più alta* (Naples, 1953); Franco Gaeta, 'Sulla lettera a Maometto di Pio II', *Bullettino dell'istituto storico italiano per il medio evo e archivio muratoriano* 77 (1965), 127–227.

called Mehmed to submit, whereas George implicitly proposed the establishment of a bipolar power structure involving the parallel coexistence of both powers within a context of harmonious collaboration. This may be deduced from the epilogue of *Eternal Glory*, where George wrote: 'For thus did Christ himself command to all: "render to Caesar the things of Caesar, and to God the things of God," in other words, worldly obedience and taxes and such things to the king, while worship and what appertains to worship to God and the Catholic Church'.[43] Did this proposal actually form an early instance of the quest to secularize the social space? If it is analysed merely as an idea pertaining to the normative social framework, then definitely not. Its application was thus not perceived in terms of systemic change of political structures, but was actually determined by the 'charismatic' personality of Mehmed as an individual. In other words, George's ideological shift of emphasis was not founded on a conviction of the need of political transformation or the dynamics of the time, but on the merits and grace attributed to Mehmed as the prospective converted emperor of the Christian world. Within the apocalyptic context of George's mind, this proposition partially clarified his vision of the ideal balance of power between the temporal and the religious spheres, under certain conditions and for fulfilling the plan of salvation. The underlying presuppositions of this scheme, which entailed partial loss of power on both sides, explain why it was politically rejected. Apart from its obviously naive character, it required both that the Ottoman side would accept the subordination of the caliph (the representative of God's message) to papal power and that the pope would relinquish his right of political rule. These concessions were both unimaginable. George's discourse, therefore, could not become hegemonic in his contemporary world. Its content, deconstructing the stereotypical negative images of Islam, could neither be accepted as 'truth' nor form the basis of consensus in the West. Neither, in the long run, could his approach influence the political behaviour of the Islamic East, since this was represented as theologically inferior.

---

43 Monfasani, *Collectanea*, 525 (*On the Eternal Glory*).

Conclusion

The main thesis of this essay is that the concept of universalism, particularly in the form of enlightened autocracy, was the actual political aim of George of Trebizond. His project for the establishment of unified political governance in both the West and the East was based on ideas which had a high symbolic significance for the theological conscience of both his interlocutors, Catholic Rome and Ottoman Constantinople. However, in practical terms the abstract nature of his discourse regarding the ways in which the fusion between the two polities would become feasible left the door open for the establishment of a bipolar system between the temporal and the religious spheres. Although it is highly unlikely that he had any such intentions at the theoretical level, it might be argued that George had implicitly called for the partial separation of these two spheres, and in that sense a practical outworking of his vision would have represented a step towards the secularity of social space.

From a political perspective, the implementation of such ideas was unthinkable for either political actor during that period. Within the contemporary context, however, George's intellectual legacy concerning Islam might be useful at a time when the cleavage between East and West represented in symbolic terms as reflecting an alleged cultural divide between a dominant and an inferior religious group, has come to dominate the public agenda.[44] Despite its serious theological misunderstandings, therefore, some aspects of George's treatment of Christian-Muslim relations, such as his analysis of Trinitarian doctrine, might offer a possible basis from which religious bias might be transcended and a spirit of mutual understanding between the two communities established.

University of Luxembourg

---

[44] The influence of the 'clash of civilizations' thesis is germane to this point: Samuel P. Huntington, *The Clash of Civilizations and the Remaking of World Order* (New York, 1996); cf. Edward W. Said, 'The Clash of Ignorance', *The Nation*, 4 October 2001, online at: <http://www.thenation.com/article/clash-ignorance#>; Jonathan Fox, 'Paradigm Lost: Huntington's unfulfilled Clash of Civilizations Prediction into the 21st Century', *International Politics* 42 (2005), 428–57.

REARTICULATING A CHRISTIAN-MUSLIM UNDERSTANDING: GENNADIOS SCHOLARIOS AND GEORGE AMIROUTZES ON ISLAM

by ANGELIKI ZIAKA

From the eighth century, the Eastern Orthodox Churches engaged in various forms of theological dialogue and debate with newly emergent Islam. Although scholars have tended to study Islamic-Christian relations in terms of confrontation and direct conflict,[1] this aspect, dominant as it may be, must not lead us to overlook another aspect of the relationship, that of attempts at rapprochement and understanding. Despite the acerbity of Byzantium's anti-heretical and apologetic literature against Islam, there were also attempts at communication and mutual understanding between Christianity and Islam. These efforts became more tangible after the fall of Constantinople (1453), which marked a partial change in Orthodoxy's theological stance towards Islam. The polemical approach, which had prevailed during Byzantine times, gave way in part to an innovative and more conciliatory theological discourse towards Islam. Modern Greek research categorizes the theological discourse that was articulated during this period according to two diametrically opposing models: the model of conciliation and rapprochement with Islam, which was not widely influential,[2] and that of messianic utopian discourse developed by Christians who had turned to God and sought divine intervention to save the community.[3]

---

[1] Spyros Vryonis, 'Byzantium and Islam: Seventh-Seventeenth Century', *East European Quarterly* 2 (1968), 205–40; Daniel Sahas, 'Eighth-Century Byzantine anti-Islamic Literature: Context and Forces', *Byzantinoslavica* 57 (1996), 229–38; Michael Bonner, *Arab-Byzantine Relations in Early Islamic Times*, (London, 2004); Asterios Argyriou, 'Perception de l'Islam et traductions du Coran dans le monde byzantin grec', *Byzantion* 75 (2005), 25–69.

[2] Anastasios Yannoulatos, 'Byzantine and Contemporary Orthodox Approaches to Islam', in George C. Papademetriou, ed., *Two Traditions, One Space: Orthodox Christians and Muslims in Dialogue* (Boston, MA, 2011), 147–77 (first publ. in *Journal of Ecumenical Studies* 33 [1996], 512–27); Angeliki Ziaka, 'La recherche grecque contemporaine et l'Islam' (doctoral thesis, Université de Strasbourg, 2002), 108–211, at 106–9.

[3] Asterios Argyriou, 'Les Exégèses grecques de l'Apocalypse à l'époque turque (1453–1821). Esquisse d'une histoire des courants idéologiques au sein du peuple grec asservi', 2 vols (doctoral thesis, Université de Strasbourg, 1977); idem, 'Nationalismes et

The pioneers of the new Christian attitude towards Islam, whose works and arguments will be explored in this essay, were the influential patriarch George Gennadios (Gennadios II), and the diplomat George Amiroutzes. Unlike George of Trebizond, who also presented a conciliatory demeanour towards Islam after 1453, these figures continued to live in the *Dār al-Islam*, the territory of the Ottoman Empire, and did not flee to the West.[4]

Analysing their theological and literary discourse, this essay will highlight their attitude to their historical and political context, exploring how they entered into conversation with a powerful Islam; it will conclude with an evaluation of how such approaches to religious plurality could be utilized today in official Orthodox discourse.

HISTORICAL TRANSFORMATION AND A NEW DISCOURSE ON ISLAM

Supported by Sultan Mehmed II, Gennadios Scholarios (*c.*1400–*c.*1473) developed a dialogue with victorious Ottoman Islam. Scholarios's works, which were deeply theological, are examples of an unusually conciliatory type of Orthodox ecclesiastical discourse which might today be appropriated in order to rearticulate Christian-Muslim understanding. Gennadios wrote three works, of which the first two were drawn from conversations he had with Mehmed II himself, in 1455 or early 1456, and the third with Turkish officers in Ferres around 1470: *On the Only Way for the Salvation of Mankind*; *Brief Confession of the Christian Faith*; and *Questions and Answers on the Divinity of our Lord Jesus Christ*. Originally written in Greek, the texts were translated into Ottoman and Arabic.[5]

---

supranationalisme dans l'Église orthodoxe à l'époque turque', in *Aspects de l'Orthodoxie: structures et spiritualité*, Colloque de Strasbourg, novembre 1978 (Paris, 1981), 135–52; Nicolas Pissis, 'Apokalyptik und Zeitwahrnehmung in griechischen Texten der osmanischen Zeit', in Andreas Helmedach et al., eds, *Das Osmanische Europa: Methoden und Perspektiven der Frühneuzeitforschung zu Südosteuropa* (Leipzig, 2013), 463–86.

 4   On George of Trebizond, see, in this volume, Konstantinos Papastathis, 'Christian-Muslim Encounters: George of Trebizond and the 'Inversion' of Eastern Discourse regarding Islam in the Fifteenth Century', 137–49.

 5   Much later, they were edited and published: Louis Petit, X. A. Sideridès and Martin Jugie, eds, *Œuvres complètes de Georges (Gennade) Scholarios*, 8 vols (Paris, 1928–36), 3: 434–75. The first text was published for the first time by Christos Papaioannou in ʾ*Εκκλησιαστικὴ Ἀλήθεια* 16 (1896), 203–96, at 210–12, 219–22, 227–9. The text in PG 160, cols 319A–332C, is that of a pseudo-Athanasian work, edited by W. Gass, *Gennadius und Pletho: Aristotelismus und Platonismus in der Griechischen Kirche, nebst einer*

In none of these writings does Gennadios cite or refer to preceding Byzantine apologetic literature against Islam, which was characterized by an intense aversion towards the figure of Muḥammad and a rejection of his prophethood. Orthodox generally identified the Muslim or so-called 'Mohammedan' with the Ottoman or Turk; Byzantine apologetics continually returned to stereotypical themes such as Muhammad's epilepsy[6] or his control of a demon,[7] and referred to him as a harbinger of the Antichrist, a seducer of the people, the son of a slave woman,[8] and impious and manic.[9] The Byzantines referred to Muslims also as Hagarenes, Saracens and Ishmaelites.[10]

In accordance with the sultan's instructions, Gennadios began composing his works. They were aimed at Muslims, especially those who belonged in the circles of the Sublime Porte, who through reading them would be informed about the Orthodox faith. They remain of enduring value for those who wish to engage in a mutually respectful dialogue between Christianity and Islam which does not in any way affect the core of these two religions. Gennadios's works offer a pastoral example of reconciliation, which promotes a form of religious diplomacy directed towards harmonious symbiosis rather than polemical confrontation. Gennadios's standpoint was reinforced by the politics of Sultan Mehmed II, who was in favour of good communication with the heads of the *ahl al-Kitāb* (Jews and Christians) and their communities.

Gennadios's life and works have been a subject of interest to many writers. Some have examined and presented his work within the interpretative framework of Orthodoxy as the 'true faith' and its testimony to people of other faiths.[11] Others, following the

---

Abhandlung über die Bestreitung des Islam im Mittelalter, 2 vols in 1 (Breslau, 1844), 2: 16–30. The genuine text in PG is the following one, entitled *Confessio Fidei Posterior*. PG 160, 333A–352A. See the critical edition of the original text: Petit, Sideridès and Jugie, eds, *Œuvres*, 3: 453–8.

6   Theophanes the Confessor, *Chronicle* (PG 108, cols 684B–685B).

7   Theodore Abū Qurrah, *Opuscula ascetica* (PG 97, cols 1545–8).

8   Bartholomew of Edessa, *Elechus et Confutation Agareni* (PG 104, cols 1383A–1448A, at 1421C).

9   George the Monk, *Chronicon Breve* (PG 110, cols 869C–872A).

10   Ziaka, 'La recherche grecque', 37–200.

11   The life and work of Gennadios are examined in Theodoros N. Zissis, *Γεννάδιος Β' Σχολάριος, Βίος – Συγγράμματα – Διδασκαλία* (Thessaloniki, 1988). Zissis's massive work has been described as 'controversial' by John Monfasani, and challenged as arbitrary, unprofessional, and 'bigoted' by leading Byzantinists such as Jean Darrouzès, in

opinion of the editor of the *Patriarchal History*, which was published in *Turcograecia*,[12] restate the belief that Gennadios had a friendly relationship with the sultan,[13] which a number of later writers have rejected as a legend.[14] Gennadios's personality and works, both theological and philosophical, have dominated research into his theology, and particularly his Christian Aristotelianism; there have been no major studies on his presentation of the Christian faith to Muslims. The few articles and references to this theme which exist do, however, present a clear picture of the historical circumstances and of Gennadios's general attitude towards Islam.[15] A perusal of the historiography on Gennadios also reveals intense interest in his anti-Latin stance and the way in which this position was used by the sultan to serve his political dealings with Rome, as well as how it led to intra-Christian disagreements 'on the limits of intimacy with the "Turks"'.[16]

Particularly interesting for our theme are the theological elements within Gennadios's discourse that refer firstly to Muslims and secondly to Jews and Gentiles. His moderation and even-handedness offer an excellent pastoral example of firmness on matters of Christian faith and theology coupled with respect for his Muslim interlocutor. In order to understand this divergence

---

Revue des études byzantines 39 (1981), 350–5; Jean Gill, in *Sobornost* 3 (1981), 240–3; George Podskalsky, in *Byzantinische Zeitschrift* 77 (1984), 59–60: see Monfasani's review of Montague Christopher Woodhouse, *George Gemistos Plethon: The Last of the Hellenes* (Oxford, 1986), in *Renaissance Quarterly* 41 (1988), 116–19, at 118.

[12] Gennadios's second work was published by Martin Crusius (1526–1607), in both Greek and Ottoman (*turcarabicam linguam*): *Turcograecia*, Book 2 (Basle, 1584), 108–20. *Turcograecia* is an eight-volume work with all the information that the German humanist managed to gather about the life of post-Byzantine Greek Christians in the Ottoman Empire. It belonged to the wider efforts made by Lutheran theologians of Tübingen, under the aegis of Martin Crusius, to engage in dialogue with the Orthodox Patriarchate of Constantinople. See Dorothea Wendebourg, *Reformation und Orthodoxie: Der ökumenische Briefwechsel zwischen der Leitung der Württembergische Kirche und Patriarch Jeremias II. von Konstantinopel in den Jahren 1573–1581* (Göttingen, 1986).

[13] Paraskevas Konortas, Ὀθωμανικές θεωρήσεις γιά τό Οἰκουμενικό Πατριαρχεῖο *(17ος ἀρχές 20ου αἰώνα)* (Athens, 1998).

[14] Tijana Krstić, *Contested Conversions to Islam: Narratives of Religious Change in the Early Modern Ottoman Empire* (Stanford, CA, 2011), 63. On the legend, she refers to Halil Inalcik, 'The Status of the Greek Orthodox Patriarch under the Ottomans', *Turcica* 21–3 (1991), 407–36, at 409–10. Inalcik believes that by recognizing the spiritual leaders of the Greeks, the Armenians and the Jews, Mehmed II 'attempted to make Istanbul a universal metropolis'.

[15] Yannoulatos, 'Approaches to Islam', 156–7; Ziaka, 'La recherche grecque', 106–9.

[16] Krstić, *Contested Conversions*, 63.

from the dominant contemporary theological discourse, it is necessary to bear in mind literature against Islam, and in particular the way Islam was examined and presented by the Byzantines. The next section of this essay will argue that Gennadios shaped and re-presented Christian identity within its historical context, between the poles of *Dār al-Islam* (the abode or territory of Islam) and *Dār al-Harb* (the abode or territory of war). The Christians of the newly founded Ottoman Empire, who lived within the geographical and spiritual territory of the *Dār al-Islam*, were seeking political compromises that would assure them freedom of religion and harmonious cohabitation with Muslims in a context of religious plurality.

The second figure to be considered was a supporter of Graeco-Ottoman cooperation, George Amiroutzes from Trebizond (d. *c.*1470). Amiroutzes' work *Dialogue on Faith in Christ* could be seen as a political approach which uses religious and doctrinal differences, but also convergences, in order to facilitate the social inclusion of Christians in the new order. The *Dialogue* with the sultan should be dated to around 1470; it is Amiroutzes' last and most important work, both in size and content. The history of the text and its publication mostly in Western circles during the sixteenth century indicates that the Muslims did not attribute much importance to it;[17] rather, they viewed Islam's victory over Christianity as proof of the expansion and superiority of the *Dār al-Islam*.

Amiroutzes was one of the most fervent apologists for this kind of Graeco-Ottoman cooperation, oscillating between political realism and a conciliatory but idealistic spirit towards the opposing political and religious powers of his day. Among the intellectuals from Trebizond who were moved to Constantinople and Adrianople when Mehmed conquered the empire of Trebizond in 1461, George Amiroutzes was named *protovestiarios* (in charge of the Byzantine emperor's wardrobe) and *megas logothetes* (supervisor of fiscal matters) to the Emperor David. Intelligent and a man of many skills, Amiroutzes seems to have been a supporter of Graeco-Turkish friendship and peaceful coexistence; he was,

[17] John Monfasani, 'The "Lost" Final Part of George Amiroutzes' *Dialogus de Fide in Christum* and Zanobi Acciaiuoli', in *Humanism and Creativity in the Renaissance: Essays in Honor of Ronald G. Witt*, ed. Christopher S. Celenza and Kenneth Gouwens (Leiden, 2006), 197–229, at 204.

after all, a diplomat. The relevant research seems less interested in the content of his work than in his life, and whether or not he converted to Islam.[18] From 1461 until around 1470, he lived in Constantinople, where he had a friendly connection with the sultan himself and enjoyed special privileges until the time of his sudden death. Balivet, commenting on Amiroutzes' special relationship with Mehmed II, deduced that he aspired to be 'the Aristotle of the new Alexander'.[19] Amiroutzes was an exceptional personality, who provoked sympathy and animosity both among his contemporaries and later researchers. Some considered him a traitor, mainly because he negotiated the surrender of Trebizond to the Ottomans in 1461, and others thought him a man of wisdom and intelligence who, in the face of changing political power, counselled the emperor as well the Church, winning at the same time the sympathy and friendship of the sultan and the interest of the Vatican. For this reason, he has been seen as favouring union with Rome. However, although he took part in the Council of Ferrara-Florence in 1438–9 as a secular counsellor of the emperor, it is said that on returning to Constantinople he supported the anti-union party.[20]

Analysing the relevant treatises of Gennadios and Amiroutzes and their theological and social discourse concerning Islam, we will explore how these Orthodox thinkers shaped and re-presented Christian identity within their historical context and between the poles of *Dār al-Islam* and *Dār al-Harb*. Thereafter, we will seek to assess the probable influence of their approach upon the dominant contemporary Orthodox ecclesiastical discourse about Islam.

---

[18] Whether or not he converted to Islam remains unknown. Some scholars maintain that he remained a Christian until the end of his life. For the argument against conversion, see Nicolaos Tomadakis, "Ετούρκευσεν ὁ Γεώργιος Ἀμιρούτζης;", ’Επετηρίς ’Εταιρείας Βυζαντινῶν Σπουδῶν 17 (1948), 99–143; Anna Frangedaki, 'On Fifteenth-Century Cryptochristianity: A Letter to George Amoiroutzes from Michael Apostolis', *Byzantine and Modern Greek Studies* 9 (1984–5), 221–4. On his supposed conversion to Islam, see Ali Ezzati, *The Spread of Islam: The Contributing Factors* (London, 2002), 149. In *Martyrology of Blessed Andreas of Chios*, George of Trebizond accused Amiroutzes of apostasy: John Monfasani, *George of Trebizond: A Biography and a Study of his Rhetoric and Logic* (Leiden, 1976), 187 n. 37, citing PG 161, cols 883B–890.

[19] Michel Balivet, *Byzantins et Ottomans: Relations, interactions, succession* (Istanbul, 1999), 139–50, at 149.

[20] Martin Jugie, 'La Lettre de Georges Amiroutzès au Duc de Nauplie Demetrius sur le Concile de Florence', Βυζάντιον 14 (1939), 77–93; Ziaka, 'La Recherche grecque', 113–15.

REARTICULATING A CHRISTIAN-MUSLIM UNDERSTANDING

In his first work, *On the Only Way for the Salvation of Mankind*, Gennadios did not attempt a critique of Islam, nor did he even mention it by name.[21] Rather, he systematized the whole of Orthodox dogmatic theology in twenty-one paragraphs. Only hints addressed to the 'non-initiated' imply that he might have in mind the Muslims, whom he accused of 'altering' the gospel.[22] Gennadios was aware of Muslim teaching, according to which the Qur'ān is the perfect and original revelation of God to humankind, and because humankind had forgotten this revelation God had re-sent it through the last of his prophets, Muḥammad.[23] Throughout the apology, Gennadios's concern was to prove that the perfect law was given to the people through 'our Lord Jesus Christ', and that this law does not contradict Moses' law but rather completes it.[24] He structured his argument as follows: the necessity of law is based on the recognition that God, who is the first truth and the ultimate good, had to give human beings a law in order that they might be governed properly.[25] They thus first received the unwritten natural law from God. However, their incomplete state rendered them unable to keep the natural law, which drove them into sin and ignorance of the good.[26] Gennadios referred to pre-Christian religious beliefs, peoples and deities,

[21] According to the footnotes of the first version of the text, Gennadios began to write it after an unexpected visit by Mehmed to the Pammakaristos monastery, to which the patriarchate had moved its seat. Eventually, during 1599–1600, the patriarchate was moved to the monastery of St Georgios, in the heart of the Fanari neighbourhood, where it remains: Manuel Gedeon, Χρονικά τοῦ Πατριαρχικοῦ Οἴκου καί Ναοῦ (Constantinople, [1894?]); Germanos Sardeon, "Ὁ πατριαρχικός οἶκος καί ναός ἀπό τοῦ 1453 καί ἑξῆς", Ὀρθοδοξία 14 (1939), 110–15, 264–7, 299–305; Aristeidis Pasadaios, Ὁ Πατριαρχικός Οἶκος τοῦ Οἰκουμενικοῦ Θρόνου (Thessaloniki, 1976).

[22] According to Muslim belief, God re-sent his eternal word, the Qur'ān, to his messenger Muḥammad due to the alteration of the Gospel by Jews and Christians: Sūra al-Maida (Q 5: 15).

[23] The Qur'ān is written on an eternal tablet (al-Lauh al-Mahfūz) which is kept next to God (Q 85: 21–2). This is the archetype, the 'Mother of the Bible' (Umm al-Kitāb), and is the prototype not only of the Qur'ān but also of all forms of revelation, particularly the Pentateuch and the gospel. It is the eternal Word of God, his speech: Gregorios Ziakas, Ἰσλάμ. Θρησκεία καί Πολιτεία (Thessaloniki, 2001), 37; Francis Edward Peters, *The Monotheists: Jews, Christians, and Muslims in Conflict and Competition, 2: The Words and Will of God* (Princeton, NJ, 2003), 52.

[24] Petit, Sidéridès and Jugie, eds, *Œuvres*, 3: 441, 442, 443.

[25] Ibid. 436–7.

[26] Ibid. 438.

such as Zoroastrianism, the Egyptians, Hermes and the contemporaries of Abraham, in order to demonstrate the perversion that humankind suffered, which generally led to 'demonic apostasy'.[27] A few paragraphs later, he returned to the issue of God's natural law, which was given as a preparation for receiving the perfect law, adding that all people are journeying on the path to eternal life.[28] For this reason, God gave a written law through the virtuous and true prophet Moses, which was not only for the Jews, but for all humankind.[29] Gennadios was positively disposed towards the great Greek philosophers (*hoi akroi tōn Hellēnōn philosophoî*) Pythagoras, Plato and Aristotle, who, he said, praised the divine and benefitted from the Jewish books.[30] This argument helped him to prove that all of humanity had received God's blessing, which was the common understanding of most Church fathers in their effort to legitimize pagan philosophy as a means of God's providence or *spermatikos logos* (seminal or divine word).[31] Indeed, Yannoulatos has noted how Gennadios regarded both the Sibylline oracles and the ancient Greek oracles as means of divine communication.[32]

The following section of the text is devoted to Jesus Christ and the law of the gospel.[33] In the same way that the Muslims understood the Qur'ān to be law, Gennadios wrote of the gospel law and the word (*Logos*) of God, concluding with the statement that there could not be a law more perfect than the law of the gospel.[34] Here, obviously, he was hinting at and countering Muslim beliefs about the Qur'ān and in particular the necessity of its message for humanity. His comments became more pointed when he referred to it as misinterpreting the persons of the Holy Trinity, saying 'do not destroy the unity of the doctrine of the Trinity', but without

---

[27] Ibid.
[28] Ibid. 440.
[29] Ibid. 439.
[30] Ibid. 440.
[31] According to Justin Martyr, all truths to which pre-Christian humanity adhered constituted the message of the seminal divine word, emerging from his illumination of, and presence with, every human being, provided they do not fall into darkness deriving from their passions and desires: *1 Apol.* 46 (PG 6, col. 397C); see George Martzelos, ʻΗ Θεολογία του σπερματικού λόγου και η σημασία της για τους θεολογικούς και διαθρησκειακούς διαλόγουςʼ, *Θεολογία* 84/2 (2013), 69–80, at 71.
[32] Yannoulatos, 'Approaches to Islam', 157–8.
[33] Petit, Sideridès and Jugie, eds, *Œuvres*, 3: 441–52.
[34] Ibid. 449.

using the word 'hypostases'.[35] This suggests that in writing for a Muslim audience he was using language that was accessible rather than strictly dogmatic, and which could accommodate understanding and promote continued discussion.[36]

Gennadios followed the same approach in his second text, *Brief Confession of the Christian Faith*.[37] This text constitutes an abbreviation and explanation of the first. It seems that Mehmed II organized a second and a third conversation in the presence of Muslim spiritual teachers and others close to him. The sultan asked Scholarios to make his exposition short and simple, so as to be 'meaningful and easy to understand by the non-initiated'. The patriarch systematically expounded aspects of Orthodox belief such as the Trinity and the divinity of Christ as Word (*Logos*) of God. In accordance with the style of the apology and its ultimate recipient (the sultan), Gennadios was very careful not to criticize Islam in either text. His references to ancient Greek thought and philosophy add authority to his discourse and help his apologetic goal of demonstrating the need to spread the new law of God to all humanity. The essence of his writings, however, is to argue for the completeness of the gospel, thus rejecting implicitly – and indirectly – the revelation of the Qur'ān. However, Gennadios was not engaging in direct theological debate as his predecessor, the Orthodox theologian and archbishop of Thessaloniki Gregory Palamas (1296/7–1359), had done. For Palamas, the fact that Muslims accepted that the word and spirit of God was Jesus (*Īsā*),[38] justified the doctrine that God had a Word (*Logos*) and Spirit (*Pneuma*), which coexisted eternally with him. According to Palamas, if Muslims maintained the opposite, it would imply that they believed that God was *a-logos* (without reason) and *a-pnous* (without breath), that is, effectively a dead essence.[39]

The third text bears the title *Questions and Answers on the Divinity of our Lord Jesus Christ*, and includes twelve questions and

---

35   Ibid. 452.
36   Yannoulatos, 'Approaches to Islam', 157.
37   Petit, Sideridès and Jugie, eds, *Œuvres*, 3: 453–8.
38   Q 4: 171.
39   See Γρηγορίου τοῦ Παλαμᾶ, 'Διάλεξις πρός τούς ἀθέους Χιόνας', in Panayotis K. Christou, ed., *Γρηγορίου Παλαμᾶ, Συγγράμματα*, 5 vols (Thessaloniki, 1962–91), 4: 109–65, at 151–2.

their answers.[40] It purports to be a conversation that Gennadios had with Muslim officials in the city of Ferres in 1470, when, after his resignation from the Ecumenical Throne, he lived in the monastery of the Honourable Forerunner. The dialogue begins with the controversial issue of understanding Christ as *theanthropos* (God-Man). The subjects that interest Gennadios's Muslim interlocutors are clear and very specialized. It seems, as they themselves suggest at one point, that they are aware of Gennadios's conversations with the sultan, and that they have come to him in order to discuss further some of the most theologically abstruse problems raised for Islam by Orthodox belief.

Gennadios's references to the teaching of Islam are more direct here than in his previous writings, although he still refuses to name either Muslims or Islam directly. The most interesting are the questions put in the mouths of the Muslims themselves, which highlight Islam's theological difficulties with Christianity. Their questions concern proof of the divine nature of Christ,[41] the divinity of Jesus,[42] the supremacy of God,[43] Moses' status as a prophet in relation to that of Jesus,[44] the Christian view of Moses, with the Muslim interlocutor referring specifically to Deuteronomy 18: 15–17,[45] the hypostatic union of the Trinity,[46] the incarnation, and why God did not send an angel to bring his law to humankind,[47] the *theanthropos* or 'God-Man', and the (to Muslims) incomprehensible union of the two natures, human and divine,[48] the indispensability of Christian faith in the theanthropic nature of Christ,[49] the Second Coming and Jesus's messianic role,[50] and the difficulty of following the Christian law, even for Christians.[51] The Muslim interlocutor's response is accompanied by an avalanche of

---

[40] Petit, Sideridès and Jugie, eds, *Œuvres*, 3: 458–75.
[41] Ibid. 458.
[42] Ibid. 458–9.
[43] Ibid. 461–3, 464–7.
[44] Ibid. 468.
[45] Ibid. 468–70.
[46] Ibid. 470–1.
[47] Referring to Islam's belief that the Qur'ān was given to Muhammad through God's messenger, the archangel Jibrīl.
[48] Petit, Sideridès and Jugie, eds, *Œuvres*, 3: 472–3.
[49] Ibid. 471–2.
[50] Ibid. 473–5.
[51] Ibid. 475.

questions, such as why Christ has not yet come again in glory,[52] why God did not give an easier law rather than such an unrealistic one – something which Christians themselves acknowledge to be problematic – which renders the number of those harmed by the law greater than those who benefit from it. Finally, he concludes by asking whether Gennadios had already been asked these questions, to which Gennadios responds affirmatively, saying that he has answered them sufficiently.[53]

Gennadios's answers manifest an apologetic attitude that is not apparent in his previous dialogues. Specifically, he refers to the importance of the concept of martyrdom for Christians and the role of crypto-Christians in the dissemination of the faith from early Roman times until the reign of Constantine; Constantine had, in Gennadios's reading, legalized Christianity because of the many martyrdoms for the sake of Christ, and had thereafter become much more open to the faith of Christ.[54] Gennadios also refers to Constantine's son Constantine Crispus, who had secretly converted to Christianity before his father, and other examples of crypto-Christian scholars who on the basis of their studies had turned to the true philosophy of Christianity.[55] In the cause of Christian-Muslim relations, Gennadios regurgitates some stereotypical anti-Jewish opinions, recalling the Muslim reserve toward the Jews whilst stressing that 'you too (the Muslims) have a good faith towards him (Jesus), because you consider him a holy human and a prophet, word (*logos*) and spirit of God, and many more glorifying things that you say about him'.[56] He reiterates the Christian thesis that faith in Jesus had already been revealed through the prophets, arguing that among Jews the coming of Jesus was foretold through the prophets and among Romans and Greeks through the oracles.[57] He then describes the dual nature of humankind, as both soul and body. The body is corruptible and material, while the soul is incorporeal and immaterial, simple and noetic, separate from the body and immortal. Gennadios uses an Aristotelian analogical argument to refute his Muslim interlocu-

---

[52] Ibid.
[53] Ibid. 459.
[54] Ibid. 466.
[55] Ibid. 467.
[56] Ibid. 461.
[57] Ibid. 467.

tors' position that it was not possible for Christ to be both God and man. He replies that, just as man is both soul and body, so Christ is both God and man.[58] He selects as his starting point the self-consciousness of Jesus Christ, whom the Qur'ān acknowledges as *logos* and spirit of God,[59] and he rejects the Muslim allegation that the gospel had been altered.[60] In a rhetorical apostrophe, Gennadios affirms that faith in God is much higher than 'submission' to him, a direct allusion to the Islamic understanding.[61]

Amiroutzes' *Dialogue on Faith in Christ* was also based on conversations that he had with the sultan. The Greek original is lost, but the contents were preserved in a Latin translation of 1518, *Dialogus de fide in Christum habitus cum rege Turcarum* (*Dialogue on Faith in Christ held with the King of the Turks*).[62] It is a very interesting text in terms both of its theological and its philosophical content: the writer — even though he does not seem to harbour any delusions about the sultan's converting to Christianity — hopes for peaceful coexistence between the two religions. The main issues Amiroutzes addresses are the possibility of the incarnation and its necessity, the prophets, and whether or not they foretold the incarnation, the Trinity and the unity of God, and the Christian understanding of the resurrection of the body. The quality of his apology is undoubted, and Monfasani observes: 'Amiroutzes skil-

---

[58] Ibid. 473.
[59] Ibid. 461.
[60] Ibid. 461–4.
[61] Ibid. 473.
[62] Paris, BN, MS Latinus 3395, fols 83–144. Emile Legrand published Amiroutzes' preface in *Bibliographie Hellénique ou description raisonnée des ouvrages publiés par des grecs aux XV⁰ et XVI⁰ siècles*, 4 vols (Paris, 1885–1906), 3: 197. Asterios Argyriou and Georges Lagarrigue published the text of MS Latinus 3395 with a French translation: 'Georges Amiroutzès et son *Dialogue sur la foi au Christ tenu avec le Sultan des Turcs*', *Byzantinische Forschungen* 11 (1987), 29–222. The most recent edition and translation were done in Spanish by Oscar de la Cruz Palma (2000), who reedited the Latin text, correcting the translation by Argyriou and Lagarrigue wherever the sixteenth-century Latin copyist referred to the Greek original in the margins: *Jorge Ameruzes de Trebisonda. El diálogo de la fe con el sultán de los turcos*, Nueva Roma: Bibliotheca Graeca et Latina Aevi Posterioris 9 (Madrid, 2000); reviewed by John Monfasani, *Speculum* 79 (2004), 1024–5. In 2006, Monfasani published an article concerning the conclusion of Amiroutzes' work, supporting the theory that three manuscripts which had been attributed to an anonymous author (Vat. Lat. 3469, 5619, 8603) were in fact the continuation of Amiroutzes' work and that 'this missing part helps us follow Amiroutzes' argument in detail'. The three manuscripts date from sixteenth-century Rome and are independent of MS Latinus 3395: Monfasani, 'Final Part'.

fully defends the Christian positions on the basis of reason in a sort of a Greek mini-*Summa Contra Gentiles* on these issues.'[63]

The tone of the conversation is very different from Gennadios's work. The questions and answers between the interlocutors (Amiroutzes and the sultan) are direct, as to some extent in Gennadios's third work. Amiroutzes articulates the questions and answers in an atmosphere of friendliness between the two men. It is true that the sultan is often presented as being offensive: he mocks Amiroutzes, calling him an 'old fox',[64] accusing him of 'saying nothing' and suggesting that 'even a child would have a better argument'.[65] However, despite the sultan's objections, he prompts Amiroutzes to continue by posing new questions for him to answer. Amiroutzes responds with patience and firmness, focusing on the fact that the gospel has not been altered,[66] and on the divine and human nature of Jesus. Scattered throughout the text are analogical – albeit tacit – references to the Muslim faith, aimed at better explaining Christian positions. At several points Amiroutzes refers to beliefs held by both religions, affirming that these do not admit of logical proof, but rather constitute a common faith; these include, for instance, creation *ex nihilo* at a specific moment of time, and the miracles of Christ.[67] Even though the issues discussed are mostly theological, the interlocutors also make lengthy references to philosophical ideas, as well as to subjects of wider historical and hermeneutical import.

Amiroutzes does not appear to be dismissing or reducing the Christian faith; his argumentation, however, is unique. Even though he tackles theological subjects, his arguments are mostly personal, based on his understanding of themes such as history in general and the history of the Church in particular,[68] and the history of the Church in particular, Jesus Christ as the *Logos* of God,[69] the Virgin Mary and the distinction between logical proof of natural

---

[63] Monfasani, review of de la Cruz Palma, 1024.

[64] MS Latinus 3395, fol. 114A (Argyriou and Lagarrigue, 'Amiroutzès', 137).

[65] Ibid., fol. 121A (Argyriou and Lagarrigue, 'Amiroutzès', 155–7).

[66] Ibid., fol. 114A (Argyriou and Lagarrigue, 'Amiroutzès', 128–37).

[67] Ibid., fol. 96B (Argyriou and Lagarrigue, 'Amiroutzès', 93–5). See also Q 3: 49; 5: 112–14.

[68] Ibid., fol. 84B (Argyriou and Lagarrigue, 'Amiroutzès', 65).

[69] Ibid., fols 86A–91B, 112B–113B, 118A–118B (Argyriou and Lagarrigue, 'Amiroutzès', 69–81); cf. for example, fols 135–7, 149 (Argyriou and Lagarrigue, 'Amiroutzès', 193–201).

principles and divine providence,[70] the prophets,[71] the Scriptures and the writing of the gospel,[72] the meaning of martyrdom for the faith, the resurrection of the dead, eternity and the Holy Spirit.[73]

We could elaborate more on the content of each section, as well as on Amiroutzes' combination of an original approach to familiar issues with faithfulness to the Church's dogmas. An example is his comment on the words of the prophets, answering the sultan: 'we use the Prophets when we are in need of their authority. We do not use them in any other case'.[74] He describes Christ's passion in a deeply human manner and explains how Christ tries to fulfil Jewish eternal law. It is interesting to note here the way Amiroutzes understands the Scriptures and how he decides to criticize certain points which he regards as superstitions, such as the Jewish Sabbath. He also advocates certain supersessionist ideas, claiming that Jewish perspectives have been replaced by (or reconstructed as) Christian ones, such as the priority of faith over the Law.[75] He concludes this section: 'Christ did not disparage the Jewish laws, but instead he perfected them, by making them at the same time more suitable and acceptable.'[76] Later Amiroutzes seeks to prove Christ's divinity by saying: 'if he was not actually "Son of God", as he was saying, he would be a blasphemer. But how can a blasphemer make miracles happen, as you (Muslims) also accept? So, you accept everything he did. Therefore the gospel is something which was neither invented nor tangled up with lies' (implying that this is what they are suggesting).[77] Furthermore, Amiroutzes presents the sultan's descriptions of Christ in a manner amenable – up to a point – to Christian understanding. The sultan recognizes Christ's righteousness and prophetic gift, and at the same time accepts everything the prophets had foretold, but refuses to accept his divinity.[78]

In the prologue to his work, Amiroutzes notes that many have

[70] Ibid., fols 91B–97A (Argyriou and Lagarrigue, 'Amiroutzès', 81–89, 91–5).
[71] Ibid., fols 97A–100B, 122B–126A (Argyriou and Lagarrigue, 'Amiroutzès', 96–105, 159–69).
[72] Ibid., fols 100B–118B (Argyriou and Lagarrigue, 'Amiroutzès', 105–49).
[73] Ibid., fols 122B–141B (Argyriou and Lagarrigue, 'Amiroutzès', 175–209).
[74] Ibid., fol. 100B (Argyriou and Lagarrigue, 'Amiroutzès', 105).
[75] Ibid., fol. 102B (Argyriou and Lagarrigue, 'Amiroutzès', 109).
[76] Ibid., fols 104B–105A (Argyriou and Lagarrigue, 'Amiroutzès', 115).
[77] Ibid., fols 107A–107B (Argyriou and Lagarrigue, 'Amiroutzès', 121–3).
[78] Ibid., fols 126A–127A (Argyriou and Lagarrigue, 'Amiroutzès', 169–71).

written on the false faith of 'these people', that is, the Muslims, in such a way that he really has nothing more to add. However, he also claims that before him nobody had defended Christian dogmas with serious arguments directed at the accusations made. Each Christian, he believes, must respond to these questions, examining each issue individually.[79]

Amiroutzes is evidently deconstructing Christian polemical stereotypes regarding Islam and offering a new discourse, which was later criticized by many Christians. Amiroutzes does not relativize the Christian faith in favour of Islam; however, he does try to emphasize certain common traditions and religious beliefs, in order to overcome conflict and ensure the peaceful coexistence of Christians with victorious Islam.

CONCLUSION

Patriarch Gennadios and George Amiroutzes could be seen as the chief proponents of a school of thought which advocated Christian conciliation and rapprochement with Islam. Gennadios was distinguished for his theological pragmatism; he combined the religious and political demands of his time with a vision of the universality of revelation. Amiroutzes proposed a non-polemical approach to understanding Islam, defending Christian teaching in a way that is not apologetic but rather based on personal commitment, firmness of argument, and the use of philosophical discourse to support theological argumentation.

Taking a more optimistic stance than that of Amiroutzes in his prologue, where he states that his detailed record of dialogue with the sultan is not aimed at the enslaved Greeks, who are not interested any longer in knowledge or philosophy due to their unbearable subjection,[80] it can be argued that these texts might contribute today to Christian-Muslim understanding, offering examples of a friendlier manner of debating theological matters. In this approach, contemporary Orthodox Churches would utilize the theological

---

[79] Ibid., fols 84B–85 (Argyriou and Lagarrigue, 'Amiroutzès', 65).

[80] Ibid., fols 83A–83B (Argyriou and Lagarrigue, 'Amiroutzès', 63). Here he refers to Ottoman rule without clearly naming it. Later, however, he mentions that there is one element which fuels hatred and leads to the Greeks' unbearable subjection. This element is not political difference, which Greeks had faced in the past with other peoples, such as the Scythians and the Romans, and had managed to overcome, but religious difference: ibid., fol. 84B (Argyriou and Lagarrigue, 'Amiroutzès', 65).

inheritance of past ages in constructive and not divisive terms, and stand against a dominant ecclesiastical narrative that still reproduces, even in the twentieth-first century, stereotypical arguments against 'other faiths'. This would mean, in theological terms, rethinking 'how Christianity has defined itself through its contacts with Others'[81] and how modern Orthodox theology deals with issues of religious otherness and plurality. Part of this involves serious re-examination of the texts analysed here; this brief study has not exhausted them, and they deserve further study, especially for what they can tell us about other religions, traditions, philosophies and theologies. Religious pluralism, even though it is omnipresent in modern societies, nevertheless seems to be an unresolved issue in ecclesiastical discourse, often unaddressed in official statements regarding religious diversity. For such reasons, these texts can help foster an understanding of religious plurality and contribute to a constructive dialogue, which – without ignoring differences – can at least mitigate religious divisions, moving towards mutual rapprochement and peaceful coexistence.

Aristotle University of Thessaloniki

---

[81] Kwok Pui-Lan, *Postcolonial Imagination and Feminist Theology* (Louisville, KY, 2005), 67.

'AND OUR MUḤAMMAD GOES WITH THE ARCHANGEL GABRIEL TO CHOIR': SIXTEENTH-CENTURY GERMAN ACCOUNTS OF LIFE UNDER THE TURKS*

by CHARLOTTE METHUEN

In the German lands of the sixteenth century, the threat of Turkish invasion coloured perceptions of religious diversity. As the Turkish threat became more real to Western Europeans, the experiences of Christians under the Turks, and the responses of the Turks – who were of course Muslims – to encounters with the Christian faith became topics of considerable concern. In 1539, a pamphlet purporting to offer a German translation of a letter from Constantinople was printed in Augsburg, Magdeburg and possibly Nuremberg. Its title hints at the unexpected story it has to tell:

> Copy of a letter from Constantinople from which one can learn how the Grand Turk had his Priests and Doctors killed for the reasons that they on good grounds confessed and proved that the Christian law and faith are true, and the Mohammedan false. And the great signs that appeared at the place where this murder took place.[1]

* Research for this paper was made possible by my status as Guest Researcher at the Herzog August Bibliothek, Wolfenbüttel. I am very grateful to Alexandra Walsham for her comments on an earlier draft. Particular thanks are due to David Thomas who elucidated references to the Qur'ān and offered insights from his deep knowledge of the history of Christian-Muslim relations. Unless otherwise stated, translations are my own

[1] *Abschrifft eines brieffs von Constantinopel | auss welichem man zuouernemen hat | welcher gestalt der Groß Türck | seine Priester und Dotores hat lassen umbbringen | auß ursachen | das sie bestendiger weyß bekannt | und mit ursachen bekrefftiget haben | Das christlich Gesetz und Glaube warhafftig | Das Machometisch aber falsch sey | Und was für grosse zeychen erschynen sein in den selbigen Stellen des beuebten Todtschlags | Im Jar do mal zalt MDXXXIX.* Carl Göllner identifies the German version as a translation of an Italian work of the same year, probably printed in Venice: *Copia di una lettera da Constantinopoli, per la quale s'ha adviso della grande occisione che ha fatto il grand signor di Turchi delli suoi Sacerdoti & Dottori ... :* Carl Göllner, *Turcica: Die europäischen Türkendrucke des 16. Jahrhunderts,* 1: *1501–1550* (Bucharest and Berlin, 1961), 310–13 (nos 648, 649 [German], 653, 654 [Italian]).

The pamphlet's account is dramatic. During a celebratory banquet at his court, the Grand Turk enquires of 'Arbeo, his Waschka', that is, one of his generals, what he knows about Christianity. The *Waschka* replies that he is a soldier and knows nothing of religion. Accepting this as a wise answer, the Grand Turk calls his 'priests' and asks them the same question. They too affirm that they know nothing of Christianity: 'As servants of God, all our work and profession is directed towards the reading of our holy law, the Alcoran, with great diligence and without ceasing, for we will not sully this holy law with the study of a foreign law which is forbidden to us.'[2] The Grand Turk takes issue with this attitude: soldiers need to know and understand their enemies in order to defeat them, he says, and in the same way the priests should also know and understand theirs. The priests concede that this might be true, and the youngest observes that the Qur'ān includes a strange word: 'HJCEHJCEALMAS &c.' which he thinks refers to 'Jesus Christ Messiah and the word of God and God's Holy Spirit'.[3] 'If that is the case,' says the Grand Turk, 'the Christian faith is the best.' 'That is the truth', his priests reply.[4] The Grand Turk sends them away to discover whether it is indeed true. Some time later, he summons them to give an account of their findings. 'Which is

---

[2] *Abschrifft eines brieffs*, fol. Aii[v].

[3] Ibid., fol. Aiii[r]. David Thomas observes that this sequence of letters could be a garbled recollection of some of the so-called 'mystical letters' that preface a number of chapters of the Qur'ān. In his 'Letter to a Muslim Friend', the twelfth-century Melkite bishop Paul of Antioch refers to the letters before chapters 2 and 3, ALM, as referring to AL-MASIH, 'the Messiah'. Paul of Antioch's letter was edited in the fourteenth century by a Christian in Cyprus, who – surprisingly for his time – 'ingeniously suggests a communion of spirit between the two faiths in their ascendancy over the Jews, and also finds a place for the Prophet and the Quran within a divine economy centered on Christianity', whilst still concluding 'the ascendancy of Christianity over Islam': David Thomas, 'Idealism and Intransigence: A Christian-Muslim Encounter in Early Mamluk Times', *Mamluk Studies Review* 13 (2009), 85–103, esp. 86 (quotations at 89, 91), online at: <http://mamluk.uchicago.edu/MSR_XIII-2_2009-Thomas_pp85-103.pdf>, last accessed 8 August 2014; cf. idem, 'Paul of Antioch's *Letter to a Muslim Friend* and the *Letter to Cyprus*', in idem, ed., *Syrian Christians under Islam: The First Thousand Years* (Leiden, 2001), 203–21, esp. 209. Moreover, Thomas points out that the interpretation placed in the mouth of the youngest Turkish 'priest' recalls Q 4: 171, which Christians routinely cited as offering support for the divinity of Jesus, and sometimes for the Trinity: see, for example, Samir K. Samir, 'The Prophet Muḥammad as seen by Timothy I and some other Christian Authors', in Thomas, ed., *Syrian Christians under Islam*, 75–106, at 85–6.

[4] *Abschrifft eines brieffs*, fol. Aiii[r].

the best faith?' he asks, 'The Christian or the Mohammedan?'[5] The priests give a surprising answer:

> Invincible Lord, we have read in the Qur'ān that Christ is in the seventh heaven with the great God, and that our Muḥammad goes with the Archangel Gabriel to choir and greets him humbly and shows him great honour and worship, and offers himself to him as his Lord and master. In masses he also asks John the Baptist and Moses and the other prophets for their intercessions to their great God and Jesus Christ. So Muḥammad gives the sign that Christ is greater than him and his Lord. From these words in the Qur'ān we conclude that Christ is alive and in the seventh heaven. But we know that our Muḥammad is dead and lies in Mecca.[6]

Christianity, they conclude, is the true religion. The Grand Turk is not impressed. Calling his guards, he has the priests taken away and executed. The people of Constantinople are shocked by his response, and the Grand Turk's remaining priests confirm their view that Christianity is the better religion. The story spreads secretly across Turkey and Greece. Perhaps, comments the author hopefully, 'this might be the beginning of the planting of Christian faith in these lands', and the end of the war with the Turks.[7]

In his survey of sixteenth-century *Turcica*, Carl Göllner categorizes this extraordinary account as one of a genre of 'neue Zeitungen' recording 'great signs' in Constantinople which were meant to presage the hoped-for fall of the Ottoman Empire and to encourage Europeans to continue resisting its incursions.[8] The *Turcica* or *Türkenbüchlein* ('little books about the Turks') were popular pamphlets, written in the vernacular and capable of being printed very quickly: they were intended to shape public opinion.[9] These pamphlets appeared in irregular waves roughly associ-

---

5   Ibid., fol. [Aiv]ᵛ.
6   Ibid., fols [Aiv]ᵛ–Bʳ. Thomas notes that that the reference to Christ's being in the seventh heaven 'looks like a reminiscence of Q 4: 157–8, in which God saves Jesus from being crucified by causing him to ascend into heaven'. The reference to Muḥammad being buried in Mecca (his tomb is in fact in Medina) is a common mistake in medieval and early modern Christian polemics: David Thomas to Charlotte Methuen, private correspondence, 27 July 2013.
7   *Abschrifft eines brieffs*, fols Bʳ–[Bii]ʳ.
8   Göllner, *Turcica*, 1: 310.
9   Göllner, *Turcica*, 3: *Die Türkenfrage in der öffentlichen Meinung Europas im 16.*

ated with the wars against the Turks. Göllner calculates that 259 pamphlets relating to the Turks were printed between 1526 and 1532, the period of the battle of Mohács, the siege of Vienna and Charles V's campaign; a further 134 appeared between 1540 and 1542, during Suleiman's campaigns; and 148 were published in 1565–6, a period which witnessed the siege of Malta and the battle of Szigetvár, Hungary.[10]

With the incursions of the Turks, a situation of religious plurality had become a lived reality in much of Eastern Europe, and a real possibility further west. 'Never before', as Francisco observes, 'had the Latin West ... been so close in physical proximity to the Muslim world.'[11] Faced with the possibility of Turkish invasion, many Christian authors characterized the Turks as violent, blood-thirsty child-murderers who were messengers of the devil.[12] Yet this did not necessarily mean that their pamphlets incited readers to war. In 1518 Luther had suggested that it was wrong to fight the Turks: their incursions were a divine punishment imposed by God, and consequently to be accepted.[13] Once the military threat became greater, Luther changed his mind and conceded that armed resistance to the Ottoman threat was necessary.[14] By 1541 he had concluded that '[w]e are fighting that the Turk may not put his devilish filth and the blasphemous Muhammad in the place of our dear Lord, Jesus Christ', and that the Turks and the papacy were 'the last two plagues of the wrath of God', as described in

Jahrhundert (Bucharest and Berlin, 1978), 16–17, 21–6.

10   Ibid. 18–19. Adam S. Francisco, *Martin Luther and Islam: A Study in Sixteenth-Century Polemics and Apologetics* (Leiden, 2007), 53–65, offers a useful survey of the literature.

11   Francisco, *Luther and Islam*, 64.

12   See, for instance, Andrei Pippidi, *Visions of the Ottoman World in Renaissance Europe* (London, 2012), 69–76; cf. Göllner, *Turcica*, 3: 173–98.

13   Martin Luther, 'Explanations of the Ninety-Five Theses' (1518), *WA* 1, 529–628, at 535; *LW* 31, 77–252, at 91–2. In 'On War against the Turk' (1529), Luther comments that since the situation had now changed, this no longer held: *WA* 30/2, 107–48, at 108; *LW* 46, 155–205, at 162.

14   Luther, 'On War against the Turk'. He reinforced his position in a sermon against the Turks of the same year: *WA* 30/2, 149–65; cf. Pippidi, *Visions of the Ottoman World*, 81. The complexities of Luther's attitudes towards the Turks and Islam are explored by Francisco, *Luther and Islam*; Johannes Ehmann, *Luther, Türken und Islam: eine Untersuchung zum Türken- und Islambild Martin Luthers (1515–1546)* (Gütersloh, 2008); Ian Almond, 'Deconstructing Luther's Islam: The Turk as Curse or Cure?', in Jørgen S. Nielsen et al., eds, *Yearbook of Muslims in Europe*, 3 (Leiden, 2011), 619–54.

Revelation.[15] In similarly apocalyptic vein, Justus Jonas proclaimed that the Ottoman Empire was one fulfilment of the apocalyptic prophecies found in Daniel 7, and that the 'Alcoran' presented 'unashamed lies and terrible blasphemy', denying the divinity of Christ, the doctrine of grace and the forgiveness of sins.[16] Johannes Brenz affirmed that a Turkish conquest would inevitably give rise to a godless government, and that preachers should call for resistance, 'for their Muḥammad has commanded that they should keep on attacking and conquering lands and peoples'.[17] After 1529, there were many accounts of the siege of Vienna, including harrowing tales of the Turks' behaviour or alarming reports of their military strength.[18] But other texts, including the 'Copy of a letter from Constantinople', although they had a sting in their tail, were subtler, witnessing, at least to some extent, to the influence of the somewhat more positive attitude towards Islam and the Turks which Göllner suggests emerged from the mid-sixteenth century, and which Andrei Pippidi proposes was associated with the approach taken by Erasmus and other humanists.[19] In her study of Renaissance accounts of the history of Islam, Margaret Meserve argues that during the course of the sixteenth century, 'the fear and fascination Westerners continued to feel regarding the "Turkish menace"' began to find 'new expression in accounts of the Turks' culture and institutions'.[20] Indeed, despite his polemic, Jonas conceded that despite what he saw as the stranger habits of the

---

[15] Luther, 'Appeal for Prayer against the Turks' (1541), *WA* 51, 585–625, at 620; *LW* 43, 213–41, at 238.

[16] Justus Jonas, *Das siebend Capitel Danielis, von des Türcken Gottes lesterung und schrecklicher Morderey* (Wittemberg, 1530), quotation at fol. Eii^r. Norman Daniel, *Islam and the West: The Making of an Image* (Oxford, 1997), 67–99, documents the medieval background to such attacks on Islam in general, and the Qur'ān in particular, as pseudo-prophecy.

[17] Johannes Brenz, *Wie sich Prediger vnd Leyen halten sollen so der Turck das deutsche land vberfalle[n] wuerde Christliche vnd notturfftige vnterricht* (Wittemberg, 1531), quotation at fol. Aiii^v.

[18] Two examples amongst many are *Warhafftige Newe zeytung von der Stat Wien[n], wie sie von der erschröckenlichen … Macht des Thürcken … belegert [et]c im M.D.xxviij. Jar. Jtem. Ein Sentbrieff so Emerich Wascha … Auch ein schöner Spruch wie graussamlich der wüetrich mit den ellenden Christen … umbgangen ist* (Regensburg, 1529); *Türcken belegerung der Statt Wien. Auch wie ein Tuerkischer Herr ynn eynen guelden stuckgefangen | was der gefragt und darauff geantwort hab* (n.pl., 1529).

[19] Göllner, *Turcica*, 3: 29; Pippidi, *Visions of the Ottoman World*, 80–90.

[20] Margaret Meserve, *Empires of Islam in Renaissance Historical Thought* (Cambridge, MA, 2008), 242.

Turks and their religion (some of which were clearly apocryphal), such as monks who went naked in winter, fasted and claimed to speak with angels, the followers of Muḥammad could nonetheless demonstrate their moral rectitude: providing water to those who were thirsty and caring for the poor who were hungry or had no shelter.[21] German authors in this period showed some awareness of different types of Islam, contrasting Persian culture and faith positively with those of the Ottoman Empire.[22] And yet Erasmus, a strong proponent of peace with the Turks, could still claim that Christendom was 'sinking into a state of Turkish barbarism', and argue that the conversion of the Turks to Christianity would be a sure way of ensuring lasting peace.[23] The metaphors associated with Turkishness did not foster hopes of a positive interreligious or intercultural interaction.

Against this backdrop, the views of the Turks, of their religion, and of their attitudes to those of other faiths, offered in a restricted set of those vernacular texts which purported to have been written either in Constantinople or in the wider Ottoman context, are particularly interesting for their more complex presentations of religious diversity. This essay will consider four such German-language texts: a '*Turcken puechlein*', 'A useful discussion composed … for the improvement of Christian order and life' (probably printed in Basel in 1522);[24] an 'Extract from a letter from one living in Turkey written to his friend in this country [i.e. Germany]' (printed in Augsburg, Nuremberg and Würzburg

---

[21]   Jonas, *Das siebend Capitel Danielis*, fol. Eii[v]. Daniel notes that an 'appreciation of practical virtue among Muslims' was quite widespread even in the medieval period, and that 'there was in the West some knowledge that Islam was a system of positive requirements, and not only a series of relaxations': *Islam and the West*, 228. However, this emphasis on moral virtue was regarded critically by Protestants, who were suspicious of anything that suggested justification by works. Jonas remarked that the Qur'ān 'setzet etliche viel gebot von eusserlichen wercken und Gottes diensten': *Das siebend Capitel Danielis*, fol. Eii[r].

[22]   See, for instance, *Warhaffte beschreibung | wie der Sophi auß Persia den Türcken erlegt | die Statt Babilonia eingenōmen | auch was Glauben | Sitten | und Kriegsrüstung er im brauch habe. Item wie der Türck | nach dem der Barbarossa auß Aphrica vertriben | all sein macht wider die Christen zusetzen willens ist | Auch auß was ursach er sein fürnämsten Hauptman Abraim Bassa erstochen hatt* ([Augsburg]?, 1536).

[23]   Pippidi, *Visions of the Ottoman World*, 80–1.

[24]   *Turcken puechlein. Ein Nutzlich Gesprech oder vnnderrede etlicher personen zu besserung Cristlicher ordenung vn[d] lebens gedichtet. Jn die schweren leüff dieser vnser zeyt dienstlich* ([Basel]?. 1522). Göllner lists three editions, all printed in 1522: *Turcica*, 1: 102–5 (nos 172–4).

in 1526);[25] 'A disputation or conversation between two stable-boys who were with the ambassador of the king's majesty to the Turkish emperor in Constantinople … describing all the normal habits, usages, faith, order and landscape' (possibly printed in Augsburg, perhaps in 1531);[26] and the 'Copy of a letter from Constantinople' (1539) introduced above. All were popular texts written for a German-speaking (and -reading) audience; they are distinctive in their claims to offer direct knowledge of the Turks, and in particular of how the Turks treat those of other faiths.

The *Turcken puechlein*, first published 1522, is set in the environs of 'Greek Wissenburg' (Belgrade), which had been conquered by the Turks on 28 August 1521. It takes the form of a discussion between four protagonists: a Turk, a Gypsy (*Zigeuner*), a Hermit (*Einsiedler*) and a Hungarian. The Turk and the Gypsy are walking together when they encounter the Hermit and the Hungarian. The Turk suggests to the Gypsy that they should tell the other two how well treated Christians will be under the Turks. The Gypsy objects: 'Is that true? I would be surprised if his majesty has been merciful to the Christian dogs.' But the Turk responds that on the recommendation of the sultan's 'wise men' he wants to offer a positive account: 'so that a rumour will be heard and spread amongst Christians that his majesty is not so hard and tyrannical to the Christian as they are often told'.[27] The Christians should be led to believe that if the Turks were to take over they would be left to live and practise their faith in peace. The Gypsy protests that it is the powerful who have the say in Turkish lands. 'You should not say that to the Christians', responds the Turk: 'If you want to

---

[25] *Auszug eines Briefes wie einer so in der Türckey wonhafft seinem Freund in dise land geschrieben und angezeygt was das Türckich regiment und wesen sey uñ wie er es mit den landen so er erobert zuhaltenn pfligt: kürtzlich in Teutsch sprach gepracht, nutzlich diser zeyt zu wissen* ([Würzburg]?, 1526). Göllner lists four editions printed in 1526 with a further two printed in 1543 and 1547: *Turcica*, 1: 136–8, 381, 409 (nos 246–9, 813, 874).

[26] Benedict Curipeschitz, *Ein Disputation oder Gesprech zwayer Stalbüben, So mit Künigklicher Maye. Botschafft bey dem Türckischen Keyser zù Constantinopel gewesen* ([Augsburg, 1531]?). A facsimile edition with transcript of the text, introduction and commentary by Gerhard Neweklowsky (Klagenfurt, 1998) has also been consulted. References are to the folios of the sixteenth-century edition, followed by the page numbers of the facsimile/transcript in brackets.

[27] *Turcken puechlein*, fol. A3^{r-v}. For the sake of clarity, I have translated 'Maiestat' and 'Keyser' as 'sultan' when it is referring to the Turkish leader, and 'emperor' when it refers to the German.

catch birds, you do not frighten them first.'[28] The remainder of the depicted discussion is presumably intended to be read in the light of this initial dialogue which establishes that not all that the Turk and the Gypsy are saying to the Hermit and the Hungarian – that is, to the Christians – can be trusted.[29]

Offered this rosy vision of Christian life under the Turks, the two Christians are in any case not persuaded. The Turkish emperor and his predecessors, protests the Hungarian, have already destroyed two Christian empires, based in Trebizond and in Constantinople, and ten Christian kingdoms, the homes of 'the Greeks and other oriental Christians'.[30] The Hermit recounts his experience of being a prisoner of the Turks for ten years, and the contradiction between the 'good words and many promises' made to the prisoners and the actual treatment of them.[31] After some inconclusive debate about the situation of Christians under the Turks, the protagonists turn to history, and the Turk explains how wars against the Turks had helped 'Emperor Conrad, the second of that name and Emperor Frederick the first ... and also other emperors' to establish their territories.[32] 'Oh God', replies the Hermit, 'that is the truth, for all our history books also tell of it.'[33] The Gypsy criticizes the pope and other bishops for leading Christians into war. The Hermit acknowledges that clergy and religious are meant to exercise patience, although he sees no reason why Christians should not take up the sword when necessary.

Pushed by the Turk to explain the reasons for wars between Christians, the Hungarian praises the skill of Christian soldiers, particularly the Germans.[34] The Gypsy suggests that the Bohemians were defeated by the Turks because 'a hundred years ago

---

[28] Ibid., fol. A3^v.

[29] This pamphlet thus introduces its readers first to the twist in the tale, in a manner reminiscent of much Renaissance drama. Its rhetorical structure has proved too complex for some commentators: thus in the *LW* introduction to Luther's treatise 'On War against the Turk', Robert C. Schultz holds it to argue that 'if Europeans did not resist, they would find that the Turks were gentle masters': *LW* 46, 157. Schultz seems here to have misread the *WA* introduction to 'On War against the Turk': *WA* 30/2, 85–6.

[30] *Turcken puechlein*, fol. B^r.

[31] Ibid., fol. Bii^r .

[32] Ibid., fol. [Biv]^r.

[33] Ibid., fol. [Biv]^v.

[34] Ibid., fols [Biv]^v–C^r.

they fell away from Christian obedience'. The Hungarian disagrees: they simply adopted – or returned to – practices which other Christians had always retained, so that 'today, like the Oriental and Greek Orthodox churches, they still enjoy the Holy Sacraments in both kinds', have abandoned fasting on Fridays, and do not accept the authority of the pope above that of the other patriarchs.[35] The Turk and the Hungarian agree that 'disloyal Venetians' and the former crusading orders have caused more problems amongst the peoples of the Mediterranean than the Turks,[36] and the Hungarian admits that their 'divisions' do the Christians no favours.[37] The Hermit concludes that it would be better in sermons to call for Christian unity and morality than for war against the Turks.[38]

This is a complex text, offering its reader insights – albeit somewhat idiosyncratic – into the history and military capabilities of both the European and Mediterranean lands. Its underlying message is that Christian Europe, disunited and weakened by religious strife, should unite. The depiction of the Turks is not unambiguously negative, although the introductory section alerts the reader to the lack of sincerity in the Turk's claim about the tolerance of his countrymen and their authorities. There is real concern with the situation of Christians living under Turkish rule. The text is concerned to dismiss as a rumour what Fraser and others believe to represent reality: 'usually the Ottomans respected the customs and institutions of subject communities, which were ruled with the aid of their own authorities'.[39] A striking aspect is the presentation of the Turk and the Gypsy as closely allied, an association which is consistent with Crowe's observation that in the face of the Turkish threat, Romani and Gypsies were 'increasingly seen as spies and something of a Turkish fifth column' or as 'incendiaries, soldiers or spies'.[40]

[35] Ibid., fols Cᵛ–Diiiᵛ.
[36] Ibid., fols Diiiᵛ–[Div]ʳ.
[37] Ibid., fol. Gᵛ.
[38] Ibid., fols Giiʳ–ᵛ.
[39] Angus Fraser, *The Gypsies* (Oxford, 1992), 173; cf. also David M. Crowe, *A History of the Gypsies of Eastern Europe and Russia*, 2nd edn (Basingstoke, 2007), 2–3.
[40] Crowe, *History*, xvii, 71; cf. Fraser, *Gypsies*, 85–6. There has been little historical research on the Gypsies; what exists often 'views Gypsies and other itinerant groups as criminal, marginal and poor': Luc Lucassen, Wim Willems and Annemarie Cottaar, *Gypsies and other Itinerant Groups: A Socio-Historical Approach* (London, 1998), 1–2, quotation at 2.

This association between Turks and Gypsies also features in the relatively short 'Letter from one living in Turkey', published in 1526. The letter claims to be written by a craftsman who, after serving his apprenticeship in Ulm, had travelled to Hungary and thence to Turkey. There he found work with a 'stalwart man, whom I served so well that he gave me the hand of one of his daughters in marriage'; he also served the emperor's captains so well that he acquired significant wealth.[41] This, however, means that he is trapped in Turkey, for under Turkish law, he claims, '[n]either I, nor any man in Turkey, can claim that his goods are his; rather they belong to our Lord the Emperor and are only for the use of the owner.'[42] The purported author writes of his interest in Turkey and the Turks, but observes that his attempts to learn about Turkish customs have not been appreciated: 'In the German land you have freedom', he comments; 'I wish to God that I could have such freedom.'[43] Moreover, whilst he affirms that in Turkey everyone is allowed to believe what they like, in practice preaching or gatherings of those of other faiths are not allowed; children have to be brought up in the 'Turkish faith'; and Christians are so hated and persecuted that 'in time the Christian faith will be entirely extinguished and eradicated amongst young and old'.[44] On the positive side, however, he claims that there is no robbery in Turkey, and the emperor's subjects are obedient – even to the point of death. Up to this point, the letter offers fictionalized evidence for the possibility of some form of Christian and Turkish coexistence.

In the final section of the letter, its mood changes. The author reports on the Turkish strategy for conquest: rather than killing local people themselves, the Turks encourage the natives' 'historic enemies' to do so. Consequently, he urges his readers to beware of those who live in their country, who might be roused by the Turks to kill them: 'I would grant to the German lands and Christendom, that they should not put up with the Gypsies or unknown people of whom no one knows what they do, or who are idle, but should hang them from the trees, for they are nothing but your traitors.'[45]

---

[41] *Auszug eines Briefes*, fol. Aii^r.
[42] Ibid.
[43] Ibid., fol. Aii^v.
[44] Ibid., fols Aii^v–Aiii.
[45] Ibid., fols B^v–Bii^r.

This text not only offers a largely negative picture of the situation of Christians living under the Turks but also, like the *Turcken puechlein*, presents the Gypsies as both complicit with the Turks and a potential threat to Western Christians. This reflects prevailing attitudes to a group which had introduced a certain measure of pluralism into the societies of the Holy Roman Empire. Legislation against the Gypsies was promulgated across the German empire from 1497 onwards, indicating the growing concerns about the role played by Gypsies.[46] It may have been known that under the Turks some Gypsies had converted to Islam.[47] Fear of the external other – the Turks – shades into an exhortation to exterminate the internal other – the Gypsies.

The author of the 'Disputation … between two stable-boys' is named as Benedict Curipeschitz, a historical figure who served as interpreter to a Hungarian and Bohemian embassy to Constantinople.[48] Here, he claims to report on a conversation he had overheard on his travels. In his introduction Curipeschitz asserts that he found that 'most of the subjects of the Turks are Christians over whom the Turks reign with great tyranny'; that Christian children are brought up in the Turkish faith; and that the Turk 'builds and holds his land with Christians and the children of Christians', a situation which he views as 'a rightful punishment by God' for the sins of the Christians.[49] The conversation between the stable-boys – referred to as the elder and the younger – opens with a discussion of just how many 'true Turks' there really are: they conclude that there are not many, and that the rest of the

---

[46] Fraser, *Gypsies*, 85–6; 90–1, citing sanctions issued by the Holy Roman Empire in 1497, 1498 and 1500, and local ordinances promulgated in the empire, the Swiss Confederation and Geneva in the early sixteenth century; cf. Donald Kenrick, *Historical Dictionary of the Gypsies (Romanies)*, 2nd edn (Lanham, MD, 2007), xxi, xxxviii–xxxix, 96, 271; also Crowe, *History*, who documents anti-Gypsy legislation in Moravia in 1538 (34) and the 'institution of Gypsy slavery' in fifteenth- and sixteenth-century Romania (109–10). In Royal or Imperial Hungary, although Gypsies became increasingly isolated, there was some appreciation of Gypsy talents as smiths, as musicians and as soldiers (71).

[47] Crowe notes that in Bulgaria, 'the Turks divided the Gypsies into nomadic Moslems and settled Christians': *History*, 2.

[48] This is historically plausible. Neweklowsky notes that Curipeschitz was matriculated in Vienna in 1508 and in 1525 appears as a public lawyer in Ljubljana: Gerhard Neweklowsky, 'Einführung', in Curipeschitz, *Ein Disputation*, 13–14. He also gives details of the embassy, including other participants and its route: ibid. 14–18.

[49] Curipeschitz, *Ein Disputation*, fols [A]ᵛ–Aiiʳ ([2]–[4])

population, and particularly 'the farmers and the subjects' – not to mention most of the Janissaries, the sultan's household troops – are really Christians.[50] However, the children of Christians in lands conquered by Turkey, for instance Bosnia, have been brought up in the 'Turkish faith' and have no knowledge of Christianity.[51] They observe that children fathered by Turkish men with captured Christian women are valued and Christian women are held to be 'much more faithful' than Turkish women.[52] 'How many wives may a Turk have?' asks the younger. 'As many as he can support', replies the elder. The sultan has 'several hundred'.[53]

The grooms consider whether the peoples from the lands bordering Turkey, including Wallachians, Serbs, Bulgarians and Greeks, are really Christians. The younger objects that '[t]hey only have St Paul's faith, and therefore I do not hold them to be true Christians.' The elder, in contrast, offers a credal affirmation: 'They believe in God, who created heaven and earth, and in Jesus Christ, that he was born of Mary; they have their churches and priests and there is no difference in the mass: I hold them to be good Christians.'[54] The grooms conclude that the disunity of the Christians is one of the reasons for their inability to repel the Turkish invasion: the Christians have too many leaders, and their subjects are not obedient, but they are also not practised in war and too used to a comfortable life.[55] Moreover, the divisions amongst the Christians, particularly over Luther's teachings, have moved God to punishment:

> The younger: May God give Luther a bad year, for he is the cause of our misfortunes. If the errors of faith were not so great, I would have hope that the Christians could do something about the powerful Turkish advance, as they did in Austria and Hungary.

[50]   Ibid., fols Aii[v]–Aiii[v], Biii[v] ([5]–[7], [14]).

[51]   Ibid., fol. [Aiv][v] ([8]).

[52]   Ibid. fols C[v]–Cii[r] ([18]–[19]).

[53]   Ibid. fol. Cii[r] ([19]).

[54]   Ibid., fols [Aiiii][v]–B[r] ([8]–[9]).

[55]   Ibid., fol. C[r] ([17]). The boys list the kings of Constantinople and Bulgaria (Wulgaria), the Despot ('König Dispoten') of Serbia, Duke Pavolvić of East Bosnia, and the kings of Bosnia (Wossen) and Croatia (Krabathen) as having been defeated; now Hungary is threatened: ibid., fol. C[v] ([18]). For the identification of the rulers, see Neweklowsky, 'Einführung', 39.

The elder. It is true. Had the pope and our clergy had the word of God and paid more attention to trying to bring salvation to poor Christian souls than to filling their purses, Luther would have had no reason to write against them.

The younger: If Luther had stopped at that, and written about clerical abuses and not against the faith, he would have been much praised; but now he is causing a lot of trouble.

The elder: In sum, God is plaguing us, and is angry with the Christians, so the punishment will not stop yet.[56]

Instead, Christians should stand together: in theory, the stable boys think, 'Every emperor is the defender of the whole of Christendom', but the emperor has betrayed this responsibility by allowing Christians to be defeated in Belgrade, Rhodes and Hungary.[57] And although, as the younger observes, '[t]hose who are of Lutheran faith still hold together', in the opinion of the elder, they do this in the wrong way and for the wrong reasons:

How [do they hold together]? In that they try to drive out the priests and the bishops, but when have they ever thought out of Christian love, which is what their faith is about, to help the poor suffering Christians in Turkey or to help prevent so many Christians being driven out of their homes, away from their goods, wives and children?[58]

The boys also discuss the Turks' faith. The elder reports that the Turks believe in God, who has created heaven and earth, and that Muḥammad is a prophet. Their '*pfaffen*' ('pastors') 'shout every day from the tower', in the morning, at nine, at noon, 'at the time of vespers and in the evening at the time of the Ave Maria', to remind 'the people and the Turks' that they should think of God and pray for the extermination of the Christians. They also pray every day in their 'churches' and particularly on Thursdays and Fridays, 'crying strange cries and swaying with their bodies'. Confession, he explains, takes the form of a ritual bathing or washing. The Turks do good works: they build hostels or caravanserai for travellers, and

---

[56] Curipeschitz, *Ein Disputation*, fol. D^r ([25]).
[57] Ibid., fol. D^v ([26]).
[58] Ibid., fols D^v–Dii^r ([26]–[27]).

wells, besides roads, good bridges and beautiful baths.[59] 'But none of that helps', comments the younger stable-boy, 'for they do not believe in Christ, the only Son of God. And so their tyrannical nature will have to suffer in hell.' The elder boy agrees, but reminds the younger: 'We are evil, and that is why God punishes us with evil.'[60] The grooms observe also that for the Turks, the conquering of Christian lands, and particularly the conversion of a Christian to Islam, are good works.[61]

Curipeschitz's account is written by someone who had been to the Turkish court and had some understanding of what he had seen. And yet, as in the *Turcken puechlein*, the underlying message of Curipeschitz's dialogue is clear: Christians should forget their differences, whether between Lutherans and Catholics or Eastern and Western Christianity, hold together and focus on their shared faith. This will help them to oppose the conquering campaigns of the Turks.

Although these four texts are less overtly polemical than many of the anti-Turkish pamphlets, and despite their purported intention of communicating information about the Turks, their faith and their interactions with Christians, none of them yields much actual knowledge about the Turks and their religion. All suggest that Christianity will be suppressed under the Turks. The details of the Turks' faith appear to be of no interest to the authors of either the *Turcken puechlein* or the 'Letter from one living in Turkey', whilst the 'Letter from Constantinople' presents an idealized image of a Qur'ān which if read properly will show the truth of Christianity. Only Curipeschitz's dialogue makes any attempt to describe the faith of the Turks, and this is not the central interest. Rather, the texts serve to warn Christian readers of their fate under the Turks. That in two of the texts, the *Turcken puechlein* and the 'Letter from one living in Turkey', the enemy without – the Turks – is associated with a stranger within – the Gypsies – serves only to increase their polemical impact, highlighting the dangers to which Christians are exposed when they seek to live together with those of other faiths or from other cultures. To some extent, then, these texts do, as Göllner suggests, exhort the Christians to resist the

---

[59] Ibid., fols Cii^r–^v ([19]–[20]).
[60] Ibid., fol. Cii^v ([20]).
[61] Ibid., fols Cii^v–Ciii^r ([20]–[21]).

Turks, but this is not a simple message of war, for the Christians are also encouraged to trust in their own faith: God will either assist them to overcome and perhaps convert the Turkish invaders, or will give the Turks victory as a sign of his wrath. They are negative but not purely so; there are hints here of the beginnings of a cultural interest in Turkey and in Islam which might transcend the merely polemical and antagonistic. Perhaps most significantly, these texts hold up a mirror to their Christian readers, demanding that they look beyond their theological and religious differences and find unity. For only then can they stand firm against the Turkish invasion. Religious diversity, all four of these texts suggest, fosters weakness in the face of the invader, particularly an invader of another faith.

University of Glasgow

ENGLAND AND RELIGIOUS PLURALITY: HENRY STUBBE, JOHN LOCKE AND ISLAM

by NABIL MATAR

The Elizabethan Settlement identified religious conformity with political allegiance. Not unlike the *cuius regio eius religio* of the 1555 Peace of Augsburg in the Holy Roman Empire, from 1559 onwards subjects in England had to subscribe to the two Acts of Supremacy and Uniformity, the first declaring the monarch as head of the state and the second determining worship under the monarch as head of the Church. In such an Anglican monarchy, there could be no legal space for the non-Anglican subject, let alone for the non-Christian. The few Marranos (Jews forcibly converted to Christianity) lived as Portuguese immigrants, at the same time that Protestant Dutch and Walloon traders congregated in stranger churches, and whilst they were allowed to worship in their own languages, they remained outsiders to the English/Anglican polity.[1]

After the Restoration of Charles II in 1660, the old religious order was restored with a vengeance, as parliamentary acts curtailed the freedom and livelihood of Dissenters: the Corporation Act (1661), the Act of Uniformity (1662, resulting in the St Bartholomew ejection), the Conventicle Act (1664), the Five Mile Act (1665) and the Second Conventicle Act (1670).[2] In the shadow of this 'Great Persecution', clergy and laymen struggled to redefine the relationship between the Anglican monarchy and

---

[1] For a collection of essays on 'strangers' in England, see Randolph Vigne and Charles Littleton, eds, *From Strangers to Citizens: The Integration of Immigrant Communities in Britain, Ireland, and Colonial America 1550–1750* (London, 2001); the essays in parts I and II focus on the stranger churches; the essays in part V focus on the non-Christian 'others'. See also Alexandra Walsham, *Charitable Hatred: Tolerance and Intolerance in England, 1500–1700* (Manchester, 2006); Andrew Spicer, '"Of no church": Immigrants, *liefhebbers* and Confessional Diversity in Elizabethan London, *c.*1568–1581', in Isabel Karremann, Cornel Zwierlein and Inga Mai Groote, eds, *Forgetting Faith? Negotiating Confessional Conflict in Early Modern Europe* (Berlin, 2012), 199–220; and references in Matthew Dimmock, 'Converting and Not Converting "Strangers" in Early Modern London', *Journal of Early Modern History* 17 (2013), 457–78.
[2] For a summary of 'the Principal Penal and Test Acts, 1660–1714', see A. A. Skeaton, *The Theory of Toleration under the Later Stuarts* (Cambridge, 1911), 335–40.

Dissenters.[3] Whether there was a move towards an 'open society', as John Coffey suggests, is not clear, since whatever toleration or comprehension was discussed was nearly always in regard to Christian denominations and not to religious groups outside Christianity.[4] In the 1640s there had been some calls for tolerating non-Christians,[5] but opposition had been strong, and in an imaginary dialogue, *Liberty of Conscience confuted,* an anonymous writer pitted the French anti-papal jurist Jean Bodin (1530–96) against the Ottoman sultan. Bodin had accepted the principle of religious plurality in his *Colloquium heptaplomeres* (*Colloquium of the Seven, c.*1588), in which men of seven religions recognize their similarity, but he was more interested in theological harmony than political rights. The author of the dialogue, putting words into the mouth of Ottoman policy, disagreed: 'Where there are two factions for Religion, there must of necessity be two heads to enliven and dispence sence and motion to the two bodies … [but] a Kingdome at the same time cannot have two absolute Kings, much lesse two Religions.'[6]

Nonetheless, a few years later, in 1655, Oliver Cromwell admitted some Jews to England, raising millenarian expectations among those eager to convert them.[7] At the same time, British trade in the Islamic Mediterranean was flourishing, with large maritime

---

3   The best history of toleration in England until 1660 remains W. K. Jordan, *The Development of Religious Toleration in England,* 3 volumes (Gloucester, MA, 1965; first publ. 1932). See also John Coffey, *Persecution and Toleration in Protestant England, 1558–1689* (New York, 2000); Walsham, *Charitable Hatred.*

4   Coffey, *Persecution and Toleration,* 179–82.

5   Leonard Busher's treatise *Religious Peace: Or a Plea for Liberty of Conscience,* which had first appeared in 1614, was republished in 1646. The treatise had included a request to King James and to Parliament 'to permit all sorts of Christians; yea, Jews, Turks, and pagans, so long as they are peaceable', to live in Britain: ibid. 6. Although the Presbyterian establishment denounced such toleration, there was support from sectaries and other non-establishment groups. A few months after the publication of the treatise, William Walwyn, one of the leaders of the Leveller movement, proposed toleration of all religions, including 'Turks' and pagans: William Walwyn, *A Demurre to the Bill for Preventing the Growth and Spreading of Heresie* ([London], 1646), 3.

6   Anon., *Liberty of Conscience Confuted: By Arguments of Reason and Policie. Delivered in a Discourse betwixt a Turke, and a Christian. Occasioned by a Letter written to a Peere of this Realme* ([London], 1648), 15. Bodin's Muslim interlocutor, Octavius, suggested the need for adjustment. As Marion Leathers Daniels Kuntz notes, the manuscript of the *Colloquium* was rare in the seventeenth century, but John Milton had a copy: *Colloquium of the Seven about Secrets of the Sublime* (Princeton, NJ, 1975), lxix.

7   The most complete study remains David Katz, *Philo-Semitism and the Readmission of the Jews to England, 1603–1655* (Oxford, 1982).

and commercial investments by the East Levant Company. Various Ottoman and Moroccan ambassadors, and a few charlatans, visited England, and there were treaties with the North African regencies stipulating that as Englishmen could practise their Christianity freely in Tripoli or Algiers, so could Muslims practise Islam in Portsmouth or London.[8] Furthermore, publications about the Ottoman polity by both visitors and chroniclers described the secure place determined by Qur'ānic law for Christians and Jews to live, work and worship. In the light of these developments, the question came to the fore of whether or not Jews and Muslims could be tolerated in the Anglican polity; until 1685 and the revocation of the Edict of Nantes, France was 'the only country in western Europe to have constitutionally guaranteed toleration of religious minorities'.[9] Could non-Christians have legal rights in England, and not just the protection of the ruler, be that Cromwell or the Stuart monarch?

Two writers furnished original and different answers to the question: Henry Stubbe and John Locke. The two men were exact contemporaries: both were born in 1632, studied at Westminster School, matriculated at Christ Church, Oxford, and were pupils of the orientalist Edward Pococke; indeed, both were at Christ Church between 1656 and 1660, Stubbe as a librarian at the Bodleian, and Locke from 1652 as the beneficiary of a studentship (effectively a life fellowship), taking his BA in 1656 and his MA in 1658. In 1659, Stubbe published *An Essay in Defence of the good old Cause*, a treatise in which he argued for the toleration of Quakers and Catholics. Locke liked it, although he disagreed over the toleration of Catholics, and he wrote to Stubbe, praising him for showing how 'men of different professions may quietly unite under the same government and unanimously carry the same civil interest and hand in hand march to the same end of peace and

---

[8]   For some of the treaties, see *Articles of Peace between his Sacred Majesty Charles II, King of Great Britain, France and Ireland, and the City and Kingdom of Algiers* (London, 1664); *Articles of Peace between the Most Serene and Mighty Prince Charles II … and the Most Excellent Signors, Mahomet Bashaw, the Duan of the Noble City of Tunis … the fifth of October 1662* (London, 1677); *Articles of Peace & Commerce between the most Serene and Mighty Prince Charles II … and the most illustrious Lords, the Bashaw, Dey, Aga, and Governours of the Famous City and Kingdom of Algiers in Barbary* (London, 1682).

[9]   Henry Kamen, *The Rise of Toleration* (New York, 1967), 197, although the Edict of Nantes was specific to French Protestants.

mutual society though they take different ways towards heaven'.[10] He signed off as his 'admirer'.

Locke first mentioned Muslims after reading an anonymous treatise by Edward Bagshaw (also of Westminster School and Christ Church), *The Great Question concerning Things Indifferent in Religious Worship* (1660). As an Independent, Bagshaw hoped that the restored king would confirm the toleration he had promised in the Declaration of Breda (4 April 1660). Bagshaw feared that toleration would extend to the Presbyterians who would be enticed into the Anglican establishment (if not into its communion) and leave out smaller groups, so he stated at the outset of the treatise that just as the magistrate did not force the Muslims or the Jews to forsake their religion, so he should not force Dissenters away from their practices and beliefs. In his reply to Bagshaw in December 1660, *Whether the Civil Magistrate may lawfully impose and determine the Use of Indifferent Things in reference to Religious Worship*, Locke accepted the political logic in regard to non-Christian subjects: he believed that no man could 'be required to believe what was not presented to him to believe'. But whilst the magistrate had no authority in determining religion, Locke thought that he did have authority in 'indifferent' matters, those rites and ceremonies that were neither part of natural law nor of divine revelation.[11] Logically, therefore, it would not be 'unlawful' for the magistrate 'to prescribe either time or place or habit to a Mahomedan for his worship if his Alcoran hath left them undetermined'.[12]

Locke was trying to bring Islamic and Dissenting practices under one authority in the area of matters he believed to be theologically 'indifferent'. The reference to time and place clearly points to worship in an Anglican church, rather than a conventicle whose members determined when and where they wanted to worship; the reference to habit is to the surplice which the Anglican priest wore and which Nonconformists decried as popish. That Locke should compare these 'indifferent' matters with the 'Mahomedan' code reveals his limited knowledge of Muslim worship: whilst the

---

[10] John Locke, *Essays on the Law of Nature*, ed. W. von Leyden (Oxford, 1965), 243.

[11] See the discussion of the history of 'indifferent things' in John Locke, *Epistola de Tolerantia: A Letter on Toleration*, ed. Raymond Klibansky, transl. J. W. Gough (Oxford, 1968), 157–9.

[12] John Locke, *Two Tracts, on Government*, ed. and intro. Philip Abrams (Cambridge, 1967), 130.

Qur'ān does not restrict 'place', except in direction to Mecca, the Sunna, the secondary but equally important source of law in Islam, enjoins worship with the community in the mosque; whilst the Qur'ān does not establish a firm schedule of worship ('time'), the Sunna does. Neither the Qur'ān nor the Sunna mentions a prayer 'habit', although the Qur'ān prescribes ablution and the Sunna prostration.[13] Locke equated the authority of the Bible in Christian worship with the authority of the Qur'ān in Muslim worship. Either he was being a purist – arguing for the sole authority of the Qur'ān in the manner that Protestants argued for *sola scriptura* without the accretions of (Catholic) traditions – or he was ignorant of the place of the Sunna in Islamic theology. In either case, he was consistent in his argument: the magistrate did not control religion, only 'indifferent' practices.[14]

In 1667 Locke changed his views to favour the toleration of Dissenters. In his *Essay on Toleration*, which he did not publish, he used Bagshaw's exact premises to defend Dissenters and to separate 'religious form from civil performances'.[15] Since non-Christians (in this case Locke was referring to the Jews) were tolerated in England, so should Dissenters be.[16] Jewish immigrants had already begun to organize their religious life in London,[17] and so he continued by

---

[13] See, however, Richard Simon, who had mentioned 'habit' specifically: *The Critical History of the Religions and Customs of the Eastern Nations, written in French by the learned Father Simon* (London, 1685), 161.

[14] The most recent discussion of Locke and Muslims appears in Denise A. Spellberg, *Thomas Jefferson's Qur'an: Islam and the Founders* (New York, 2013), ch. 2. Spellberg points out that my statement in 'John Locke and the "Turbanned Nations"', *Journal of Islamic Studies* 2 (1991), 67–77, at 76, about Locke presenting the 'first favorable pronouncement about the status of Muslims in Christian England', should be qualified and should take account of Thomas Helwys (*c.*1550–1616), the Baptist minister, in his *A Short Declaration of the Mystery of Iniquity* (Amsterdam, 1612), and Roger Williams (1603–83) in his *The Bloody Tenet of Persecution* (London, 1644): both these works made passing remarks to 'Turks'. See the discussion of English writers advocating toleration for Muslims in my 'The Toleration of Muslims in Renaissance England: Practice and Theory', in John C. Laursen, ed., *Religious Toleration from Cyrus to Defoe: The Variety of Rites* (New York, 1999), 127–46. Spellberg also engages with John Marshall, *John Locke, Toleration and Early Enlightenment Culture* (Cambridge, 2006), 371–96.

[15] John Gerald Anglim, *Locke and Toleration* (Cambridge, MA, 1975), 108.

[16] Carlo Augusto Viano, ed., *Scritti editi e inediti sulla toleranza* (Turin, 1961), 86. Bagshaw, however, had come to realize that the parallel between non-Christians and Dissenters was risky and in his sequel, *The Second Part of the Great Question concerning Things Indifferent in Religious Worship* (London, 1661), he disregarded it.

[17] H. S. Q. Henriques, *The Jews and the English Law* (Clifton, NJ, 1974; first publ. 1908), 126; see also my 'John Locke and the Jews', *JEH* 44 (1993), 45–62.

denouncing religious persecution, alluding to the ineffectiveness of force in matters of faith. As an example, he mentioned English captives who returned from galley slavery among the 'Mahometans', having obstinately defied all pressures to convert.[18] Two years later, in 1669, Locke wrote the constitution for the new colony of Carolina, which laid down that conversionary effort should be meek and humble, especially towards Jews and the heathens.[19]

As Locke became active in London's political and colonial affairs, his old correspondent Henry Stubbe began writing his treatise on *The Originall & Progress of Mahometanism* (c. 1671–5).[20] Times in England were turbulent, especially after King Charles II had issued his Declaration of Indulgence in March 1672, granting toleration to Dissenters and Catholics, bringing on him the disaffection of the Anglican establishment. In support of the king, Stubbe published a lengthy treatise, *A Justification of the Present War against the United Netherlands wherein the Declaration of His Majesty is vindicated*, in which he showed the parallels between King Charles and Emperors Constantine and Theodosius, and particularly how all three rulers had the authority and right to determine religion in the state. In similar manner, staunch Anglicans such as Edward Stillingfleet and John Tillotson defended the magistrate's supremacy over Dissenters and Catholics (depending on the political climate). However, having been forced by the opposition to break the Great Seal of the Indulgence a year later (7 March 1673), and giving up on toleration, Charles began to gravitate toward the Anglican party created by the Earl of Danby, which 'necessarily involved the strict enforcement of uniformity in religion and [granted] no toleration either for Roman Catholics or for Protestant dissenters'.[21]

In reaction, Stubbe turned to the Islamic model of polity as first established in Medina. In *The Originall & Progress of Mahometanism*, he showed how Muḥammad, combining religion with political power, prepared the ground for an Islamic empire that allowed for coexistence with Christians and Jews. Uniquely among European writers debating toleration, Stubbe invoked the 'great Prophet'

---

[18] Viano, ed., *Scritti sulla toleranza*, 98.

[19] *The Constitutions of Carolina* (London, 1670).

[20] See my introduction to *Henry Stubbe and the Beginnings of Islam* (New York, 2013). The first edition of Stubbe's work appeared in Lahore in 1911, edited by Mahmud Khan Shairani.

[21] Richard Boyer, *English Declarations of Indulgence, 1687 and 1688* (The Hague, 1968), 24.

Muḥammad, who had consolidated the power of the state without undermining religious plurality. Having read the Old and New Testaments in the light of the Higher Criticism of scholars such as Isaac Casaubon, Claude Salmasius, Gerard Vossius and others, which emphasized textual accuracy and historical content, Stubbe argued that the post-Constantinian doctrines of the Christian Church had not stemmed from the teachings of the gospels but from impe-rial decrees. Epiphanius, whose *Panarion* Stubbe often mentioned, showed how rife with heresy the Jewish and Christian communi-ties were in the centuries before Muḥammad. To make toleration of Muslims possible, Stubbe realized that Christians would have to make theological adjustments: only when the two theologies and their scriptures were drawn closer together would political destabi-lization and civil war, engendered by difference in denominations and religions, come to an end. As Bishop Samuel Parker wrote in *A Discourse of Ecclesiastical Politie* (1670), 'How vain is it to expect Peace and Settlement in a Commonwealth, where their Religion keeps men in a State of War, where Zeal is arm'd against Zeal, and Conscience encounters Conscience'.[22] For Parker, only the authority of the Anglican monarch could ensure religious submis-sion and subsequent peace.

For an alternative, Stubbe turned to Islamic history. Aware that Christians had lived in the Muslim dominions as far back as the beginnings of Islam, Stubbe explained Islam's toleration of Chris-tians by reference to Muḥammad's admiration of Jesus, or as he called him throughout his treatise, 'Isā, the Qur'ānic name. Muḥammad, wrote Stubbe, 'was undoubtedly a great admirer of Isa as a prophet or apostle of God, and of this he makes so great and frequent declarations, and that Isa was his predecessor and taught the same doctrine that it is but justice to style him a Christian'.[23] Indeed, on two occasions in his treatise Stubbe referred to Muḥammad as the 'great Prophet', exactly the same phrase as was used about Jesus in the King James translation of Luke 7: 16. Having shown Islamic acceptance of Jesus (in a non-Trinitarian interpretation), Stubbe turned to examine the two religions of Christianity and Islam from a comparative angle, arguing not that one was superior to the other, but that there was continuity and propinquity between

---

[22] Samuel Parker, *A Discourse of Ecclesiastical Politie* (London, 1670), 158.
[23] *Henry Stubbe*, ed. Matar, 190.

them. Lancelot Addison, who had served as chaplain in Tangier, and who in 1671 published a book about *West Barbary* which Stubbe read, had noted numerous similarities in Jewish, Christian and Muslim religious practices, so much so that he feared that if he elaborated too much on such similarities, 'I might make all Mahumeds Institutions yield some probable Resemblances of those ancient Customs & Ordinances in usage among Jews and Christians'.[24] Stubbe went ahead and showed how many of these 'Institutions' had already been present in Jewish and Christian scriptures.[25]

Stubbe did not stop at this exploration of historical continuity, but turned to examine the scriptural canon which was coming under scholarly scrutiny from the 'Criticks' of the Bible. He had learned from the work of John Gregory, another student of Pococke's at Christ Church and an Arabist, that there were, for instance, early Arabic sources of Christian texts. 'The Mahometans', wrote Gregory, 'have another Lord's Prayer, called by them the Prayer of Jesu the Son of Mary'.[26] This prayer, he explained, appeared in the 'Gospel of the Nazarites, or that secundum Hebraes; (as it used to be called)'.[27] Stubbe concluded that the Arabic texts belonged in a history of an alternative Christian canon: were there other texts, in other languages, that also belonged to the canon, but had been ignored or suppressed?

The answer came in a text that bridged the gap between the Qur'ānic view of the human Christ and the human-divine view of Christian doctrine. These are Stubbe's words at the very end of the first surviving manuscript of the treatise:

> Lastly whereas it is said in the Gospel, 'Except I go hence, the comforter shall not come', this they interpret about Mahomet, and it is one of the names of Mahomet among the Saracens viz, the Comforter.

---

[24] Lancelot Addison, *West Barbary, or, A Short Narrative of the Revolutions of the Kingdoms of Fez and Morocco* (Oxford, 1671), 216.

[25] These included the multiple wives of Solomon, the exterminatory violence of the Israelites against the Amalekites, and the descriptions of the 144,000 virgins in the kingdom of heaven: *Henry Stubbe*, ed. Matar, 201–4.

[26] *The Works of the reverend and learned Mr. John Gregory* (London, 1665), 161.

[27] Ibid.

They say also that the Christians have corrupted their gospels and expunged many passages which gave credit to Mahomet, and that a Christian priest showed them in a true copy to that purpose and said there was another unsophisticated preserved at Paris.[28]

Stubbe does not mention the gospel by name. So to what was he alluding? The association between the Paraclete of John 14: 16 (and elsewhere) and its prophetic application to Muḥammad could be found in the eighth-century *Sīra* or biography of Ibn Hishām and in the work of numerous other Muslim exegetes, and these were known to Pococke and other European scholars. Stubbe, however, knows not just of a reference to Muḥammad as the Paraclete but of a 'gospel': and the only 'gospel' which emphasizes the association between Muḥammad and the Paraclete was the Gospel of Barnabas. Only the *Vero Evangelio die Jesu* (as its Italian title reads) makes that association its theological foundation.

If, therefore, the words of Stubbe refer to the Gospel of Barnabas, he would be the first English writer to mention it before John Toland, and by more than two decades. As Justin Champion has shown, Toland knew of it in the late 1690s, but he only mentioned its discovery in 1707, and then used it extensively in his *Nazarenus* in 1718.[29] In the course of recording references in European texts to the Gospel of Barnabas, Toland wrote: 'The Gospel of BARNABAS is likewise quoted in the Index of the Scriptures, which COTELERIUS has publish'd from the 1789th manuscript of the French King's library'.[30] In 1672 Johannes Baptista Cotelerius had published in Paris *SS Patrum qui temporibus apostolicis*, in the first volume of which he argued for the canonicity of the Epistle of Barnabas, including the 'Evangelium inscriptum nomine Barnabae'.[31] In invoking the Gospel of Barnabas, Stubbe applied the strategy that the Andalusian authors in Spain had used at the end of the sixteenth century. In their fear of expulsion from their homeland, they forged Arabic writings, inscribing them on lead leaves, and claimed that they had been revealed in the first

---

[28] *Henry Stubbe*, ed. Matar, 211.
[29] John Toland, *Nazarenus*, ed. Justin A. I. Champion (Oxford, 1999), 58–9.
[30] Ibid. 137.
[31] Johannes Baptista Cotelerius, *SS Patrum qui temporibus apostolicis*, 2 vols (Paris, 1972), 1: 9.

century and then 'discovered' in the area that came to be known as Sacro Monte, in Granada. These were the 'Lead Books', consisting of a number of gospels, in which Mary and Peter described a Christ without incarnation. Although not among the 'Lead Books', the Gospel of Barnabas was another forgery which presented a Qur'ānic Christ of miracles and power, without incarnation or crucifixion, who spoke openly of the advent of Muḥammad.[32] The authors of these works hoped that by showing Muslim veneration of Mary and Jesus, and by showing that Muḥammad had been prophesied by Jesus, they would create an accommodation that would protect them from expulsion. It did not, and between 1609 and 1614 all Andalusians, derisively called 'Moriscos', were violently driven out from Spain.

With the history of the expulsion of the Andalusians in mind, Stubbe cast his eye on the Christian populations in the Ottoman polity, noting a striking contrast. While Muslims had been expelled from the Christian dominions, the Greeks enjoyed more freedom under Ottoman rulers than they had under previous Byzantine potentates:

> [Y]et it is observed by [Joseph] Scaliger – and it is an assured truth – that the vulgar Greeks live in a better condition under the Turk at present than they did under their own emperors when there were perpetual murders practiced on their princes and tyranny on their people. But they are now secure from injury if they pay their taxes, and it is more the interest of the princes and nobles than of the people at present which keeps all Europe from submitting to the Turks.[33]

Such toleration had been possible because of Islam's recognition

---

[32] The *Libros Plumbeos* were plates of lead on which was inscribed Arabic writing. Only in 1682 did the Vatican officially declare them forgeries: for the history of these books, see L. P. Harvey, 'The Literary Culture of the Moriscos, 1492–1609' (DPhil thesis, Oxford University, 1958); see also T. D. Kendrick, *St. James in Spain* (London, 1960), ch. 5. For the translation and the controversy surrounding them, see L. P. Harvey and G. A. Weigers, 'The Translation from Arabic of the Sacromonte Tablets and the Archbishop of Granada: An Illuminating Correspondence', *Qurtuba* 1 (1996), 59–78. Although the story goes that a priest, Fra Marino, found the Gospel of Barnabas in the library of Pope Pius V (1566–72), there was no reference to it until 1634, when the Andalusian exile Ibrahim al-Tayibi mentioned it, as Harvey and Weigers show.

[33] *Henry Stubbe*, ed. Matar, 179. Joseph Scaliger (1540–1609) was a Protestant biblical and classical scholar whose writings Stubbe consulted regularly.

of Jesus. By making a similar place for Muḥammad in the religious history of monotheism, Stubbe defined the premises for tolerating Muslims in the Christian polity: since veneration of Jesus inspired the Qur'ānic protection of Christians in the Islamic polity, some form of veneration of Muḥammad should open the door for protection of Muslims in the Christian polity. Whether Stubbe would have followed up on this theological approach with a political formulation cannot be determined. He died soon after finishing (but not publishing) his treatise.

No earlier writing had furnished as detailed a history of Islam and its toleration as Stubbe's *Originall* had. Stubbe was the first European writer to show how fundamental religious plurality had been in Islam's foundational theology and how much non-Muslims, Jews and Christians alike, had been accommodated in the peace treaties between the early Arab-Muslim armies and the peoples of the Byzantine Empire. Like Stubbe, Locke had become interested in Islam under the guidance of Edward Pococke. While tutoring Pococke's son, Locke acquired numerous works about Islam, ranging from the French 1647 translation of the Qur'ān to Pococke's own 1663 translation of Abu al-Faraj's *Historia compendiosa dynastiarum*, and numerous other books about the East, including the Latin translation of *Hayy ibn Yaqzan* by the younger Pococke.[34] So when, some time in the mid-1680s, Locke began working on his *Epistola de Tolerantia*, he brought in Muslims in a manner that he had not done in his earlier writings. Although he included them with the non-Christian Jews and pagans, he had to approach them differently given the complexity of their international status.

Locke wrote *Epistola* soon after the accession of the Catholic James II to the throne in 1685.[35] Two years later, James issued the Act of Indulgence, which gave freedom to subjects to 'meet and

[34] He also owned Sir Henry Blount, *Voyage into the Levant* (London, 1650 edn); Francis Osborne, *Political Reflections upon the Government of the Turks* (London, 1656); Addison, *West Barbary*; Sir Paul Rycaut, *L'État present de l'Empire Ottomane* (Rouen, 1677); and Humphrey Prideaux, *The True Nature of Imposture fully display'd in the Life of Mahomet* (London, 1697). See also John Harrison and Peter Laslett, *The Library of John Locke*, Oxford Bibliographical Society (Oxford, 1965), entries 2008, 2064, 2073, 2075, 2128, 2145. Locke also had among his manuscripts 'The Questions of Abdalla Ebn Salam the Jew and answers of Mahomet, written in Arabicke by Abdalla Ebn Abbas, and translated into English by J. G.' (Oxford, Bodl., MS Locke c.27, fols 3ʳ–9ʳ). John Greaves was Locke's friend and another pupil of Pococke's.

[35] It was published anonymously after the Revolution in 1689.

serve God after their own way and manner' as long as they did not 'alienate the hearts of our people from us or our government'. As Houston and Pincus have observed, the Act 'broke the equation of dissent with disloyalty'.[36] So disaffected was the Anglican establishment with this Act that one Anglican writer criticized the king in 1688, saying that the Act had opened the door for the toleration of Muslims,[37] the same toleration for which Locke argued in his yet unpublished *Epistola*. As his treatise shows, Locke was aware that large Christian populations lived in the Islamic world (chiefly in the Ottoman East): Henry Blount included in his travelogue of 1634 a whole section on the varieties of Christian communities in the sultan's dominions; as did Paul Rycaut in his very popular history of the Ottoman Empire of 1668. Many writers, especially Dissenters, described such toleration in glowing terms, including the Quaker William Penn, whose works Locke owned.[38]

In *Epistola*, Locke began the argument for the legalization of the status of Muslims, Jews and pagans in England – began because it was an argument that would gradually develop and reach its conclusion a few years later, in 1692. That he brought the 'pagans' into the picture is important: they had not received significant mention anywhere in his previous writings on toleration, but, as noted above, in the Carolina constitution of 1669 Locke had argued for accommodating them, suggesting that, 'heathen' as they were, they believed in some kind of God. He linked them with the Jews and the Dissenters in the hope of converting them to

---

[36] Alain Craig Houston and Steven C. A. Pincus, *A Nation Transformed: England after the Restoration* (New York, 2001), 15.

[37] See the references to the Anglican documents *An Answer to the City Ministers Letter from his Country Friend* (1688) and *Some Queries concerning Liberty of Conscience* (1688?) in Scott Sowerby, *Making Toleration: The Repealers and the Glorious Revolution* (Cambridge, MA, 2013), 171, 320 n. 65.

[38] In 1670, and writing in defence of toleration, Penn appealed to the examples of 'the very Mahometans of Turkey and Persia' where there was 'variety of opinions', yet they enjoyed 'unity and concord in matters … of a civil importance': 'The Great Case of Liberty of Conscience', in *Select Works of William Penn*, 4th edn, 3 vols (London, 1825), 2: 128–64, at 155. 'The Turks themselves show us', added Penn in 1686, 'that both other religions, and divers sects of their own, are very tolerable with security to their government': 'A Persuasive to Moderation to Church Dissenters', ibid. 2: 504–42, at 539. 'Where do you read', wrote George Fox in 1677, 'that ever the Turks forced any Christians to observe any of their Holy-Dayes, Fasts, or Feasts?': *The Hypocrites Fast and Feast not God's Holyday. Hat-Honour to Men Man's Institution, not God's* (London, 1677), 10. For an overall view of Quakers and Islam, see Justin Meggitt, *Early Quakers and Islam* (Uppsala, 2013), especially ch. 6.

Anglican Christianity.[39] Locke also included Muslims in the toleration debate, although they were unique among the three groups:
only among Muslims did large numbers of Christians live, and
not the other way round, as in the case of Jews and pagans. He
called for the toleration of Muslims as an act of reciprocity: since
Muslims tolerate Christians in the Islamic world, so should Christians tolerate Muslims. Non-toleration of Muslims in Christian
polities, he warned, could have serious ramifications for Christians
in Muslim lands: '[W]hat if to a pagan or a Mahometan prince
the Christian religion seems false and offensive to God? May
not Christians too be extirpated for the same reason and in the
same manner?'[40] As another author put it in the same year (1689),
neither Jews nor 'Mahometans in the Dominions of Christian
Princes' ought to be 'compelled to hear reasons for convincing
and perswading them to embrace' Christianity because 'Christians
would not like to be so treated by them'.[41] Therefore, as a logical
conclusion to his argument in support of toleration of Dissenters,
and in the last pages of his *Epistola*, Locke openly urged the acceptance of 'Pagan', 'Mahometan' and 'Jew': all must be included in the
commonwealth and, along with Socinians, Lutherans and others,
allowed 'assemblies, solemn meetings, celebrations of feast days,
sermons, and public worship'.[42]

The logic of his conclusion infuriated an Oxford don by the
name of Jonas Proast, who promptly wrote a rebuttal attacking
Locke's toleration of the 'different Professions of [the Christian]
Religion'. More objectionable to Proast, however, was Locke's
concluding remarks in regard to non-Christians, and he opened his
treatise, *Argument of the Letter Concerning Toleration, Briefly Consider'd*

---

[39]   *Constitutions of Carolina*, articles 95 and 97, cf. article 96: 'that Jews, heathens, and
other dissenters from the Purity of Christian Religion, may not be scared and kept
at a distance from it, but, by having an Opportunity of acquainting themselves with
the truth and Reasonableness of its Doctrines, and the Peaceableness and inoffensive-
ness of its Professors, may, by good Usage and Perswasion, and all those convincing
Methods of Gentleness and Meekness, suitable to the Rules and Design of the Gospel,
be won ever to embrace and unfeignedly receive the Truth'. For Locke and Native
Indians, see John Farr, 'Locke, "Some Americans", and the Discourse on "Carolina"',
Locke Studies 9 (2009), 19–96; for a discussion of Locke's views on slavery (of North
American pagans), see Mary Nyquist, *Arbitrary Rule: Slavery, Tyranny, and the Power of
Life and Death* (Chicago, IL, and London, 2013), ch. 10.
[40]   Locke, *Epistola*, ed. Klibansky, 115.
[41]   Anon., *Liberty of Conscience* (London, 1689), 11.
[42]   Locke, *Epistola*, ed. Klibansky, 143.

and Answer'd, by showing that Locke wanted to extend toleration to everyone who held 'no Opinions contrary to Civil Society' and who concurred on 'the Duty of tolerating all men in matters of meer religion'.[43] Although the main thrust of his argument was to reject toleration of Dissenters, in his first two pages Proast attacked Locke's call for toleration of non-Christians.[44] Locke, he claimed, had put forward a dangerous view: that 'neither Pagan, nor Mahumetan, nor Jew ought to be excluded from the Civil Rights of the Commonwealth'.[45]

The statement shows that Proast had read William Popple's English translation of Locke's treatise, in which the phrases *jura civilia* and *jus civile* had been rendered as 'civil rights'. Although Locke had not used that phrase in the context of non-Christians – it was Proast who applied it to Muslims and others[46] – he promptly adopted it in his rebuttal of Proast, the *Second Letter Concerning Toleration* (licensed on 24 June 1690). Locke confirmed the 'Civil Rights of the Commonwealth' for 'Pagan, Mahumetan, or Jew',[47] but instead of continuing the discussion of rights, he appealed to a commonly invoked argument: that toleration was the best means to a conversionary end, and admitting non-Christians to live in the Christian polity (of England) would be conducive to their conversion. This was the same argument that he had used in regard to pagans and Jews in the Carolina constitution. But

---

[43] Jonas Proast, *Argument of the Letter Concerning Toleration, Briefly Consider'd and Answer'd* (Oxford, 1690), 1–2.

[44] Curiously, the 'Minister of the Church of England' who published a treatise at the same time as Proast defended toleration, if only by association. In his collection of references and citations from major Anglican divines, the author included Isaac Barrow's treatise on the 'Unity of the Church', in which the latter called for 'general Charity towards all good Christians [Dissenters] and for the pursuit of 'peace with all, without any exception, with men of all Nations, Jewes, and Greeks, and Barbarians': *The Conformists Sayings: or, the Opinion and Arguments of Kings, Bishops; and severall Divines lately assembled in Convocation in Favour of those who Dissent from the present Ceremonies of Publick Worship* (London, 1690), 35.

[45] Proast, *Argument*, 1.

[46] William Popple, *A Letter concerning Toleration* (London, 1689), imprimatur 3 October, 40 ('civil rights'), 46 ('civil right'). For a discussion of the translation of this phrase in the *Epistola*, see Spellberg, *Jefferson's Qur'an*, 76. See Milton's *Readie and Easy Way* (1660): 'The other part of our freedom consists in the civil rights and advanc'ments of every person according to his merit', cited in the *New Oxford English Dictionary*. For Proast's use of the English version, see John Locke, *A Letter concerning Toleration*, ed. and intro. James H. Tully (Indianapolis, IN, 1983), 33, 43.

[47] 'A Second Letter Concerning Toleration', in *The Works of John Locke*, 10 vols (London, 1823, repr. 1963), 6: 59–137, at 62. Locke finished it on 27 May 1690.

now he pushed the argument further: toleration not only allowed non-Christians living in our midst to convert, it also allowed us to preach the doctrines of the 'church of England' in any 'Mahometan, or pagan country'.[48]

Henceforth, in the replies to Proast, Locke focused on Muslims since they constituted the majority population in the countries in which Eastern Christians lived. Locke knew about Anglican missionary efforts already under way in the Levant: Pococke had translated Hugo Grotius's *De Veritate Religionis Christianae* into Arabic in 1660 (*Kitāb al-sharīʿa al-masīḥiyya*), and in 1674 he had translated the Book of Common Prayer too, after which copies were sent to the Ottoman East.[49] However, there had been resistance to the books from Catholic missionaries. As Robert Huntington, the Levant Company chaplain in Aleppo, noted in September 1673: 'I have several of the Grotius's yet by me, rather out of the apprehension I have of the malice of some Christians … than from the unprompted accusation and downright danger by the Turks'.[50] Still, for Locke, toleration in England would open up toleration elsewhere which could prove 'advantageous to true religion', that is, (Anglican) Christianity. How seriously Locke took this missionary effort is not clear, given his later statements about the fragmented nature of Christian communities.[51] But sensing the strength of the toleration-for-conversion argument, he was not unwilling to go along with the possibility of converting Muslims, at least those in England, by using 'civil rights' as inducement.

Finding himself out-argued, Proast decided on blunt confronta-

---

[48] Ibid. 64–5.

[49] See G. J. Toomer, 'Edward Pococke's Arabic Translation of Grotius, *De Veritate*', *Grotiana* 33 (2012), 88–105. Locke owned a copy of the 1680 edition of *De Veritate*, published in Amsterdam.

[50] Quoted by Shireen Khairallah, 'Arabic Studies in England in the Late Seventeenth and Early Eighteenth Centuries' (PhD thesis, University of London, 1972), 50.

[51] Later, in his *Third Letter* to Proast, he reminded the cleric that Christians had to unite: with all the rifts among Protestants in England, and with the polarization that Anglicans such as Proast and others generated, creating thereby a kind of exclusionary national Christianity, Locke recognized the limitedness of the appeal of Christianity to Muslims. A 'rational Turk or infidel', he wrote, could not be expected to convert to a Christianity that was expressed so differently by different denominations. Furthermore, it was not possible to practise 'Des Cartes's way of doubting': no man, asserted Locke, could divest himself of his intellectual background and examine the truth of his religion without bias. For the Muslim was as convinced of his 'Koran' as his 'divine revelation' as the Christian was of his Bible: Locke, 'A Third Letter for Toleration: to the Author of the Third Letter Concerning Toleration', in *Works*, 7: 139–546, at 239.

tion. Granted the imprimatur to publish his *Third Letter Concerning Toleration* on 20 April 1691, Proast stated that the author of *Epistola* (he knew it was Locke although he never mentioned him by name) was asking for nothing less than the endenization of Muslims, using the term for the first time in the exchange: 'endenizen'd'. Significantly, Proast did not use the term 'naturalized' as naturalization was granted through an Act of Parliament, while endenization was by letter patent from the monarch.[52] Still, Proast realized that bringing to the debate the prospect of Muslim and other non-Christian endenization would position Locke against the English writers who were criticizing the endenization and naturalization of foreigners (in many pamphlets, the terms were used together). As in the case of the phrase 'civil rights', so in the case of endenization: Locke latched on to it as a logical conclusion to his argument. Inadvertently, Proast now forced Locke to move the discussion beyond the social parameters of toleration to the legal framework of citizenship.

Discussion of naturalization had begun in England soon after the accession to the throne of the Scottish king, James I. Although naturalization of non-Christians went against the statute of 7 Jacobi, c. 2,[53] during the reign of Charles II some Jews were endenizened, resulting in vociferous opposition, as Samuel Hayne showed in his letter to James II decades later.[54] In 1669, 'The Act for Naturali-

---

[52] 'The king without parliament could not turn an alien into a subject for all purposes. He might for some, but not for all. This doctrine gave rise to the class of persons known as denizens – intermediate between subjects and aliens. The denizen was so made by the king's letters patent, i.e. by an act done by the king without parliament. The limit to the royal power (as I understand it) was this: the person whom the king made a denizen of his realm became capable of acquiring lands by purchase or devise, and of holding them when acquired, and in general he became a subject of the realm, but the king could not make him capable of inheriting. An act of parliament might of course do even this, and Naturalization Acts (I believe) usually did it, but the king could not do it': F. W. Maitland, *The Constitutional History of England* (Cambridge, 1926), 427. See also Max Kohler, 'The Doctrine that "Christianity is a part of the Common Law," and its recent Judicial Overthrow in England, with Particular Reference to Jewish Rights', *Publication of the American Jewish Historical Society* 31 (1928), 105–34, at 119. The most recent discussion of this subject is Irene Scouloudi, ed., *Returns of Strangers in the Metropolis 1593, 1627, 1635, 1639: A Study of an Active Minority*, Huguenot Society Quarto Series 57 (London, 1985).

[53] See the reference in Anon., *The History of Naturalization, with some Remarques upon the Effects thereof, in respect to the Religion, Trade and Safety of his Majesties Dominions* (London, 1680), 1.

[54] S. H[ayne]., *An Abstract of all the Statutes made concerning Aliens trading in England from the first Year of K. Henry VII* (London, 1685), the opening letter to 'Dread Sove-

zation of Strangers' (interestingly issued in Scotland) allowed 'all Strangers, being of the Protestant Religion ... residence within this Kingdom',[55] after which both Charles II and his brother issued letters patent to Protestants and Catholics.[56] This seemingly open-door policy to immigrants precipitated wide anxiety: a petition to King Charles in the early 1660s complained about the 'strangers both Christians and Jews who live here obscurely',[57] and in 1667 John Owen, the former Independent leader, writing anonymously, declaimed against 'the French and Dutch churches here in England', who were openly tolerated.[58] By the early 1680s, and as the conditions of Huguenots worsened in France, there was fear over the potentially large number of foreign Protestants who were 'forced to quit their Native Countrey, and shall desire to shelter themselves under His Majesties Royal Protection'.[59] In 1685 the Edict of Nantes was revoked, and with the accession to the throne of Dutch William III in 1688 the debate over strangers intensified as large numbers of Dutch merchants and Huguenot refugees arrived in England. The reaction was mixed: while some traders argued in favour of naturalization on the grounds of economic benefit, others opposed it: 'it should seem great Prudence for all

raign'. As Hayne points out, he had planned to address the letter to Charles II. See also the lampoon against King Charles, [John Wilmot?], *History of Insipids* (London, 1676), stanza 4: 'He like a politick Prince and pious | gives liberty of conscience tender, | And doth to no Religion tye us | Jews, Christians, Turks, Papists, he'll please us | With Moses, Mahomet or J------'. For a history of English views on Jews, see Marshall, *John Locke*, ch. 12.

55 *Act for Naturalization of Strangers* (Edinburgh, 1669).

56 In 1687, for instance, King James endenizened 'several French ... lately got out of France': Narcissus Luttrell, 'Diary', in idem, *A Brief Historical Relation of State Affairs, from September 1678 to April 1714*, 6 vols (London, 1857), 1: 404.

57 Lucien Wolf, 'Status of the Jews in England after the Re-Settlement', *Jewish Historical Society of England Transactions* 4 (1899–1901), 177–93, at 186.

58 Anon., *Indulgence and Toleration considered: In a Letter unto a Person of Honour* (London, 1667), 29. For the stranger churches in seventeenth-century England, see Nigel Goose, 'The Dutch in Colchester in the 16th and 17th Centuries', and Jean Tsushima, 'Melting into the Landscape: The Story of the 17th-Century Walloons in the Fens', in Vigne and Littleton, eds, *From Strangers to Citizens*, 88–98, 106–16 respectively; Ole Peter Grell, *Dutch Calvinists in Early Stuart London: The Dutch Church in Austin Friars, 1603–1642* (Leiden, 1989). For developments after 1685, see Robin D. Gwynn, 'Disorder and Innovation: The Reshaping of the French Churches of London after the Glorious Revolution', in Ole Peter Grell, Jonathan I. Israel and Nicholas Tyacke, eds, *From Persecution to Toleration: The Glorious Revolution and Religion in England* (Oxford, 1991), 251–73.

59 *At the Court at Hampton-Court the 28th day of July 1681* (London, 1681).

English Subjects', a broadsheet read, 'to use all discreet and lawful means to prevent the future Naturalization of Aliens'.[60] At the same time, and while some theologians argued for giving shelter to Protestants, others feared that Protestants from France were really Catholics in disguise, as an anonymous author wrote in *The History of Naturalization*.[61] And there was danger from naturalized non-Christians, too, especially Jews: they were a potential threat to the security of the realm. Josiah Child of the East India Company summarized the general opposition to Jewish naturalization, although he himself saw its benefit.[62]

In opposing the endenization of non-Christians, Proast did not wade into the discussion about economic advantage or disadvantage. He was an ordained don and from inside the walls of Oxford University more concerned about God than mammon. He opposed the endenization of non-Christians on religious grounds: non-Christians would seduce pious Anglicans away from their 'national Church'. As early as 1681, an anonymous writer had emphasized the danger to the Protestant religion when non-Christians (in this case, Jews) were naturalized:

> Naturalization hath been a great cause of our distraction in Religion ... [for] contempt of our Religion brings in Judaism, and this pretence of the enlargement of Trade, as [unclear in original] of the Causes, it being ... true of the English, that their good [unclear in original] prompts them to look and think favourably of such things as they see in request with other, [unclear in original] they proceed to affect the Novelty, or at least become unstable in their own Religion. And when the said Usurpers thought it convenient to make England an Amsterdam of all Religions, the admission of Foreiners was a most effectual means to introduce the great diversity of Opinions amongst us, which hath ever since abated mens zeal for, and reverence of our Established Religion.[63]

Proast made the same point but applied it to the three groups that Locke had included in his discussion: if Jews, Muslims, and Pagans

---

[60] Anon., *A Brief and Summary Narrative of the many Mischiefs and Inconveniences in former Times as well as of late Years, occasioned by Naturalizing of Aliens* (London, 1690).

[61] Anon., *The History of Naturalization* (London, 1680), 2 (article II).

[62] Josiah Child, *A Discourse about Trade* (London, 1690), 122–7.

[63] Anon., *History of Naturalization*, 2.

were 'endenizen'd', they would seduce Protestants to their religions rather than the other way round, as Locke had argued. Englishmen would desert Christianity without having to fear the consequence of forfeiting their civil rights as subjects. Proast feared that granting the security of endenization to non-Christians would encourage apostasy in England: after all, 'even God's own peculiar People ... receive[d] that mortal Infection, notwithstanding all that he did to keep them from it'.[64]

Detecting inconsistency, Locke wrote his *Third Letter* (finishing it on 20 June 1692), invoking Islam in the discussion: 'To learn some moderation', he advised Proast, look at Muslims, even pagans, how they treat outsiders.[65] Locke continued: if 'Jews, Mahometans, and pagans' were to be denied civil rights in the commonwealth because they could seduce followers of the 'national church', then so should 'Socinians, papists, anabaptists, quakers, presbyterians', who posed more of a danger than the non-Christians because 'danger is most from that religion which comes nearest to it, and most resembles it'.[66] There was less danger in non-Christians, such as Jews and Muslims, simply because they were alien in their customs and social habits. They were, to Locke, foreign, and therefore would remain unintegrated in the social fabric, abiding without 'the advantage of truth or interest to prevail by'.[67] English non-Anglicans were more dangerous than them because they were part of the historical culture of England: and since these non-Anglicans were 'admitted to the rights of the commonwealth', then there was no logical argument that Proast could make to prevent 'Jews, pagans, and Mahometans' from enjoying the same rights. 'Why',

---

[64] Jonas Proast, *A Third Letter Concerning Toleration* (Oxford, 1691), 2–3: 'If therefore a just care of the Flock of Christ, requires us to *exclude Jews, Mahometans, and Pagans* from the *Civil Rights of the Commonwealth, because of their Religion;* 'tis plain, we may *pray in earnest for their Conversion,* though we so *exclude them:* Because though we are bound to desire their Conversion, and so to *pray* for it; yet we are bound to *seek* it, no further than we can do it, without endangering the Subjects of Christs Kingdom, to whom he has a special regard'. The italicized words are direct quotations from Locke's treatise.

[65] John Locke, 'A Third Letter for Toleration', in *Works*, 6: 139–546, at 390.

[66] Ibid. 229–30. A treatise of 1689 had argued that it was an error for 'a National Church' to 'compel all their Subjects to hear Instruction, and after a competent time, to conform their Professions to the Church', Anon., *Liberty of Conscience Explicated and Vindicated, and the Just Limits betwixt it and Authority, Sacred and Civil, Cleared* (London, 1689), 9.

[67] Locke, 'Third Letter', 230.

asked Locke, 'this common pravity of human nature should make Judaism, Mahometanism, or paganism more catching than any sort of non-conformity, which hinders men from embracing the true religion; so that Jews, Mahometans, and pagans must, for fear of infecting others, be shut out from the commonwealth, where others are not'.[68] Unlike Proast, Locke did not fear that Christians in England would be 'infected' by the disease of the two other monotheisms. There was no historical proof that when Christians met members of the other two religions 'on equal terms', they lost: Christians could not be defeated.[69]

Locke kept the discussion within the religious sphere and like Proast did not bring in economic or commercial factors in regard to the advantages of endenization.[70] He wanted to defeat Proast on his own ground. But he was aware, at the same time, of the strength of the national security argument against naturalization or endenization. As one author warned, naturalized foreigners never forgot their allegiances and could prove 'dangerous to the Government'.[71] Danger to the polity was sufficient reason not only to deny endenization and naturalization, but toleration, too. That is why Locke denied toleration to three communities in England: Catholics, whom he feared were in obedience to an infallible foreign power, the pope; atheists, because they feared no account-ability; and enthusiasts – the fringe millenarians – because they threatened law and order. But writing just a few years after the defeat of the Ottomans at Vienna, Locke could not have been oblivious to Ottoman military might. In March 1684, less than six months after the battle (and the multitude of London ballads that celebrated the defeat), and a year or so before beginning work on his *Epistola*, he wrote to Edward Clarke expressing the hope that Christian Europe would unite against the Ottoman enemy.[72]

In the discussion of endenization, however, Locke did not allude to Ottoman danger: after all, Paul Rycaut had assured Britons in

---

[68] Ibid. 231.

[69] Ibid. 232.

[70] In 1693, Locke wrote about the economic advantages of naturalization in 'For a generall naturalization'. 'Naturalization is the strength & easiest way of increasing yr people', and will encourage 'Trade … manifacture [*sic*] … Carriage or Navigation': Cambridge, MA, Harvard University, Houghton Library, MS Eng. 818.

[71] Anon., *History of Naturalization*, 3.

[72] Esmond S. de Beer, ed., *The Correspondence of John Locke*, 8 vols (Oxford, 1976–82), 2: 612.

the last pages of his often-published *The Present State of the Ottoman Empire* that the Ottomans were too weak to venture against them. But while there was no military danger in Muslims, Rycaut had warned that danger lay in the alleged authority of the 'Mufti of Constantinople' over them:

> The Mufti is the principal head of the Mahometan Religion or Oracle of all doubtful questions in the Law, and is a person of great esteem and reverence amongst the Turks; his election is soly in the Grand Signior, who chuses a man to that office always famous for his Learning in the Law, and eminent for his vertues and strictness of Life; his Authority is so great amongst them, that when he passes judgment or determination in any point, the Grand Signior himself will in no wise contradict or oppose it.[73]

Rycaut's description of the power of the mufti was inaccurate, although during the reign of Murad IV (1623–40), there had been an earnest policy of converting minorities. But after reading the passage in Rycaut, Locke felt the need to take account of the 'Mufti factor' and stated that whatever 'rights' Muslims were to be given in England, including endenization, should be conditional on their renunciation of the authority of 'the Mufti of Constantinople, who himself is entirely obedient to the Ottoman Emperor'.[74] Locke confirmed the viability of Muslims as subjects, but he wanted to make sure that they would not form a fifth column of traitors, in the same way that Henry VIII had made treasonous the defence of papal supremacy, thereby equating patriotism with religious obedience. Once Muslims denied their allegiance to the mufti, they could be safely endenized.

In urging Muslims to renounce their (non-existent) allegiance to the 'Mufti', Locke deviated from his usual logical consistency. Christians in the Ottoman Empire were not viewed by the authorities as subversive and were not forced to deny their allegiance to the pope (in the case of the Catholics), even though the pope was relentlessly sending missionaries and trying to undermine the faith

---

73 Paul Rycaut, *The Present State of the Ottoman Empire* (London, 1668), 105. Locke had also read Robert Withers, *A Description of the Grand Signor's Seraglio, or Turkish Emperor's Court*, ed. John Greaves (London, 1650), of which he owned a copy.

74 Locke, *Epistola*, ed. Klibansky, 135.

of the subjects of the sultan. At the same time, Locke did not criticize English missionary publications which were being sent to the
Ottoman Levant to gain converts to Anglicanism. These publications included prayers for the British monarchs, not the Ottoman
sultans: while Muslims in England were to forgo allegiance to the
mufti as a foreign potentate, Ottoman converts to the Church of
England were told to pray, in Arabic and in Aleppo or Istanbul,
for the safety of Sultan Qarlos (i.e. the foreign King Charles). In
the translation prepared by Pococke of the Book of Common
Prayer into Arabic, the Muslim (or Orthodox Christian) convert
to Anglicanism was to repeat the following invocation: 'Listen to
us, Lord, and preserve and bless our gracious queen | And the
king's brother | And the rest of the Sultan's household' – the sultan
being 'Qarlos'.[75]

By the time he finished the *Third Letter*, Locke had confuted
the arguments of Proast and demonstrated the legality of Muslims,
Jews and pagans becoming subjects of the Crown. But Locke's call
for the endenization of Muslims remained hypothetical: there is
no record that Muslims were either endenized or naturalized in
the Anglican polity, unless they were willing to convert to Christianity.[76] Actually, in the polarized climate of post-1688 Britain,
there was vociferous opposition even to the possibility of naturalizing foreign Protestants, as the defeat of the 1708 Act shows, and
in 1754 popular anger forced the British Parliament to repeal the
Jewish Naturalization Act, which had been passed a year earlier.
No similar proposals for naturalizing Muslims were put forward.

Using two different approaches, Henry Stubbe and John Locke
challenged England's theological and political status quo in regard
to Muslims. Uniquely in early modern debates about toleration,
Stubbe appealed to the historical model of Islamic polity, while Locke
included in his defence of the toleration of Dissenters the call for
endenization of Muslims, Jews and pagans. Locke formulated the
legal basis for determining the status of the subject in the Anglican
monarchy. Although the *Epistola* 'was neither as original nor as liberal

[75] *Liturgiae Ecclesiae Anglicanae, partes praecipuae … in linguam Arabicam traductae*
(Oxford, 1674), no pagination.

[76] Alexandra Walsham rightly criticizes the treatment of toleration in England
from the exclusive angle of 'history of ideas' in *Charitable Hatred*; see also John Coffey's
review, 'Milton, Locke and the New History of Toleration', *Modern Intellectual History*
3 (2008), 619–32.

as defenses of toleration penned by other European writers who had preceded Locke', and although 'its main arguments were labored restatements of old positions',[77] it was quite revolutionary in moving the debate beyond its traditional intra-Christian parameters to the non-Christian, and in doing so, not out of moral conscientiousness, but on the basis of logic. Having rescued the state from the Church, as one critic put it,[78] Locke was able to argue for an early modern plurality in the state: his inclusion of non-Christians in the Christian polity reveals a conceptualization of the state that is wide enough for those who deny the religion (and not just the denomination – as with the Huguenots) of the monarch, but do not threaten state security.[79] His observations on Muslims and Jews and pagans constitute the first argument in European political theory for granting the non-Christian 'Civil Rights' by means of endenization. In so doing, Locke went beyond all other writers on toleration, including Pierre Bayle, often viewed as holding broader views on toleration than Locke.[80] It is true that Locke conceived of toleration in a Stuart state that was like 'a limited liability company, the ringholder in a laissez-faire business community', as Christopher Hill put it.[81] But it was the first company in European political history that did not, in principle, discriminate against its members on the basis of Islamic or Jewish or pagan religion. And so after thirty years of reflecting on toleration, and moving from opposition to legal acceptance, Locke concluded that there was no reason why Muslims, Jews and pagans should live in Christian polities – in England and its colonies – but be denied endenization: 'Live amongst you then Jews, Mahometans, and pagans may; but endenized they must not be',[82] as his *Third Letter* expressed it. It was simply illogical. And illegal.

University of Minnesota

---

[77] Kamen, *Rise*, 231.

[78] Richard S. Dunn, *The Age of Religious Wars, 1559–1689* (New York, 1970), 218.

[79] See, however, Duncan Ivison, 'The Nature of Rights and the History of Empire', in David Armitage, ed., *British Political Thought in History, Literature and Theory, 1500–1800* (Cambridge, 2006), 191–212, at 200: 'Locke's argument for toleration is not addressed to the kind of pluralism we find in multicultural societies today'.

[80] Harry M. Bracken, 'Toleration Theories: Bayle, Jurieu, Locke', in idem, *Mind and Language: Essays on Descartes and Chomsky* (Dordrecht, 1983), 83–96, at 91.

[81] Christopher Hill, *The Century of Revolution 1603–1714* (London, 1974; first publ. 1961), 257.

[82] Locke, 'Third Letter', 229.

CHRISTIANS AND MUSLIMS ON MALTA IN THE SIXTEENTH TO EIGHTEENTH CENTURIES

by FRANS CIAPPARA

Samuel P. Huntington has described the encounter between Christianity and Islam as the 'clash of civilizations',[1] and so have Norman Daniel and R. W. Southern.[2] This Manichean vision is the result partly of political and religious rivalry which demonizes 'the other'. Such an interpretation has been challenged by scholars who emphasize a more complex reality and refer to 'a shared discourse of the Ottoman and European worlds'.[3]

This essay explores such conceptions with reference to Malta, focusing on the ability or otherwise of the island's Catholic population to coexist with the minority of Muslim slaves. Did the Maltese accept the 'enemy within'? Was Malta a place of acculturation, which Jonathan Riley-Smith claims is a recurring theme in frontier societies?[4] Did the Government and the Church follow a policy of peaceful coexistence and mutual toleration, a 'shared world', as Molly Greene has found on Crete after the island was conquered by the Ottomans from the Venetians in 1669?[5] Or was there, as in Spain, a policy of religious homogeneity marked by disrespect for other cultures?

Located in the centre of the Mediterranean, Malta is well situated for examining the nature of cultural interaction in this inland sea. No doubt it was a 'shield to Sicily, a bulwark to Italy, and a

---

[1] Samuel P. Huntington, 'The Clash of Civilizations?', *Foreign Affairs* 72 (1993), 22–49.

[2] Norman Daniel, *Islam and the West: The Making of an Image* (Oxford, 2000), 308; R. W. Southern, *Western Views of Islam in the Middle Ages* (Cambridge, 1962).

[3] Cemal Kafadar, 'The Ottomans and Europe', in Thomas A. Brady, Jr, Heiko A. Oberman and James D. Tracy, eds, *Handbook of European History, 1400–1600: Late Middle Ages, Renaissance and Reformation*, 1: *Structures and Assertions* (Leiden, 1994), 589–636, at 620.

[4] Jonathan Riley-Smith, 'Government and the Indigenous in the Latin Kingdom of Jerusalem', in David Abulafia and Nora Berend, eds, *Medieval Frontiers: Concepts and Practices* (Aldershot, 2002), 121–31.

[5] Molly Greene, *A Shared World: Christians and Muslims in the Early Modern Mediterranean* (Princeton, NJ, 2000). Ronald C. Jennings draws a similar conclusion for Cyprus: *Christians and Muslims in Ottoman Cyprus and the Mediterranean World, 1571–1640* (New York, 1993).

hindrance to the infidels', which was how an Augustinian friar referred to Malta when he preached a sermon on the occasion of the laying of the foundation stone of the new city of Valletta in 1566.[6] If Malta were to be conquered, it would serve as an ideal place for the conquest of the Christian West, 'a disaster for Christendom', according to Fernand Braudel.[7]

However, its bastions, as Balard has observed for medieval Caffa, were only a symbolic boundary; they were formidable and awe-inspiring but they were porous to every influence.[8] For one thing, ransoming imperatives, as was the case for instance with Sicily,[9] obliged the two groups, Christians and Muslims, to maintain constant relations.[10] Besides, Malta, like Genoa,[11] carried on a considerable trade direct with the Barbary regencies.[12] They preyed on each other's shipping but it cannot be said that they were irreconcilable enemies. Maltese merchants went to trade at Sfax, Tunis or Tripoli and Muslims came to Malta to sell their

[6] Cited in Giovanni Francesco Abela, *Della Descrittione di Malta Isola nel Mare Siciliano* (Malta, 1647), 12.

[7] Fernand Braudel, *The Mediterranean and the Mediterranean World in the Age of Philip II*, transl. Siân Reynolds, 2 vols (London, 1973), 2: 1017.

[8] Michel Balard, '*Genuensis civitas in extremo Europae*: Caffa from the Fourteenth to the Fifteenth Century', in Abulafia and Berend, eds, *Medieval Frontiers*, 143–51, at 147–50.

[9] For the redemption of Sicilian slaves, see Giuseppe Bonaffini's two books, *Sicilia e Tunisia nel Secolo XVII* (Palermo, 1984); *La Sicilia e i Barbareschi. Incursioni corsare e riscatto degli schiavi, 1570–1606* (Palermo, 1983).

[10] Frans Ciappara, *Society and the Inquisition in Early Modern Malta* (Malta, 2001), 234–50.

[11] For the Franco-Genoese Salt Company, which operated from Zarzis (Tunis), see S. Boubaker, 'Les relations économiques entre gênes et la Régence de Tunis au début du XVIIIème siècle: La Compagnie du Sel Gergis, 1714–1724', in R. Belvederi, ed., *Rapporti Genova-Mediterraneo-Atlantico nell'Età Moderna. Atti del IV Congresso Internazionale di Studi Storici* (Genoa, 1990), 123–39.

[12] On this topic, see, among other works, Anne Brogini, *Malte, frontier de chrétienté 1530–1670* (Rome, 2006), 358–70; L. Valensi, 'Les relations commerciales entre la Régence de Tunis et Malte au XVIIIe siècle', *Cahiers de Tunesie* 43 (1963), 71–83; Jean Mathiex, 'Le ravitaillement moghrebin de Malte au XVIII siècle', *Cahiers de Tunesie* 6 (1954), 191–202; Jean Marie Roland de la Platière, *Lettres écrites de Suisse, d'Italie, de Sicile et de Malte*, 6 vols (Amsterdam, 1780), 3: 36, 71. For Muslims in Venice and Ancona in the sixteenth century, see Cemal Kafadar, 'A Death in Venice (1575): Anatolian Muslim Merchants Trading in the Serenissima', *Journal of Turkish Studies* 10 (1986), 191–218. For Venetians in Constantinople, see Eric R. Dursteler, *Venetians in Constantinople: Nation, Identity, and Coexistence in the Early Modern Mediterranean* (Baltimore, MD, 2006).

'several kinds of merchandise of Barbary'.[13] Commercial relations were paralleled by diplomatic relations. In 1748 the Bey of Tunis was killed and his son requested the help of the Hospitallers, who sent a galley under the command of Fra Laparelli.[14]

Even so, the Maltese identify the 'Turk' (as Muslims are still called) with whatever is maleficent and malignant.[15] Hasan epitomizes those Turks who abducted beautiful maidens from Malta. Ugliness is expressed by the phrase *Tork ta' Barbarija* (as black as a 'Turk' from Barbary), and parents frighten their children with the bogey Turk. Turks were 'enemies of the Christian name' so that their defeat on land or at sea occasioned great festivities.[16] But popular opinion identified the 'Turk' best with unbelief. Muslims were 'dogs' or followers of the 'sect of the wicked and damned Muhammad'.[17] One finds also reference to the 'false laws of Mahomet' and the 'fortunate impostor'.[18]

These are revealing words which show how sharply the boundary between the Catholic Maltese and the 'others' was perceived. The extraordinary expression of violence that accompanied the uprising of the slaves in 1749 underlines the deep cultural divide between the two civilizations. Only long repressed anger mixed with a hatred of an alien religion can explain the vicious behaviour that accompanied the revolt's collapse: red-hot pincers

[13] Mdina, Archives of the Inquisition, Malta, Proceedings 74, fol. 75[r] [hereafter: AIM, Proc.]; ibid. 75B, fol. 585[r]; Valletta, National Library of Malta, Archives 6528, fol. 664[r] [hereafter: NLM, Arch.]; ibid. 459, fol. 333[r]. The only condition was that they made use of Christian vessels. The object of this kind of foreign relations was to subject the economy of the Muslims to the merchant navy of the Christian states: Valensi, 'Les relations commerciales', 82.

[14] Vatican City, Archivio della Congregazione per la Dottrina della Fede, Stanza Storica HH4–d, unnumbered, Gualtieri to the cardinal inquisitors, 25 October 1748.

[15] For perceptions of Muslims in Maltese literature, see Joe Vella Gauci, *Christian-Muslim Relations as a Topos in Maltese Historiography and Literature* (Malta, 2010); Marco Galea, 'Renewing an Enemy Ship: Turk Sightings in Nineteenth-Century Maltese Literature', *Sacra Militia* 5 (2006), 29–34.

[16] NLM, Library 738, p. 238 [hereafter: Libr.]. For the celebrations held in Valletta and the harbour on the lifting of the siege of Vienna in 1683, see NLM, Arch. 262, fol. 159[v]. In 1685 there were again great festivities following a memorable campaign' by the Order of St John's vessels 'against the common enemy': ibid., fol. 233[r]. Thanks are due to Manuel Buttigieg for both these references.

[17] Francesco Balbi di Correggio, *The Siege of Malta 1565*, transl. Henry Alexander Balbi (Copenhagen, 1961), 138; for the menace they presented to the Catholic West, see Jean Delumeau, *La peur en occident* (Paris, 1978), 342–55.

[18] Godfrey Wettinger, *Slavery in the Islands of Malta and Gozo ca.1000–1812* (Malta, 2002), 438; M. A. Vassalli, *Ktyb yl Klym Målti* (Rome, 1796), xii.

tore the flesh and boiling pitch was poured into the wounds of the rebels before they were quartered and burnt.[19]

But despite this real antagonism, Muslims on Malta, instead of having to attend sermons designed to convert them, as in Spain,[20] were allowed to practise their faith freely and had some claim to the protection of the government. This policy was based on the principle of reciprocity. As Salvatore Bono has observed for Italy,[21] so too for Malta: if Muslim slaves were harassed, the same fate would befall Maltese captives held in Turkish lands.[22] As at Leghorn, Civitavecchia and Genoa (although not at Naples), in Malta the Muslims had a mosque in which to worship.[23] Patrick Brydone, a Scot on the Grand Tour, was surprised to find in 1770 one in each of the three *bagnos* (slave prisons) 'notwithstanding the supposed bigotry of the Maltese'.[24] These must have been simple rooms furnished for the purpose, like the one used as a synagogue by the Jews.[25] However, not later than 1738, the Muslims had a much better building, specially built as a mosque, just outside the town bastions and adjoining the Muslim

---

[19] Carmel Testa, *The Life and Times of Grand Master Pinto 1741–1773* (Malta, 1989), 119–27. There are several contemporary accounts of the event, but see especially Michele Acciard, *Mustafá Bassá di Rodi schiavo in Malta, o sia la di lui Congiura all'Occupazione di Malta* (Naples, 1751). For the polemic about who was the true author of this book, the Neapolitan Acciard or the Maltese Francesco Agius de Soldanis, see Robert Thake, *Patriotism, Deception and Censorship: De Soldanis and the 1751 Account of the Uprising of the Slaves* (Malta, 2013).

[20] For the sermons delivered by the Jesuit Tirso Gonzáles in seventeenth-century Spain, see Emanuele Colombo, *Convertire i musulmani. L'esperienza di un gesuita spagnolo del seicento* (Milan, 2007).

[21] Salvatore Bono, 'Schiavi maghrebini in Italia e cristiani nel Maghreb. Proteste e attestazioni per la 'reciprocità' di trattamento', *Africa* 49 (1994), 331–51.

[22] NLM, Arch. 452, fols 277ᵛ–284ᵛ; Salvatore Bono, 'Schiavi musulmani a Malta nei secoli xvii–xviii. Connessioni fra Maghreb e Italia', in *Karissime Gotifride. Historical Essays presented to Professor Godfrey Wettinger on his Seventieth Birthday*, ed. Paul Xuereb (Malta, 1999), 89–96. For the religious festivities held in north Africa by Christian slaves, see Ellen G. Friedman, *Spanish Captives in North Africa in the Early Modern Age* (Madison, WI, 1983).

[23] Salvatore Bono, *Lumi e corsari. Europa e Maghreb nel Settecento* (Perugia, 2005), 74–5; Raffaella Sarti, 'Bolognesi schiavi dei "Turchi" e schiavi "Turchi" a Bologna tra cinque e settecento: Alterità etnico-religiosa e riduzione in schiavitù', *Quaderni Storici* 107, anno 36 (2001), 437–71, at 450.

[24] Patrick Brydone, *A Tour through Sicily and Malta in a Series of Letters to William Beckford*, 2 vols (London, 1773), I: 331 (letter 16, 7 June 1770).

[25] Frans Ciappara, 'The Roman Inquisition and the Jews in Seventeenth- and Eighteenth-Century Malta', in *Le inquisizioni cristiane e gli ebrei. Tavola rotonda nell'ambito della Conferenza Annuale della Ricerca (Roma, 20–21 dicembre 2001)*, Atti del Convegno Lincei 191 (Rome, 2003), 449–70, at 455.

cemetery at Marsa. Here, led by their imam, they met for prayers, for instance on *laylatu l-gumgha* (Friday night).[26] The government helped them keep these places in good condition, providing the beams and other timber, as (for example) in 1702.[27] It supplied them with oil for the night lights 'as their Lent is approaching, during which they are obliged to stay awake throughout the night'.[28] It allowed them, too, to celebrate their *'id al-fitr* (the three days following Ramadan) and protected them during prayer, to the extent that 'some boys had been sent to prison for disturbing the poor slaves at their devotions'.[29]

Muslims received Islamic burial rites when they died. The body first received the customary ablutions consisting mainly of pouring hot water over it. The corpse was then borne to the burial place by four slaves accompanied by the imam, who observed whether it showed any bruises or other signs of ill treatment for an inquiry to be made.[30] Anyone who molested the body on its way to the grave was liable to be jailed.[31]

But could not the presence of these infidels among Christians serve as a source of corruption and pose a threat to the Catholic identity of the island?[32] Inquisitor Lazzaro Pallavicini had no doubt that they could undermine Christianity and make it seem fragile. He recorded in his memoirs in 1715 that Malta was 'exposed to the violent whirlwind of the wicked opinions of the Muslims' and warned his successors to guard against the 'tiring tempests sustained by the great quantity of infidel slaves'.[33]

This challenge to the moral ordering of Malta was real enough because these captives constituted a significant number. In 1582 a papal official had reported that more than 600 belonged to the Order of St John and 200 to private owners.[34] Of a population of about 35,000 this equated to 2.3 per cent. This was a smaller percentage than, say, Seville, where the proportion was 3.3 per cent in 1565, but higher than in Sicily, where it was 1 per cent

---

[26] Wettinger, *Slavery*, 446.
[27] NLM, Arch. 647, fol. 205^v.
[28] NLM, Università 338, 30 October 1741.
[29] NLM, Arch. 672, pp. 33–7; Brydone, *Tour*, 1: 331 (letter 16, 7 June 1770).
[30] NLM, Arch. 6570, fols 3^r–4^r.
[31] NLM, Libr. 666, 3 January 1743.
[32] Julia A. Clancy-Smith, *Mediterraneans: North Africa and Europe in an Age of Migration c.1800–1900* (Berkeley, CA, 2011), 76.
[33] AIM, Memorie 3, fol. 2^r.
[34] NLM, Libr. 1306, fol. 8^r.

for the same period.[35] By 1630 the number of slaves in Malta had increased to 3,000 (5.9 per cent of the population),[36] but by the end of the eighteenth century it had fallen to 1,000 or 1.0 per cent.[37]

Furthermore, if slaves did not share the same religion and worldview with the inhabitants, this could not be said for their language. The Maltese spoke a variant of Maghribī Arabic, which made it possible for the two groups to mix freely. Moreover, as in Genoa,[38] captives were allowed to engage in trade on their own account and to earn money from a variety of crafts; the only condition was that they must pay their owner a fee known as the *giornata*. They wandered about the streets of the towns and villages hawking cloth, leather goods, ironware, vegetables and fruit.[39] They were also hairdressers, tailors, shoemakers, shoe repairers, tooth-drawers, woodcarvers, water- and oil-sellers. They repaired carpets and made rush baskets, and also engaged in pawnbroking.[40]

This communication worried the civil and religious authorities because the Maltese also sought the services of slaves to find treasure or lost objects, win the hand of a lover, identify thieves, make a husband impotent, cast a spell *ad mortem* on an enemy, become wise and virtuous and (since slaves claimed to undo as well as to cast spells) to be cured from a malefice. Were not the fumigations, magical circles and numbers, Arabic texts, charms, talismans and potions which were utilized in these experiments a real threat to correct Christian practice and true doctrine?[41] Were not blessed water, incense, candles, oil and the eucharistic host to be employed only to worship God? Did not their use imply, as St Thomas Aquinas had outlined in the thirteenth century, reverence towards a power other than God himself?[42] And by attributing to the devil powers that were God's alone, would not that mean

35 Salvatore Bono, *Corsari nel Mediterraneo. Cristiani e musulmani fra guerra, schiavitù e commercio* (Milan, 1993), 194–5.

36 Alexander Bonnici, 'Aspetti della vita cristiana nell'Isola di Malta verso la metà del seicento', *Maltese Folklore Review* 1 (1974), 305–35, at 315 n. 46.

37 Figures based on data in Wettinger, *Slavery*, 553–62.

38 Bono, 'Schiavi Musulmani', 90.

39 Philip Skippon, *A Journey thro' Part of the Low Countries, Germany, Italy and France*, ed. Awnsham Churchill (London, 1732), 621.

40 Wettinger, *Slavery*, 411–38.

41 On this topic, see Ciappara, *Society and the Inquisition*, 261–320.

42 David Gentilcore, *Healers and Healing in Early Modern Italy* (Manchester, 1998), 45.

placing the devil on a par with God? Could he, for example, foresee the future? Was not divination a sacrilegious wish to take from God the mastery over time?[43] And did not unknown characters written on pieces of paper represent the names of devils?[44]

Therefore, lest they should contaminate the inhabitants with their beliefs and error creep into the ways of society, the divide between Christians and Muslims had to be marked in a number of ways. Slaves were 'forced into a sort of internal exile', confined within *bagnos*.[45] And since 'one should know with whom one is talking' they wore distinctive marks to be distinguished from Christians.[46] A law of 1593 ordered iron rings for all of them, worn visibly on the foot and weighing twelve ounces,[47] while from 1663 they all had their hair cut except for a pigtail (*ciuffo*).[48] A great deal of attention was dedicated to matters of sexual purity. In a document from 1658 we read that Grand Master de Redin issued a proclamation against sexual intercourse between Christians and infidels and decreed the stiffest penalties against 'mixing the blood of dogs with that of Christians which has been redeemed by the blood of Jesus Christ'. Slaves who were caught with women could be whipped and have their ears and nose cut off.[49] These laws must have proved largely ineffectual, because in 1667 Grand Master Nicholas Cottoner prohibited the slaves from hawking their wares around the streets of Valletta in order to 'prevent as much as possible the offence given to His Divine Majesty by the intercourse of infidels with Christian women'.[50]

As a response to the crossing of one another's thresholds the Maltese Church also sought to construct the parameters of Christian-Muslim relations. The diocesan synod of 1620 legislated to

---

[43] Muriel Verbeeck-Verhelst, 'Magie et curiosité au XVIIᵉ siècle', *Revue d'histoire ecclésiastique* 83 (1988), 349–68; Jean-Claude Schmitt, *Medioevo 'Superstizioso'* (Rome and Bari, 1987), 86.

[44] On the condemnation of beneficent magic as originating from the devil, just like maleficent magic, see S. Clark and P. T. Morgan, 'Religion and Magic in Elizabethan Wales: Robert Holland's Dialogue on Witchcraft', *JEH* 27 (1976), 31–46.

[45] *Decreta Melivetanae Synodi Actae in Cathedrali Melitensi* (Rome, 1647), 17–18. See also NLM, Libr. 5, pp. 236–7. For the various possible origins of the term *bagno*, see G. Audisio, 'Recherches sur l'origine et la signification du mot *bagne*', *Revue Africaine* 101 (1957), 363–80.

[46] AIM, Memorie 3, fol. 7ᵛ.

[47] NLM, Libr. 704, fol. 101ᵛ.

[48] NLM, Libr. 738, 299–300.

[49] Ibid. 234–9.

[50] NLM, Libr. 740, part C, fols 91ʳ–ᵛ.

mark the social distance between the Muslims and the rest of civil society. Christians were not to go to their festivities, receive medicines from them or take their sick to them to be cured.[51]

Furthermore, in principle Muslims were outside the jurisdiction of the inquisition, but the fear of contamination was a real threat. Muslims had a right to protection, but they lost this when they crossed the bounds of acceptable behaviour and challenged communal discipline.[52] Dabblers in sorcery and witchcraft were humiliated publicly to serve as a warning to others. Heralded by the government's trumpeter,[53] they were lashed and paraded through the city on an ass or a donkey, seated backwards and with their hands tied, wearing a mitre on their head and an ignominious placard proclaiming their crime on their breast.[54]

But were Muslims to be made to recant the faith into which they had been born?[55] Was there any mechanism for their assimilation in the culture of their masters? According to the Council of Trent, 'as in baptism we all die to sin and resolve to live a new life so it is fit that it be administered only to those who receive it of their own free will and accord'.[56] However, is it not a good thing to win a soul for God? Benedict XIV, ignoring the opinion of theologians like Aquinas who prohibited baptism *invitis parentibus* (against the wish of the parents), claimed that baptizing an infidel infant in danger of death 'is without doubt a praiseworthy and meritorious thing'. The principle of *favor fidei* (in faith's favour) prevailed over any other consideration and even if this was an illicit baptism and the perpetrator was to be punished, the sacrament was still valid.[57] Cases from the proceedings of the inquisition provide examples of children baptized in secret. One such instance refers to Pulcra of

[51] Wettinger, *Slavery*, 451.

[52] For the case of the Jews of Ferrara, see Adriano Prosperi, *Tribunali della coscienza. Inquisitori, confessori, missionari* (Turin, 1996), 192.

[53] ACDF, Stanza Storica HH 4–d, unnumbered; AIM, Corrispondenza [hereafter: Corr.] 95, fol. 270ᵛ, Inquisitor Salviati to Cardinal Corsini, 10 January 1756.

[54] AIM, Proc. 28A, fol. 66ʳ; AIM, Proc. 125C, fol. 1405ʳ.

[55] For a full treatment of the subject, see Francesco Russo, 'Schiavitù e conversioni a Malta in età moderna: nuove fonti e percorsi di ricerca', in Sara Cabibbo and Maria Lupi, eds, *Relazioni religiose nel Mediterraneo. Schiavi, redentori, mediatori, secc. XVI–XIX* (Rome, 2012), 135–58.

[56] *The Catechism of the Council of Trent*, transl. John A. McHugh and Charles J. Callan (Rockford, IL, 1982), 180.

[57] Marina Caffiero, *Battesimi forzati. Storie di ebrei, cristiani e convertiti nella Roma dei papi* (Rome, 2004), 81.

Valletta who, believing it a 'piece of meritorious work', baptized a fifteen-month-old Muslim girl in 1784, pouring the water on the child's head and reciting the usual words: 'I baptize you in the name of the Father and of the Son and of the Holy Spirit. Amen'.[58] Another case concerned a nine-year-old slave whom his master 'feared would die of an epileptic stroke'. He was baptized in 1768 at a shoemaker's shop at St Nicholas (Siġġiewi) even though, according to his master, he had always lived as a Muslim and never wanted to become a Christian.[59] However, these sporadic examples cannot be compared to the forced baptisms of Jews at Rome about which Marina Caffiero has written.[60]

Winning children over to Christianity was also the professed aim of the Order of St John. Thus, when a party of Moors were captured in 1549, the grand master and council prohibited the sale of any who were under fourteen years old 'in the hope … that they would turn Christian, as in fact it is quite frequent that baptism of such children takes place'.[61] In 1593 Grand Master de Verdalle prohibited for the same reason the sale of children to non-Christians.[62] And a proclamation of 28 September 1661 declared that no child born or conceived in captivity could be sold to infidels; nor could it be ransomed, set free or allowed to return to its parents' country, even in its parents' company, before it reached the age of ten. The proclamation ended with an exhortation to all owners of such children 'to admonish and instruct them in all charity in our Holy Faith so that they might be illuminated by the Holy Spirit to embrace it and receive Holy Baptism'.[63]

Pressure was also exerted on slaves awaiting execution to secure their last-minute conversion.[64] They did not always comply,

---

[58] AIM, Proc. 133A, fols 365ʳ–367ᵛ.

[59] AIM, Proc. 129, fols 51ʳ–52ᵛ.

[60] Besides Caffiero, *Battesimi forzati*, see also eadem, "'Il Pianto di Rachele". Ebrei, Neofiti e Giudaizzanti a Roma in etá moderna', in *L'Inquisizione e gli storici: Un cantiere aperto* (Rome, 2000), 306–28; eadem, "'La caccia agli ebrei". Inquisizione, casa dei catecumeni e battesimi forzati nella Roma moderna', in *Le inquisizioni cristiane e gli ebrei*, 503–37.

[61] Giacomo Bosio, *Dell'istoria della Sacra Religione et Illustrissima Militia di San Giovanni Gerosolimitano*, 3 vols (Naples, 1684), 3: 263.

[62] NLM, Libr. 704, fol. 101ʳ.

[63] NLM, Libr. 740, fols 48ʳ–ᵛ.

[64] For one such conversion in 1654, see AIM, Proc. 69A, fols 86ʳ–91ᵛ.

however, and an eighteenth-century account of the last days of a Muslim condemned to death is worth quoting:

> From the moment when judgement had been pronounced on him, he was assigned a confessor, who did not quit his side for an instant during the succeeding three days and nights. He was absolutely determined to have him die a Christian. When the slave was on his way to execution, he … stuck to his side, with crucifix in hand and ceaselessly exhorting him. The *Salve* was sung, holy water was sprinkled on this son of Muhammad, but nothing could shake him … The confessor called him brother and friend and described to him vividly the Christian heaven. … The Turk remained a Turk. When the confessor saw him dangling in the air, he quickly forgot that he had just called him friend and brother. He now spat at him, called him a dog, and consigned him to all the devils.[65]

Likewise, galley chaplains in their daily round of the infirmary lovingly exhorted sick infidels to be baptized. They explained to them that they would either enjoy eternal life in heaven if they embraced the Christian religion or eternal damnation in hell if they continued in their infidelity. The chaplains commended them to God and asked his divine goodness to provide them with ardent words to enable them to gain the soul already on the point of eternal loss through its own fault.[66]

Besides, there were various enticements for slaves to embrace Christianity, although these did not include manumission.[67] Although baptism did not necessarily 'break the bond of slavery', baptized slaves were entitled to money allowances. They could ransom themselves for much less than the current market price and (which slaves appreciated most) they were allowed to marry and live with their families in their own homes.[68] In addition,

[65] M. Carasi, *The Order of Malta exposed or a Voyage to Malta*, transl. Thomas Freller (Malta, 2010), 158–9.

[66] NLM, Arch. 1927, fols 136^r–137^v.

[67] For the case of Teresa, the fifty-year-old slave of the Barbaros of Valletta, whose brother and two sisters offered unavailingly to pay 300 scudi for her ransom, see AIM, Corr. 65, fols 158^r–160^v, Cardinal Pallavicini to Inquisitor Zondadari, 6 October 1778. For the juridical status of baptized slaves, see Lucia Rostagno, *Mi faccio Turco. Esperienze ed immagini dell'Islam nell'Italia moderna* (Rome, 1983), 19–20; Frans Ciappara, *The Roman Inquisition in Enlightened Malta* (Malta, 2000), 57–8.

[68] Wettinger, *Slavery*, 464–70.

the inquisitors, who considered piracy to be 'so odious to God's and man's laws',[69] could pay for their ransom[70] or offer them help whenever their masters ill-treated them.[71]

The number of Muslims who were baptized was at first considerable. In the two Valletta parishes of St Dominic and St Paul, there were no less than 375 between 1595 and 1605. The phenomenon continued until the end of the order on Malta in the late eighteenth century, even though corsairing had diminished considerably in importance by then, with a consequent reduction in the number of slaves.[72] In the period 1777–86 at St Paul's there were only 36, amounting to 1.3 per cent of the total of 2,813 baptisms.[73] Yet this is a higher ratio than that in Madrid for 1650–1700, which registered a rate of only 0.6 per cent.[74] In Malta, unlike in Rome,[75] there was no *casa dei catecumeni* (house of converts) for Muslims to learn their Catholic catechism, even though Inquisitor Salviati had proposed setting one up in 1756.[76] However, baptized slaves were kept in a separate place from the other captives in the *bagno*, so as to avoid exposing them to unchristian beliefs and practices.[77]

To conclude, it has been argued that in border territories like the Mediterranean, where historical and geographical circumstances brought Christians and Muslims together, cultural contact was not impossible. Constant religious and ideological confrontation did not prevent connection between the two groups. They interacted with each other in a variety of social contexts, so that we can speak of a shared 'Islamo-Christian' civilization or 'a shared

[69] AIM, Memorie 16, fol. 11[v].

[70] For the case of Eiza, for whose redemption Mgr Zondadari in 1779 disbursed 25 Roman scudi, see AIM, Corr. 66, fols 104[r]–[v], Cardinal Pallavicino to Inquisitor Zondadari, 16 February 1779.

[71] For the case of the female slave of Teresa Manduca who was beaten with the bridle and had to beg for her food, see AIM, Atti Civili 488, fols 404[r]–409[v]; see also Ciappara, *Roman Inquisition*, 57–8.

[72] Molly Greene, *Catholic Pirates and Greek Merchants: A Maritime History of the Mediterranean* (Princeton, NJ, 2010). This reduction was evident in all Christian lands with a Muslim population: Bono, *Lumi e corsari*, 68–70.

[73] Valletta, St Paul's Parish Archives, Liber Baptizatorum 12 (1777–1787).

[74] Calculated from data in C. Larquié, 'Les esclaves de Madrid à l'époque de la décadence (1650–1700)', *Revue historique* 244/1 (1970), 141–74, at 151–2.

[75] Caffiero, *Battesimi forzati*, 21–6.

[76] Vatican City, Archivio Storico di Propaganda Fidei, Fondo Scritture Riferite nei Congressi, fols 103[r]–110[v].

[77] NLM, Arch. 647, fol. 175[r].

political community'.[78] To put it differently, although the process of boundary-making strove to separate the two communities it involved at the same time the recognition of the rights of the 'other'. However, it must not be imagined that Christians and Muslims considered each other as 'fellow pilgrims towards the truth'.[79] Muslims were not allowed to corrupt Christian practice, while pressure could be put on them to change their faith.

University of Malta

---

[78]   See, respectively, Molly Greene, 'Resurgent Islam: 1500–1700', in David Abulafia, ed., *The Mediterranean in History* (London, 2003), 219–49; Richard W. Bulliet, *The Case for Islamo-Christian Civilization* (New York, 2004); Janina M. Safran, *Defining Boundaries in Al-Andalus: Muslims, Christians, and Jews in Islamic Iberia* (Ithaca, NY, and London, 2013), 169.

[79]   Hugh Goddard, *A History of Christian-Muslim Relations* (Chicago, IL, 2000), 194.

WILLIAM JOWETT'S *CHRISTIAN RESEARCHES*: BRITISH PROTESTANTS AND RELIGIOUS PLURALITY IN THE MEDITERRANEAN, SYRIA AND THE HOLY LAND, 1815–30[*]

by GARETH ATKINS

[Acre,] Sunday, Nov. 2, 1823 – This morning, in the Consul's room, we held Divine Service, with a congregation of ten souls – as promiscuous an assembly as could well be expected within the compass of so small a number. The individuals who composed it were, a British Consul – his Dragoman, a native of the country – a Maronite Priest – a Roman Physician – one Greek – one Jew – an English captain of a merchant vessel then in port – my servant, who is under French protection – an American Brother-Missionary – and myself, of the Church of England ... The whole Service was in Italian.[1]

This picture of religious diversity on the coast of Ottoman Syria serves to introduce an important yet seldom examined aspect of the nineteenth-century British missionary interest in other religions. The writer was the Reverend William Jowett, sometime Cambridge fellow but now Church Missionary Society (CMS) agent in the Mediterranean. Jowett had ranged widely around the Levant, visiting Corfu, Greece and Egypt. Now, on his second tour of duty, he headed for Syria and the Holy Land. Much of what he saw delighted him. Like many nineteenth-century travellers he revelled in the associations of the Sea of Galilee: 'yonder ... must have been the very spot; where ... the Disciples were affrighted at seeing Jesus walk on the water'.[2] At the Mount of Beatitudes he and his travelling companions could not discern the lilies of the field, but found instead an autumn crocus that conjured up suitable scriptural reflections.[3] Elsewhere,

---

[*]   I am deeply indebted to Simeon Wallis for his valuable insights into this subject.
[1]   William Jowett, *Christian Researches in Syria and the Holy Land, from MDCCCXV to MDCCCXX* (London, 1825), 145.
[2]   Ibid. 176.
[3]   Ibid. 188.

the ruins of Tyre prompted sombre thoughts about the fulfilment of prophecy. Reading from Isaiah and Ezekiel the party marvelled at the completeness of its fall. 'I have seen the ruins of Athens, and the innumerable memorials of Egyptian glory in Thebes', enthused Jowett. 'But, on this deserted shore, not one sight, not one sound remains, to bear witness to her former joyousness and pride.'[4] Most interesting, however, to Jowett and his companions was the current religious state of the places that they passed through. In Nazareth, for instance, they met Franciscan friars, Greek priests and native Maronite Christians, but were depressed by the minaret that stood in the centre of the town: 'Jesus of Nazareth is not here the exclusive, or the dominant master'.[5] Jerusalem elicited still more mixed feelings: while initially sent into raptures by its beauty as seen from afar, closer acquaintance left Jowett struck by its 'meanness, and filth and misery'.[6] 'These are not the Towers or the Temple of ancient times', he sighed on departure.[7]

This essay will argue that Jowett's work in the Mediterranean represents a foundational phase of modern Protestant engagement both with other forms of Christianity and with other religions. While the Society for the Propagation of Christian Knowledge and the Society for the Propagation of the Gospel in Foreign Parts had long worked to spread Christianity within and round about British possessions, in the closing decades of the eighteenth century Evangelicals in particular began to think more systematically about how to reach the unconverted masses.[8] Scientific exploration was a key catalyst – the Baptist William Carey had his imagination fired by reading about the voyages of Captain Cook – but newly founded bodies like the Baptist, London and Church Missionary Societies in their turn sought further, more specific information about the nature and beliefs of those they sought to convert.[9] Initially they garnered such data on an ad hoc

---

4   Ibid. 136.
5   Ibid. 158.
6   Ibid. 208.
7   Ibid. 270.
8   Among recent works, see Rowan Strong, *Anglicanism and the British Empire, c.1700–1850* (Oxford, 2007); Bob Tennant, *Corporate Holiness: Pulpit Preaching and the Church of England Missionary Societies, 1760–1870* (Oxford, 2013), 92–166; Andrew Porter, *Religion versus Empire? British Protestant Missionaries and Overseas Expansion, 1700–1914* (Manchester, 2004), 39–63.
9   Eustace Carey, *Memoir of William Carey, D.D.* (London, 1836), 18.

basis from travellers, merchants and published accounts, but as their incomes boomed in the 1800s and 1810s their ambitions grew, and they began to sponsor agents of their own. What follows contends that the early decades of the nineteenth century form a period of exploration and information-gathering characterized by 'Christian researches', a phrase that describes a distinct missionary strategy and the publishing genre that sprang from it.[10] Its progenitor was the East India Company chaplain Claudius Buchanan (1766–1815), whose celebrated *Christian Researches in Asia* (1811) went through nine editions in two years.[11] Less well known are Buchanan's imitators, of whom Jowett was one of the most faithful. Buchanan gave Jowett 'highly desirable counsel' prior to his departure, and the younger man's publications, as we shall see, followed closely the model his colleague had set out, in particular in his careful taxonomy of different religious groups.[12]

Jowett's activities have especial relevance for historians of mission in the Middle East, for although a great deal of work exists on encounters with the so-called 'heathen' in North America, Africa, Asia and the Pacific, historians of mission are only just beginning to consider how British agents abroad dealt with the multifarious religions and sects of the region.[13] In part this is because recent work has often focused on missions to the Jews, an endeavour that Jowett supported enthusiastically, but which was hardly his or his society's main remit.[14] Their chief interest was in the allegedly moribund Eastern Churches: the Greeks, Jacobites, Copts, Abyssinians, Armenians, Nestorians and others, real and imagined.[15] Of crucial significance here were Henry Martyn's translation of the

---

[10] A similar point is made in Porter, *Religion*, 116–35.

[11] Allan K. Davidson, *Evangelicals and Attitudes to India, 1786–1813* (Sutton Courtenay, 1990), 151–63.

[12] 'Christian Researches in the Mediterranean', *Christian Observer* 22 (1823), 30–45, at 30.

[13] An exception is Paul Sedra, *From Mission to Modernity* (London, 2011), which focuses on education in nineteenth-century Egypt. The American Board of Commissioners for Foreign Missions, by contrast, has received considerable recent coverage: see Heleen Murre-van den Berg, ed., *New Faith in Ancient Lands* (Leiden, 2006); Heather Sharkey, *American Evangelicals in Egypt: Missionary Encounters in an Age of Empire* (Princeton, NJ, and Oxford, 2008); Samir Khalaf, *Protestant Missionaries in the Levant: Ungodly Puritans, 1820–1860* (London, 2012). Lyle L. Vander Werff, *Christian Mission to Muslims: The Record* (Pasadena, CA, 1977), 153–4, discusses Jowett briefly.

[14] Donald M. Lewis, *The Origins of Christian Zionism* (Cambridge, 2010), 214–20.

[15] 'Appendix V', *Proceedings of the CMS* (1817), 141–55, at 143–4.

New Testament into Persian, his heroic travels and his untimely death at Tokat in 1812, all of which sparked a widespread interest among British religious thinkers in missions to Muslims.[16]

The desire to revive the ancient Eastern Churches through the Mediterranean was a reflex of the same urge. Only through them could Western agents hope to reach the wider Muslim world. The tactic was dictated as much by pragmatism as by any deliberate principle: direct proselytism was frowned upon, and British missionary societies, the CMS in particular, were chronically short of volunteers. But there was nothing to stop Western Protestants from preaching to the converted, reminding believers in the East that they occupied the cradle of Christianity and that it was their duty to win it back. Whether or not they believed their Eastern brethren were genuinely 'converted', of course, was sometimes a moot point, but this essay advances the premise that there was genuine excitement among Evangelicals in the early decades of the nineteenth century about the possibilities of reviving those Churches, rather than simply making Protestants in a Western mould. Jowett, then, occupied a crucial position in the 1810s and 1820s. He was deeply influential both in the 'rediscovery' of the Eastern Churches and in the networks and institutions developed in order to evangelize the multifarious religious groups that existed within and around them.[17] Put simply, he was part of an attempt to tailor missionary endeavour to a pluralistic setting. This essay examines how.

Jowett seemed an unlikely pioneer. One contemporary reckoned him to be 'about five feet four or five inches in height … partially bald … quiet and gentle in speaking, although not inanimate'.[18] A member of a prominent evangelical family, he attended St John's

---

[16]   The documents Martyn had been working on were swiftly published, including his Persian New Testament (St Petersburg, 1815) and his Arabic New Testament (Calcutta, 1816): see John Sargent, *Memoir of the Rev. Henry Martyn, B.D.* (London, 1816); Samuel Lee, ed., *Controversial Tracts on Christianity and Mohammedanism, by the late Rev. Henry Martyn, B.D.* (Cambridge, 1824); see also Brian Stanley, '"An ardour of devotion": The Spiritual Legacy of Henry Martyn', in *India and the Indianness of Christianity: Essays on Understanding – Historical, Theological, and Bibliographical – in Honor of Robert Eric Frykenberg*, ed. Richard Fox Young, SHCM (Grand Rapids, MI, 2009), 108–26.

[17]   The best overview and bibliography of this area is Heleen Murre-van den Berg, 'The Middle East: Western Missions and the Eastern Churches, Islam and Judaism', in Sheridan Gilley and Brian Stanley, eds, *CHC*, 8: *World Christianities, c.1815–c.1914* (Cambridge, 2006), 458–72.

[18]   Anon., *Random Recollections of Exeter Hall* (London, 1838), 116–17.

College, Cambridge, graduating twelfth wrangler in 1810 and winning the prestigious Hulsean Prize the same year. He was a fellow of St John's from 1811 to 1816, during which time he was also priested, and in 1813 became the first Anglican clergyman to volunteer for CMS service abroad, although not without reservations on his part.[19] Intensive preparation followed, and marriage to Mary Whiting, a resident of his uncle's Norfolk parish, later memorialized in her own right as a 'Heroine of the Mission Field'.[20] Despite his own less-than-heroic credentials, Jowett was chosen by the society to be its literary representative. It was an unusual title, but, as the committee made clear in a highly detailed set of instructions imparted on the eve of his departure, it was an unusual post, one which would demand learning, courage and imagination. The CMS secretary was the London clergyman Josiah Pratt, Jowett's brother-in-law and a leading missionary publicist; the instructions seem to have been chiefly of his making. 'Your path is new;' Pratt warned, 'and you must become … qualified on the spot for your labour.'[21] Instead of preaching the gospel himself, he was to prepare the way for others to do so. He was to do this, the instructions explained, in two ways. First, he should ascertain the state of religion in the regions surrounding the Mediterranean, directing his travels, his correspondence, his linguistic study and his acquisition of manuscripts towards the 'ROMAN CHURCH' of southern Europe, 'MAHOMEDANS', 'various classes of Christians', 'JEWS' and 'HEATHEN', enquiring in each case into the best means of circulating Bibles and tracts and tracts among them. Second, he was to become, in time, agent for 'the PROPAGATION OF CHRISTIAN KNOWLEDGE' in the region, via education, journeys and publications. Crucially, they reminded him, he was being sent to an area that

---

[19] Charles Hole, *The Early History of the Church Missionary Society for Africa and the East, to the End of A.D. 1814* (London, 1896), 297, 306, 417–18. The date of Jowett's deaconing is unclear, but he was licensed as curate of St James's, Nottingham, in March 1811 and priested by the archbishop of York in December: Clergy of the Church of England Database, online at:<http://www.theclergydatabase.org.uk/jsp/search/index.jsp>, accessed 11 July 2014.

[20] Charles F. Childe, *The Finished Course: Brief Notices of Departed Church Missionaries* (London, 1865), 169–83; Emma Raymond Pitman, *Heroines of the Mission Field* (London, 1880), 322–9.

[21] 'Appendix V', 141.

was mostly outside British control; one where Ottoman sensitivities called for the utmost circumspection.

The Jowetts set sail from Deal on 4 September 1815. It seemed a propitious point for new endeavours in the Levant. As early as 1802, the CMS had entertained the idea of sending 'a man of the right stamp' to kindle 'Spiritual and Evangelical Religion' in the Greek Church.[22] But despite appeals to 'zealous young clergymen' versed in the classics and Christianity, there was no flood of clerical volunteers for this, or indeed for any other, missionary post. The Committee's vision of another Pentecost, when 'Parthians and Medes and Elamites, and the dwellers in Mesopotamia, and in Judaea – in Egypt – and Arabians' would 'speak in their own tongues the wonderful works of God', looked like a pipedream.[23] Impetus came from an unexpected direction. Dr Cleardo Naudi, a Maltese physician, had written to the society in 1811 regarding the collapse of Roman Catholic Propaganda missions to the Coptic Christians of Egypt.[24] Although Naudi was himself a Catholic, both the British and Foreign Bible Society (BFBS) and the CMS recognized a kindred spirit, and his appointment as their correspondent helped to crystallize a growing sense that Protestant missions would supplant Catholic ones. The final defeat of Napoleon at Waterloo a matter of weeks before the Jowetts departed helped to convince mission-minded Protestants that the French had been used to clear the way for them.

This mood was intensified by the fact that the Jowetts were heading for Christianity's original heartlands. If the Mediterranean teemed with religious associations, Malta seemed peculiarly apt as a headquarters:

> The ancient Sees of Augustin [*sic*] and of Cyprian – the Holy Land with the City of Jerusalem – Aleppo and Syria – the Lesser Asia with the Seven Churches – Constantinople and her subjected Greece – in truth, almost the whole sphere of

---

[22] 'Appendix III', *Proceedings* (1803), 238.
[23] Eugene Stock, *The History of the Church Missionary Society*, 4 vols (1899–1916), 1: 223.
[24] An interesting, although highly coloured, account of Naudi is given in Joseph Wolff, *Travels and Adventures of the Rev. Joseph Wolff; D.D., LL.D.* (London, 1861), 101–3.

the travels and labours of the Apostles is within a few days' sail.[25]

Predictably, the CMS Committee recommended that Jowett study the Epistles of St Paul, 'the great Evangelist of the Mediterranean', to Timothy and Titus. Paul's 'instructions', just as much as those delivered by the committee, 'will form a code of rules and a body of encouragement for you at this day'.[26] (Later missionaries were exhorted to treat the 'benighted and corrupted' Churches they encountered with moderation, taking the apostles' treatment of their Jewish countrymen and of Gentile converts as their model.)[27] The committee neglected to mention that the technology had not always changed much in the intervening period. Travel, Stock observed, was 'almost as difficult and fatiguing as in the time of St Paul', one voyage from Malta to Constantinople taking sixty-nine days.[28] This sense of a region where time had stood still both drew on and helped to fuel the growing Protestant fascination with the Eastern Churches. While Buchanan's *Researches* are often quoted for their colourful accounts of Hindu religious ceremonies, one of their most significant results had been to inform British readers about the Syrian Church in Malabar. Here was a community that claimed descent from the Apostle Thomas, preserved scriptural manuscripts of great antiquity and, Buchanan claimed, spoke the same language that Christ had.[29] The same urge that drove Protestants to seek primeval Christianity on the coast of India impelled them to find similar 'missing links' in the Middle East. Such ideas were made all the more credible by the standard works of contemporary religious history. Those familiar with Mosheim's widely read *Institutes* would readily recognize the sectarian geography of the Levant from accounts of the councils and controversies of the early Church, while Joseph Milner's influential *History of the Church of Christ* (1794–1809) conditioned readers to think of the elect as small, persevering groups scattered amid errors and idolatry.[30] These ideas in turn were part of a much broader sense

---

[25] 'Appendix V', 147.
[26] Ibid. 153.
[27] *Proceedings* (1828), 142.
[28] Stock, *History*, 1: 227.
[29] Claudius Buchanan, *Christian Researches in Asia* (Cambridge, 1811), 88–123.
[30] Milner would help Jowett in distinguishing between 'visible' and 'true' members

among nineteenth-century British people that the Mediterranean was a place where time stood still; where antique artefacts, peoples and cultures were miraculously preserved from the days of the Bible and of classical antiquity.[31]

Yet the chief reasons for choosing Malta were practical. Its post-war retention as a British military base was hailed as a heaven-sent opportunity, a 'bridge between the Oriental and the Occidental world'.[32] Ever since Britain had acquired it in 1800, missionaries had eyed it as a place to acclimatize to Mediterranean weather, culture and languages. The Jowetts spent their first winter studying Italian, Arabic and Maltese.[33] It was also well placed for communication with ports like Leghorn, Trieste, Smyrna, Acre and Alexandria, all of which had significant expatriate communities who might act as agents or patrons.[34] But Malta was not without its problems. Some of the most amusing papers among Jowett's letters to the BFBS detail the salty abuse hurled at eager tract distributors by local sailors.[35] More seriously, being a young colony, the British authorities were anxious not to offend Catholic sensitivities, and direct proselytization was banned under the 1814 Treaty of Paris.[36] Naudi was a helpful coadjutor and go-between, making translations into Maltese and Italian, but as Wolff's account of him attests, British colleagues sometimes found his changes of religious opinion alarming.[37] Correspondence flew to and fro between Jowett and the London secretaries of the CMS and BFBS regarding a variety of sensitive issues: whether or not to distribute Maltese Bible translations, most notably Naudi's Gospel of St John; and how to secure permission for a shop selling tracts and vernacular Bibles.[38] Nevertheless, Malta provided a safe centre of operations for those sponsored by British organizations, many of the CMS

---

of the Church of Christ: 'Appendix V', 144.

[31] David Gange and Michael Ledger-Lomas, eds, *Cities of God: The Bible and Archaeology in Nineteenth-Century Britain* (Cambridge, 2013).

[32] W. F. Ainsworth, *The Claims of the Christian Aborigines* (London, 1843), 6.

[33] Childe, *Finished Course*, 173.

[34] *Missionary Register* (1816), 246.

[35] Cambridge, University Library, British and Foreign Bible Society [hereafter: BFBS] Archives, BSA/D1/2, Abstract of Scriptures in Depository, 1830.

[36] Stefan Goodwin, *Malta, Mediterranean Bridge* (Westport, CT, 2002), 78–80.

[37] Wolff, *Travels*, 101–3.

[38] For which it was necessary to send a deputation to lean on Earl Bathurst: BFBS Archives, BSA/D1/2, Robert Pinkerton to Jowett, 26 April 1825.

agents, like Samuel Gobat, Christian Kugler, J. L. Krapf and K. W. Isenberg, being drawn from the Basle *Evangelische Missionsgesellschaft*.[39] It was also a haven for their American counterparts, whose Syrian mission and press withdrew there in 1828 during the Russo-Turkish war.[40] By the mid-1820s, then, a visitor would have encountered a thriving book depot, an active press, a women's Bible class (run by Martha Jowett), several young Jowetts, and, among the British residents, auxiliaries of the Bible Society, the CMS and the London Society for Promoting Christianity among the Jews.

Most important was the printing press. With its aid, mused Jowett in 1818, 'we may excite and enlighten three Continents'. Without one, 'we might almost as well be living in one of the fixed stars'.[41] His instructions on the subject were ambitious in the extreme.

> The Christian and Mahomedan Pilgrims might perhaps be supplied, as cheap articles of commerce, with the Scriptures and Tracts, at the places to which they resort, on their respective pilgrimages to Jerusalem and Mecca – the Christians at Alexandria, Rosetta, Damietta, and other towns: and the Mahomedans at Cairo, which is the great resort of the African Pilgrims; and at Damascus, which is the place of meeting of those of Europe and Asia. Arabic and other Bibles and Tracts might, by these caravans, be conveyed, on the one side, into the interior of Africa, to the kingdom of Fezzan, and even to Darfur; and, on the other, to all parts of Europe and Asia from which the pilgrims resort.[42]

Yet this was not as unlikely as it seemed. Regular readers of the *Missionary Register* in the 1810s and 1820s could hardly have been unaware that Jowett at Malta fitted into a rapidly developing global missionary strategy. Through the Reverend Henry Leeves, BFBS representative at Constantinople, and Robert Pinkerton, its travelling agent, he touched hands with John Paterson and the St Peters-

---

[39] Timothy C. F. Stunt, *From Awakening to Secession: Radical Evangelicals in Switzerland and Britain 1815–35* (Edinburgh, 2000), 122–33.

[40] A. L. Tibawi, 'The Genesis and Early History of the Syrian Protestant College', *Middle East Journal* 21 (1967), 1–15, at 6.

[41] *Missionary Register* (1818), 292.

[42] 'Appendix V', 149.

burg Bible Society, and with the Scottish 'Astrachan' Mission.[43] Through Gobat and Kugler in Egypt and Abyssinia, the route to the African interior lay open. Through Karl Gottlieb Pfander, based at Shusha in Persia, the gates of Central Asia seemed to be opening.[44] Further afield, the London Missionary Society (LMS) had carved out areas of influence in South Africa and the Pacific, while the American Board of Commissioners for Foreign Missions had agents in British India, Ceylon and the Far East, as well as Zululand and the Middle East.[45] By 1825 the depot at Valletta stocked Bibles in all the major Mediterranean languages and turnover had reached several thousand books a year, prompting frequent notes to London for extra supplies: 'Christian Travellers now increasing in number, and sometimes taking us by surprize. We could wish for at least 1000 Arabic Testaments and the same number of Psalters, without delay', as well as Armenian, English, Syrian, Spanish and Slavonian versions.[46] Had the art of printing been known in the days of the apostles, Jowett speculated, history might have turned out differently. The heresies that sapped the resilience of the Eastern Churches and laid them open to Muslim expansion could well have been averted from the outset. Now the latest technology might rekindle miraculous scenes from the apostolic age.[47]

In 1821, on his first furlough, Jowett became the youngest man ever to preach the CMS Anniversary sermon. His text was Revelation 3: 22, 'he that hath an ear, let him hear what the Spirit saith unto the churches', and he applied the message not just to the seven historic churches of Asia Minor, a frequent destination for pious British travellers keen to discern how providential warnings

---

[43] John Paterson, *The Book for Every Land: Reminiscences of Labour and Adventure in the Work of Bible Circulation in the north of Europe and in Russia* (London, 1858), 288–393.

[44] Avril Powell, *Muslims and Missionaries in Pre-Mutiny India* (Abingdon, 1993), 132–57.

[45] For details of these developing areas of influence, see Elizabeth Elbourne, *Blood Ground: Colonialism, Missions, and the Contest for Christianity in the Cape Colony and Britain, 1799–1853* (Montreal, ON, 2002); Donald Philip Corr, *'The Field Is the World': Proclaiming, Translating and Serving by the American Board of Commissioners for Foreign Missions, 1810–40* (Pasadena, CA, 2009).

[46] BFBS Archives, BSA/D1/2, Jowett and Cleardo Naudi to 'BFBS Secretary', 24 September 1822.

[47] William Jowett, *Christian Researches in the Mediterranean, from MDCCCXV to MDCCCXX*, 3rd edn (London, 1824), 284, 293.

had come true, but also to the supposed lineal descendants of those churches across the Levant.[48]

> Humble yourselves, ye churches of Greece, of Armenia, of Syria, of Egypt, and of Abyssinia! ... There was a time when ye endured a great fight of afflictions, but surmounted all by the triumphant powers of Divine grace. That time is long gone by. Your unblest sufferings of a thousand years bespeak now your sinful condition; and the judgments of God are made manifest.[49]

Yet the message was not without hope. If the Eastern Churches had been authors of their own downfall, Jowett held out the possibility that their revival was to be part of the moral and religious revival of the region around them. The point was pragmatic – the missionary organizations simply did not have the funds or personnel to set up Churches from scratch – but there was a deeper sense of providential symmetry to Jowett's rhetoric, revolving as it did around the vision of a biblically inspired return to primitive faith. Such post-millennial confidence helped to ensure that his writings were warmly received by British and American Protestants. His *Christian Researches in the Mediterranean* (1822) went into at least three editions; the sequel, *Christian Researches in Syria and the Holy Land* (1825), into four. In truth they were little more than hasty compilations from Jowett's journals and correspondence, much of which had been published already in the CMS *Annual Reports* and Pratt's *Missionary Register*. Nevertheless, their publication still generated considerable interest. On one level they were part of the boom in oriental travelogues that followed Napoleon's retreat from Acre in 1799.[50] But the fascination they awakened among evangelical readers had as much to do with present-day realities as with half-imagined past glories. The first volume, wrote one observer, 'seemed to arouse the attention of many in Europe and in America to scenes long held in almost religious reverence, but of the real

---

[48] For one example of this, see John Hartley, 'Visit to the Apocalyptic Churches, in the Year 1826', in idem, *Researches in Greece and the Levant*, 2nd edn (London, 1833), 223–304; see also Michael Ledger-Lomas, 'Ephesus', in Gange and Ledger-Lomas, eds, *Cities of God*, 254–84.

[49] Cited in 'Church Missionary Society', *Christian Observer* 20 (1821), 831–9, at 834.

[50] Eitan Bar-Yosef, *The Holy Land in English Culture, 1799–1917* (Oxford, 2005), 18–60.

condition of which little had hitherto been known'.[51] 'No similar work has ever made such deep impression on my mind and heart as this', an American correspondent wrote. 'I feel my soul expand, and seem to realise the latter-day glory.'[52]

There were indeed grounds for optimism. Letters of recommendation from the Coptic patriarch in Egypt commending Jowett's translation to his congregations meant that the CMS agent ran out of Bibles long before the end of his 1819 visit.[53] Meanwhile, Greek patriarchs and bishops were assisting in the formation of Bible Societies at Malta, Smyrna, Athens, on Corfu and in the Ionian Islands, with New Testament translations in modern Greek, Albanian, Turkish and Maltese all in progress. A signal moment was the well-publicized visit to London in 1819 of the Maronite archbishop of Jerusalem, Gregory Peter Giarve, seeking funds for printing educational texts and Bibles.[54] 'The revival of religion is unquestionably begun', trumpeted the CMS report.[55] Most encouraging for Jowett were avenues opening up for work in Abyssinia. In particular he was excited about acquiring translations of the Scriptures. The CMS already had manuscripts written in Ethiopic, the ecclesiastical language, but a ready-made version in Amharic, one of the vernacular tongues, conjured up visions of an enlightened Africa. The translation, carried out by an aged monk, Abu Rumi, under the sponsorship of the French Consul at Cairo, had taken ten years. That it came to light at such an opportune moment gave its creation a providential aspect, and Jowett deemed the cost of its purchase – 4,762 Spanish dollars, about £1,250 – to be warranted.[56] The manuscript was reviewed by Samuel Lee, Professor of Arabic at Cambridge and a key member of the CMS, before being published between 1824 and 1840 by another of Jowett's Cambridge friends, the linguist Thomas Pell Platt.[57] Its publication, prophesied Jowett, would be 'as the lighting of a Pharos on the inhospitable shores of the Red Sea!'[58] If the Greek

[51] Josiah and John Henry Pratt, *Memoir of the Rev. Josiah Pratt* (London, 1849), 185.
[52] Ibid.
[53] *Proceedings* (1820), 109.
[54] *Missionary Register* (1819), 134.
[55] Ibid. (1820), 477.
[56] BFBS Archives, BSA/D1/2, Jowett to BFBS Secretary, 17 April 1820.
[57] Edward Ullendorff, *Ethiopia and the Bible* (London, 1968), 162–72.
[58] Jowett, *Mediterranean*, 203.

War of Independence and consequent hardening of Ottoman attitudes represented the closing of one door, another appeared to be opening for work among the Copts and Abyssinians.[59] Ethiopia and East Africa would become a central CMS concern in succeeding decades.

As Leslie Howsam has argued, cheap Bibles, preferably sold rather than given away, became seen as the missionary key that would unlock every door.[60] Jowett took much the same view, offering Scriptures to Jews, Muslims and Christians wherever he travelled. His first volume in particular provided a systematic taxonomy to this end. Dividing 'Professed Christians' into four classes – the superstitious, the hypocritical, the covert infidel and the sincere enquirer – he went on to discuss 'Latins', 'Greeks', 'Coptic Christians' and 'Abyssinians'. Many individuals he found welcoming, but although he found vestiges of past glory and pockets of fervent belief, the overwhelming impression was of 'superstition' and lamentable deficiencies in scriptural knowledge. Jews he had seldom encountered, but he warned would-be missionaries that they were stubborn and self-righteous. Muslims, too, suffered from ignorance of the Bible, especially when it came to acknowledging their sinfulness and need for a saviour. 'The Mahomedan Religion', he pronounced, 'leaves all its votaries PROFOUNDLY IGNORANT OF THE NATURE OF THE HUMAN HEART.'[61] Drawing on developing tropes about oriental backwardness, he insisted that spiritual blindness went hand-in-hand with intellectual darkness.[62] This false religion, he argued, was protected by a despotic polity. There were noticeable parallels, therefore, to be drawn between 'Mahomedanism' and 'Popery', whose origins, Jowett noted earnestly, were

---

[59] Stock, *History*, 1: 231.

[60] Leslie Howsam, *Cheap Bibles: Nineteenth-Century Publishing and the British and Foreign Bible Society* (Cambridge, 1991).

[61] Jowett, *Mediterranean*, 249.

[62] Ibid. 250–2. It is worth making clear that Evangelicals were far from being mere prejudiced 'Orientalists' in the Saidian mode. Nile Green, 'Parnassus of the Evangelical Empire: Orientalism and the English Universities, 1800–50', *Journal of Imperial and Commonwealth History* 40 (2012), 337–55, argues that they shared much of the positivity of academic Orientalists such as Sir William Jones, whose enlightened study of Indo-European languages and culture influenced biblical and philological scholarship. At the same time, missionary preachers and publicists were apt to paint alien religious practices as barbarous and backward: see, for instance, Brian K. Pennington, *Was Hinduism Invented? Britons, Indians, and the Colonial Construction of Religion* (Oxford, 2005), 23–100.

coeval.[63] But where preaching was impossible, the circulation of Bibles and the encouragement of literacy might help to cast off the veil. Important, too, was the development of vernacular liturgies: for, anticipating a brighter future, how else could Eastern Christians imbibe the truth that would set them and their Muslim neighbours free? The second volume acted as a continuation, using Jowett's later travels to flesh out local details and providing further hints for those whom he hoped would come after him.

If Buchanan was the originator of the genre, Jowett's publications marked an influential second step, issuing from correspondence with the parent society by an agent specifically commissioned for that purpose. Others followed suit. James Connor's *Visit ... to Candia, Rhodes, Cyprus, and Various Parts of Syria and Palestine* (1822), Joseph Greaves's *Journal of a Visit to Some Parts of Tunis* (1825) and John Hartley's *Researches in Greece and the Levant* (1831) were all by CMS colleagues, and were published alongside Jowett's works. The genre also attracted American writers, Eli Smith and H. G. O. Dwight mirroring the CMS writers in structuring *Missionary Researches in Armenia* (London, 1834) in 'letters' and purposing to extend missionary knowledge into areas of the Levant that Jowett and his colleagues had not yet explored.[64] The author Joseph Wolff's eccentric attempt to find the lost tribes of Israel took him overland from Anatolia to Bombay and elicited *Researches and Missionary Labours among the Jews, Mohammedans, and Other Sects* (1835). Further afield, the LMS missionary John Philip produced two volumes of *Researches in South Africa* (1828), and William Ellis's two-volume *Polynesian Researches* was published the following year, both arguing that although much accurate information was available regarding exotic locations, Christians had more specific motives in garnering data. Pinkerton's *Russia* and Karl Gutzlaff's *Journal of Three Voyages along the Coast of China* both emerged in 1833. Although highly idiosyncratic, George Borrow's hugely popular three volumes on *The Bible in Spain* (1843) can on one level be placed in a similar category. Borrow's brief, at least, was undoubtedly a similar one: while he distributed copies of the Bible, he reminded readers that he had been sent 'more to explore

---

[63] Jowett, *Mediterranean*, 258.
[64] Eli Smith and H. G. O. Dwight, *Missionary Researches in Armenia including a Journey through Asia Minor, and into Georgia and Persia* (London, 1834), ix–xii.

the country, and to ascertain how far the minds of the people were prepared to receive the truths of Christianity, than for any other object'.[65] The most famous of all titles in this genre was David Livingstone's *Missionary Researches and Travels in South Africa* (1857); Livingstone's chapters, like theirs, combined travel accounts with religious taxonomy. Jowett, then, was one among many roughly contemporary writers concerned with similar questions but, as one of the earliest, he helped to establish both a set agenda for missionary travellers and a set of conventions for writing it up, being frequently quoted among the exemplars and remaining especially important for those concerned with the Mediterranean.

Although Jowett returned to Britain for good in 1830, following the death of his wife, Malta remained an important missionary centre. The Malta Protestant College, founded in 1846 by the earl of Shaftesbury and a consortium of London philanthropists, recycled familiar rhetoric. By training 'youthful orientals of good character and of fair abilities' as missionaries, Scripture-readers and interpreters, the college aimed to become 'A GREAT NURSERY AND STOREHOUSE' for evangelistic activity in the region.[66] Its deputation to 'the East' in 1849 revisited familiar ground, combining data-gathering with forging new networks. The inevitable published report weighed in at 1,228 pages of minute observation spread across two volumes, profits from the sale of which were to be ploughed back into the college. This essay has shown that such ideas and methods marked an important stage in the development of Protestant missionary endeavour. On one level they bore the hallmarks of Enlightenment thinking: the mapping of peoples and religions and the confident application of resources based on the data gathered. Yet all this had a dual purpose, too. It was also intended to enthuse those at home; to encourage them to pray, to participate, to give. It follows, therefore, that this was a highly 'modern' phenomenon too; one that drew on and helped to define the middle-class participatory 'public sphere' of activity, philanthropy and good works. How this fusion of research and publicity became a central plank of missionary strategy in the first half of the nineteenth century warrants sustained scholarly atten-

---

[65] George Borrow, *The Bible in Spain*, 3 vols (London, 1843), 1: xx.
[66] *Journal of a Deputation sent to the East by the Committee of the Malta Protestant College, in 1849*, 2 vols (London, 1854), 1: xiii.

tion: Pratt, for instance, is a key figure whose role in planning and projecting missionary influence from London has yet to be appreciated fully. We need to be aware, moreover, that Jowett was only one among many globetrotting agents who travelled the trade and later tourist routes, establishing depots, making connections and taking notes as they went. How such networks worked and overlapped is not yet fully appreciated: while recent attention has, for instance, been given to the German activities of Robert Pinkerton (1780–1859) of the Bible Society, he travelled much further afield and corresponded with individuals in Scandinavia, Central Asia and the Ottoman Empire.[67] Yet Jowett's work in particular was, and is, especially fascinating. His writings sought to pave the way for missionary endeavour in a region that seemed at once deeply familiar and unexpectedly strange. Here, as nowhere else, the Bible was not just a means of salvation but a conceptual map of the area's religious past and its present geography and culture. It shaped the way missionary agents dealt with the beliefs they found there, and in turn shaped local perceptions of how British people acted and what they expected to do. That the Eastern Churches continued to intrigue and baffle British Christians was, in large part, due to Jowett's pioneering work and his insistence that they were the key that would unlock a region of perplexing religious plurality.[68]

University of Cambridge

[67] Wayne Detzler, 'Robert Pinkerton: Principal Agent of the BFBS in the Kingdoms of Germany', in Stephen Batalden, Kathleen Cann and John Dean, eds, *Sowing the Word: the Cultural Impact of the British and Foreign Bible Society* (Sheffield, 2004), 268–85.

[68] See J. F. Coakley, *The Church of the East and the Church of England* (Oxford, 1992); W. H. Taylor, *Antioch and Canterbury* (Piscataway, NJ, 2005).

PLURALITY IN THE CAPITAL: THE CHRISTIAN RESPONSES TO LONDON'S RELIGIOUS MINORITIES SINCE 1800

by JOHN WOLFFE

On a late spring day in 1856 Prince Albert carried out one of the less routine royal engagements of the Victorian era, by laying the foundation stone of what was to become 'The Strangers' Home for Asiatics, Africans and South Sea Islanders', located at Limehouse in the London docklands. The deputation receiving the prince was headed by the earl of Chichester, who was the First Church Estates Commissioner and president of the Church Missionary Society, and included Thomas Carr, formerly bishop of Bombay, Maharajah Duleep Singh, a Sikh convert to Christianity and a favourite of Queen Victoria, and William Henry Sykes, MP and chairman of the East India Company. According to *The Times*,

> several other distinguished Orientals were in attendance in their magnificent costumes, including Ishore Singh Buhadur, Rajah of Benares; Nawab Meer Jaffier Alee Khan, Buhadur of Surat; the Syrian Archbishop and many others. The young Princess of Coorg was also present and witnessed the ceremony. On each side of the covered avenue leading to the marquee were arranged 50 Hindoos, an equal number of Chinese and Lascars, and several Arabs, Africans, islanders from the South Pacific, from the Malaccas, the Mozambique, and other countries, all in native costume.

In his speech Lord Chichester explained the purpose of the building, which was to provide a temporary home for visitors to London from Africa, India, the Far East and the Pacific, especially the so-called 'lascars' who manned ships arriving in the port, and who were often left stranded and destitute after they had spent or been robbed of their wages. These men, he said, were told that 'our laws and institutions were the admiration and envy of other nations', and they knew that 'the people of England were a people professing the Christian religion'. 'It was therefore', he went on, 'a most painful thing, and one most degrading to the character of the country, to find that no better welcome was accorded to the poor and helpless natives of other countries who visited our shores.'[1]

The Strangers' Home and the lascars have hitherto attracted some attention from historians of Asian communities in Britain,[2] but very little from historians of Christianity, despite the fact that there was substantial Christian involvement in the early history of the institution. Hence the laying of its foundation stone seems an apt point of departure for this essay, which explores the wider theme of the volume through a case study of Christian responses to religious minorities in London since the early nineteenth century, culminating in the enormous diversity that character-izes the contemporary metropolis. In the 2011 Census, while 48.4 per cent of the population of the capital described themselves as Christians, professed adherents of religions other than Christianity totalled 22.3 per cent of the population of London, a proportion somewhat exceeding the 20.7 per cent who declared themselves of 'no religion'.[3] That statistic implies that in London at least the dominant narrative in the religious history of the last fifty years has been quite as much one of pluralization as of secularization.

This essay falls into three somewhat unequal sections. First, it sets the scene by briefly surveying the growth of religions other than Christianity in Britain and the current historiography of these developments. Second, in the central and longest section, it explores two specific Christian responses to religious minorities in nineteenth-century London: missions to the Jews, and the Stran-gers' Home and the associated work of the London City Mission (LCM). An extended conclusion then surveys some twentieth-century developments in the context of that earlier history.

Non-Christian religions in Britain have in some respects been well studied by academics, especially since the terrorist attacks of 11 September 2001 in the United States and 7 July 2005 in London, which excited considerable research interest in Muslims,

---

[1]   *The Times*, 2 June 1856, 10.
[2]   For example, Rosina Visram, *Asians in Britain: 400 Years of History* (London, 2002), 59–61; Humayun Ansari, *'The Infidel Within': Muslims in Britain since 1800* (London, 2004), 67–8; Diane Robinson-Dunne, *The Harem, Slavery and British Imperial Culture: Anglo-Muslim Relations in the Late Nineteenth Century* (Manchester, 2006), 155–9.
[3]   2011 Census, Table KS209EW, 'Religion: Local Authorities in England and Wales', online at: <http://www.ons.gov.uk>, accessed 11 March 2014.

Islamophobia and the prevention of radicalization.[4] However the perception that the presence of minority religions in Britain is primarily contemporary rather than historical has meant that this work has been undertaken predominantly by social scientists rather than historians. Judaism is of course a significant exception to this pattern, with a long tradition of scholarly historical study dating back at least to the formation of the Jewish Historical Society of England in 1893. Otherwise, however, the only systematic scholarly histories of minority religious traditions in Britain are Humayun Ansari's study of Muslims and John Hinnells's of Zoroastrians.[5] There are also some significant monographs on British attitudes to Islam and relations with the Islamic world in earlier periods, notably Nabil Matar's *Islam in Britain 1558–1685*.[6] Anne Kershen's study of Huguenots, Jews and Bangladeshis in Spitalfields is a fascinating exploration of successive religious minorities in the East End from the seventeenth century to the twenty-first, their presence symbolized by the building in Brick Lane which began life as a French Huguenot temple and subsequently became a synagogue and then a mosque.[7] A recent collection edited by Jane Garnett and Alana Harris includes substantial material relating to religious minorities in London.[8]

Nevertheless, especially if one is concerned not so much with the internal history of religious minorities, but with their interactions with Christianity, there is still much to be explored. Even if one were concerned only with the history of minority religious communities since the mass migrations of the post-Second World War period, there is now a span of over fifty years to examine, the earlier parts of which are now moving to the fringes of living

---

[4]   For a variety of recent perspectives on these issues, see Marc Helbling, ed., *Islamophobia in the West: Measuring and Explaining Individual Attitudes* (London, 2012); Basia Spalek, *Terror Crime Prevention with Communities* (London 2013); Stacey Gutkowski, *Secular War: Myths of Religion, Politics and Violence* (London, 2014).

[5]   Ansari, *Muslims in Britain*; John R. Hinnells, *Zoroastrians in Britain* (Oxford, 1996).

[6]   Nabil Matar, *Islam in Britain 1558–1685* (Cambridge, 2008); see also Shahin Kuli Kahn Khattak, *Islam and the Victorians: Nineteenth Century Perceptions of Muslim Practices and Beliefs* (London, 2008); Robinson-Dunne, *Harem, Slavery and British Imperial Culture*, 154–96.

[7]   Anne J. Kershen, *Strangers, Aliens and Asians: Huguenots, Jews and Bangladeshis in Spitalfields 1660–2000* (London, 2005).

[8]   Jane Garnett and Alana Harris, eds, *Rescripting Religion in the City: Migration and Religious Identity in the Modern Metropolis* (Farnham, 2013), especially chs 8, 14, 16.

memory and hence certainly worthy of the attention of historians as well as social scientists. However, these histories are in fact
substantially longer ones, even if the scale of earlier activity was
relatively limited. In other fields of ecclesiastical history, marginality
has not been a disincentive to study, especially when a long chronological perspective indicates that groups that may have seemed
insignificant in their time were to acquire major importance in
a later period. In this respect research on non-Christian religious
groups in pre-twentieth-century Britain might, for example, be
seen in a similar light to work on the byways of medieval religious
and intellectual life by scholars seeking to understand the long-
term roots of the Reformation.[9] Moreover, to pursue the analogy
for a moment, much of the interest of such enquiry surely lies
in exploring the reactions of the dominant religious tradition of
the day in the endeavour to understand the origins of subsequent
patterns of behaviour.

Research on the early modern era has yielded intriguing hints
of the long-standing religious diversity of London. The capital's importance as a political and trading centre always attracted
short-term visitors and longer-term settlers to the extent that its
population was probably never exclusively Christian. Even in the
sixteenth century, when Jews were still in theory excluded from
the country, a small number of *conversos* lived in the city, outwardly
conforming to the Church of England, but probably maintaining
Jewish worship in secret.[10] Following Cromwell's readmission of
the Jews to England in 1655/6, a community several hundred strong
had established itself by the end of the seventeenth century, and
the first Great Synagogue in Duke's Place was built around 1690.
By the mid-nineteenth century the Jewish population of England
had grown to around fifty thousand, the majority of whom lived in
London. There was already considerable internal ethnic and social

---

[9] For example K. B. McFarlane, *John Wycliffe and the Beginnings of English Nonconformity* (London, 1966); Alister McGrath, *The Intellectual Origins of the European Reformation* (Oxford, 1987); G. R. Evans, *The Roots of the Reformation: Tradition, Emergence
and Rupture* (Downers Grove, IL, 2012).

[10] Beverley Nenk, 'Public Worship, Private Devotion: The Crypto-Jews of Refor-
mation England', in David Gainster and Roberta Gilchrist, eds, *The Archaeology of
Reformation* (Leeds, 2003), 204–20; Andrew Spicer '"Of no church", Immigrants,
liefhebbers and Confessional Diversity in Elizabethan London, *c.*1568–1581', in Isabel
Karremann, Cornel Zwierlein and Inga Mai Groote, eds, *Forgetting Faith? Negotiating
Confessional Conflict in Early Modern Europe* (Berlin, 2012), 199–220, at 213–14.

diversity, with Sephardim originating from the Iberian peninsula constituting a wealthy and influential elite, but finding themselves increasingly outnumbered by poorer Ashkenazim immigrants from central Europe.[11] Levels of religious practice were low: the 1851 Census of Religious Worship recorded only 2,824 sabbath attendances for the London registration division, probably no more than 10 per cent of the Jews living in the capital at that time, a much lower proportion of worshippers than for the nominally Christian population.[12]

Other minority religious groups initially lacked any organizational or physical focus of their own, although these emerged at an earlier date than is sometimes appreciated. The London Zoroastrian Association was formed in 1861, and the Woking Mosque built in 1889.[13] Regular Islamic worship was conducted in central London from the early twentieth century, initially in a variety of rented premises, until property was acquired in Commercial Road, Whitechapel, where the East London Mosque opened in 1941.[14] The first Sikh gurdwara opened in Putney in 1911 before moving to Shepherds Bush in 1913,[15] and the London Buddhist Vihara was established in 1926.[16] Hence by the time of the Second World War only Hinduism among the major world faiths lacked a place of worship in London: the first *mandir*, in Islington, eventually opened in 1970.[17]

Adherents of these religions were, however, present in London long before they acquired places of worship. A few Muslim travellers visited London in the sixteenth and seventeenth centuries, and a few conversions to Christianity, such as those of Chinano, 'a Turk, born at Negropontus', in 1586 and his compatriot Isuf

---

[11] For the development of Anglo-Jewry, see Todd M. Endelman, *The Jews of Georgian England 1714–1830: Tradition and Change in a Liberal Society* (Philadelphia, PA, 1979); David S. Katz, *The Jews in the History of England 1485–1850* (Oxford, 1994).

[12] *Census of Great Britain, 1851, Religious Worship, England and Wales, Report and Tables* (London, 1853), clxxxiv.

[13] Hinnells, *Zoroastrians in Britain*, 85; Ansari, *Muslims in Britain*, 15.

[14] Humayun Ansari, ed., *The Making of the East London Mosque, 1910–1951*, Camden 5th ser. 38 (Cambridge, 2011), 4–29.

[15] See <http://www.centralgurdwara.org.uk/history.htm>, accessed 11 March 2014; Visram, *Asians in Britain*, 104.

[16] See <http://www.londonbuddhistvihara.org/aboutus.htm>, accessed 11 March 2014.

[17] See <http://www.mandir.org/baps_uk/history.htm>, accessed 11 March 2014.

in 1659, were prominently trumpeted.[18] During this period the authorities were also much exercised by cases of returned English seamen and other travellers who had converted to Islam, sometimes but not necessarily under duress. By the early eighteenth century Londoners had become 'pretty well accustomed' to seeing Muslim visitors in the streets.[19] The growth of trading and political links with India in the eighteenth century increased the flow of visitors to London, both impoverished lascars recruited in the subcontinent to man the East India Company's ships, and higher status individuals with commercial, financial or scholarly interests. In 1810 Shaykh Din Muhammad opened the capital's first Indian restaurant, and although the venture was ahead of the tastes of its time and did not succeed, it was a sign of things to come.[20] By 1865 the religious diversity of London was such that the leading Baptist preacher, Charles Haddon Spurgeon, observed in a sermon:

> You may go on a mission to the heathen without going out of this huge town of ours. You might almost preach to every sort of literal heathen within the bounds of London – to Parthians, Medes, and Elamites and the dwellers in Mesopotamia. There are men of every colour, speaking every language under heaven, in London; and if you want to convert Mahommedans, Turks, Chinese, men from Bengal, Java, or Borneo, you may find them all here. There are always representatives of every nation close at our door.[21]

When in the 1870s the religious journalist Charles Maurice Davies visited the Unitarian South Place Chapel in Finsbury to hear a sermon by a representative of the Bramo Samaj,[22] he noticed how 'the well-filled chapel was dotted over here and over there with bright-eyed Asiatics, who had come to witness the once-rare phenomenon of a countryman delivering himself in an English pulpit'.[23] As South Asians were primarily only transient residents

---

[18] Matar, *Islam in Britain*, 126–8, 146–9.
[19] Quoted ibid. 151.
[20] Sophie Gilliat-Ray, *Muslims in Britain: An Introduction* (Cambridge, 2010), 25.
[21] Charles Haddon Spurgeon, 'The Great Itinerant', in idem, *Metropolitan Tabernacle Pulpit*, vol. 11, Sermon 655 (delivered 22 October 1865), 6, online at: <http://www.spurgeongems.org>, accessed 11 March 2014.
[22] A Hindu reform movement, influential in mid-nineteenth-century India.
[23] C. Maurice Davies, *Unorthodox London, or Phases of Religious Life in the Metrop-*

in London, it is impossible to establish a firm figure for their numbers at any one time, but there were probably several thousand temporary visitors in the later Victorian period as well as a few hundred more permanent settlers. Like Jews they were socially highly diverse. At one extreme were princely visitors, residing in the West End and moving in aristocratic and court circles; at the other the homeless and starving lascars of the docklands, and those former servants brought back from India by East India Company officials who found themselves destitute when their employers died or dismissed them. In between were members of princely retinues, and also traders and a growing number of students, including such subsequently famous names as Mohandas Gandhi, Mohammed Jinnah and Jawaharlal Nehru.[24]

Against this backdrop we turn, secondly, to more specific case studies of nineteenth-century London. The earliest and most sustained Christian response to a specific non-Christian minority was the London Society for Promoting Christianity amongst the Jews (LSPCJ), founded in 1808.[25] It followed a few years of small-scale work under the auspices of the London Missionary Society (LMS) by a German convert from Judaism, Joseph Frey.[26] In May 1806 David Bogue, a leading Independent minister, who had trained Frey for the work, preached for the LMS on 'The Duty of Christians to Seek the Salvation of the Jews'.[27] His sermon was,

olis, Series II (London, 1875), 194–5.

[24] Visram, *Asians in Britain*, 44–104.

[25] The LSPCJ (now The Church's Ministry among Jewish People) has yet to receive systematic scholarly attention, although its rich archives are deposited in the Bodleian Library (shelfmark Dep. CMJ), but see R. H. Martin, 'United Conversionist Activities among the Jews in Great Britain 1795–1815: Pan-Evangelicalism and the London Society for Promoting Christianity amongst the Jews', *ChH* 46 (1977), 437–52; Mel Scult, *Millennial Expectations and Jewish Liberties: A Study of Efforts to Convert the Jews in Britain up to the mid Nineteenth Century* (Leiden, 1978). In the absence of a subsequent full narrative history, the Edwardian centenary volume, W. T. Gidney, *The History of the London Society for Promoting Christianity amongst the Jews from 1808 to 1908* (London, 1908), remains an essential point of departure, supplemented for more recent developments by Walter Barker, *A Fountain Opened: A Short History of the Church's Ministry Among the Jews* (London, 1983).

[26] On Frey, see Donald M. Lewis, ed., *The Blackwell Dictionary of Evangelical Biography*, 2 vols (Oxford, 1995), 1: 410–11, and his own autobiographical pamphlet, *Narrative of the Rev. J. S. C. F. Frey, A Converted Jew* (Newcastle, 1810), which was subsequently expanded, notably in *The Converted Jew* (Boston, MA, 1815).

[27] In *Four Sermons Preached in London at the Twelfth Anniversary of the Missionary Society* (London, 1806).

however, more a critique of the behaviour of professed Christians and of their attitudes towards the Jews than the launching of an aggressive missionary campaign. Bogue argued that Christians had profound obligations to the Jews, but were themselves placing stumbling blocks in the way of their conversion. Roman Catholic worship was, he believed, 'disgustful and revolting … in the extreme' to those who were taught to eschew idolatry. It was true that Jews did not have to witness such things in England, but 'do they not see what is as bad, or worse? Do they not hear blasphemies, and oaths, and imprecations, every hour ascend to heaven? Do they not behold intemperance, lewdness, injustice, nay, every crime committed that can offend God, or render man guilty?'[28] The primary means to the conversion of the Jews was thus 'the display of a truly Christian temper and conduct before their eyes'.[29] This was the necessary context for prayer and efforts 'to communicate the knowledge of the Gospel to the Jews'.[30] On the other hand, persecution would be entirely counterproductive: 'For oppressors to engage in the work of converting the oppressed, is the very height of absurdity'.[31] The freedom of settlement and worship enjoyed by Jews in England gave 'reason to hope that they will listen to what we say, because it can be done without force or constraint'.[32]

Bogue's sermon highlights an emphasis that recurred in subsequent responses to religious minorities in London: a caution regarding provocative or oppressive evangelism, coupled with a concern to exhibit 'true' Christianity to non-Christian neighbours. Unfortunately, however, the development of the Jewish mission over the next decade showed scant regard for his advice. Already in 1808 his relations with his protégé Frey were becoming seriously strained, and he was uneasy about some of the latter's schemes. He wrote to him:

> Your plan of setting up a <u>boarding School</u> for Jewish children, and supporting everyone who professed to have a regard to Christianity, I could not approve − it is bribing people to

---

[28] Bogue, 'Duty of Christians', in *Four Sermons*, 84–5.
[29] Ibid. 91.
[30] Ibid. 95.
[31] Ibid. 99.
[32] Ibid. 100.

become Christians. I do not believe the apostle Paul ever gave all Jews unconverted forty shillings to make them Christians; and it would have filled your society with hypocrites.[33]

When the LSPCJ, initially dominated by Frey, began active operations the following year it provoked a hostile pamphlet from a Jewish preacher and teacher, Tobias Goodman, who also took particular exception to plans to establish a school for Jewish children, as 'ill-applied benevolence' which he feared would divide families. He challenged the society:

> Shew us on what authority you dare attempt to change our religion; give us a better form, a form more beneficial to man; and more to the glory of God: do not delude your proselytes; state your reasons, but lay aside temptations, for the unprincipled will always catch the bait; be at unity with yourselves first.[34]

If a subsequent pamphlet denouncing the society by its former printer, B. R. Goakman, is to be believed, fears that its methods would lead to insincere conversions proved entirely justified. In Goakman's view, the supposed converts given employment in his printing works showed little sign of genuine Christianity and had only embraced it 'to flee from distress and poverty'.[35] Moreover Frey himself was accused by Goakman and others of high-handed behaviour, mismanagement and misappropriation of the society's funds and even of an adulterous relationship with a female convert. When the committee enquired into the allegations they decided to dismiss him, but gave him financial assistance to emigrate to the United States in July 1816, where in 1820 he helped to found the American Society for Meliorating the Condition of the Jews.[36]

---

[33] Quoted in B. R. Goakman, *The London Society for Promoting Christianity Amongst the Jews; and the Pretension of the Converted Jew, Investigated* (London, 1816), 14. The LSPCJ employed Goakman from July 1810 until he resigned in October 1814: Oxford, Bodl., Dep. CMJ, c.5, 194; c.6, 406.

[34] Tobias Goodman, *An Address to the Committee of the London Society for Promoting Christianity Among the Jews* (London, 1809), 26.

[35] Goakman, *London Society*, 45.

[36] Dep. CMJ, c.7, minute 507, 28 May 1816; minute 532, 25 June 1816; cf. Scult, *Millennial Expectations*, 90–123; Michael R. Darby, *The Emergence of the Hebrew Christian Movement in Nineteenth-Century Britain* (Leiden, 2010), 45–57; Endelman, *Jews of Georgian England*, 71–6.

The LSPCJ had initially been set up on an interdenominational basis, but by 1815 it was apparent that it was ahead of the
times in its endeavour to manifest Christian unity in mission to
Jews, and its Dissenting supporters, recognizing that their presence
deterred Anglican donors, withdrew 'for the sake of the cause'.[37]
There was a frank acknowledgement of past failings, notably by
Charles Simeon, the leading Cambridge Evangelical, a prominent supporter, who recommended that 'as little as possible be
said of our early converts'. He drily observed 'Pharoah was not
more cruel to infant Hebrews than we are to adults. He drowned
his victims, and we hug them to death.'[38] The society had clearly
learnt the hard way that its initial well-intentioned policy of giving
material support to Jews as well as seeking to convert them to
Christianity was open to abuse and misrepresentation, and in 1819
it changed its rules to define its purpose as being purely spiritual.[39]
However, the new policy had its own difficulties, as it made it easy
for critics, both Jewish and non-Jewish, to allege that the LSPCJ
was only interested in securing converts and not in their subsequent well-being. Hence the policy was again modified in 1829
with the formation of the Operative Jewish Converts Institution,
which housed converts for a maximum of three years and trained
them in printing and bookbinding, and in 1844 with the creation
of a separate 'Temporal Relief Fund For Baptized and Enquiring
Jews'.[40] At the end of the century, in response to the large-scale
migration of East European Jews to the East End, the society
opened a surgery and dispensary for them at its mission hall in
Whitechapel and between 1892 and 1899 recorded nearly 90,000
attendances. Those waiting to be seen by the medical staff were
a captive audience for the Scripture readings, prayers and weekly
addresses in Yiddish provided by one of the society's missionaries.[41] There was clearly a precarious tightrope to walk and, as the
society's centenary historian acknowledged in 1908, '[t]he whole
subject of Temporal Relief is beset with difficulties.'[42]

---

[37] Dep. CMJ, c.6, 501–4, 27 December 1814; 508–10, 6 February 1815.
[38] Quoted by Gidney, *History*, 78.
[39] Ibid. 218.
[40] Ibid. 76–7, 218.
[41] Ibid. 533; Dep. CMJ, d.38/2, report from missionary, 2 June 1896, 18 Darnley
Rd, Hackney (signature illegible).
[42] Gidney, *History*, 218.

The LSPCJ was a substantial institution with impressive premises at Palestine Place in Bethnal Green, which housed a chapel,
training college, schools and the Operative Jewish Converts Institution. Much of its activity was among Jewish communities in
continental Europe, North Africa and Middle East, although it was
also active in English provincial cities. By the time of its centenary in 1908 it claimed to have carried out 2,110 baptisms in
the London mission alone.[43] Many of these were meticulously
recorded in the extant manuscript records. A typical page of the
register records eleven baptisms between January and October
1881, of which all but one (of an infant) were of young adult
males, with birth dates ranging from 1855 to 1866. A few of their
parents had local addresses, but most of them resided in eastern
Europe, including Galicia, Poland, Pomerania and Silesia. It would
appear therefore that the typical convert was a recent single male
migrant, isolated from immediate family ties and influences and
very probably lacking links to any synagogue or worshipping
Jewish community.[44]

The LSPCJ's income of £11,000 in 1820 and of £46,000 in
1900 bears comparison with that of the LCM and the major overseas missionary societies.[45] Its key lay supporters, such as William
Wilberforce and the seventh earl of Shaftesbury, were predominantly evangelical, but the patronage of most of the diocesan
bishops suggests broad-based Anglican sympathy for its work. The
most expansive Christian critic of the LSPCJ in its early years,
the Hackney Phalanx high churchman Henry Handley Norris,
questioned the society's methods and the prioritizing of substantial
expenditure on mission to Jews over remedying the 'deplorably
defective' 'means of public worship and of religious instruction' for
the nominally Christian population. However Norris was at pains
to emphasize that he agreed with its over-arching objective, and
considered 'that the conversion of the Jews remains … an object
of most intense interest, left in charge to the Christian Church,
as one of its most imperative obligations, and to be promoted by

---

43 Ibid. 592.
44 Dep. CMJ, c.249/1.
45 Gidney, *History*, Appendix II; for some comparative figures, see Andrew Porter,
Religion versus Empire: British Protestant Missionaries and Overseas Expansion 1700–1914
(Manchester, 2004), 55, 91; Donald M. Lewis, *Lighten their Darkness: The Evangelical
Mission to Working-Class London, 1828–1860* (Westport, CT, 1986), Appendix C.

its ministry, whenever the scripturally appointed means shall be pursued'.[46]

When at the turn of the twentieth century the LSPCJ sent a circular to the bishops, most of them were encouraging, albeit sometimes rather guarded in their responses. George Browne of Bristol (who had formerly been suffragan bishop of Stepney) was the most specific:

> I heartily approve of a moderate forward movement towards the instruction of poor Jews in London. I intentionally use the word 'instruction' instead of 'conversion,' believing that that puts the emphasis in the proper place. And I say 'moderate,' because I believe that action of a large type might stir animosities of a racial character.[47]

Bishop Mandell Creighton of London was a warm supporter, although he noted that 'some people' say, 'Why don't you leave the Jews alone?' His answer was that there was an imperative to give them knowledge of Christ, but then to 'leave God to do the rest'. He thought that 'we have to use all our wisdom and our caution to see that we do it well, so that there may be no reproach'. However, from conversations with LSPCJ workers he was reassured that 'their methods are right'.[48]

A similar moderation was apparent in the approach of the LCM, which began specific work among Jews in 1841 by distributing a circular letter to them. This acknowledged their understandable prejudices against Christianity, founded in 'the bitter persecution your forefathers endured from ungodly people who called themselves Christians' and the ungodliness of many professed Christians. Such actions, however, were 'quite contrary to the example and precepts of Jesus of Nazareth'.[49] Subsequent reports from their agents suggest that although they encountered considerable initial suspicion and even hostility from Jews, this was largely overcome on closer acquaintance, even if actual conversions were not numerous. One example illustrates something of the grassroots

---

[46] H. H. Norris, *The Origin, Progress, and existing Circumstances of the London Society for Promoting Christianity amongst the Jews: An Historical Enquiry* (London, 1825), 1–4.

[47] Quoted by Gidney, *History*, 526.

[48] Quoted ibid. 502.

[49] Quoted by Irene Howat and John Nicholls, *Streets Paved with Gold: The Story of the London City Mission* (Fearn, 2003), 171–2.

dynamics of such encounters. One autumn afternoon in 1855 the LCM missionary was sheltering from the rain under a gateway when he began a conversation with a young Jew who had been involved in the revolutionary movement in Germany in 1848, 'lost the little religion he had, and became ... a careless infidel'. Subsequently he fled to England, but his inadequate English had prevented him from obtaining employment and he was now on the verge of starvation. Visiting him at his lodgings a couple of days later, the missionary found him sick in bed, but being nursed by his landlady, 'a pious old Scotchwoman'. He laughed at the missionary's attempts to convert him, but the latter nevertheless helped him to obtain a job with a fellow German. When his circumstances improved, he moved to better accommodation, but kept in contact both with his former landlady and with the missionary. When the old lady became dangerously ill the missionary visited her, and met the German Jew by her bedside. His subsequent observation of the comfort brought to her by her Christian faith proved to be a trigger for his conversion, which he professed to the missionary while they were both attending her funeral. The salient features of this case would seem to be the convert's previous rootlessness and lack of active practice of Judaism, and the development of genuine and supportive friendships with both the LCM missionary and his Christian landlady.[50]

The Philo-Judaean Society, formed in 1826 as an offshoot of the LSPCJ, articulated a different Christian response to London's Jews. Rather than seeking individual conversions they were motivated by their understanding of biblical prophecy to promote the wider welfare of the Jews in the belief that 'upon their restoration to his [God's] favour, and to their own land, a great measure of blessedness will come upon all the nations of the earth'. This organization thus combined a liberal vision for the promotion of Jewish emancipation with radical premillennialist Evangelicalism, represented by Henry Drummond (1786–1860), who hosted the Albury prophetic conferences from 1826 to 1830, and by Hugh McNeile (1795–1879), who was commissioned to preach a series of sermons at St Clement Danes on the biblical prophecies relating to the Jews. In this context philo-Semitism was closely bound up with anti-Catholicism, and the society, whose president Viscount

---

[50] *London City Mission Magazine* [hereafter: *LCMM*] 39 (1874), 39–41.

Mandeville was also president of the British Society for Promoting the Religious Principles of the Reformation, vigorously denounced the 'grand apostasy of Rome' for renewing its 'persecutions and insults towards the favoured nation of Jehovah'. The Philo-Judaean Society was instrumental in securing the ending of a ban on Jews being admitted to the freedom of the City of London, a restriction that had severely hampered their prospects in business.[51] It was still in operation in 1842, albeit with only a modest income of £365 in the preceding year. The majority of this was spent on apparently unconditional financial support to 'distressed' Jews and converts from Judaism.[52]

The legacy of nineteenth-century Christian engagement with London's Jews was a complex one. The LSPCJ's early mistakes left an abiding sour taste, with the perception of unscrupulous missionary methods and hypocritical converts. However the ongoing reality was rather one of a slow trickle of sincere conversions, albeit usually of ethnic Jews who were not actively practising their religion, and of significant practical Christian support for Jewish people and their aspirations. Some converts were given substantial long-term support, as is apparent from a meticulous record kept by an LSPCJ worker in the early 1850s. His patience was put to the test particularly by one Lewis Nathan, who, despite 'annoying, threatening and demanding' behaviour and imprisonment for assault in 1851, received ongoing financial assistance and other support, and was eventually assisted in emigrating to the United States in 1853.[53] There was also specific concern for Jewish women, articulated for example in an appeal on behalf of the LSPCJ in 1810[54] and in the formation of female branches of the Philo-Judaean Society. Arguably too, awareness of competition and critique from Christians had a positive impact on Jewish religious life, in helping to stimulate the movement that led to Reform Judaism and in encouraging the Orthodox to be more purposeful

---

[51] *The First Report of the Philo-Judaean Society read at the General Meeting at Freemasons' Hall May 18 1827* (London, 1827), 10, 13; Endelman, *Jews of Georgian England*, 78–83; Darby, *Hebrew Christian Movement*, 77–81.

[52] *An Appeal in behalf of the Philo-Judaean Society including the Fifteenth Annual Report* (London, 1842).

[53] Dep. CMJ, d.12, especially 30, 39, 222–3.

[54] *An Address to Females on behalf of the London Society for the Promotion of Christianity amongst the Jews* (London, 1810).

in ministering to their own people. It also seems that a sense of the positive potentialities of Jews mitigated and limited the anti-Semitic tendencies evident in some of the arguments used against Jewish emancipation by conservative Christians. In general anti-Catholicism was a more prominent feature of religious life in Victorian London than anti-Semitism.

What then of other religious minorities, especially Muslims and Hindus, much less numerous than the Jews in London in the nineteenth century, but greatly exceeding their numbers by the beginning of the twenty-first? Shortly after the formation of the LSPCJ the LMS also became concerned about the lascars, of whom it was estimated that around 2,500 visited the country annually,[55] and in 1812 it set up a committee of supporters resident in east London to consider what measures might be taken. It recommended that missionaries be sought who either already spoke Asian languages or were willing to learn them.[56] In 1814 an appeal to that effect addressed to 'young men' was published. The anonymous author was unequivocal in his dismissal of Hinduism and Islam as 'the senseless worshippers of dumb idols, or the deluded followers of the licentious doctrines of a false prophet', and hence saw it as 'the incumbent duty of all who have time and opportunity to seek the eternal salvation of their immortal souls'.[57] As they had been exposed to oppression and wickedness at the hands of nominal Christians, it was imperative that they should be taught to 'distinguish between false and true professors' of Christianity.[58] Some Christian worship had already been held for them in Bengali and Hindustani, and had attracted up to seventy lascars.[59]

This initiative does not appear to have been sustained, and in 1842, James Peggs, formerly a Baptist missionary in Orissa, reawakened concern with a letter to the *Evangelical Magazine*, arguing that 'on every principle of policy, philanthropy and Christian zeal, we should not overlook that which is near, in our ardent prosecution of that which is distant'.[60] Peggs's intervention was supported by

[55] *Lascars and Chinese: A Short Address to Young Men of the several Orthodox Denominations of Christians* (London, 1814), 4–5.
[56] Ibid. 18–19.
[57] Ibid. 3, 9.
[58] Ibid. 11.
[59] Ibid. 14.
[60] James Peggs, *The Lascars' Cry to Britain: An Appeal to British Christians in Behalf*

George Smith, minister of Trinity Independent Chapel in Poplar, who emphasized that 'in any endeavour to benefit the Lascars prominent regard should be had to the alleviation of their physical sufferings', through the provision of accommodation, and medical and legal assistance. If this were done first, Smith thought, 'the way would be plain to endeavour to lead these degraded outcasts to the Friend of Sinners'.[61] Peggs republished the correspondence in a pamphlet in 1844, in which he highlighted his sense that Christian ministry to the lascars in London was of considerable strategic importance for the wider overseas missionary effort, because of the impressions they would carry with them when they returned home: 'The favourable or unfavourable report which they bring of our country, laws and religion is evidently of the utmost importance to the success of Christian missionaries and the propagation of the gospel of Christ.'[62] Again, however, no action was taken.

In 1854, however, there was at last a decisive step forward when Henry Venn, secretary of the Church Missionary Society, encouraged by a pledge of £500 from Maharajah Duleep Singh, took a personal interest and brought together an interdenominational board of management on which the other major missionary societies were also represented.[63] The resulting plan for a 'Strangers' Home for Asiatics, Africans and South Sea Islanders' was a product of a *prima facie* improbable collaboration between the missionary societies, the East India Company, returned Indian civil servants and soldiers, and the Indian princes. All of them, however, shared a concern for the physical well-being of the lascars. As described above, the foundation stone was laid in 1856, and the home, located close to Limehouse Church, opened a year later, on 3 June 1857. The trust deed summarized its objects as being:

> to provide, at a moderate charge, a temporary home, or lodging and board, under adequate superintendence, for strangers in any part of the United Kingdom, being natives of any part of the continent or islands of Africa (including Madagascar), or any part of the continents or islands of Asia, or New Zealand,

of the Asiatic Sailors, who Resort to the Ports of London, Liverpool &c. (London, 1844), 5.
[61] Ibid. 10–11.
[62] Ibid. 29.
[63] R. Marsh Hughes and Joseph Salter, *The Asiatic in England: Sketches of Sixteen Years' Work among Orientals* (London, 1873), 6–10.

or any of the islands of the China Sea, or Indian, or North Pacific Ocean; and in other ways to offer protection and aid, with Christian instruction, to such natives occasionally resident in this country.[64]

The home protected residents from robbers and swindlers by looking after their money and valuables. It provided general advice and information, and served in effect as an employment agency, both for obtaining work on shore and for seamen seeking a ship on which to return to Africa or Asia. Those able to pay were charged for their board and lodging, but the destitute were accommodated free of charge.[65] As the very name of the Strangers' Home implied, the underlying assumption was that its residents were temporary visitors to London, who would in due course return to their homelands.

The muted reference to 'Christian instruction' was presumably a compromise between the diverse individuals and agencies who funded the home. It was, however, too much for the Parsi firm of Cama and Company who in 1863 offered to discharge an outstanding debt of £4,000 if it were removed.[66] The Cama brothers were leading members of the small Zoroastrian community: both had travelled to London on business, but Karshedji Rustomji had returned to Bombay in 1855, where he played a central role in articulating a Zoroastrian response to the Christian missionary critique. His brother Muncherji Hormusji remained in England and in 1861 was the founding chairman of the London Zoroastrian Association.[67] They were therefore particularly sensitive to any hint of Christian proselytism. In response, Colonel Marsh Hughes, the secretary of the home, pointed out that the trust deed did 'not enforce upon foreigners Christian instruction, but *offer[ed]* it to those *willing* to receive it'. There was no wish 'to interfere with the prejudices of the natives of the East' but those who could read and so desired were given a copy of the Bible in their own language and were given instruction 'in the truths of the Gospel'. This response was deemed 'very unsatisfactory' by the Camas, who withdrew their conditional donation, but interest-

---

[64] Quoted ibid. 296.
[65] *Strangers' Home: Annual Report for the Year 1887* (London, 1888), back cover.
[66] Hughes and Salter, *Asiatic in England*, 296.
[67] Hinnells, *Zoroastrians in Britain*, 69, 85.

ingly it did not deter other wealthy non-Christian Indians from providing substantial financial support.[68]

The 'Christian instruction' in question was provided by Joseph Salter, employed by the LCM, working closely with the Strangers' Home and also visiting other lodging houses and ships in port. Over the next forty years extensive reports of Salter's work appeared in the LCM magazine, and he also published two books, *The Asiatic in England* (to which Hughes contributed accounts of the Strangers' Home itself) in 1873 and *The East in the West* in 1896. These provide valuable sources for scholars interested in the early history of British Asian communities. Salter was a zealous Evangelical, with what must have been an irritating facility for seeing opportunities to preach the gospel in the most unlikely contexts. For example he joined a group of Muslims celebrating Eid, listened to a song about a rajah whose son had been carried away to fairyland, and then sought to gain their attention with his own account of the heavenly rajah who sent his son into the world of men.[69] Nevertheless, he displayed a significant degree of cultural sensitivity, and, by his own accounts at least, was often given a respectful hearing. Many were willing to receive, or even to help distribute, his tracts, even if they did not profess conversion to Christianity.[70] Although he could dismiss Muslims as collectively 'bigoted' he was nevertheless aware of their internal diversity, and capable of engaging in reasoned theological debate with the better informed among them.[71] The extent of his activity was impressive; for example in the single year 1887 he reported that he had made 104 visits to 68 different vessels, spoken to a total of 2,805 people on board ship, in the Strangers' Home and in other lodging houses, and distributed well over 2,000 tracts and gospels, including publications in Arabic, Armenian, Bengali, Chinese, Gujarati, Hindi, Japanese, Malay, Malayalam, Marathi, Persian, Singhalese, Tamil and Turkish, as well as English and several other European languages.[72]

---

[68] Hughes and Salter, *Asiatic in England*, 297–301.

[69] Joseph Salter, *The East in the West or Work among the Asiatics and Africans in London* (London, 1896), 21–2.

[70] Ibid. 77.

[71] Ibid. 67, 72–4.

[72] *Strangers' Home ... Annual Report for the Year 1887* (London, 1888), 13–14, online at: <http://webarchive.nationalarchives.gov.uk/+/http://www.movinghere.org.uk/search/>, last accessed 1 September 2014.

JOHN WOLFFE

The generally positive reception Salter received was no doubt founded on an awareness of his substantial practical support and compassion for lascars, for example in ensuring that their medical needs were attended to, or intervening with the police and magistrates to assist those who, sometimes unjustly, found themselves on the wrong side of the law.[73] He was sometimes in physical danger, not from the lascars themselves, but from local criminals and unscrupulous landlords who found their livelihoods threatened by his endeavours to protect less streetwise visitors from theft and exploitation. He claimed credit for the closure of local opium dens, and raising the moral tone of the neighbourhood.[74] In later years he supplemented the work of the Strangers' Home and provided a substitute for less reputable places of recreation by setting up his own Asiatic Rest near the East India Dockyard gates to provide 'drop in' facilities, refreshments and a library, in which the Qur'ān as well as the Bible was available.[75]

Assessment of Salter's achievement depends on the criteria applied. He made few, if any, converts and acknowledged that the response to his public preaching, especially on board ship, was limited, because men were reluctant to show interest in Christianity in front of their peers. However, he reported that many subsequently sought him out at the Asiatic Rest for further instruction.[76] A few encounters suggested genuine spiritual searching: for example a young Hindu seaman asked him for a gospel in Hindustani, and was very disappointed when he only had one available in English. The young man said 'he had long wished to become a Christian' and had attended places of worship at every port hoping to get 'the influence', but did not feel any more a Christian. 'What he required', Salter wrote, 'was not an "influence" to feel but an object to trust – to know Whom to believe; and on pointing him to the Saviour his hunger seemed satisfied.'[77] More commonly, it seems, Salter merely awakened the diffuse spiritual interest of transient visitors remote from any organized provision for teaching or worship in their own faith. They may have felt edified and comforted by his ministry and some of their misun-

73 Salter, *East in the West*, 111–6.
74 Marsh and Salter, *Asiatic in England*, 272–94.
75 Salter, *East in the West*, 150–67.
76 Ibid. 150–1.
77 Ibid. 79–80.

derstandings about Christianity were mitigated, but they were not yet persuaded to change their religion. Salter wrote: 'It is one of the saddest things about our work among these birds of passage that, however hopeful we may be, we are so often unable to speak of the results.'[78] Nevertheless, it is arguable that Salter's energetic ministry over four decades and his readiness to offer practical help as well as spiritual exhortation had a significant impact in mitigating prejudice on both sides. He presented Christianity with a human face to numerous non-Christian visitors to London and through his reports and writings helped his Christian readers gain a sympathetic understanding of religious and cultural worlds in their own city that would otherwise have been entirely closed to them.

Salter's world was primarily a male one, but not exclusively so. He wrote of English women, such as 'Chinese Emma' and 'Lascar Sally', who formed long-term relationships with non-European men who had became semi-permanent settlers and set up lodging-houses and opium dens to provide for more transient visitors.[79] Salter was especially concerned for Chinese Emma's welfare and was delighted to be able eventually to report that she had married her partner Appoo and that they had shut down their disreputable establishment and signed on as stewardess and cook respectively on a transatlantic passenger vessel. Salter sent them off with Testaments in English and Chinese 'directing their attention once more to the sacrifice for sin'.[80]

India Office files illustrate the practical problems the Strangers' Home sought to address in responding to the human casualties of empire. In 1897 they housed Mahomed Khan, who had come to London from Karachi after having been dismissed from an Indian army regiment. After refusing two offers of employment he had been asked to leave the home, and was now threatening to squat at a Windsor railway station and petition the queen. He was deemed 'excitable' and 'likely to give trouble' and his threats were taken sufficiently seriously for warnings to be passed on to the Metropolitan Police and the queen's private secretary.[81] In 1908 the home

---

78   Ibid. 79.
79   Marsh and Salter, *Asiatic in England*, 27.
80   Ibid. 284–5.
81   London, BL, India Office Records [hereafter: IOR], L/PJ/440/File 346, letters of 22 February, 6 March 1897.

looked after six Punjabis who had attempted to emigrate from India to the United States but had been refused admission by the American authorities and returned destitute to Southampton.[82]

The Strangers' Home, intended primarily for visiting seamen, was complemented by the Ayahs' Home, established in Aldgate as a privately-run hostel, possibly as early as 1825, although its provision initially appears to have been precarious and inadequate.[83] It housed Indian women employed as nannies on board ship by families returning to England, but then paid off and requiring accommodation until re-employed by other families going out to India. Salter subsequently became closely involved with its work and it was eventually, in 1900, taken over by the LCM, which placed it on a more secure footing and moved it to larger premises in Hackney.[84] A further initiative was the St Luke's Lascar Mission, which from 1887 to 1905 employed a Bengali Christian, the Revd E. B. Bhose, as its chaplain. Like Salter, Bhose organized social and leisure facilities as well as engaging in evangelistic work.[85]

The twentieth century – and more particularly its later decades – saw the transformation of London from a city in which only small minorities of the population adhered to faiths other than Christianity to one in which, by 2011, less than half of the population professed to be Christians and more than a fifth professed other religions.[86] The implications of this profoundly significant change merit much more extensive attention from researchers than they have yet received, but in concluding this essay some exploratory observations can be made against the background of the nineteenth-century developments described above.

Initially there were naturally significant continuities with the Victorian era. A printed report in 1902 listed numerous agencies

---

[82] Ibid. L/PJ/6/861/File 1297.

[83] *The Times*, 3 December 1868, 3. This advertisement, claiming the home was set up in 1825, is widely cited on websites relating to the history of Muslim and Asian communities, but I have not found any further evidence of its existence prior to 1879, when Salter reported visiting it: *The Times*, 2 June 1879, 6. Visram notes the 'disreputable' living conditions experienced by ayahs in London in the 1850s: *Asians in Britain*, 51.

[84] Salter, *East in the West*, 165; <http://www.open.ac.uk/researchprojects/makingbritain/content/ayahs-home>, accessed 15 July 2014; Visram, *Asians in Britain*, 51–4.

[85] Ibid. 61–2.

[86] Peter Brierley, *Capital Growth: What the 2012 London Church Census Reveals* (Tonbridge, 2013), 41.

involved in missions to Jews in London, with the longstanding
labours of the LSPCJ and the LCM complemented by local and
personal initiatives such as the East London Fund for the Jews
and Mr Henry Barnett's Mission.[87] Although Salter's successors
lacked the public profile he achieved through his two books, the
LCM maintained what it called its 'mission to Orientals'. During
the inter-war period its missionary, Mr Bugby, was based at the
Lascar Institute in Tilbury, which like Salter's Asiatic Rest in earlier
years provided social and recreational facilities for visiting seamen.
Bugby also engaged in assiduous visitation, both on board ship
and in lodging houses around east London. He usually met with
a favourable reception from Hindus, Muslims and Sikhs who
welcomed his personal interest in them and were willing to discuss
religion, but much more reluctant to convert to Christianity.[88]
The Strangers' Home, now known as the Asiatic and Overseas
Home, continued to provide accommodation that was recognized
by official inspections in the 1920s to be of a superior standard
to that available in other lodging houses.[89] Similarly the Ayahs'
Home, by the 1930s under the charge of LCM missionaries Mr
and Mrs William Fletcher, continued to provide essential support
for vulnerable Asian women stranded in London with little or
no knowledge of English and no immediate means of returning
home.[90]

By this period the increasing visibility of London's religious
minorities, with the beginnings of permanent settlement, was
prompting a different kind of broadly Christian response, which
was to offer limited public recognition and seek to provide facilities for non-Christian worship. Thus in 1920, at the instigation of
Lord Curzon, considerable efforts were made to obtain Muslim
and Sikh representation at the dedication of the Cenotaph and the
funeral of the Unknown Warrior.[91] In the meantime a number of
prominent non-Muslims, such as Sir William Bull, a Conservative
MP, and Lord Ampthill, a former governor of Madras, were active

---

[87] Dep. CMJ, d.38/5.
[88] *LCMM* 99 (1934), 11–12, 123; 101 (1936), 142; J. E. Bugby, 'Moslems in London',
MW 28 (1938), 76–9.
[89] IOR, L/E/7/1152, fols 554–8, London County Council Public Health Department, 15 June 1922; L/E/7/1360, File 3847, report by E. W. Hudleston, 7 January 1926.
[90] William Chambers, 'A Haven for Oriental Women', *LCMM* 101 (1936), 143–4.
[91] Kew, TNA, Cabinet Office Papers, CAB 27/99, 52.

members of the London Mosque Fund, which raised funds to support provision for Muslim worship and the eventual opening of the East London Mosque in 1941. They found common ground with Anglophile Indian Muslims, led by Saiyid Ameer Ali, who perceived the project for a London mosque as a means of affirming the loyalty of their co-religionists to the British Empire. This movement reached its culmination in the early years of the Second World War, when the government provided funds for the purchase of the land on the edge of Regents Park that was subsequently to become the site of the London Central Mosque.[92]

There was, however, no clear-cut distinction between Christian mission and acceptance of religious plurality. In the 1920s, the Christian ethos of the Asiatic and Overseas Home was no barrier to its providing appropriate facilities for Muslim prayers, in contrast to private lodging houses, which did not offer these. Muslim residents were also allowed to kill their own halal meat at a local slaughter house.[93] Although the social and material support provided by the LCM through the Lascar Institute and the Ayahs' Home was part of an underlying evangelistic strategy, it was given without preconditions. Meanwhile, missions to Jews were associated more with philo-Semitism than with anti-Semitism. Indeed, Donald Lewis has argued that the Balfour Declaration of 1917 was in part attributable to the legacy of Victorian religious interest in the Jews.[94] Certainly in the 1930s the LSPCJ and the LCM readily articulated concern for the plight of German Jews: for example, in 1934 the LSPCJ urged its members to take every opportunity to show kindness to Jews 'for even in this country rudimentary forms of anti-Semitism are becoming common'.[95] An LCM missionary wrote in 1939: 'our endeavour is always to show the Jews Christian kindness in order that they may see and know that whatever treatment they may receive in other countries, the great heart of Christian England goes out in loving sympathy to the Jewish race'.[96] There was little evidence, however, of practical action commensu-

---

[92] Ansari, ed., *East London Mosque*.

[93] IOR, L/E/7/1152, fols 554–8; L/E/7/1360, File 3847, report by E. W. Hudleston, 7 January 1926.

[94] Donald M. Lewis, *The Origins of Christian Zionism: Lord Shaftesbury and Evangelical Support for a Jewish Homeland* (New York, 2010).

[95] *Jewish Missionary Intelligence*, August 1934, 95.

[96] Quoted by Howat and Nicholls, *London City Mission*, 169.

rate with the rhetoric. Nevertheless, although organizations with an ethos of inter-faith dialogue rather than of mission, notably the London Society for Jews and Christians (formed in 1927) and the Council of Christians and Jews (1942), marked a new departure in Christian-Jewish relations, there was more continuity in spirit with earlier activity than is sometimes appreciated.[97]

Victorian institutions finally faltered in the late 1930s and 1940s, due in large part to disruption consequent on the Depression, unrest in India and the Second World War. By the early 1930s the Asiatic and Overseas Home was suffering heavy annual losses and in 1935, seventy-nine years after its opening, it was decided to close it, despite an expression of 'grave concern' from the Muslim Association of East London, testimony to its success in overcoming earlier religious suspicions.[98] The Ayahs' Home survived a few more years but closed during the Second World War.[99] The LCM maintained its presence at Tilbury under Bugby's dedicated leadership and replaced him when he retired in 1967, but the primary focus on visiting seamen twenty miles downriver was marginal to the religious life of London itself.[100] Meanwhile the legacy of the Holocaust transformed the dynamic of Christian-Jewish relations, and the LSPCJ similarly scaled back its activities. It followed the migration of London's Jews themselves, and now concentrated its work in Hampstead and Finchley.[101]

It is thus a significant irony that when, in the late 1950s, London began to receive substantial numbers of Asian migrants, there was probably less active practical Christian engagement with people of other faiths in the metropolis than at any time in the previous century. Initially the issue was seen, even by the churches, to be essentially one of race rather than religion, a perception that was understandable in light of the low levels of religious practice among early migrants, but still a noticeable concession to secular thinking that is a neglected aspect of what Hugh McLeod has

---

[97] Marcus Braybrooke, *Children of One God: A History of the Council of Christians and Jews* (London 1991), 3, 12.

[98] IOR, L/E/9/967, letters from F. J. Adams (Indian High Commissioner's Office), 28 February 1935; Syed Fazal Shah, 26 April 1935.

[99] See <http://www.20thcenturylondon.org.uk/indian-london>, accessed 19 May 2014.

[100] *LCMM* 116 (1951), 59–62. Bugby was succeeded at Tilbury by a Mr J. Colby: *LCMM* 131 (1967), 52. Around 1976 the LCM missionary there was a Dutchman, Teus Kuppers (information from Tim Grass).

[101] Barker, *Fountain Opened*, 17.

called 'the religious crisis of the 1960s'.[102] In 1970, the *London City Mission Magazine* struck a rather despairing and implicitly racist note: 'The invasion of London by many thousands of immigrants has introduced patterns of life that could retard our progress. These visitors have brought with them their own religions; their own peculiar ideologies'.[103]

The 1970s, however, saw a growing recognition at a national level, notably by the British Council of Churches, of the need to respond constructively to the growth of non-Christian minority religions, but in this decade there was little active engagement by the churches in London.[104] One revealing case is that of David Sheppard, who, despite working for twenty years between the mid-1950s and the mid-1970s on the cutting edge of inner-city ministry in east and south-east London, does not appear to have become alert to the religious implications of the Asian presence in Britain until the early 1980s when, already bishop of Liverpool and a member of the Archbishops' Commission on Urban Priority Areas, he sought some 'education' through a visit to Southall.[105] Even in the early 1980s, it was unusual and controversial for a London church – such as that of Sheppard's host at St George's, Southall, Mano Ramulshah – actively to engage with other religious groups.[106] Nevertheless this period saw a gradual change in attitudes: the LCM's approach became more engaged and cultur-

---

[102] Hugh McLeod, *The Religious Crisis of the 1960s* (Oxford, 2007); in this volume, Peter Webster, 'Race, Religion and National Identity in Sixties Britain: Michael Ramsey, Archbishop of Canterbury, and his Encounter with other Faiths', 385–98.

[103] *LCMM* 134 (1970), 261.

[104] John Wolffe, 'How many Ways to God? Christians and Religious Pluralism', in Gerald Parsons, ed., *The Growth of Religious Diversity: Britain from 1945*, 2: *Issues* (London, 1994), 25–53; Matthew Grimley, 'The Church of England, Race and Multi-Culturalism, 1962–2012', in Garnett and Harris, eds, *Rescripting Religion*, 207–21. This provisional conclusion is, however, very much open to testing by further research, drawing particularly on oral history and on records relating to the sale of former Christian buildings to other religious groups. For case studies from other parts of the country of the actual or proposed use of Christian buildings by other faiths, see, in this volume, John Maiden, '"What could be more Christian than to allow the Sikhs to use it?" Church Redundancy and Minority Religion in Bedford, 1977–8', 399–411; Gillian Carver, *A Place to Meet: The Use of Church Property and the New Religious Minorities in Britain* (London, 1978), 29–35; Andrew Chandler, *The Church of England in the Twentieth Century: The Church Commissioners and the Politics of Reform* (Woodbridge, 2006), 229–39, 290–4.

[105] David Sheppard, *Steps Along Hope Street: My Life in Cricket, the Church and the Inner City* (London, 2002), 283.

[106] Ibid. 284.

ally sensitive, although still unashamedly evangelistic, while clergy working in East London during this period recall increasing contacts with other faiths, arising primarily from shared community concerns.[107]

Although by the early 2000s there was more extensive institutionalized activity, in London at least much of it was still of only recent development. The London Inter-Faith Centre in Brondesbury was established in 1998, St Ethelburga's Centre for Reconciliation and Peace in the City of London in 2003, and the Contextual Theology Centre at the Royal Foundation of St Katherine in Limehouse in 2005; this hosts the London Presence and Engagement Network, established in 2009.[108] A book published in 2008 presented numerous case studies of London churches and their members engaging with people of other faiths, but almost all the initiatives described had only emerged since the turn of the millennium. As the coordinator of a multi-faith chaplaincy at the O2 dome put it, 'In 2000 we were Christian chaplains. In 2007 we were Muslim, Sikh and Christian. The world has changed.'[109] Nevertheless, change remained uneven. Kenneth Leech, whose initial anti-racist concerns had increasingly led him into inter-faith activity in the East End, still thought in 2006 that 'Christians are very divided and confused about how they relate to other faiths'.[110]

Although religious plurality remains controversial and sometimes difficult to negotiate at a local level, the London experience prompts the concluding reflection that Christianity may actually thrive better in a context of religious plurality rather than in one of monopoly. The upsurge in recent years of practical cooperation and good neighbourliness reflects a recovery of the awareness, apparent in the practical support for Jews provided by the LSPCJ

[107] *LCMM* 147 (1983), 22, 48; 149 (1985), 26; e-mail from the Rt Revd Clive Young, 9 June 2014; telephone conversation with the Revd Richard Bentley, 15 July 2014.

[108] See <http://www.londoninterfaith.org.uk/about/purpose-and-history>; <http://www.stethelburgas.org/history>; <http://www.theology-centre.org.uk/about-us/>; <http://www.londonpen.org/>; <http://rowanwilliams.archbishopofcanterbury.org/articles.php/1038/archbishop-to-launch-greater-london-presence-and-engagement-network>, accessed 19, 29 May 2014.

[109] Malcolm Torry and Sarah Thorley, eds, *Together and Different: Christians Engaging with People of Other Faiths* (Norwich, 2008), 21. There are further such case studies on the London Presence and Engagement Network website, <http://www.londonpen.org/?page_id=276>, accessed 19 May 2014.

[110] Kenneth Leech, *Doing Theology in Altab Ali Park* (London, 2006), 125.

and in the building of the Strangers' Home, that effective Christian witness involved much more than confrontational mission.[111] Moreover, one of the prominent features of the rhetoric of those in nineteenth-century London promoting missions to Jews and Asiatics was the need to promote moral and spiritual renewal among the nominally Christian population as a witness to their non-Christian neighbours. In this context recent trends in London are fascinating and significant: although the 2011 Census indicates that only 48.4 per cent of the population of the capital profess to be Christians, 10 per cent or so less than the national average, the 2012 Church Census suggests that 8.8 per cent of the total population of Greater London, or nearly 20 per cent of the nominally Christian population, are churchgoers, a much higher proportion than in the country as a whole. That figure has risen substantially in recent years.[112] In London at least, pluralization may indeed be a more accurate way of thinking about the religious trends of the last two centuries than secularization.

The Open University

---

[111] Cf. Michael Keith, 'Discovering Faith? The Hidden Contours of Political Participation and Devotional Practice in Contemporary East London', in Garnett and Harris, eds, *Rescripting Religion*, 223–33.
[112] Brierley, *Capital Growth*, 67.

ANGLICAN CLERGY RESPONSES TO JEWISH MIGRATION IN LATE NINETEENTH-CENTURY LONDON

by W. M. JACOB

When, yearly, on Good Friday, Church of England clergymen prayed: 'Have mercy upon all Jews, Turks, Infidels and Hereticks, and take from them all ignorance, hardness of heart and contempt of thy Word: and so fetch them home blessed Lord, to thy flock, that they may be saved among the remnant of the Israelites', 99.9 per cent of them in the late nineteenth century had little expectation of encountering a Jew, Turk or Infidel. This paper seeks to explore how the few Church of England clergy in London who in the 1890s did have a significant presence of Jews in their parishes responded as ministers of the established Church, with a charge to be responsible for the spiritual well-being of all the inhabitants of their parishes, including the call to save the Jews 'among the remnant of the Israelites'.[1]

Even in London there were not many 'Infidels',[2] but there were a minority of Jews who were relatively significant because they were concentrated in a very limited area: Sephardic Jews from Spain and Portugal and Ashkenazi Jews from Central and Eastern Europe had settled in London since the mid-seventeenth century, mostly in the City of London and neighbouring parishes in Tower Hamlets. In 1858 it was estimated that there were about 36,000 Jews in Britain, about 90 per cent of whom were British-born, and about two-thirds of whom lived in London.[3]

The east side of the City and the adjoining Tower Hamlets parishes were long-standing areas of settlement for earlier migrant

---

[1] Book of Common Prayer, Third Collect for Good Friday.
[2] See G. Beckerlegge, 'Followers of "Mohammed, Kalee and Dada Nanuk": The Presence of Islam and South Asian Religions in Victorian Britain', in John Wolffe, ed., *Religion in Victorian Britain*, 5: *Culture and Empire* (Manchester, 1997), 221–67; Humayun Ansari, *The Infidel Within: Muslims in Britain since 1800* (London, 2004), 35, 68; in this volume, John Wolffe, 'Plurality in the Capital: The Christian Response to London's Religious Minorities since 1800', 232–58.
[3] Vivian D. Lipman, *A History of the Jews in Britain since 1858* (Leicester, 1990), 12–14.

communities which had been Christian: Huguenots in the late seventeenth century, and Irish from the late eighteenth century. The Huguenots, as Protestants, had mostly assimilated into English and Anglican society. The Irish, especially Catholics, had remained as distinct communities, strongly resisting attempts to convert them to Anglicanism, even if they had lapsed from Catholic practice.[4] At the end of the nineteenth century there were also Norwegian, Swedish and German seamen's missions, and a German church for the significant numbers of German settlers in east London.[5]

British Jews, apart from their religious practices, had like Huguenots sought assimilation into British society. The British were largely indifferent to them, and had not excluded them from political, economic or social life.[6] A significant proportion of the Jewish population were successful professional men and city brokers, and merchants. The Anglo-Jewish elite saw themselves as well integrated into the culture and institutions of the London propertied classes.[7] They had formed their religious institutions on English (and most particularly Church of England, models) with the office of chief rabbi paralleling that of archbishop of Canterbury, and had reformed the rabbinate in Britain on the model of Anglican and Nonconformist clergy, which involved undertaking pastoral, preaching and teaching roles, preaching in English and mixing on equal terms with other clergy. Lord Rothschild expected a 'minister' to live 'like a Christian gentleman in the midst of his flock'.[8]

---

[4]   See Lynn Hollen Lees, *Exiles of Erin: Irish Immigrants in Victorian London* (Manchester, 1979).

[5]   Richard Mudie Smith, ed., *The Religious Life of London* (London, 1904), 53.

[6]   For the background of Jews in London and Britain, see David Englander, 'Anglicized not Anglican: Jews and Judaism in Victorian Britain', in Gerald Parsons, ed., *Religion in Victorian Britain*, 1: *Traditions* (Manchester, 1988), 235–73; Lipman, *History*. For the settlement of Jews in the East End of London, see Vivian D. Lipman, 'Jewish Settlement in the East End, 1840–1940', in Aubrey Newman, ed., *The Jewish East End, 1840–1939*, Jewish Historical Society (London, 1981), 17–40.

[7]   David Feldman, 'The Importance of Being English: Jewish Immigration and the Decay of Liberal England', in idem and Gareth Stedman Jones, eds, *Metropolis London: Histories and Representations since 1800* (London, 1989), 56–84, at 62. For an account of the reaction to Jewish migrants in the East End, see William J. Fishman, *The Streets of East London* (London, 1979), ch. 4.

[8]   Englander, 'Anglicized not Anglican', 252, quoting S. Sharot, 'Religious Change in Native Orthodoxy in London 1870–1914: Rabbinate and Clergy', *Jewish Journal of Sociology* 15 (1973), 167–87, at 177–8.

From the 1860s new waves of Jewish migration from eastern Europe challenged this assimilation. In 1881 it was estimated that there were at least 60,000 Jews in Britain, an increase of 24,000 in just over twenty years.⁹ The influx increased in the 1880s and 1890s following pogroms in Russia and Poland, and the expulsion of Jews from the land and larger cities.¹⁰ Immigration intensified settlement in existing Jewish quarters, and spread into neighbouring areas. It was reckoned that about 80 per cent of migrants settling in London settled in the parishes of Whitechapel, Spitalfields, St George's-in-the-East and Bethnal Green. In 1900 it was claimed that almost half the population of Whitechapel and St George's-in-the-East was Jewish, that nearly all streets had at least half the population Jewish, and that in about a quarter of the streets 95 per cent of the population was Jewish.¹¹ In 1902–3, thirty-four of the sixty-two synagogues in London were in Stepney, with four in Hackney and four in the City.¹²

Anglo-Jewry was hesitant about this influx of strangely dressed, Yiddish-speaking paupers, fearing that their arrival would be deleterious for the existing Jewish poor. Often the established London Jewish community actively encouraged migrants to return whence they had come, or to continue to North America. The migrants were not easily assimilated into Anglo-Jewry. They brought their heritage, cultural life and work skills with them, and established their own self-contained street communities, keeping as close as possible to the family, friends and neighbours who had migrated with them. They suspected Anglo-Jewry's accommodation with the establishment as heretical, and resented the chief rabbi's opposition to their traditional customs and their use of Yiddish. They felt excluded by pew rents in synagogues, and established their own small synagogues, often in disused chapels or mission halls. They aroused hostility in the already deprived areas where they settled, tending to be employed by co-religionists, thought to be willing to work for lower wages, and accepting overcrowded accommodation, where they were thought to live at a low standard.

There are similarities with the responses to earlier generations

---

⁹ Lipman, *History*, 12, 50.
¹⁰ There was no restriction on entry into Britain until the Aliens Act 1905.
¹¹ Feldman, 'Importance of Being Jewish', 56.
¹² Mudie-Smith, *Religious Life of London*, 265.

of immigrant communities from the seventeenth century onwards, especially the Irish, who also had their own language and religious practices, who strongly resisted Anglican and Nonconformist proselytizing, and who were not easily assimilated into 'old' English Catholicism. However, Jews aroused less animosity than Irish Catholics, who, in addition to their alienness, were feared as agents of 'popery', the traditional enemy of Protestant England, and were subjected to persistent attempts to convert them from what were regarded as their errors. The arrival of increasing numbers of poor Jews into east London from the 1860s aroused less fear and anxiety, for, although there was considerable hostility towards migrants and 'aliens' in east London, this does not seem to have been linked to anti-Semitic sentiment.[13]

As John Wolffe has shown, English Christians were generally reluctant to engage in aggressive evangelism of English Jews.[14] The pages of the *London Diocesan Magazine* suggest that the Jewish migration into London made little impact on the wider diocese. There were very occasional references to the presence of Jews during the 1890s. In May 1892 an article on 'The Jews' described the work of the Parochial and Foreign Mission to the Jews.[15] Lectures at the Hebrew Missionary College at Palestine Place, Cambridge Heath, were occasionally advertised. In January 1893 it was noted that 'Alien immigration' had been debated in Whitechapel 'four or five times' in the past six years, with 'always the same result', opposition to restraint on immigration.[16] In September 1893 a report from the *East End News* was noted of 'an anniversary service of the Hebrew Guild of Intercession, one of the chief branches of Mr Rosenthal's East London Mission to the Jews', at which letters were read from Jewish converts at home and abroad testifying to the help that they had received.[17] Michael Rosenthal was a Jewish convert, ordained in 1877 as curate of St Paul's, Haggerston; he became a missioner with the East London Mission to the Jews in 1890, and

---

[13] See Anne J. Kershen, *Strangers, Aliens and Asians: Huguenots, Jews and Bangladeshis in Spitalfields 1660–2000* (London, 2005), 200–7.

[14] Wolffe, 'Plurality in the Capital', 238–46. The energies and substantial income of the London Society for Promoting Christianity amongst the Jews seem largely to have been directed towards Jews in Europe, North Africa and the Middle East.

[15] *London Diocesan Magazine* 7 (1892), 175.

[16] Ibid. 8 (1893), 13.

[17] Ibid. 273.

in 1900 vicar of St Mark's, Whitechapel.[18] However, in December 1894 it was noted that '[p]oorer parishes of East London are daily becoming still poorer owing to the continued exodus of the most respectable inhabitants to Upton Park and Leytonstone', and that '[t]he place of these inhabitants is being taken by Jews', the author adding: 'They are coming in on us like a flood'.[19] Amongst the many challenges that bishops of London from the 1860s addressed in visitation charges, the small but increasing Jewish presence in some East End parishes did not feature, nor was it the subject of any correspondence between bishops and the clergy of those parishes. Nor did the Jewish presence in east London attract interest in the great survey *The Religious Life of London*, undertaken in 1902–3. The only point noted by Percy Alden in writing about 'The Problem of East London' was that 'Jewish services [in Stepney] are invariably attended by more men than women'.[20] A much more significant issue for everyone was the ritualistic practices of some of the Church of England clergy.

From the early 1880s incumbents of some parishes in Spitalfields, Whitechapel, Stepney, Mile End and St George's-in-the-East comment in their answers to questions in bishops' visitations about increasing numbers of Jewish migrants in their parishes. In 1883 the incumbents of St Olave, Hanbury Street, Christ Church, Spitalfields, St Mary, Spital Square, St Mark's, Whitechapel, St Paul's, Whitechapel, St George's-in-the-East, Christ Church, Watling Street, St Matthew's, Pell Street, St Augustine's, Settle Street, St Benet's, Mile End and St Peter's, Stepney all note that there are many Jews in their parishes, and some, such as Christ Church, Spitalfields, St Mary's, Spital Square and St Olave, Hanbury Street, suggest that their parishes are largely Jewish, with empty houses being bought up by Jews. None comment on how this affects their pastoral practice, except the rector of St George's-in-the-East, who states that Jewish families are not visited.[21] In the summary of Bishop Temple's visitation returns for 1891 only nine incumbents are noted as including the presence of Jews, along with indiffer-

[18] For Rosenthal, see 'Biographies – Rabbis who followed Yeshua', online at: <http://www.ha-gefen.org>, accessed 30 June 2013; I am grateful to Sarah Flew for this reference. See also *Crockford's Clerical Directory*, 1900.

[19] *London Diocesan Magazine* 9 (1894), 394.

[20] Mudie-Smith, *Religious Life of London*, 36.

[21] London, LPL, Fulham Papers, Jackson Papers, vol. 2, Visitation Returns 1883.

ence, Roman Catholicism, Dissent, heathenism and immorality, amongst the hindrances to ministry in their parishes, and only six are noted as mentioning the presence of Jews in 1895.[22] In the answers to Bishop Mandell Creighton's visitation returns in 1900 only eleven incumbents mention Jews in their parishes.[23]

As Anne Kershen has noted, the poverty-stricken Jewish migrants from Russia and Poland brought with them their culture and religion; established their own butchers, grocery, fried fish shops and dairies, and their own 'sweat shops' in which Yiddish, not English, was the common language; and founded *chevrots*, or small synagogues, often drawing their membership from kinship or geographical groups or trades, in small rooms which became second homes and social centres for men. They had no desire to be assimilated with British Jewry, let alone with English society.[24] Effectively they established closed, largely self-sustaining communities, with little or no contact with their English neighbours. Some incumbents in their visitation replies give a sense that they felt they lived in alien territory. For example, the incumbent of St Olave's, Hanbury Street noted in his 1883 visitation return: 'The Church was built 89 years ago in a District which will soon be entirely Jewish', and the incumbent of St Paul's, Whitechapel commented: 'The population consists of Roman Catholics, Jews and foreigners'.[25] A degree of despondency amongst incumbents with large proportions of Jewish residents in the parishes is perhaps understandable when the figures for church attendance in 1902–3 are considered.[26] None, except the ritualist St Augustine's and the ancient parish churches of St Dunstan's, Stepney and St Mary's, Whitechapel had particularly good attendances: these three recorded total Sunday attendances of over 800, nearly 900 and over 1,100 respectively in Mudie Smith's census, but St Olave's, Hanbury Street had a total attendance of 85, with only eight men in the morning, and Christ Church, Spitalfields and St Stephen's,

---

[22] Fulham Papers, Temple Papers, vol. 44, Summary of Visitation Returns 1891 and 1895.
[23] Fulham Papers, Mandell Creighton Papers, Visitation 1900, Archdeaconry of London Deaneries I–VIII.
[24] Kershen, *Strangers, Aliens and Asians*, 85–90, 118–19.
[25] Jackson Papers, vol. 2, Visitation Returns 1883.
[26] Mudie-Smith, *Religious Life of London*, 49–53, 55–8, for Stepney and Bethnal Green.

Spitalfields only had twenty-five and ten men respectively on the Sunday morning. By comparison, the 7,959 Jewish men who were recorded as attending synagogues in Stepney must have seemed a large number.

The only detailed evidence about the reactions of incumbents of these parishes in Whitechapel, Spitalfields, Stepney, Mile End and St George's-in-the-East to this unprecedented development of diversity in their parishes is found in the notes of Charles Booth's researchers' interviews of 1898 with incumbents of parishes containing significant Jewish settlement, conducted as part of his research project on the religious life of London.[27] Fifteen incumbents spoke about Jews in their parishes, and they provide an interesting insight into clergy in London's East End. Thirteen of them appear in *Crockford's Clerical Directory* for 1899. Five had been at Cambridge, including two at Trinity, one who had been an exhibitioner at Clare and senior *optime* in his year, and another a scholar of Jesus; three had been at Oxford, including one who was a fellow of New College; one had been at Trinity College, Dublin; two at King's College, London; and only one was a non-graduate, from St Bees. They were all experienced priests, having been ordained between ten and forty-four years. Seven had served in their current parishes for between five and twenty-eight years. Only two had been in post less than two years. Nine had previously served in London. Of those whose gross benefice incomes can be identified, only one had an income under £200 a year.[28] The others had comparatively good incomes, including one with £600 a year. Despite working in one of the most poverty-stricken parts of the East End, they were a sample of well-educated and experienced clergy, and only one had a seriously low income. They reflect the full range of Anglican churchmanship. Harry Wilson, vicar of

---

[27] Rosemary O'Day and David Englander, *Mr Charles Booth's Inquiry:* Life and Labour of the People of London *Reconsidered* (London, 1993); for the Religious Influences Series, see ibid., ch. 3, and David Englander, 'Booth's Jews: The Presentation of Jews and Judaism in *Life and Labour of the People of London*', in David Englander and Rosemary O'Day, eds, *Retrieved Riches: Social Investigation in Britain 1840–1914* (London, 1995), 289–322. Booth employed 'trained' interviewers, using a set of open-ended questions with clergy to gather information about religious influences in London. The researchers' verbatim records of their interviews are in notebooks deposited in the library of the London School of Economics and Political Science, Booth Collections.

[28] Henry Dinsdale at Christ Church, Watney Street, formerly curate at Eton College's mission at Hackney Wick.

St Augustine's, Stepney, a well-known ritualist, was described as wearing a cassock and biretta, while Thomas Richardson at St Benet's, Mile End was described as a 'Bible Christian', employing a Church Pastoral Aid Society lay agent and having sent missionaries to 'Uganda, China, and I know not where'.[29] All the parishes were well staffed on the conventional late nineteenth-century urban parochial model, with numbers of curates, deaconesses, Bible and mission women, Scripture readers, paid and unpaid lady workers, temperance workers and Sunday school teachers.[30]

Booth's interviewers described being shown round the parishes by two Metropolitan Police officers. Inspector Reid conducted a tour of St Mary's, St Augustine's and St John's, Whitechapel. The interviewer noted the 'absorption of districts by Jews', describing some streets as 'wholly English', and in others, where there was a mixture of English and Jews, he observed 'frictions and quarrels [to be] … the inevitable result', and that '[t]he repulsion felt of one for the other is mutual'. A 'great mess' was noted in Jewish streets – 'fishes heads, paper of all colours, bread (not a great abundance of this), orange peel in abundance', and '[t]he constant whir of the sewing machines or tap of the hammer as you pass through the streets; women with dark abundant hair, olive complexions, not hats but shawls. Children [were] well fed and dressed'. 'Men with 'dark beards, fur caps and long boots' were noted. He commented: 'The feeling is of being in a foreign country'. In St John's parish the interviewers noted: 'Everard Street and Boyd Street are almost entirely foreign: many can neither speak nor understand English'. However, a week later an interviewer shown round by Sergeant French noted: 'Betterment is noticeable in some of the larger streets such as Hanbury and Church Street owing to the incoming of well-to-do Jews and also in the courts of Old Montague Street, owing to the displacement of rough English and Irish by poor but quiet Jews'. The conversion of the Wesleyan chapel in Fournier Street to a synagogue was noted as 'characteristic of the change that has taken place in the neighbourhood'.[31]

Ten incumbents commented on increasing numbers of Jews, two claiming that Jews were the dominant group in their parishes,

---

[29] Booth Collections, B182.
[30] Ibid., B182, B221.
[31] Ibid., B350.

and three that Jews were buying up property in their parishes; one commented on the insanitary conditions arising from over-crowding amongst Jews. One noted good relations with the Jews, and only one, Walter Bourchier of St Olave's, Hanbury Street, made disparaging remarks.[32]

Jewish migration into East End parishes reinforced incumbents' sense of loss of artisan and middle-class church-going parishioners to more distant and salubrious suburbs. Arthur Dalton, rector of St Dunstan's, Stepney, where he thought 'the Jewish element is increasing at a great pace', noted that the middle classes, and the 'respectable young who marry, move to less crowded areas'.[33] James Greaves, vicar of Holy Trinity, Tredegar Square, noted it was an 'area of migratoriness; with an efflux of better class and an influx of Jews'. He thought that Jews 'monopolised houses in Bow Road and Tredegar Square' and often built workshops over back gardens, and that they 'generally buy the fag end of a lease that a Christian would not look at'.[34] Henry Dinsdale, at Christ Church, Watney Street, with, he estimated, 2,000 Jews in a population of 10,000, thought that 'people were usually driven out by their house being bought by a Jewish landlord, or by a general raising of rents due to the Jewish invasion'.[35] John Draper at St Mary's, Whitechapel, where he reckoned two-thirds of the population was Jewish, said that they had 'long ago driven out all but the poorest gentiles from the side streets and are driving out the middle-class shopkeepers from the High Street, as Jews mainly go to Jewish shops, and the gentiles cannot make a living in the neighbour-hood. The parish has grown poorer and more overcrowded.' The overcrowding amongst the Jews was appalling, he thought, because 'the authorities' could not be sure how many people slept in a house.[36] Walter Bourchier at St Olave's, Hanbury Street thought that it had become almost a 'Jewish quarter, with only 600 gentiles left in a population of 6,000'. The interviewer commented: 'His is practically a Hebrew parish' and 'he has almost given it up in despair'. Bourchier regretted the 'filth and insanitary habits of his

---

32 Ibid., B221.
33 Ibid., B182.
34 Ibid.
35 Ibid., B221.
36 Ibid.

Jewish parishioners, habits which make it impossible for even the poorest gentiles to live in the same house with them'. He said that he had moved from his vicarage to live elsewhere, regarding the neighbourhood as 'absolutely impossible' for his children, if not for his wife.[37] Wilfred Davies, rector of Christ Church, Spitalfields, claimed his gentile population was 'of the lowest semi-criminal class', but thought that '[n]o gentile with a shred of decency would live in the parish'. Alfred Allen, vicar of St Stephen's, Spitalfields, claimed his parish was rapidly becoming 'judaized', but noted 'English drink. Jews do not. Jewish children are most regular and the tidiest at school. The Jews are turning out the prostitutes'.[38] In 1900 Michael Rosenthal at St Mark's, Whitechapel noted 'there is but little drunkenness and immorality in the parish owing to the preponderance of the Jewish population, who belong to the strictly orthodox class'.[39]

There usually seems to have been a tacit agreement among the clergy themselves not to evangelize Jews, apart from exhibiting true Christianity to non-Christian neighbours, an approach endorsed by George Browne, who had been bishop of Stepney.[40] However, eight incumbents reported attempts to convert Jews. At St Augustine's, Stepney, Harry Wilson mentioned a Jewish Mission Hall where Michael Rosenthal, the East London Mission to the Jews missionary, 'carries on his excellent work', which 'has met with much success'. Wilson thought work amongst Jews 'must be left to their own race', for 'their minds work quite differently from ours'.[41] Draper at St Mary's, Whitechapel had three special workers amongst the Jews, whom he thought were well received. He had services for Jewish men attracting 'as many as 200 Jews', most, he thought, as enquirers but some as 'sceptics'. He thought that 'outwardly, at all events, the rabbis were very friendly', but he admitted that there was 'no doubt' that they resented attempts to proselytize. He mentioned a Medical Mission for the Jews where receiving relief was contingent on listening to the gospel,[42] but

---

37 Ibid. *Crockford's*, 1899, however, gives his address as St Olave's Vicarage.
38 Booth Collections, B221.
39 Mandell Creighton Papers, Visitation 1900, Archdeaconry of London, Deaneries I–VIII, Deanery VIII–24.
40 Wolffe, 'Plurality in the Capital', 243.
41 Booth Collections, B221.
42 Wolffe, 'Plurality in the Capital', 241.

in response 'the Jewish authorities' had started a free dispensary. His policy was always to refer Jewish applicants for relief to the Jewish Board of Guardians, 'otherwise we should be swamped'.[43] The Sunday attendances in 1902–3 at the various missions to Jews in Stepney – the Anglican Jewish Mission in Goulston Street (22 attenders for the day), the Presbyterian Jewish Mission (19), the Mildmay Mission to Jews (51) and the Hebrew Christian Testimony to Israel (123) – do not suggest that Christian missionary activities attracted many Jews.[44]

Bourchier at St Olave's, Hanbury Street was unenthusiastic about converts. He claimed to leave Jews alone, adding: 'I hate a converted Jew. He's usually a mean sneaking brute'. He recounted that for some years he had had a converted Jew as a curate, which he concluded was the worst possible plan, 'for not only are the converted Jews poor creatures, but they are looked upon with intense hatred by their race as renegades'. The Jews, he said, 'used to spit at the curate in the streets, and hiss the most horrid blasphemies through the door of the vicarage where he lived'. He had also had a curate who was a 'fanatic' on the question, but whom he thought had only made 'a slight impression on a few'. He concluded that 'on the whole all the work among the Jews is totally without effect, and that such conversions as take place are not sincere'. He gave as his 'non-clerical opinion' that 'their religion is just as good as ours, and better for them'.[45] Dinsdale at Christ Church, Watney Street commented: 'Work among Jews is quite hopeless', for 'We don't understand them'. He too had had a Jewish curate, A. W. Schapira, from the Parochial Mission to the Jews, who, he claimed, in two years had brought one Jew to baptism who had 'remained firm'. He concluded: 'All this work among the Jews is thoroughly unsatisfactory: it is simply bribery'.[46] Alfred Allen at St Stephen's, Spitalfields also suspected that his previous London City Missionary, who had worked among the Jews, had bribed them.

[43] Booth Collections, B221.

[44] Mudie-Smith, *Religious Life of London*, 49, 51, 52.

[45] Booth Collections, B221.

[46] Alexander Wilhelm Schapira had studied at St David's College, Lampeter, and had been ordained in 1873 as Professor of Hebrew and Theology at Fourah Bay College, Sierra Leone. He was subsequently a missionary in Gaza, Syria (1878–84); curate of St Mark's, Whitechapel (1887–90); missionary at Haifa (1890–5); and curate of Christ Church, Watney Street (1895–7): *Crockford's*, 1899.

He currently had a Jewish missionary, funded by the Society for the Propagation of Christianity among Jews. Rosenthal seems to have been the only convert who had been ordained or worked as a missioner who was thought well of. Allen, however, suggested that 'the great difficulty in dealing with Jews was the exclusiveness of the English against Jews'.[47]

At All Saints, Buxton Street, the vicar, J. Basil Rust, thought that nearly half the population was Jewish, but that his Jewish Mission and Dispensary had made a great advance in conversions. He claimed that Jewish children 'glide into Christianity'.[48] He had provided instruction in Yiddish and in Hebrew and Hebrew history to promote mission among Jews. [49] F. J. Hobbins at Christ Church, Jamaica Street, where Jews were 'numerous', described himself as 'an old fashioned low churchman' and claimed the feeling towards the church among Jews was 'of the friendliest', and that he was 'on the best of terms' with the Jews and their rabbi. He had been invited to give the prizes at the Jewish school. However, he reported that he did no direct work among the Jews, but encouraged a Jewish convert missionary who worked in the parish.[50] Davies at Christ Church, Spitalfields, whom the interviewer thought had 'little religious fervour', reported that work among Jews there was mainly social and educational, with the religious motive 'at the back'. Only the Old Testament was read at meetings and classes, and 'carefully taught, especially with reference to the Messiah, in the hope that when the attributes to be expected of the Messiah were pointed out the minds of the Jews might be awakened, and they may be led by enquiry to recognise that Jesus was the Messiah'. He was surprised by Jews' 'ignorance' on religious matters, not knowing whether Moses lived twenty or two thousand years ago, or that the Bible contained their Scriptures, and generally believing that Christians worshipped a different God to them. He concluded 'they have religious sentiment, but no religious knowledge'.[51] Ronald Bayne, vicar of St

---

[47]   Booth Collections, B221. The Society for the Propagation of Christianity among Jews was founded in 1842. It has subsequently united with the Barbican Mission to Jews, as Christian Witness to Israel.

[48]   Ibid.

[49]   *London Diocesan Magazine* 14 (1899), 404.

[50]   Booth Collections, B221.

[51]   Ibid.

Jude's, Whitechapel, thought that his parish was mainly Jewish, and criticized the policy of his distinguished predecessor, the broad churchman Samuel Barnett, of leaving Jews entirely alone. Bayne thought that they ought to be converted but confided that 'he had no call to it'. However, he had a mission woman who 'was consumed with a great desire to bring the Gospel to her Jewish neighbours' and, although a 'quite uncultured woman', was learning Yiddish for the purpose.[52]

Respondents to Mandell Creighton's questionnaire in 1900 were no more enthusiastic about evangelizing their Jewish parishioners. The vicar of St Saviour's, Hoxton, R. M. Carrick, commented: 'We are fortunate in not having many Jews'. Allen at St Stephen's, Spitalfields again noted '[t]he great prejudice of one against the other between Christian and Jews'. Michael Rosenthal, now vicar of St Mark's, Whitechapel, also noted '[t]he intense hostility of the Jews and the lukewarmness of the Christians'. R. W. Harris, incumbent of St George's-in-the-East, noted '[t]he constant displacing of Christians by foreign Jews, the true method of evangelising whom I have not discovered'. H. C. Dinsdale, vicar of Christ Church, Watney Street, requested: 'I shall be grateful for advice about meeting the indifference of men and the conversion of Jews'. Thomas Richardson, vicar of St Benet's, Stepney, reported '[a] large number of Jews whom we try to reach … nearly every house is visited weekly with Christian literature. All accepted.'[53] Otherwise only two other incumbents noted attempts to evangelize Jews.

The only incumbent of a parish to which better-off Jews had moved who commented on their presence was Canon Robinson Duckworth at St Mark's, Hamilton Terrace, in St John's Wood. He noted: 'The crucial fact about us is that we are rapidly becoming Hebrew' and that part of his parish was rapidly 'going down' because wealthy Christians were leaving, and being replaced by Jews, resulting in a loss of pew rents. However, he also complained that church pew renters were 'of the class who have now taken to late dinners on Sundays', and criticized those who wanted 'free and open churches' as people who 'want their religion for

---

[52] Ibid.
[53] Visitation 1900, Archdeaconry of London Deaneries I–VIII, Deaneries VI-21, VII-21, II-24, VIII-20, VIII-32.

nothing'.[54] In 1900, however, he reported: 'I am on friendly terms with the Presbyterian Minister and the Jewish rabbis', but noted '[i]ncreasing immigration of Jews, many of whom are agnostics and help neither Church nor synagogue'.[55] Across Maida Vale the ultra-ritualist Fr Kirkpatrick at St Augustine's, Kilburn noted many Jews in the parish. He was more positive, perhaps because his church had no pews to rent. Its flourishing boys' schools made special provision for Jewish teaching, providing three Jewish teachers who only gave religious teaching to the Jews. He noted that just two Jewish parents had withdrawn their children from New Testament lessons before the Jewish masters were appointed.[56] The vicar of St Matthew's, Bayswater, where the magnificent New West End Synagogue had been built almost opposite the regularly packed church, noted in 1891 that the presence of Jews and Greeks was a hindrance to his parochial work.[57] When interviewed in 1899, his successor merely noted that Jews had begun to move in 'about two years ago', and in his 1900 visitation return recorded the presence of a synagogue in the parish and complained of the indifference and idleness of the wealthy.[58]

This limited evidence from the interview notes of Booth's researchers and the visitation questionnaires suggests that the few incumbents with large Jewish populations in their parishes expressed little interest in the religious diversity among their parishioners. They showed no awareness of migration as part of a continuum, or of the experience of earlier generations of clergy who had failed to convert Irish settlers from popery. They did not protest against migration, but expressed conventional popular concerns about the impact of migration on the housing and well-being of their Gentile parishioners. They recognized that Anglo-Jewry was providing for the welfare of Jewish migrants, and were sensitive to the risk that provision of social welfare for Jews might lead to accusations of bribery to win converts. Clergy of

---

[54] Booth Collections, B219.

[55] Visitation 1900, Archdeaconry of London, Deaneries XXI–XXVIII Deanery XXI 17.

[56] Booth Collections, B219.

[57] The Greek church of St Sophia had moved from Soho to near St Matthew's in this very rich and cosmopolitan part of Bayswater in 1877.

[58] Temple Papers, vol. 44, Summary of Visitation Returns 1891; Booth Collections, B250; Visitation 1900, Deaneries XV–XVIII, Deanery XVII–18.

all churchmanships showed little interest in evangelizing amongst their new parishioners, probably because of the closed nature of the Jewish communities in their parishes. The only obvious anti-Semitism was in complaints by some incumbents about squalor in some Jewish streets, which were refuted by others, and the negative views of some incumbents about Jewish converts. This small sample of incumbents showed little interest in either the social or religious implications of the new religious diversity in their parishes. Their interest seemed to be largely in the Christian populations of their parishes, and on the loss of the middle-class and upper working-class elements, from which their congregations were drawn. Their enthusiasm to fulfil actively the Good Friday prayer to 'fetch [Jews] home blessed Lord, to thy flock, that they may be saved among the remnant of the Israelites', was limited. Implicitly, at least, their policy was coexistence.

King's College, London

RAMA OR AHIMSA? TERROR OR PASSIVE RESISTANCE? REVOLUTIONARY METHODS OF HINDU STUDENTS FROM LONDON UNIVERSITY AND THE CHRISTIAN RESPONSE, 1909–17

by STUART MEWS

The assassination in London on the evening of 1 July 1909 of Sir Curzon Wyllie, aide-de-camp to the Secretary of State for India, by a twenty-six-year-old Indian student named Madar Lal Dhingra stunned the nation. The background to the shooting and its consequences shed light on the attitudes of British Christians to Indian Hindus. In turn light is shed on the response of Hindus, most crucially that of the eventual leader of the successful campaign for Indian independence, Mohandas Karam-chand Gandhi, in the crucial decade before the First World War.

India cast a spell on late Victorian British Christians, especially Anglican high churchmen. Charles Gore, who was to become bishop of Oxford and an outstanding theologian in the early twen-tieth-century Church of England, was drawn 'from Cuddesdon to Calcutta' in 1884 to support the three-years-old Oxford Mission.[1] From Cambridge B. K. Cunningham, later principal of Westcott House, an important moulder of two generations of bishops, went as a layman from Trinity College, Cambridge, to St Stephen's College, Delhi, in 1893.[2] In both cases their short visits made lifelong impressions. But if English Christians were enchanted by India, what was happening in reverse?

It is no coincidence that both Gandhi (in 1888) and Dhingra (in 1906) were students at University College, London, an institution with no official ties to a Christian denomination but situated in the capital of the British Empire. Eric Hobsbawm has suggested that 'the most powerful cultural legacy of imperialism' was an educa-tion in Western ways 'for the favoured few who became literate'.[3] But that is an oversimplification.

---

[1] G. L. Prestige, *The Life of Charles Gore: A Great Englishman* (London, 1935), 54, 60–5.

[2] J. R. H. Moorman, *B. K. Cunningham: A Memoir* (London, 1947), 18–31.

[3] Eric Hobsbawm, *The Age of Empire 1875–1914* (London, 1991), 79.

The use which students made of that education depended on their experience in Britain (as much outside as inside the lecture room), their receptivity to British culture and the overall effect of the student experience on their worldview. Gandhi's autobiography has a section entitled 'Playing the English Gentleman' in which he recalls his adoption in the late 1880s of Western dress (bought at the Army and Navy stores), learning to wear a tie and purchasing a mirror to check that he was neat. He was told that to become an English gentleman it was necessary to play the violin, take lessons in dancing, French and elocution. He soon discovered that French and ballroom dancing were not for him but only after serious attempts to acquire both skills. The first wave of Indian students admired England, Western ways and ideas. They aspired like Gandhi to become English gentlemen.[4] That phase ended in 1904–5. The external factor behind this change was, as we shall see, the totally unexpected defeat of Russia by the Japanese, the first time the white man had been beaten by Asiatics. The internal factor was the partition of Bengal by the British viceroy, which could be portrayed as an anti-nationalist move. Now Indian students still came to England to obtain qualifications but they were suspicious of the British government and susceptible to anti-imperial teaching.

The first decade of the twentieth century saw a significant expansion of higher education in Britain.[5] University College was formally incorporated into London University in 1905 and was an obvious magnet for ambitious young men from South Asia. The arrival of students whose native language was not English brought a speedy response from the Student Christian Movement (SCM).[6] Founded in the 1890s, primarily to encourage missionary vocations, the SCM soon broadened into an interdenominational movement of and for students. However a global perspective remained throughout the pre-First World War period. An article on 'Oriental Students in England' appeared in *The Student Move-*

---

4   Mahatma Gandhi, *My Experiments with Truth: An Autobiography* (New Delhi, 2010), 68–71.

5   G. R. Searle, *A New England? Peace and War 1886–1918* (Oxford, 2004), 630; James Parkes, 'The Stirring in the Universities', in G. Stephens Spinks, ed., *Religion in Britain since 1900* (London, 1952), 90–124.

6   Tissington Tatlow, *The Story of the Student Christian Movement of Great Britain and Ireland* (London, 1933), 549–71.

ment magazine in December 1904,[7] and its message was powerfully exemplified by Robert Wilder, an American firebrand from Princeton, who after three years' missionary work in India joined the staff of the British SCM in 1905 as its London secretary.

India burst into the consciousness of British student Christians most powerfully as the result of an address by an Indian former medical student, S. K. Datta (now a travelling secretary for the SCM), at the movement's Conishead conference in 1907; it led to fervent intercession for that country. The sense of walking with divine destiny was reinforced the very next day when a telegram from Calcutta was read out to the conference: 'India's students her greatest peril and highest hope. Our Movement appeals to yours for leaders. – Azariah, Andrews, Carter'.[8] V. S. Azariah, having started as a YMCA evangelist, was to become the first Indian to be consecrated a bishop in the Anglican communion in 1912, but C. F. Andrews was to become so disillusioned with the Anglican imperial mission that in 1914 he resigned and devoted his formidable energies to the campaign for Indian independence. That same year he urged Gandhi to return to India from South Africa, which was to provide the independence movement with a strategist and figurehead. The American E. C. Carter, the third of the signatories to the telegram, was General Secretary of the YMCA of India, an organization which provided leadership opportunities for Indian Christians such as the dynamic K. T. Paul, who was both a Christian and a nationalist.[9]

The workload for the London secretary of the SCM and the rising numbers of students soon necessitated the appointment of another officer specifically for overseas students. A high church layman, Kenneth Kirk, was selected. His first task was to conduct a survey into the problems faced in Britain by students from abroad. His investigation, published in 1910, revealed about 1,500 Asian

---

7   Ibid. 550.
8   Ibid. 298.
9   Susan Billington Harper. *In the Shadow of the Mahatma: Bishop V. S. Azariah and the Travail of Christianity in British India*, SHCM (Grand Rapids, MI, 2000); Hugh Tinker, *The Ordeal of Love: C. F. Andrews and India* (Oxford, 1979), Daniel O'Connor, *Gospel, Raj and Swaraj: The Missionary Years of C. F. Andrews* (Frankfurt-am-Main, 1990); Jeffery Cox, 'C. F. Andrews and the Failure of the Modern Missionary Movement', in Stuart Mews, ed., *Modern Religious Rebels* (London, 1993), 226–44.

students in Britain.[10] As secretary for foreign students in London, Kirk busied himself helping new arrivals cope in a strange land. He met them at the docks, helped them find adequate lodgings, checked their papers, organized leisure-time activities and set up invitations into the homes of English families.[11] He was therefore well placed to give an informed response when the predictable outcry against foreign students was unleashed by the assassination of Sir Curzon Wyllie.[12]

The event was tragic enough. Wyllie had been born in Cheltenham into a family devoted to India. He followed his two elder brothers in joining the Indian army and later the Raj administration. After service with the Gurkhas and in Afghanistan, he became military secretary to his brother-in-law, the governor of Madras. The rest of his time in India was spent in the princely states, particularly Rajputana, where the worst effects of the famine of 1899–1900 were mitigated by his skilful organization of relief. Back in England, he advised secretaries of state for India on military matters and kept an eye on Indian students, whom he often invited to his home. In November 1908 he attended a meeting to discuss the 'Indian Student Problem', which to his chagrin was taken over by an Indian militant, Bipin Chandra Pal, later to be known as 'the Father of Revolutionary Thought in India' and to be remembered as part of the rebel trinity of 'Lal, Pal and Bal'.[13] It was while attending a social evening at the Imperial Institute in South Kensington that Wyllie was shot dead in front of his wife. A Parsi doctor, Cawas Lalcaca, who tried to intervene, also received wounds, from which he died.[14]

The India Secretary, Viscount Morley, was distraught. 'It is indeed horrible', he wrote to Lord Minto, the viceroy. 'Wyllie was one of the most attractive men I have ever worked with – always good tempered and good-natured, obliging and helpful,

---

[10] Eric W. Kemp, *The Life and Letters of Kenneth Escott Kirk* (London, 1959), 17; Tatlow, *Student Christian Movement*, 550; *Foreign Students in British Universities*, February 1910.

[11] Kemp, *Kirk*, 17; Tatlow, *Student Christian Movement*, 550.

[12] *ODNB, s.n.* 'Wyllie, Sir William Huff Curzon (1848–1909)'.

[13] Lala Rajpat Rai, Bipin Chandra Pal, Bal Ganghadur Tilak: Nicholas Owen, 'The Soft Heart of the British Empire: Indian Radicals in Edwardian London', *Past & Present*, no. 220 (2013), 143–84, at 156. I owe this reference to Hugh McLeod.

[14] *The Times*, 3, 4, 5, 7 July 1909.

and thoroughly master of the delicate matters that come within his province'.[15] The assassin, Madan Lal Dhingra, was overpowered before he could turn his pistol on himself. At his trial at the Old Bailey, he refused to recognize the authority of the court and when sentenced to death announced: 'I am proud to have the honour of laying down my life for the cause of my motherland'. He was hanged at Pentonville on 17 August 1909.

But who was Dhingra and what were his motives in shooting Wyllie?[16] It seems that he was from an upwardly mobile professional background; his father and brother were medical doctors, who were loyal to the British crown, and his family disowned his actions. Dhingra himself was an early convert to Swadeshi, the movement for self-sufficiency and economic boycott of British goods which was part of the reaction to the viceroy Lord Curzon's partition of Bengal (the nation's largest province),which came into effect in October 1905. The partition, although long advocated on the grounds of administrative efficiency, was seen by most Indians as a British plan to divide and frustrate the development of an Indian national or proto-national consciousness. Opposition took the form either of the economic boycott of British goods like Lancashire cotton or by direct action by secret societies of terrorists.[17]

One of the architects of partition was Andrew Fraser. Born in Bombay, he was the son of a Scottish missionary and grandson of a parish minister in Skye. After an education in Edinburgh he devoted his working life to India. A solid but plodding career was followed by rapid promotion in the Indian Civil Service when Lord Curzon became viceroy. This led to his unexpected appointment as lieutenant-governor of Bengal, with a knighthood in 1903. Fraser was a committed Presbyterian and in 1907 took pride in being elected moderator of the General Assembly of the United

---

[15] Morley to Minto, 2 July 1909, in John, Viscount Morley, *Recollections*, 2 vols (London, 1917), 2: 211.

[16] On Dhingra, see S. N. Datta, *Madra Lal Dhingra and the Revolutionary Movement* (New Delhi, 1978); *ODNB, s.n.* 'Dhingra, Madan Lal (1883–1909)'; *The Times*, 24 July, 18, 20 August 1909.

[17] John R. McLane, 'The Decision to Partition Bengal in 1905', *Indian Economic and Social History Review* 2 (1965), 221–37; David Dilks, *Curzon in India* (London, 1970), 200–1; David Gilmour, *Curzon* (London and Basingstoke, 1995), 273; Peter Heehs, 'Foreign Influences on Bengali Revolutionary Terrorism 1902–1908', *Modern Asian Studies* 28 (1994), 533–56.

Free Church of Scotland in India.[18] C. A. Bayly has described
the years 1905–10 as 'the revolutionary period', and the historian
of imperial intelligence has stated that 'the opening shot in the
terrorist campaign came in 1907 with the unsuccessful attempt to
assassinate Sir Andrew Fraser'.[19] Despite several attempts on his
life Fraser resisted calls for repression. He could never believe that
what was to him a commonsense act of partition could be the
cause of the unrest, or that the Indians he had known and loved
and served could be unable to see the benefits of the Raj. In his
memoirs, published in 1911, he dismissed talk of a Hindu revival,
especially when it was associated with political activism. In his
view, the effect of 'sham supporters of the Hindu religion [had]
been to induce thoughtless fanatical and half-trained youths to
associate their religion with particular forms of violence and sedition which are really inconsistent with its true teaching'.[20] Both
Fraser's children went to Oxford and Mary Fraser subsequently
became the wife of her brother's friend from Trinity College,
Oxford, J. H. Oldham.[21] A Scottish layman, Oldham after a short
stint as a missionary in India found his niche as a visionary church
bureaucrat, becoming secretary of the World Missionary Conference at Edinburgh in 1910, which Fraser also attended.[22]

Indian Christians who embraced nationalism rejected violence
and chose to work for greater participation in government through
constitutional methods of discussion and persuasion. National
cultural consciousness required a change in the presentation of
the Christian gospel and in December 1904 a National Missionary
Society had been formed which emphasized indigenous expressions of worship and sought to bring Indians to Indian Christianity
and not to an exported British denomination. The foundations
were being laid for church union in South India.[23]

---

[18] *ODNB, s.n.* 'Fraser, Sir Andrew Henderson Leith (1848–1919)'; A. H. L. Fraser,
Among Indian Rajahs and Ryots (London, 1911), 276.

[19] C. A. Bayly, *The Origins of Nationality in South Asia: Patriotism and Ethical Government in the Making of Modern India* (Oxford, 1998), 118; Richard J. Popplewell. *Intelligence and Imperial Defence: British Intelligence and the Defence of the Indian Empire 1904–24*
(London, 1995), 125.

[20] Fraser, *Among Indian Rajahs*, 276.

[21] *ODNB, s.n.* 'Fraser, Alexander Garden (1873–1962)'; Keith Clements, *Faith on
the Frontier: A Life of J. H. Oldham* (Edinburgh, 1999), 26–7.

[22] Clements, *Faith on the Frontier*, 52.

[23] Bengt Sundkler, *The Church of South India: The Movement towards Union 1900–*

Before 1909 the 'Indian Unrest' was confined to the subcontinent, although a base for fostering subversive sentiments among Indian students was secured in 1905 by Shyamji Krishna Varma, a rich merchant who bought a mansion in Highgate which he called India House and opened as a student hostel. It was there that he started printing the *Indian Sociologist*, which was banned as seditious by the British Raj and has been described as 'the prototype for all anti-British newspapers published by Indians abroad'.[24] Student talk was turned into action by the arrival at India House of a young law student, Vinayek Damodhar Savarkar, who wrote of the 1857 Indian Mutiny as India's war of independence and (according to a Special Branch plant) made a Sunday evening speech in India House calling for an immediate rebellion in India. He was considered by the Special Branch to be a threat to national security and was ultimately detained in the Andaman Islands. Savokar is believed to have exercised an influence over Madan Lal Dhingra and probably wrote for him the speech which he wanted to read at his trial, which was admired by Winston Churchill, a member of the British cabinet.

'The horrible murders of Sir William Curzon Wyllie and Dr. Lalcaca have brought the sedition of India to the very doorstep of the British public', wrote J. A. Sharrock, a former missionary. 'It is often assumed', he continued, 'that the people of India as a whole are disaffected, but that the few violent Anarchists who will stop at no deeds however outrageous to carry out their vile purpose have no important backing'. He thought it would be more accurate to divide the nation into two: 'a small educated minority who are speaking broadly disloyal, and a large uneducated majority who are as a whole, loyal'.[25]

An assassination in the centre of London was a shock to post-Victorians like Edward Dicey, a Resident Bencher of Gray's Inn and brother of A. V. Dicey, the eminent constitutional lawyer. In a journal article prompted by the Wyllie murder, Dicey suggested

---

1947, rev. edn (London, 1965), 34–5; Daniel O'Connor et al., *Three Centuries of Mission: The United Society for the Propagation of the Gospel 1701–2000* (London and New York, 2000), 9; Robert Eric Frykenberg, *Christianity in India: From Beginnings to the Present*, Oxford History of the Christian Church (Oxford, 2008), 239.

[24] Popplewell, *Intelligence and Imperial Defence*, 125.

[25] J. A. Sharrock, 'Some Misconceptions about the Unrest in India', *Nineteenth Century and After* 56 (July–December 1909), 361–76, at 372.

a tightening of the admissions requirements at the Inns of Court. He had observed that the Japanese victory over the Russians in the war of 1904–5 had changed perceptions of the military capacity of Asians, producing a new self-confidence and releasing nationalist aspirations. In a not entirely logical leap he suggested that 'one of the indirect, if not the direct, results of the Russian defeat was a rapid increase in the number of Indian students, who arrived in England ... to study as barristers and be called to the English Bar'.[26]

Most of them returned home after being called, but there were some who settled permanently in London. 'The best known member of this category', wrote Dicey, 'is Mr. Krishnavarma [*sic*], who started a boarding home known as India House, where Indian students are boarded and lodged and receive instruction in law.'[27] Dicey thought it only natural for overseas students to prefer their fellow countrymen instead of mixing with Englishmen. Apart from dietary rules – Hindus not eating beef – he well understood that cultural customs and taboos built barriers. To the best of his knowledge, in London only Sir Curzon Wyllie kept open house for Indian students. Consequently, Dicey was quite certain that 'meeting-places such as India House, which are, in plain English, schools of sedition, must be put down by the strong arm of the law'.[28]

It was Kirk who offered 'Indian Students in England: Another Point of View', which he described as a gloss on Dicey's negative article. Kirk was evidently appalled by Dicey's contention that '[t]he truth is that England won India by the sword; that she holds it by the sword; and that if she wishes to retain possession of India she must continue to hold it by the sword.'[29] Drawing on his experiences with Indian students, Kirk thought Dicey's article ill informed and far too pessimistic. He accepted that Dicey was

---

[26] Edward Dicey, 'Hindu Students in England', *Nineteenth Century and After* 56 (July–December 1909), 349–60, quotation at 350; *ODNB*, *s.n.* 'Dicey, Edward James Stephen (1832–1911)'. On the freedom – personal and intellectual – enjoyed by Indian students in Britain, see Nicholas Owen, *The British Left and India: Metropolitan Anti-Imperialism 1885–1947* (Oxford, 2007), 64.

[27] Dicey, 'Hindu Students', 352.

[28] Ibid. 358.

[29] Kenneth E. Kirk, 'Indian Students: Another Point of View', *Nineteenth Century and After* 56 (July–December 1909), 598–606, at 601.

right in focusing on the loneliness of Indian students, many of whom lived in sordid lodgings. Dicey was also right in pointing to different cultural assumptions and inhibitions which inhibited friendship between Englishmen and Indians. Dicey's article had ignored Kirk's efforts and achievements. Kirk knew that the sports field was one place where students of all backgrounds could meet and mix. From visiting student flats he could write that those who had 'the privilege of entertaining or being entertained by an Indian will not deny that he is both an agreeable and an interesting table companion'.[30] He concluded 'by putting on record the experience of many Englishmen of the last forty years, and of a growing body of English students to-day, that a close and equal friendship with Indian students' was both possible and desirable, in order to remove the 'racial suspicion to which the present sedition is so largely due'.[31]

The assassination of Wyllie as a British extension of the Indian unrest was world news. It provided the background to the mission to London on behalf of the Indian community in South Africa led by Gandhi in July 1909. Gandhi had moved to South Africa in 1893. There he was transformed into a public figure as he championed the fight of Indian migrants for racial justice. Though influenced by the theories of Tolstoy and Ruskin, he found the most effective model for direct action in the campaign of passive resistance mounted by the English Free Churches against the rate levied by the Education Act of 1902. Gandhi had been impressed by what he had been told about this movement by Baptist ministers in Johannesburg and by an English Free Church leader, the Baptist Dr F. B. Meyer, who visited South Africa in 1908. In 1909, after spending three months in prison, Gandhi headed for London in an attempt to influence the shaping of the constitution of the new Union of South Africa.[32]

On board ship he had heard the news of the assassination of Curzon Wyllie. In *Indian Opinion*, the newspaper which he founded in Johannesburg, Gandhi commented that the assassination 'was a terrible thing'. The social gathering had been 'arranged with the

---

[30] Ibid. 604.
[31] Ibid. 606.
[32] James D. Hunt, *Gandhi and the Nonconformists: Encounters in South Africa* (New Delhi, 1986), 119–20.

object of bringing Indian students into contact with Englishmen, who therefore attended as the guests of Indians. Sir Curzon Wyllie was thus a guest of the assassin. From this point of view Mr. Madanial Dhingra murdered his guest in his own house'. Gandhi pressed the point: 'If I kill someone in my own house without a warning – someone who has done me no harm – I cannot but be called a coward'. He rejected the view that Dhingra had shown exceptional courage, because it seemed to have been a courage fuelled by alcohol. 'I must say', wrote Gandhi, 'that those who believe and argue that such murders may do good to India are ignorant men indeed. No act of treachery can ever profit a nation'. 'Every Indian should reflect thoughtfully on this murder', he wrote. 'It has done India much harm; the deputation's efforts have also received a setback'.[33]

Whenever he visited London Gandhi called at India House and had discussions with Savarkar, but there was no meeting of minds. More congenial were the Free Church supporters of passive resistance, John Clifford, F. B. Meyer and Robertson Nicoll, who met Gandhi on his 1909 visit and advised on the development of the campaign in South Africa.[34] But it was the Wyllie murder and reactions to it which confirmed Gandhi in his rejection of violence.[35]

The murder by a student in Kensington produced different responses. It presented Indians with a choice: – between reenacting with Savarkar Prince Rama's destruction of the demon king Ravana or with Gandhi choosing *ahimsa* and *satyagraha* or 'firmness in truth' which took the form of nonviolent disobedience.[36] Gandhi was confirmed in his opposition to bloodshed, but Savarkar sought national independence through the bomb and the bullet. The SCM was convinced that to prevent another India House there was a need for a more permanent international hall of

[33] *Indian Opinion*, 14 August 1909, in *Collected Works of Mahatma Gandhi*, 9: *September 1908 – November 1909* (New Delhi, 1963), 302–3.

[34] Dhanannjay Keer, *Veer Savarkar*, 2nd edn (Bombay, 1966) 62–3; Wikipedia, *s.v.* 'India House', online at: <http://en.wikipedia.org/wiki/India_House>, accessed 1 June 2013.

[35] Owen, *British Left*, 75.

[36] John Moffitt, *Journey to Dorakhpur: Reflections on Hindu Spirituality* (London, 1973), 19–20; Judith M. Brown, *Gandhian Non-Violence: Vision and Reality* (Oxford, 1993).

residence for students. Shortage of funds and the outbreak of the
First World War delayed matters, but in November 1917, although
the war was still raging, Student Movement House was opened in
Russell Square, London.[37]

If we fast forward to 1947 we find that India achieved its independence but that Gandhi was assassinated. Almost certainly one of
the conspirators was V. S. Savarkar. Coinciding with the birth of the
new republic was the inauguration of the Church of South India.
It was a development which was fiercely resisted by a high church
faction in the Church of England led by the bishop of Oxford, the
former champion of Indian students, Kenneth Kirk.

It is important to set this essay in its religio-political context.
As Mark Juergensmeyer has observed: 'in traditional India there
was no clear distinction between the spheres of religion and politics ... In the twentieth century religion and politics continued
to interact'.[38] That interaction was clearly to be found in 1909
in the use of Hindu epics and hymns to encourage, support and
justify nationalist terrorists or freedom fighters amongst university
students in London. To counter this mood the SCM provided
opportunities for the meeting of Hindus and Christians so that
faith could meet faith. Sharing the goals of the Hindu nationalists
and the means of the Indian Christians was the enigmatic Gandhi,
whose own outlook and methods had been decisively affected by
the atrocity of 1909.[39] Thus the pluralisms of Christianity – British
and Indian, imperial and nationalist – met the many pluralisms of
Hinduism.

Grantchester

[37] Tatlow, *Student Christian Movement*, 565.

[38] Mark Juergensmeyer, 'India', in Stuart Mews, ed., *Religion in Politics: A World Guide* (Harlow and Chicago, IL, 1989), 98–107, at 98–9.

[39] Eric J. Sharpe, *Faith meets Faith: Some Christian Attitudes to Hinduism in the Nineteenth and Twentieth Centuries* (London, 1977), 46–7.

SYMPATHY FOR MUSSULMANS, LOVE FOR JEWS: EMILIE LOYSON-MERIMAN (1833–1909), HYACINTHE LOYSON (1827–1912) AND THEIR EFFORTS TOWARDS INTERRELIGIOUS ENCOUNTER[*]

by ANGELA BERLIS

In 1905, Madame Hyacinthe Loyson published her travelogue *To Jerusalem through the Lands of Islam among Jews, Christians, and Moslems.*[1] In this work, Emilie Loyson, who had some experience as a journalist, described the couple's travels in the Orient and their encounters with those of other religions, which – unusually for the time – took place on a footing of equality. This essay will first introduce the author, before turning to the religious and interreligious commitment of Emilie Loyson and her husband. Whilst in the 1870s they were engaged in 'ecumenical' efforts, over time their interest in interreligious encounter developed. The essay will examine – primarily from Emilie's point of view – how the couple perceived Islam, and in particular Muslim women, as well as their understanding of Judaism and Eastern Christianity. Finally, it will ask what the couple were able to achieve.

Emilie Loyson is considerably less well known than her famous husband Père Hyacinthe Loyson. Until very recently, information about her amounted to little more than stereotypical judgements: for example, that she was a 'pathological American widow'[2] or an 'eccentric American' who married a former monk.[3] However, in 2012 extensive source materials became fully available; these offer

[*] I would like to thank Martin della Valle and Charlotte Methuen for their translation of, and comments on, earlier versions of this essay, and to my student assistant Nadja Heimlicher for her preparatory work.

[1] Madame Hyacinthe Loyson, *To Jerusalem through the Lands of Islam among Jews, Christians, and Moslems* (Chicago, IL, and London, 1905).

[2] So, in their index of persons, Charles Stephen Dessain and Thomas Gornall, eds, *The Letters and Diaries of John Henry Newman*, 24: A Grammar of Assent, *January 1868 – December 1869* (Oxford, 1973), 419.

[3] As, for example, in a frequently cited recent encyclopaedia article: 'His marriage to the eccentric American Emilie Meriman deepened the break' [i.e. with his order and the Roman Catholic Church]: Victor Corzemius, 'Loyson, Charles', in *Lexikon für Theologie und Kirche*, 3rd edn, 11 vols (Freiburg im Breisgau, 1993–2001), 6, col. 1074.

a very different picture of Emilie, her relationship to Hyacinthe Loyson, and her significance to the ecumenical and interreligious cause.[4]

EMILIE BUTTERFIELD: 'THE EVOLUTION OF A SOUL'[5]

Emilie Butterfield was born on 2 June 1833 in Oswego in western New York. Her ancestors had been religious refugees to the New World,[6] and the puritan frontier spirit of the Pilgrim Fathers lived on in the family. Emilie's father, Amroy Butterfield, was a Presbyterian pastor; her mother, Mary Lamb, the descendent of a fifth-generation puritan pastor, was seen by her daughter as a woman of 'strong moral character'.[7] After Amroy was killed in 1836 – when Emilie was not yet three years old – in an accident during the building of a church, Mary was left to raise the children on her own.

In 1851, when she was eighteen, Emilie married Captain Edwin Ruthven Meriman (d. 1867), son of an affluent Presbyterian family. The couple had two children, Ralph (b. 1854), who would die as a young man, and Mary (1859–64), who died in childhood. In 1854 Emilie also started writing political and religious articles for local newspapers; later she also wrote for the *New York Times*. In 1863 and 1867 she travelled to Europe. While she was away on her second trip, her husband, who had remained in the USA, died.

During her time in Paris, where she visited the 1867 *Exposition universelle*, through a mutual friend, the Roman Catholic convert from Anglicanism Rosalind Margaret Phillimore, née Knight-

---

4   Between 1948 and 1957, the Loyson Papers were donated to the Bibliothèque de Genève by Laura Loyson, née Bucknell, the widow of Paul-Hyacinthe Loyson, the couple's son, but some were embargoed until 2012. They include important correspondence by both Hyacinthe and Emilie, Hyacinthe Loyson's journal, and an unpublished autobiography written by Emilie Loyson: see Marie-Pierre Gilliéron-Graber, 'Un prêtre marié à la BPU: Charles Hyacinthe Loyson', in *Bibliothèque publique et universitaire. Bibliothèque musicale. Institut et Musée Voltaire: Rapport annuel* 2004 (Geneva, 2005), 43–6. I am currently preparing an annotated edition of Emilie's autobiography for publication.

5   For what follows, see Geneva, Bibliothèque de Genève, Loyson Papers, MS fr. 3906, Madame Hyacinthe Loyson, 'Autobiography, 1: The Evolution of a Soul. From the Great American Forest to the Vatican Council', n.d. Planned additional volumes did not materialize due to Emilie's death in 1909. See also Georges Zwianzek, 'Emilie Loyson. Die Wandlung einer Seele', *Christkatholisches Kirchenblatt* 122 (1999), 222–4.

6   Loyson, 'Autobiography', 16.

7   Ibid. 19.

Bruce (d. 1871), Emilie met the famous preacher Père Hyacinthe Loyson.[8] Initially she did not take to him. A monk did not seem to her to be in keeping with the times; indeed, after their second encounter, she remarked: 'Well, I think he is a good man, ... a very religious man, and, I will believe, a devout Christian, but ... I think he is woefully wrong and sadly out of place in the nineteenth century and in this age of Christianity!'[9] Additionally, it was utterly incomprehensible to Emilie, who had been familiar with the Bible ever since childhood, that the Roman Catholic faithful did not have access to Holy Scripture.[10]

Over time, however, Emilie and Père Hyacinthe came to know and appreciate each other better, and through many conversations they discovered their spiritual kinship. After extensive soul-searching, Emilie decided to convert to Roman Catholicism. Her free spirit, her liberal views and her open heart – her Protestant legacy – appealed to Père Hyacinthe, and he told her that in his eyes they were truly suited to Catholicism.[11]

Père Hyacinthe was a strong advocate of the equality of Catholicism, Protestantism and Judaism. In 1869, two years after he met Emilie, he left the Carmelite Order, and in 1870 he protested against the papal dogmas of the First Vatican Council. He joined the resulting Old Catholic movement, published treatises about it in France, and during the winter of 1871/2 visited Munich, where for a time he not only stayed with its spiritual leader, the church historian Ignaz von Döllinger (1799–1890), but collaborated with him closely.[12] In September 1872, Hyacinthe Loyson and Emilie

8   For a detailed biography and additional relevant literature, see Angela Berlis, 'Hyacinthe Loyson (1827–1912) dans le vieux-catholicisme: un esprit libéré des frontières religieuses', in Frédéric Amsler and Sarah Scholl, eds, *L'Apprentissage du pluralisme religieux au XIXe siècle (1815–1907). Le cas genevois dans son contexte suisse* (Geneva, 2013), 189–214.
9   Loyson, 'Autobiography', 268–9.
10   Ibid. 266.
11   Hyacinthe Loyson to Emilie Meriman, 17 July 1868, cited in Albert Houtin and Paul-Louis Couchod, *Du Sacerdoce au mariage. Le Père Hyacinthe (1867–1870)* (Paris, 1927) [hereafter: *Du Sacerdoce* I], 80.
12   On Döllinger, see Angela Berlis, 'Ignaz von Döllinger and the Anglicans', in Stewart J. Brown and Peter Nockles, eds, *The Oxford Movement: Europe and the Wider World, c.1830 – c.1930* (Cambridge, 2012), 236–48. On the Old Catholic movement, see Angela Berlis, *Frauen im Prozess der Kirchwerdung. Eine historisch-theologische Studie nach der Anfangsphase des deutschen Altkatholizismus (1850–1890)* (Frankfurt, 1998); in English, see Urs von Arx, 'The Old Catholic Churches of the Union of Utrecht', in Paul Avis,

Meriman married in London.[13] Both viewed their love and their marriage as a first step in reforming the Church.[14]

In 1873, they moved to Geneva, where the local liberal Catholics (the future Old Catholics) elected Hyacinthe rector the following autumn,[15] although he resigned from his position only one year later. 1873 also saw the birth of their son, Paul-Emmanuel Hyacinthe (1873–1921), who would later become a well-known writer. The family initially remained in Geneva, but in spring 1878 they returned to France, where in 1879, with Anglican support, Hyacinthe founded the Catholic Gallican parish in Paris, which remained under his leadership until 1893.[16] After his with-

ed., *The Christian Church: An Introduction to the Major Traditions* (London, 2002), 157–85; compare also (albeit somewhat outdated) C. B. Moss, *The Old Catholic Movement, its Origins and History* (London, 1948; repr. 2005).

[13] Cf. Albert Houtin and Paul-Louis Couchod, *Du Sacerdoce au mariage, Gratry et Loyson (1870–1872). Lettres et journaux intimes* (Paris, 1927) [hereafter: *Du Sacerdoce* II], 268–9; see also Angela Berlis, 'Père Hyacinthe Loyson und Emilie Meriman-Loyson: ihre Begegnung, ihr Einfluss aufeinander und ihre Zusammenarbeit' (provisional title), forthcoming in *Internationale Kirchliche Zeitschrift* 105 (2015).

[14] For instance, on 16 June 1869 Hyacinthe Loyson wrote in his diary that Emilie Meriman had told him that she felt 'that she, I and GOD together are one, and that we are working towards the birth of a new church': Houtin and Couchod, *Du Sacerdoce* I, 141. The sense that God was revealing himself through their love, that their relationship might be the precursor to the birth of a new Church, or that their marriage offered a clear sign of the reform of the Church was also portrayed by the couple in their public utterances: ibid. 85, 141, 169; Houtin and Couchod, *Du Sacerdoce* II, 244–8. On 25 August 1872, just a few days before his marriage to Emilie in London, Hyacinthe Loyson published in *Le Temps* a justification for his decision, 'Pourquoi je me marie', which would frequently be reprinted. In English: 'Concerning my Marriage', in Father Hyacinthe, *Catholic Reform: Letters, Fragments, Discourses*, transl. Madame Hyacinthe-Loyson [*sic*] (London, 1874), 114–26.

[15] See Sarah Scholl, 'Le *Kulturkampf* comme tentative d'intégration des catholiques à la nation. Le projet des catholiques libéraux genevois', in Amsler and Scholl, eds, *L'Apprentissage*, 97–114; compare also eadem, *En quête d'une modernité chrétienne. La Création de l'Église catholique-chrétienne de Genève au coeur du Kulturkampf (1870–1907)* (Neuchâtel, 2014). For the *Kulturkampf* in Switzerland in general, see Heidi Bossard-Borner, 'Village Quarrels and National Controversies', in Christopher Clark and Wolfram Kaiser, eds, *Culture Wars: Secular-Catholic Conflict in Nineteenth-Century Europe* (Cambridge 2003), 255–84.

[16] For this period, see Anthony John Cross, 'Père Hyacinthe Loyson, the Église Catholique Gallicane (1879–1893) and the Anglican Reform Mission' (PhD thesis, University of Reading, 2011). This otherwise careful work, which makes ample use of Hyacinthe Loyson's diaries and is based on solid archival research, unfortunately does not draw on the sources held in Old Catholic archives. Cross depends for his knowledge of Old Catholicism on Moss's now outdated work (ibid. 350; see n. 12 above), and does not refer to any more recent studies, which leads him to draw a number of erroneous conclusions. For instance, the 'culte public libre' which Loyson founded in

drawal from the Paris congregation, Hyacinthe dedicated himself primarily to his lectures and publications. Encouraged by Emilie, who was very fond of travelling, the couple also undertook several journeys to Constantinople and the Orient, where the question of the reconciliation of the three monotheistic faiths interested them increasingly.

The relationship between Emilie and Hyacinthe, which had brought together Protestantism and Catholicism, constituted the foundation for the subsequent development of their ideas. They continuously expanded the idea of 'reunification', from reuni-fication or reunion within Christianity (which we now call 'ecumenism') to the reunification of different faiths, and especially the three monotheistic religions. In their approach, the Loysons were certainly influenced by Ignaz von Döllinger's far-sighted *Lectures on the Reunion of the Churches*, given in 1872, which were welcomed by Old Catholics and Anglicans and fiercely criticized by ultramontane Roman Catholics. Hyacinthe had been staying with Döllinger in Munich at the time that he gave the lectures, and after their marriage Emilie translated them into French, so she was very

Geneva in 1874 had nothing to do with the liberal 'national Catholics'; by then he had ceased to be a pastor for the Église *catholique nationale* (which later became part of the 'Christian Catholic Church', as the Old Catholic Church is known in Switzerland). In spring 1874, when Loyson travelled through the Netherlands, he was not welcome in Amersfoort. Until 1893 when, after his resignation, the Gallican Catholic congregation in Paris came under the jurisdiction of the archbishop of Utrecht, as a former monk and priest his marriage (and, indeed, his self-confident wife!) represented an insurmountable impediment to deeper relations with the Church of Utrecht. Consequently, he was unable to enter into negotiations with the Dutch Old Catholics about 'episcopal assistance' (ibid. 98). Cross's depiction of the relationship between Loyson and the Swiss Old Catholic bishop Eduard Herzog, and of the relationship between the Old Catholics and Loyson's *Église Catholique Gallicane* (ECG) would also have profited from reference to Old Catholic archives in Switzerland and the Netherlands. However, Cross does have interesting things to say about Emilie Loyson's prominent role 'in the work of the ECG' (ibid. 206–21, 286–7, quotation at 221) and the Anglican disapproval (which was shared by Old Catholics) of Emilie's unwillingness 'to play the discreet, supporting role of parson's wife', of her role as an intermediary in Loyson's English correspondence, and of her perception of herself – which was shared by her husband – as a partner in ministry (ibid. 220). For a more detailed consideration of Loyson's relationship to the Old Catholic movement and Church, see Angela Berlis, 'Père Hyacinthe Loyson (1827–1912). Ein Vertreter Frankreichs im Altkatholizismus', in *Meester in kerk en recht. Vriendenbundel voor Jan Hallebeek bij zijn 25-jarig jubileum als docent kerkelijk recht*, ed. Lidwien van Buuren and Peter-Ben Smit, Publicatieserie Stichting Oud-Katholiek Seminarie 50 (Amersfoort, 2013), 187–206.

familiar with their content.[17] In his lectures, Döllinger discussed the problems which prevented the 'reunion' of the Churches, and the 'Grounds of Hope'.[18] He referred repeatedly to the Eastern Churches and to Islam, reminding his audience that it had been customary since the time of St John of Damascus (*c*.676–749) to view Islam as a Christian heresy.[19] Döllinger lamented the poor persuasive power of a disunited, fragmented Christianity, particularly in its encounters with Islam, which he viewed as a religion of the sword and a '*falsa religio*',[20] although he thought that – like Ishmael – it was a legitimate bearer of the divine promise.[21] The elderly theologian's assessment of Judaism was much more positive than his attitude towards Islam.[22] Through his engagement for the reunion of the Churches – manifested in his lectures on reunion and in the Bonn Union Conferences in 1874 and 1875 – Döllinger's 'tolerance for and understanding of those holding other religious conviction' had been strengthened.[23] Elsewhere he

[17] Ignaz von Döllinger, *Conférences sur la réunion des églises*, transl. Madame Hyacinthe Loyson (Paris, [1880]).

[18] 'Difficulties and Grounds of Hope' is the title of his last lecture. Here he mentions also Pusey's *Eirenicon* and the Oxford Movement as agents for unity: John J. I. von Döllinger, *Lectures on the Reunion of the Churches* (London, Oxford and Cambridge, 1872), 146–7.

[19] Ibid. 7.

[20] Ibid. 33.

[21] Döllinger engaged with Islam, at least theoretically, at several points during his life. His view of Islam was influenced by the Catholic theologian Johann Adam Möhler (1796–1838), the most influential representative of the Catholic 'Tübingen School' of the early nineteenth-century, whose works Döllinger subsequently edited; however (and unsurprisingly), Döllinger's view of Islam remained bound by the polemics of his age: see Hartmut Bobzin, 'Döllingers Sicht des Islam', in *Geschichtlichkeit und Glaube: Gedenkschrift zum 100. Todestag Ignaz von Döllingers*, ed. Georg Denzler and Ernst Ludwig Grasmück (Munich, 1990), 459–75.

[22] Döllinger's views on Judaism changed significantly between his early and later writings. In the 1820s he was against the emancipation of Jews in Bavaria: Jews would not be granted equal rights there until the late 1860s. Towards the end of his life, in 1881, in response to the debate on the so-called *Judenfrage* (the 'question of the Jews') in the German *Kaiserreich*, which had been initiated in 1879 by the conservative Prussian historian and member of the *Reichstag*, Heinrich von Treitschke – the so-called *Berliner Antisemitismusstreit* – Döllinger gave his ground-breaking lecture, 'Die Juden in Europa': I. von Döllinger, *Akademische Vorträge*, I (Nördlingen, 1888), 209–41. For the development of his ideas, see Rudolf Bulin, 'Ablehnung des Antisemitismus bei Döllinger und Reinkens. Ein Vergleich', part I, *Internationale Kirchliche Zeitschrift* 87 (1997), 16–42.

[23] Bulin, 'Ablehnung', 33.

would suggest that the Jews were *Gottes Lieblingsvolk* ('God's most beloved people').[24]

In their explorations of the relationships between the religions, and on the basis not only of their own story but also of their encounters with Islam, the Loysons went much further than Döllinger.[25] Ample proof of this is offered by their openness not only to different Christian traditions, but also to other religious forms, including Spiritualism, and also by the way in which they sought encounters with Judaism and Islam during their travels.[26]

TRAVELS TO THE ORIENT (1894–6)

The Loysons undertook two journeys to Northern Africa and Palestine: the first, from December 1894 to spring 1895, to Algiers; the second, from 29 October 1895 until May 1896, to Algiers, Tunis, Malta, Egypt and Palestine. The regions they visited were under French (Algiers) and British (Malta, Palestine) sovereignty. Emilie published her accounts of these travels about ten years later. At the staging points of their journey, Hyacinthe gave lectures to audiences which included Protestants, Catholics, Freethinkers and Muslims, and in Tunis also Jews.[27] In general, he took as his theme 'The Reconciliation of Religions and the Unity of Races'.[28] These lectures were intended to communicate the trav-

---

[24] Döllinger, 'Die Juden in Europa', 236.

[25] In 1910, at a congress organized by the International Council of Unitarian and other Liberal Religious Thinkers, Hyacinthe Loyson said of Döllinger: 'With him we dreamt of the unification of all Christian churches; now we have become wiser and we seek a rapprochement and alliance of all religions which are worthy of this name … The true Church includes all people': Hyacinthe Loyson, 'Die Allianz der Religionen', in Max Fischer and Friedrich Michael Schiele, eds, *Fünfter Weltkongress für freies Christentum und religiösen Fortschritt. Protokoll der Verhandlungen* (Berlin, 1910), 737–44, at 743. The same sentiment is found in the French inscription on Hyacinthe Loyson's gravestone in the Père Lachaise cemetery, Paris: 'The strata inhabited by my soul are so high that I can be simultaneously Catholic and Protestant, Greek and Latin, Christian and Jew or even Mussulman. These different forms of faith are beautiful in different ways. None is absolutely true under these different names.'

[26] Further research is needed to establish the people and religious trends to which the Loysons were linked. For instance, the extent of their connection to the 1893 World Parliament of Religions in Chicago is currently an open question. In an obituary published in the magazine *The Open Court*, the editor remarks that 'Father Hyacinthe came into connection with *The Open Court* soon after the Religious Parliament, held in Chicago in 1893': *Open Court* 26 (1912), 129.

[27] Loyson, *Jerusalem*, 26, 100.

[28] See, for example, ibid. 77.

ellers' ideas, but they also helped to finance the Loysons' journey.[29] With the help of the local authorities, the lectures were carefully prepared and publicized in advance. For example, in Jerusalem Emilie – who managed the journey as 'agent' – enlisted the support of the governor to print two thousand broadsheets with an invitation to the lecture in French, Arabic and Hebrew.[30] Looking back, she reported enthusiastic responses to the idea of a 'rapprochement between two great religions'.[31] Emilie developed a truly missionary zeal for this concept, and was careful to avoid giving the impression that the members of her audience should all convert to Christianity.

The travellers did not view themselves as tourists or as globetrotters who accidentally encountered people of other faiths in an unfamiliar country. Rather, their journeys were inspired by their perception of the important role of religion in establishing international peace. At the time, there were about 300 million Muslims worldwide, and Emilie observed that 'France has thirty million Moslem subjects in Africa alone'.[32] With considerable vision, she saw that that such reconciliation would be essential to calm or settle the differences and tensions between the religions. As she explained in the introduction to her book:

> I am convinced after a long life of careful observation and unusual experience, that the … strain upon humanity may manifest itself on the surface of political events any day … and that the long impending catastrophe can only be averted by careful observation and timely action in the domain of religion, which is to humanity what the atmosphere is to the earth.[33]

The Loysons' journeys were undertaken in the spirit of 'seeking our fellow-men whom we knew not' and of 'looking everywhere for new manifestations of nature's beauty and God's love'.[34] The result of this 'pilgrimage', which allowed the travellers to walk in

---

[29] See, for example, ibid. 88, 100 (in Tunis).

[30] Ibid. 300.

[31] Ibid. 117. Emilie observed that 'rapprochement' means 'strictly speaking: "A coming together in friendly relations"': ibid.

[32] Ibid. 8.

[33] Ibid. 2.

[34] Ibid. 7.

the footsteps of Paul and Jesus, was, Emilie wrote, 'the ineffable joy of the Infinite Presence'.[35]

The Loysons regarded proselytizing and evangelization very critically. Instead, they sought the peaceful coexistence not only of different religions but also of different Christian denominations and confessions. For that reason they rejected the interference of the Roman Catholic Church in the Coptic Church and the creation of the Coptic Catholic Church under Rome's jurisdiction, arguing that, as Emilie put it, such interference was 'disloyal to [the Church's] Divine Founder' and 'illegal in the ecclesiastical realm'; moreover, such interference had resulted in 'dissension, bitterness, hatred, war, and massacre'.[36] In her book Emilie emphasized the unity of God above all: this is directly connected with the Loysons' desire for a reconciliation of the religions.[37] They nevertheless remained steadfast in their own belief in the significance of Jesus Christ as Saviour.[38]

Ultimately, the aim of the Loysons' travels was nothing less than the reunification of the children of God: Jews, Christians and Muslims.[39] In their attempt to achieve this goal, on arrival in a new town the Loysons sought out the local religious leaders – who were often highly educated – in order to enter into conversation. Achieving this usually proved unproblematic.[40] Emilie also had access to women and she tried to make contact with common people.[41] Along the way, the train journeys the couple undertook could also offer possibilities for conversations: 'Our railway compartment became a Monotheistic and Ecumenical Council – for the whole world's true faith was represented here: by Jews,

---

[35] Ibid. 8.

[36] Ibid. 254. Emilie objected to the fact that Roman Catholic missionaries had persuaded around 100,000 Copts to leave their Church, thus creating a schism. She understood mission in terms of help and support of local Churches, rather than proselytizing.

[37] It is significant that their primary interlocutors shared a monotheistic faith. Thus Emilie Loyson points out that Muslims are amongst the 'firmest monotheists': Loyson, *Jerusalem*, 8.

[38] It would be interesting to explore the extent to which Emilie's puritan family history played a part in her thinking. The couple's contacts with the Unitarian movement also deserve further investigation.

[39] Loyson, *Jerusalem*, 63.

[40] One exception was their visit to Hebron: ibid. 290–1.

[41] Ibid. 185.

Christians and Moslems.'[42] For the Loysons, the 'unity of God' was the only foundation for a lasting peace between Christians and Muslims.[43]

With their journeys – and also with the subsequent travelogue – both Loysons were seeking to fulfil a mission. The people at home were to be enlightened: 'we had come to learn as much as possible, not only for our own satisfaction, but also for the purpose of rectifying many errors in Europe concerning Islam.'[44]

ISLAM AND MUSLIM WOMEN

Even in the preface to her book, Emilie Loyson anticipated critical reactions: 'I may be suspected of unusual sympathy for Mussulmans … . Yet, my sympathy for Islam does not prevent me from deploring their polygamy, their lack of energy, and the unwarranted seclusion of their women.'[45] On a more positive note, she commended the fact that Muslims did not drink alcohol (with this prohibition, she wrote, Muhammad had bestowed 'a permanent blessing on his religion'[46]) or use drugs.[47] Muslims were also more hospitable than Christians. In contrast to the fragmented state of Christianity, she (mistakenly) saw Islam as unified.[48] For Emilie, Islam was a lived religion characterized by high moral norms and practices.

Emilie was particularly interested in the role of women in Islam. Her first encounter with Muslim women took place in Algiers, when she was offered a glimpse of harem life, which, as she observed, was normally 'a closed and hermetically sealed domain'.[49] She noted – in contrast to the stories which circulated in Europe and North America – that the women in the harem, and in particular the more upper-class women, had nothing in common with slaves,[50] and she defended the Muslim practice of

---

[42] Ibid. 134.
[43] Ibid. 107.
[44] Ibid. 214.
[45] Ibid. 9–10.
[46] Ibid. 101.
[47] Ibid. 121–2.
[48] Ibid. 319.
[49] Ibid. 35. For another visit to a harem, see ibid. 163–6.
[50] Ibid. 142. Compare Döllinger, *Lectures on Reunion*, 25: 'The woman is a being of lower grade, so that throughout the East it is commonly supposed that only men have souls, and accordingly women are oppressed, maltreated, shut out from all means of

arranged marriages.[51] Emilie was also very enthusiastic about the fact that Muslim women did not wear corsets, which she saw as dangerous to women's health.[52] In Cairo she visited two schools for girls, observing that these were the only such schools in the whole of Egypt.[53] Her account of these schools is a strong plea for an improvement in the education of girls. For Emilie, however, the 'seclusion of woman and her consequent exclusion from intellectual development' remained one of the fundamental evils of Islam.[54]

Judaism and Eastern Christianity

Emilie Loyson also observed the 'profound resentment for the Jews' expressed by both Muslims and Christians, while noting that in many places the legal status of the Jews had changed during the course of the nineteenth century, and in many places quite recently, from 'pariah' to 'citizen'.[55] Emilie saw the Jews as a 'living and continuous miracle', because they had kept their faith through all persecutions and tribulations.[56] She understood Jews to be 'our brethren' whom 'we should love', but for Christians also 'our fathers', who had given to Christians both the 'divine book' (in her view not only the Old Testament but also the New) and the Saviour himself.[57] She had no doubt that 'the Jews are to become more and more a powerful and beneficent factor among the people of the earth'.[58] Emilie wrote this at the time of the Dreyfus affair – which between 1894 and 1906 caused uproar in France – in a period of growing French anti-Semitism.[59]

education, bought and sold like merchandise, and surrendered to the arbitrary caprice of men like slaves or beasts of burden'.

[51] Cf. Loyson, *Jerusalem*, 60: 'I believe their marriages are as happy, taking it all in all, as among so called Christians'.

[52] As a young woman in the United States, she had invented an alternative to the corset: Zwianzek, 'Emilie Loyson', 222; see also Loyson, *Jerusalem*, 97.

[53] Loyson, *Jerusalem*, 201–5.

[54] Ibid. 205. Another evil, in her eyes, was 'the augmented Oriental somnolence and inactivity resulting from the general use of tobacco – by both sexes': ibid. Emilie Loyson was a real apostle against smoking.

[55] Ibid. 61.

[56] Ibid.

[57] Ibid. 62.

[58] Ibid.

[59] Emilie Loyson makes explicit reference to the Dreyfus affair in her introduction: ibid. 10. For a recent account, see Louis Begley, *Why the Dreyfus Affair matters* (New

In Malta and Alexandria the Loysons also encountered a range of Christian communities. In Roman Catholic Malta, Emilie reported, 'the presence of the married monk and his wife had been noised about, and the advisability of our visiting the churches was discussed'.[60] In Egypt, where Coptic Christians then numbered about 700,000,[61] the Loysons observed that, as a minority in a majority Islamic culture, Egyptian Christians had adopted many Islamic customs. There Emilie found the position of Christian women to be very similar to that of their Muslim sisters.[62] However, both Loysons were made very welcome: indeed, during a visit to the Coptic patriarch, they told him that they came from 'the ancient Church of Gaul, believing in One Only Church', and asked him if they might 'show our belief in this unity by partaking of the Holy Communion'.[63] During the liturgy that followed, the preacher interrupted his Arabic sermon, asking the Loysons in Italian to confirm their belief in Christ: 'Crede Lei in Nostro Signore Gesu Cristo?'[64] The Loysons responded with a public confession – 'Si, lo credo' – after which they were officially given leave to receive communion. The same would happen later in the Armenian parish in Jerusalem.[65] To participate in the celebration of the eucharist and to receive communion 'in the ancient Church of Egypt' – that is, in the Coptic Church, although no agreement concerning intercommunion with any Western Church existed, was for Emilie Loyson an intense experience.[66] However, she remarked, it was reported all over the world that 'Père Hyacinthe has become a Copt!'[67]

Haven, CT, 2009). See also the views of Judaism expressed in Döllinger, 'Die Juden in Europa', as well as Bulin, 'Ablehnung'.

[60] Loyson, *Jerusalem*, 120–6, quotation at 122 (Malta), 127–31 (Alexandria).

[61] Ibid. 226.

[62] Ibid. 167.

[63] Ibid. 232.

[64] Ibid. 236.

[65] Ibid. 282–3. The Coptic and Armenian Churches belong to the family of so-called Oriental Orthodox Churches, which do not accept the Chalcedonian Christological definition of 451.

[66] Loyson, *Jerusalem*, 231–9, cf. 267–70.

[67] Ibid. 239. She also records that several Egyptian newspapers published Hyacinthe's correction of this story: ibid. The Loysons' own confessional allegiance at this time was somewhat ambiguous.

What did the Loysons achieve with their Journeys?

Emilie Loyson's travel account is notable for its focus on religion and for its portrayal of the active role of women. Indeed, it was quite unusual at that time for married women to appear in public or to play a role in a religious debate, as she did.[68] She comes across as a highly articulate disputant on religious questions. The Grand Mufti of Hebron, into whose house she was the first Christian woman to enter, asked her why, if she was so positive about Islam and the truth of the Qur'ān, she did not convert. She responded that it had been God's will that she be born in the United States, 'in the religion of my fathers', and that she would remain loyal and obedient to that religion.[69] Given her own conversion from the Protestant religion of her own parents to Catholicism, this response indicates that Emilie understood her own religious position as holding together Protestantism and Catholicism in an 'ecumenical' Christianity. Her interlocutor, who presumably did not know her story, was pleased by this answer and called her 'a holy woman'.[70]

Emilie had much more freedom of movement and many more privileges than local women, whether Muslim or Christian, in the countries she visited. She was allowed to enter the al-Azhar Mosque in Cairo whenever she wished, and in the Coptic Cathedral she was not only not obliged to sit in the women's area, but was even allowed to enter the sanctuary:

> Knowing that no woman enters there, I was filled with aston-
> ishment when, the next moment, the High Priest returned
> and beckoned me to enter also! … then kneeling beside
> my husband at the High Altar, the High Priest gave to Père
> Hyacinthe and then to me, the Most Holy Communion of
> our Lord.[71]

Emilie used the opportunities available to her and her experience as a journalist to try to further her concerns, particularly
in relation to the position of women. Thus, in a lecture given in
the Coptic Cathedral and college in Alexandria, attended by the
archbishop of Alexandria and about two hundred male teachers

---

[68] Ibid. 214.
[69] Ibid. 296.
[70] Ibid. 297.
[71] Ibid. 236–7.

and clergy, and at which Emilie was the only female present, she pleaded for better education and training opportunities for women and for their participation in society. Her lecture was subsequently published in an Arabic newspaper in Beirut.[72] In order to further these aims, and also to bring Eastern and Western women together, Emilie founded the 'Alliance des Femmes Orientales et Occidentales pour le Progrès des Relations amicales entre toutes les Nations', of which she became the first president. Its aim was 'to create a bond of sympathy, both religious and human, between women of the Orient and the Occident, or even the whole world, without consideration of differences of cult and civilization'.[73] Men were welcome to join the alliance, too. Emilie would continue to promote the alliance and its aims until her death.[74]

In many ways, the Loysons were ahead of their time. Their commitment to the reconciliation of religions arose from deeply held conviction, which also led them to propose the building of a mosque in Paris – a plan that was only realized in 1926.[75] But the Loysons also remained children of their own time and of their own cultural – and indeed national – contexts.[76] Their sometimes very critical observations were informed by comparisons with their own culture. Islamic culture remained foreign to them, as did its language (they spoke only French and English), and they demonstrated some tendency to idealize the Orient.[77] Nevertheless, the

---

[72] Ibid. 263–4.

[73] [Emilie Loyson], *Alliance des Femmes Orientales et Occidentales pour le Progrès des Relation amicales entre toutes les Nations* (Paris, 1903), 17. The brochure contains a list of members and donors, amongst whom was the widow of the late French president, Felix Faure (ibid. 34–6). Princess Nazli of Egypt was honorary president of the alliance: Loyson Papers, MS fr. 2960, fol. 164. Her involvement and the high social status of the other women on the board, and of those women and men sympathetic to the association, indicate that the organization was potentially influential.

[74] See, for example, her two letters (under the letterhead of the alliance) to world peace and woman's rights activist May Wright Sewall (1844–1920): Indianapolis, IN, Indianapolis Public Library, May Wright Sewall Papers, online at: <http://digital-library.imcpl.org/cdm/landingpage/collection/mws>, accessed 1 July 2014. On 17 September 1900 Emilie Loyson invited Sewall to take part in a 'glorious pilgrimage' to Jerusalem, in order to build 'the tent of the new covenant of peace'.

[75] Loyson, *Jerusalem*, 46. The mosque was built in the fifth *arrondissement* (the *Quartier Latin*). Its construction was in part an expression of French gratitude for Muslim support against the German Reich during the First World War.

[76] Emilie was well aware of this: Loyson, *Jerusalem*, 8.

[77] For an example, see ibid. 181.

Loysons sought and found an entry to Islam and to Arab culture.[78] They experienced real hospitality and high regard. One indication of this is the 'Avant-Propos', or preface, written for Emilie's book by the former governor of Palestine, the Arab intellectual Youssef Zia Pacha El Khalidy (1829–1907). Another was the fact that Emilie and Hyacinthe were admitted to communion by both the Copts and the Armenians,[79] which was widely understood as a public act and a symbol of friendship, as can be seen from obituaries in Armenian newspapers after Hyacinthe's death in 1912.[80]

Emilie Loyson often wrote of the 'Unity of the True Faith of man' which she had experienced, particularly in Jerusalem: 'Patriarchs, Prophets, Jewish High Priests, Christian Apostles, and Moslems, all unite in the Cosmic Truth of the One and Only God – who was, and is, and ever shall be proclaimed here!'[81] The title of her book should probably be understood symbolically: it offers an account of two Christians travelling *To Jerusalem through the Lands of Islam among Jews, Christians, and Moslems*. However, it is difficult to judge what the Loysons really achieved. How effective were their endeavours? Their attitudes and demeanour must have seemed strange, unusual and novel to many in Europe – even those to whom they were close.

Emilie Loyson was aware that reactions to their travels differed widely. She wrote: 'Then the newspapers … were kind or unkind, according to their religious convictions.'[82] Old Catholic responses to the Loysons' interreligious involvement ranged from reserved to openly critical. The Swiss Old Catholic bishop Eduard Herzog (1841–1924), for example, emphasized that Hyacinthe Loyson's new 'profession of faith' went much too far for his taste: 'He went to Algier last winter, where he encountered Islam. And now he'd

---

[78] Ibid. 223–4.

[79] On their travels, the Loysons also had contact with other Churches, Eastern and Western: ibid. 284–6.

[80] According to the Armenian journal Ժամանակ ('Times'), he was 'the last great ally of the Armenian Church': Geneva, Archives of the Paroisse Catholique-Chrétienne, 'Hyacinthe Loyson devant l'histoire 1912–1913'. The archives include obituaries from across the world.

[81] Loyson, *Jerusalem*, 281; cf. Döllinger, *Lectures on Reunion*, 30; for him Palestine and Jerusalem were 'the meeting-place of Churches that hate one another'. Therefore he pleaded for praying 'for a fresh outpouring of the Spirit of Unity, that we may keep a new Pentecost of enlightenment, peace, and brotherly love': ibid. 31.

[82] Loyson, *Jerusalem*, 82–3.

like to merge Christianity with Islam: let's be Islamic Christians and evangelical Mussulmans!'[83] The ultramontane media were delighted by these differences amongst those they considered to be Old Catholics, and, Herzog complained, they 'scornfully exploited [Loyson's] new programme, "Let's be Islamic Christians", against us'.[84] That was, they wrote, 'what Old Catholicism was leading to!'[85]

Despite these contemporary criticisms, Hyacinthe and Emilie Loyson can be considered pioneers of the twentieth-century ecumenical movement and of a budding interreligious openness. This openness did not lead to structural reform, but largely remained that of two individuals on their own spiritual journey. However, because of the significant media coverage they generated, the Loysons' travels and their implications for interreligious encounter attracted significant attention in early twentieth-century Europe. While the Loysons did extend their hands to others, they did so as travellers and observers with European values and standards. Nevertheless, the encounter with representatives of other faiths happened in ways that were extraordinary for their time. Emilie Loyson also shone a light on the role of women in religious practice; she was fascinated by this question and repeatedly and explicitly referred to it in her addresses and publications.[86] Through their partnership, therefore, Hyacinthe and Emilie Loyson not only

---

[83] Bern, Bischöfliches Archiv, AH 71, E. Herzog to J. H. Reinkens, 8 April 1895 (transcription of the German text by Ewald Kessler).

[84] Ibid., AH 74, E. Herzog to R. Jenkins Nevin, 5 April 1897 (transcription of the German text by Hubert Huppertz). According to Herzog, Loyson was by this time no longer to be considered an Old Catholic (Berlis, 'Hyacinthe Loyson', 213), although outsiders still saw him as such. As noted above, Loyson's ecclesiastical identity is hard to define; as Nigel Yates has put it, he moved within 'an exceedingly complicated ecclesiastical triangle' made up of the Church of England and the Dutch and the German-speaking Old Catholic Churches: 'Old Catholics and Reformed Catholics in late Nineteenth-Century Europe', in Brown and Nockles, eds, *Oxford Movement*, 249–65, at 262. Loyson, especially in the last phase of his life, would probably have defined himself in a quite different way, answering questions of belonging by claiming a universal religious identity – 'simultaneously Catholic and Protestant, Greek and Latin, Christian and Jew or even Mussulman' – as his epitaph shows (see n. 25). In his final years, he was frequently in Geneva. Nonetheless, and contrary to the impression given by Bishop Herzog, the Old Catholic Church in Switzerland later reappropriated Hyacinthe: in 1928 the Old Catholic parish of Geneva held a public celebration to mark the unveiling of a plaque in his memory in the Church of St Germain. The inscription reads: 'Agir comme s'il n'y avait au monde que sa conscience et Dieu.'

[85] Herzog to Nevin, 5 April 1897.

[86] Cf. for instance, Madame Hyacinthe Loyson, *The Religious Condition of Oriental*

inspired reflection on relationships between Christians and other faiths but also a reassessment of the relationship between the sexes.

Universität Bern

Women: Address given at the International Congress of Monotheistic Religions in Geneva, Switzerland, 30 August 1905 (Geneva, 1905).

CHRISTIANITY, PLURALITY AND VERNACULAR RELIGION IN EARLY TWENTIETH-CENTURY GLASTONBURY: A SIGN OF THINGS TO COME?*

by MARION BOWMAN

This essay focuses upon a significant place, Glastonbury, at an important time during the early twentieth century, in order to shed light on a particular aspect of Christianity which is frequently overlooked: its *internal* plurality. This is not simply denominational diversity, but the considerable heterogeneity which exists at both institutional and individual level *within* denominations, and which often escapes articulation, awareness or comment. This is significant because failure to apprehend a more detailed, granular picture of religion can lead to an incomplete view of events in the past and, by extension, a partial understanding of later phenomena. This essay argues that by using the concept of vernacular religion a more nuanced picture of religion as it is – or has been – lived can be achieved.[1]

Presenting a brief account of inter-related events and people in Glastonbury at the turn of the twentieth century will underline the importance of folklore and the power of invented tradition, and raise questions about the extent to which the 'orthodoxy' and 'orthopraxy' of church personnel and laity can be assumed. It will also highlight the extent to which seemingly 'alternative' practitioners (who might be neglected or rejected as outside the Christian frame) can prove to be significant in relation to Chris-

* I would like to thank Brendan Macnamara, whose paper at the Irish Society for the Academic Study of Religion Conference, Dublin, 10–12 May 2013, 'Wellesley Tudor Pole and the Glastonbury Phenomenon: The "Celtic" Dimension of Pre-First World War Religious Discourse in Britain', renewed my interest in this period of Glastonbury's history and Paul Fletcher, Archivist, Chalice Well, Glastonbury for his invaluable assistance in relation to Tudor Pole's contribution to the Dean's Yard Meeting.
[1] Articles that outline and advocate this broader, more inclusive view of religion include Don Yoder, 'Toward a Definition of Folk Religion', *Western Folklore* 33 (1974), 2–15; Leonard Primiano, 'Vernacular Religion and the Search for Method in Religious Folklife', *Western Folklore* 54 (1995), 37–56; Marion Bowman and Ülo Valk, 'Introduction: Vernacular Relion, Generic Expressions and the Dynamics of Belief', in eidem, eds, *Vernacular Religion in Everyday Life: Expressions of Belief* (Sheffield, 2012), 1–19.

tian plurality and may in fact self-identify as Christians. Boundaries between official and folk, orthodox and alternative tend to be fuzzier and far more permeable than commonly acknowledged, both popularly and in the academy. While the ferment of 'alternative' ideas in the late nineteenth and early twentieth centuries has been chronicled elsewhere in relation to Glastonbury and characters mentioned in this essay,[2] their framing through the lens of vernacular religion offers a helpful perspective in relation to internal diversity and the ramifications of Christian plurality.

VERNACULAR RELIGION

Don Yoder, drawing heavily upon the German tradition of scholarship, succinctly describes folk religion as 'the totality of all those views and practices of religion that exist among the people apart from and alongside the strictly theological and liturgical forms of the official religion', highlighting a huge and frequently understudied area of religious life.[3] Some years ago I suggested within the context of Religious Studies that to obtain a realistic view of religion, it should be viewed in terms of three interacting components: official religion (meaning what is accepted orthodoxy at any given time within institutional religion, although this is subject to change), folk religion (meaning that which is generally accepted and transmitted belief and practice, regardless of the institutional view) and individual religion (the combination of received tradition, folk and official, and personal interpretations of this 'package' in response to personal beliefs and insights gained from experience).[4] The significance of this is that different components interact to produce what, for each person, constitutes religion. These are not 'neat' compartments: folk religion is not a

---

[2]   See especially Brendan McNamara, 'The "Celtic" Dimension of Pre-First World War Religious Discourse in Britain: Wellesley Tudor Pole and the Glastonbury Phenomenon', *Journal of the Irish Society for the Academic Study of Religion* 1/1 (2014), 90–104; Tim Hopkinson-Ball, *The Rediscovery of Glastonbury: Frederick Bligh Bond, Architect of the New Age* (London, 2007); James Carley, *Glastonbury Abbey: The Holy House at the Head of the Moors Adventurous* (Glastonbury, 1996); Patrick Benham, *The Avalonians* (Glastonbury, 1993).

[3]   Yoder, *Definition*, 14.

[4]   Marion Bowman, 'Phenomenology, Fieldwork and Folk Religion', repr. with additional 'Afterword' in Steven Sutcliffe, ed., *Religion: Empirical Studies* (Aldershot, 2004), 3–18; first publ. as *Phenomenology, Fieldwork and Folk Religion*, British Association for the Study of Religions, Occasional Paper 6 (London, 1992).

tidy and easily recognizable category separate from (and inferior to) official religion, and folk and individual religion are not the result of people getting 'pure' religion wrong.

Yoder shows how the term 'folk religion' has been used both by religious professionals and by scholars to make judgements about 'lived religion' in relation or in contradistinction to 'proper' or official religion. For example, on the basis of a study of the diocese of Bath and Wells, Geoffrey Walker has argued that the term 'folk religion' is used in some Anglican circles as an umbrella term for 'things we don't approve of', such as evolving popular forms of memorialization.[5]

'Vernacular religion' is the term and approach increasingly used by scholars working at the interstices of folklore/ethnology and religious studies, and this fits well also with the study of religion in historical context. Whereas, as Yoder and others have shown, there have been many debates over, and conceptualizations of, folk religion, Leonard Primiano problematizes the category of official religion, rightly stating the obvious, namely that institutional religion 'is itself conflicted and not monolithic'.[6] Primiano, claiming that '[r]eligious belief takes as many forms in a tradition as there are individual believers',[7] asserts that no one, including members of institutional hierarchies, 'lives an "officially" religious life in a pure unadulterated form'.[8] Vernacular religion is not just another term for folk religion; it is not simply the 'dichotomous or dialectical partner of "institutional" religious forms'.[9] Primiano describes vernacular religious theory as 'an interdisciplinary approach to the study of the religious lives of individuals with special attention to the process of religious belief, the verbal, behavioral, and material expressions of religious belief, and the ultimate object of religious belief'.[10] The emphasis of vernacular religion is on the need to study religion 'as it is lived: as human beings encounter, under-

---

[5]   See Geoffrey Walker, 'Clergy Attitudes to Folk Religion in the Diocese of Bath and Wells' (PhD thesis, University of Bristol, 2001).
[6]   Leonard Primiano, 'Afterword – Manifestations of the Religious Vernacular: Ambiguity, Power and Creativity', in Bowman and Valk, eds, *Vernacular Religion in Everyday Life*, 382–94, at 384.
[7]   Primiano, 'Vernacular Religion', 51.
[8]   Ibid. 46.
[9]   Primiano, 'Afterword', 384.
[10]   Primiano, 'Vernacular Religion', 44.

stand, interpret, and practice it'.[11] Its conceptual value lies in the fact that it 'highlights the power of the individual and communities of individuals to create and re-create their own religion'.[12]

If we accept that 'All religion is both subtly and vibrantly marked by continuous interpretation even after it has been reified in expressive or structured forms',[13] the study of both contemporary and historical religion can be enriched by anticipating and recognizing heterogeneity, individual creativity and non-conformity. The study of material culture, narrative, tradition and 'the totality of all those views and practices of religion that exist among the people apart from and alongside the strictly theological and liturgical forms of the official religion' can reveal a much more nuanced and realistic account of religion as it is, and as it has been, lived.[14] For these reasons, vernacular religion as an approach has much to offer the study of Glastonbury, past and present.

THREE GLASTONBURY LEGENDS

Religious Studies scholar Kim Knott claims that '[t]he particularity of a place arises from the complexity of its social relations and the sum of the stories told about it'.[15] In the case of Glastonbury, much of the complexity of its social relations has arisen from the sheer quantity and variety of the stories told about and within it, and the key to understanding the 'ongoing interpretations and negotiations of religion' lies in myth.[16] The Religious Studies usage of myth is employed here, namely that a myth is a 'significant story', regardless of issues of truth or proof.[17] Also helpful in understanding aspects of historical and contemporary religiosity in Glastonbury is the concept of the multifunctional 'belief story', characterized by folklorist Gillian Bennett as an informal story which enunciates and validates the current beliefs and experiences of a given community.[18]

---

[11] Ibid.

[12] Primiano, 'Afterword', 383.

[13] Ibid. 384.

[14] Yoder, 'Definition', 14.

[15] Kim Knott, *The Location of Religion: A Spatial Analysis* (London, 2005), 33.

[16] Primiano, 'Vernacular Religion'.

[17] Ninian Smart, *The Science of Religion and the Sociology of Knowledge* (Princeton, NJ, 1973); idem, *The Religious Experience of Mankind* (New York, 1969).

[18] Gillian Bennett, '"Belief Stories": The Forgotten Genre', *Western Folklore* 48 (1989), 289–311, at 291.

In Glastonbury there are three legends in particular, current at the turn of the nineteenth and twentieth centuries and persisting today, which gave, and still give, rise to considerable speculation, experimentation and occasional confrontation. These relate to alleged visits to Glastonbury of St Joseph of Arimathea, Jesus and St Brigit.

For many Christians, past and present, Glastonbury's status has rested on the legend that Joseph of Arimathea established the first Christian church in the British Isles there.[19] On arriving at Glastonbury, Joseph is said to have thrust his staff into the ground at Wearyall Hill, and according to local tradition this became the Holy Thorn that blossoms twice a year, in spring and around Christmas.[20] Joseph also reputedly brought with him the Grail, that mysterious artefact regarded variously as the chalice used at the Last Supper, the blood of Christ in some form, or (as depicted in the fifteenth century stained glass fragment in St John the Baptist Church, Glastonbury) two containers, one of Christ's blood and one of his sweat.[21] Chalice Well in Glastonbury is connected by some with the chalice allegedly hidden there, accounting for the red stain of its chalybeate waters. The idea that Joseph founded an early 'pure' Church in Britain has been and remains extremely important to Christians of various denominations.[22] There is also the myth that Jesus may have accompanied Joseph (in popular tradition characterized as a merchant) on trading trips before his ministry began, visiting Glastonbury and perhaps even spending

---

[19] The age, provenance and veracity of this legend are all hotly debated and are not the focus of this essay; see Deborah Crawford, 'St Joseph in Britain: Reconsidering the Legends', *Folklore* 104 (1993), 86–98; ibid. 105 (1994), 51–9; Carley, *Glastonbury Abbey*.

[20] Marion Bowman, 'The Holy Thorn Ceremony: Revival, Rivalry and Civil Religion in Glastonbury', *Folklore* 117 (2006), 123–40.

[21] See, for example, C. L. Marson, *Glastonbury: The Historic Guide to the 'English Jerusalem'* (London, 1909), 5–8.

[22] St Joseph of Arimathea is depicted in both the Anglican Church of St John the Baptist and the Roman Catholic Shrine of Our Lady of Glastonbury at St Mary's Church, Glastonbury, and both mention the myth in their literature and on their websites. The Celtic Orthodox Church dates the foundation of the Celtic Church to 37 CE and the arrival of St Joseph in Glastonbury. In interviews, contemporary participants in the Anglican pilgrimage and non-conformist Christian visitors to the town have stressed the significance of St Joseph bringing Christianity directly to England and the later 'imposition' of Roman Catholicism.

some time living there.[23] Many believe that by coming to Glastonbury they are literally walking in Christ's footsteps.

Additionally, St Brigit and other Celtic saints such as St Patrick and St David reputedly visited Glastonbury.[24] According to legend, the Irish saint Brigit (458–523) – also referred to as Brigid or Bride – visited Glastonbury in 488 and spent time at Beckery or Bride's Mound, an elevated area on the edge of Glastonbury. An earlier chapel on this site dedicated to St Mary Magdalene was replaced in the tenth century by a larger church erected by St Dunstan and dedicated to St Brigit.[25] There was also a nearby spring known as Bride's Well, which some claim was known for its powers of healing and fertility. A carving of St Brigit milking a cow appears on the tower of St Michael's on Glastonbury Tor, all that remains of a fourteenth-century chapel.

GLASTONBURY: THE LATE NINETEENTH- AND EARLY TWENTIETH-CENTURY CONTEXT

In the late nineteenth and early twentieth centuries, a number of trends and events had an impact upon religious life and spiritual speculation in, and in relation to, Glastonbury.

Glastonbury's religious history had been brought to the forefront by some significant events. At the time of the dissolution of Glastonbury Abbey in 1539, Abbot Richard Whiting and two monks, John Thorne and Roger James, had been hanged as traitors on Glastonbury Tor for resisting the suppression of their house, and the abbey buildings were confiscated and later sold by the crown. Whiting, Thorne and James were beatified by Pope Leo XIII in 1895, and a Roman Catholic pilgrimage to Glastonbury Tor was held that year in celebration.[26] In 1897 the 1300th anniversary of the arrival of St Augustine in England was commemorated by 'an

---

[23] For example, a detailed 'account' of Jesus's life in Glastonbury can be found in Kirsten Parson, *Reflections on Glastonbury* (London, 1965).

[24] Carley, *Glastonbury Abbey*, 109–10.

[25] John L. Robinson, 'St. Brigid and Glastonbury', *Journal of the Royal Society of Antiquaries of Ireland* 83 (1953), 97–9, at 98.

[26] Benedictines Dom Francis Aidan Gasquet and Dom Bede Camm actively promoted interest in and devotion to English Catholic Martyrs; Camm edited the *Lives of the English Martyrs declared Blessed by Pope Leo XIII*, 2 vols (London, 1904–5). Pope Leo XIII also raised the nearby Benedictine Downside Priory to the status of abbey in 1899, Downside taking on the titular abbacy of Glastonbury; Blessed Richard Whiting appears on the abbot of Downside's seal: *Catholic Encyclopedia* (New York,

international pilgrimage' to Glastonbury Abbey led by the arch-bishop of Canterbury.[27]

The abbey site was sold by auction in 1907 to Ernest Jardine and ownership passed to the Bath and Wells Diocesan Trust in 1908.[28] Excavations of the site aroused considerable public interest. In 1911, for example, Albany F. Major reported in a communication to the journal *Folklore* two phenomena noted since the excavations started: the strong smell of incense at various points in the abbey (which some dismissed as the result of deposits of incense being disturbed by the excavation) and the claims that people had started to hear a peal of twelve bells at night, and that 'an examination of old records showed that the Abbey had a peal of twelve bells'. Major concluded that 'the halo of legend, which has always hung round Glastonbury, is proof against modern scepticism'.[29] An annual Anglican pilgrimage to Glastonbury Abbey was established in 1924; that year's service included penitence for the desecration of the abbey, and thanksgiving for its return to Christian ownership which had given the opportunity for religious use. The constitution of the West of England Pilgrimage Association, founded in 1926 to administer the annual pilgrimage, included the following among its purposes:

> To declare our adherence to the Catholic Faith as received by the Church of England and to deepen the community of faith and love with those who lived and worshipped at Glastonbury Abbey and other religious sites in past centuries.

1909), *s.v.* 'Downside Abbey', online at: <http://www.newadvent.org/cathen/05149a. htm>, accessed 10 July 2014.

[27] 'Glastonbury: Town', in R. W. Dunning, ed., *Victoria History of the Counties of England. A History of the County of Somerset,* 9: *Glastonbury and Street* (London, 2006), 16–43, online at: <http://www.british-history.ac.uk/report.aspx?compid=117175>, accessed 22 January 2014.

[28] The precise circumstances of the sale and subsequent acquisition of the abbey by the Bath and Wells Diocesan Trust tend to be contested (Carley, *Glastonbury Abbey*; Benham, *Avalonians*), but there appears to have been a feeling that the site, once on the market, should be acquired by the Anglican Church in some form – possibly in response to the strong Catholic presence (including a convent and a seminary) in the town, as well as Downside's titular claim on Glastonbury.

[29] Albany F. Major, 'Somersetshire Folklore', *Folklore* 22 (1911), 495–6, at 495.

> To support the Glastonbury Abbey trustees by any means in the development and use of the Abbey as a sanctuary for Christians of all denominations and as a centre of pilgrimage.[30]

In these statements we see a desire for continuity with Glastonbury's pre-Reformation Christian tradition, to which the Anglican Church was claiming to be rightful heir, but also an aspiration that Glastonbury Abbey might become a multi-denominational Christian pilgrimage centre. However, Glastonbury and the abbey site were to become the foci of far broader interests and speculations.

In a broader context, the turn of the nineteenth and twentieth centuries was another period of Celtic revival, with burgeoning interest in Celtic art, culture and spirituality.[31] Breton scholar Ernest Renan (1823–92) had influentially characterized the Celts as 'spiritual beings and visionary dreamers',[32] claiming that they had displayed an enlightened approach to the integration of paganism and Christianity. Interest in Druidry, renewed in an earlier eighteenth-century Celtic revival, continued apace.[33] An important contribution to the spiritual milieu at that time was also being made by Theosophy.[34] Among the ideas put forward by H. P. Blavatsky and her followers were the existence of an ancient wisdom tradition, esoteric in character but manifest through exoteric religious traditions; the existence of adepts or masters of the wisdom; channelling of this wisdom to those attuned to receive it; a rather Westernized understanding of reincarnation and karma which portrayed a generally positive view of spiritual progression ('in every life a lesson'); humanity's spiritual as well as physical evolution; and a vision of universal brotherhood. However, some thought it more appropriate to seek a native British form of mysticism than to pursue those of India or Tibet. As the British mystic Lewis Spence wrote in 1905:

---

[30] See Marion Bowman, 'Drawn to Glastonbury', in Ian Reader and Tony Walter, eds, *Pilgrimage in Popular Culture* (Basingstoke, 1993), 29–62, at 43–5.

[31] See McNamara, 'Religious Discourse'.

[32] Donald E. Meek, *The Quest for Celtic Christianity* (Edinburgh, 2000), 46.

[33] See Stuart Piggott, *Ancient Britons and the Antiquarian Imagination* (London, 1989); idem, *The Druids* (London, 1993; first publ. 1968).

[34] See Kevin Tingay, 'Madame Blavatsky's Children: Theosophy and its Heirs', in Steven Sutcliffe and Marion Bowman, eds, *Beyond New Age: Exploring Alternative Spirituality* (Edinburgh, 2000), 37–50.

We Britons are much too prone to look for excellence outside of the boundaries of our own island … That we should so weakly rely on alien systems of thought while it is possible for us to re-establish our own is surely miserable. In no individual born in these islands does there not flow the blood of Druid priests and seers, and I confidently rely on British mystics, whatever their particular predilections, to unite in this greatest of all possible quests, the restoration of our native Secret Tradition.[35]

Many figures involved in the Celtic revival of the late nineteenth and early twentieth centuries had Theosophical connections, including the poet W. B. Yeats (who edited a collection of *Fairy and Folk Tales of Ireland* and wrote *The Celtic Twilight*), the Celtic revival artist John Duncan[36] and William Sharp (who wrote mystical prose and verse under the pseudonym Fiona Macleod).[37]

FIVE GLASTONBURY TALES[38]

This section will look at five individuals, with complex interconnected stories, who were of great significance in the twentieth-century development of Glastonbury as a special, spiritual place. These snapshots of people and events in Glastonbury demonstrate various aspects of vernacular religion: the influence of place on people and people on place; the role of folklore, in particular myth and belief story; and the invention of tradition. The stories highlight instances of Christian plurality, diversity within institutional Christianity (in this context Anglicanism in particular) and the Christian aspects of seemingly alternative views.

In the late nineteenth century John Arthur Goodchild (1851–1914), a psychic, author and physician, connected with the Hermetic

---

[35] Lewis Spence, *The Mysteries of Britain: Secret Rites and Traditions of Ancient Britain* (London, 1993; first publ. 1905), 256.

[36] John Duncan's 1913 painting *Saint Bride* can be viewed at: <http://www.nationalgalleries.org/collection/artists-a-z/D/3210/artist_name/John%20Duncan/record_id/2464>.

[37] For instance, the blessing, 'Deep peace of the running wave to you, Deep peace of the flowing air to you, Deep peace of the quiet earth to you', frequently presented as an 'ancient Celtic blessing', was in fact written by William Sharp under the name Fiona Macleod, and published in the *Pagan Review* during 1895.

[38] Much of the information for this section comes from Benham's *Avalonians*, a classic account of the early 'alternative' history of Glastonbury; McNamara's 'Religious Discourse' adds valuably to the scholarship of this period.

Order of the Golden Dawn, the British Israelites and the Freemasons, developed a keen interest in Glastonbury. Very much inspired
by the Celtic revival, in his book *The Light of the West* (1898) he
put forward the theory that 'ancient Ireland had been the centre
of a cult venerating the female aspect of the Deity'.[39] He came
to believe that a remnant of this cult had survived in Glastonbury,
attached to the figure of St Bride,[40] and could be revived. In 1885
he purchased a glass bowl (later usually referred to as the Cup) and
platter of unknown provenance in Bordighera, Italy.[41] He subsequently claimed that in 1897 he had a psychic experience in which
it was revealed to him that the Cup 'had once been carried by
Jesus' and that it would be instrumental in reviving feminine-based
spirituality in Glastonbury.[42] In September 1898 he concealed the
Cup in the muddy waters of a sluice in the area of Bride's Well
in Glastonbury, where he anticipated it would be discovered by a
woman. Goodchild's Cup provides the link with the next character
to be considered, Wellesley Tudor Pole (1884–1968).

Tudor Pole was brought up by socially aware Anglican parents
in Weston-super-Mare and later lived in Bristol. At the age of
eighteen, in 1902, he claimed to have had a vision in which it
was revealed to him that in a previous existence he had been a
monk at Glastonbury Abbey. After this he spent as much time
as possible at Glastonbury, becoming very interested in Chalice
Well and developing a pilgrimage route around the town which
included Bride's Well. In 1905 Janet and Christine Allen,[43] friends
of Wellesley Tudor Pole and his sister Kitty, first visited Glastonbury. The following year, at Tudor Pole's prompting, the sisters
searched the Bride's Well area and found the Cup, but left it
there. Kitty subsequently retrieved the Cup, and took it home
to Clifton, Bristol, where an 'Oratory' was set up in the Tudor
Pole house. Although, as McNamara notes, 'Goodchild and Tudor
Pole were adamant that there was no collusion in the independent

---

[39] Benham, *Avalonians*, 15.

[40] St Brigit is also known as St Brigid and St Bride; in the Glastonbury context,
those who specifically connect her with the pre-Christian Celtic goddess tend to refer
to her as Bride.

[41] Benham, *Avalonians*, 6; although McNamara dates this to 1887: 'Religious
Discourse', 96.

[42] Benham, *Avalonians*, 16–17.

[43] Christine Allen married John Duncan in 1912.

recovery of the vessel in 1906',[44] naturally there has been speculation concerning the contact which had undoubtedly occurred
between Tudor Pole and the Allen sisters with Goodchild, and thus
the extent to which the parties had influenced each other in the
'independent' discovery of the bowl.

People were invited to meditate in the presence of the Cup or
receive 'healing' from it.[45] At their oratory the Tudor Poles and
Allens developed distinctive services (including a communion
service involving the Cup as chalice), giving rise to, as Benham
puts it, 'a church in which woman was in the ascendant and Bride,
the Celtic embodiment of the Universal Feminine, was restored
and harmonized with a mystical understanding of the tenets of the
Christian faith'.[46]

In 1907 Tudor Pole showed the Cup to various people, from
Dom Aidan Gasquet, abbot president of the English Benedictines, to the Theosophist Annie Besant. He also consulted Archdeacon Basil Wilberforce, a canon of Westminster Abbey who was
connected with the temperance and anti-vivisectionist movements
and known to attend séances.[47] Although criticized by some for
his openness in religious matters, particularly his connections with
the Bahá'í movement, Wilberforce was nevertheless at the heart
of the Anglican establishment. He initially seemed sympathetic to
the idea that the Holy Grail had been found at Glastonbury and
on 20 July 1907 convened what became known as the Dean's Yard
Meeting, a gathering of scholars, religious leaders and other interested parties, to enable Tudor Pole to tell his story and display the
bowl. Although Wilberforce had expressly declared the meeting
'strictly private', the *Daily Express* got hold of the information,
resulting in the headline on 26 July, 'Mystery of a "Relic" – Finder
Believes It to Be the Holy Grail – Two "Visions" – Great Scientists
Puzzled – Discovered at Glastonbury', and almost two full front-
page columns on the story.[48] The report concluded, in relation to
'this astonishing story on the statements made by Mr Tudor Pole

[44] McNamara, 'Religious Discourse', 96.

[45] Benham, *Avalonians*, 50.

[46] Ibid. 50–1.

[47] As McNamara ('Religious Discourse', 92) points out, Wilberforce's biographer
G. W. E. Russell recorded that '[h]e communed with "Spooks" and "Swamis" and
"Controls"': *Basil Wilberforce: A Memoir* (London, 1918), 120.

[48] *Daily Express*, 26 July 1907, 1.

and Dr Goodchild' that '[w]hatever the cup may be, the story has succeeded in stirring the greatest interest in the minds of men and women of distinction'.[49] Wilberforce convened another meeting about the Cup in January 1908, but declined Tudor Pole's request to place it in St John's, Westminster, and appeared to retreat from his earlier enthusiasm.

What was not reported in the *Daily Express* account of the Dean's Yard Meeting, however, were Tudor Pole's predictions about Glastonbury and his appeals to 'all Christian leaders of thought'. The following gives a flavour of his rhetoric:

> Glastonbury will become the centre of healing as at Lourdes, a centre of healing, not only of physical but also of spiritual healing. Just as Glastonbury was the spot at which Christianity first touched Britain, so through Glastonbury is Christianity to be renewed here in England in the future ...
>
> I would like to say that all Christian leaders of thought, official or unofficial, will find that by making a pilgrimage to Glastonbury, by coming into contact with the point at which Christianity first touched England, they will be given the necessary force and power to carry out this great work that lies ahead of them. If the leaders of Christian thought will go down there, as I have seen in a vision at Glastonbury, merely with the idea of praying for the greater unity of the Christian Churches, they will be given power which will enable them to be used as this great channel of Divine force which is imminent [*sic*] in the world at the present.
>
> If the English Christian Churches are going to be made the great centre of the Divine outpouring of the Holy Spirit, they must unite. And by that I do not mean corporate unity but spiritual. There must be closer sympathy and closer concord between them, and if this does not take place, then the work will be passed on to other hands, to other agencies, and the English Christian Churches of all denominations and all sects will have lost the most stupendous and the most marvellous opportunity of working for the greater evolution of the world.[50]

[49] Ibid.
[50] Glastonbury, Chalice Well Trust Archive, Dean's Yard transcript, 1907, 10–12. Handwritten title on cover page: '20 Dean's Yard July 20 1907'. Authorship of transcript unknown, but believed to have been donated to Chalice Well by Rosamond

Tudor Pole was most emphatically drawing on the vernacular traditions of Glastonbury as the earliest site of Christianity in England, highlighting pilgrimage to Glastonbury as an important source of spiritual insight, and presenting a vision for a spiritually united Christianity for a new age.

Tudor Pole became a prolific writer and respectable businessman. With his own London-based company, run on ethical principles, he remained part of the establishment, influential if in some respects unconventional. He had a distinguished record during the First World War,[51] and during the Second World War (allegedly having broached the matter with Churchill), he was instrumental in establishing the Silent Minute at nine o'clock each evening, when people were urged to unite and be silent in prayer and contemplation.[52] He remained convinced of Glastonbury's status as a highly significant spiritual centre, and of the existence and importance of the Watchers of Avalon, the community of souls formerly connected with the abbey who continue to influence people and events there. In 1958 he purchased Chalice Well in Glastonbury and established the Chalice Well Trust 'to preserve and safeguard it for the public good in perpetuity'.[53] The Cup remains in the care of the Trustees of the Chalice Well. Until the mid-1980s, it was occasionally displayed there in the Upper Room set up for quiet contemplation, modelled on a vision Tudor Pole had of the upper room of the Last Supper. It is still accessible by appointment and at the discretion of the trustees.[54]

The Cup also provides a link with Alice Buckton (1867–1944), a pioneering educationalist, poet, Arts and Crafts enthusiast and dramatist, who settled in Glastonbury in 1913 and lived at Chalice Well until just before her death in 1944, exerting considerable

Lehmann, with whom Tudor Pole co-authored *A Man Seen Afar* (London, 1968): personal communication from Paul Fletcher.

[51]   This included helping to save Abdul Baha, the eldest son of the founder of the Bahá'í Faith, contributing to an important ongoing link between Bahá'ís and Glastonbury: see Lil Abdo, 'The Bahá'í Faith and Wicca – A Comparison of Relevance in Two Emerging Religions', *Pomegranate: The International Journal of Pagan Studies* 11 (2009), 124–48.

[52]   This continued on the BBC Home Service until the mid-1950s.

[53]   Quotation from Chalice Well website: <http://www.chalicewell.org.uk/index.cfm/glastonbury/HistoricalArchive.Articles/category_id/2>, accessed 24 November 2013.

[54]   Personal communication from Paul Fletcher.

influence on artistic and religious life in and beyond Glastonbury.[55] Buckton had visited the Tudor Pole oratory in Clifton and was at the 1907 meeting convened by Wilberforce; some believe that Buckton's purchase of Chalice Well in 1913 was encouraged by Wilberforce. In 1904 Buckton had first produced probably her best known and widely acclaimed play, the spiritually radical *Eager Heart, A Christmas Mystery Play.* In 1914, her pageant play *The Coming of Bride* was performed in Glastonbury.[56] The play starts with Bride spending seven years on Iona learning herbal lore and other wisdom from friendly Druids; the scene then shifts to Ireland, and finally Bride comes to Glastonbury with an entourage of maidens, where she is welcomed and consecrated by St Patrick, before going to Beckery to live with her companions. The play's focus on Bride has obvious connections with Goodchild's ideas, and seems to reflect plans, with which Buckton was involved, to bring about the spiritual renewal of Britain by 'reactivating' sacred sites in Iona, Ireland and Glastonbury through pilgrimage.[57] Despite her considerable interest in the Bahá'í movement and her tendencies towards 'mystical pantheism', she appears to have considered herself an Anglican.[58] Her funeral service was conducted by Lionel Smithett Lewis, vicar of Glastonbury, and her ashes were scattered on Glastonbury Tor, which she had purchased and handed over to the National Trust to ensure perpetual public access to an ancient pilgrimage site. There is a memorial plaque to her in St John the Baptist Church, Glastonbury.

Tudor Pole had believed that Glastonbury was a sacred site, in some way watched over and in contact with monks from Glastonbury's past, a concept developed and made more public by Frederick Bligh Bond (1864–1945), antiquary, expert on church architecture and restoration, archaeologist, psychical researcher and son of an Anglican cleric.[59] As noted above, the Glastonbury Abbey site, formerly in private hands, was acquired by the Church of

---

[55]   For a full account of Buckton's life, see Tracy Cutting, *Beneath the Silent Tor: The Life and Work of Alice Buckton* (Glastonbury, 2004).

[56]   Ibid. 63–77.

[57]   Ibid. 99–101.

[58]   Ibid. 20; Benham, *Avalonians,* 149.

[59]   For full accounts of Bligh Bond's career and connection with Glastonbury, see Hopkinson-Ball, *Rediscovery of Glastonbury;* W. Kenawell, *The Quest at Glastonbury: A Biographical Study of Frederick Bligh Bond* (New York, 1965); Benham, *Avalonians.*

England in 1907 and the following year Bligh Bond was appointed director of excavations. In 1918, in *The Gate of Remembrance*, Bligh Bond revealed that he had used psychic methods to guide his excavations, in particular channelling information (including a ground plan of the Edgar Chapel) from former monks of Glastonbury via automatic writing received by a medium.[60] In 1924 Bligh Bond wrote of the Company of Avalon as 'a group of souls who are impregnated with the devotional ideal which was translated into architectural symbol by the Benedictine brethren of old time'.[61] Bligh Bond made enemies who wished to remove him from the abbey excavations, including the dean of Wells, Joseph Armitage Robinson, and eventually his books and his unconventional beliefs and methods came to be considered incompatible with his post. Despite losing his formal connection with Glastonbury, Bligh Bond remained passionate about it, writing in *The Mystery of Glastonbury* (1930):

> We, as Christians, believe that Joseph took down from the Cross the body of the Master Jesus. It is no stretch of imagination that he would have taken the utmost pains to secure for all time that most precious relic of all, a phial of His Blood. And this he brought to Glaston, where, by tradition, it lies buried beneath the soil – not to reappear until the time is ripe for its revelation.[62]

As Benham points out: 'Notwithstanding his psychical and metaphysical leanings, Bond saw everything he did within the context of the Christian tradition. But the Church he had in mind was something larger and more universal than the modern denominational divisions.'[63]

---

[60] Frederick Bligh Bond, *The Gate of Remembrance: The Story of the Psychological Experiment which resulted in the Discovery of the Edgar Chapel at Glastonbury* (Oxford, 1918). In addition, Bligh Bond published, with Thomas Simcox Lea (an Anglican cleric best known as a naturalist), *A Preliminary Investigation of the Cabala contained in the Coptic Gnostic books and of a similar Gematria in the Greek text of the New Testament …* (Oxford, 1917) and *The Hill of Vision: A Forecast of the Great War and of Social Revolution with the Coming of the New Race, gathered from Automatic Writings obtained between 1909 and 1912, and also, in 1918, through the Hand of John Alleyne, under the Supervision of the Author* (Oxford, 1918).

[61] Preface to Bligh Bond, *Company of Avalon*, quoted in Benham, *Avalonians*, 206.

[62] Bligh Bond, *The Mystery of Glastonbury* (1930), quoted in John Matthews, ed., *A Glastonbury Reader* (London, 1991), 209.

[63] Benham, *Avalonians*, 220.

The final Glastonbury character to be considered is Lionel Smithett Lewis (1867–1953), anti-vivisectionist, animal welfare campaigner and Anglo-Catholic vicar of Glastonbury from 1921 to 1950. Lewis was friendly with Bligh Bond and oversaw the erection of the memorial to Alice Buckton in St John the Baptist Church.[64] He was passionate about Glastonbury's Christian legends, particularly those of Joseph of Arimathea and Jesus, as he demonstrated in his books *St. Joseph of Arimathea at Glastonbury; or, The Apostolic Church of Britain* and *Glastonbury, 'The Mother of Saints' – Her Saints, A.D. 37–1539*. Clearly Lewis was celebrating Glastonbury's vernacular Christian traditions at a time when there was renewed interest in the associated legends and considerable esoteric and experimental Christian activity relating to them. At the same time, however, Armitage Robinson was scathing in his dismissal of the Glastonbury legends, and his disagreement with Lewis on that topic was played out publicly in print with Armitage Robinson's *Two Glastonbury Legends* and Lewis's rebuttal of the dean in the foreword to the second edition of *Glastonbury, 'The Mother of Saints'* in 1927. This well illustrates why it is unsatisfactory to consider that there is any straightforward division between 'folk' and 'official' religion. Both Armitage Robinson and Lewis were ostensibly representatives of 'official' religion, but their public feud underlines Primiano's point that institutional religion 'is itself conflicted and not monolithic'.[65]

In December 1929, very much in the spirit of 'invented tradition' that was rife at the period,[66] Lewis sent a sprig of the Glastonbury Thorn to Queen Mary, claiming that he was 'reviving' the tradition of sending sprigs of the Christmas flowering thorn to members of the Royal Family.[67] From this developed the Holy Thorn ceremony, held annually in December at St John the Baptist Church, with the mayor and other civic dignitaries in attendance, during which a sprig of the Glastonbury Thorn tree in the grounds of

---

[64] Ibid. xvii.

[65] Primiano, 'Afterword', 384.

[66] See Eric Hobsbawm and Terence Ranger, eds, *The Invention of Tradition* (Cambridge, 1983), especially David Cannadine, 'The Context, Performance and Meaning of Ritual: The British Monarchy and the "Invention of Tradition", c.1820–1977', 101–64.

[67] See Marion Bowman, 'The Holy Thorn Ceremony: Revival, Rivalry and Civil Religion in Glastonbury', *Folklore* 117 (2006), 123-40, for debate about earlier practices Lewis was claiming to revive.

the church is cut in the presence of children from St John's Infant School and subsequently sent to the monarch.[68] Hobsbawm cites 'the inculcation of beliefs' as one aspect of invented tradition.[69] For Lewis, the Glastonbury Thorn was an 'ever-present testimony to the story of St. Joseph',[70] and the so-called revival gave him a vehicle through which to champion Glastonbury's status as the location of the first church in England and to perpetuate her legends. It has ensured that generations of Glastonbury children have heard the legend annually and learned the Holy Thorn song composed for the occasion, as well as attracting media attention. Adults attending the ceremony, many of whom participated as children, confidently attest the antiquity of the tradition. Through this invented tradition, Lewis trumped Armitage Robinson and perpetuated vernacular Christian myth.

Conclusion

Contemporary Glastonbury is unique in Britain as a multivalent pilgrimage site, attracting a range of pilgrims, spiritual tourists and spiritual seekers from Europe, America, Australia and elsewhere.[71] Religious plurality in modern Glastonbury is not the multicultural plurality of a city; it is in many ways harder to quantify and identify, usually described by catch-all terms such as 'alternative', 'non-aligned' or 'contemporary' spirituality. This plurality results from creative engagement with existing Christian vernacular myth, and an ever widening conceptualization of Christianity, influenced by popular esotericism and growing awareness of, and interest in, other religions. As we have seen, however, the seeds of many contemporary features of Glastonbury were actually sown in the late nineteenth and early twentieth centuries. They were fed by religious trends and phenomena that are still influential today, in particular the vernacular Christian legends of

---

[68] For fuller detail of the history and development of this ceremony, see ibid.

[69] Eric Hobsbawn, 'Introduction: Inventing Traditions', in idem and Ranger, eds, *Invention of Tradition*, 1–14, at 9.

[70] Lionel Smithett Lewis, *Glastonbury, 'The Mother of Saints' – Her Saints, A.D. 37–1539*, 2nd edn (Orpington, 1985; first publ. 1927), 5.

[71] Marion Bowman, 'Ancient Avalon, New Jerusalem, Heart Chakra of Planet Earth: Localisation and Globalisation in Glastonbury', *Numen* 52 (2005), 157–90; eadem, 'Going with the Flow: Contemporary Pilgrimage in Glastonbury', in Peter Jan Margy, ed., *Shrines and Pilgrimage in the Modern World: New Itineraries into the Sacred* (Amsterdam, 2008), 241–80.

St Joseph of Arimathea, St Brigit and Jesus in Glastonbury, and endless speculation upon Glastonbury's Christian, pre-Christian and future significance.

My point in drawing attention in this essay to vernacular religion, the Glastonbury legends and these snapshots of events and characters in Glastonbury in the late nineteenth and early twentieth centuries has been to highlight the fact that we see then the stirrings of the plurality with which the town is now associated. Looking in the round at these people and this period in Glastonbury highlights both the age and variegated nature of Christian plurality. Accounts of some significant people directly or indirectly involved with Glastonbury at this earlier period demonstrate that eclectic spiritual seekers and those now described as 'Christaquarians' – people who are happy to use insights from alternative spirituality to enhance their understanding and experience of Christianity – were already recognizable characters then.[72] While late twentieth- and early twenty-first-century media focus, internet access, relativism and neoliberal economics may have accentuated and accelerated such trends, they are not novel. Furthermore, as some of these people discussed were intimately connected with mainstream Christianity, indeed part of the establishment, their alternative nature and capacity for undermining Christian hegemony may not have been fully recognized by historians.

Glastonbury's significant Christian plurality arose and arises from differing views of Glastonbury's vernacular legends (some continue to believe passionately that Jesus and Joseph came to Glastonbury, while others find such myths useful metaphors at best, an embarrassment at worst); from esoteric and mystical readings of Glastonbury's past, clues to which reside in its historic material culture (such as the abbey) and natural phenomena (such as Chalice Well),and its present and future global significance; and from expanding, universalistic views of what Christianity is and might encompass. Belief stories continue to circulate in support of such speculations about Glastonbury's unique role and special nature. Through fieldwork and informal conversation, for example, I know a number of people currently residing in Glastonbury who feel they were drawn there by the Watchers of Avalon or the

---

[72] For the concept of Christaquarians, see Daren Kemp, *The Christaquarians? A Sociology of Christians in the New Age* (London, 2003).

Company of Avalon, with whom they are in active communication, and in whose service they believe themselves to be working.

Ironically, at present one of the few things that the myriad groups and individuals on diverse spiritual paths in Glastonbury can agree on is that Christ came to Glastonbury.[73] This vernacular Christian myth is reworked creatively to support diverse claims. Many Druids would say that he came to attend the great druidic university which some believe operated there; healers and energy workers would say that he came to gain healing powers from the energy generated by the node of ley lines found there; and so on. The legend of Brigit in Glastonbury has similarly broad currency. Working on the theory that '[w]here we find St Bridget we know that the Goddess Bridie was once honoured',[74] some in the Glastonbury Goddess movement feel they have restored the Goddess Bride to her rightful, pre-Christian eminence in Glastonbury.[75] Others, however, believe that the Celtic Christian Church anticipated and welcomed the coming of the 'new' religion of Christianity, incorporating insights and praxis from Druidry, and in this light Bride is seen as a bridge-builder between traditions. Pilgrimage to Glastonbury, the revival of which was so important to characters such as Tudor Pole and Buckton, has expanded to encompass organized denominationally based events such as the Anglican and Roman Catholic annual pilgrimages, individual and small group pilgrimages by an array of visitors, ecumenical and inter-faith pilgrimage, the annual Glastonbury Goddess procession, and pagan and earth energy pilgrimage.[76] The Glastonbury Reception Centre and Sanctuary (formerly Glastonbury Pilgrim Reception Centre) caters specifically for this pilgrimage boom. Denominational differences do remain significant, however. The annual Catholic Pilgrimage has traditionally started from the foot of the Tor, preserving the memory of the three Glastonbury martyrs, although the stress now tends to be on Glastonbury's past

---

[73] Marion Bowman, 'Taking Stories Seriously: Vernacular Religion, Contemporary Spirituality and the Myth of Jesus in Glastonbury', *Temenos* 39–40 (2003–4), 125–42.

[74] Kathy Jones, *In the Nature of Avalon: Goddess Pilgrimages in Glastonbury's Sacred Landscape* (Glastonbury, 2000), 16.

[75] Marion Bowman, 'Restoring/Restorying Arthur and Bridget: Vernacular Religion and Contemporary Spirituality in Glastonbury', in eadem and Valk, eds, *Vernacular Religion in Everyday Life*, 328–48.

[76] See Bowman, 'Ancient Avalon'; eadem, 'Contemporary Pilgrimage'.

and present status as a centre of Marian devotion. The Anglican Pilgrimage has been emblematic of diversity within Anglicanism, as, after the refusal of its organizers to acknowledge female priests, St John's Church no longer felt able to host or participate in it.[77]

The methodology of vernacular religion encourages a broad and encompassing view of religion that recognizes its diversity and creativity. Examining religion as it has been lived, with all its complexity, fuzzy boundaries and messiness, helps to give us a better grasp of what was actually happening. As a corollary, it is also necessary to see contemporary religion in its historical perspective. If we look beyond the myth of institutional hegemony, we need to question what made attendance at séances, empathy for the universalism of Bahá'ís, or belief in Glastonbury's vernacular legends acceptable for some, such as Archdeacon Wilberforce or the Revd Lionel Smithett Lewis, and unacceptable in others. We need to think carefully about Christianity and plurality, or perhaps articulate a more nuanced spectrum of definitions of Christian belonging. Characters such as Wellesley Tudor Pole, Alice Buckton and Frederick Bligh Bond felt they were at the dawning of a new age of Christianity: they thought of themselves as Christians, albeit of a more enlightened, universalistic, mystically inclined turn than was common within institutional Christianity. While these people appear exceptional for their time, at least in the extent to which they wrote about and expressed their ideas publicly, they may offer clues to broader societal trends at the time, and indeed to contemporary phenomena such as the high percentage of people who self-identify as Christians while not belonging formally to institutional Christianity.[78]

Concentrating on this exceptional place and these seemingly exceptional people can help to make sense of more general trends historically and in the present day, particularly in relation to plurality. If we adopt the insights from, and expectations of, individual creativity and heterogeneity provided by vernacular religion, we can see in Glastonbury in the early twentieth century the sign of things to come.

The Open University

---

[77] Marion Bowman, 'Procession and Possession in Glastonbury: Continuity, Change and the Manipulation of Tradition', *Folklore* 115 (2004), 273–85.

[78] 71.6% self-identified as Christians in England and Wales in the 2001 Census; 59% in the 2011 Census.

'AN EXTREMELY DANGEROUS BOOK'?
JAMES HOPE MOULTON'S *RELIGIONS AND RELIGION* (1913)

by MARTIN WELLINGS

On 4 April 1917 the British steamship SS *City of Paris* was torpedoed by a German submarine in the Gulf of Lions, and sank with considerable loss of life. Among the passengers was the Wesleyan Methodist scholar James Hope Moulton.[1] Paying tribute to his friend and colleague, Arthur Samuel Peake recorded the 'tragic irony' of the death under such circumstances of an eloquent advocate of peace and of a scholar whose international reputation in New Testament studies was signalled by plaudits from Harnack, a doctorate from the University of Berlin and a longstanding academic friendship with Adolf Deissmann.[2] Moulton, however, was more than a New Testament scholar. His presence in the Mediterranean in the spring of 1917 came about through his expertise in the history and thought of Zoroastrianism, which had taken him to India for eighteen months' work with the Parsee community under the auspices of the Indian YMCA.[3] Moulton brought together biblical scholarship, a fascination with the evolution of religion and a passionate enthusiasm for Christian missions. These commitments combined in his Fernley Lecture of 1913, *Religions and Religion*, and this essay will situate Moulton's lecture in its contexts and explore the significance of the book and its reception in capturing the varied and evolving attitudes of early twentieth-century Methodists to other faith-communities.

The first context for *Religions and Religion* was the centenary of the Wesleyan Methodist Missionary Society (WMMS), due to be

---

[1] William F. Moulton, *James Hope Moulton: By his Brother* (London, 1919), 193–5; Harold K. Moulton, ed., *James Hope Moulton, 11 October 1863 – 7 April 1917* (London, 1963), 20; *Methodist Recorder* [hereafter: *MR*], 12 April 1917, 4; *The Times*, 11 April 1917, 8.

[2] A. S. Peake, 'A Record of Professor J. H. Moulton's Work', *BJRL* 4 (1917–18), 18–23. The Moulton MSS in the Methodist Archives and Research Centre, John Rylands Library, Manchester, include many letters from Deissmann.

[3] W. F. Moulton, *James Hope Moulton*, 134, 139–45; James Hope Moulton, *The Treasure of the Magi* (London, 1917), ix–x.

celebrated in 1913.[4] Mindful of this, the Fernley trustees invited the distinguished missionary statesman W. H. Findlay to give their prestigious annual lecture, but Findlay eventually declined due to ill-health.[5] At comparatively short notice, therefore, J. H. Moulton took on the commission, writing 'in a hayloft on a lakeland holiday, with occasional intermissions to feed the pony in the stable below'.[6] The WMMS approached its centenary in good heart. After a period of ecclesiastical and financial crises, Conference in 1902 resolved to adopt 'a more energetic and aggressive policy with regard to Foreign Missionary Work', and over the next decade the society was revitalized.[7] William Goudie, an experienced missionary, was appointed to supervise the 'Centenary movement',[8] and he contributed weekly updates to the *Methodist Recorder*. This was the immediate background to Moulton's 1913 Fernley Lecture.

If the WMMS centenary gave Moulton an occasion, the theme and treatment of *Religions and Religion* reflected Moulton's own expertise, the burgeoning interest in comparative religion in the late Victorian and Edwardian period and the backdrop of the World Missionary Conference of 1910. Turning first to the author's expertise, one reviewer observed that Moulton's name was 'not generally associated with missionary enterprise', a reservation acknowledged by Moulton himself.[9] Moulton, however, brought a rare combination of gifts to his task.[10] Born in 1863 into a Wesleyan family of impeccable connections, high culture and undoubted missionary credentials,[11] he was educated at the Leys School, Cambridge, where his father was the first headmaster. He

---

4   For the history of the WMMS, see N. Allen Birtwhistle, 'Methodist Missions', in Rupert Davies, A. Raymond George and Gordon Rupp, eds, *A History of the Methodist Church in Great Britain*, 4 vols (London, 1965–88), 3: 1–116.

5   G. S. W[akefield]. and W. L[eary]., 'Fernley-Hartley Lecture', in John A. Vickers, ed., *A Dictionary of Methodism in Great Britain and Ireland* (Peterborough, 2000), 119.

6   James Hope Moulton, *Religions and Religion* (London, 1913), vii–viii; H. K. Moulton, ed., *James Hope Moulton*, 18.

7   *Minutes of the Wesleyan Methodist Conference*, 1902, 12–13; Birtwhistle, 'Methodist Missions', 113–14.

8   *Minutes of Conference*, 1912, 648; *Minutes of Conference*, 1922, 119–20.

9   [H. B. Kendall], 'Current Literature', *Holborn Review* 120 (1913), 727; Moulton, *Religions and Religion*, vii.

10   *ODNB*, *s.n.* 'Moulton, James Hope (1863–1917)'.

11   Moulton, *Religions and Religion*, x, pays homage to the author's uncle, James Egan Moulton, a missionary in the South Seas, although without the explicit dedica-

proceeded to King's College, Cambridge, where work on Indo-European philology as part of the Classical tripos laid the foundation both for New Testament scholarship and for a growing interest in Zoroastrianism, fostered by study with 'that Prince of Orientalists', E. B. Cowell, the professor of Sanskrit.[12] Cambridge also brought friendship with J. G. Frazer.[13] In 1902 Moulton left Cambridge for Manchester, teaching New Testament at Didsbury College and holding the Greenwood Chair of Hellenistic Greek and Indo-European Philology in the University. He was an outspoken champion of the values at the heart of Edwardian Nonconformity, as happy preaching in a rural chapel, speaking on Christian apologetics for Samuel Collier's Manchester Mission or writing an indignant letter to the *Manchester Guardian* as when poring over the papyri.[14]

Moulton described his own intellectual formation in a letter to Peake in 1904: 'a comparative philologist at Cambridge, a classic mostly for teaching purposes, a NT [*sic*] student from the grammar side ... and a Zendist as a philologue originally, finally a disciple of Frazer from the growing taste for comparative religion'.[15] The last phrase was particularly significant: both the theme of *Religions and Religion* and its treatment owed much to the developing discipline of comparative religion and to the assimilation of its conclusions by theologians and missionaries.

The discipline variously denoted the 'science of religion', the 'comparative study of religion' or 'comparative religion' drew its raw materials and methodology from many sources.[16] From the late eighteenth century, however, scholars and learned societies began to publish editions of Eastern sacred texts, comparative philologists

---

tion of the volume to J. E. Moulton, F. W. Kellett and W. C. Tucker implied in *MR*, 31 July 1913, 23.

[12] H. K. Moulton, ed., *James Hope Moulton*, 24; Moulton, *Religions and Religion*, viii. For Cowell, see *ODNB*, *s.n.* 'Cowell, Edward Byles (1826–1903)'.

[13] Moulton, *Religions and Religion*, viii. Several letters from Frazer survive in the Moulton MSS.

[14] *MR*, 12 April 1917, 4, referring to Moulton as a 'stalwart agitator'; W. F. Moulton, *James Hope Moulton*, 97–103; *British Weekly*, 17 July 1919, 363.

[15] W. F. Moulton, *James Hope Moulton*, 75.

[16] For the development of the discipline and for the chief protagonists, see Eric J. Sharpe, *Comparative Religion: A History* (London, 1986); Hans G. Kippenberg, *Discovering Religious History in the Modern Age* (Princeton, NJ, 2002); Margaret Wheeler-Barclay, *The Science of Religion in Britain, 1860–1915* (Charlottesville, VA, 2010).

started to tease out connections between languages, and archaeologists brought ancient civilizations to light. Above all, the historical sense promoted by Romanticism, and the mechanism of evolution, offered students of religion a method of organization and interpretation for a growing body of data.[17] Evolution became the master theory accounting for religious development. A traditional Christian scheme of original divine revelation to humanity followed by fall, degeneration and a fresh revelation of truth in the gospel gave way to an understanding of religion advancing in conjunction with the evolution of culture and civilization. The leading exponents of the new discipline – Max Müller, E. B. Tylor, William Robertson Smith and James Frazer – differed in their approaches and their religious commitments. Each, however, made the point that religion was not – or was not solely – a divine revelation: it was also an element of human culture, open to scientific investigation.

Wesleyan responses to the first ventures in comparative religion were very wary. Modern scholarship has drawn attention to theological resources in John Wesley's works for constructive engagement with other faiths,[18] but the tenor of Wesleyan commentary in the first two-thirds of the nineteenth century largely assumed that non-Christian religions represented a fall from primitive revelation and constituted a field of endeavour for missionaries. Thus in the first chapters of his *Theological Institutes* Richard Watson laboured to show that 'those Truths which are found in the Writings and Religious Systems of the Heathen' must derive from the biblical patriarchs.[19] Sixty years later, in his *Compendium of Christian Theology*, William Burt Pope criticized 'the Science of Religion' for comparing Christianity – 'the one only religion that the world has received directly from heaven' – with other faiths.[20] A similar criticism was offered by John Shaw Banks in his Fernley Lecture of 1880, *Christianity and the Science of Religion*. By the end of the century, however, A. S. Geden could acknowledge

---

[17] Sharpe, *Comparative Religion*, 27.

[18] Randy L. Maddox, 'Wesley and the Question of Truth or Salvation through other Religions', *Wesleyan Theological Journal* 27 (1992), 7–29; Philip R. Meadows, '"Candidates for Heaven": Wesleyan Resources for a Theology of Religions', *Wesleyan Theological Journal* 35 (2000), 99–129.

[19] Richard Watson, *Theological Institutes*, 3 vols (London, 1831), 1: 33.

[20] William Burt Pope, *A Compendium of Christian Theology*, 3 vols (London, 1880), 1: 57.

the value of comparative religion as 'a systematic endeavour to classify the various religions of the world, to ascertain their mutual relationship … and to present an orderly and historical account of human belief and practice with regard to the supernatural and the unseen'.[21] Geden insisted on 'the unapproached excellence' of Christianity, and repeated the point fifteen years later, while acknowledging that 'in all the more important systems of religion there is a measure of truth … which … has made it *live*, a vital force in the hearts and lives of its professors'.[22] Geden gave credit to Max Müller and the scholars of comparative religion for helping Christian thinkers to approach 'alien faiths' with 'sympathy and intelligent appreciation' rather than 'mere denunciation of error'.[23] As will be seen below, Moulton took a similar position.

J. H. Moulton's first-hand experience of foreign missions before 1913 was limited to a brief tour of the West Indies in the summer of 1911.[24] A year earlier, however, he had attended the Edinburgh World Missionary Conference, where he found his enthusiasm for mission strengthened and his theology of religion reinforced.[25] Writing in the *Methodist Recorder* in the immediate aftermath of the conference, he described it as more significant even than the Council of Nicaea.[26] Moulton drew heavily in *Religions and Religion* on the report of the fourth preparatory commission for the conference, *The Missionary Message in Relation to Non-Christian Religions*, taking from the material submitted by missionaries and from the analysis offered by the commission strong evidence in support of a sympathetic understanding of other faiths. Brian Stanley's recent study of the conference shows that the commission wrestled with the task of reconciling the traditional imperative of Christian missions with the challenge of comparative religion.

---

[21] Alfred S. Geden, *Studies in Comparative Religion* (London, 1898), 6.

[22] Ibid. 3; Alfred S. Geden, *Studies in the Religions of the East* (London, 1913), 9.

[23] Geden, *Religions of the East*, 9.

[24] Moulton, *Religions and Religion*, ix.

[25] *World Missionary Conference Edinburgh 1910 Official Handbook* (Edinburgh, 1910), 72, 106. Moulton was one of thirty-eight delegates appointed by the WMMS. For the conference, see Brian Stanley, *The World Missionary Conference, Edinburgh 1910*, SHCM (Cambridge, 2009); for Moulton and the conference, Kenneth Cracknell, *Justice, Courtesy and Love: Theologians and Missionaries encountering World Religions 1846–1914* (London, 1995), 271–82.

[26] J. H. Moulton, 'Into all the World: What the World Missionary Conference is doing', *MR*, 23 June 1910, 5.

The position taken by the commission – sometimes in defiance of the missionaries' evidence – was to arrange the world's religions in an evolutionary hierarchy, with Christianity as the crowning revelation gathering up the partial insights of other traditions. This theology of fulfilment foresaw a gradual absorption of other faiths into Christianity and suggested that Christian missions would be most effective in engaging with the 'higher' religions of India, Japan and China.[27] Moulton took up this argument with enthusiasm. It echoed his own understanding of Zoroastrianism and his admiration of the Parsees, 'this little community … so honest and truth-loving, so free from the accumulated burdens which ages of superstition and the manifold horrors of the caste system have imposed on the Hindu'.[28] The conviction that 'Christ comes not to destroy but to fulfil … to complete and crown the broken arch of truth, reared by the seekers after God in many lands'[29] ensured that the commission's report received a warm endorsement in *Religions and Religion*, to which attention may now be turned.

In its printed form *Religions and Religion* comprised four chapters. In the first, 'A Century and its Lessons', Moulton set the missionary task in context by describing the principal changes of the 'wonderful' nineteenth century.[30] Passing quickly over social improvements, Moulton turned to intellectual developments, highlighting biblical criticism, the impact of Darwinism and the application of evolution to the science of language.[31] In Moulton's view, 'a revelation of the Reign of Law invaded every field of thought'.[32] He welcomed this development, asserting that it placed theology and the study of religion on a proper scientific basis. At the end of the chapter Moulton turned to comparative religion, citing the monumental works of Frazer and the fifty volumes of *The Sacred Books of the East*. Such studies, he claimed, did not undermine the missionary enterprise, but brought a new motivation, based on 'a wider and truer view of God'.[33]

---

[27] Stanley, *World Missionary Conference*, 205–47, esp. 246–7.
[28] J. H. Moulton, 'Parseeism and Christianity', *The East and the West* 5 (1907), 408–18, quotation at 418.
[29] Ibid. 418.
[30] Moulton, *Religions and Religion*, 1.
[31] Ibid. 5, 6, 11.
[32] Ibid. 7.
[33] Ibid. 13, 16.

The second chapter of *Religions and Religion* discussed 'Comparative Religion and Christian Origins', looking at claims that beliefs and practices hitherto regarded as distinctively or uniquely Christian might have derived from other faiths. Moulton gave short shrift to suggestions that Jesus was a wholly mythical figure or that gospel stories were borrowed from Greek or Persian sources,[34] taking from the work of Frazer and of Tylor not a reductionist explaining away of Judaeo-Christian religion as mere natural evolution, but a confidence in 'the upward progress' of humanity's religious awareness, with God choosing to work in 'the evolutionary mode'.[35] Moulton could quote Rendel Harris's dictum that 'for us the infallibilities are gone', while believing that the discoveries of biblical criticism, comparative philology and anthropology had placed Christianity on a much firmer foundation than the discredited former authorities of Church, pope or Bible.[36]

The third chapter turned to 'Christianity and Other Religions'. Moulton cheerfully acknowledged that Christianity had borrowed from other faiths, praising the linking of Christmas to the winter solstice as a 'stroke of genius'.[37] Sometimes, however, the Church had been unwise in its accommodation of existing practices, and here Moulton's severest strictures were reserved for Roman Catholicism.[38] Moving from Christian history to the contemporary mission field, Moulton drew on *The Missionary Message* to show that missionaries increasingly recognized in other faiths both elements of truth and points of contact with Christianity. The missionary method, argued Moulton, was no longer to destroy other faiths, but to understand them.[39] This did not mean undermining the supremacy of Christianity, because whatever valuable insights could be found elsewhere were brought to completion and fuller integration in Christianity: 'the more carefully and sympathetically we study other religions, the more clearly does it appear that Christ completes and crowns them all'. The

---

[34] Ibid. 23–6.

[35] Ibid. 49–53.

[36] Ibid. 47; cf. James Hope Moulton, 'How stands the Bible: Three Lectures on Biblical Apologetics', in idem, *The Christian Religion in the Study and the Street* (London, 1919), 1–60, at 1, 4, attributing the phrase about 'the infallibilities' to Harris.

[37] Moulton, *Religions and Religion*, 86.

[38] Ibid. 87–8.

[39] Ibid. 91.

missionary task became one of 'bringing out the latent possibilities of backward tribes and developing to their highest ethical level the life of the more advanced races'.[40] Moulton suggested that this sympathetic appreciation of other faiths provoked Christians to rethink and restate inherited doctrines, discarding 'some venerable lumber' and some inadequate dogmatic formulations, like the 'practical tritheism' of much popular Trinitarian theology.[41] He recognized the need for a new motivation to persuade Western Christians to support missions, given the decline of the belief that adherents of other faiths were destined for hell. He hoped for a growing sense of Christians' responsibility to share the benefits of the gospel with others and for a realization that a commitment to foreign missions would revitalize and reform the Church in the West and lead to 'a Golden Age for all the world'.[42]

In the fourth and longest chapter of *Religions and Religion*, 'The Christ that is to be', Moulton returned to earlier themes, urging that Christians were 'bound by the very fundamental law of our religion to pass it on to every man who does not yet possess it, *because* it is incomparably the mightiest power in enabling weak humanity to achieve the life that God demands'.[43] Emphasizing the unifying 'central and fundamental doctrines' and 'the vital elements in religion' – for him, the Fatherhood of God, the deity of Jesus and his supremacy as Saviour – Moulton called for toleration of diversity of opinions on such matters as biblical inspiration, higher criticism, church organization and the sacraments.[44] After a rapid tour of the opportunities and challenges facing the modern missionary movement, Moulton concluded with a peroration urging greater support for foreign missions and reminding his readers of the other-worldly orientation of the Christian hope.[45]

Three broad reactions to *Religions and Religion* may be identified. In the Methodist and Free Church world, and among the supporters of the Edinburgh movement, the response was overwhelmingly positive. A leading article in the *Methodist Times* called the book valuable and timely, and welcomed it as an effective

---

[40] Ibid. 123.
[41] Ibid. 99–100.
[42] Ibid. 98, 123.
[43] Ibid. 132.
[44] Ibid. 128, 131, 147–8, 154–5.
[45] Ibid. 209.

restatement of the case for foreign missions in the light of modern knowledge.[46] Writing in the *Methodist Recorder*, W. T. Davison, a leading Wesleyan theologian and trenchant critic of Max Müller, noted Moulton's 'contagious enthusiasm' and praised his demolition of the 'anarchists of criticism' like Drews and Robertson who deployed comparative religion to discredit Christian origins. Davison hailed *Religions and Religion* as 'a rare combination … of scholarship and zeal, learning and enthusiasm'.[47] Beyond Wesleyan Methodism, Moulton's book was also welcomed by H. B. Kendall in the Primitive Methodist *Holborn Review*,[48] and by the Scottish theologian James Denney in the *British Weekly*. Denney was no admirer of Frazer, but he described *Religions and Religion* as 'a much-needed Tract for the Times', rescuing missionary motivation from the perplexities created by comparative religion.[49] Moulton's combination of scholarship and missionary zeal was praised by J. H. Oldham in the *International Review of Missions*. Oldham, the principal organizer of the World Missionary Conference, not unnaturally saw *Religions and Religion* as 'a striking revelation of the impression made by that conference on a highly cultured and unusually living mind'.[50]

Davison, Denney, Kendall and Oldham were not entirely uncritical of *Religions and Religion*. Each wondered if Moulton gave too much ground to syncretism in Christian origins, and several regretted his tendency to make provocative asides about contemporary politics. A more weighty criticism came in the *Methodist Times* leading article, which noted the absence of any treatment of such important topics as sin, atonement, forgiveness and regeneration.[51]

Moulton admitted in the preface to *Religions and Religion* that he had written in haste. The *Methodist Times* regretted this; other reviewers were less inhibited in their criticisms. 'G. A. C.' in the

---

[46] 'A New Plea for Missions', *Methodist Times*, 21 August 1913, 3.

[47] W. T. D[avison], 'Religions and Religion. Dr Moulton's Fernley Lecture', *MR*, 7 August 1913, 3–4. For Davison's critique of Max Müller, see 'Max Müller on Natural Religion', *London Quarterly Review* 73 (1889–90), 73–94.

[48] [Kendall], 'Current Literature', 727–9.

[49] James Denney, 'Religions and the True Religion', *British Weekly*, 21 August 1913, 501–2; cf. Denney's comments on Frazer: *British Weekly*, 4 September 1913, 548.

[50] J. H. Oldham, 'Religions and Religion', *IRM* 2 (1913), 804–6.

[51] 'New Plea for Missions', 3.

Irish Church Quarterly was sorry that Moulton had produced his book 'in a few weeks, on a holiday, and *currente calamo*'.[52] Henry Preserved Smith, reviewing 'Works on the History of Religion' in the *American Journal of Theology*, noted inaccuracies of fact and errors of interpretation.[53] Most damning of all, Ambrose Vernon in the *Harvard Theological Review* called *Religions and Religion* 'ineffective as an argument, slipshod in construction, ordinary in style'.[54]

The final response, and the most splenetic, came from the ultra-conservatives of the Wesley Bible Union. Moulton's immediate predecessor as Fernley Lecturer, George Jackson, alarmed and antagonized conservative Wesleyans by his lecture of 1912 on *The Preacher and the Modern Mind*, with its enthusiastic endorsement of modern biblical scholarship. For much of the connexional year 1912–13 conservative forces were being marshalled to condemn Jackson's lecture and to prevent his appointment to a chair at Didsbury College. The campaign came to a head at the Plymouth Conference, where Jackson was vindicated by an overwhelming majority, but the consequence was that Moulton, who as a tutor at Didsbury must have been aware of it, prepared and delivered his lecture against a background of theological controversy.[55] It was significant, therefore, that Samuel Chadwick, principal of Cliff College and a standard-bearer of constructive conservatism, praised Moulton and his lecture in the conservative weekly *Joyful News*, and that the *Methodist Recorder* made a point of reporting this endorsement.[56] Jackson's critics, outmanoeuvred in Conference, coalesced in the autumn of 1913 in the Wesley Bible Union (WBU), and it was the union's *Journal* that denounced *Religions and Religion* as 'an extremely dangerous book'. For G. A. Bennetts, Moulton's worst offence was 'thorough-going acceptance of the doctrine of evolution as the ruling principle of all created being

---

[52] G. A. C., 'Religions and Religion', *Irish Church Quarterly* 7 (1914), 175.

[53] Henry Preserved Smith, 'Works on the History of Religion', *American Journal of Theology* 18 (1914), 415–20, at 417.

[54] Ambrose W. Vernon, 'Religions and Religion', *Harvard Theological Review* 8 (1915), 267.

[55] D. W. Bebbington, 'The Persecution of George Jackson: A British Fundamentalist Controversy', in W. J. Sheils, ed., *Persecution and Toleration*, SCH 21 (Oxford, 1984), 421–33; Martin Wellings, 'Methodist Fundamentalism before and after the First World War', in David W. Bebbington and David Ceri Jones, eds, *Evangelicalism & Fundamentalism in the United Kingdom during the Twentieth Century* (Oxford, 2013), 76–94.

[56] 'Mr Chadwick and the new Fernley Lecture', *MR*, 4 September 1913, 3.

and of every province of thought'.[57] The undermining of revelation, the claim that Christ might be reduced to a product of evolution and the assertion that 'the infallibilities are gone' recurred in WBU strictures against Moulton for several years.[58] Bennetts was happy, however, to acknowledge that 'elements of truth are to be found in the non-Christian religions', and he linked this recognition to 'the doctrine of universal redemption, upon which John Wesley and John Fletcher laid so much stress', continuing that this emphasis had 'led Wesleyan Methodist theologians to a specially clear apprehension of this aspect of truth'.[59]

Scholars far removed from the outlook of the WBU have agreed with Bennetts in drawing attention to the contribution of Wesleyan and Methodist theologians to the study of other religions and to inter-faith dialogue, suggesting a connection between Wesleyan theology and openness to other faiths.[60] But Moulton nowhere acknowledged a debt to Wesley in *Religions and Religion*: his outlook demonstrated rather the transforming effect of contemporary currents of thought on Methodist Evangelicalism. However, *Religions and Religion* was not a work of original scholarship in the field of comparative religion. Moulton lacked the first-hand experience of encounter and dialogue with practitioners of other major world faiths enjoyed, for instance, by his contemporary A. S. Geden, whose massive volume *Studies in the Religions of the East* also appeared in 1913.[61] He wrote in haste, for a popular audience, on a topic some distance from his field of academic expertise. *Religions and Religion* therefore offered a synthesis of progressive scholarship, an apologia for Christian missions in an era of apparent opportunity and underlying anxiety about the missionary enterprise, and a call to commitment addressed to rank

---

[57]   G. Armstrong Bennetts, 'The Fernley Lecture of 1913', *Journal of the Wesley Bible Union* [hereafter: *JWBU*], July 1914, 103–5.

[58]   H. C. Morton, '*The Chief Corner Stone*: An Attempt to lull Methodists into False Security', *JWBU*, October 1914, 127–34, at 133–4; G. Armstrong Bennetts, 'What is the Present Message of the Wesleyan Methodist Conference to Mankind?', *JWBU*, October 1915, 217–21, at 220; 'Book Notices', *JWBU*, August 1916, 189.

[59]   Bennetts, 'Fernley Lecture', 103.

[60]   Frank Whaling, 'John Wesley's Premonitions of Inter-Faith Discourse', in Tim Macquiban, ed., *Pure, Universal Love: Reflections on the Wesleys and Inter-Faith Dialogue* (Oxford, 1995), 15–31, at 17.

[61]   Geden's work ran to over nine hundred pages and retailed at 12s. 6d.; *Religions and Religion* sold for 3s. 6d.: *Methodist Times*, 24 July 1913, 1.

and file supporters of the missionary societies. As a student of religion, an advocate of missions and a practitioner of dialogue, espousing and expressing an understanding of faiths fulfilled in Christ, James Hope Moulton occupied a representative and significant place in the evolution of Methodist theology and missionary practice in the heyday of the Protestant missionary movement, and served as an inspiration to later generations of scholars in the field of comparative religion and inter-faith dialogue.

Oxford

JERUSALEM'S EMPIRE STATE? THE CONTEXT AND SYMBOLISM OF A TWENTIETH-CENTURY BUILDING*

by CLYDE BINFIELD

My theme is religious encounter in the crucible of three faiths. Its focus is a building and its impact. The encounter as yet has no conclusion. The faiths are Christianity, Islam and Judaism. The building is one of two belonging to the Young Men's Christian Association (YMCA) now in Jerusalem. It expresses the personalities who shaped it and the events which surrounded it. It is an essay in imperial Christian mission, inter-faith dialogue and the chemistry of human personality. Religious pluralism is the name of its game, community its watchword, as caught in a streamlined and golden expression of Bible-Land Deco. It is rich in the symbolism of faith, integrated in stone; but what does such pluralism signify?

The scene might be set by two long letters written by an American, Waldo H. Heinrichs, General Secretary of Jerusalem YMCA. The first letter, 28 January 1933, was addressed to the Revd Everett R. Clinchy of the Federal Council of the Churches of Christ in America, and copied to twelve others. It anticipated a weighty readership since its recipients included Justice Brandeis, Rabbi Stephen S. Wise, Dr Emerson Fosdick, and Dr John R. Mott. Mott (1865–1955), a Methodist and missionary ecumenist, was a household name in YMCA and student Christian circles. Louis D. Brandeis (1856–1941), the first Jew to be appointed to the United States Supreme Court (1916) and a liberal in his social and political attitudes, was a Zionist. His support for the Balfour Declaration (1917) was influential in shaping American attitudes to Palestine. Rabbi Wise, of New York's Free Synagogue, shared his views. Harry Emerson Fosdick (1878–1969), who knew all three, had recently navigated the sort of minefield that Heinrichs was currently experiencing. Fosdick was an evangelical liberal, a Baptist minister with an international reputation as a preacher.[1] A recent

* I must acknowledge the unfailing help of Andrea Hinding and Dagmar K. Getz, archivists of the YMCA of the USA Archives (now the YMCA/Kautz Archive) at the University of Minnesota, Twin Cities Campus, St Paul, and of Claude Alain Danthe, archivist of the World Alliance of YMCAs, Clos Belmont, Geneva, during my visits

sabbatical, spent partly in Palestine, had resulted in *A Pilgrimage to Palestine* (1928), first serialized in the *Ladies' Home Journal* (1926–7). Palestine's biblical associations enthralled him, its Christian actuality appalled him, but his expression of what he saw offended contemporary Jewish sensitivities and convinced his American Zionist friends that he was opposed to their views. There was, however, another point of contact, this time a building. Fosdick's Riverside Church, New York, had been dedicated in February 1931. Its tower (400 feet high, with a 72-bell carillon) was a skyscraper in Gothic dress; its iconography celebrated the evolution of religion; its magnificence was the gift of John D. Rockefeller Jr.[2] The enthusiasms and influence of such men explain why Heinrichs, writing from his own fine new building, with tower and carillon, copied his letter to them. The following extracts indicate its length and its tenor. They suggest the tensions between faiths and races, as well as within its own faith, with which a lay, mission-minded, youth-focused, Protestant movement had to contend.

> As long as the Y.M.C.A. was located in small and insignificant quarters the non-Christians and certain sects of the Christians could treat it condescendingly. As soon however as the new building neared completion the reactionary elements of the Moslems (particularly the Grand Mufti's Party), the Roman Catholics – as represented by the Latin Patriarch, and those Jewish elements who are out for an exclusively Jewish Palestine were united to their opposition to the Y.M.C.A. by the fear that ... their youth ... would become too liberalised by the Y.M.C.A. The one word which they all seized upon ... was 'proselytizing' ... .

> The Latin Patriarch started the whole fracas: the old position of the Roman Catholic Church ... is well known, and is based on the Pope's encyclical of 1921.[3] ... [T]here are very strong elements,

---

to their collections. The YMCA/Kautz Archive was accumulated by the International Committee of the YMCAs of the USA and Canada.

[1] For Fosdick, see R. M. Miller, *Harry Emerson Fosdick: Preacher, Pastor, Prophet* (New York, 1985), 179–99.

[2] For a contemporary assessment, see A. L. Drummond, *The Church Architecture of Protestantism* (Edinburgh, 1934), 118–20. The architects were Pelton and Collens, of New York and Boston.

[3] The official Catholic position with regard to the YMCA had in fact been formulated by Cardinal Merry Del Val, Secretary of the Holy Office, in a warning dated November 1920. Its subsequent modification can be followed in Clyde Binfield,

very strong indeed, within the Roman Catholic Church which oppose the Latin Patriarch's ban. This includes the Franciscans, Dominicans, and certain very high officials under the Patriarch ... whose names I am not allowed to mention. It did not affect our membership: in fact it increased the Roman Catholic membership ...

The Nationalistic Arab press seized upon this ... and made a furore ... about ... our President who is also Director of Education, under the headline 'Is he Director of Education or a missionary'.

Some weeks after this Jewish friends ... told us that the Jewish Vaad Leumi – an organization centralizing the Jewish interests of Jerusalem, was about to make a statement in opposition ...

One difficulty was the arrival of the new Anglican Bishop, a very staunch Evangelical ... He comes from Wycliffe Hall at Oxford, and with the English University prejudice against the Y.M.C.A. as opposed to the American programme and also with the rather secluded point of view of the average University man ... In the heat of the battle we were tremendously amused that a Y.M.C.A. programme should unite in opposition against us the Grand Mufti, the Latin Patriarch, the Chief Rabbi, and the Anglican Bishop. Dr. Magnes said 'You have achieved something even in this, for it is the first time in history that that group has ever united on any subject.'[4]

There are several clues here. A building is referred to. Its construction has an impact on men of different faiths whose stereotypes cannot be entirely taken for granted. The writer, who has executive responsibility for that building, is both politically sensitive and detached. His attitudes are liberal, diverging from the sort of Evangelicalism, expressed by the newly arrived bishop, which had characterized the YMCA when it began in London in 1844. The English YMCA had tradition-

---

'"An Artisan of Christian Unity": Sir Frank Willis, Rome and the YMCA', in R. N. Swanson, ed., *Unity and Diversity in the Church*, SCH 32 (Oxford, 1996), 489–505.

4   YMCA/Kautz Archive, Heinrichs to Clinchy, 28 January, 1933. Dr Judah L. Magnes was founder and first chancellor of the Hebrew University; the newly arrived (1932) bishop was George Francis Graham Brown (1891–1942), on whom see Andrew Atherstone, 'Evangelical Pilgrims to the Holy Land: Wycliffe Hall's Encounter with the Eastern Churches, 1927–37', *Sobornost* 30/2 (2008), 37–58. I am indebted to Charlotte Methuen for this reference.

ally concentrated on young commercial men. Its international dimension reflected the expansion of an imperial nation; it provided homes from home for expatriates. The American YMCA had extended its appeal to young university men. Its associations were more complex; its vocational training was more professional. It had taken the Social Gospel into its system and its internationalism reflected that of the World Student Christian Federation, whose dominant figure, Mott, had been formed by the American YMCA.[5] The American and English YMCAs were the chief exemplars of an international movement. Heinrichs had served both, notably in India, where his work in the predominantly Muslim city of Lahore had paved the way for his service in Jerusalem. That is indicated by another long letter to New York, sent the following November, this time to a YMCA colleague, copied to four others.[6] Crisis had been reached, precipitated by such minutiae as no historian should ignore: composition of staff, clashes of personality and jealousies about status; finance came into it, too. Heinrichs was naturally keen to stress his achievements, but what had succeeded in Lahore was harder to achieve in Jerusalem:

> From the very first the appeal of the Jerusalem work ... was the fact that it was to be more in the line of a Community Center to bring all the various conflicting groups of Jerusalem's population together. ... Jerusalem has no common meeting ground ... The Sports Club is exclusive, the Rotary Club similarly so, the Masonic organizations are all divided by business or racial groups. The University club is the nearest approach, and their totally inadequate quarters make no appeal.

> My ideal ... is something similar to what we were trying to do in Lahore with a totally inadequate building, but where 52 different organizations used that building for the common meeting center for the whole city ...

> Our musical programmes have won an increasing number of Jews of the best class ... In addition ... the Association has won increasing respect from the British community ... Today we have the High Commissioner, many of the leading Government offi-

---

[5] For Mott, see C. H. Hopkins, *John R. Mott, 1865–1955: A Biography* (Grand Rapids, MI, 1979).
[6] YMCA/Kautz Archive, Waldo H. Heinrichs to Wilbert B. Smith, 7 November 1933.

cials, many military, Air Force and other officers, as well as their men. ... Previous to the opening of this building we had no contacts with the German Colony or German community. ... [T]oday we have over 70 of the best Germans in the Colony in our membership, the German Consul ... and other similar leaders. This is my idea of what a Y.M.C.A. can do. ... This is what the staff wants, ... but this is being blocked by a group of reactionary Arab nationalists on our Board.[7]

Although the thrust of Heinrichs's complaints lay with business practices and unsatisfactory local ways of doing things, there was a further dimension which it is impossible to ignore. He identified this as 'The Arab Nationalist drive' and 'Political tensity' and enclosed accounts of riots in Jerusalem, Jaffa and Nablus, extracted from his diary for October and early November 1933.[8]

Heinrichs's days in Jerusalem were numbered. The building to which he referred, however, survives. Field Marshal Lord Plumer had laid the cornerstone in July 1928; Field Marshal Lord Allenby officiated at the opening on Easter Sunday 1933.[9] No wonder the British community was beginning to show an active interest and no wonder so many tensions had come into play.

Jerusalem's International YMCA, as it quickly became known, is one of the most prominent twentieth-century buildings in that city. The Jerusalem association which it houses was British in origin but American in development. It began in 1876–8 but was transformed in the wake of General Allenby's entry into the city in 1917.[10] Its building celebrates that transformation. It also marks a shift from British to American accents, a process that was by no means complete in the 1930s.

The building itself was the work of Arthur Loomis Harmon (1878–1958), a New York architect who in the course of its construction became the design director of Shreve, Lamb, and Harmon, the practice responsible for New York's Empire State

---

7   Ibid. This letter and related correspondence give no indication as to what 'best Germans' might mean in November 1933.

8   YMCA/Kautz Archive, 'Extracts from Diary of Waldo H. Heinrichs, Referring to the Political Situation in Palestine', 13, 14, 27–31 October, 1–3 November 1933.

9   *The Jerusalem Young Men's Christian Association* (Jerusalem, 1933), 23, 25, 47.

10   Ibid. 19–22.

Building, completed in 1931.[11] The Empire State, conceived as an upright pencil, was the work of William Lamb, but Lamb, Richmond Shreve and Arthur Harmon were indistinguishable in their mastery of the needs and ways of corporate America. Harmon owed his Jerusalem commission to American generosity.

In this respect his YMCA building was representative of building schemes in Jerusalem between the wars. Although the most interesting work, stamped increasingly by International Modernism, came from Jewish immigrants, an egregious note was struck by the YMCA's closest neighbour and near contemporary on Julian's Way, the King David Hotel (1929–31), a luxury block in pink limestone, financed by Jewish bankers from Cairo. Its architect, Emil Vogt, was Swiss. His hotels in Lucerne, St Moritz, Athens and Cairo were models of their kind, European in plan, cosmopolitan in comfort, reflecting their surroundings in decor rather than essence. Vogt's hotel had carefully cosmetic Near Eastern touches, any echoes of Byzantium were discreet, and Vogt had an expert on the spot: Benjamin Chaikin (1883–1950), Russian-born, English-trained, who had practised in Jerusalem since 1920.[12]

A contrasting approach was that of Antonio Barluzzi (1884–1960), an Italian architect who tested his Franciscan vocation and perfected his skills, chiefly between the wars, in Jordan, Lebanon and Palestine. Barluzzi's specialism was ecclesiastical and primarily Franciscan architecture. His Church of All Nations, Gethsemane (1919–24), and his Church of the Transfiguration, Mount Tabor (1921–4), expressed the mood and associations of tradition without historicism and without Vogt's cosmopolitan fitness-for-purpose veneered to suggest a local vernacular.[13]

Harmon's YMCA fits between Vogt's efficiency and Barluzzi's free style. His formative years in practice had been with the preeminent firm of McKim, Mead & White (and it is hard not to see the interior of White's exquisite but short-lived Madison Square

[11] Paul Goldberger, *The City Observed: New York. A Guide to the Architecture of Manhattan* (New York, 1979), 118–19; New York City Landmarks Preservation Commission, *Guide to New York City Landmarks*, 4th edn (New York, 2009), 82–3.

[12] For Vogt, Chaikin and the King David, see David Kroyanker, *Jerusalem Architecture* (New York, 1994), 154.

[13] For Barluzzi, the printed source remains a book for young people: Daniel M. Madden, *Monuments to Glory: The Story of Antonio Barluzzi, Architect of the Holy Land* (New York, 1964).

Presbyterian Church in some of Harmon's Jerusalem interiors).[14] In independent practice he developed a line in hotels for professional men. His Shelton Hotel and Club (1924), thirty-five storeys deftly massed and stepped back from Lexington Avenue in obedience to recent building regulations, set the pace for such towers.[15]

Although he visited Jerusalem, Harmon operated from New York, relying on the local spadework of an American and a German. The American, A. Q. Adamson, had the title of Construction Executive or Engineer-in-Charge, nomenclature which hides a world of bruised *amour-propre*. Mercifully for the building saga, Adamson combined professional efficiency with almost unflappable humour; nothing surprised him. The German, Herman Glunkler, was underestimated by all who first encountered him. He was a dependable dogsbody, as meticulous as he was unimaginative, who had built several YMCAs in India. The national, indeed racial, stereotypes are already gathering in best Hollywood style.[16]

The financing of the enterprise, discreetly topped up by Rockefeller money, came largely from James Newbegin Jarvie (1850–1929), an Anglo-Scottish immigrant to New York and New Jersey whose five-year involvement with this ever-expanding scheme committed him to four times his original outlay.[17] Jarvie's sudden death, crossing the Atlantic on SS *Homeric* to revisit his country of birth, occurred in the wash of the Wall Street crash and before building had properly begun, but his obligations were honoured by a nephew, a niece and George W. Davison of New York's Central Hanover Bank & Trust Co. Davison was a banker for whom Harmon had undertaken some private work and he had been a friend since youth of the man whose vision was to be expressed by Harmon's building.

The visionary behind the project was Archibald Clinton Harte (1865–1946), the American Methodist son of Jewish immigrants.[18]

---

[14] Stanford White's short-lived (1906–19) but architecturally influential Madison Square Presbyterian Church, New York, is described in L. M. Roth, *McKim, Mead & White Architects* (London, 1984) 275–9; its interior is illustrated: ibid. 278.

[15] The Shelton, much altered, became the Marriott East Side in 1990.

[16] This and subsequent paragraphs are drawn from the exhaustive correspondence about the evolution of the Jerusalem YMCA building in the YMCA/Kautz Archive.

[17] Anon., 'James Newbegin Jarvie', *Tower Views International: A Quarterly Bulletin published by the Jerusalem International YMCA*, April–June 1992, 2.

[18] This account of Harte is drawn from correspondence and other material in the YMCA/Kautz Archive, especially K. Brooke Andrews, 'Dr. Archie C. Harte. 1865–1926' (typescript, 1964); Alvah L. Miller, 'My Recollections of Archibald Clinton

He never spoke of that, although his father is said to have been a rabbi. Harte's YMCA career had ranged from the Deep South (Mobile, Alabama), through India and Ceylon, to wartime Central Europe and revolutionary Russia. He moved as easily in skyscraper circles as among kings, princes and proconsuls. In Jerusalem, driven by Otto, his handsome chauffeur, his motor car was a Chrysler, the gift of Walter Chrysler (the Empire State Building, was by contrast a flagship for General Motors). Harte was oblivious of danger. His sangfroid in Palestine at explosive points in the 1920s and 1930s alarmed the most seasoned visitors. In Europe during the First World War he had crossed national boundaries and enemy lines to help prisoners of war of all nationalities and had continued to slip unmolested into Germany after the United States had entered the war. Thanks to the good offices of the Swedish crown princess and the English Princess Helena Victoria, he secured introductions to the German and Russian empresses and signed photographs of imperial and royal personages were displayed in his quarters. The boardroom of Jerusalem's new YMCA housed a museum of his prisoner of war work.

Harte's commitment to Palestine began with his arrival in Jerusalem in 1920, but his passion had been fired by a Cook's tour in 1888. Connoisseurs of evangelical, missionary and YMCA history will sense that a narrative is taking shape. The families of Thomas Cook (1808–92), the travel agent, and George Williams (1821–1905), the wholesale draper who had founded the London YMCA, were connected by marriage as well as missionary sentiment. Their London headquarters were within easy reach of each other.[19] Williams became the president of the nascent Jerusalem YMCA and when Harte, whose determination to serve in Palestine had been thwarted more than once, at last came to Jerusalem's YMCA he saw to it that a replica of the London room in which the movement had started on 6 June 1844 should be an inte-

---

(Archie) Harte' (typescript, 10 February 1964); Christina H. Jones, 'Dr Archie Harte' (typescript, 24 April 1965); Paul B. Anderson to Joel E. Nystrom, 6 September 1965.

[19] Thomas Cook's headquarters on Ludgate Circus and George Williams's in St Paul's Churchyard were within ten minutes' walk. For Holy Land connections, see Timothy Larsen, 'Thomas Cook, Holy Land Pilgrims and the Dawn of the Modern Tourist Industry', in R. N. Swanson, ed., *The Holy Land, Holy Lands and Christian History*, SCH 36 (Woodbridge, 2000), 329–42.

gral part of its new premises.[20] Commerce, mission, pilgrimage, adventurous travel and self-improvement together expressed the YMCA mindset. Harte secured a prime site on which to build his vision. In subsequent years he ensured that Bethlehem's Field of Shepherds, a plot on Mount Olivet acquired for his own house, and another overlooking the Sea of Galilee for a camp, retreat centre and summer house, should come into YMCA hands. The last, which he called Peniel, faced the cliff from which, as he liked to think, the Gadarene swine had hurled themselves. Harte was gripped by story, symbol and association; he had a rare gift for communicating his enthusiasms and convincing sensible men of their feasibility.

Harte was universally admired and impossible to work with. The saga of his relations with English assistants, British Mandate officials, Palestinian Christians, Jewish immigrants and religious leaders of all shades and grades, gnashing their teeth at the determination of this charismatic American, is vividly illuminated by the YMCA/Kautz Archive.[21] This enlarges our dramatis personae to include Mott, with whom Harte had crossed swords during the First World War; Mott is ever present yet judiciously distant in this archive. Increasingly to the fore is Fred W. Ramsey, the Cleveland businessman who switched careers to steer the American YMCA through the Depression. The hero is Neil Macmillan Jr, the American Scot who ran the American movement's Architectural Bureau. These men exemplified the liberal Protestant Social Gospel at its most expertly optimistic. They fought to shape, discipline and contain Harte's dream. They kept the show on the road. They ensured that Harte's vision was built despite Harte.

Jerusalem's new YMCA, like the neighbouring King David Hotel, was bound to be a Holy Land gloss on a Western frame, as alien as the temples of the Decapolis and the Crusader castles, but that testifies to its interest. It would be at home in California; it is wholly at home in Jerusalem. Its colouring, texture and massing are integral to its setting and its detailing is integral to a secular building intended 'to convey ... the Christian message'.[22] Braced

[20]   *Jerusalem YMCA*, 35, 37, 48.
[21]   YMCA/Kautz Archive; this covers especially the years 1914–33, and is voluminous from 1925.
[22]   *Jerusalem YMCA*, 25–6; the following paragraphs are drawn from this source, esp. 25–46.

by Harte, steadied by Ramsey and Macmillan, Harmon combined the strengths of Vogt and Barluzzi.

His building had to meet the requirements of an American YMCA upgraded to suit the expectations of tourists. It must be home, hotel and clubhouse. Consequently its main block contained lounges, offices and a cafeteria, and housed equipment for refrigeration, central heating and ventilation, as well as 'men's photographic dark room, barber shop and Turkish baths'. The bedroom floors confirmed the impression: sixty-four single, eighteen double, 'adequate toilet and bath facilities', running water 'supplied to a number'. 'Complete room service, laundry chutes, trunk storage, vacuum sweepers, valet shop, and telephone on each floor assure every comfort'. There was more: on each floor were reception rooms where 'hostesses, acting as floor mothers, may entertain and give the home-touch so essential to the lives of young men'. This hostel-hotel was also college hall: its library, with 'the latest fireproof shelving', had room for 50,000 volumes; its lecture hall had 'stereopticon lantern and cinematograph'.

These amenities extended to the flanking auditorium and gymnasium blocks. In the former the 'Golden Hall of Friendship', treated with 'acoustical plaster for good tone properties', seated 672 people. It was equipped for plays, films, and concerts with space for 'ticket office, telephone booth, check room, lavatories, lounges, and carpenter shop'. Its ambition was announced by 'the great four-manual organ presented by the Juilliard Musical Foundation for the encouragement of musical appreciation in the Near East'. The other block housed the physical education unit. The gymnasium (its ceilings lined with 'acoustical' plaster) could seat 750 and catered for a thousand members. It had the latest equipment. There was provision for boxing, wrestling, squash, handball and tennis, and a five-acre athletic field, with quarter-mile cinder track, boasted a concrete stand for 1,500 spectators. The whole catered for men, women and boys, 'on a carefully scheduled basis'. There remained the swimming pool, conserving rainwater 'caught from every roof and from the athletic field', held in cisterns, chlorinated and constantly filtered. This was to the gymnasium what the Juilliard organ was to the Golden Hall of Friendship. There could be no finer common meeting ground.

This could be in Chicago or Seattle. What distinguished it? Harmon took great care with his furnishings, but these tended to have a sturdy Spanish-Renaissance air. Greater authenticity was provided by the seventeenth-century Persian rug, 'Damascus divan' and 'low oriental table' placed in a tower room, or the early seventeenth-century ceiling from Damascus, again fitted into the tower, or the marble copy of 'an early Arabic fireplace' in a lounge, but what went beyond decor and truly authenticated and integrated this building were its style, massing, detailing and the narrative which it developed.

It belonged to its site, from which its stone had been largely quarried. Its massing (each block was allowed 'its own individuality and function' while blending 'into a unified whole') symbolized the Trinity (Three in One and One in Three) and also the YMCA's threefold purpose (the development of mind, body and spirit). The style ('Byzantine ... typical of many of the early churches in the Near East') allowed for a domed tower (Fig. 1), domed auditorium (Fig. 2), domed gymnasium, and appropriate carving in stone and wood. Bas-reliefs expressed reconciliation and forgiveness, those preconditions of worship, in the tower's oratory, and the Last Supper in its upper room. Capitals represented biblical fauna, flora and rustic duties: a goatherd, a camel driver, a donkey boy, a shepherd.

There were further layers of understanding. The tower (Harmon's Palestine pencil in exchange for Lamb's Empire State pencil?) was the Jesus Tower, but its main decorative feature was a bas-relief, sixteen feet high, of the seraph in Isaiah's vision. Its vestibule floor contained a transparent Star of Bethlehem, which lit the altar of the oratory beneath. That altar was a cairn of twelve rough stones from Bethel, such 'as the early Israelites used to commemorate notable incidents'. The tower rose to an observation gallery, commanding 'the highest view of Jerusalem except ... from the German and Russian churches on the Mount of Olives'. Here were heads of the twelve apostles and eight inscriptions about Jerusalem, chosen by Harmon. At the very top was a domed room for silent prayer. Its 'star-studded blue vault' conveyed 'the infinitude of God'.

Such symbolism, suggestive rather than prescriptive, was everywhere. (It had a contemporary Gothic parallel in the iconography of Fosdick's Riverside Church.) The Social Room 'with its crown shaped decorative dome ... beyond the cross shaped threshold' suggested 'that there is no crown without its cross'. The auditorium's balcony was backed by twelve arches, its dome was lit

Fig. 1: Tower (the Jesus Tower), Jerusalem YMCA building.

by twelve windows, its apse had five windows and seven arches: twelve for the tribes of Israel and the disciples of Jesus, five for the four evangelists and Jesus, seven for the days of creation. There were forty forecourt and cloister columns, for the Jews' years in the wilderness and Jesus's days of temptation; the capitals of those linking the gymnasium were carved with animals, the strong protecting the weak.

These emphases were Judaeo-Christian: the Upper Room commemorated Jesus's Last Passover Supper; the numbers spoke equally to Jew and Christian; the room for silent prayer was cruciform but it also recalled King David's upper room, 'where he closed the shutters and was alone with his God'. This YMCA's instinctively male Christianity (no woman, not even Mary, was represented apart from the woman from Samaria) was rooted in Jewish soil. The cross was suggested but nowhere was it shown.

Fig. 2: Auditorium, housing the Golden Hall of Friendship, Jerusalem YMCA building.

There was no representation of the crucifixion. Had there been a failure of nerve?

There was, however, another dimension, less insistent but present nonetheless. The central façade had three inscriptions, one each from Hebrew and Christian Scriptures and one from the Qur'ān. It was hoped that the library would become a centre for the study of Islam and Judaism as well as Christianity. The auditorium's windows and arches also represented Muḥammad's twelve followers. Lord Allenby seized on this in his dedicatory address at the building's opening: 'The entire project is a gesture of friendship by British and American citizens towards Moslems, Jews, and their own Palestinian co-religionists intended and calculated to promote a better understanding of each other; in the city which is Holy to all three faiths.'[23] This Christian building embraced people of all faiths.

The building has been described as it appeared on Easter Sunday 1933, viewed perhaps with the eyes of Lord Allenby, perhaps with those of the Americans who came in considerable numbers on touristic pilgrimage for the occasion.[24] We cannot see it with the

---

23 Ibid. 48.
24 See the brochure/itinerary in the YMCA/Kautz Archive, *Pilgrimage to Palestine*

eyes of Archibald Harte, for he had left the Jerusalem association, although not the YMCA in Palestine. He had retired prematurely to nurture a sense of noble grievance in Peniel, and it was to be several years before he set foot in his Jerusalem creation.[25]

Remarkably, and thanks primarily to Harmon, Adamson, Glunkler, Macmillan and Ramsey, the building remained Harte's creation. After seven years of shaping, enlarging, altering and latterly of trimming in the wake of world depression, what was inaugurated was almost miraculously in line with Harmon's original plans and Harte's matured scheme. The classical Roman building briefly contemplated had evolved into a Byzantine palace, perhaps a cathedral (its tower was a belfry with a carillon cast in England but given by Jarvie's New England niece), although more a business-like monastery (it had cloisters) with Saracenic accents (there were kiosks) and American standards. Here was building as symbol, an infinity of movement, pluralism to be celebrated and orchestrated into harmony.

The scene is set. It remains to suggest the encounter which this building was designed to promote. As Heinrichs's correspondence makes clear, Harmon's YMCA was from the first in the eye of several storms. In this it was like Vogt's hotel. From 1938 until its partial destruction by Irgun in July 1946, a wing of the King David housed the offices of the British Mandate. In 1948 the YMCA housed Count Bernadotte's United Nations Mediation Commission, and Bernadotte's body lay in state there after his assassination on 17 September. It was not solely its amenities that brought Jerusalem's YMCA into such political play. The Bernadottes were the European royal family most closely associated with the YMCA and kindred movements. Folke Bernadotte (1895–1948), grandson and nephew of kings of Sweden, was president of the Swedish Red Cross and Boy Scouts; he had an impressive record in refugee and prisoner of war work.[26] His sister and brother-in-law, Elsa (1893–1996) and Hugo Cedergren (1891–1971) were commanding figures in the Swedish and World YWCAs and YMCAs respectively; they played the sorts of role in the Second World War that

to attend Dedication Services, New YMCA Building, Easter, April 16th 1933 (New York, 1933).

[25] Miller, 'My Recollections', 7–8.

[26] 'The Story of Count Bernadotte', *World Communique* 7/6 (1948), 106–7; Sune Persson, *Escape from the Third Reich: Folke Bernadotte and the White Buses* (London, 2009).

Harte had played in the First.[27] The building was bound to be a focus for international YMCA concerns with the Middle East.

There were YMCAs in Syria, Lebanon, Jordan, Iraq and Egypt. The movement had experienced in long overview what happened when Christian understandings of mission (and Christian care for expatriates) met Christian understandings of ecumenism and confronted several varieties of fundamentalism, not least amongst the Middle East's squeezed Christian minorities. It provoked questions about the dialogue and partnership needed to help people of different faiths address what faced them. The YMCA's refugee work raised more pointed concerns. Jerusalem's other YMCA, the East Jerusalem YMCA, close to St George's Anglican Cathedral, began in a Palestinian refugee camp in 1948/9. Thanks to partition it was part of the Jordanian YMCA. The creation of the state of Israel and the assimilation of the International YMCA into the American movement deflected that YMCA's multi-faith development. The Jewish/Christian thrust of West Jerusalem's International YMCA and the Muslim/Christian thrust of East Jerusalem's YMCA were never wholly polarizing (and their outworking cannot be explored here) but it took another sixty years for the logic of Harmon and Harte's symbolism to be reflected in a judiciously radical executive appointment. Forsan Hussein, who became West Jerusalem YMCA's chief executive in 2009, was well qualified. He had been educated at Johns Hopkins, Brandeis and Harvard Business School. He was also an Israeli-Arab Muslim.[28] Justice Brandeis, to whom Heinrichs's letter of January 1933 had been copied, would have approved.

That appointment offers a late but relevant commentary to a report written fifty years earlier. Tracy Strong, an American Congregationalist, had been general secretary of the World's Alliance of YMCAs between 1937 and 1953. He was a longstanding friend and colleague of Harte, Heinrichs and the Cedergrens, and his predecessor, Walter Gethman, had been another recipient of Heinrichs's letter of January 1933. In 1958–9 Strong visited thirty-four countries where Islam had an important influence on youth. The

[27] 'The Royal Families of Sweden (b) House of Bernadotte', *Burke's Royal Families of the World*, 1: *Europe and Latin America* (London, 1977), 513–14.

[28] David Horowitz, 'In the exceptional Rise of a gutsy Arab Kid from the Galilee, many Harsh Truths for Israel', *The Times of Israel*, 24 August 2012. I am indebted to Mr K. Montgomery for this reference.

resulting report, carefully worded, bypassing political complexities, begging too many questions, was nonetheless perceptive and comprehensive. It included a visit to Jerusalem's YMCA:

> As a centre of fellowship and service it respects a man's freedom of religion and the communal loyalties which are closely linked to the family, the history and the traditional heritage of faith. There is much silence about the inner meaning of each other's faiths between Christian and Muslim often because it might be a divisive controversial subject, often because of lack of knowledge of one's own faith and often because nationalism, secularism, [and] the hunger for security supersede the essential place of religion. How can the YMCA fellowship encourage a deeper understanding and obedience to the will of God in the youth of Jerusalem is a major problem.[29]

It is easier to ask questions than to answer them but answers are not the immediate purpose of reports. Strong was writing primarily about East Jerusalem's YMCA, then in the Hashemite Kingdom of Jordan, but his comments applied equally to the International YMCA, now in Israel, and they were memorialized in the building – that essay in mission, dialogue and community, integrated in stone – which Harmon had created, in what was briefly a British Mandate, to enshrine Harte's vision.

University of Sheffield

---

[29] Tracy Strong, *A Pilgrimage into the World of Islam: A Personal Report* (Geneva, c.1960), 23–4.

CHARLES MALIK AND THE ORIGINS OF A CHRISTIAN CRITIQUE OF ORIENTALISM IN LEBANON AND BRITAIN

by TODD M. THOMPSON

The field of Oriental studies was the main context in which amateur and professional scholars developed the academic study of Islam before World War II.[1] The role of religion in the rise of this discipline is now widely acknowledged, but the role of religion, particularly Christianity, in the critique and transformation of Orientalism after World War II has never been explored.[2] Given the prevalence of Christian scholars in Islamic studies after 1945, why has this been the case?[3]

The research agenda has been driven, in part, by the assumption that critique itself is a secular enterprise.[4] The last decade has witnessed a 'historical turn' in the study of Orientalism. Despite growing appreciation for the plural nature of the critiques of Orientalism, there has been little study of the Christian critique of the discipline or discourse. Genealogies of varieties of Marxist and post-structuralist critiques have hitherto attracted the most attention.[5]

This essay will question assumptions about the secular nature of critique by providing an outline of the Christian critique of

---

[1]   Historically, the term 'Orientalism' has referred variously to a scholarly discipline, an imperial educational policy, a tradition of art and architecture and a discourse of imperial power: see John M. MacKenzie, *Orientalism: History, Theory and the Arts* (Manchester, 1995), xii–xiii. In this essay, I use it, like Malik, to refer to a scholarly discipline. While geographical terms like 'the West' appear in quotation marks in this essay only when they reflect the exact language of the cited material, the reader should note that I consider such designations to be historical constructs rather than natural entities.

[2]   Urs App, *The Birth of Orientalism* (Philadelphia, PA, 2010).

[3]   Norman Daniel, 'Some Recent Developments in the Attitude of Christians Towards Islam', in *Re-discovering Eastern Christendom: Essays in Commemoration of Dom Bede Winslow*, ed. A. H. Armstrong and E. J. B. Fry (London, 1963), 154–66, at 165.

[4]   Talal Asad et al., *Is Critique Secular? Blasphemy, Injury and Free Speech* (Berkeley, CA, 2009).

[5]   Edmund Burke III and David Prochaska, 'Introduction: Orientalism from Post-Colonial Theory to World History', in eidem, eds, *Genealogies of Orientalism: History, Theory, Politics* (Lincoln, NE, 2008), 1–71, at 1–2, 4–6, 10, 46.

Orientalism after 1945. The focus will be on the main progenitor of this tradition, the Lebanese philosopher and diplomat Charles Malik, and the development of his ideas between the end of World War II and the beginning of the Suez crisis. It will argue that, while Edward Said's well-known critique of Orientalism centred on the problem of discourse, Malik's work highlighted the importance of the pre-discursive. By doing so, the essay will demonstrate the formative role Christian scholars played in reshaping the agenda of Islamic studies.

LOVE AND THE LIMITS OF ORIENTALIST SCHOLARSHIP

Charles Malik (1906–87) was an American-educated Christian intellectual from Lebanon. After completing an undergraduate degree at the American University in Beirut (AUB), where he concentrated on natural science and mathematics, Malik went on to study under Alfred North Whitehead at Harvard and Martin Heidegger in Freiburg, before obtaining his PhD in philosophy from Harvard in 1937.[6] In order to understand Malik's approach to the problem of Orientalist scholarship, it is important to place his concern with Islam within the context of wider Christian experience in the Arab world and to sketch briefly his broader critique of positivistic approaches to science and reason in the West.

At mid-century, native Christians of the Middle East like Malik could look back on a troubled history and forward to an uncertain future in the region. For centuries after the Muslim conquests of the Arabian peninsula and what has come to be referred to as the wider 'Middle East' in the seventh and eighth centuries, Christian communities maintained a robust presence and remained extraordinarily influential in the cultural and intellectual life of the new Muslim polity. It was only in the course of Europe's late medieval era that Christians in the Middle East lost their numerical edge over the soon-to-be Muslim majority. A further blow to Middle Eastern Christian communities came in the late nineteenth and early twentieth centuries, particularly during and after World War I, when hundreds of thousands of Christians in the Ottoman Empire were forced to migrate from their homes and were later killed. Two of the most prominent cases of this concerned the Assyrian

---

6 Cecil Hourani, *An Unfinished Odyssey: Lebanon and Beyond* (London, 1984), 77.

and Armenian communities. These events, in part, prompted the lawyer Raphael Lemkin to coin the term 'genocide' in international law in the early 1940s. Against this backdrop, the French, who considered themselves protectors of the Maronite Christians in the Arab world, set apart territory in their League of Nations mandate in Syria for the establishment of the separate state of Lebanon, which was to house a Christian majority.[7]

The spread of nationalist ideals in the Arab world in the late nineteenth and early twentieth centuries challenged Middle Eastern Christians to grapple intensively with their own relationship to Arab culture and to the religion of the Arab majority, Islam. While Maronite Christians in the greater Syrian region were more likely to identify with 'Western' than with Arab culture, Greek Orthodox Christians like Malik, who would have witnessed the ministry of native Arab clergy in the see of Antioch since the late nineteenth century, made significant contributions to Arab nationalist discourse. In the process, Greek Orthodox Arab intellectuals helped shape public debate concerning the relationship between Arab identity and Islam. In the 1930s and 1940s, to take two of the most prominent examples, both Constantine Zurayq, a key theorist of Arab nationalism, and Michel 'Aflaq, one of the principal architects of the Ba'ath party, argued that Islam was of vital importance to all Arabs regardless of their religious affiliation.[8] In a similar manner, Malik would later affirm that 'Moslem culture' was 'in a deep sense' also the culture of Arab Christians.[9] In Malik's view, Arab Christians could not 'be too deeply interested in the development of their common heritage' with Muslims.[10] The future of Islam, and the understanding of Islam cultivated in the West, were thus of great importance to Arab Christians such as Malik.

For Malik's criticism of the scientific rationalism of the West, his interaction with the thought of Whitehead and Heidegger during his graduate studies in the 1930s was crucial. As a student of science

---

  7 Philip Jenkins, *The Lost History of Christianity: The Thousand-Year Golden Age of the Church in the Middle East, Africa and Asia – and how it died* (New York, 2009), 4, 8, 16, 18, 24, 140–1, 164–5.

  8 Sylvia Haim, 'Introduction', in eadem, ed., *Arab Nationalism: An Anthology* (Berkeley, CA, 1962), 3–72, at 57–65.

  9 Charles Malik, 'The Near East: The Search for Truth', *Foreign Affairs* 30 (1951–2), 231–64, at 255.

  10 Ibid.

with, as he put it himself, 'an irrepressible leaning towards fundamental theory and … a strong personal religious background', Malik was attracted to the writings of philosophers who sought to be systematic and did not consider the question of God's relationship to science beneath their dignity.[11] He found such a thinker in Whitehead and spent the summer of 1929 in Cairo working through the latter's major writings.[12] In 1932, Malik joined Whitehead in Cambridge, Massachusetts to deepen his studies. Throughout this period he expressed admiration for Whitehead's attempt, uncommon amongst the most notable philosophers of the day, to break away from rationalistic presuppositions.[13]

Malik found an equally congenial critique of rationalism in the thought of Heidegger.[14] He came to Heidegger's work as a thinker troubled, not just by the relationship of religion and science, but also by problems concerning his own identity as a Christian caught between the Arab world and the West. Ultimately, he came to believe that Heidegger's writing only had meaning to individuals, like him, whose existence had 'become a problem' to themselves.[15] Of all the material in Heidegger's early opus, *Sein und Zeit* (1927), Malik found the sections concerning the themes of authenticity, heritage, tradition and the future the 'most inspiring'.[16] He wrote that Heidegger's remarks concerning these issues 'served to open my eyes disturbingly to myself and to lots of things in the Western World'.[17] To be more specific, Heidegger's critique of the shortcomings of Western rationalism, especially as it stressed the abstract over the particular, resounded with Malik.[18] Although Whitehead

---

[11]   Charles Malik, 'An Appreciation of Professor Whitehead with Special Reference to his Metaphysics and to his Ethical and Educational Significance', *Journal of Philosophy* 45 (1948), 572–82, at 573.

[12]   Ibid. 572–3.

[13]   Charles Malik, 'Review: Collected Papers of Charles Sanders Pierce', *Isis* 23 (1935), 477–83, at 480, 483.

[14]   Ibid. 480.

[15]   Washington DC, Library of Congress, Manuscript Division, Charles Habib Malik Papers, Box 256, Folder 1, Charles Malik, draft PhD thesis, ch. 8, 'Man and Temporality', 317.

[16]   Ibid. 324.

[17]   Ibid. 329.

[18]   Martin Woessner, 'Provincializing Human Rights? The Heideggerian Legacy from Charles Malik to Dipesh Chakrabarty', in Jose-Manuel Barreto, ed., *Human Rights from a Third World Perspective: Critique, History and International Law* (Newcastle upon Tyne, 2013), 65–101, at 72.

had been Malik's primary mentor at Harvard, Malik expressed a genuine preference for the thought of Heidegger. In a draft of his PhD thesis, Malik revealed:

> I *find myself* more truly in Professor Heidegger's than in Professor Whitehead's philosophy. The former, just because it is more personal than the latter, gives me a deeper grasp on my own being, and therefore affords me a more 'self-relieving' possibility of expression, than does the latter …[19]

Malik also found Heidegger more conversant than Whitehead with the whole span of what he called the 'great tradition' of Western thought stretching from Plato to Kant and encompassing such Christian luminaries as Augustine and Aquinas.[20] However, Heidegger's influence on Malik, whilst significant, should not be overstated.[21] 'I would not be a man', Malik went on to explain later in the same passage, 'if I did not here add that I do not quite *find myself* in either philosophy'.[22] While Heidegger helped Malik refine his search for his own Arab Christian identity and his relationship with the Western tradition, Malik would draw on a broader array of sources to flesh out his critique of Orientalist scholarship.

It is easy to find in Malik's critical reflections on Western understandings of Islam and the Arab world a Heideggerian

---

[19]   Malik, thesis draft, ch. 9, 'The Existential Basis of the Cosmology of Process', 338.

[20]   Charles Malik, 'Introduction', in idem, ed., *Readings in Philosophy: Selections from the Great Masters*, 1: *Ancient Philosophy* (Beirut, 1939), i–xliii, at xiii; idem, 'Introduction', in idem, ed., *God and Man in Contemporary Islamic Thought* (Beirut, 1972), 1–100, at 26.

[21]   This is the main problem I find in Woessner's otherwise illuminating and valuable account. He makes the strange argument that in the 1930s Malik sought to advance a critique of the dominant paradigm in the philosophy of science, drawing primarily upon 'Heidegger's existential analytic – all without necessarily relying upon religion'. He goes on to draw the untenable conclusion that Malik's dependence on Christian teaching would only become 'more explicit' much later, suggesting that this was possibly motivated by a delayed recognition of the dangers of Heidegger's thought: Woessner, 'Provincializing Human Rights', 76. For an alternative perspective, more in line with my own, that emphasizes the continuity in Malik's Christian philosophical project and his immersion in the work of Christian thinkers such as Augustine and Aquinas both prior to, and alongside, his engagement with Heidegger in the 1930s, see Habib C. Malik, 'The Arab World: The Reception of Kierkegaard in the Arab World', in Jon Stewart, ed., *Kierkegaard's International Reception: The Near East, Asia, Australia and the Americas*, 3 vols (Farnham, 2009), 3: 39–96, at 41, 43.

[22]   Malik, thesis draft, ch. 9.

disdain for the danger posed by scholarship prone to abstraction, but there is much more at work. In fact, in the development of his unique criticism of Orientalism (more narrowly) and of Western rationalism (more broadly), Malik owed his greatest debt to the Thomist revival of the early twentieth century. During this period the French Roman Catholic philosopher Jacques Maritain helped renew interest in the work of Thomas Aquinas and the Thomistic notion of poetic knowledge.[23] According to Maritain, Thomistic realism was distinct amongst other philosophies in acknowledging the existence of metaphysical realities while also recognizing the limits of discursive or conceptual forms of knowledge.[24] Aquinas had in fact taken pains to highlight the genuine value of a 'non-conceptual' way of knowing, which he called *poetica scientia* or 'poetic knowledge'.[25] In a poetic encounter, Maritain explained, one could gain real, though pre-discursive and pre-conceptual, knowledge of something or someone through the agency of the affections, which produced a form of intuitive intellectual union more obscure, but also more intimate, than anything produced by philosophical reasoning.[26] For Maritain, poetic knowledge through love had priority over conceptual knowledge through discursive reasoning.

If Maritain helped recover the Thomistic concept of poetic knowledge for the twentieth century, Malik applied it to the problem of cross-cultural engagement with the Arab world. Although Greek Orthodox, Malik had been influenced by Protestant Evangelicalism.[27] He also admired Roman Catholicism, and, after completing his PhD at Harvard, returned to AUB, where he hoped to establish a new philosophy curriculum incorporating the work of Augustine and Aquinas.[28] The recent revival of Thomism

[23] James S. Taylor, *Poetic Knowledge: The Recovery of Education* (New York, 1998), 6, 40, 57, 65, 67, 71–2, 176.

[24] Jacques Maritain, *The Degrees of Knowledge*, transl. Bernard Wall (London, 1937; first publ. as *Distingue pour unir ou Les degrés du savoir*, Paris, 1932), ix, xi, 7–12, 17–18, 132, 321, 323.

[25] Jacques Maritain, *The Range of Reason* (New York, 1952; first publ. as *Raison et raisons*, Paris, 1948), 25–6.

[26] Ibid. 26.

[27] Oxford, St Antony's College, Middle East Centre Archive, Sir Illtyd Clayton Collection, Box 1, Charles Malik, 'The Problem of Lebanon: An Interpretation in Three Parts', 20 October 1943, fol. 106.

[28] Minneapolis, University of Minnesota, Immigration History Research Center,

struck him as one of the most significant philosophical movements of the era and he considered Maritain to be one of the greatest minds of the age.[29]

Malik first considered the problem of the 'Orientalist' scholar in the early 1940s while teaching at AUB.[30] As Lebanon would gain its independence from France in 1943, the immediate concern prompting Malik's initial thoughts was the 'Problem of Lebanon'. The problem for Malik, in this case, consisted in the difficulty of defending the concept of Lebanon as an independent 'Christian-European-Arab state' in the face of those who would conceive of Lebanon purely as a Christian European entity separate from the Arab world or, by contrast, a strictly Arab entity inseparable from a greater Syria dominated by Sunni Islam.[31] Malik found his vision of Lebanon was one which European Orientalist scholars, obsessed with cultural difference rather than hybridity and more sympathetic to Western imperialism than Arab self-determination, were unable to conceive.[32] After 1945, Malik continued to ponder the broader problem of understanding between 'Asia' and 'the West' as a Lebanese delegate to the United Nations.[33] Ultimately, he found the cause of misunderstanding in the absence of equality between regions and in the West's reliance on abstract knowledge over proper affection to inform its engagement.[34] Whilst his daily duties prevented him from writing a formal treatise on the topic, it came up repeatedly in his speeches and published essays.

Malik's criticism of Orientalism was part of his broader criticism of conventional understandings of science. For Malik, science was 'not merely technique' or 'the clever utilization and exploitation of nature'.[35] Nor was it to be restricted to the natural sciences. In this regard, like Maritain, Malik preferred the medieval Chris-

---

Near Eastern Collection, Philip Khuri Hitti Papers, Box 10, Folder 13, Charles Malik, 'Annual Report of the Department of Philosophy for 1941–1942'.

[29]   Malik, 'Introduction' in idem, ed., *Readings in Philosophy*, xxxviii; Malik Papers, Box 21, Folder 3, Charles Malik to William Elliot, 9 July 1953.

[30]   Clayton Collection, Box 1, fol. 120, Charles Malik to I. N. Clayton, 22 March 1944.

[31]   Ibid., fol. 48, Charles Malik to I. N. Clayton, 11 January 1944.

[32]   Ibid.

[33]   Charles Malik, 'Understanding each other: "Idolatry of Gadgets" cannot convert Asia', *Vital Speeches of the Day* 17 (1950), 66–7, at 66.

[34]   Ibid. 67.

[35]   Charles Malik, 'Appeal to Asia', *Thought* 26 (1951), 8–24, at 14.

tian notion of *scientia*, which encompassed a much broader field of knowledge and did not discount the importance of affection.[36] Malik sketched his vision of authentic scientific inquiry:

> To use, you must be able to understand; and to understand, you must be able to see. But to see is precisely what is meant by theory, and you must love that which you rest your sight upon if you are really to understand it. It is this loving vision of nature, this ecstatic oneness with her powers that constitutes the essence of the scientific culture.[37]

Poetic knowledge provided the foundation for Malik's conception of *scientia*.

Instead of simply encouraging the collection of more accurate knowledge about other cultures, Malik pointed out the fundamental importance of joining the proper affections to understanding.[38] He explained:

> Enemies make it a point to understand each other perfectly, and yet they aim at destroying each other … there is something beyond understanding, something which converts understanding into peace … this saviour of understanding from being an instrument of death, is love … Only in love, a love that is not sentimental, a love that is grounded and established in the truth, can the present profound anxieties of the world be resolved and surmounted.[39]

The affections were of primary importance to Malik because they yielded a form of knowledge more immediate and more conducive to right action than conceptual reasoning. For this reason, Malik would later emphasize the importance in public affairs of those who helped cultivate proper emotions, such as poets.[40]

In 1948, Malik provided a more general critique of the limits of 'Western' scientific understanding of the 'Near East' in an article for the American Academy of Political Science.[41] By contrast with

---

[36] Ibid. 15.

[37] Ibid.

[38] Malik, 'Understanding each other', 67.

[39] Ibid.

[40] Charles Malik, 'Domestic Public Affairs: International Impacts', *Vital Speeches of the Day* 33 (1967), 538–41, at 541.

[41] Charles Malik, 'The Basic Issues of the Near East', *Annals of the American Academy*

abstract understanding, which because of its 'external and utilitarian' approach was prone to instrumentalizing the 'Near East'
and therefore to missing its inner reality, he stressed the need for
Westerners to develop an acquaintance with the 'intrinsic being
and character' of the region.[42] He warned this would require no
less than 'a total revolution of perspective'. For Malik, Westerners
were merely spectators of the Near East who sought to use the
region as a means to achieve their own ends, a malady no amount
of careful discursive analysis could correct. As an alternative to
conceptual reflection, Malik recommended the importance of
knowing the Near East through 'a radical and serious self-positing
within the inner crisis' of the region. This sympathetic and loving
vicarious experience, or what Aquinas and Maritain had called
'connaturality', was a way to gain poetic knowledge, which would
help Westerners to know the true inner being of the Near East as
'an end' in itself.[43]

In the early 1950s, Malik sharpened his contrast of the different
ways of knowing. 'How much good and how much harm has
Orientalism done', he asked.[44] Regardless of its scholarly accom-
plishments, academic interest in the 'Near East' had not prevented
the 'West' from basing its relationship with the region on 'strategy,
commerce, exploitation', the search for 'an imperial route' and
'immense racial arrogance', rather than love.[45] The 'West' valued
the 'Near East' only for what it offered and not for its inherent
value.[46] 'Now reason and nature are wonderful things', Malik
argued, 'but without love they are nothing'. As a solution to this
'contraction in the order of love', Malik commended the cultivation of the affections as a way to anchor Orientalism in a non-
utilitarian way of knowing.[47]

Given the influence of Aristotle and Aquinas, Malik thus insisted
on 'the natural lucidity of things to … reason' as a fundamental

---

of Political and Social Science 258 (1948), 1–7.
[42] Ibid. 1.
[43] Ibid. 2.
[44] Malik, 'Near East', 257.
[45] Ibid. 263.
[46] Ibid. 259.
[47] Charles Malik, 'The Relations of East and West', *Proceedings of the American Philosophical Society* 97 (1953), 1–7, at 7.

axiom.[48] Not surprisingly, he also reckoned the true inner reality of the Near East as intimately connected with God's providential purposes. 'He alone loves the East', Malik proclaimed, 'who has a sure vision of all of us as potential children of God'. Yet he did not consider this vision as something that originated in human reason, but as a supernatural gift 'from above'. Malik also reckoned poetic knowledge in unambiguously Christocentric terms: 'he loves East and West most who, despite all his weaknesses, loves Jesus Christ first'. Thus his critique of Western views of the Near East was rooted not only in philosophical realism but also in a distinctly Christian form of philosophical realism. This allowed him to distinguish the sort of love he advocated from romanticism, which he considered too subjective, and humanitarian sentiment, which he considered too limited.[49] For Malik, neither tradition of thought cultivated the sort of affections that accorded with the true nature of reality in all its fullness.

In the era following World War II, as Europe's formal empires crumbled and new nations emerged, Malik's critique of Western views of the Near East had a profound impact on the thought of key Christian intellectuals, including the British scholars Albert Hourani, one of the founders of the discipline of modern Middle Eastern history, and Kenneth Cragg, one of the most influential twentieth-century Protestant scholars of Islam.[50] Both individuals first encountered Malik at AUB, in the late 1930s and early 1940s respectively, and came to share his concern for the plight of Arab Christians in the Middle East. Hourani was there to teach English history, literature and international relations, and Cragg to teach philosophy.[51] During their time at the university, both became enamoured with Malik's vision of Christian intellectual vocation to the Arab world. Attending Malik's introductory philosophy lectures,

[48] Charles Malik, 'Natural Law and the Problem of Asia', in John D. Wild, ed., *Return to Reason* (Chicago, IL, 1953), 333–53, at 335.

[49] Malik, 'Relations', 7.

[50] For Hourani's legacy, see Roger Owen, 'Albert Hourani the Historian', in Ilan Pappe and Moshe Ma'oz, eds, *Middle Eastern Politics and Ideas: A History from Within* (London, 1997), 7–19. For Cragg, see Christopher Lamb, *The Call to Retrieval: Kenneth Cragg's Christian Vocation to Islam* (London, 1997).

[51] 'Albert Hourani', in Nancy E. Gallagher, ed., *Approaches to the History of the Middle East: Interviews with Leading Middle East Historians* (Reading, 1994), 19–45, at 23–4; Kenneth Cragg, *Faith and Life negotiate: A Christian Story-Study* (Norwich, 1994), 98.

Cragg found that he 'brought to life the thrill of study and the pursuit of meaning'.[52] 'To listen to Charles Malik in full cry was what it must have been like to attend on Demosthenes', Cragg explained; '[h]e was still youthful, often dramatic, always challenging, cajoling, exciting'.[53] When Malik left to take up an official posting for Lebanon at the United Nations, Cragg succeeded him as the acting head of the philosophy department.[54] In the early 1950s he praised Malik for providing 'outstanding spiritual and Christian leadership' in the Arab world.[55]

Hourani's admiration for Malik went even deeper. In a report for British officials in Egypt during World War II, he called Malik 'undoubtedly the greatest intellectual figure in the Arab world today'.[56] Shortly after that war's conclusion, he suggested that one heard 'the authentic voice of humanity' in Malik's speeches.[57] He also counted Malik as his most significant intellectual and spiritual influence. Hourani considered his time reading Augustine with Malik in the late 1930s as a decisive factor in his eventual conversion to Roman Catholicism in the 1950s and confessed 'my mind was formed in a way more by Charles than by anybody else'.[58] Such was the profound debt Hourani owed to Malik.

Before moving on to discuss Hourani and Cragg, it is worth observing that Malik was known simply as 'Uncle Charles' to the intellectual who did the most to put the criticism of Orientalism on the scholarly map, Edward Said.[59] Said's critique of Orientalism makes an interesting contrast with the Christian critique shaped by Malik. As a child in Cairo in the 1940s and an undergraduate at Princeton in the 1950s, Said counted Malik as his most significant early intellectual influence.[60] Despite this debt, Said grew distant

[52] Kenneth Cragg, *The Arab Christian: A History in the Middle East* (Louisville, KY, 1991), 231.

[53] Cragg, *Faith and Life*, 102.

[54] Ibid. 98.

[55] Kenneth Cragg, 'The Arab World and the Christian Debt', *IRM* 42 (1953), 151–61, at 159.

[56] Kew, TNA, FO 141/866/149/44/43, Albert Hourani, 'Great Britain and Arab Nationalism', March 1943, 17.

[57] Albert Hourani, 'Islam and the West', *Listener* 48 (1952), 501–2, at 502.

[58] Malik Papers, Box 21, Folder 3, Albert Hourani to Charles Malik, 28 November [early 1950s]; 'Hourani', in Gallagher, ed., *Approaches*, 24.

[59] Edward Said, *Out of Place: A Memoir* (London, 1999), 263, 265. Malik married Said's mother's first cousin, Eva.

[60] Ibid. 265–6, 276, 280–2.

from Malik in the 1960s as their viewpoints on Arab nationalism diverged.[61] Though the details of Said's break with Malik need not concern us here, we should note how their respective critiques of Orientalism came to differ. In sharp contrast to Malik, who highlighted the importance of pre-discursive knowledge obtained through the affections, Said denied the existence of knowledge outside the context of discourse. Said's well-known critique of Orientalism was rooted in the post-structuralist assumption that there was 'no such thing as plain, or unadorned, or brute, or naive reality', and that therefore 'all meaning and value-systems' were 'man-made' rather than rooted in the nature of things.[62] This supposition made for a very different starting point than did Malik's Christian realism.

Even though Said's critical work diverged considerably from that of his uncle, Malik's approach found important disciples elsewhere, namely in Hourani and Cragg. During the 1940s, first within the context of the British Foreign Office and later under the auspices of the Arab League's Arab Office, Hourani had been amongst the foremost advocates of Arab nationalism and Palestinian self-determination.[63] As a result, he was well acquainted with the policy-making establishment and the Orientalist scholarly elite in Britain, and familiar with the extent and limits of their interaction. He shared Malik's admiration for Maritain and concern for Arab Christians, and drew on Malik's ideas concerning the importance of affective knowledge to critique British views of the Arab world.[64]

In 1948, fuelled by bitter disappointment over Britain's lack of support for Palestinian Arabs, Hourani left politics and returned to Oxford where he became one of the first historians of the 'Middle East' in Britain.[65] At Magdalen College, Hourani set out to explain why the Arabs had been shunned as 'wholly outside' the West and Arab nationalism had been dismissed as a 'mass of irrational feeling'

---

[61] Ibid. 264, 268–9, 281–2.

[62] Edward Said, 'Shattered Myths', in Naseer Aruri, ed., *Middle East Crucible: Studies on the Arab-Israeli War of October 1973* (Wilmette, IL, 1975), 408–47, at 438, 441.

[63] Hourani, *Unfinished Odyssey*, 57–8, 69–75.

[64] Albert Hourani, *Minorities in the Arab World* (London, 1947), 125.

[65] London, Royal Institute of International Affairs Archives, 8/1332, Albert Hourani, 'Palestine after the Report', 17 May 1946, 7; Owen, 'Hourani the Historian', 7–19.

by the British.[66] He gave his answer in a two-part essay entitled 'The Decline of the West in the Middle East', which began as a talk for the Royal Institute of International Affairs in 1951. In his view, the West was not just guilty of 'a failure of understanding but also a failure of virtue, a lack of love'.[67] In the talk and the essay, he attempted to lay bare the imperial power realities affecting human relationships to 'see things as they really are'.[68] 'The essence of imperialism', Hourani explained, was 'to be found in a moral relationship ... of power and powerlessness'.[69] No matter what officials might say, he continued, Britain's imperial relationship with Arabs was not one of equality or even paternal friendship, but 'one of self-confident force imposing itself on resentful weakness'.[70] It was the nature of this irregular relationship that had warped Britain's affections towards Arabs, distorted their understanding of history and encouraged the pursuit of unjust policies.[71] Hourani believed these policies had also been disastrous for Christian-Muslim relations.[72]

For Hourani, the solution to this relational estrangement was not to be found in the 'realm of theoretical reason' or abstract understanding. Formal imperial withdrawal was necessary, but not sufficient. Instead, he believed that the estrangement could only be resolved in the sphere of 'the confrontation of hearts and souls: of witness, of love, and of faith'.[73] If one loved the Arabs, one would see their desire for self-determination as it really was, not 'the emanation of a diseased society, so much as a natural movement of self-respect, individual and communal' to normalize relations with the West.[74] However, whilst Hourani considered the Arab achievement of formal independence a 'good in itself', he believed the

[66] Albert Hourani, 'The Decline of the West in the Middle East, Part I', *International Affairs* 29 (1953), 22–42, at 31, 22 respectively.

[67] Royal Institute of International Affairs Archives, 8/1966, Albert Hourani, 'The Decline of Europe in the Middle East', 20 November 1951, fol. 5.

[68] Hourani, 'Decline, Part I', 22.

[69] Ibid. 31.

[70] Ibid. 33.

[71] Ibid. 29–33; Albert Hourani, 'Review: The Middle East in the War: Survey of International Affairs, 1939–1946', *International Affairs* 29 (1953), 204–5, at 205.

[72] Hourani, 'Decline of Europe', 5.

[73] Malik Papers, Box 21, Folder 3, Albert Hourani, untitled document [Part I, Ford Foundation], 1954.

[74] Albert Hourani, 'The Decline of the West in the Middle East, Part II', *International Affairs* 29 (1953), 156–83, at 174.

desire for autonomy carried within itself 'the danger of premature attempts at cultural independence'.[75] For him, the normalizing of relations was a two-way street: the West needed to love Arabs in the hope that there would be no unnecessary barriers preventing Arabs from loving the best that the West had to offer. Improper affections were the root of cross-cultural conflict and proper affections were the cure.[76]

By contrast with Hourani, who had spent the Second World War embroiled in Arab politics, Cragg had ministered to an English-speaking Anglican congregation in Beirut and had taught philosophy as Malik's temporary replacement. He returned to Oxford in 1947 to pursue a doctorate, which he finished in 1950.[77] In his thesis, which had been inspired by his work at AUB with Arab students from a variety of religious backgrounds, Cragg began to sketch out his vision for the renewal of Western scholarship on Islam through the infusion of explicit Christian concern.[78]

In his work, Cragg tried to take Malik's summons to develop an inward, non-utilitarian understanding of Islam and the Arab world seriously. Instead of simply setting out to add to the general store of Western knowledge about Islam, Cragg believed it imperative for Christians to look for 'a basis of genuine fellowship' between Christians and Muslims.[79] He believed he had found the basis for this fellowship in their common theological predicament with 'modernity'.[80] To understand Islam truly, it was thus imperative for Christians to 'try and see from within Islam itself the challenge of its modern problems and to leave in abeyance the usual themes and points of direct controversy'.[81] In his view, cultivation of this type of 'connatural' knowledge would require 'religious commitment' and a searching sympathy.[82]

Cragg elaborated on his criticism of the shortcomings of Orientalism upon his appointment at Hartford Seminary, Connecticut

[75] Hourani, untitled document.
[76] Hourani, 'Decline, Part II', 183, 181.
[77] Kenneth Cragg, 'Islam in the Twentieth Century: The Relevance of Christian Theology and the Relation of the Christian Mission to its Problems' (DPhil thesis, University of Oxford, 1950).
[78] Ibid. 39.
[79] Ibid. ii.
[80] Ibid. ii, 3.
[81] Ibid. 22–3.
[82] Ibid. 23–4.

in 1951. Key to his approach was the conviction that 'merely academic interest in Islam' was indicative of the corrupting influence of secularism.[83] Secular Orientalism was insufficient, he believed, because it had failed to come 'into fruitful intercourse with Muslims at the central points of Muslim genius and life'.[84] He warned that as long as Orientalist scholarship sought to avoid the requirements of a 'religious relationship', it would remain 'a study about Islam, not a meeting of mind with Muslims'.[85] Thus it was imperative that Christians study Islam 'in close, intellectual and spiritual partnership with Muslims', in order to cultivate the sort of genuine fellowship that was essential for authentic personal encounter.[86] Cragg believed that scholarship on Islam was best pursued as a communal, confessional endeavour rooted in affection and not simply as abstract reasoning.

In this way, a coherent, philosophically sophisticated 'Christian' approach to the problem of Orientalism existed which was developed well before Marxists or post-structuralists had worked out their own approaches. This Christian critique makes a fascinating contrast with Said's later work. While Said focused on discourse, Malik and his disciples pointed to the importance of the pre-discursive affections. It is perhaps easier to appreciate Malik's critique today, given the seriousness with which the field of political philosophy is now taking the emotions.[87] Moreover, with the decline of religion in the modern era no longer a foregone conclusion, the emphasis on the religious dimensions of intellectual engagement in the thought of Malik and his disciples seems less like special pleading and more like realistic pragmatism. While there remains much to explore concerning the interplay of religion and Oriental studies in Britain, the influence of Christianity on Islamic studies in Britain after 1945 is clear. Given the important role religion played in the criticism of Orientalism in the work of Malik, perhaps future discussions of the evolution of

---

[83] Kenneth Cragg, 'The Christian Church and Islam Today: The Spur of the Moment, III', *MW* 42 (1952), 207–17, at 217.

[84] Kenneth Cragg, '"Each Other's Face": Some Thoughts on Muslim-Christian Colloquy Today', *MW* 45 (1955), 172–82, at 174.

[85] Ibid.

[86] Ibid. 175.

[87] See, for example, Martha Nussbaum, *Political Emotions: Why Love Matters to Justice* (Cambridge, MA, 2013); Joshua Hordern, *Political Affections: Civic Participation and Moral Theology* (New York, 2013).

Western study of Islam and the Arab world will one day attend not just to the influence of Marx, Gramsci and Foucault, but also to figures like Aquinas and Maritain as well.

Biola University

'TO LIVE WITHIN ISLAM':
THE CHALDEAN CATHOLIC CHURCH IN
MODERN IRAQ, 1958–2003

by KRISTIAN GIRLING

Since June 2014 the Chaldean Catholic Church has faced an existential crisis. The recent attacks of the terrorist forces of the so-called Islamic State of Iraq and the Levant in the northern Iraqi provinces of Duhok, Erbil, Mosul and Sulaymaniya have resulted in increasing levels of persecution and forced displacement. This essay reflects on a more secure period in Chaldean history, during which the community made a strong contribution to the development of the modern state of Iraq, established in 1921. Although proportionally small in size, the essay will show that the Chaldean community contributed in ways which far outweighed their numbers, especially in the sphere of inter-communal relations.

In 2003, Antoine Audo SJ, Chaldean bishop of Aleppo, suggested that the Chaldeans must 'live within Islam', hinting at innovative ways in which Christians have had to adapt in order to survive and maintain their social position within majority Muslim societies.[1] This essay will consider the nature of this innovative approach in Iraq and will delineate three levels of engagement – national, local and institutional – at which the Chaldeans have been involved and which they themselves helped to develop. It is intended that this framework of understanding should provide a foundation for further discussion of the historical role of Christians as a distinct and alternative voice in religious and communal dialogue in the Arab Middle East. Since this is an emerging area of academic enquiry with little prior critical analysis of these engagements in Iraq, what follows should not be considered as an authoritative account, but rather as an effort to introduce into scholarship themes concerning the specific relationship between churches, the state and Muslim communities in Iraq, and especially to consider

---

[1]   Antoine Audo SJ, statement at the Asian Synod of Catholic Bishops, February 2003, quoted in Anthony O'Mahony, 'The Chaldean Catholic Church: The Politics of Church-State Relations in Modern Iraq', *Heythrop Journal* 45 (2004), 435–50, at 447.

how Ba'athism and the rule of Saddam Husain affected Christian daily life.[2]

The Chaldean community originated as a distinct ecclesiastical body from its progenitor community, the Church of the East, in the mid-sixteenth century.[3] The Church of the East had separated from other parts of the Christian communion following the condemnation of the Christological views of Nestorius at the Council of Ephesus in 431, and had consolidated itself in Mesopotamia. This emerging community existed in an environment independent of the Roman Empire under Persian Sasanid rule, where it found it politically expedient to assert a more independent policy of church governance than that of the rest of the Christian *oikumene*. Because they were associated with the faith of the Romans, the Christians of the Sasanid Empire were subject to

---

[2] For recent consideration of Christianity in Iraq, see David Wilmshurst, *The Martyred Church: A History of the Church of the East* (Sawbridgeworth, 2011); Suha Rassam, *Christianity in Iraq: Its Origins and Development to the Present Day*, new edn (Leominster, 2010); Anthony O'Mahony, 'Patriarchs and Politics: The Chaldean Catholic Church in Modern Iraq', in idem, ed., *Christianity in the Middle East: Studies in Modern History, Theology and Politics* (Sawbridgeworth, 2008), 105–42; Herman Teule, 'Christianity in Iraq: The Development of Secular Christian Political Thinking', *One in Christ* 45 (2011), 312–20.

[3] Disputes had arisen over the most appropriate explanation of the relationship between the human and divine natures of Christ. The Christian community in Mesopotamia was influenced by the theological views of the Antiochene School and especially those of Nestorius, archbishop of Constantinople (428–31), Diodore of Tarsus (d. *c.*392) and Theodore of Mopsuestia (350–428), which the Council of Ephesus condemned as a heretical, dyophysite Christology denying the title of Mother of God to the Blessed Virgin Mary. Whether or not Nestorius was heretical or indeed professed the beliefs ascribed to him came under scrutiny during the twentieth century. Dyophysitism is far from an alien concept, being a cornerstone of the Christology of the Roman Catholic and Orthodox Churches: that Christ exists with two natures, human and divine, in one person. What came to be of concern was as to the arguments of Nestorius and others regarding the moment of hypostatic union in Christ and as to whether he could be regarded as in effect taking on his divinity at some point subsequent to his birth. See, for instance, M. J. Birnie, 'The Church of the East and Theodore of Mopsuestia: The Commitment to his Writings and its Implications for Dialogue', *Journal of Assyrian Academic Studies* 10/1 (1996), 14–19, at 14–15; John Chapman, 'Nestorius and Nestorianism', *The Catholic Encyclopedia*, 15 vols (New York, NY, 1911), 10: 755–9; Milton V. Anastos, 'Nestorius Was Orthodox', *DOP* 16 (1962), 117–40; Sebastian P. Brock, 'The "Nestorian" Church: A Lamentable Misnomer', *BJRL* 78 (1996), 23–35.

scrutiny of their political loyalties. Although it initiated extensive, and very successful, missionary efforts across south-west and central Asia between the fifth and the thirteenth centuries, the Church of the East declined rapidly following the invasions of Tamerlane (*c.*1370–1405), and withdrew to form a few active dioceses in and around northern Mesopotamia. In the mid-fifteenth century, in an attempt to consolidate the remaining community, hereditary accession to the patriarchate was introduced by the leading clerical family, a principle which was in contravention of accepted tradition. Gradually criticism of this principle grew and, in the mid-sixteenth century, a group led by the monk Yohannan Sulaqa emerged, resisting the patriarchal family. Entrusted with seeking an alternative form of ecclesiastical authority and consecration as the head of the nascent community, he presented its case to Pope Julius III in 1553 and saw the formal establishment of the Chaldean Catholic rite.[4] However, in the short to medium term, this new patriarchal line also proved insecure. Disputes over power and position, geographical separation from the Latin missionaries operating in Mesopotamia and military conflict between the Ottoman and Persian Empires all led to decline and confrontation. Such was the extent of factional disputes that from the 1670s there were three patriarchal lines purporting to assert their legitimate claim to the heritage of the Church of the East: a new Chaldean line in union with the Holy See, which was established in 1681 following the conversion of the Church of the East's metropolitan of Amid in 1672; the Sulaqite line, which had originated after Yohannan Sulaqa's meetings with Pope Julius III but which broke union with the Holy See in the late seventeenth century; and the original legitimist Church of the East line from which the Sulaqites had separated. The Sulaqite line, which had been the first community of the Church of the East to enter into union with the Holy See,

---

[4]   Jerome Labourt, 'Note sur les schismes de l'Église nestorienne du XVIᵉ au XIXᵉ siècle', *Journal Asiatique* 11 (1908), 227–35, at 231. The first return of a bishop of the Church of the East to a Chalcedonian confession of faith was towards the end of the seventh century when a bishop, Sahdona, entered into communion with the Church at Antioch: Jerome Labourt, 'Chaldean Christians', *Catholic Encyclopedia*, 3: 559–61, at 559. Metropolitan Elias of Cyprus entered into union with the Holy See in 1340, but the term Chaldean was not used to describe him: David Wilmshurst, *The Ecclesiastical Organisation of the Church of the East 1318–1913*, Corpus Scriptorum Christianorum Orientalium 582 (Louvain, 2000), 22, 63.

later returned to its previous ecclesiological and Christological beliefs; today it is regarded as the contemporary Church of the East. The legitimist line of the Church of the East, from which the Sulaqites separated, maintained its independence from the Holy See until the nineteenth century, and is one ancestor of the current Chaldean patriarchal line. The essential unity of the Chaldean community was recovered during the 1830s, a decade which saw the merging of the Amidite and legitimist lines; under the leadership of Patriarch Joseph VI Audo (d. 1878) a widespread and well defined Chaldean Catholic ecclesiological identity began to emerge.[5] This unification followed nearly a century of debates, not only between the communities themselves, but also with the Holy See and with Latin missionaries in Mesopotamia, regarding which group could be considered the true heir to the heritage of the Church of the East. Stability within the Chaldean Church greatly increased from the 1840s with strong contributions from several Catholic religious orders including the Vincentians, Dominicans and Capuchin Franciscans in parochial schools, the construction of seminaries for native Chaldean clergy and the provision of Catholic literature in Syriac and Arabic.[6] Since then, even when faced by conflict, population displacement or political upheaval, the Chaldean community has remained without further ecclesial division.

From its initial establishment in the sixteenth century until the mid-twentieth century increase in urbanization, the Chaldean population was mainly located in northern Iraq, with its patriarchal headquarters in or in close proximity to Mosul.[7] Extensive Chaldean migration southwards to the major industrialized cities

---

5   To date, the only major study of Audo's life and his work in the sphere of Chaldean ecclesiology, which was vital to the formation of modern Chaldean identity, is Joseph Habbi's unpublished PhD thesis, 'Mar Joseph Audo et le pouvoir patriarcal. Étude historico-juridique' (Lateran University, 1966).

6   Amir Harrak, 'Seminary of St John (Mosul)', in Sebastian Brock et al., eds, *Gorgias Encyclopedic Dictionary of the Syriac Heritage* (Piscataway, NJ, 2011), 612; J. F. Coakley, 'The Vincentian Mission Press in Urmia, Persia: A preliminary Bibliography', *Orientalia Christiana Periodica* 79 (2013), 209–26, at 212.

7   The northern provinces of Iraq contained perhaps one of the most diverse collections of ethnic and religious groups anywhere in the country, with significant populations of Sunni Arabs, Sunni and Shia Kurds, Shabaks, Zoroastrians, Sunni Turkmen and Yazidis, along with members of the Church of the East and of the Syrian Catholic and Syrian Orthodox Churches.

of Baghdad, Basra and Kirkuk led to an increasing level of interaction with Muslims and, in the 1950s, the patriarchal administration was relocated from Mosul to Baghdad. The Chaldean patriarch came to be considered the ultimate point of contact with the state for all Christians in Iraq due to the size of his community, which represented by far the largest proportion of the Christian population.[8] The patriarch thus largely assumed overall responsibility for the direction of Christian-Muslim relations in Iraq, and for determining how best to assert a confident Christian presence without being viewed as interfering with day-to-day Muslim religious or social activities.

The three other main Christian Churches present in Iraq are the Syrian Catholic and Syrian Orthodox Churches[9] and the Church of the East. All these churches had had large communities in eastern Asia Minor and the Levant, of which many subsequently migrated to Mesopotamia. The region was regarded as offering relative security, whether from persecution from Byzantine forces, in the case of the Syrian Orthodox after the Council of Chalcedon in 451, or (nearly 1500 years later) in the wake of the Ottoman-led massacres during the First World War, in the case of the Church of the East. The Chaldeans shared a closer ecclesiological and theological bond with the Syrian Catholics since both Churches were in union with the Holy See and thus affirmed Catholic orthodoxy. Nevertheless, the Christians of Iraq were largely similar in their social and cultural activities, whilst at the same time affirming a distinctive communal identity and generally living in different villages and towns.

From the foundation of modern Iraq in 1921, and in practical terms until the mid-1960s and the growth in commitment to modern ecumenical dialogue, the Churches continued for the most part to operate independently. Ecumenical discussions

---

8   During the twentieth century the Chaldean Church was led by patriarchs Emmanuel II Thomas (1900–47), Joseph VII Ghanima (1947–58), Paul II Cheikho (1958–89) and Raphael I Bidawid (1989–2003).

9   The Syrian Orthodox Church maintains a pre-Chalcedonian confession of faith, shared with the Copts, Armenians and Ethiopians. The Syrian Catholics are the descendants of that group of Syrian Orthodox faithful who entered into union with the Holy See in the 1780s. For a discussion of their origins and relationship with the Syrian Orthodox, see, for example, Anthony O'Mahony, 'The Syrian Catholic Church: A Study in History and Ecclesiology', *Sobornost* 28/2 (2006), 28–50.

of theology grew to encompass shared areas of pastoral concern, which increased in significance during the decline of the socio-economic order from the mid-1980s with the continued effects of a period of near-perpetual conflict in Iraq. This should not imply that shared activities never occurred prior to the 1960s; educational projects existed, often under the aegis of the Latin religious orders, such as the schools in Baghdad run by Jesuits and Dominicans, which were open to all regardless of their religion.

INTER-COMMUNAL DISCOURSE AND CHALDEAN RELATIONS WITH THE STATE

The impetus for organizing and developing inter-communal discourse in a formal sense came predominantly from the Chaldeans' recognition that as a numerically minor presence they lacked the influence to secure their position in Iraq without acquiescing to some of the prerogatives of the government of the day. Consequently they could not overtly shape and frame political life as they would have desired. During the period from 1921 to 2003 the Chaldeans formed perhaps as much as 70 per cent of the entire Christian population (but no more than a few per cent of the total population), with at least 300,000 Chaldeans still living in Iraq in the 1990s.[10] Their ultimate security derived both from their perceived usefulness to Iraqi society and from the acknowledgement of this value by the dominant power groups. Therefore they placed considerable emphasis on providing examples of Christian lives well lived.

Alongside these concerns, the Chaldeans also considered the promotion of inter-communal engagement a means of restricting sectarianism and facilitating better interaction with the Sunnī and Shī'a religious communities. The Shī'a made up over half the population, yet it was the Sunnī who were most present in the political and military elites.[11] The Chaldeans thus relied upon maintaining a level of relations with both Muslim communities which reflected their relative significance to Iraqi society. However, they were not

[10] Ronald Roberson, 'The Eastern Catholic Churches 2010', online at: <http://www.cnewa.org/source-images/Roberson-eastcath-statistics/eastcatholic-stat10.pdf>, accessed 11 March 2013.

[11] Michael Eppel, 'The Elite, the Effendiyya, and the Growth of Nationalism and Pan-Arabism in Hashemite Iraq, 1921–1958', *International Journal of Middle East Studies* 30 (1998), 227–50, at 236–9.

the only non-Muslim religious group found in Iraq: Jews, Yezidis and Mandaeans, together with a few smaller groups, completed the non-Muslim religious presence.[12] By supporting the binding together of the nation as a whole through their presence and their witness to an alternative metaphysical perspective, the Chaldeans hoped to help prevent the stratification of Iraqi society.

For the Christians, some basic starting points of engagement with Muslim communities were in their apparent affinities to Islamic and Arabic culture, both theologically, in their adherence to a monotheistic tradition, and also often through use of the same language (Arabic), and similar customs in dress, food or literature. The identification of these points of contact arose from the necessity to ensure that Christians were not further set apart from other Iraqis than via their religious identity and that the door to dialogue remained open.

We can suggest that inter-communal engagements proceeded, in the main, on three levels: National-Political, Local-Social and Institutional-Formal.

NATIONAL-POLITICAL

This level focused on attempts to align the leadership of secular and spiritual powers better with the intention of maintaining a long-term working relationship. Successive Iraqi governments, whether monarchist, republican or Ba'athist, had no need to alienate the Chaldean leadership, especially given the disproportionately high number of professionals who were members of the Church. Chaldeans had vital links to the West, economically, socially and politically, and through their involvement in these areas helped inform the wider Iraqi population of relevant advances. This support for the development of Iraq and encouragement to be loyal to the established authority was led by the patriarch, Emmanuel II Thomas, who fostered an excellent working relationship with the monarchy.[13]

In the newly formed state and an era of social uncertainty, the Chaldean commitment to a stable order was very welcome to a new ruling elite which lacked legitimacy. The ruling Sunnī Hash-

---

[12] Thabit A. J. Abdullah, *A Short History of Iraq from 636 to the Present* (Harlow, 2003), 110.

[13] Ali A. Allawi, *Faisal I of Iraq* (New Haven, CT, and London, 2014), 155–6, 373.

emite family had its origins in the western, Hijaz, region of the Arabian peninsula and had been installed as de facto client rulers of the British Empire in the aftermath of the division of the Ottoman Empire at the end of the First World War.[14] This precedent for Chaldean loyalty to the contemporary ruler stemmed largely from the recognition of the need for a social order which was at worst ambivalent to Christians and at best included them within the government of the day or consulted with them on issues of mutual concern. One sign of the recognition of Chaldean influence was the formal position of their patriarch in the Iraqi senate from 1921 to 1958, which, even before the patriarchate moved to Baghdad, permitted him to advise on matters of state. This relatively free presence within a society coloured by Islamic social norms went only so far, however; for example, an Iraqi law of 1947 gave the Minister of Justice the right to oversee the religious courts of both Christians and Jews.[15]

Chaldean Political Identity and Religious Practice

The growth of popular support for the Iraqi Communist and Ba'ath parties among many Iraqis from the mid-twentieth century stemmed from the genuine desire to see a more equitable social order, which it was believed could be achieved through a more representative form of government. The leaders of the 1958 republican coup which overthrew the monarchy sought complete economic independence from Britain and the formation of a more Arab-centred political outlook.[16] Stability did not result: there was a rapid turnover of four militarily-backed governments in the following ten years. It is not clear whether the Chaldean leadership had defined strategies for responding to the changes in political discourse which they witnessed between 1958 and 1968, but the presence of the Chaldean patriarch in Baghdad from 1950 must have made it easier for him to intervene with the government on behalf of his community during this crucial period. What is clear is that the Chaldeans had been to some extent dependent

[14]   The Iraqi kings were Feisel I (1921–33), Ghazi (1933–9) and Feisel II (1939–58).
[15]   John Joseph, *The Nestorians and their Muslim Neighbors: A Study of Western Influence on their Relations*, Princeton Oriental Studies 20 (Princeton, NJ, 1961), 216.
[16]   Amatzia Baram, Achim Rohde and Ronen Zeidel, 'Iraq: History Reconsidered, Present Reassessed', in eidem, eds, *Iraq between Occupations: Perspectives from 1920 to the Present* (Basingstoke, 2010), 1–12, at 6.

on the good will of the monarchy to retain their position within the social order; therefore, with the removal of the monarchy the Chaldeans faced an uncertain outcome and were challenged to develop a new relationship with the new state.

In general, by the early 1960s Christian political identity appears to have rested on the hopes for socio-economic change which were derived from the highly organized and increasingly influential Ba'ath party, but it also retained a religious aspect which was generally dependent on personal ties and on encouragement from clergy that individual Christians should remain committed to their faith. This may indicate that the formation of national-political engagement at this time moved out of the hands of the Chaldean hierarchy and into those of the laity.

Ba'athism was attractive to Christians, at least in part, due to the emphasis on economic development aside from a Marxist-Socialist paradigm. Mansfield, for example, suggests: 'The socialist content in Ba'thism is not very specific. It is less a set of socio-economic principles than a rather vague means of national improvement … only certain broad basic conditions need to be fulfilled for a system to be called socialist.'[17] Consequently, the potentially dangerous effects of overtly anti-religious policies favoured by the communist political groupings, with which Christians had historically been involved, could be avoided within the Ba'ath party. At the same time, the vision of overall improvement for the poorer urban and rural classes which the Christian intelligentsia favoured could still be acted upon. The increase of stability in social relations which the Ba'ath appeared to offer following their successful coup in 1968 was not, therefore, opposed. This coup settled the question of the political status quo in Iraq until 2003, with Saddam Husain taking power as president in 1979.

Once the Ba'ath government became fully cognizant of the power it wielded over Iraqi society following consolidation of its position, secularization and coercive Arabization of society became more widespread. From 1968, the Ministry of Endowment and Religious Affairs oversaw nationalization of all non-government schools with a view to ensuring the overall unification of Arab

---

[17] Peter Mansfield, 'Saddam Husain's Political Thinking: The Comparison with Nasser', in Tim Niblock, ed., *Iraq: The Contemporary State* (Beckenham, 1982), 62–73, at 69.

nationalist political thought among Iraqis.[18] Nevertheless, religion was not something that particularly needed to be hidden under the Ba'ath government, for it was acceptable, so long as it was not political, in which case it was suppressed.[19] Thus the connections between the Shī'a in Iraq and in Iran led the Ba'ath to limit their role in public life through the preferential selection for office of party members deemed to have a suitable ethnic and religious background. However, the importance of religious identity declined over the years of Ba'athist rule; loyalty to the state and to Husain proved far more important than religion in determining social position and access to employment.[20]

Under the Ba'ath, the Chaldean hierarchy sought political neutrality and avoided engaging in behaviour which might have been considered critical of the government. They conformed to the party's official expectation that they acknowledge the authority of its leadership, which, after his accession to power, was accomplished through at least token loyalty to Saddam Husain. Nevertheless, despite the limited threat which the Chaldeans posed to the maintenance of government authority, in northern Iraq coercion of sections of the Chaldean population did occur, to the extent of forced displacement. The Chaldeans also suffered physical persecution during the infamous Anfal campaign of the 1980s.[21] The north was home to a large Kurdish minority, which since the formation of Iraq had agitated for political independence. This demand ran counter to the Ba'ath political outlook, which sought to enforce the Arabization of the region through the transfer of Iraqis from the central and southern regions of the country. The campaign was an attempt to drive the Kurds further to the edges of Iraq both politically and geographically, but it also impacted on the significant Christian proportion of the resident population and led some to question their allegiance to the government. Arguably, these measures therefore contributed to a desire to advance a more Syriac-based cultural identity, which differed from the mainstream

[18] Shak Hanish, 'Christians, Yazidis, and Mandaeans in Iraq: A Survival Issue', *Digest of Middle East Studies* 18 (2009), 1–16, at 3.

[19] Anthony O'Mahony, 'Iraq in the Melting Pot', *The Tablet*, 17 May 2003, 4–5, at 4.

[20] Joseph Sassoon, *Saddam Hussein's Ba'ath Party: Inside an Authoritarian Regime* (New York, NY, 2012), 3.

[21] Wilmshurst, *Martyred Church*, 438.

Arabist narrative: Syriac had functioned as a means of sustaining Christian identity in northern Mesopotamia prior to the formation of Iraq and in the migration of the community to central and southern Iraq.

Justification for a greater cultural separation from the state, to some extent a strategy for distancing themselves from the ideal of the Iraqi Arab nation, derived in part from the attacks in northern Iraq, which appeared to belie the state's apparent interest in continuing its relationship with the Chaldean community. At a local level the relationship was severely damaged, and entire villages were destroyed to ensure displacement of the population, leaving the Chaldeans with little alternative but to consider permanent emigration, whether internally to central or southern Iraq – particularly Baghdad – or further afield to the Levant, Europe or the USA.

Ba'athist Iraq and the International Community

From the end of the Gulf War, the Chaldeans became one of the Iraqi government's strongest links with the West, via the Holy See, which has had diplomatic links with the ruling governments of Mesopotamia-Iraq since the nineteenth century. The link to such an international organization with extensive influence – albeit through soft power – was vital for a state which, particularly after 1990, had pariah status among many of the dominant Western and Middle Eastern powers,[22] and state attempts to interfere with Chaldean religious life were to the long-term disadvantage of the national interest. The Holy See also had a strong and genuine sense of responsibility towards the Iraqi population as a whole.[23] The opposition of the international Catholic community to war in Iraq and subsequent sanctions influenced Husain to the extent that he considered a state visit by John Paul II in 2000. Tariq Aziz, the Ba'ath deputy prime minister and foreign minister (1979–2003), was the apparent contact for such meetings, he being the most

---

[22] A fact which is increasingly recognized among government elites internationally: Laura Gotti Tedeschi, 'Vatican Is an "Enormous Soft Power", Says MP after Visit', *Catholic Herald*, 25 October 2013, online at: <http://www.catholicherald.co.uk/news/2013/10/25/vatican-is-an-enormous-soft-power-says-mp-after-parliamentary-visit/>, accessed 15 November 2013.

[23] Clyde Haberman, 'Pope, in Christmas Message, Warns on a Gulf War', *New York Times*, 26 December 1990, online at: <http://www.nytimes.com/1990/12/26/world/pope-in-christmas-message-warns-on-a-gulf-war.html>, accessed 28 November 2013.

senior Chaldean member of government. Yet it appears that his
religious allegiance had declined from his early adult years, as he
became involved in political activity; he applied himself to affairs
of state; and he offered no preferment to the Chaldeans in their
formal relationship with the government.[24] However, whilst it is
impossible to determine Aziz's exact religious affiliations or beliefs,
he seems to have retained at least an affection for Chaldean identity, as he could have converted to Islam very easily to pursue
further his own political career: whilst Ba'athism was often applied
to advance a more secularist cultural paradigm the longstanding
and close relationship of Iraqi cultural customs and social mores
to Shī'a and Sunnī Islam could not in practice be removed from
Iraq, nor did the Ba'athist leadership seek to do so.

Consolidation of the Ba'athist State and Chaldean Emigration

Direct Christian involvement in Ba'ath political activities in
general began to decline from the 1970s. As Ba'ath methods of
governance and direction of the future of the state departed from
the ideals to which the party had adhered for reducing social
and economic inequalities a passive approach to the party and
its ideology emerged. However, in practice it proved impossible
for Christians to distance themselves from the Ba'ath entirely, as
the views of the party aggregated to define the outlook of all
Iraqis. Christians relied on the Ba'athist paradigm severely limiting
Islamism. But whilst formally the Chaldean hierarchy and laity
accepted the rule of Husain – having little practical alternative
– unofficially opinion was far more divided as to the best future
political direction for Iraq. A distinctive Chaldean political identity had limited potential under the Ba'ath, and the majority of
the Chaldean population, especially in urban areas of central and
southern Iraq, perceived Husain as the least bad option for the
security of the Christian population as a whole.[25] This limited

[24] Despite Aziz's prominent position within the government there is, as yet, no
comprehensive study of his life. Closest to a biography is the extended interview
conducted by Béatrice Bouvet and Patrick Denaud, *Tarek Aziz: le diplomate de Saddam
Hussein*, Des hommes et des conflits (Paris, 2000). However, this contains only a few
comments on his religious background and no discussion of how this affected his
political views or government policy. Currently Aziz remains in prison in Baghdad.
[25] As indicated above, for Chaldeans resident in rural northern Iraq, the situation
was complicated by the effects of war between the Kurds and the Iraqi armed forces.

development of a Chaldean political identity among the laity was due also to the community's having come to be reliant on their clerical hierarchy to act as the mediator between them and the state. This was largely a legacy of the Ottoman *millet* system which had enforced the position of religious leaders – whether Jewish, Muslim or Christian – as the arbiters of political, social and legal relations between their communities and the state, and which had not greatly altered under the authoritarian governments which had ruled Iraq since British occupation in 1921.

By the mid-1980s the Chaldeans followed two main paths: migration or the adoption of a wait-and-see approach regarding their future in Iraq. The psychological burden of the Iran-Iraq War on the entire Iraqi population was considerable. The future direction of Iraq was unclear, although despite the growing Western diaspora of Christians and Muslims it appears that a degree of confidence was retained in the likely ability of the government to restore living standards, as evidenced by a relatively low level of emigration by Chaldeans until after 1991. This is perhaps surprising in view of the war's devastating effects in terms of casualties and material destruction in Iraq. Husain expended much of the country's economic output on sustaining the Iran-Iraq War, significantly decreasing the financial reserves which had been built up since the 1960s from the consolidation of petroleum production.[26] Subsequent defeat in the Gulf War of 1990–1 led to an even greater shock to the economic and social systems of Iraq. Power output was reduced to 4 per cent of pre-conflict levels and the standards of available health services were lowered to a level not seen for several decades.[27] Had sanctions not been imposed, recovery could perhaps have taken hold, but the sanctions crushed the ability of the state to respond to the needs of the people. They also deepened resentment towards those Western and Gulf states who had taken part in Operation Desert Storm, and engendered suspicions about the supposedly treacherous nature of the Iraqi Christian population through its connections with the West. These factors all served to inhibit Chaldean relations on the national-political level, as Christians came to be regarded as an alien if not threatening presence.

---

[26] By the end of the war 200,000 Iraqis had been killed, 400,000 wounded and 70,000 taken prisoner: Efraim Karsh, *The Iran-Iraq War 1980–1988*, Essential Histories 20 (Oxford, 2002), 89.

[27] Abbas Alnasrawi, 'Iraq: Economic Sanctions and Consequences, 1990–2000', *Third World Quarterly* 22 (2001), 205–18, at 210, 214.

LOCAL-SOCIAL

The second level of inter-communal engagement existed in the realities of day-to-day life. Chaldean laity in particular played a role as intermediaries and representatives of Christian life to the Muslim population.[28] Audo suggests that Christian experiences can function as 'living icons', or as windows into the realities of Christian religion expressed through the distinctive situation of Christians as both members of Middle Eastern societies and bearers of a paradigm which develops within, but is set apart from, the dominant Islamic environment.[29]

On a personal level, between neighbours and work colleagues there was awareness of one another's religious background and of the consequent – but often unstated – implications and delineations of communal boundaries. This awareness of difference did not generally lead to the adoption of antagonistic positions in communal relations. However, underlying differences did exist, and Islam placed restrictions upon those who entered into closer personal relationships. Consequently the marriage of an Iraqi Christian to a Muslim invariably led to difficulties, with one or both communities ostracizing the non-member. The marriage of a Christian woman to a Muslim man often entailed the woman's conversion to Islam, whilst those who sought conversion to Christianity or who actually converted faced at best social and cultural prohibitions and at worst physical abuse or death threats. These effects were well known and both mixed marriages and conversions occurred only infrequently; however, they were far from unheard of and indeed could not feasibly be prevented.[30]

Social Pluralism

The generally benign day-to-day relations between communities as a whole derived in part from the support for a plural religious society initiated under King Feisel I and his successors, which continued for the most part under both republican and Ba'ath governments. The

[28] Antoine Audo SJ, 'Eastern Christian Identity: A Catholic Perspective', in Anthony O'Mahony and John Flannery, eds, *The Catholic Church in the Contemporary Middle East: Studies for the Synod for the Middle East* (London, 2010), 19–35, at 31.

[29] Ibid. 29.

[30] See, for example, the account of conversion from Islam by the Iraqi Joseph Fadelle, *The Price to Pay: A Muslim risks all to follow Christ* (San Francisco, CA, 2012).

latter, however, attempted to maintain a politically neutral popular society through the increasing use of internal security services to curtail any threat to the maintenance of Ba'ath power. Blanket attempts at excluding non-Ba'athist influence from public life were clear from the outset of their rule, for instance with the complete nationalization of the education system. The homogenization of cultural affairs was also attempted through the encouragement of an all-encompassing association of Iraqi life with Arabness and with the Semitic empires of ancient history such as the Akkadians and Babylonians.[31] These attempts could not be sustained in every aspect of life, and the deliberate Arabization of Iraq which republican governments attempted and Ba'athism enacted did not prevent the maintenance of many specifically Christian facets of cultural life.

Language and dialect have been key identifying features across all religious communities in Iraq, and are of particular importance to the Chaldeans through their use of Syriac as the closest expression of their relation with the original language of Christ. Relations between Christians and Muslims in some areas developed to the extent of mixed language use in areas where the two populations lived side by side. Following the migration of large numbers of Christians to Baghdad from northern Iraq during the 1950s and 1960s, Muslim communities in proximity to Christians showed widespread use of colloquial Syriac, which had sustained Christian identity in northern Mesopotamia prior to the formation of Iraq and in the migration of the community to central and southern Iraq. The use of the language by Muslims should not be thought of as a syncretistic religious phenomenon but as a pragmatic necessity for the conducting of daily business. The strength of Syriac as a marker of Chaldean identity is notable, however, and that Muslims were willing to learn it suggests that relations and social connections between the two communities were fluid.

INSTITUTIONAL-FORMAL

We now turn to the third level of engagement between the leaders of each denomination or religious group, which was conducted extraneously to the state and often apart from the day-to-day lives of many within the communities. This type of discourse

---

[31] Amatzia Baram, 'Mespotamian Identity in Ba'thi Iraq', *Middle Eastern Studies* 19 (1983), 426–55, at 435–7.

permitted not only the maintenance of working relations on issues of common concern and interest but also apparently simple practices such as meeting and greeting each other on festive occasions such as Easter or Eid. The presence of Christian leaders at Muslim events was important as emphasizing their acknowledgement of the status of the culture of the majority; similarly a Muslim elite presence at Christian occasions indicated the respect in which they held the Christian communities.

From the 1960s, the landscape of interreligious communication changed dramatically. From the Chaldean perspective, of primary importance was the Second Vatican Council declaration *Nostra Aetate*, and the associated changes in Roman Catholic teaching regarding non-Catholic Christianity and other religions.[32] In many ways the declaration abandoned a traditional understanding of the unique nature of the Roman Catholic faith, emphasizing instead the importance of openness to the experience of other religions in their seeking after the truth, particularly those of the Abrahamic tradition (i.e. Judaism and Islam). In practical terms this had little resonance with Christian Iraqis insofar as they were already living an integrated life of engagement. However, *Nostra Aetate* offered some clergy an opportunity to reassess their opinions concerning the best way to engage with Muslims. Moving away from concerns about the theological difficulties which the Muslim denial of Christ's divinity presented, and despite the strong reservations of those who feared that such an approach would lead to syncretism and the rise of religious relativism, it offered an opportunity, for example, to develop areas of theological exploration regarding shared acknowledgement of monotheism and the role of the prophets (considered by both Christians and Muslims to be bearers of divine revelation).

This was a new area of discussion for many Chaldeans, although they recognized its importance and had a genuine concern for stable relations with their Muslim friends and neighbours. It was widely known that on occasion Muslims sought Christian aid, whether temporal or spiritual, as in seeking the blessing of a priest

---

[32] Paul VI, 'Declaration on the Relation of the Church to Non-Christian Religions – Nostra Aetate' (1965), §3, online at: <http://www.vatican.va/archive/hist_councils/ii_vatican-council/documents/vat-ii-decl-19651028-nostra-aetate_en.html>, accessed 15 July 2013.

prior to surgery or visiting a shrine to the Blessed Virgin Mary. Concerned to bring about a direct improvement of relations, Joseph Habbi, a senior Chaldean priest, established the Encounter of Wisdom inter-faith discussion group. Meetings were held to explore issues of concern to both Muslims and Christians and to seek an approach to the common good which could be expressed in terms supported by all.[33] Yet despite the significance of such efforts it was difficult to form a consensus among the communities as to how to sustain these activities. Many of the laity were struggling to get by in their own working lives, and had little opportunity to engage in such theological activities. Nor was there a greatly developed interest on the part of many Muslim leaders to extend interaction. This should not, however, detract from the importance of these efforts; such attempts to work through disputes were key to diffusing tensions.[34]

CONCLUSION

The Decline of Intercommunal Relationships

Throughout the period from 1958 to 2003 opportunities for Chaldean leaders to enter into reflective engagement on theological issues and to maintain friendly relations with their Muslim countrymen existed because in the main they did not encounter Islamist movements on an extended basis. Many such movements which developed in neighbouring states gravely influenced popular opinion concerning non-Muslim communities. That Iraq initially retained a pluralist or secularist character in its national political life meant that the Chaldean actors were largely spared the need to tackle the difficulties which such parties could cause. This situation changed after the Gulf War: from 1991 a change in

---

[33] Rassam, *Christianity in Iraq*, 175–6.

[34] This period also witnessed direct interaction between the Chaldeans and the Church of the East, with the intention of reconciling Christological beliefs and presenting a more unified Christian witness. Since the mid-1990s this has borne considerable fruit. Encouraged by the Holy See, which had instigated discussions with the Church of the East, these discussions culminated in a joint Christological statement in 1994. Subsequent discussions produced remarkable documents encouraging pastoral cooperation and offering eucharistic hospitality to members of the Church of the East at the Chaldean liturgy: see Kristian Girling, 'Engaging "the Martyred Church" – The Chaldean Catholic Church, Assyrian Church of the East and the Holy See in Ecumenical Dialogue 1994–2012 and the Influence of the Second Vatican Council', in Mary Grey et al., eds, *Living Stones Yearbook 2012* (London, 2012), 38–64.

mindset emerged among the Chaldeans as they lacked the means and the opportunity to be as committed to the nation as they once had been.[35] During the 1990s Husain increasingly turned to Islamist groups for support, and as a result localized persecution of, and attacks on, Christians throughout Iraq increased in frequency. Denied the opportunity to act freely through the loss of the state's commitment to a broadly secularist paradigm, Chaldean migration to the West increased; those who remained relied heavily on the deepening of mutually supportive relationships between the Christian communities.

The establishment of the charity 'Caritas Iraq', with the backing of the Chaldean patriarch, Raphael I Bidawid, as an attempt to alleviate the material situation of all Iraqis, was a key measure in efforts to reinvigorate Christian life.[36] One focus of its work was on the construction of sufficiently good-quality housing to encourage young families to remain instead of emigrating, but the decline in healthcare and lack of job opportunities were such that ever greater numbers chose or were forced to leave. This led to a further problem: whilst it was clearly desirable to retain continued links at all levels with Muslim neighbours in order to sustain a stable level of interaction, in practice, especially following the invasion of 2003, rapid demographic shifts appear instead to have led to a focus on maintaining mutual support between Christians as a means to survive.

Reconsolidating Intercommunal Relationships

From the 1920s informal day-to-day relationships and more formal inter-communal discussions were important – indeed integral – as a means to ensure the Chaldeans were not relegated to a secondary level of participation in Iraqi society. Consequently, they are still encouraged among church members, even since the fragmentation of Iraq from 2003.[37] Nevertheless, during the twentieth century

35   Philippe Fargues, 'Demography and Politics in the Arab World', *Population: An English Selection* 5 (1993), 1–20, at 7–9.

36   'Caritas Iraq', *Caritas Internationalis* (n.d.), online at: <http://www.caritas.org/worldmap/mona/iraq.html>, accessed 15 April 2013.

37   Within the growing Iraqi diaspora of Muslims and Christians, such activities have continued in those places where both communities live. The ties which hold them together outside Iraq impact upon the future of reconciliation inside the country: see, for example, Habib Jajou, 'Christian Muslim Relations [text of a speech given by the Chaldean Catholic Chaplain in Britain at the Al-Khoei Benevolent Islamic

a paradoxical relationship developed: the Chaldeans were often politically marginal in the shaping of society, yet they played a vital role in the sustainment of a stable socio-economic order. That the Chaldeans were able to continue to preserve a cohesive presence in Iraq is testimony to the resilience of their own communities in the face of a state and society which neither comprehended nor consistently welcomed their presence within its cultural milieu.

Looking at the destruction within Iraq since 2003 and especially the surge in violence in 2014, we can recognize the reasons why pursuing dialogue was viewed as an essential strategy in the attempt to prevent the development of an entirely sectarian discourse in twentieth-century Iraqi religious life. The Chaldeans were able to offer a counter-narrative from a particular Christian perspective which not only supported their own position but also facilitated enrichment of Iraqi life. Whether welcomed, dismissed or viewed with ambivalence by many non-Christians, it could not be ignored entirely. This counter-narrative meant that the Chaldeans once again became more than a minority voice, as a witness within Arabic culture disavowing the notion that Islam is a monolithic structure or that Muslim communities cannot be constructively engaged by Christians. Nonetheless, although the three levels of engagement offer an effective means to highlight Chaldean contributions and their vertical integration in Iraq at all levels of society, it is apparent that the consistent emphasis has been on Christian initiation of such engagement. Given their smaller size and lesser influence, for Christians to live within a modern environment of predominantly Islamic culture requires a politically and social stable society, with constant application, effort and charity by both Christians and Muslims: this is a situation which, tragically, appears unlikely to be reinstated in Iraq within a time frame which will enable the presence of the Chaldeans in the long term to be secured.

Heythrop College, London

Foundation, London, 3 November 2008]', *Mesopotamia: Eastern Christians Newspaper* 2/13 (December 2008), 5.

RACE, RELIGION AND NATIONAL IDENTITY IN SIXTIES BRITAIN: MICHAEL RAMSEY, ARCHBISHOP OF CANTERBURY, AND HIS ENCOUNTER WITH OTHER FAITHS[*]

by PETER WEBSTER

The twentieth century saw the opening of wider spaces in which the settled historic Christianity of the UK could encounter other faiths. By the time Michael Ramsey became archbishop of Canterbury in 1961, developments both in England and in the international Anglican Communion made the task more present and more urgent. Ramsey was enabled by the expansion of air travel to visit more of the countries of the former empire in which Anglicans still worshipped, as Geoffrey Fisher before him had begun to do.[1] Added to this was his willingness to intervene in international affairs, whether the war in Vietnam or the apartheid regime in South Africa.[2] As such, there were new opportunities for Ramsey to come into contact with leaders of the other world faiths, and with local conflicts in other nations that had religious elements to them.

At home, the post-war English generation was the first that had widespread experience of having neighbours who practised other faiths.[3] There had of course long been significant Jewish communities in the UK, and some smaller concentrations of Muslims. However, the immigrants from the New Commonwealth after 1945 were much more widely spread and in much greater numbers. Ramsey therefore headed a Church engaged in national debates about the appropriate levels of immigration and the means of fostering what is now called social cohesion, and whose clergy worked in precisely those local communities that

---

[*] I am grateful to the editors and peer reviewer of Studies in Church History, and to Clare Brown, Graham Macklin, John Maiden and Stephen Parker for their comments on this essay.
[1] Andrew Chandler and David Hein, *Archbishop Fisher, 1945–1961* (Farnham, 2012), 76–91.
[2] See Peter Webster, *Archbishop Ramsey, 1961–74* (Farnham, 2015), ch. 5.
[3] See Zig Layton-Henry, *The Politics of Immigration* (London, 1992).

struggled to adapt successfully to cultural difference, which had wrapped up in it a strong religious element.[4]

Perhaps surprisingly, this interaction of race, religion and national identity has hitherto been relatively marginal to scholarly concern, particularly in the case of work on the Church of England.[5] Historical work on the extreme political right has tended to concentrate on the question of race and colour to the exclusion of the religious element in national identity.[6] The growing body of scholarship on secularization and the sixties has been more concerned with the weakening of the historic Christianity of white Anglo-Saxon English people; the major competitor for allegiance was not the faiths of the newly arrived immigrant communities, but a more general unbelief.[7] There has been important work on the role of the Church of England in the dechristianization of the moral law on capital punishment, divorce and homosexuality, but little on the sequence of legislative changes in relation to immigration and race relations.[8] Such work as there is has focused on the Church's interventions in matters of racial and social justice, and not on the interactions of the faiths as faiths.[9]

This essay explores two main themes, one major and one minor. After an examination of Ramsey's own engagement with inter-

---

[4] See Nira Yuval-Davis and Philip Marfleet, eds, *Secularism, Racism and the Politics of Belonging* (London, 2012).

[5] Most recently, see Matthew Grimley, 'The Church of England, Race and Multi-Culturalism, 1962–2012', in Jane Garnett and Alana Harris, eds, *Rescripting Religion in the City: Migration and Religious Identity in the Modern Metropolis* (Farnham, 2013), 207–21. See also Hugh McLeod, *The Religious Crisis of the 1960s* (Oxford, 2007), 120–2, 239; Callum G. Brown, *Religion and Society in Twentieth-Century Britain* (Harlow, 2006), 256–7. There are several useful essays in Gerald Parsons, ed., *The Growth of Religious Diversity: Britain from 1945*, 2 vols (London, 1993–4). Issues of race and immigration are largely absent from older studies such as Paul Welsby, *A History of the Church of England 1945–1980* (Oxford, 1984).

[6] See, for instance, Richard Thurlow, *Fascism in Britain: From Oswald Mosley's Blackshirts to the National Front*, rev. edn (London, 1998), 230–57.

[7] The non-Christian religions feature only marginally in Callum G. Brown, *The Death of Christian Britain: Understanding Secularisation, 1800–2000*, 2nd edn (London, 2009).

[8] Matthew Grimley, 'Law, Morality and Secularisation: The Church of England and the Wolfenden Report, 1954–1967', *JEH* 60 (2009), 725–41; Harry Potter, *Hanging in Judgment: Religion and the Death Penalty in England* (New York, 1993); Jane Lewis and Patrick Wallis, 'Fault, Breakdown and the Church of England's Involvement in the 1969 Divorce Reform', *Twentieth Century British History* 11 (2000), 308–32.

[9] See, for example, G. I. T. Machin, *Churches and Social Issues in Twentieth-Century Britain* (Oxford, 1998), 205–9.

faith theology in the abstract, it briefly considers his interventions on behalf of Anglican minorities caught up in religiously inflected conflict overseas. The main preoccupation of the essay, however, is with the interaction between the Church of England and the emerging non-Christian minorities in the UK. It examines the role of the archbishop in the diplomatic interaction between faiths nationally, and also his interventions on behalf of religious minorities, whether in relation to the admission of immigrants or to their lot once they arrived. Whilst Ramsey was no syncretist in his theology, he knew that the mission situation both at home and abroad required that the Church of England became less and less the embodiment of Protestant Englishness, and (to borrow a phrase) more and more the defender of faiths.

The SS *Empire Windrush* arrived at Tilbury in 1948, an event that has come to symbolize the beginning of mass post-war immigration to the UK from the New Commonwealth. In 1948 Ramsey was already forty-three years of age, professor of divinity in the University of Durham, consultant to the World Council of Churches and identified as one of the leading theologians of a self-confident Anglo-Catholicism. Ramsey's theological formation had required little in the way of theological engagement with the fact of the other world religions, either abroad or at home.[10] It was a younger generation of theologians who by the mid-sixties were beginning to grapple with the substantive theological issues involved.[11] Some of that work could be seen in the collection of *Lambeth Essays on Faith*, commissioned by Ramsey for the 1968 Lambeth Conference. In it Henry Chadwick and Kenneth Cragg attempted to chart the spaces available for genuine interchange between the world faiths whilst asserting, gently but firmly, the ultimate superiority of the Christian revelation.[12] The conference itself recommended the committal of people and money to the task of inter-faith dialogue, and called for serious study of other faiths and for cooperation in 'economic, social and moral action'.[13]

---

[10]   Owen Chadwick, *Michael Ramsey: A Life* (Oxford, 1991), 26–78.

[11]   Myrtle S. Langley, 'The Challenge of the Religions', in Rupert Davies, ed., *The Testing of the Churches, 1932–1982* (London, 1982), 132–44.

[12]   Henry Chadwick, 'The "Finality" of the Christian Faith', and Kenneth Cragg, 'Dialogue with other Faiths', in [Michael Ramsey], ed., *Lambeth Essays on Faith: Essays written for the Lambeth Conference, 1968* (London, 1969), 22–31, 32–9 respectively.

[13]   *The Lambeth Conference 1968: Resolutions and Reports* (London, 1968), 31–2.

Ramsey's own view was summed up in two short addresses, both given in 1969: one in St Paul's Cathedral in commemoration of Mahatma Gandhi, and the second at a quincentenary celebration of Guru Nanak at the Royal Albert Hall. 'Now, I am a Christian', he told the Sikh audience, 'and you know that means I believe Jesus Christ to be the only perfect, complete revelation of God. No Christian can surrender the uniqueness of Jesus Christ.'[14] However, Christians 'reverence the divine image in every man' and the divine light had shone 'in good men of other religions' such as Gandhi. Gandhi had shown forth important things: he 'made non-violence his ideal, put simplicity of life before wealth and comfort, put the things of the spirit before material things, made the cause of the poor and outcast his own, and sealed it all by a martyr's death'. Ramsey prayed that 'to us the same light will shine and we shall follow it'.[15]

If Ramsey was not himself greatly influenced by contemporary trends in inter-faith theology, there were other forces in play. As an undergraduate he had been active in Liberal politics in Cambridge, and although the path to a political career that he seriously considered was not the one he took, the task of interpreting his actions involves separating out political motivation from religious, while recognizing that often the two ran together, and inseparably.[16] His liberalism meant that, even if he had not had occasion to engage theologically with other faiths, he had long since been exercised by the issue of racial discrimination. At the assembly of the World Council of Churches at Evanston, Illinois, in 1954, he had noted the visible struggles of conscience in a delegate from the Dutch Reformed Church over apartheid, and the situation in South Africa was to exercise him throughout his time as archbishop.[17]

Equally important was the religious element in Ramsey's family background. Unlike many of his predecessors, Ramsey was not a son of the established Church, but had grown up within Congregationalism, a background which gave him an acute sensitivity to

---

[14] London, LPL, Ramsey Papers, vol. 169, fols 243–4, typescript of speech given at a dinner connected with the event on 6 November 1969. The Ramsey Papers are cited by kind permission of the Librarian of Lambeth Palace.

[15] Michael Ramsey, 'Gandhi', in idem, *Canterbury Pilgrim* (London, 1974), at 137–8.

[16] Owen Chadwick, *Ramsey*, 18–21.

[17] Michael Ramsey, 'Evanston', in idem, *Durham Essays and Addresses* (London, 1956), 81–4, at 83; see also Webster, *Ramsey*, ch. 5.

the position of the religious minority in a hostile environment.[18] The history of British Nonconformity had much to teach those seeking to understand the position of the non-Christian faiths in a changed Britain. Finally, Ramsey's interventions were in no small part motivated by a simple Christian compassion; the same compassion that he felt for homosexual men vulnerable to blackmail by dint of their criminality under the law at that time, or for couples in damaging marriages that could not be dissolved without the services of a pliant chambermaid.[19]

There was an older strain of inter-faith endeavour which lacked the rigour and realism of Cragg or Chadwick, and which Ramsey knew was a dead end. Ramsey was approached for an interview by the World Fellowship of Religions, but the advice of his Council on Foreign Relations was that the organization was dubious, and so the invitation was politely declined.[20] Rather more respectable was the World Congress of Faiths, which counted as its president Edward Carpenter, later dean of Westminster.[21] Ramsey nonetheless refused invitations to services and meetings held under its auspices, citing a basic disagreement with the approach: 'I do not believe that "religion" is a kind of banner under which we should all unite as if it contained the essence of what is good versus "irreligion" as its opposite.'[22]

There was also an attempt to create a national Council of Faiths, mirroring the British Council of Churches, and it was the Oxford philosopher Michael Dummett, himself a Roman Catholic, who contacted Ramsey about this in 1967. In a secularized context, Dummett argued, the threat to any one faith was not conversion from one to another, but unbelief. Muslim, Hindu and Sikh

---

[18] I am indebted to Clyde Binfield for discussions on this point; see also Peter Webster, 'Archbishop Michael Ramsey and Evangelicals in the Church of England', in Andrew Atherstone and John Maiden, eds, *Evangelicalism and the Church of England in the Twentieth Century: Reform, Resistance and Renewal* (Woodbridge, 2014), 162–82, at 170–2.

[19] On Ramsey's involvement in efforts to reform the various elements of the moral law, see Webster, *Ramsey*; Owen Chadwick, *Ramsey*, 145–7, 150.

[20] Ramsey Papers, vol. 90, fol. 40, William Theobald Frary von Blomberg to Ramsey, 5 October 1965; ibid., fol. 45, John Satterthwaite to Robert Beloe (Ramsey's lay secretary), 11 October 1965. The Council for Foreign Relations was the department at Lambeth charged with handling relationships with overseas Churches, and with religious affairs in other countries more generally.

[21] Alan Webster, obituary of Carpenter, *Independent*, 28 August 1998.

[22] Ramsey to Carpenter, late 1969, quoted by Owen Chadwick, *Ramsey*, 407.

arrivals from the Commonwealth were particularly vulnerable to losing their historic faith as they sought to integrate, and so it was in the interest of all the faiths to support each other against a common enemy.[23] Ramsey thought the idea of securing the official support of the Churches nationally to be hopelessly unrealistic, and favoured local cooperation on matters of integration, and joint study and exchange of ideas.[24]

There were some matters on which the religions could unite. February 1968 saw a remarkable joint statement on the war in Vietnam, initiated by the British Council of Churches and signed by Ramsey and John Heenan, cardinal archbishop of Westminster, along with the chief rabbi Immanuel Jakobovits and the president of the Friends of the Western Buddhist Order. It called for an end to the 'intolerable suffering [of] the people of Vietnam' and for religious people both to pray for peace and to give aid.[25] This matched the mood of the Lambeth Conference in July and August of the same year, which asked Ramsey to look into the possibility of a conference of world faith leaders 'at which in concert they would speak in the interests of humanity on behalf of world peace'.[26]

As well as this type of joint humanitarian action, there were troubled parts of the world where Ramsey had a more direct interest as head of the Anglican Communion. In 1967 civil war in Nigeria led to its disintegration into a Muslim majority north and a mostly Christian east; the latter seceded and renamed itself Biafra, but the Labour government of Harold Wilson continued to arm Nigeria's federal government. Faced with incredulity in Biafra that the archbishop of Canterbury had not prevented the British government aiding the wrong side in an apparently religious war, Ramsey spoke against the supply of arms in the House of Lords, tried to promote fundraising for aid, and sent delegations to both sides to intercede.[27] Another failed state in which Anglicans were at risk was Sudan, which in 1965 collapsed into civil war between Muslim north and partly Christian south, cutting off the Chris-

---

[23] Ramsey Papers, vol. 134, fols 281–3, Dummett to Ramsey, 1 January 1968.
[24] Ibid., fols 279–80, Ramsey to Dummett, 31 January 1968.
[25] Ibid., vol. 148, fol. 161, appeal dated 13 February 1968.
[26] *Lambeth Conference 1968*, 31.
[27] Owen Chadwick, *Ramsey*, 250–5.

tians in the south from their bishop in Khartoum. Ramsey met with the Sudanese ambassador to London and spoke out against the 'terrible and relentless persecution of Christians'.[28] Ramsey had often intervened internationally on the side of peace, but in these cases the balance was hard to strike between seeking to be on one hand a disinterested peacemaker and on the other the confidant of religious leaders on one side of the conflict.

Perhaps the faith which had made least impression on the British consciousness at this point was Buddhism. Since few of the immigrants to Britain were Buddhists, contact with them remained always as with visitors from overseas, and retained a touch of the exotic. George Appleton, rector of St Botolph, Aldgate, had a particular association with British and international Buddhism, formed during two decades' work in Burma, and it was he who accompanied a delegation of Burmese Buddhists to Lambeth Palace in 1961 at the behest of the British Council.[29] The group had met with Lord Lansdowne at the Foreign Office to discuss the religious situation in China and Burma, and with Ramsey they spoke and strolled in the palace gardens.[30]

If there was some contact between Anglican and Muslim in other countries, there was in Ramsey's time little direct contact in Britain at national level. David Feldman has highlighted the solidifying effect that the establishment of 'usual channels' tended to have on internal politics within faith communities.[31] However, there was little in the way of such national representative bodies for British Muslims, and it was through such channels that inter-faith diplomacy tended to be conducted. In the later sixties, the preponderant community amongst immigrants from south Asia

[28] Owen Chadwick, *Ramsey*, 267–71.

[29] Appleton had been a missionary with the Society for the Propagation of the Gospel (which in 1965 became the United Society for the Propagation of the Gospel) and then archdeacon of Rangoon; he was later to be archbishop of Perth and then in Jerusalem: see, *inter alia*, his *The Christian Approach to the Buddhist* (London, 1958).

[30] Ramsey Papers, vol. 4, fol. 244, press release from the Church Information Office about the visit, 2 August 1961; ibid., fols 241–3, typescript memorandum of meeting with Lansdowne.

[31] David Feldman, 'Why the English like Turbans: Multicultural Politics in British History', in *Structures and Transformations in Modern British History: Essays for Gareth Stedman Jones*, ed. David Feldman and Jon Lawrence (Cambridge, 2011), 281–302, at 302; see also, in this volume, John Maiden, '"What could be more Christian than to allow the Sikhs to use it?" Church Redundancy and Minority Religion in Bedford, 1977–8', 399–411.

was that of the Sikhs, making up more than three-quarters of the total, and it was Sikhs who were first to establish national community representation, in the form of Shromani Khalsa Dal UK (The Supreme Body of Sikhs in Britain). The Supreme Body invited Ramsey, as head of the National Committee for Commonwealth Immigrants (of which more below), to address its first national conference, as it began 'to prepare the Sikh Community to integrate properly into this multiracial society … thus making it a healthier and more productive organ of this very adopted country [*sic*]'.[32] Ramsey was otherwise engaged, but hoped that 'this plan will set forward the happiness and welfare of the Sikh community in this country'.[33] Even then, it was not always easy to know with whom the Church should be dealing. In 1969, the lay chaplain to Donald Coggan, archbishop of York, wrote to Lambeth in some confusion as Coggan had been invited to two rival events to mark the quincentenary of Guru Nanak and did not know which was the official one.[34] This particular confusion was resolved through contact between Lambeth and the Community Relations Commission, set up by the Race Relations Act of 1968;[35] but it was certainly easier if Lambeth knew with whom it should work.

One faith connected to Christianity in a unique way, and for which 'usual channels' did exist, was Judaism. The Council of Christians and Jews had been set up in 1942 by a joint initiative involving William Temple.[36] Since that point, the archbishops of Canterbury and York had been joint presidents of the Council, along with the chief rabbi, the moderator of the Church of Scotland and the moderator of the Free Church Federal Council, and Ramsey gladly accepted the role in his turn. Ramsey was also on friendly terms of long standing with Sir Bernard Waley-Cohen, Lord Mayor of London and friend of the Council, whose father Robert had been involved in its inception.[37] Ramsey also sought

---

[32] Ramsey Papers., vol. 145, fol. 213, Joginder Singh Sadhu (president) to Ramsey, 27 July 1968.

[33] Ibid., fol. 214, Ramsey to Sadhu, 30 July 1968.

[34] Ibid., vol. 169, fol. 241, David Blunt to Geoffrey Tiarks, 6 October 1969.

[35] Ibid., fol. 242, Hugh Whitworth to Blunt, 10 October 1969.

[36] Marcus Braybrooke, *Children of One God: A History of the Council of Christians and Jews* (London, 1991), 13–14.

[37] Ramsey Papers, vol. 6, fol. 312, W. W. Simpson (general secretary) to Ramsey, 20 January 1960; Ramsey's reply is at ibid., fol. 313.

to involve representatives of British Jewry in international religio-diplomatic discourse, such as the meeting with the patriarch of Moscow in 1964: the chief rabbi Israel Brodie was invited but was unable to attend.[38]

As the reflexive superiority of English Christians waned with the empire that had engendered it, there were signs of changing attitudes towards the other faiths. In 1962 the London Society for Promoting Christianity amongst the Jews, of which Ramsey was patron, proposed to drop the word 'missions' from the long version of its name in favour of 'ministry', a change which Ramsey supported.[39] Awareness of the Holocaust had set Christians to thinking more seriously about the Christian roots of European anti-Semitism.[40] Ahead of Holy Week 1964, Ramsey was approached by Martin Sullivan, archdeacon of London and in charge of the London Diocesan Council for Christian-Jewish Understanding, who was concerned that the gospel narrative of Good Friday was often presented to the detriment of the Jews. Ramsey responded with a short statement. It could not be right to lay blame upon the Jews, he argued, since the Roman governor had been no less responsible. Ultimately, the crucifixion had been a clash between the love of God and the sinfulness of the whole human race, in which those who crucified him stood as true representatives of all humankind: 'We must all see ourselves judged by the crucifixion of Christ.'[41] The statement caused some concern overseas. Najib Cuba'in, the Arab bishop of Jordan, Lebanon and Syria, feared the consequences for Israel's relations with its Arab neighbours if the West was seen to exonerate the Jews of a responsibility long attributed to them.[42] As the speed at which news could travel increased, statements from the archbishop had repercussions in places and situations far away from Lambeth.

Religious diplomacy of the kind so far examined had been

---

[38] Ibid., vol. 59, fol. 269, Brodie to Ramsey, 23 September 1964.

[39] The proposed change was from 'Church Missions to Jews' to 'Church Ministry to the Jews': ibid., vol.18, fols 104–5, W.A. Curtis (secretary) to Ramsey, 23 May 1962, and Ramsey's reply.

[40] Owen Chadwick, *Ramsey*, 221.

[41] Ramsey Papers, vol. 59, fols 264–5, Ramsey to Sullivan, 18 March 1964. On the reaction, see ibid., fols 266–7. The text is reproduced at Braybrooke, *Children of One God*, 53.

[42] Owen Chadwick, *Ramsey*, 222.

part and parcel of the work of the archbishops for many years, a game with established rules by which it should be played. There were however broader issues of identity at stake, in which conceptions of Englishness in all its racial, cultural and religious aspects interacted with brute economic and social fact in local neighbourhoods. The sixties saw two related series of legislation, one which dismayed liberal opinion and a second which pleased it. Successive Acts, beginning with the Commonwealth Immigrants Act of 1962, limited for the first time the total number of immigrants to Britain and introduced what amounted to a racial qualification for that entry. In parallel, mounting social tension from west London to the west Midlands was the catalyst for legislation to protect the immigrant population from discrimination once they had reached and settled in the UK.[43] Ramsey was in the thick of these matters in a very public way: Cantuar the gentle but insistent prodder of the national conscience.

On the matter of immigration, Ramsey denounced the 1962 Act in the House of Lords in the strongest terms, as both a reneging on historic responsibilities of Britain to its former colonies and an offence against basic Christian belief in the equality of all in the eyes of God.[44] The rapid introduction in 1968 of legislation to deny entry to the UK to Kenyans of Asian descent fleeing the government of Jomo Kenyatta was, for Ramsey, a similar abrogation of national duty, but also threatened to upset the precarious balance of community relations by creating mistrust amongst the immigrant communities behind whom it was intended that the door be shut.[45]

Not all interventions by peers in the House of Lords are based on first-hand experience of the issues involved; but Ramsey had just such experience. Prime Minister Wilson had asked Ramsey to chair the new National Committee for Commonwealth Immigrants (NCCI), set up by the government to monitor the situation of immigrants in the UK.[46] The NCCI was for some an unwarranted interference with the right of Englishmen to discriminate

---

[43] Layton-Henry, *Politics of Immigration*, 51–6, 71–6.
[44] *House of Lords Debates*, vol. 238, cols 25–6, 12 March 1962.
[45] Ramsey, 'Kenya Asians', in *Canterbury Pilgrim*, 148–52, at 150.
[46] Owen Chadwick, *Ramsey*, 166–76.

against the outsider as they pleased, while for others – including Ramsey – it was nothing like as powerful as it needed to be.

One element of Ramsey's work with the NCCI was its collaboration with an attempt to outlaw discrimination on religious grounds. In 1966 the Labour peer Fenner Brockway introduced a Racial and Religious Discrimination Bill, which sought to extend the general principle of the 1965 Race Relations Act to close a possible loophole, in the words of the bishop of Winchester, 'for those who might claim that they are ready to serve coloured people but are not ready to serve Hindus, Moslems or Sikhs'. Amending the 1965 Act in this way was essential, the bishop continued, to protect the Jews 'as a religious, rather than as a racial group' and because 'religious discrimination is as unjustified in principle as racial discrimination'.[47] The NCCI had been through the bill clause by clause, but Ramsey himself was not able to be present in the Lords to debate it, although he had wished to.[48] It failed at second reading, although it was supported by the bishops of Winchester, Truro and Southwark; but the process shows the Church of England using its position to act on behalf not only of other Christian groups, but of other faiths.

At a local level, the archbishops were often in demand to make visits and to cut ribbons on new buildings. In 1968 Ramsey declined an invitation to open a new gurdwara at Gravesend (in his own diocese), as he was otherwise engaged, but he did visit the Hindu temple at Golders Green in 1970.[49] However, he had gained a reputation as a friend of the minority, which made him the subject of direct appeals for help in specific situations. He was approached by the Ealing Community Relations Council on behalf of the Muslim community of Greenford, outraged not only at the levelling of Muslim graves in Greenford cemetery but at the brusque response of Ealing Borough Council to their complaint.[50] In 1969 Michael Dummett called on him to intervene in the then public dispute regarding discrimination over the wearing by Sikhs of turbans and beards while working for Wolver-

---

[47] *House of Lords Debates*, vol. 278, cols 1855, 1857, 19 December 1966.

[48] Ramsey Papers, vol. 104, fol. 272, Beloe to Brockway, 16 December 1966.

[49] Ibid., vol. 145, fol. 218, Ramsey to Charles Revis, 24 September 1968; Owen Chadwick, *Ramsey*, 407.

[50] Ramsey Papers, vol. 277, fol. 215, memorandum from Hugh Whitworth, 23 April 1974.

hampton Transport. No other religious leader had acted publicly, and for Dummett it was time for Ramsey to 'speak out loudly and clearly on this issue'.[51] Some such approaches came from local religious communities themselves. Ramsey was asked by a Sikh leader from Amritsar to intervene with Hammersmith Borough Council in 1967 in a dispute over the siting of a new gurdwara in the borough, over which there were injured feelings.[52] In none of these particular cases did Ramsey allow himself to become involved, but together they indicate the degree to which he as archbishop was viewed as an honest broker in difficult matters, and as a friend of the minority, whether Christian or not.

In the summer of 1968 the Conservative cabinet minister Enoch Powell made an infamous speech to a party meeting in Wolverhampton, now commonly known as the 'rivers of blood' speech. In it he accused all the elites in the UK of sleepwalking into disaster, as uncontrolled immigration led to the gradual dilution and extinction of the native English. To what extent could the Church of England, and Ramsey in particular, be held culpable as the nation engaged, in Powell's phrase, in 'heaping up its own funeral pyre'?[53] It was not only Powell who thought that the Church should have accommodated less, and resisted more, the process of assimilation of aliens in culture, language and religion. Ramsey was under police protection for a time in June 1968, in the aftermath of Powell's speech. In September supporters of the National Front marched to Lambeth, and others disrupted a meeting in a church in Essex in December, at which Ramsey spoke, with cries of 'Traitor!'[54] There was also limited but notable support amongst Anglican clergy and more widely amongst laity for a view of Britishness in which both whiteness and Christian religion were key. For those who held this view, Ramsey represented precisely the dangerous liberalizing tide that had moved the established Church away from its 'traditional' role in supporting such a view of Britishness.[55]

---

[51] Ibid., vol. 169, fols 238–9, Michael Dummett to Ramsey, 9 April 1969. On the affair, see Feldman, 'Why the English like Turbans', 281–2.

[52] Ramsey Papers, vol.121, fol. 260, Beloe to Sant Fateh Singh, 17 April 1967.

[53] Roy Lewis, *Enoch Powell* (London, 1979), 105–9.

[54] Owen Chadwick, *Ramsey*, 174–6.

[55] Paul Jackson, 'Extremes of Faith and Nation: British Fascism and Christianity', *Religion Compass* 4 (2010), 507–27, esp. 513–16; Owen Chadwick, *Ramsey*, 167.

By and large Ramsey was not much exercised by apparent symbolic defeats for the established Church in relation to other faiths. Andrew Chandler has documented the case of St Mary, Savile Town, a chapel of ease in Dewsbury in the diocese of Wakefield, in which local Christian and Muslim communities, along with the diocese and the national Church, wrestled with the prospect of allowing a redundant building to be taken over for Muslim use.[56] Ramsey intervened through the Church Commissioners, in whose hands the decision lay, to allow such a use, as opposed to demolition. 'I should regret the making of a contrary decision', he wrote, 'having regard to the whole missionary situation in this country and overseas'.[57]

This phrase is the key to understanding Ramsey's view of the changing position of the Church of England. He knew that Christian minorities overseas found their freedom to worship under pressure from governments which conceived of national identity as religious in character. The safety and peace of Anglicans elsewhere was partly dependent on how the established Church in a Christian nation dealt with its own religious minorities. And the situation in the UK was a missionary one too, no longer one in which an easy congruence of Church, nation and people could be assumed, as some were wont to do, particularly when confronted with the fact of Britons adhering to other faiths.

Feldman has recently described the recurrence of a conservative pluralism in British history: a form of adaptation that created space for religious minorities within the British and imperial polity which was at the same time structurally conservative and which 'buttresses the position of an otherwise beleaguered Anglican establishment'.[58] Whilst this was the effect of Ramsey's work, he would have articulated its purpose in rather more positive terms. Ramsey oversaw the freeing of the Church of England from parliamentary control of its worship and doctrine, and the decisive separation of the moral law from Christian discipline, with regard

---

[56] Andrew Chandler, *The Church of England in the Twentieth Century: The Church Commissioners and the Politics of Reform, 1948–1998* (Woodbridge, 2006), 231–9; see also Maiden, 'Church Redundancy and Minority Religion'.

[57] Ramsey Papers, vol. 210, fol. 47, Ramsey to Kenneth Ryle, 14 October 1971.

[58] Feldman, 'Why the English like Turbans', 302; see also idem, 'Conservative Pluralism and the Politics of Multiculturalism', in Yuval-Davis and Marfleet, eds, *Secularism*, 10–12.

to divorce, abortion and homosexuality, amongst other matters. He did what he could to support the civil rights of religious minorities, and to aid constructive religious dialogue that was at the same time realistic about the real claims to uniqueness and finality of each faith. Without quite being a programme of work, all this had a coherence. The Church of England was, in its own eyes if not in law, becoming less established and more national; a Church less bound to the state but retaining a national dimension in its sense of its own mission. This strongly implied a more equal partnership with other Christian Churches, but also that the Church of England needed to act, in an embryonic but significant way, as a defender of faith.

Chichester

'WHAT COULD BE MORE CHRISTIAN THAN TO ALLOW THE SIKHS TO USE IT?' CHURCH REDUNDANCY AND MINORITY RELIGION IN BEDFORD, 1977–8

by JOHN MAIDEN

In 1985, *Faith in the City*, the Church of England's report on Urban Priority Areas, commented that Christians frequently had an excess of church buildings, while 'people of other faiths are often exceedingly short of places in which to meet and worship'.[1] The challenge of securing sacred space has been common to migrant groups in Britain,[2] and during the 1970s sharing of space between national historic denominations and migrant religious groups was identified by the British Council of Churches (BCC) and its Community and Race Relations Unit as a leading issue for interreligious relations.[3] In the case of the Church of England, ancillary parish buildings were occasionally shared with non-Christian religious congregations for limited use: for example, later that decade the church halls of All Saints, Gravelly Hill, Birmingham, were being used by Muslims and Hindus for festivals and clubs.[4] Furthermore, buildings were sometimes shared with, or sold to, the emerging 'Black-led' Christian congregations, particularly in London and Birmingham.[5]

However, the Church of England was not of one mind on transferring redundant consecrated church buildings, formerly used for worship, to non-Christian religious groups. A handful of local cases brought the issue of church redundancy and religious plurality sharply into focus. Andrew Chandler's important account of the unsuccessful attempt to transfer St Mary's, Savile Town, Dewsbury, to Muslims in 1972 has demonstrated the controversial nature of

---

[1]   *Faith in the City: a Call for Action by Church and Nation* (London, 1985), 145.

[2]   See, for example, Humayun Ansari, ed., *The Making of the East London Mosque, 1910–1951*, Camden 5th ser. 38 (Cambridge, 2011).

[3]   See, for example, *The Community Orientation of the Church* (London, 1974).

[4]   Gillian Carver, *A Place to Meet: The Use of Church Property and the New Religious Minorities in Britain* (London, 1978), 29–31.

[5]   *Building Together in Christ: A Report on the Sharing and Transfer of Church Buildings: The Joint Working Party between White-led and Black-led Churches* (London, 1979).

the issue.[6] This essay examines the rather different specificities of another case – St Leonard's, Bedford, five years later. Highlighting the relevance of the themes of theology, community relations and diaspora in the decision making of the Church Commissioners, it explores the relationship between a local controversy and a wider debate in the Church.

CONTEXT AND BACKGROUND

The BCC took a leading role in the Christian response to religious plurality and in 1971 set up a working party on the use of church properties in 'multi-racial' areas. The following year, an interim report included the recommendation that redundant churches 'should be made available on appropriate terms to those of other Faiths for any purpose for which they may require them'.[7] This was highly contentious, probably most of all in the Church of England. The Church Commissioners' Redundant Churches Committee (RCC) was agreed that redundant buildings could be purchased by Christian groups (provided that they were either members of, associated with, or aspiring to become members of the World Council of Churches), but sales to non-Christian religious groups were recognized as problematic. In 1971, the Redundant Churches Uses Committee of the diocese of Wakefield approved the conversion of St Mary's, Savile Town, Dewsbury, to a mosque, a proposal which the RCC investigated, and which became a high-profile 'test case'. There was serious controversy locally, seemingly accompanied at times by a whiff of 'racial' politics.[8] General Synod also debated the issue, but was completely divided: J. N. D. Anderson, a leading evangelical layman and Professor of Oriental Laws at the University of London, expressed the view that such sales 'could only give rise to the wishy-washy idea that the two faiths were alternative ways to God', while the Revd I. Smith-Cameron asserted that the Church had 'the opportunity to show the width

---

[6]   Andrew Chandler, *The Church of England in the Twentieth Century: The Church Commissioners and the Politics of Reform, 1948–1998* (Woodbridge, 2006), 231–9. On the case, see, in this volume, Peter Webster, 'Race, Religion and National Identity in Sixties Britain: Michael Ramsey, Archbishop of Canterbury, and his Encounter with other Faiths', 385–98, esp. 396–7.

[7]   *The Use of Church Properties for Community Activities in Multi-Racial Areas* (London, 1972), §56.

[8]   Chandler, *Church of England*, 236–8.

of its charity'.[9] The controversy concluded the following year when it was decided to demolish the church, but no clear policy on redundancy and non-Christian religious groups had emerged.

During the course of the controversy, various positions on the matter became clear. Some Christians perceived a 'lowering the flag' of Christianity, or were particularly sensitive to the holiness of consecrated buildings; in the Church of England, although the Pastoral Measure of 1968 legitimized the sale of consecrated buildings for other uses, sales to a non-Christian group raised special dilemmas. Other Christians related the quality of holiness to people rather than buildings, or were more sensitive to the colonial past, or defended what they saw as practical 'loving service' towards the non-Christian neighbour.[10] Amongst the most articulate presentations of the case 'for' came from the Revd Canon Douglas Webster of the Church Missionary Society, who argued: 'The effectiveness of the Christian mission rests on the truth of the Christian Gospel, not on privileges for the Church or on restriction of its opponents.' He added: 'Two things need to be remembered. The Gospel was launched in a highly competitive world (from a religious point of view); the truth needs proclaiming rather than protecting.'[11] Generally speaking, Free Church denominations seemed less troubled by the issue than the Anglicans. At least two Methodist chapels had been sold to Muslim groups by 1972, one in Purlwell, close to St Mary's, Savile Town;[12] by 1978 seven redundant Nonconformist churches had been sold to Sikh groups in Birmingham alone.[13] Such cooperation, a BCC report asserted, could be of 'great value in building racial and religious harmony', but it recognized that '[d]ifficulties have been experienced in the Church of England when what is in question is the sale of a church, which has been consecrated and used for Christian worship, to members of other

---

9   Ibid. 238; London, LPL, Ramsey Papers, vol. 236, fol. 177, 'Muslim Offer splits Church', *Guardian*, 10 July 1972. The papers of Archbishops Ramsey and Coggan are used with permission of the Trustees of Lambeth Palace Library.

10   See *Community Orientation of the Church*, Appendix B.

11   London, Church of England Record Centre, British Council of Churches papers, Division of Community Affairs, Community and Race Relations Unit, 7/4/7, Douglas Webster, 'Should a redundant Church be disposed of to People of another Faith?', March 1972.

12   Chandler, *Church of England*, 238.

13   Carver, *A Place to Meet*, 23.

faiths', although it underlined that the Church Commissioners did not 'rule out' the sale of a redundant church.[14]

The next Anglican 'test case' occurred in Bedford in 1977, five years after the St Mary's episode. In 1975 the benefices and parishes of St John and St Leonard, Bedford had been united. The St Leonard's church building, erected only in 1913, and now in an area where an estimated 60 per cent of the population were immigrants, was declared redundant. In 1976, St John's, a church of a conservative evangelical flavour,[15] began to use the St Leonard's church hall as a mission base to evangelize the local immigrant population. With the assistance of Operation Mobilisation, an inter-denominational evangelical mission agency, they had undertaken at least two visits to every home in the area.[16] The hall became a venue for a multiracial Sunday school which appears to have attracted Sikh children.[17] The expansion of such missionary activity may have been a reason behind the ending of the Ramgarhia Sikh Society's tenancy of the church hall in 1976.[18] This society had been formed in 1969 and was made up of around 350 Sikhs, mostly from East Africa. On leaving St Leonard's, they began to use a local house as a temple instead, but shortly afterwards made a bid to the diocese for the main St Leonard's sanctuary building. Their confidence was perhaps enhanced by the recent sale of a Methodist chapel to another Sikh group in Bedford.[19] A previous bid by the Regional Health Authority had apparently received serious consideration, but negotiations had not been concluded, and the diocesan hierarchy felt some sense of moral obligation towards the Ramgarhias. The Bedford Deanery Synod debated the sale of the building, voting by 40 votes to 7 in favour of a motion which

[14] Ibid. 28.

[15] The incumbent, the Revd D. F. Strong, appeared on the list of council members for the Protestant Truth Society in 1975–6: Protestant Truth Society, *Annual Report 1975–76* (London, 1976).

[16] Redundant Churches Committee Agenda and Papers [hereafter: RCCAP], part 15, RC (78) 100, Annex A, 8. All Church Commissioners archive material cited in this essay is held at the Church of England Record Centre, Bermondsey, London. The papers of the Church Commissioners are used with their permission.

[17] RCCAP, part 15, RC (78) 100, Annex E, 10.

[18] 'Church Sale is given more Backing', *Bedfordshire Times* [hereafter: *BT*], 7 April 1978, 1.

[19] RCCAP, part 15, RC (78) 100, Annex A, 10.

was interpreted as giving a green light for sale to the Sikhs.[20] The Diocesan Uses Committee, which decided on the future of redundant church buildings in Bedford, recommended the sale of St Leonard's church building to the Ramgarhia Sikh Society.[21]

This was the beginning of a complex and extended process which required the approval of the Church Commissioners' RCC and Board of Governors. The RCC in June 1977 agreed, 'on the basis of their own varied experiences of dealing with Sikhs', in principle to recommend to the board that the church building be sold to Sikhs for religious purposes.[22] The situation was complicated, however, by another bid, by the Guru Nanak Gurdwara, a larger group of 1,200, also in need of a building.[23] The RCC thus felt obliged to delve into local Sikh politics. It did so carefully, concerned lest local disagreement between the Ramgarhias and the Guru Nanak Gurdwara might have repercussions, not only in Bedford but also in Leicester, and indeed in Kenya and the Punjab.[24] The decision was left to the bishop of St Albans, Robert Runcie. He felt obliged to follow the advice of the deanery synod, whom he understood felt a 'moral commitment' to the Ramgarhia Sikhs.[25] However, he also indicated openness to the Guru Nanak Gurdwara suggestion that, if their own bid was rejected, they might be willing to purchase St Leonard's in conjunction with the Ramgarhias. The RCC felt that Runcie's recommendation 'was not very decisive' but agreed to propose a draft redundancy scheme recommending sale to the Ramgarhia Sikhs but also leaving open the possibility of joint purchase and use.[26] The Board of Governors approved the issuing of this scheme for appropriating the church building for use as a Sikh temple by

---

[20]   Ibid., Annex E, 2. Some claimed, however, that the motion did not give clear approval to such a sale.

[21]   RCCAP, part 13, RC (77) 75, S. E. Gray to Bishop Robert Runcie, 11 September 1977, 2–3.

[22]   Minutes of the Church Commissioners' Redundant Churches Committee [hereafter: RCC Minutes], vol. 2 (May 1973 – November 1977), RC (77) 3rd meeting, 8 June 1977, 8.

[23]   Gray to Runcie, 11 September 1977, 2–3.

[24]   RCCAP, part 15, RC (78) 100, Annex E, 2.

[25]   RCCAP, part 13, RC (77) 75, Bishop Robert Runcie to S. E. Gray, 3 November 1977, 4.

[26]   RCC Minutes, vol. 3 (October 1977 – June 1981), RC (77) 5th meeting, 15 November 1977, 7; ibid., RC (78) 3rd meeting, 10 May 1978, 8.

10 votes to 3.[27] The RCC now entered a period of consultation with local groups. Two issues were central: should St Leonard's be sold for non-Christian worship; and, if so, to which Sikh group?

THEOLOGY, COMMUNITY AND DIASPORAS

On the publication of the draft scheme, the *Bedfordshire Times* reported: 'The plan to sell St Leonard's Church to the Sikhs has sparked off strong reactions both for and against.'[28] The consultation phase brought a range of issues for the RCC to negotiate, centring around four main themes: theology, Christian identity and community relations, local politics of the Sikh diaspora, and relations between Indian Christians and Sikhs.

Questions of theology figured largely in the debate, with the broad argument 'for' based on the idea of Christian neighbourliness. The Revd Christopher Hamel Cooke, vicar of St Andrew's, Bedford, asked: 'What could be more Christian than to allow the Sikhs to use it?'[29] Another vicar even suggested that to demolish the redundant church, and so prevent or hinder non-Christian worship, was a form of religious persecution.[30] Robert Runcie argued that the sale was 'an act of charity',[31] but rejected the accusation of theological relativism, as offering the building 'did not mean that their beliefs were accepted'.[32] The wider context was one of increasing openness towards theological dialogue with other faiths, with the inauguration of the World Council of Churches Dialogue with People of Living Faiths and Ideologies sub-unit (1971) and the appointment of the Archbishops' Consultants on Inter-faith Relations (1975).[33]

The opposing arguments came largely from the local and national evangelical constituency. The parish of St John and St Leonard was regarded by Bishop Runcie as strong on 'the Gospel' and 'conversion', and had a 'stronger sense of the "Gathered Church" than

[27] Ibid., RC (78) 1st meeting, 14 March 1978, 5.
[28] 'To Sell or Not to Sell', *BT*, 31 March 1978, 5.
[29] Ibid.
[30] RCCAP, part 15, RC (78) 100, Annex E, 4.
[31] 'To Sell or Not to Sell'.
[32] RCC Minutes, vol. 3, RC (78) 8th meeting, 13 December 1978, 3–6.
[33] On this, see Douglas Pratt, *The Church and other Faiths: The World Council of Churches, the Vatican and Interreligious Dialogue* (Bern, 2010), 63; John Wolffe, 'How Many Ways to God? Christians and Religious Pluralism', in Gerald Parsons, ed., *The Growth of Religious Diversity: Britain from 1945*, 2: *Issues* (London, 1994), 23–53, at 38–40.

of a "Body of Christ" theology'.[34] The vice-chairman of the St John's and St Leonard's Parochial Church Council (PCC) reported opposition to the sale on the grounds that it would not further the re-establishing of Christian witness to the area.[35] According to the RCC, many parishioners regarded the draft scheme as ill-conceived, and resisted the sale because they were 'fundamentally opposed to the spirit of syncretism' and the sale of a church, dedicated to Christ, to non-Christians.[36]

Similar attitudes were expressed in the local press: 'Does the Church of England hierarchy take seriously the idea of Christ as being the one mediator?' enquired one of many similar letters.[37] This response, driven by exclusivist ideas of salvation, was echoed by conservative Evangelicals more widely. One outburst in the Calvinistic *English Churchman* condemned the Church Commissioners for selling St Leonard's 'for the worship of devils!'[38] More tempered national evangelical responses, such as those by Norman Anderson, contended that the sale would undermine the uniqueness of Christ and missionary activity in his name.[39]

The boundaries of theology sometimes blurred with wider concerns over Christian identity, and these, along with the practice of evangelism, touched on issues of community and 'race' relations. The Bedford Community Relations Association and the Bedford Society believed the sale would foster stronger community relations.[40] The RCC took from a conversation with one local official that their decision 'would be an important precedent in the field of community relations' as there 'would be disappointment, discouragement and frustration if the redundant church was not sold to another faith. Conversely, it would be a great encouragement that such foreign groups were not regarded as second-class citizens.'[41] Those against the sale tended to distance themselves very definitely from any racial prejudice: One PCC member stressed: 'We

---

34 RCC Minutes, vol. 3, RC (78) 8th meeting, 13 December 1978, 4.

35 'Objections flood in over Sale of Church', *BT*, 28 April 1978, 3.

36 RCCAP, part 15, RC (78) 100, Annex E, 5.

37 'Letters to the Editor', *BT*, 7 April 1978, 6.

38 'Redundant Churches', *English Churchman*, 5–12 May 1978, 2.

39 RCCAP, part 15, RC (78) 100, Annex E, 6. The evangelical Church Society also opposed the sale: 'Notes and Comments', *English Churchman*, 5–12 May 1978, 4.

40 'Church Sale is given more Backing'; RCCAP, part 15, RC (78) 100, Annex E, 4.

41 Ibid. 10.

have good relations with both groups of Sikhs and they appreciate our situation. We have every sympathy with them',[42] while one long-standing member of St Leonard's explained in the local press that she had cordial relations with Sikhs and was 'not against their colour'.[43] Coggan's estimate was that the views being expressed by local Anglicans seemed 'responsible'.[44]

Some local discourse reflected a concern for local Christian hegemony. 'May it never be said of John Bunyan's own town', declared the former St Leonard's organist, 'that, in this year 1978, a Christian Church … was sold to unbelievers. Where, I ask, is Progress.'[45] 'It is a sure sign of defeat', argued another, 'when the faith of our ancestors is renounced in this way by handing over our centres of worship.'[46] However, the Anglican deanery chaplain, the Revd Ted Nadkarni, believed that the sale would ultimately improve community relations, although he admitted that 'some English people would feel bewildered and perhaps resentful that the church might be sold to an ethnic minority'.[47] The RCC did not have to deal with some of the racial tensions seemingly evident in the case of St Mary's, Savile Town, where there were allegations that Muslims sacrificed chickens and 'delighted in appearing to outwit authority or the local residents'.[48] However, in a sensitive political climate, both locally and nationally, it was difficult for the RCC to deal with concerns regarding Christian privilege discretely from wider concerns about community and race relations.

The controversy also brought into sharp relief the heterogeneity of the Sikh diaspora in Bedford. The offer from the Guru Nanak Gurdwara, and the possibility of joint usage, made the matter more complex. The chairman of the RCC informed Coggan that it would be 'necessary to try to evaluate the relative claims of the two groups to the church'.[49] In the course of the consulta-

[42] 'Objections flood in over Sale of Church'.

[43] 'To Sell or Not to Sell'.

[44] Coggan Papers, vol. 73, fol. 100, Coggan to Betty Ridley, 18 April 1978.

[45] 'Church Sale: Ten-Day Deadline for Protest', *BT*, 14 April 1978, 6.

[46] 'Letters to the Editor'.

[47] 'Sikhs Church should be for "worship not a squash centre"', *BT*, 14 April 1978, 14.

[48] RCC report, quoted in Chandler, *Church of England*, 238.

[49] Coggan Papers, vol. 73, fols 102–3, William Harris to Coggan, 20 April 1978.

tion, the issue of caste – and which group might be the most 'inclusive' – entered discussions.[50] It appears that the Community Relations Officer attempted to broker a meeting between the groups regarding possible joint use, but was unable to bring them together.[51] There was disagreement in local newspapers regarding the perceived characteristics of Ramgarhia Sikhism. Some asserted that the Ramgarhias were based on an old caste system 'fundamentally against the principles of Sikhism', and expressed alarm that an 'exclusive minority' were to take ownership of the building.[52] One prominent Ramgarhia Sikh would later deny this strongly, asserting that they 'deplore[d] the caste system' and 'very strongly believe[d] in the unity of Sikh organisations'.[53] Ultimately no agreement based on joint use or ownership was reached, although the bishop of St Albans later reminded the RCC that if the Sikhs lacked unity, so too did Anglicans![54]

The politics of diaspora brought additional complications. An Asian Christian Fellowship numbering nearly one hundred members, mostly from North India, was a regular user of St Leonard's church hall. Their robust response to the proposed sale of the adjacent main building to Sikhs was based on a strong sense of Christ's uniqueness and a theology of consecrated space.[55] The RCC report noted their amazement that 'British Christians, who have sent missionaries to India, could so readily aid and encourage the propagation of a non-Christian philosophy in a building solemnly consecrated for Christian worship'.[56] 'Church', wrote one Indian Christian in the *Bedfordshire Times*, 'means the body of Christ and when we dedicate a building as a church, that means it is the body of Christ. If we are to sell it to the gentiles that means we are taking the place of Judas Iscariot.'[57] Such concerns, and also what appears to have been a sense of betrayal, were partly

[50]   RCCAP, part 15, RC (78) 100, Annex E, 2.
[51]   'Church Sale is given more Backing'; Sikh Groups in Deadlock over Church Sale', *BT*, 21 April 1978, 17.
[52]   'Church Sale: Ten-Day Deadline'. The background of the authors of these letters – and whether or not they had any association with the Guru Nanak Gurdwara – is unknown and should not be assumed.
[53]   'Temples are open to All', *BT*, 5 May 1978, 6.
[54]   RCC Minutes, vol. 3, RC (78) 8th meeting, 13 December 1978, 4.
[55]   RCCAP, part 15, RC (78) 100, Annex E, 7–8.
[56]   Ibid. 5.
[57]   'Church Sale: Ten-Day Deadline'.

shaped by perceptions of ongoing religious rivalries in North India, and anxiety that the sale would undermine the activities of Christian missionaries. 'To the westerner', the RCC reported, 'such a proposal might be viewed with cool logic, but to the Asian Christian they were issues of burning relevance to his beliefs.'[58] There was sympathy amongst others in the locality for such arguments, with one letter claiming the proposal was not 'an exercise in community relations' but 'a direct kick in the teeth to those many Christian missionaries who have and are spending a lifetime in privation and hardship in Indian and other lands in order to spread the word of Christ'.[59]

The RCC took the anxieties of the Asian Christians seriously. They contacted the India Secretary of the BCC, who shared the view that Punjabi Christians in Pakistan, especially, were a 'frightened and very defensive group' and suggested that '[t]here would probably be a considerable amount of bewilderment on the part of many Christians in the Punjab' over a decision to sell to another religion, confirming also that it would receive publicity in the region. However, the secretary also argued that Indian Christians 'who had visited England and knew the situation here' would react less strongly.[60] Bishop Runcie confessed concern over the 'loss of face that a sale to the Sikhs would entail' for the Asian Christians, although he felt repercussions in the Indian sub-continent would not be severe.[61] The presence of this Christian diaspora complicated the decision faced by the Church.

At a meeting in December 1978 the RCC came together to discuss the consultation, with Bishop Runcie invited. Before his arrival, it had been commented that the case had taken on 'wide-ranging public relations aspects' and that either way 'disappointment was going to be felt and criticism levelled at the Commissioners'.[62] The bishop justified the principle of the sale, commenting on the monotheism of Sikhism, remarking that the religion was 'egalitarian in ideal if not in practice', and asserting that a Sikh temple was a holy place. Quoting Archbishop Ramsey, he said: 'There is

---

[58] RCCAP, part 15, RC (78) 100, Annex E, 6.
[59] 'Church sale: Ten-Day Deadline'.
[60] RCCAP, part 15, RC (78) 100, Annex E, 11.
[61] RCC Minutes, vol. 3, RC (78) 8th meeting, 13 December 1978, 4.
[62] Ibid. 3.

not all darkness in such faiths. There is a light which Christ is the completion and fulfilment of.'[63] While he admitted that opposition within the parish was 'very powerful', he asserted that the central problem was the position of the Asian Christians, who he admitted made him 'most undecided'. Nevertheless, he advised selling to the Sikhs.[64] The RCC voted 5–4 in favour, recommending to the Board of Governors of the Church Commissioners that the Ramgarhia offer should be accepted.[65] However, the levels of controversy surrounding the case were now considerable, not only locally but nationally – ninety letters against the sale had been received from around the country and a question had been raised in the House of Laity earlier that year.[66] When the Board of Governors took a deciding vote in December, they rejected Sikh use of the building by 13 votes to 10.[67] Their statement made reference to the view that 'use of the building would seriously hinder the work of the Christians in the parish and also be particularly hurtful to the local Christian Asians who worship in the adjacent hall'.[68] While the vice-chairman of the PCC had previously suggested that selling to the Regional Health Authority 'would be a good way to meet the needs of the whole community',[69] in subsequent months, the diocese, following consultation with the PCC, agreed to keep the building open in the expectation that in three or four years' time it might be used once again for parochial purposes.[70] Some years later it was destroyed by fire, although the church hall remains in use for worship by the parish of St John's and St Leonard's today.

CONCLUSION

In his discussion of the Church of England and 'multiculturalism', David Feldman convincingly characterizes the national Church as an institution broadly inclined towards a pragmatic accommo-

---

[63] Ramsey expressed such views at the commemoration of Gandhi at St Paul's Cathedral in 1969: Michael Ramsey, 'Gandhi', in idem, *Canterbury Pilgrim* (London, 1974), 137–8.

[64] RCC Minutes, vol. 3, RC (78) 8th meeting, 13 December 1978, 4.

[65] Ibid. 6.

[66] RCCAP, part 15, RC (78) 100, Annex E, 3.

[67] RCC Minutes, vol. 3, RC (79) 1st meeting, 7 February 1979, 1.

[68] Coggan Papers, vol. 73, fol. 106, 'Statement concerning the Commissioners' Decision on Draft Redundancy Scheme'.

[69] 'Objections Flood in over Sale of Church'.

[70] RCC Minutes, vol. 3, RC (79) 2nd meeting, 14 March 1979, 3.

dation of minority religious groups, for example in education.[71] The case of St Leonard's further illustrates the inclination towards accommodation on the part of many within the Church. However, it also demonstrates the extent to which controversial and complex considerations could arise where matters of religious plurality were concerned. As described earlier, religious policymakers during the 1970s realized that the negotiation of sacred space was a vital aspect of interreligious relations. While the case of St Leonard's had its own unique circumstances, it exhibited a range of issues bound up with the question of the sale of church buildings to religious minorities. The decision facing the Church Commissioners was complicated by conflicting theologies of pluralism and consecrated space within the Church; tension between notions of Christian hegemony and community and 'race' relations; differences within heterogeneous religious communities, which the Church might need to adjudicate; and the international dimensions of local controversies.

The case of St Leonard's did not bring clarity in the Church of England regarding the sale of redundant churches to minority non-Christian religions. When the archdeacon of St Albans tabled a question for General Synod on whether the commissioners' decision – made in spite of diocesan and deanery recommendations – meant that such sales should not be pursued in principle, the RCC resolved to reply that the situation had 'been reached in the circumstances of the particular case and should not be regarded as one of general application'.[72] In 1983, the Church Commissioners agreed to sell St Luke's, Southampton, to a Sikh group.[73] In this case, there was far less local controversy, and the sale had a respected, vocal theological proponent in the form of John Taylor, bishop of Winchester.[74] However, with regard to its general position on the matter the Church remained divided. When General Synod that year debated a motion to sell St Luke's to the Sikhs, the majority were in favour, but the House of Clergy and the

---

[71] David Feldman, 'Why the English like Turbans: Multicultural Politics in British History', in *Structures and Transformations in Modern British History: Essays for Gareth Stedman Jones*, ed. David Feldman and Jon Lawrence (Cambridge, 2011), 288–95.

[72] RCC Minutes, vol. 3, RC (79) 4th meeting, 13 June 1979, 1–2.

[73] Clifford Longley, 'Redundant Church to be Sold to Sikhs', *The Times*, 25 February 1983, 2.

[74] Chandler, *Church of England*, 293–4.

House of Laity were both narrowly divided.[75] In 1984 guidelines on the sale of redundant buildings to Christian and other religious groups were drawn up by the Church Commissioners. These were rather ambiguous, stressing that sale for 'worship by adherents of a non-Christian faith is not to be regarded as an evidently suitable use', but stating also that with the support of the bishop the commissioners would still examine such cases, 'taking into account all the relevant circumstances'.[76] Considerations included the 'belief, practices and attitudes' of the group in question; heritage and architectural implications; the views of local Anglicans and other Christians; the opinions of local leaders and residents; and the possibility of alternative use, particularly by another Christian denomination.[77]

The Church of England finally published an official report on the issue in 1996. *Communities and Buildings: Church of England Premises and Other Faiths* remained rather ambiguous on the matter, stressing the significance of consecration to many Anglicans, prioritizing Christian mission and recognizing the potential impact on churches abroad, but also recognizing the damaging effect on interreligious relations of refusal to sell.[78] No doubt the protracted nature of the redundancy process itself, with its requirement for extended consultation, as well as legal issues associated with individual buildings, contributed to the Church's conservative position. However, issues of canon law, or legal complications with regard to individual buildings, were not regarded as key factors in the cases of St Mary's, Savile Town, St Leonard's, Bedford, or St Luke's, Southampton. While it is difficult to establish exactly the present situation, it would appear that since 1983, no consecrated Church of England buildings have been sold to a non-Christian faith group for the purpose of worship.

The Open University

---

75   Ibid. 292.
76   On this, see Board of Mission, *Communities and Buildings: Church of England Premises and Other Faiths* (London, 1996), §2.47.
77   Ibid.
78   Ibid., §§7.132–3.

CHRISTIANS, MUSLIMS AND THE STATE
IN TWENTIETH-CENTURY EGYPT AND
INDONESIA

by BRIAN STANLEY

Surveys of the historical relationship between Christianity and other faiths often suggest that through a process of theological enlightenment the churches have moved from crusade to cooperation and from diatribe to dialogue. This trajectory is most marked in studies of Christian-Muslim relations, overshadowed as they are by the legacy of the Crusades. Hugh Goddard's *A History of Christian-Muslim Relations* proceeds from a focus on the frequently confrontational inter-communal relations of earlier periods to attempts by Western theologians over the last two centuries to define a more irenic stance towards Islam.[1] For liberal-minded Western Christians this is an attractive thesis: who would not wish to assert that we have left bigotry and antagonism behind, and moved on to stances of mutual respect and tolerance? However laudable the concern to promote harmonious inter-communal relations today, dangers arise from trawling the oceans of history in order to catch in our nets only those episodes that will be most morally edifying for the present. What Herbert Butterfield famously labelled 'the Whig interpretation of history' is not irrelevant to the history of interreligious relations.[2] In this essay I shall use the experience of Christian communities in twentieth-century Egypt and Indonesia to argue that the determinative influences on Christian-Muslim relations in the modern world have not been the progressive liberalization of stances among academic theologians but rather the changing views taken by governments in Muslim majority states towards both their majority and minority religious communities. Questions of the balance of power, and of the territorial integrity of the state, have affected Christian-

---

[1] Hugh Goddard, *A History of Christian-Muslim Relations* (Edinburgh, 2000).

[2] Herbert Butterfield, *The Whig Interpretation of History* (London, 1931). For examples of this approach, see Goddard, *Christian-Muslim Relations*, 4, 177–94; Sidney H. Griffith, *The Church in the Shadow of the Mosque: Christians and Muslims in the World of Islam* (Princeton, NJ, and Oxford, 2008), 3–4, 22, 176–9.

Muslim relations more deeply than questions of religious truth and concerns for interreligious dialogue.

Egypt in the early twentieth century was the intellectual and publishing hub of the Muslim world, and was thus regarded by Western Christians as the key to its regeneration by the gospel and 'modern' ideas of reform.[3] It was also the home of Africa's oldest church, the Coptic Orthodox Church. Until the tenth century, the Copts formed the majority community. Estimates of the size of the Coptic population today vary widely according to their provenance, from 6 to 16 million, and from 6 to 20 per cent of the total population. The Copts have had to come to terms with their attenuated and vulnerable status as a statistical minority, even if they still decline to rank themselves among the 'religious minorities' of the Middle East and so to accept the implication of marginality. Rather, they regard themselves as the true Egyptians, descended from the Pharaohs and of one blood with the steady stream of their fellow countrymen who over the centuries have abandoned their Christian heritage and conformed to the increasingly dominant Islamic identity.[4]

The church in Indonesia is a much younger Christian community within a younger nation. The vast and ethnically diverse archipelago of Indonesia does not only contain more Muslims than live in the whole of the Arab world, but also has a larger Christian population than South Korea.[5] In some parts of Indonesia Christians form a majority of the regional or 'Outer Island' population. Interreligious relations involve Hindu and Buddhist communities as well as Christians and Muslims. The new nation of Indonesia was constructed between 1945 and 1950 from disparate components of the Dutch colonial empire. It remained in a real sense an empire, but one ruled from Jakarta. For much of its short history, the primary question has been, not how Islamic the state should

---

3 See Samuel M. Zwemer, 'The City of Cairo', *MW* 10 (1920), 266–73.

4 The French Orientalist Louis Massignon estimated that *c*.95% of Egyptian Muslims are of Coptic ancestry: see Anthony O'Mahony, 'The Coptic Orthodox Church in Modern Egypt', in idem and Emma Loosley, eds, *Eastern Christianity in the Modern Middle East* (London and New York, 2010), 56–77, at 62.

5 Todd M. Johnston and Kenneth R. Ross, eds, *Atlas of Global Christianity* (Edinburgh, 2009), 135, estimates the Christian population of Indonesia in 2010 at 28.99 million, in comparison with South Korea's 20.15 million.

be, but how viable and permanent this new nation would prove to be.

In the Egyptian case, by contrast, there was never any serious possibility of the dismemberment of the nation on religious lines. The challenge for the churches was starker: in both the colonial and post-independence eras the state appeared to privilege Muslims over Christians. In all Islamic contexts British colonial governments, while prepared to treat missionaries with courtesy, took a sceptical line towards native converts from the majority religious community, frequently regarding them as opportunists and cultural deviants.[6] The British government of Egypt in 1913 instituted a register for recording 'the names of those who change their religion in Egypt', but the decree, in conformity with Islamic precedent, made provision only for those who wished to embrace Islam.[7] Whereas conversion to Islam was something to be carefully monitored, genuine conversion from Islam was simply too disturbing a possibility to be given recognition in official records. Protestant missions recognized that this disjunction mirrored *sharīʿa* law, and in 1921 tried in vain to persuade the Foreign Office to ensure that the forthcoming new constitution of Egypt should contain legal protection for converts.[8] The British Empire in the late 1920s ruled over more than 100 million of the world's 233 million Muslims. As Samuel Zwemer, the American Protestant 'Apostle to Islam', observed in 1929, the British crown claimed to be the Defender of the Faith, but in its imperial capacity it was (in his view) defending the wrong variety of faith.[9]

The Egyptian case study also highlights the dissonance between the post-Enlightenment philosophy of individual rights and freedom of religion that undergirds Western discourse on the subject and the markedly different concept of religious toleration that prevails in Muslim majority states. Modern Islamic views

[6]   Heather J. Sharkey, *American Evangelicals in Egypt: Missionary Encounters in an Age of Empire* (Princeton, NJ, and Oxford, 2008), 65.

[7]   Decree no. 2466, 28 February 1913, in Helen Clarkson Miller Davis, comp., *Some Aspects of Religious Liberty in the Near East: A Collection of Documents* (New York and London, 1938), 104.

[8]   New Haven, CT, Yale Divinity School Library, Minutes of Egypt Inter-Mission Council, 1921, Appendices II and III.

[9]   Samuel M. Zwemer, *Across the World of Islam: Studies in Aspects of the Mohammedan Faith and in the Present Awakening of the Moslem Multitudes* (New York, 1929), 33, 48–50.

of religious toleration are shaped by the *dhimma* system of the Islamic empire, instituted by the Pact of 'Umar, often attributed to the second caliph, 'Umar II (682–720), and generally dated to the eighth century. As 'people of the book', Jews and Christians could expect protection from the Islamic state on condition that they accepted its fundamental rationale, paid their *jizya* taxes in lieu of military service, and respected both the dictates of *sharī'a* law and the religious sensitivities of Muslims. In the later Ottoman Empire, the toleration of *dhimmī* implied, not the separation of religion from the state, but the state's agreement to grant conditional acceptance to *millets* – self-governing minority communities who did not share its religious values but who agreed to abide by its authority.

From the early nineteenth century, as the Ottoman Empire entered its long decline, Eastern Christians came under the influence of ideas of religious toleration shaped by the Enlightenment and the French and American Revolutions. As a result, they were emboldened to claim the status of *citizens* of a religiously neutral or 'secular' state, with individual human rights. By the mid-nineteenth century, the increasingly fissiparous Ottoman state was not unresponsive to the cohesive potential of these ideas: the *tanzimat* (reform) decrees issued in 1839 and 1856 proclaimed such a separation of Ottoman citizenship from religious identity.[10] For many Muslim subjects of the empire, however, this revolutionary principle of political organisation destabilized the covenantal character of the *dhimma* system, just as for conservative Anglicans in the 1830s similar ideas of a religiously neutral state appeared to threaten the very foundations of political order.[11] It thus provoked in reaction more frequent instances of anti-Christian violence than had ever been known during the centuries of Ottoman rule, notably in the Balkans, Anatolia and Syria.[12] The demise of the Ottoman Empire after the First World War left the Western idea

---

[10]   For the Hatt-ı Şerif decrees of 1839 and the more radical Hatt-ı Hümayûn decrees of 1856, see Bruce Masters, *Christians and Jews in the Ottoman World: The Roots of Sectarianism* (Cambridge, 2001), 134–41; Fiona McCallum, *Christian Religious Leadership in the Middle East: The Political Role of the Patriarch* (Lewiston, NY, Queenston, ON, and Lampeter, 2010), 69–70.

[11]   See Peter B. Nockles, *The Oxford Movement in Context: Anglican High Churchmanship, 1760–1857* (Cambridge, 1994), 44–79.

[12]   Masters, *Christians and Jews*, 195.

of the nation-state as the only obvious political option on the table, but it was rarely obvious either what the boundaries of the nations should be or that new national identities would obliterate older religious ones. 'The principle of nationality has come to rule', reflected the American missionary scholar, Duncan Black Macdonald, in January 1919; 'Pan-Islam has now no meaning but one of sentiment and religion'.[13] Despite such optimism, the story of Christian-Muslim relations in the Islamic world in the twentieth century is one of the uneven progress made by Western and 'modern' notions of citizenship in eroding older Islamic concepts of the limited toleration that could be granted to *millet* communities.[14]

COPTIC CHRISTIANITY IN EGYPT

The Coptic community in Egypt has experienced a steady decline in numbers over many centuries. Since the mid-twentieth century a major contributor to that decline has been the process of emigration, especially to the United States. But in a longer perspective the predominant cause has been conversion to Islam, a process that is still continuing.[15] The few converts in the other direction have often found themselves shunned by the Coptic Orthodox Church or being shunted on hurriedly to one of the Protestant churches; the ancient Eastern Churches have, not without reason, tended to fear the convert as an infiltrator and potential cause of trouble.[16] The preference of the Coptic Church for communal survival over evangelistic expansion branded it in Protestant eyes as an institution almost as spiritually moribund as Islam itself: one American missionary likened the Church in its unreformed state

---

[13] D. B. Macdonald, 'Anno Domini 1919', *MW* 9 (1919), 1–3, at 1.

[14] Samir Khalil Samir, 'The Christian Communities, Active Members of Arab Society throughout History', in Andrea Pacini, ed., *Christian Communities in the Arab Middle East: The Challenge of the Future* (Oxford, 1998), 67–91; Yvonne Y. Haddad, 'Christians in a Muslim State: The Recent Egyptian Debate', in eadem and Wadi Z. Haddad, eds, *Christian-Muslim Encounters* (Gainesville, FL, 1995), 381–95.

[15] Fiona McCallum, 'Muslim-Christian Relations in Egypt: Challenges for the Twenty-First Century', in O'Mahony and Loosley, eds, *Christian Responses to Islam*, 66–104, at 74.

[16] W. H. Temple Gairdner, 'The Christian Church as a Home for Christ's Converts from Islam', *MW* 14 (1924), 235–46, at 238; Sharkey, *American Evangelicals*, 67–8; Constance E. Padwick, *Temple Gairdner of Cairo*, 2nd edn (London, 1929), 264.

to a mummified body taken out of the tombs.[17] Nevertheless, the missionaries hoped for a biblically inspired reformation of this ancient Church, and used their influence to promote its renewal.

The Church Missionary Society (CMS) began work in Egypt in 1825, and after an interval from 1865 to 1882 resumed its activities following the British occupation. It took the view that it was no part of its commission to seek the conversion of Copts to Anglicanism. CMS missionaries such as W. H. Temple Gairdner cultivated the friendship of those in the Coptic Church who appeared committed to its reformation, and encouraged them in their efforts.[18] While the reformation tarried for which missionaries longed, they saw it as their duty to lead the way by directing evangelistic endeavours towards the Muslim population. Yet they were consistently frustrated by the fact that, to employ Samuel Zwemer's graphic image, 'the doors of this vast temple reared by the Arabian Prophet swing only inward, not outward'.[19] A member of the Reformed Church of America, Zwemer served the United Presbyterian Church of North America mission in Egypt from 1913 to 1929. He saw Islam as a dying religion of ritual and tradition, a stagnant creed that would be unable to withstand the onset of modernity.[20] The Presbyterian mission in Egypt had won few converts from Islam since its inception in 1854; the majority of the adherents of the Coptic Evangelical Church planted by the Presbyterians were Copts from Upper (southern) Egypt.[21] Mission societies blamed the British government for the paucity of conversions. Even before he began work in Egypt, Zwemer had imbibed

---

[17] Andrew Watson, *The American Mission in Egypt, 1854–1896*, 2nd edn (Pittsburgh, PA, 1904), 58, cited in Heather J. Sharkey, 'American Missionaries, the Arabic Bible, and Coptic Reform in Late Nineteenth-Century Egypt', in eadem, ed., *American Missionaries and the Middle East: Foundational Encounters* (Salt Lake City, UT, 2011), 239.

[18] See Padwick, *Temple Gairdner*, 267–8; Eugene Stock, *The History of the Church Missionary Society*, 4 vols (London, 1899–1916), 4: 113–14.

[19] Samuel M. Zwemer, *The Law of Apostasy in Islam: Answering the Question Why there are so Few Moslem Converts, and Giving Examples of their Moral Courage and Martyrdom* (London, [1924]), 18.

[20] See Todd M. Thompson, 'J. N. D. Anderson, Nationalism, and the "Modernisation" of Islamic Law, 1932–1984' (PhD thesis, University of Cambridge, 2010), 88–9; Thomas S. Kidd, *American Christians and Islam: Evangelical Culture and Muslims from the Colonial Period to the Age of Terrorism* (Princeton, NJ, and Oxford, 2009), 71.

[21] Sharkey, *American Evangelicals*, 71, 77.

the evangelical view that the professed religious neutrality of the British colonial administration was a sham.[22]

If colonial policy was intended to keep Christians and Muslims safely apart, the nationalist reaction against British rule proved capable of bringing them together. Christian-Muslim relations in the first decade of the century were at a low ebb, reaching their nadir in April 1910 with the assassination by a Muslim extremist of the first Coptic Prime Minister, Boutros Ghali Pasha. Yet the ensuing period from about 1911 until the foundation in 1928 by Hasan al-Banna of the Muslim Brotherhood was the golden age of Christian-Muslim cooperation in Egypt in the common cause of a nationalist movement, the goal of which was the creation of a secular Arab state.[23] March 1919 saw the outbreak of a tumultuous revolution against British control. American and British mission aries feared for their lives, but the revolution was not fundamentally anti-Christian. Missionary sources focused on the disorder, while downplaying the part played by Copts in the revolution.[24] In Cairo Copts and Muslims marched together to the mosque at the heart of the world's oldest university, al-Azhar, in protest against the British exiling of four leaders of the nationalist party, the Wafd. The Grand Mufti, Muhammad Bakhit, paid a friendly visit to the Coptic patriarch; Muslims spoke in Coptic churches on the subject of national independence; attendance by Muslims at Christian services increased; while for fifty-nine consecutive days in March and April 1919, a Coptic priest, Malti Sergius, addressed Muslim congregations from the al-Azhar pulpit – the first Christian ever to be granted that privilege.[25] The American evangelist George Sherwood Eddy conducted campaigns in Cairo, Tanta and

---

[22] Samuel M. Zwemer, *Islam: A Challenge to Faith. Studies on the Mohammedan Religion and the Needs and Opportunities of the Mohammedan World from the Standpoint of Christian Missions* (New York, 1907), 172; idem, *Across the World of Islam*, 48.

[23] McCallum, *Christian Religious Leadership*, 74–5.

[24] *United Presbyterian*, 12, 26 June, 3 July 1919; *Triennial Report of the Board of Foreign Missions of the United Presbyterian Church of North America, 1919–1921* (Philadelphia, PA, 1922), 64–5, 81, 84. Missionary sources implied that all non-Muslims were under attack; for a retrospective account, see Earl E. Elder, *Vindicating a Vision: The Story of the American Mission in Egypt 1854–1954* (Philadelphia, PA, 1958), 151–4, 195–6.

[25] For a Muslim eye-witness account, see Arthur Goldschmidt Jr, ed., *The Memoirs and Diaries of Muhammad Farid, an Egyptian Nationalist Leader (1868–1919)* (San Francisco, CA, 1992), 507–9. See also Leland Bowie, 'The Copts, the Wafd, and Religious Issues in Egyptian Politics', *MW* 67 (1977), 106–26, at 108; Vivian Ibrahim, *The Copts of Egypt: Challenges of Modernisation and Identity* (London and New York, 2011), 64–5; S.

Assiut in October 1920. In Tanta, which he described as 'the most bigotted [*sic*] Muhammedan centre in Egypt', he attracted a thousand hearers a night, among them Muslims who listened quietly, even when Eddy, in unashamed contradiction of the Qur'ān, spoke at length of the death of Christ. In Assiut, Muslims 'almost fought to get copies of the Gospels', and signed cards pledging that they would read them.[26] One American Presbyterian missionary even reported that a Muslim sheikh to whom he had refused the elements at a communion service, had complained: 'Why not let me have a share in your blessing? Are we not all one now?'[27] In 1924 Copts won a considerable number of seats for the Wafd in the first parliamentary election held under the 1923 constitution, which gave Egypt limited independence under British suzerainty. The emblem of the Wafd party displayed the cross interlinked with the crescent – a political symbol that would be unthinkable in the Islamized Arab world of the postcolonial era.

The interreligious cooperation that characterized this phase of the nationalist movement was not generally extended to Christians associated with Western missions and was short-lived. It failed to survive the decline of the Wafd in the 1930s and the growth of overtly Islamist styles of nationalism after the revolution of 1952. Nasser's pan-Arabist regime of the Free Officers which ruled Egypt from 1952 to 1970 was officially secular. Nasser nearly lost his life to an assassin from the Muslim Brotherhood in 1954, and in the absence of reliable support from Islamist sources found it prudent to cultivate good relations with Pope Kyrillos VI (1959–71). He therefore authorized the building of a new cathedral in the Abbassiyah district of Cairo, and promised the patriarch that licences for the building of twenty-five new churches would be issued annually.[28] However, Egypt's humiliation at the hands of Israel in the Six Days' War of 1967 strengthened the hands of the Islamists. In practice the Nasser years witnessed the steady erosion

S. Hasan, *Christians versus Muslims in Modern Egypt: The Century-Long Struggle for Coptic Equality* (New York, 2003), 36.

[26] New Haven, CT, Yale Divinity School, Special Collections, G. S. Eddy Papers, RG 32–3–67, report letter, 21 October 1920.

[27] *Triennial Report, 1919–1921*, 64; W. T. Fairman, 'Nationalism and Evangelism in Egypt', *MW* 13 (1923), 231–5, at 234.

[28] McCallum, *Christian Religious Leadership*, 81–3; Hasan, *Christians versus Muslims*, 104.

both of the influence of Copts in national life and of the inter-religious nationalism that had characterized the period from 1919 to the 1930s.

Even while it lasted, Coptic-Muslim collaboration in the nationalist cause was largely confined to the political elite and was not a reliable indicator of inter-communal relations among the populace at large. The most lasting contribution of Western missions to Egyptian Christianity in the twentieth century lay in the fillip they gave to the renewal and modernization of the Orthodox tradition. In the course of the century, the reformation for which they had prayed did, to an extent, come to pass. The laity found a voice through the institution in 1874 of the Coptic communal council, the *Majlis al-Milli*, which owed a debt to the Presbyterian model introduced by the Coptic Evangelical Church.[29] As an elected body it posed a challenge to the existing control of Coptic affairs by the patriarch and bishops. The low standard of education of Coptic priests was raised following the foundation of a Coptic seminary in 1893. The face of lay piety and Christian education was gradually transformed by the institution of the Sunday school. The first was opened in Cairo in 1908 by Habīb Girgīs, professor of theology and subsequently principal of the Coptic seminary; from 1918 Girgīs organized Sunday schools on a national basis.[30] The Sunday school movement was regarded by its lay promoters as a revival for modern times of the catechetical methods of the church in third-century Alexandria, but its genesis owed more to contemporary Protestant example than to patristic precedent.[31] The Sunday schools were concerned to renew Coptic tradition through a revival of the Coptic language and ancient hymnody, yet also fostered a new puritan style of lay spirituality, more biblically based, and more strident in its demands for reform and in its articulation of Coptic interests.[32] For Copts, evangelization of the unchurched population was almost unthinkable; the only hope for church renewal lay in the

---

[29] Hasan, *Christians versus Muslims*, 71–3; Sharkey, *American Evangelicals*, 45.

[30] On Girgīs, see Metropolitan Bishoy, 'Revival of the Egyptian Church since the Middle of the Nineteenth Century', in Habib Badr, ed., *Christianity: A History in the Middle East* (Beirut, 2005), 775–96, at 781.

[31] Hasan, *Christians versus Muslims*, 73–5.

[32] The parallel with radical puritanism is implicit in Hasan's book. Hasan, a secular Muslim, acknowledges her debt to her teacher in political science at Harvard, Michael Walzer, and alludes to his study of puritan politics, *The Revolution of the Saints: A Study in the Origins of Radical Politics* (London, 1966): Hasan, *Christians versus Muslims*, x, 82, 85.

religious socialization of their own youth.[33] By 1950 some 85,000 young Copts were graduating annually from the Sunday schools.[34] One of the leaders of the Sunday school movement in the Shubra suburb of Cairo, and the chief editor of the movement's national magazine from 1947 to 1950, was Nazir Gayed, who later became a monk and in 1971 was elected Pope Shenouda III.[35] Protestant precedent also lay behind the adoption by the clergy from the 1940s of the practice of preaching sermons at the eucharist, whilst the practice of catechizing the young was borrowed from the French Catholic missions introduced during the Napoleonic period.

Nazir Gayed's progression from Sunday school organizer to monk to patriarch points to another important ingredient of the Coptic revival that owed less to Western missions than it did to the symbolic power of the ancient tradition of desert monasticism. The monastic revival was pioneered under Kyrillos VI by the same educated laymen, often university graduates, who were the architects of the Sunday school movement. Decaying monasteries were rebuilt, new ones founded, and the number of monks expanded from 200 in 1971 to at least 1,200 in 2001. Parties of the faithful, including schoolchildren, were bussed into the desert to give them a taste of the religious life, inspect relics and ancient manuscripts, and learn about the lives of the saints.[36] The desert monks became invested with almost angelic significance as those who mediated between the heavenly realm and the temporal sphere in which the faithful endured oppression.[37] The monastic revival validated the suffering of the Copts at the hands of militant Islam through encouraging remembrance of the early Christian saints and martyrs. The Coptic community dates its solar calendar from the beginning of the age of the martyrs on the original '9/11', 11 September 284 in the Gregorian calendar, the date of the accession

---

[33] McCallum, *Christian Religious Leadership*, 132.

[34] Dina El Khawaga, 'The Political Dynamics of the Copts: Giving the Community an Active Role', in Pacini, ed., *Christian Communities*, 172–90, at 179.

[35] Ibid. 183 n.; J. D. Pennington, 'The Copts in Modern Egypt', *Middle Eastern Studies* 18 (1982), 158–79, at 162, 167.

[36] Hasan, *Christians versus Muslims*, 216–19; O'Mahony, 'Coptic Orthodox Church', 75; McCallum, *Christian Religious Leadership*, 130–1, follows John W. Watson in estimating the number of monks at 2,000 in 2004.

[37] Mark Francis Gruber, 'The Monastery as the Nexus of Coptic Cosmology', in Nelly van Doorn-Harder and Kari Vogt, eds, *Between Desert and City: The Coptic Orthodox Church Today* (Oslo, 1997), 67–82.

of the emperor Diocletian.[38] Those who have lost their property or lives to militant Islamists are joined to the company of martyrs killed under Diocletian, and take their place among the perfect symbolic number of 144,000 martyred saints mentioned in the book of Revelation, a figure that is said also to represent both the number of children murdered by Herod in Bethlehem, and the number of martyrs under Diocletian.[39]

Under Anwar Sadat's presidency from 1970 to 1981 Christian-Muslim relations deteriorated markedly. Sadat cultivated the image of a devoutly Muslim president, and relied increasingly on Islamist support, although he always fell short of the expectations of the militants. Episodes of sectarian violence multiplied, and Sadat did little other than issue vague pleas for reconciliation. Pope Shenouda saw his role as one of mobilizing Copts to defend the secular character of the Egyptian state, and in 1977 convened a Coptic Conference to demand freedom of worship and government protection against Islamic attacks.[40] Shenouda was also determined not to allow his people to play their allotted role within Sadat's grand design to normalize relations between Israel and Egypt following the Camp David agreement of 1978. Whilst Sadat urged Copts to satisfy the desire of the Israeli government to see Egyptian tourists flocking to Israel, the Coptic pope, in a striking reversal of crusading precedent, banned Christians from participating in pilgrimages to Jerusalem until such time as the holy city was again under Arab control, and promised not to enter the city until he could do so walking hand in hand with the Palestinian leader, Yasser Arafat. Any Copt who persisted in such pilgrimages was threatened with excommunication. Shenouda maintained this stance even in the Mubarak era, vowing in 2000 that 'we will not enter Jerusalem except with our Muslim brethren'.[41]

In 1980 Shenouda took the dramatic step of cancelling the public

[38] Hasan, *Christians versus Muslims*, 22–5; Otto F. A. Meinardus, *Christian Egypt Ancient and Modern*, 2nd edn (Cairo, 1977), 75.

[39] Nora Stene, 'Becoming a Copt: The Integration of Coptic Children into the Church Community', in van Doorn-Harder and Vogt, eds, *Between Desert and City*, 191–212, at 205, 210; Edward Wakin, *A Lonely Minority: The Story of Egypt's Copts*, 2nd edn (Lincoln, NE, 2000), 7.

[40] McCallum, 'Muslim-Christian Relations', 69.

[41] Hasan, *Christians versus Muslims*, 108–9; McCallum, *Christian Religious Leadership*, 127; eadem, 'Muslim-Christian Relations', 79.

celebrations of Easter, in which state representatives had traditionally played a part, and withdrew in protest with his bishops into the
seclusion of a remote monastery. Sadat retaliated the following year
by sending Shenouda into internment in a desert monastery, and
appointing a five-man panel of bishops to run the Church in his
absence – an extraordinary Islamic example of high-handed Eras-
tianism. Sadat knew that he could count on some influential Christian supporters. Shenouda's high-profile tactics and dictatorial style,
whilst they had support among the young and the middle classes,
caused anxiety among the Coptic aristocracy and among the episcopate, some of whom feared that politics were supplanting spirituality, and preferred quiet diplomacy as a way of defending Christian
interests.[42] The five bishops co-opted by Sadat seemed happy to play
his game, while the more pietistic segment of the Coptic community, led by the abbot of the great monastery of St Macarius, Father
Matta El Meskeen (renowned internationally as 'Father Matthew the
Poor'), 'stood firmly on the touchline'; so did the global ecumenical
community.[43] In January 1983 Archbishop Runcie sent the bishop
of London, Graham Leonard, to investigate the Egyptian church
struggle; Leonard met both Shenouda and one of the five, Bishop
Athanasius, but advised against siding openly with Shenouda.[44] The
only consistent international support Shenouda received was from
the American Coptic Association, formed in 1974 by the growing
Coptic emigré community in the United States to report on human
rights abuses in Egypt.[45] The pope remained in detention for 1,213
days, only being released in January 1985 by President Mubarak on
condition that he avoided political statements, returned regularly to
his desert residence, and should never be present in Cairo on Fridays
for fear of inflaming Muslim opinion.[46]

The final period of Shenouda's long patriarchate from his rein-
statement in 1985 until his death in March 2012 was marked by
a quieter tone. Once freed from his long incarceration, Shenouda
appeared to abandon political confrontation for conciliation of
the Mubarak regime, and repeatedly urged cooperation with

---

[42] Hasan, *Christians versus Muslims*, 105–13; McCallum, *Christian Religious Leadership*, 133.
[43] John W. Watson, *Among the Copts* (Brighton, 2000), 103, 109.
[44] Ibid. 113–14.
[45] Ibid. 104–5.
[46] Ibid. 116.

Muslims. He appeared on public platforms alongside the Grand Mufti, Muhammad Sayyid Tantawi, himself a consistent advocate of fraternal intercommunal relations. Such high-profile collaboration was intended to demonstrate that Copts had a recognized place alongside Muslims in national life; it was a reversion to the communal politics of the Ottoman *millet*. Once again, however, it did not signify that at the local level, Christian-Muslim relations were any more amicable.[47] The vessel of the modern Egyptian state had taken another tack in its zigzagging course, sometimes choosing to run with the prevailing winds of Islamic militancy, at other times attempting to make headway against them; Shenouda had simply adjusted his tiller accordingly.

THE CHURCH IN INDONESIA

Although Indonesia boasts the largest Muslim population of any nation, it witnessed, in contrast to Egypt, a steady growth in the size of the Christian community during the course of the twentieth century. Between 1900 and 2003, the Catholic community grew from 26,000 to 6 million and the numbers of indigenous Protestants rose from 285,000 to 16 million. What is more, it is estimated that perhaps 1 million of the Christians converted in the course of the century were of a Muslim rather than a traditional religious background.[48] Whereas Protestant church growth took place without any substantial increase in missionary numbers, Catholic growth was related to a sustained expansion in the numbers of missionaries sent by male and female religious orders to Indonesia. Missionaries of the Sacred Heart, Capuchins and members of the Society of the Divine Word increasingly took the place of the Jesuits who had pioneered Catholic evangelization in the Dutch East Indies; many were involved in education, which became the main Catholic weapon in the race with Islam for the conversion of traditional religionists.[49]

---

[47] McCallum, *Christian Religious Leadership*, 147; on Tantawi, Grand Mufti from 1986 to 1996, and rector of al-Azhar University from 1996 until his death in 2010, see Peter E. Makari, *Conflict and Co-operation: Christian-Muslim Relations in Contemporary Egypt* (New York, 2007), 98–104.

[48] '1800–2005: A National Overview', in Jan Sihar Aritonang and Karel Steenbrink, eds, *A History of Christianity in Indonesia* (Leiden and Boston, MA, 2008), 135–228, at 165. Although this book presents itself as an edited volume, the authors of the individual chapters are not identified.

[49] Ibid. 166–7, 170.

There was no direct correlation between the progress of conversion and the extension of colonial authority from Java and Sumatra to other parts of the archipelago, a process of subjugation that continued after independence, as Indonesia annexed Netherlands New Guinea (West Papua) between 1962 and 1969, and East Timor (now Timor-Leste) in 1975–6. In Batakland and Halmahera mass conversions preceded subjugation to colonial rule. In Karo, Sumba, and Torajaland in South Sulawesi mass movements followed national independence. In Flores, the educational missions of the Society of the Divine Word saw steady success after the Dutch assigned them the territory as part of a colonial strategy of pacification in 1913: 90 per cent of the population are now Catholic. In West Papua conversion of the highland Dani, a Melanesian people, began in the early 1960s, when the Dutch had barely established control of the region, and accelerated under the equally alien rule of Jakarta.[50] The Dutch took an instrumental view of conversion to Christianity: in areas that were already Islamized, it was strongly discouraged, as it was under British rule in Africa; by contrast, in outlying areas not yet subject to full colonial control the Dutch actively supported missions, viewing their provision of education and health services as useful tools in the incorporation of these marginal societies within the structures of colonial rule. The same was true of the government of independent Indonesia, especially under the 'New Order' regime of President Suharto from 1967 to 1998: mission-led development and modernization programmes were a useful antidote to the appeal of radical Islam to tribal peoples, binding them to a distant central government and the national economy.[51]

The Dutch colonial view of missionary activity as useful only when it served the interests of the state was shared by the colonial established Protestant Church, the *Indische Kerk* (Church of the Indies), which had its own missionary work in outlying regions such as the

---

[50] Ibid. 173; Susanne Schröter, 'The Indigenisation of Catholicism on Flores', in eadem, ed., *Christianity in Indonesia: Perspectives of Power* (Berlin, 2010), 137–57; Charles E. Farhadian, *Christianity, Islam, and Nationalism in Indonesia* (New York and London, 2005).

[51] Lorraine V. Aragon, *Fields of the Lord: Animism, Christian Minorities and State Development in Indonesia* (Honolulu, HI, 2000), 24–5; Rita Smith Kipp and Susan Rodgers, 'Introduction: Indonesian Religions in Society', in eaedem, eds, *Indonesian Religions in Transition* (Tucson, AZ, 1987), 1–31, at 23.

southern Moluccas, but showed no signs of wishing to evangelize the predominantly Muslim Sundanese or Javanese who formed the heart of the Dutch empire. Hendrik Kraemer, missionary with the Dutch Bible Society in Indonesia from 1922 to 1935, and the most influential Dutch missionary theorist of the twentieth century, commented in 1933 that such political opportunism had brought fatal consequences for the cause of the gospel in Java.[52] Kraemer took a dim view of the *Indische Kerk*, believing it to be so permeated by the mindset of the colonial government and so indifferent to the propagation of the faith that it did not warrant being called a church at all.[53] The Protestant missions and Catholic religious orders were in theory independent of the state, yet in practice reliant on state subsidies for their educational and medical work in the 'Outer Islands'.[54] The public face of Indonesian Christianity in the first half of the twentieth century was overwhelmingly a Dutch one, particularly in the Catholic Church. The first Indonesian Catholic priest was ordained in 1926, and the first bishop in 1940, yet at that date only sixteen of the 570 priests were Indonesians. As late as 1979, only 42 per cent of the priests were nationals.[55] As elsewhere, the progress towards indigenization belatedly made in the inter-war period made a virtue out of necessity. One of the largest Protestant agencies, the Rhenish Mission Society, which worked among the Batak people of northern Sumatra, was hit hard by the First World War and its economic aftermath in Germany. Its devolution of power in May 1930 to an autonomous Batak Church, the *Huria Kristen Batak Protestan* (HKBP), was precipitated by the widening gulf between a growing Church and an attenuating financial base in Germany. Kraemer reported later that year that '[n]otwithstanding the name of People's Church (*Huria Kristen Batak*) there is no people's church yet in actual reality. There is a people among whom Europeans are carrying out church activities, but there is no spiritual community borne by the people and rooted in their relationships.'[56] Nevertheless, the HKBP grew to be the largest Protestant Church in the country.

After the financial crash of 1929 all missions found their govern-

---

[52] Hendrik Kraemer, *From Missionfield to Independent Church: Report on a Decisive Decade in the Growth of Indigenous Churches in Indonesia* (London, 1958), 146.

[53] Ibid. 32–4.

[54] '1800–2005: A National Overview', 174.

[55] Ibid. 167.

[56] Kraemer, *Missionfield to Independent Church*, 65.

ment subsidies severely cut. During the 1930s Dutch Protestant missions followed the Rhenish Society's example in establishing autonomous Churches, though many missionaries still occupied senior leadership positions. When the Japanese occupied Indonesia in 1942, almost all missionaries were interned. In the younger Churches in the east and in many parts of Sulawesi, where missionaries had been in sole control, a few evangelists in these regions were hurriedly ordained on the eve of the Japanese takeover and were given charge of mission funds. The Japanese imposed ecumenical organization, requiring all Protestant Churches to join regional Councils of Churches in North and Central Sulawesi, South Sulawesi, Kalimantan, and the Moluccas. An attempt to include the Roman Catholic Church failed. Although these councils collapsed after the war, the foundations had been laid for Indonesian ecumenism.[57]

In view of the role of the *Indische Kerk* as the religious arm of empire and the financial dependence of voluntary missions on the colonial state, it is not surprising that the anti-colonial movement drew its religious dynamic from Islam. The Indonesian nationalist movement dates from the foundation in Java in 1911 of the first nationalist political party, Sarekat Islam. It rapidly attracted a mass following, and branches were formed throughout Indonesia. In the wake of the Russian Revolution, Marxist ideology became influential within the nationalist movement, leading to a split in 1921 between Sarekat Islam and the newly formed Indonesian Communist party, Partai Komunis Indonesia (PKI). From now on, the Islamist and the Marxist routes towards Indonesian nationhood increasingly diverged. Given the options available, many Christian sympathizers with the nationalist cause gravitated towards the Communist party. Most Indonesian Christians before the 1940s had little exposure to Islam; even in Java, where the Muslim presence was largest, many Christians lived in Christian villages.[58] The most prominent of these Christian sympathizers with Communism was a member of the HKBP named Amir Sjarifoeddin.

Amir Sjarifoeddin (1907–48) came from Medan in north Sumatra.[59] His mother was a Muslim and his father, a senior civil

---

57 '1800–2005: A National Overview', 180–7.
58 Ibid. 187.
59 There is a biography in Indonesian: Frederiek D. Wellem, *Amir Sjarifoeddin:*

servant, was a convert to Islam from nominal Christianity. Amir studied at the Law College in Batavia (Jakarta), where he joined the secular nationalist Indonesian Students Association, and was exposed to the revolutionary idea that a future independent nation would take the form, not of a federation of the different ethnic groups within the Indonesian archipelago, but rather of 'one state, Indonesia, one nation, Indonesia, and one language, Indonesian'. A single national youth organization, Indonesia Moeda, was formed, and Amir became treasurer of its organizing committee. Simultaneously with his adoption of nationalist politics, however, he had become a Christian through the influence of one of his law professors, J. M. J. Schepper, who had been raised in Amsterdam within the Exclusive Brethren, but whose Evangelicalism was now of a broader kind. Schepper deployed his Christian convictions and eminence as a jurist to interrogate the colonial government's repression of the nationalist movement. Amir was baptized into the HKBP in 1931. His mother, horrified at such apostasy, committed suicide. Schepper's grand house in Batavia was the meeting place of the infant Indonesian Student Christian Movement (SCM), where students gathered to discuss Rudolf Otto's *The Idea of the Holy*, the German Confessing Church theologian Hanns Lilje and Karl Barth.[60]

Sjarifoeddin became a leader, not simply in the Indonesian SCM, but in the Indonesian nationalist movement, becoming recognized as third in line behind Sukarno and Mohammad Hatta; another SCM contemporary, Johannes Leimena, also attained political eminence, becoming deputy prime minister under Sukarno. Sjarifoeddin's fiery oratory in the context of the Federation of Indonesian Political Parties, formed in 1939, made a deep impression on the young T. B. Simatupang, of whom I shall say more below.[61] During the Japanese occupation Sjarifoeddin was imprisoned as a result of his subversive activities against the Japanese authorities,

---

Tempatnya Dalam Kekristenan dan Perjuangan Kemerdekaan Indonesia (Jakarta, 2009).

[60] Gerry van Klinken, *Minorities, Modernity and the Emerging Nation: Christians in Indonesia, a Biographical Approach* (Leiden, 2003), 115–23. On Schepper (1887–1967), see '1800–2005: A National Overview', 178–9; Doede Nauta et al., eds, *Biografisch Lexicon voor de Geschiedenis van het Nederlands Protestantisme*, 6 vols (Kampen, 1983–2006), 6: 276–8.

[61] T. B. Simatupang, *Report from Banaran: Experiences during the People's War*, transl. Benedict R. O'G. Anderson (Ithaca, NY, 1972), 78.

and allegedly sentenced to death, only being saved by the intervention of Sukarno and Hatta.[62] Following the Indonesian declaration of independence made two days after the Japanese surrender
in August 1945, Sjarifoeddin was released from prison and given a
seat in the first independent cabinet, serving initially as Minister of
Information and then of Defence, and after July 1947 also as Prime
Minister. As Minister of Defence, he coordinated the armed forces
of the Indonesian republic in the war of independence, in which
Muslims and Christians fought side by side against the Dutch. He
remained active in church circles, and was originally proposed as
one of the Indonesian representatives at the inaugural assembly
of the World Council of Churches (WCC) due to convene in
Amsterdam on 22 August 1948. Why he was not in fact selected
is unclear, but on 31 August, to the shock of some of his fellow
Christians, he announced that he had been a Communist since
1935. When his colleagues in the Council of Churches called him
in to explain his profession of Communism, he informed them
that he was a genuine Christian who loved truth, and that there
was truth in Communism. Perhaps they should not have been
surprised. His first four children had been given biblical names but
his fifth child, born in April that year, had been named Tito, after
the Yugoslav partisan.[63] Sjarifoeddin did not live to see the Dutch
recognize the sovereignty of Indonesia on 27 December 1949.
After announcing that he was a Communist, he became involved
in the Madiun revolt, an abortive leftist rebellion against the provisional Republican government. He was captured by Republican
troops and executed in Jakarta on 19 December 1948.[64]

Amir Sjarifoeddin's ideological pilgrimage towards revolutionary
Marxism perplexed even sympathetic Christians who knew him
well, such as Simatupang.[65] But Sjarifoeddin was not alone among
Indonesian Christian intellectuals in finding in the New Testament a blueprint for the organization of an independent nation on
Communist principles. Rather, he is a graphic illustration of how
in Indonesia, to an even greater extent than in Egypt, anti-colonial
nationalism relativized the religious divide between Christianity

---

[62] Ibid. 78–9.
[63] Van Klinken, *Minorities*, 198–201.
[64] Ibid. 205.
[65] See Simatupang, *Report from Banaran*, 81–3.

and Islam. What Christianity and Islam had in common – monotheism – became the first of the 'five principles' or *Pancasila* enunciated by Sukarno in June 1945 as an ideological basis for a state that would be both secular and theistic. In their final form the *Pancasila* comprised belief in one supreme God; a just and civilized humanity; the unity of the Indonesian nation; representative democracy through consensus; and social welfare for all.[66] In a religious, ethnic and geographical context far more diverse than in Egypt, the Islamic majority, especially its predominant Javanese adherents, was willing to concede such a basis for the state. Muslims tried in 1945 to add to the first principle – belief in one God – the clause 'with the obligation for adherents of Islam to carry out the Islamic law', but had to drop this insistence when it became clear that the Christian parts of eastern Indonesia might secede in protest.[67]

Many Christians in Muslim-dominated Java and Sumatra were understandably supportive of *Pancasila* and of Sukarno's regime. One of Sukarno's closest supporters was Sjarifoeddin's one-time young admirer, T. B. Simatupang, who came from a devout second-generation Protestant family in Tapunuli, North Sumatra.[68] Trained at the Royal Dutch Military Academy at Bandung, he rose rapidly through the ranks and after the proclamation of independence became the chief military strategist planning the contest with the better-equipped Dutch forces. He also had to put down the Madiun revolt in which Amir played such a prominent role. From 1950 to 1953 he was Deputy Chief of Staff and then, at only twenty-nine, Chief of Staff in the Republic's armed forces. After falling out with Sukarno, he was removed from office in 1953, and developed a new career as a lay theologian and ecumenist. He was

---

[66] Both the order and the wording of the *Pancasila* were amended between their first enunciation by Sukarno in a speech of 1 June 1945 and their eventual embodiment in the Indonesian constitution.

[67] '1800–2005: A National Overview', 188–90; T. B. Simatupang, in John B. Taylor, ed., *Christian Presence and Witness in Relation to Muslim Neighbours* (Geneva, 1981), 30. For an argument that the Muslim acceptance of *Pancasila* was indebted to a Javanese tradition of cultural tolerance yet superiority, see Franz Magnis-Suseno, 'Pluralism under Debate: Muslim Perspectives', in Schröter, ed., *Christianity in Indonesia*, 347–59, at 353–5.

[68] For Simatupang, see his autobiography, *The Fallacy of a Myth*, transl. Peter Suwarno (Jakarta, 1996); Frank L. Cooley, 'In Memoriam: T. B. Simatupang, 1920–1990', *Indonesia* 49 (1990), 145–52.

a leading figure in the Christian Conference of Asia and the WCC, of which he served as one of the six presidents, representing Asia, from 1975 to 1983. Simatupang became the best known Christian spokesperson for Christian-Muslim relations in Indonesia, and the most articulate Christian supporter of *Pancasila*. His early interest in the writings of Marx left him with an abiding enthusiasm for the concept of revolution, but his revolutionary fervour had been moderated by subsequent reading in development studies and theology, especially in the social ethics of Reinhold Niebuhr. 'What gave me much new passion', he records, 'was that in the perspective of Christian faith the problems of freedom, justice and humanity suddenly came to be seen through more realistic glasses although with a vision that was more hopeful.'[69] As interpreted by Simatupang, the Indonesian revolution had entered a second phase in which *Pancasila* was best expressed through the creed of national development.

The relative harmony enjoyed by Christians and Muslims under Sukarno was not, however, destined to last under the 'New Order' regime of President Suharto from 1967 to 1998. Suharto deployed religion as a weapon in his drive to purge the country of Communism. Islam, Protestantism, Catholicism, Hinduism and Buddhism were now declared to be the five recognized religions that constituted the Indonesian nation. As in Communist China, Protestantism and Catholicism were regarded as separate religions, whilst, following both Dutch colonial and Islamic precedent, traditional religionists were regarded as 'people who do not yet have a religion'.[70] Soon after Suharto's assumption of power from Sukarno in March 1966, in a move designed to flush out Communists, affiliation to one of these five religions was declared obligatory on all citizens. Up to half a million Communist sympathizers were killed by Suharto's army. It was no coincidence that the Javanese churches received a flood of converts from traditional backgrounds between 1965 and 1971. Avery Willis, the Southern Baptist missionary who chronicled this movement, was in no doubt that the decree requiring adherence to one of the five religions was the primary cause of these conversions, although he did not scruple to entitle his account of the movement *Indonesian Revival: Why*

Two Million came to Christ: God could work even through political expediency to draw people to Christ.[71]

Muslims welcomed the state's campaign against atheistic Communism, and expected to obtain a dominant position in Suharto's New Order, but their expectations were disappointed. Tensions between Christians and Muslims intensified in consequence, culminating in a riot at Makassar on 1 October 1967, when a crowd of Muslim youths destroyed church buildings and injured some young Christians.[72] In response to these escalating tensions, the government convened an interreligious consultation in Jakarta. The consultation failed because the Christians refused the Muslim proposal that each community should not make the other the target of proselytism. Simatupang argued that both Christians and Muslims were bound by their scriptures to propagate their faith, and appealed to the Universal Declaration of Human Rights. A more problematic consequence of the Makassar riot was that the government began to regulate the building of places of worship, thus limiting the freedom of Christians to construct churches in Muslim areas. Buoyed by reports of the Indonesian 'revival', evangelical and Pentecostal mission agencies had poured into Indonesia after 1966, each constructing their own church buildings. Muslims felt encircled, as there was usually only one mosque per neighbourhood.[73] It is estimated that the average annual number of attacks on Christians rose from zero in the period from 1945 to 1955, to 4.6 from 1965 to 1974, and 52.5 from 1995 to 1997.[74] The deterioration in Christian-Muslim relations compelled the WCC to abandon plans to hold its fifth assembly, due to take place in 1975, in Jakarta, and relocate the event to Nairobi.[75]

The Indonesian tradition of a tolerant and inclusive form of Islam was thus weakening well before the end of Suharto's authoritarian regime in 1998. Nevertheless, the collapse of the Indonesian

---

[71] Avery T. Willis Jr, *Indonesian Revival: Why Two Million came to Christ* (South Pasadena, CA, 1977), 63–4, 103–4, 210–11. As a disciple of Donald McGavran's church growth theory, Willis was not afraid to cite political and sociological factors behind conversion movements.

[72] Aragon, *Fields of the Lord*, 14–15, 33; '1800–2005: A National Overview', 204–7.

[73] '1800–2005: A National Overview', 207–9; Cooley, 'Simatupang', 149; Rupert Shortt, *Christianophobia* (London, 2012), 135–7.

[74] K. A. Steenbrink, 'Muslim-Christian Relations in the Pancasila State of Indonesia', *MW* 88 (1998), 320–52, at 338.

[75] Simatupang, *Fallacy of a Myth*, 209–13.

economy and ensuing fall of the Suharto government precipitated a new upsurge of intercommunal violence, notably in Kalimantan, Nusa Tenggara, Sulawesi and the Moluccas. The worsening situation owed much to the growing influence of militant Salafist varieties of Islam, especially among students, and also to rumours of an international Zionist-Christian conspiracy to destroy Muslim hegemony in Indonesia, coordinated by the American government of George W. Bush. Although there were still influential liberal intellectuals within the Islamic community, particularly in the Islamic state universities, by the close of the century the prospects for a revival of the Indonesian pattern of Christian-Muslim harmonious coexistence were not good.[76]

CONCLUSION

Both the case studies examined here exemplify the fact that for Christians living as a minority community within an Islamic environment the story of Muslim-Christian relations in the twentieth century cannot be told as if it were a single narrative of two religious communities learning through a process of theological enlightenment to accept each other and live together. Both examples suggest that if there is any common trend over the century, it is broadly in the opposite direction, involving a regression from some measure of Christian-Muslim collaboration in the anti-colonial cause in the first half of the century to intensifying religious rivalry and antagonism in the post-colonial era. Furthermore, both in Egypt and in Indonesia, the responses of Christians to Islam have been shaped less by theological reflection than by the day-to-day demands imposed by the state, which itself has had to determine and periodically adjust its stance towards Muslim demands for the conformity of the legal system to Islamic norms. The juxtaposition of the two case studies highlights the role played by geography and demography: where, as in Indonesia, Christians have constituted majority or near-majority elements of particular regions within a geographically dispersed nation, they have been able to use the threat of secession to block attempts at Islamization of the state. Where, as in Egypt, the regional concentration and numerical

---

[76] See Hassan Noohaidi, 'The Radical Muslim Discourse on Jihad, and the Hatred against Christians', and Franz Magnis-Suseno, 'Pluralism under Debate', in Schröter, ed., *Christianity in Indonesia*, 323–46, 347–59 respectively.

weight of Christians has been less marked, their capacity to resist Muslim absolutism has been correspondingly reduced.

Throughout the twentieth century in both Egypt and Indonesia the dictates of survival were more powerful than theological principle in determining the stance of Christian communities towards majority Muslim populations. The deterioration in Christian-Muslim relations evident in both Egypt and Indonesia from the 1990s owed much to the growing appeal of Salafist or Wahhabist varieties of militant Islam, but the fact of their rising popularity itself requires explanation. Islamic militancy arises when Muslims feel under threat, either from a Western culture seen as morally dissolute, or from a revival of the crusading spirit in the supposedly Christian West. Crusading rhetoric, whether deployed by American presidents or by evangelical missions whenever they are oblivious to the consequences of uncoordinated and unreflective evangelistic campaigns for the viability of their own work, engenders Islamic absolutism in response. It would be a theologically cheap solution to suggest that the only ways forward for Christians in Islamic environments are either to revert to spiritual introversion, as in the unreformed Coptic Church of the early twentieth century, or to choose exile in the West, as more and more Christians from the Middle East have found themselves compelled to do in recent decades.[77] The challenge for Christianity in the Islamic world is to find ways of embodying the universal compulsion of the gospel that evoke the spirit of Christ rather than the memory of a powerful Christendom.

University of Edinburgh

---

[77] For example, the number of Christians in Iraq declined from about 1.2 million in 1990 to under 200,000 in 2012: Shortt, *Christianophobia*, 27.

DIATRIBE, DISCOURSE AND DIALOGUE: REFLECTIONS ON JESUS IN THE HISTORY OF CHRISTIAN-MUSLIM ENCOUNTERS*

by MONA SIDDIQUI

The history of Christian-Muslim encounter is a growing field in areas of Christian theology and Islamic Studies. While there is arguably no particular systematic discipline or approach, anyone who enters the history of the theological encounters between these two religions is met with a large body of work which reflects an unusual complexity and degree of nuance. These range from polemical and irenic approaches by those who were writing in response to critiques of their faith without any direct contact with one another, to those Muslim and Christian writers who lived and wrote within the shared culture and civilization of the Arab East. The other dimension is that many of the Christian writers were also writing for their co-religionists, attempting to define orthodoxy through their own treatises. Perhaps the most celebrated example is John of Damascus, who wrote against Judaism and Islam but became more famous for his dogmatic works in defence of right faith in Christology and for his opposition to the iconoclastic policy of the Byzantine emperor Leo III (717–41), who banned the veneration of icons in 726. Another well known figure writing in Arabic against his Muslim adversaries as well as defending his views amongst his co-religionists is Theodore Abu Qurrah (c.750–c.823). Here is an example of a Melkite or Chalcedonian bishop, in communion with Constantinople and Rome but whose views on Christology were branded heretical by the Oriental Churches. Many of his writings articulated his Christian faith in a milieu transformed by the spread of Islam.

Notwithstanding political and territorial conflicts, the dialogues between Christians and Muslims demonstrate how seriously each side took the other's doctrines, if only to refute them. From the

---

* Many of the names and themes in this essay appear in my earlier book, *Christians, Muslims and Jesus* (New Haven, CT, 2013).

Christian perspective, many of the treatises in the Latin West were written by Christian priests and monks who might never have met any Muslims and who understood Islam to be a growing threat to Christianity, but who appreciated Islamic thought and its intellectual traditions. Thomas Aquinas (1225–74) criticized Islam but also appreciated it as a religion of great philosophers who had transmitted, through Arabic translations, so much of the Greek heritage to the Christian West. The German philosopher and cardinal Nicholas of Cusa (1401–64) saw the Qur'ān as a work of genuine merit, but considered that even if Muḥammad's original impulse was good, his teachings had gone astray, influenced by heretical Christians and corrupt Jews. Such notable names are examples of Christian scholars who found the Muslim rejection of Christ's salvific role erroneous and lamentable and always in need of urgent correction, but their focus on this interreligious polemical discourse was only part of a more complex world of mutual perceptions and cross-fertilization of ideas. A more recent gradual movement away from sharp polemics to dialogue, both social and academic, has been a different kind of process in which the primary aim is to explore commonalities rather than question difficult beliefs and doctrines such as the incarnation, the Trinity and the finality of prophecy. While this newer form of encounter undoubtedly has some virtues, it also has intellectual limitations. Here, I wish to explore some of the theological themes and tensions which were part of the early history of both religions and which have exercised some of the greatest minds on both sides.

Both Christianity and Islam are lived religions with complex histories, not only of conflict and coexistence but also of internal schisms brought about by theological and political conflicts. In Christianity this became manifest mainly through the Orthodox, Roman Catholic and Protestant traditions; and in Islam principally through the Sunnī and Shī'a sectarian divide, although many other groups followed. These divisions remain and continue to find new ways of emerging as theological and political conflicts. Outside institutional structures, a range of different mystical dimensions retained their distinct approach to the search for God. In Islam Ṣufism became the shorthand term used for the nexus of spiritual theories and practices through which countless Muslims sought a closer personal relationship with God.[1]

Despite the recent emphasis on dialogue rather than doctrine, it is important to return to what was actually said by major thinkers on both sides, because doctrine has retained a central significance in both religions. While a variety of themes has been debated, partly in response to the internal schisms within Christianity, the fundamental bridge or gulf between Christianity and Islam has been the person of Jesus Christ, whose status, whether prophetic or divine, has been defended and contested with a particular passion. Despite the description of Jesus as rabbi or prophet amongst both Jews and Muslims, it was clear that for Christians neither definition could be adequate, because Jesus had broken out from that entire categorical system.

For many of the early Christians, the rise of Islam through Arabia was received with theological curiosity as well as political hostility:

> The rapid rise of Islam in the seventh and eighth centuries placed Christian thinkers in an unaccustomed position. From its earliest days Christianity had defined itself against classical paganism on the one hand and Judaism on the other, but the religion of Muḥammad demanded a different response, for it proclaimed itself the very culmination of Christianity.[2]

Many of the Christian writers of the East placed Islam in the broad context of a monotheistic belief but critiqued the religion for its misunderstanding or denial of Christ's salvific status. The source of controversy around Jesus in Islam is to be found in the Qur'ān itself. One of the very few modern Muslim thinkers who has written on Christianity, Hasan Askari, states that 'Islam is the only religion outside Christianity where Jesus is again really present. In other religions, Jesus is not part of their sacred scriptures.'[3] Askari is right to the extent that Jesus is present in the Qur'ān in a way that is absent from any other religious tradition. But Jesus is not

---

[1] Nile Green, 'Emerging Approaches to the Sufi Traditions of South Asia', in Lloyd Ridgeon, ed., *Sufism*, 2: *Hermeneutics and Doctrine*, Critical Concepts in Islamic Studies (Abingdon, 2008), 123–48.

[2] John Moorhead, 'The Earliest Christian Theological Response to Islam', *Religion* 11 (1981), 265–74, at 265.

[3] Cited by Gregory A. Barker, *Jesus in the World's Faiths* (New York, 2005), 142.

central to Islam's understanding of God in the same way as he is in the Christian faith. This non-centrality of Jesus but acceptance of him as a prophet with the epithet *rūh Allah* or 'spirit of God' has often created a rather peculiar theological tension between the two faiths. Nevertheless, Muslim reflection on the life and ministry of Jesus is not monolithic, and this has led to a variety of ways in which Jesus has been understood in the various Islamic intellectual and literary disciplines. A brief look at certain Qur'ānic verses shows us this complexity:

> Those who believe and those who are Jewish and Christians and who believe in Allah and the last day and work righteousness shall have their reward with the Lord, and on them will be neither fear nor will they grieve. (Q2: 62)

> Christ Jesus, the son of Mary, was no more than a messenger of Allah and his word, which he bestowed on Mary and a spirit proceeding from him. Say not three, it will be better for you; Allah is one God. (Q4: 171)

> O People of the Book, do not exaggerate in your religion, nor utter anything concerning Allah save the truth. Far is it removed from his transcendent majesty that he should have a son. (ibid.)

Early Muslim scholars took their cue from the Qur'ān's multiple allusions to the Torah, the Gospels and the Psalms to articulate a distinctly Islamic perception of the people and places mentioned in earlier scriptures. On the specific person of Jesus, even a cursory examination of these Qur'ānic verses reveals that the Qur'ānic Jesus is viewed in a fundamentally different light from the Christ of Christian faith. Jesus's death and resurrection are the cornerstones of Christianity, and his divinity is central to any Christian Christology. Thus any faith which revealed an appreciation of Jesus but a rejection of his divinity had in Christian eyes to be false, or at the very least a heresy. The Qur'ānic story of Jesus emphasizes Jesus as prophet rather than Messiah, even though it is Jesus who will return to earth in the end times. In the Qur'ān, prophecy is a historical paradigm through which God reveals and conceals, guides and warns. The Qur'ānic emphasis on prophecy and messengerhood recalls and presents biblical patriarchs but their stories lie squarely within Qur'ānic prophetology. The burdens and blessings of prophecy are a consistent theme in the Qur'ān, and there is no higher status in the Qur'ān than to be chosen by God as a prophet or messenger. It is the ultimate divine election, in that prophets speak for God at different times and in different places. Human involvement in the process of revelation is always instrumental in Islamic thought. However, while Islamic prophetology is not Christian Christology, Islam does have a Christology of sorts. Christian doctrine, Christians (*nasārā*), and Muslim attitudes to them as communities of believers are alluded to over a hundred times in the Qur'ān. Jesus, or 'Īsā as he is called in the Qur'ān, is mentioned in fifteen *sūras* of the Qur'ān and in ninety-three verses as 'sign', 'mercy' or 'example'. He is a revered prophet, but is also the Prophet, Word and Messenger of God, although there is no one particular Jesus narrative which brings together the Christic, miraculous and prophetic nature of Jesus under his most dramatic epithet, 'spirit of God' (*rūh Allah*). Yet for all this Jesus is defined as a human prophet, a precursor to Muḥammad who, according to the Qur'ān and the Islamic tradition, never claimed to be anything else but a servant of God. Indeed the Qur'ān has several examples of Jesus clarifying a misunderstanding or revealing the purpose of his message when those around him have seemingly exceeded the bounds of religion or gone astray: 'When Jesus brought clear [signs], he said, "I have come to you with wisdom and to clarify for you some of what you are differing about. So fear God and obey me. God is my Lord and your Lord, so worship Him; this is a straight path."' (Q43: 63)

This verse, like others in the Qur'ān, portrays Jesus himself as proclaiming that he is not God and that only God is the Lord of all. The Qur'ān has various instances of Jesus confirming his prophetic status, but while prophecy as a conceptual paradigm of God's purpose remained central to Islam, it had by then assumed a lesser relevance in Christianity. For Christians, in the person of Jesus God himself was present and thus the status of prophecy was eclipsed by the doctrine of the incarnation. The divine/human nature of Christ unfolded as a unique event which went far beyond prophetic mission and guidance for Christians. For Muslims, however, Christian views of Christic complexity were for the most part refuted as impinging on the very essence and purpose of God. The central theological separation between Islam and Christianity remains the person of Jesus. For this reason alone, many Eastern Christians, who were the first to witness the rise of Islam, saw in this new religion some sound teachings regarding the worship of God, but also lamented how Muslim monotheism misunderstood God himself in its rejection of Jesus's divinity.

The spread of Arabic as the language of administration by the end of the first century of Islam influenced the Christians living under Muslim rule. Not only did they embrace it as their language of business, but some used Arabic in the ecclesiastical sphere as well. Sidney Griffith claims that the Melkite community, whose liturgical and patristic tradition remained in Greek, used Arabic as their *lingua franca*.[4] Christians in the Holy Land, and especially those who belonged to a monastic order, were among the first to translate Christianity into Arabic and also compose works of theology in Arabic for an audience which was familiar with the Qur'ān. While many of the works translated were those required by the Church, such as Scripture, homilies, canon law and liturgical works, other writings responded to the new challenges which came with the rival claims of Islam. This scholarly defence of Christianity could be construed as theology in dialogue. Even though the language of Arabic was bound over to the religion of Islam, it nonetheless provided a new and challenging context for the Christian monks to expound Christian doctrines, and also to write original works in Arabic during the late eighth and ninth centuries. The translation of the Bible into Arabic served as an important catalyst for dialogue between Christians and the emerging Muslim communities. Western Christian thinkers engaged in interreligious or comparative theology between Christianity and Islam have only in recent years begun to appreciate the intellectual history of the Christians who lived for centuries in the world of Islam and who wrote Christian philosophy and theology in Syriac and Arabic. The relevance of Syriac alongside Greek and Coptic is that these were among the languages of the Christian communities living around Arabia. Griffith contends that, while Arabic was the language of the Christian communities, Syriac would have been their original liturgical and confessional language, and that echoes of Syriac can be heard in the 'very diction of the Qur'an'.[5]

4   Sidney H. Griffith, 'From Aramaic to Arabic: The Languages of the Monasteries of Palestine in the Byzantine and Early Islamic Period', *DOP* 51 (1997), 11–31.
5   See Sidney H. Griffith, *The Church in the Shadow of the Mosque: Christians and*

Some of the earliest written Christian responses to the rise of Islam took the form of apocalyptic reflections in which Christian authors applied biblical prophecies to current events in such a way that the latter became harbingers for the end of time and God's final judgement. The arrival of the Muslims was seen in the context of eschatological prophecies which provided Christian readers with an explanation for the rise of Islam.[6] Islam was viewed as a form of judgement, and the rise of Islam was God's response to Christian sin. As a result, these texts could give Christians hope that if they repented this would bring an end to Islamic rule. One of the most detailed expositions of Islam as a heresy was written by John of Damascus, a Christian monk and priest of the eighth century, who recognized that Islam was a new and powerful – albeit monotheist – threat to Arab Christianity. John understood that the concept of divine oneness was central to Muslim monotheism but he derided the Qur'ānic message of divine unity on the basis that Muḥammad's claims concerning monotheism and his own prophecy were incorrect. His famous critique is the *Heresy of the Ishmaelites*, contained in the *De Haeresibus* section of his *Pege Gnoseos*, written in Greek. Here, John scoffed at the Muslim belief in the divine origins of the Qur'ān, accusing Muḥammad of falsely claiming that a 'scripture had been brought down to him from heaven' whereas in fact the Qur'ān's pronouncements are worthy of laughter.[7] But John knew that Muḥammad's message in the Qur'ān, however understood, was one which urged people back to monotheism, to one God. Perhaps the biggest bone of contention for John was the question of monotheism, for John was well aware that Muslims saw Christian monotheism in a very different light. Christian monotheism was associated with Jesus's divine sonship, for which Christians were accused in the Qur'ān of ascribing partners to God. John was not prepared to accept the Muslim accusation that Christians were themselves actually 'Associators' (*mushrikīn*) because they saw Christ as the 'Son of God'. In a vehement theological attack he writes: 'The Muslims accuse the

Muslims in the World of Islam (Princeton, NJ, and Oxford, 2008), 8–9.

⁶ See, for example, Jessica Lee Ehinger, 'Biblical History and the End of Times: Seventh-Century Christian Accounts of the Rise of Islam', in Peter D. Clarke and Charlotte Methuen, eds, *The Church on its Past*, SCH 49 (Woodbridge, 2013), 52–62.

⁷ Daniel J. Sahas, *John of Damascus on Islam: The Heresy of the Ishmaelites* (Leiden, 1972), 133.

Christians of being "Associators" for ascribing a partner to God, by calling Christ "son of God," and "God." The Christians in turn accuse the Muslims of being 'Mutilators' by having disassociated God from His word and Spirit.'[8]

For John, if Christ is a Word and a Spirit coming from God, he must be in God and thus he must be God. When Muslims deny this they separate and place outside of God what is part of God, thus mutilating God. If one takes Word and Spirit away from God, God becomes an inanimate object like a stone or a piece of wood. While John of Damascus can be seen as one of the earliest examples of a Christian polemicist, it seems that despite some variations doctrinal discussion between Christians and Muslims has stayed on the same course throughout the centuries. For most Christians Islam had no credibility as a true religion because Muḥammad had no credibility as a true prophet. Prophecy was central to the Islamic concept of divine revelation, but Muḥammad was viewed neither as being in line with Old Testament prophets nor as a moral leader after Christ, in whom Christians had already witnessed the fullness of God and the fullness of humanity. From the earliest debates right through to medieval polemics and into modern times, Christ's divinity and Muḥammad's prophetic status have continued to present dialogical challenges for both religions.

Christian appraisals of the Qur'ān as a mixture of Jewish and Christian myths continued well into the twelfth and thirteenth centuries, when European Christendom's main mission was to retake Christian lands occupied by the infidel Moors. One of the key figures of the time, Peter the Venerable (1092–1156), Benedictine abbot of Cluny, was also of the opinion that winning access to the Holy Places was a legitimate cause but he thought that what was not legitimate was the manner in which Christians were attempting to achieve it. At Peter's insistence, the Qur'ān was translated into Latin so that Christians could have access to the Muslim scripture directly. It could be argued that, despite the limited circulation of this translated Qur'ān, Peter's greatest achievement was his insistence that the Church reappraise its attitude towards Islam. It was not the 'sword' but the 'Word' which was needed to convert people to Christ. By the time of Peter's translation

---

8 Sahas, *John of Damascus*, 75–82.

project, 'literate Muslim scholars in Baghdad and the Islamic West had seen Arabic versions of the Christian Scriptures for over two centuries'.[9] Christian scholars were by no means ignorant of the scholarship that was emerging at that time, particularly from the Islamic world. Many Christian authorities were alarmed that the best and brightest minds were not Christians, but rather heretical Muslims.[10] The medieval Christian ego was, however, assured by Peter's version of Islam, which admired much of Islamic cultural superiority but saw it against Christianity's religious superiority:

> In support of this suggestion about [the image of Islam that was created] as a response to a superior culture it is to be noted that, where the Muslim perception of Christianity empha-sized its intellectual weaknesses, the Christian perception of Islam, without neglecting the intellectual side, gave rather more weight to moral weaknesses. This meant that Christians could feel that, even if the Muslims were superior to them in various cultural matters, yet they, besides having a true and thus better religion, were in many ways morally superior to the Muslims.[11]

Muslims were known as Saracens and Islam as a heresy, and Peter was shocked that a heresy such as Islam had not been addressed much earlier by Christians. Peter's conclusion was that although Islam might have emphasized monotheism, the Qur'ān was not revealed by Gabriel to Muḥammad but formed by a combina-tion of Christian heresies and Jewish myths.[12] Islam as a religion was little known in the Latin West, and Peter tried to dispel the commonly held twelfth-century perception that Muslims were polytheists by emphasizing Muslim monotheism, although not in the way Muslims themselves understood revelation. In Peter's eyes, Islam was a heresy which had sprung up from 'the diabolical

9   Dominique Iogna-Prat, Graham Robert Edwards and Barbara H. Rosenwein, eds, *Order and Exclusion: Cluny and Christendom Face Heresy, Judaism, and Islam, 1000-1150* (New York, 2002), 326.

10   John V. Tolan, *Sons of Ishmael: Muslims through European Eyes in the Middle Ages* (Gainesville, FL, 2008), 113–23.

11   William Montgomery Watt, *Muslim-Christian Encounters: Perceptions and Misper-ceptions* (New York, 1991), 88.

12   James Kritzeck, *Peter the Venerable and Islam*, Princeton Oriental Studies 23 (Princeton, NJ, 1964), 132.

spirit' and the 'greatest error of all errors.'[13] It was obvious to most Christians of the time that while Muslims did believe in one God, their denial of the Trinity, incarnation, crucifixion and resurrection meant that they had completely distorted Christian truth.

This position was echoed in the works of the thirteenth-century Dominican friar, theologian and philosopher, Thomas Aquinas, who, as John Renard describes, 'breathed the air of Latin triumphalism and the lingering spirit of the Crusades'.[14] He was keen to stress that the 'truths' Muḥammad had brought were at root doctrines mixed with falsehoods and that there was no divine supernatural quality to his teachings. Such teachings, Thomas claimed, appealed to desert wanderers. Furthermore, the charges that concupiscence and carnal pleasure functioned as a means of enticing people to Islam featured often in Christian-Muslim polemics as a funda-mental accusation concerning how Muḥammad 'seduced' people to the faith. Islam (and Judaism), unlike Christianity, promised people sexual and other pleasures as a reward for virtue, whereas Christianity offered eternal bliss.[15] This contrast in the very essence of religions was a strong theme in Thomas's work in relation to Islam and he devotes much discussion to the assertions that human happiness does not lie in bodily pleasures, chiefly in food and sex. Islam, on the other hand, appeared to him to be a religion where even heavenly bliss was bound up with sensual fulfilment.[16] Yet, despite such views on Islam and Muḥammad, Thomas took seri-ously the works of Muslim thinkers, many of whom he saw quite simply as great rationalist contributors to the intellectual world. As Henk Schoot writes, 'They made a large contribution to Aquinas' thoughts on questions such as the attributes of God, fatalism, God's knowledge of singulars, naming the divine, the human soul, and the relation between reason and revelation.'[17]

By the time of the sixteenth century, the political landscape

---

[13] Ibid. 142–3.

[14] John Renard, 'The Dominican and the Dervish', *Journal of Ecumenical Studies* 29 (1992), 189–201, at 190.

[15] Thomas Aquinas, *Summa contra Gentiles* 4: 83. All extracts are taken from the online translation at: <http://dhspriory.org/thomas/ContraGentiles1.htm#2>.

[16] Ibid.

[17] Henk Schoot, 'Christ Crucified Contested: Thomas Aquinas', in Barbara Roggema, Marcel Poorthuis and Pim Valkenberg, eds., *The Three Rings*, Publications of the Thomas Instituut (Utrecht, 2005), 143. See also Robert Hammond, *The Philos-ophy of Al-Farābi and its Influence on Medieval Thought* (New York, 1947). This book gives

of the Islamic world had come to be seen as a territorial as well as theological threat to Christendom. The Latin West saw both the challenge and the lure of the Muslims, or Turks as they were known. The major figure of this period was Martin Luther, who wrote a substantial critique of Muslim doctrine. Like many Christians of the seventh and eighth centuries, Luther held that Islam was fundamentally a divine punishment of Christians for their sins.[18] He admired the piety of Muslims and praised much in Islamic culture, yet his critique of Muslim doctrine was based on the bedrock of his theology: the incarnation of God in Christ. Luther wrote that it was its Christological doctrines which distinguished Christianity 'from all other faiths on earth'. As Muslims did not recognize the divine personage of Christ, his sonship and coequality with God the Father and the Holy Spirit in the one divine *ousia*, Muḥammad, claimed Luther, 'is a destroyer of our Lord Christ and his kingdom'. Without recognizing the divinity and redemptive work of Christ, 'all Christian doctrine and life are gone'.[19] Like many of his predecessors Luther ridiculed Islamic preoccupation with the flesh in their understanding of sonship and wrote abrasively:

> Christians know full well how God can have a son and it is not necessary that Muḥammad teach us how God must first become a man and have a woman to produce son or a bull must have a cow to produce a calf. Oh how overpowered in the flesh of women Muḥammad is. In all his thoughts, words and deeds, he cannot speak nor do anything apart from this lust. It must always be flesh, flesh, flesh.[20]

Christian scholars during the height of the missionary movement continued to lament that Muslims had failed to appreciate the uniqueness of Christ. For this reason, in the early part of the

extensive citations in parallel columns from al-Farābī and Thomas, showing the latter's almost verbatim dependence on the former.

[18] For a translation of Luther's works, I have used Adam S. Francisco, *Martin Luther and Islam: A Study in Sixteenth-Century Polemics and Apologetics* (Leiden, 2007), especially here 208, citing Luther, *Verlegung des Alcoran* (1542), which was a translation of Ricoldus de Monte Crucis, *Confutatio Alcorani.*

[19] Luther, *Eine Heerpredigt wider den Türken* (1529), quoted in Francisco, *Martin Luther*, 113–16.

[20] Luther, *Verlegung*, quoted in Francisco, *Martin Luther*, 115.

twentieth century Samuel Zwemer (1867–1952), the noted American student of Islam and missionary in Arabia and Egypt, felt that the need to evangelize amongst Muslims was paramount. He viewed 'the dead weight of formality called tradition' as 'Islam's intolerable burden'.[21] It was, in his view, this tradition which had gradually led to the demise of Islam's glory and political power, and yet a gap had been created as a result of this demise. Zwemer saw this as an opportunity for 'a divine preparation for the evangelization of Moslem lands and the winning of Moslem hearts to a new allegiance. Jesus Christ is sufficient for them as He is for us.'[22] Zwemer's attitude to Islam changed over time, especially in regard to his own all-encompassing vision of God which was the driving force of his missiology. He was moved by the strength of Islamic theism and saw Islam's monotheism as its greatest strength. Paradoxically, for Zwemer Islamic monotheism was also Islam's greatest weakness because it did not recognize the incarnation, the greatest miracle in human history. Zwemer lamented the fact that Christ's life had been eclipsed by the life of Muḥammad for Muslims and that whatever differences there were between the various schools and sects in Islam, their position towards Christ remained essentially the same. Zwemer understood the global phenomenon that was and is Islam but often reiterated his sadness over the absence of Jesus in the life of the Muslim:

> As in a total eclipse of the sun the glory and the beauty of the heavenly orb are hidden, and only the corona appears on the edge, so in the life and thought of Mohammedans their own Prophet has almost eclipsed Jesus Christ. Whatever place He may occupy in the Koran – and the portrait there given is a sad caricature; whatever favourable critics may say about Christ's honourable place among the Moslem prophets, it is nevertheless true that the large bulk of Mohammedans know extremely little and think still less, about Jesus Christ. He has no place in their hearts nor in their lives.[23]

---

[21] Samuel Zwemer, *The Disintegration of Islam* (London, 1916). The book is based on a series of lectures Zwemer gave at Princeton, the purpose of the lectures being 'distinctly missionary': ibid. 9–10.
[22] Ibid. 10.
[23] Ibid. 181–2.

For their part, Muslims from the earliest times continued to emphasize the prophetic status of Jesus and remained determined that the Jesus of the cross was a Christian distortion of Jesus's original message. Muslim writers engaged with Christian doctrine but made little attempt to understand Christian monotheism as essentially talking about one God; nor did they have much interest in what Christ meant in Christian devotion. From the eighth to the late tenth century, Muslim theology was strong and flourishing in all dimensions. Philosophy developed under the Abbasids with the translations of Greek philosophy and science, and while it retained its non-Islamic origins, Abbasid rule witnessed the appearance of distinguished Islamic philosophers such as Al-Kindī (d. 870), Al-Farābi (d. 950) and Ibn Sīnā (d. 1037). They claimed a stake in knowledge of the divine and became leading intellects of the philosophical world, combining theology, philosophy and politics in their works. Theological apologetics included intellectual engagement with Christian doctrines. A fundamental aspect of this discourse was to argue for the legitimacy of Muḥammad as a true prophet in response to Christian critique of Muḥammad's personality and life. Aside from the defence of his prophecy, the theological refutation of Christianity by Muslim theologians focused on wrestling with the doctrines of the Trinity and the incarnation.

'Alī al-Ṭabarī was a ninth-century Persian physician of Nestorian Christian background who produced one of the first encyclopaedias of medicine. He converted to Islam very late in his life and explained in his *Book of Religion and Empire* that his reason for writing was to show those to whom revelation was previously given how they had denied Muḥammad's prophecy as foretold by previous prophets:

> They have hidden his name and changed his portrait founding the Books of their prophets [i.e. those prophets to whom revelation had been given prior to the coming of Islam] – peace be with them. I shall demonstrate this, disclose its secret, and withdraw the veil from it, in order that the reader may see it clearly and increase his conviction and his joy in the religion of Islam.[24]

---

[24] 'Ali Rabbān al-Ṭabarī, *Kitāb al-dīn wa-l-dawla, The Book of Religion and Empire*, transl. A. Mingana (Manchester, 1922), 3.

An example of an aggressive inquiry into Christian creeds can be found in the works of the tenth-century theologian and jurist al-Bāqillānī. Al-Bāqillānī asks about the Trinity, and particularly the way in which the Son and the Holy Spirit are particularities of the Father. His point is that if all three hypostases are equal then why could the Father not be a particularity of the Son and Holy Spirit?

> Say to them: If the hypostases are one substance, and the Father's substance is the substance of the Son, and the substance of the Spirit is the substance of both of them, then why are the Son and Spirit, in that they are Son and Spirit, particularities of the Father, rather than each of them being Father and the Father a particularity to them?[25]

Al-Bāqillānī further locates the discussion on the uniting of the Word with the body in the disputes between the Nestorians, Melkites and Jacobites and the analogies they offer to explain how this uniting and indwelling came about. He writes that for some the uniting of the Word with the human nature is like a 'mingling and mixing of water with wine and milk', while for others '[i]t is in the way the form of a man appears in a mirror and polished, clean objects when he is in front of them, without the man's form inhering in the mirror.' Then, he says, there are those who say that 'the Word united with the body of Christ in the sense that it inhered in it without touching, mixing or mingling in the same way that I say God almighty dwells in the heavens and does not touch or mingle with it'.[26] Al-Bāqillānī offers a rejection of each of these analogies and tries to show from within the logic of the doctrine itself its weaknesses and incoherence. Thomas concludes that al-Bāqillānī 'was not engaged in dialogue or its equivalent, nor even polemic, but in a demonstration of the errors inherent in this alternative vision of the Godhead to the one he was promoting in the work'.[27]

Furthermore, in al-Bāqillānī's view, Jesus could be viewed in the same prophetic paradigm as Moses, for he performed miracles

---

[25] David Thomas, *Christian Doctrines in Islamic Theology* (Leiden, 2008), 169–71, quoting 'Abū Bakr al-Bāqillānī, 'Refutation of the Christians', from *Kitāb al-Tamhīd*, ed. R. J. McCarthy (Beirut, 1957). Thomas provides a useful introduction to the intellectual period of the writers, as well as a synopsis of their main arguments.

[26] Quotations from Thomas, *Christian Doctrines*, 173–7.

[27] Ibid. 132.

similar to the phenomenal miracles performed by Moses. Christians, however, he says, claim that Moses prayed to God for signs whereas Jesus's miracles lay in his divinity; indeed, al-Bāqillānī states that the Christians deny that Jesus too prayed to God for signs and that if Jesus is divine in performing miracles the same should be claimed for Moses. Stretching this link further, he asks why, if the Word united with the body of Christ, it did not unite with the body of Moses or any of the other prophets. Prophetic election was always brought into such discussions by the Muslims, who were keen to show that they took Christian doctrines seriously but always placed them alongside a Muslim perspective. So while the attempt to engage with Christological doctrines was a serious or even polite area of intellectual discourse, Christian piety and devotion towards Jesus as God and Messiah was always dismissed.

While the incarnation and divinity of Jesus continued to be contested between Sunnī orthodox Muslims and Christians, not all Muslims saw the Trinity as a doctrine which divided God's unity or which separated Islam and Christianity. In the world of poetry and Ṣūfī spirituality, Jesus was given a particularly important place where his miracles and life-giving qualities were recognized. The great Andalusian mystic, poet and philosopher Ibn al 'Arabī (1165–1240) and other Persian Ṣūfī poets saw the Trinity and the incarnation as symbolic ways of speaking about the Absolute. For Ibn al-'Arabī, number did not beget multiplicity in the Divine substance. He wrote in his famous poem, *Tarjumān al-Ashwāq* (*The Translator of Desires*):

My beloved is three although he is One

Even as the three persons are made one Person in essence.

The Ultimate for Ibn al-'Arabī is the Essence, that is, God in himself, and thus unrelated to any created thing. The Essence remains ultimately unknowable but God's relationship to created entities can be articulated.[28]

The work of the thirteenth-century Turkish Persian mystic and poet-theologian, Jalāl al-din Rūmī (1207–73), includes a variety of themes which pervaded the expressions about Jesus found in

---

[28] For an in-depth analysis, see James Royster, 'Personal Transformation in Ibn al-'Arabī and Meister Eckhart', in Yvonne Y. Haddad and Wadi Z. Haddad, eds, *Christian-Muslim Encounters* (Gainesville, FL, 1995), 158–79.

mystical poetry. Rūmī, also known as *Maulana* ('Our Master'), is considered the greatest of the Persian poets and is certainly one of the most popular, his appeal reaching across religious and social divisions. While for Rūmī, Jesus is less saviour and Son of God and more the Muslim prophet, Rūmī sees in Jesus much more than a miracle worker. As a prophet, Jesus is identified by Rūmī as representing 'the perfection of humanity', a concept elaborated in his most famous poem, the *Mathnawi* (translated as *Rhyming Couplets of Spiritual Meaning*), in which Rūmī explores the concept of this perfection. The perfect man achieves cosmic consciousness because he is a microcosm of the universe. He reflects the 'universality of God' and is at the same time united to all other perfect men.[29]

In more recent works of a more dialogical nature which aim to emphasize themes of possible commonality between the two religions, Jesus is often used as a model of reconciliation. In his introduction to *The Muslim Jesus*, Tarif Khalidi refers to the collective sayings attributed to Jesus by various Muslim scholars and mystics as the 'Muslim gospel'. While the Islamic Jesus of the gospel may be a fabrication, he writes:

> Here is a Jesus who on the one hand is shorn of Christology, but who on the other is endowed with attributes which render him meta-historical and even, so to speak, meta-religious. In his Muslim habitat, Jesus becomes an object of intense devotion, reverence and love. He bears the stamp of Qur'ānic *nubuwwah*, or prophecy, but as he advances inside the Islamic tradition he ceases to be an argument and becomes a living and vital moral voice, demanding to be heard by all who seek a unity of profession and witness.[30]

The moral model of Jesus is reflected in his struggle with Satan, who wants to accuse Jesus of seeking comfort in this world:

> Satan passed by while Jesus was reclining his head upon a stone. 'So, then Jesus, you have been satisfied with a stone in this world!' Jesus removed the stone from beneath his head,

---

[29] R. Nicholson, cited in James Roy King, 'Jesus and Joseph in Rūmī's *Mathnawi*', *MW* 80 (1990), 81–95, at 85.
[30] Tarif Khalidi, *The Muslim Jesus* (Cambridge, MA, 2003), 45.

threw it at him, and said, 'Take this stone, and the world with it! I have no need of either.'[31]

It seems to me that, notwithstanding the political conflicts throughout history between Muslims and Christians, there has also been a theological conflict about doctrine which has centred specifically on Christology. Muslims argued in the context of the Qur'ānic framework of prophecy, in which Jesus was a miracle worker, born of a virgin and one who remained a human prophet par excellence. Jesus was not a rabbi in the Jewish sense or divine being in the Greek sense. The Qur'ān is not concerned with the Jewishness of Jesus and his teachings as it is with the prophetic model of his life in the long line of prophetic history.

Today, when there is so often face-to-face dialogue, Christological concerns are less pronounced. Dialogue today has a different kind of urgency which demands finding new ways of meaningful interaction by bringing people together. But, as can be seen from the above, Islam's challenge to Christianity was not the rejection of Jesus but of the Christian view of Jesus. Muslim scholars, by virtue of what was in the Qur'ān, understood Jesus according to their own interpretation of Scripture and refused to see Jesus defined only within Christian doctrine. One could plausibly argue that images of Jesus are global and that Christians must be increasingly receptive to the fact that Jesus is in various ways part of global culture, Christian as well as non-Christian. Thus Christology retains its significance even in more recent forms of dialogue. But how many Muslims will be willing to engage in serious Christology or any other Christian doctrine as a form of dialogue? And how many Christians will pay any attention to what Muslims have to say on Christology? Christology may be only one factor in dialogue but it is an extremely important factor when both Christians and Muslims speak of God.

Much of the dialogical work today focuses on the importance of understanding one's own faith within the context of the wider world, global perspectives in which interreligious discussions matter as much as intra-religious. The twentieth century saw many big names such as the Roman Catholic Hans Küng and the Tunisian Mohammad Talbi engage in dialogue, define pluralism, and exhaust the finer nuances of concepts such as inclusivism,

[31] Ibid. 118.

exclusivism and pluralism.[32] We should recognize that both Islam and Christianity have from the beginning been informed by a sort of religious plurality, but the issue of religious pluralism – in the sense of simply being aware of other religious communities and challenged by how to embrace or exclude them – is present in a new way today. One might wonder whether more and more of us are articulating a theology of religions which has a particular nuance: however much we talk of truth within our own religion, we cannot talk of a singular truth. Islam and Christianity, as the two largest faiths in the world, have a particular stake in this debate, which has a political as well as theological urgency. Many now recognize that over the last fifteen years or so, and especially after the attacks of 11 September 2001, there has been a shift in the way Islam is now often seen as a political, and not just a religious, threat to the West. It took the tragedy of 9/11 and the subsequent phenomenon of jihadist rhetoric and terrorism to create a new global political tension. It seems to me that 9/11 is not just another date. For some in the West, it has become a symbol of a fundamental tension, a symbol which pits all that is good in the West against all that is bad in the Muslim world. This is partly because we tend to replace 'Christian-Muslim' by the West and Islam, as if the two mean the same thing. Thus Islam becomes a religion, culture and civilization opposed to liberal values, which are seen as Western but with a Christian hinterland. Muslims for their part also collapse 'Christian' with 'Western'; thus any issues they may have with European or Western governments and their foreign policies erroneously identify the West with 'Christian'.

This was a particular concern with the invasion of Iraq and Afghanistan. However, if the post-9/11 world has seen a rise in jihadist rhetoric against the West, it has also seen a rise in anti-Islamic polemical literature in some parts of the world insisting that Islam is essentially a violent religion and that Christians should rise to the defence of Christianity against the increasing Islamization of Western lands. One such article analysing the situation in the USA reveals that some Christian Evangelicals, namely those who

---

[32]   It is beyond the scope of this essay to go into further detail about these concepts, but for a useful collection of articles on Islamic theologies of other religions which deals with these terms, see Muhamaad Suheyl Umar, ed., *The Religious Other: Towards a Muslim Theology of Other Religions in a Post-Prophetic Age* (Lahore, 2008).

are converts away from Islam, are keen to stress that there is little ground between Christianity and Islam and that Islam is not only a violent religion but also a wicked religion. This prejudice is not so much ethnic or racial – directed against Muslims – as much as it is against the religion of Islam.[33] In his work on anti-Islamic polemics, Cimino argues that many former Muslims who have converted to Christianity are keen to show the 'truth' of Islam, which, they argue, encourages violence and extremism as tenets of the Qur'ān. Thus the God of the Christians and the God of the Muslims cannot be the same God. But in trying to inject some balance as a Christian respondent to this debate, the American-Croatian theologian Miroslav Volf concludes that despite fundamental differences in the way God is conceptualized, the God of Muslims and Christians is the same God.[34]

Religious language remains potent and is now used ubiquitously to defend all kinds of ideological and political fanaticisms. In 2005, Abdou Filali-Ansary wondered why we allow fundamentalists who use religious language to add legitimacy to their perspectives:

> The first reflex of the fundamentalists is to withdraw from the mainstream, to build around themselves a shell that is impervious to any logic except their own. The most essential questions that humans face today – those that engender the deepest conflicts – have nothing to do with theology. They concern disputes over territory, political power, definition of rights and distribution of wealth. The means of discussing these questions is known to all and is expressed in all religions and all languages.[35]

Ansary may be right to claim that religious language is increasingly being used to mask other kinds of divisions and concerns and that religious difference is rarely the main reason behind murderous conflict. Yet political and civic environments across the world have still generated a new impetus for making dialogue

---

[33] An interesting analysis is Richard Cimino, '"No God in Common": American Evangelical Discourse on Islam after 9/11', *Review of Religious Research* 47 (2005), 162–74.

[34] See Miroslav Volf, *Allah: A Christian Response* (New York, 2011).

[35] Abdou Filali-Ansary, 'Jihad or Murder?', online at: <http://www.project-syndicate.org/commentary/jihad-or-murder>, last accessed 10 September 2014.

a more urgent task. There is no one way to engage in dialogue because dialogue involves and affects religion, politics and civil society. It looks different in peaceful societies, and one may legitimately wonder whether it serves any real purpose in areas of conflict, where people are killed simply because of their faith. But it seems to me that we have no alternative to speaking and acting together. What we say to each other, within our families and communities, in our places of work informs people's perceptions of difference. Doctrine and dogma may no longer be at the forefront of much of interreligious dialogue but it is worth remembering that how we think of God can determine how we think of our neighbour.

University of Edinburgh